Lethal Imagination

Lethal Imagination

*Violence and Brutality
in American History*

EDITED BY

Michael A. Bellesiles

New York University Press

NEW YORK AND LONDON

NEW YORK UNIVERSITY PRESS
New York and London

Library of Congress Cataloging-in-Publication Data
Lethal imagination : violence and brutality in American history /
edited by Michael A. Bellesiles.
  p. cm.
Includes bibliographical references and index.
ISBN 0-8147-1295-9 (cloth : alk. paper)
1. Violence—United States—History. 2. United States—History.
I. Bellesiles, Michael A.
E179.L44   1999
303.6'0973—dc21   98-37696
                                                                          CIP

New York University Press books are printed on acid-free paper,
and their binding materials are chosen for strength and durability.

Manufactured in the United States of America

10 9 8 7 6 5 4 3 2 1

For Elizabeth Eckford,
who met hatred with courage and dignity.

Contents

Our imagined past often has little relation to the reality. Heroic struggles against the enemy often turn out to be little more than massacres. Here a white settler slaughters some Christian Indians. The original caption reads, "Of the number thus cruelly murdered by the backwoodsmen of the upper Ohio, between fifty and sixty were women and children—some of them innocent babes." Henry Howe, *The Great West* (Cincinnati: Henry Howe, 1854), 107.

Introduction

Michael A. Bellesiles

The essential American soul is hard, isolate, stoic, and
a killer.

—D. H. Lawrence

America's violent heritage is widely assumed though, generally, only anecdotally demonstrated. The perspective of most writers on the subject is decidedly present-minded. It is well known and thoroughly documented that the United States is the most violent nation in the industrialized world. To find comparable levels of interpersonal violence, one must examine nations in the midst of civil wars or social chaos. Yet evidently the majority of Americans accept two million violent crimes a year as the price they must pay for personal freedom, resisting every suggested form of correction except those that call for more violence, whether by a reactive state or through individual acts of self-defense. It appears that many people feel hopeless to alter what they see as a fixed aspect of American character. Because what we perceive as truth often determines how we act, it is vital that we arrive at a more accurate portrait of America's historical relationship with violence.[1]

Of course, many works on modern American violence do not consider the historical context at all. These texts assume an ahistorical now and proffer proposed solutions without consideration of the deep historical roots of American violence.[2] Most others tend to offer jeremiads or simplistic history lessons, or both. Some commentators see the country's falling away from a more pacific past as a consequence of liberalism and permissive child-rearing practices.[3] Others offer a distinctive critique of an America decaying as a consequence of excess greed and individualism.[4] Such modern Jeremiahs rarely offer any historical perspective other than personal reminiscence to validate this alleged change over time. Those who do explore the origins of American violence have generally emphasized the immutability of America's frontier character.[5] Evoking images of the Wild West, such writers observe that Americans have a long tradition of settling their disputes violently. The more sophisticated scholars among this group devote their attention to America's near genocidal way of war, so unlike

European methods, it is argued, in refusing to grant quarter or to spare noncombatants.[6]

For the longest time, American intellectuals saw no reason to explain their nation's violent history and society. It seemed obvious to most scholars, and a point not even worthy of consideration, that, in this regard, the United States could hardly be thought of as unique. It was the case not that Americans are violent but that people are violent. Any reader of Genesis knew that. "Now the earth was corrupt in God's sight and was full of violence" (Gen. 6:11). This perspective, whether theological or more vaguely defined, still holds sway with vast numbers of Americans.[7] But as a secular intellectual concept, this perspective on the violent nature of man has a fairly specific origin. The half century after the American Revolution witnessed the success of a liberal theology that largely rejected the pessimistic perception of humanity preferred by Puritan Calvinism. That positive notion of human nature fed a series of reform movements in the United States based on the "perfectibility" of man. But America's sunnier Christianity gave way before the dark realities of the Civil War, and an alternative vision was offered by a coincidental encounter with Darwinian theory.

As Richard Hofstadter wrote in his seminal study of Social Darwinism, "[T]he United States during the last three decades of the nineteenth and at the beginning of the twentieth century was the Darwinian country. England gave Darwin to the world, but the United States gave to Darwinism an unusually quick and sympathetic reception."[8] After all, it was the American Philosophical Society that made Darwin an honorary member in 1869, just ten years after publication of *Origin of the Species* and three years before the French Academy of Science rejected Darwin. American intellectuals found in Darwin the explanation for the violence of their democracy and a justification for their often brutal behavior. In turning to Darwinism, they rejected early Enlightenment notions of human reason overcoming the natural passions, as well as the sentimental Christian visions of human perfectibility. Darwin taught these Americans that men are violent because they must so be by nature, and even Americans could not hope to escape their nature. It was a point repeated recently by a Speaker of the United States House of Representatives when he explained why men are better suited for combat—and for hunting giraffes.[9]

Henry Adams noted this connection between the brutality of the Civil War and Darwinism. "Such a working system for the universe suited a young man who had just helped to waste five or ten thousand million dollars and a million lives, more or less, to enforce unity and uniformity on people who objected to it; the idea was only too seductive in its perfection; it had the charm of art." Adams described Darwinism as a recognized faith, "a form of religious hope; a promise of ultimate perfection." Though he admitted that neither he nor most Americans "knew enough to verify" natural selection, they shared a sense of discovering what they had always known. Adams described himself as "a Darwinist before the letter; a predestined follower of the tide." Darwinism suited all those Americans "in search of a father."[10]

Of course, behind this popular Social Darwinist cant of "survival of the fittest" lurked self-interest. The main spokesman for this harsh vision, Herbert Spencer, wrote, "If they are not sufficiently complete to live, they die, and it is best they should die." Such a philosophy, which saw human violence as natural and inevitable while consigning masses of the weak to a deserved death, was not formulated as a justification for barroom brawls. Rather, Social Darwinism defended the violence of class against class, of industrialists grinding the poor into dust, and of aggressive nations overwhelming small ones. Or, as Nietzsche put it, "Over the whole of English Darwinism there hovers something of the ordure of humble people in need and in straits." The reality of this social connection between theory and its use is amply revealed by the Social Darwinists' rejection of violence by labor unions. Somehow the violence of natural selection was available only to business people. The same class base holds for most legitimations of violence.[11]

For many Americans at the turn of the twentieth century, the nation's history of violence appeared a positive feature. Most notable, Theodore Roosevelt saw in America's conflict-full heritage signs of manliness, vigor, and virtue. His famous essay "The Strenuous Life" set forth the general contours of the necessity of violence. In Roosevelt's vision, peace was "ignoble" and "slothful"; it was the "timid . . . over-civilized man, who has lost the great fighting, masterful virtues." Roosevelt's own histories laid out the glories of this violent past, praising those who had fought and killed for national expansion and the "winning of the West."[12]

American historians have largely accepted this portrayal of a vigorous, youthful nation that could not help but be violent as it shoved its way across the continent. Frederick Jackson Turner's renowned frontier thesis gave shape and intellectual validation to this formulation of a necessarily violent America. "The Indian was a common danger, demanding united action." As a result, the frontier "strips off the garments of civilization" from the American, "and arrays him in the hunting shirt and the moccasin. . . . Before long he . . . shouts the war cry and takes the scalp in orthodox Indian fashion. . . . Little by little he transforms the wilderness, but the outcome is not the old Europe"; it is America, a distinctive and violent culture. Turner found "the importance of the frontier, from that day to this, as a military training school, keeping alive the power of resistance to aggression, and developing the stalwart and rugged qualities of the frontiersman." Turner closed the circle back to the Darwinists by concluding that "in this progress from savage conditions lie topics for the evolutionist."[13]

Until very recently, these historical generalizations have not been carefully examined. There have been surprisingly few quantitative studies of violence in America's past, and almost no efforts at comparative evaluation, even from one region of the country to another.[14] But then it is very difficult to arrive at statistics on American violence prior to World War II. The few meticulous efforts conducted so far reveal only a handful of violent acts annually in any given county in the 250 years prior to the Civil War. Thus, in Middlesex County, Massachusetts, in the pre-Revolutionary period, there was an average of 2.3 violent acts reported per year, with one murder every three and a half years. In all of

Massachusetts in the three decades before the Civil War, there was an average of 331 violent acts per year, nine of these murders. In contrast, antebellum South Carolina, probably the subject of the most precise study to date, averaged 120 violent acts per year, with fewer than five murders a year. And, as Bruce Baird so convincingly shows, even cherished popular images, such as southern gentlemen slaughtering one another in duels, have little relation to reality.[15]

The most notable efforts at internal comparison have involved isolating the South as intrinsically more violent than the rest of the country. Again, though, these studies tend to be not comparisons but assertions, offering up an examination of southern culture with no cross-reference to any other region of the country. Wilbur Cash set the tone for this historical perception of the southern heritage in his 1941 work *The Mind of the South*. Cash wrote that southern character was marked by "the perpetuation and acceleration of the tendency to violence which had grown up in the Southern backwoods as it naturally grows up on all frontiers." In a circular formulation, Cash held that the basic character of the southerner, "the direct willfulness of his individualism" was the "decisive" cause of the greater degree of violence in the South. Southerners demanded "the immediate satisfaction . . . of a body dancing at the end of a rope or writhing in the fire—now, within the hour." Thus "the tradition of vigilante action, which normally lives and dies with the frontier, not only survived but grew . . . steadily."[16]

Oddly, Cash, like nearly all historians of southern exceptionalism, did not relate violence to the South's peculiar heritage: explicitly institutionalized racism. This omission is particularly curious because Thomas Jefferson noted the connection in his racist *Notes on the State of Virginia*.

> There must doubtless be an unhappy influence on the manners of our people produced by the existence of slavery among us. The whole commerce between master and slave is a perpetual exercise of the most boisterous passions, the most unremitting despotism on the one part, and degrading submissions on the other. Our children see this, and learn to imitate it. . . . The parent storms, the child looks on, catches the lineaments of wrath, puts on the same airs in the circle of smaller slaves, gives a loose to the worst of passions, and thus nursed, educated, and daily exercised in tyranny, cannot but be stamped by it with odious peculiarities. The man must be a prodigy who can retain his manners and morals undepraved by such circumstances.[17]

Few scholars picked up on Jefferson's hint. One significant exception to the general avoidance of race was the landmark *The Militant South* by John Hope Franklin, which identified "militant race superiority" as the source of southern violence. In a similar vein, Edward Ayers has written of racism intensifying the southern code of honor. The slightest indication of contempt or equality from a black person inflamed white men, who "literally knew no way to react other than with violence." Failure to respond violently to a perceived insult from a black man left a white man completely without personal respect or honor.[18]

But for most historians and current cultural critics, the South was and remains more violent than the rest of the country for vague cultural reasons. In 1846, the

Scottish visitor Alexander MacKay was shocked by the violence of the South, attributing their brutality to "the fiery blood" of the Southern people.[19] Curiously, many scholars now attribute this violence to the South's Scottish, or "Celtic," heritage, though it is not at all clear how this violent nature is transmitted from generation to generation. It is certainly the case that southern violence has always been racially defined, with white males largely monopolizing the extreme use of force from the brutal punishments of slaves through post–Civil War lynchings to modern drunken fights. One recent study indicates that white male southerners are twice as likely to kill as white male nonsoutherners.[20]

Even among themselves, white southerners may be violent for racial reasons rather than as a consequence of their Celtic heritage. As Bertram Wyatt-Brown argues, the southern cult of honor is based on a perverse need to express superiority through the domination of those understood as inferior, albeit in the name of family and community. Though some scholars hold otherwise, the evidence seems overwhelming that this violently hierarchical culture did not emerge from Scotland but from the experience of slavery.[21] As Sally Hadden confirms, the need to control slaves drove southern slave patrols to ever greater levels of brutality.

But in the twentieth century black Americans, South and North, somehow managed to acquire the Scottish disease as their homicide rates equaled and eventually surpassed those of southern white males. Jeff Adler offers an intriguing examination of how white racism can even feed black-on-black violence. And as Craig Pascoe so persuasively demonstrates, the threat of black violence could effectively forestall white attacks during the segregation years.

Despite the obvious large gaps still existing in the scholarship, it is possible to make a few provisional comparisons. It seems evident that prior to the twentieth century, European cities, riven by political and economic upheaval, had higher levels of interpersonal violence than did contemporary American cities.[22] There also seems little reason to suppose that the American frontier attained the same level of violence as the cities. As Bob Dykstra's research indicates, any industrial site in the United States was home to more violence and danger than the wildest street in the West.[23]

Much of the difficulty in being precise about American violence lies in problems of definition. It is not just that some types of conduct are defined as violent in some periods and not others—for instance hitting children—but also that undisputed forms of violence are not considered such in some regions and periods if directed at certain groups or individuals. Thus a Baltimore crowd that in 1803 beat the prominent Revolutionary War general Henry "Light-Horse Harry" Lee nearly to death had certainly violated every standard of normative conduct and committed criminal violence subject to arrest and prosecution by the state. Yet a crowd beating a black man to death has, on occasion been perceived by the state as justified and even heroic, and may have been led by law enforcement officers.[24] This baffling failure to perceive violence because of the warping power of racism makes it nearly impossible to make sensible comparisons. Antebellum South Carolina was, by modern standards, surprisingly nonviolent, as measured by criminal prosecutions. But then nearly all violence against black people never appeared in official records, though routinely recorded in some plantation records; and because blacks constituted the majority of the population of South Carolina, the statistics on violence were almost immediately cut in half. Further, there is evidence that white violence against blacks served to diminish white-on-white violence. If nothing else, the need to maintain racial control, as is examined in Junius Rodriguez's essay, required white unity.[25]

Chris Waldrep gets to the heart of the issue of defining violence in his essay on lynching. Too often scholars have negated the nature of American violence by focusing on the dramatic, and often imagined, gun battles of the Wild West, missing the primacy of racist violence in American history. For instance, is the beating of a slave violence? Is vigilantism violence? Hubert Howe Bancroft, author of the classic study, seemed to think not, and many modern historians share that perspective. Most people seem to connect lynching to the American West and the image of a posse hanging a horse thief, but it was primarily a southern phenomenon, and not at all limited to blacks. In Texas, white mobs lynched nearly as many Mexican Americans as African Americans.[26] Frontier violence in general is certainly more confused than the movies often portray it. As Nicole Etcheson reveals, villains and the law are difficult to determine, and vigilantes are often indistinguishable from the criminals they seek to punish. The changing character of the reporting of violent crimes became evident after the Civil War when H. V. Redfield studied homicide in the United States and found that South Carolina's homicide rate was ten times that of Massachusetts.[27]

The justification of violence in extreme circumstances, such as war, or as part of a national psychosis, such as racism, is fairly comprehensible. Much odder, and more difficult to understand, is the glorification of violence that is otherwise condemned by social norms. Certainly America is not unique in its romanticization of crime. Back in the early nineteenth century Francois de La Rochefoucauld-Liancourt observed that "there are crimes which become innocent and even glorious through their splendor, number, and excess."

But such attractive crimes tend to be singular events rather than routine exercises in mayhem. George Orwell well expressed that delight in violent transgressions and attempted to define its parameters in his essay "Decline of the English Murder." Orwell paints a portrait of "a Sunday afternoon," after a good meal of "roast beef and Yorkshire . . . have put you in just the right mood." "You put your feet up on the sofa, settle your spectacles on your nose, and open the News of the World. . . . Your pipe is drawing sweetly, the sofa cushions are soft underneath you, the fire is well alight, the air is warm and stagnant. In these blissful circumstances, what is it that you want to read about? Naturally, about a murder."

There is, as Orwell observed, something satisfying, even fulfilling, about a good murder. But lately, Orwell wrote in 1946, murders have lost their charm. Orwell attempts "to define what it is that the readers of Sunday papers mean when they say fretfully that 'you never seem to get a good murder nowadays.' " The key ingredient is the inherent respectability of the murderer. Lowlifes, brutal and coarse thugs who hack at their victims or pummel them without knowing when to stop, lower the allure of murder. Orwell links the coarsening of murder to the "brutalising effects of war." He also implies significance to the fact "that the most talked-of English murder of recent years should have been committed by an American and an English girl who had become partly americanised." The old murders would be fondly remembered because they were the "product of a stable society where the all-prevailing hypocrisy did at least ensure that crimes as serious as murder should have strong emotions behind them."[28]

But, Orwell hopefully noted, we can still be entranced by an assassin with finesse. And on both sides of the Atlantic there is a continuing and lively interest in individual acts of murders. The shelves of every bookstore are crammed with such case studies. One particularly elegant work, John Berendt's *Midnight in the Garden of Good and Evil* has been on the *New York Times* best-seller list longer than any other work of nonfiction. Clearly, the market for a murder well executed remains lively.

Yet it must also be noted that in America glorification of the violent criminal has broken all bounds of taste and reason, as any viewer of such aggressively amoral movies as *Natural Born Killers* can attest. This popular fascination may be understandable only as an almost aesthetic appreciation for the extremes of human folly and immorality. And the media certainly reinforce and even foster the attractive power of violence.[29] Lee Chambers-Schiller's essay provides an outstanding example of the emerging role of the newspaper in determining public response to a single murder.

In different periods there has been a widespread acceptance of some forms of violence, for instance, as Anne Little shows, for the preservation of patriarchy. The structure of authority legitimates violence; it is all part of the state's monopoly, as Max Weber formulated it. Others have followed Frantz Fanon in finding violence by the oppressed legitimate and redemptive. Fanon wrote that "violence alone, violence committed by the people, violence organized and educated by its leaders, makes it possible for the masses to understand social truths," freeing them from "despair and inaction." Of course, the victims of this violence from below are not always the oppressors, as is evident today in Fanon's own homeland of Algeria.[30]

The one area of historical violence most studied remains violence by the state. The Civil War is and has been the most popular area of historical writing.[31] In any bookstore, half the history section is usually devoted to the Civil War, with World War II and the Vietnam War filling many other shelves. Most readers find the history of warfare simple and straightforward, with their favored side forced into combat and the moral positions of the combatants largely unambiguous. Yet as Evan Haefeli points out in the opening essay, war can result from deep cultural misunderstandings expressed through competing "systems of violence." In such a situation, the moral agency of the combatants becomes irrelevant.

Recent years have witnessed the swing of the pendulum on the historical study of violence. Only thirty years ago the National Commission on the Causes and Prevention of Violence spoke of a "historical amnesia" when it came to

America's history of violence. Historians were roundly censured for having ignored the entire subject; an accusation well supported when the leading historian of the antebellum South could conclude his section on the "disciplining" of slaves with the observation that "by one means or another good will and affection were often evoked." My own high school text from the 1960s stated, "As for Sambo, whose wrongs moved the abolitionists to wrath and tears, there is some reason to believe that they suffered less than any other class in the South from its 'peculiar institution.' " The authors of this book, the prominent historians Samuel E. Morison and Henry S. Commager, dismissed tales of violence as so much "abolitionist cant," and noted that the slave owner treated his slaves "like his own children, as indeed they sometimes were."[32]

Historians have now made up for this earlier failure, and then some. Many students walk away from introductory history courses believing that the United States is and has been the most violent nation in modern times, with long traditions of savagery. As Richard Maxwell Brown wrote, "Violence has accompanied virtually every stage and aspect of our national existence."[33] Historians who lived in the relatively peaceful first sixty years of the twentieth century in the United States thought their society the norm; just as those who lived through the turbulent 1960s and 1970s believed their America normative.[34] Those witnessing the urban violence of the past thirty years assume that these pathological levels of homicide form a fundamental aspect of the American character. The current emphasis on America the violent is reinforced by television and movies, which overwhelm the public with visions of a ceaselessly murderous culture. For instance, the American Psychological Association recently concluded a study of the media's impact on young people with the summary: "The average American has seen 8,000 television murders and 100,000 acts of violence by the end of elementary school and has watched about 22,000 hours of TV and some 18,000 murders in the media by the end of high school."[35]

Certainly, the United States appears a nation overwhelmed by crime and violence. Its prison population has risen 239 percent from 1980 to 1997, from 501,886 people to 1,700,000 people; the United States is second only to Russia in the percentage of population behind bars. The United States has 4,700 prisons, at an annual cost of $38 billion. Yet most modern violence tends to originate close to home, as domestic disputes; is self-inflicted, as suicides; or is the product of drugs or alcohol. A recent study by the National Center on Addiction and Substance Abuse at Columbia University reports that 80 percent of the 1.7 million people in jail in the United States are incarcerated as a result of some connection to drugs. It also found that alcohol figures prominently in the majority of violent crimes.[36]

The media make violence appear easy, but there is much evidence that historically the majority of Americans do not find it so. Some scholars argue that Americans do not want to kill, and when they do, they feel terrible about it. S. L. A. Marshall first made the argument in 1947 that many if not most soldiers disliked the idea of killing so much that they fired over the enemy's heads or not at all. In a recent treatment of this theme, David Grossman writes that the military needs to train its members to repress "their innate resistance to killing their fellow human beings." Of course, this training seems easier at some times than others. Yet we have constructed an image of the violent American, and that image has consequences.[37]

Scholarship is now moving from easy and largely inaccurate generalizations to precise examinations of the role of violence in America's past. This collection of original essays seeks to make a contribution toward that more exacting exploration. A unifying theme of these essays is the manner in which Americans have misperceived the nature of violence in their society and acted upon that error. In short, perception determines response. Another key observation of most of these essays is that historians themselves have too often erred in believing that the culture of the United States has always been as it is now. To grasp the centrality of any cultural construct, it is necessary not only to compare a specific place and time within the American experience but also to get a sense of its uniqueness in contrast to other nations and cultures.

The one longstanding comparison that manifested the relative nonviolence of the American experience is the nation's founding revolution. Compared with the French, Russian, or Chinese revolutions, the American Revolution appears positively benign. As Howard Mumford Jones said in a famous formulation:

> American mobs were amenable to cunning leadership, sometimes disguised, sometimes demagogic; they pillaged, robbed, destroyed property, defied law, interfered with the normal course of justice, . . . and were now and then the cause, direct or indirect, of deaths in their own number or among those they attacked. . . . On the other hand American mobs were curiously lacking in furious, deep-seated, and bloodthirsty resentment. No royal governor was hanged or shot by a drumhead court martial. No stamp collector or customs official was summarily executed. . . . No "tyrant" was decapitated . . . and nobody's head was borne about the streets of Philadelphia or Boston on a pole.[38]

Compared to other nations, the United States was, prior to the 1960s, relatively tame, with the single exception of the Civil War. The Boston Massacre claimed five lives; London's Gordon Riots of 1780 just short of three hundred.[39]

Even within the context of American history itself, historians too often make qualitative judgments unsupported by quantitative evaluation. The leading historian of violence in America, Richard Maxwell Brown, has suggested that the three decades prior to the Civil War "may have been the era of the greatest urban violence that America has ever experienced." But this statement is just simply wrong. The New York City Draft Riots (1863) alone should make evident the invalidity of such an assertion. But there were many other post–Civil War conflicts that easily surpassed the entire urban casualty list for the whole country in the 1840s. For instance, on the single day of September 14, 1874, white racists battled the black militia for control of New Orleans, bringing a Gatling gun to bear and killing twenty people. This horrendous crime came just the year after the even worse Colfax Massacre, at which more than one hundred black Louisiana citizens attempting to exercise their right of assembly were murdered by a well-armed white mob.[40]

The armaments employed by crowds, urban or rural, in the years after the Civil War account for much of this carnage. Until the Philadelphia riots of 1844, no American militia had opened fire on an American crowd. As a number of recent studies of crowd action illustrate, the antebellum mobs tended to intimidate and break noses rather than shoot and kill. From the New York City riots of 1863 on, American military units regularly fired on crowds, and those crowds often returned fire.[41]

With no notable exceptions, crowd violence between the Civil War and World War II originated either in racism or antilabor actions. For instance, the nationwide railroad strike of 1877 led to riots in several cities, and a death toll of ninety people; the Chicago riot of 1919 saw whites and blacks battling one another for nearly a week, claiming the lives of thirty-eight people.[42]

But Americans do not confine themselves to organized violence. One thing is certain, since 1861 Americans have excelled at killing one another in a fashion unparalleled in any other industrial nation. It is difficult to establish precise figures for the years prior to World War II, but the murder rate has shown a steady rise since the Civil War, reaching new plateaus in 1870, 1910, 1940, and 1975 that remained fairly constant. Carl Bakal has estimated that there were 265,000 homicides with guns in the years from 1900 to 1965.[43] Americans are the most heavily armed people in the world, having exceeded parity, with more guns in private hands than the total population, though the FBI estimates that those guns are concentrated in half of the homes in America. It is impossible to know how many firearms are purchased every year in the United States, but the FBI estimates that five million guns are bought annually by private individuals. The final essay in this collection, by Arthur Kellermann and Philip Cook, addresses the consequences of this buying pattern.[44]

There is one constant to this story: most violence in the United States, as in the rest of the world, is and always has been committed by men. In some ways that would seem to be the end of the matter: men are violent by nature. But there is much to be learned from the particulars of gendered crime. The law is not always an objective preserver of social peace; other cultural goals are often involved, whether, as Uche Egemonye argues, the maintenance of an ideal of feminine conduct, or as Laura Edwards proposes, an expectation of family behavior determined by class and race. Violence may, as John Pettegrew argues, play a key role in the construction of social identity, most particularly masculinity. This latter point—that men are men precisely because they are violent—is supported by several of the essays in this volume.

With gender, as with other categories of analysis, the question of definitions is determinative. Most of us conceive of violence in the terms presented in the media: the villain with a gun. Yet there are many distinctive forms of violence that can have a long-term impact on the lives of their victims. As is well known, in some periods of American history, rape has either not been recognized as significant or has been held to a higher standard of evidence than required of any other crime—a standard that generally inflicted a second assault on the victim. In other times, rape has been identified as a crime against the father or husband of the woman, who has been denied use of his property.[45] Mary Odem's study of rape in the early twentieth century highlights the culturally constructed perceptions of the roots of violence and the essential indifference of the courts to the victims of this crime. In a startlingly original essay, Andrea Tone calls into question our very understanding of the meaning of violence, drawing our attention to its different forms. Industry and medical science objectify women's bodies and make them sites for violent experimentation in the name of science—and profit. Most telling of social expectations and standards is the popular response to women killers. Popular literature, as examined by Laura McCall, fashions violence by women as a rare and even unnatural exception, the product of dire circumstance and the absence of a heroic man. And as the essays of Kate Nickerson and Paula Hinton establish, the public will do backflips to disguise and justify real violence by women. These efforts to explain the inexplicable can utterly demoralize society.

Repeatedly, we return to the connection of racism and violence. The fears and false perceptions engendered by racism drove whites to levels of brutality not seen elsewhere in their society. Whites acted with outrageous barbarity in the Indian wars and the suppression of slave rebellions, real and imagined. The only mass executions in antebellum America came in the aftermath of slave rebellions. In New York City in 1712, authorities responded to a slave insurrection with a series of executions, including burning and hanging in chains. In 1741, rumors of a slave uprising in New York led to the execution of more than thirty slaves, thirteen by public burning. Gabriel's insurrection in Virginia in 1800 ended with the hanging of thirty-five suspects, about the same number as were hanged in Charleston in 1822. Whites responded to Nat Turner's rebellion with a rampage of murder that claimed at least one hundred lives. In such a context it is not surprising that many scholars have come to see violence as the core value of American culture and that a later black power advocate could declare violence "as American as cherry pie." This book seeks to test the accuracy of that contention.[46]

NOTES

I would like to thank Jennifer Hammer for her patience and support.

1. For statistics on annual crime rates in the United States, see the annual *Uniform Crime Reports for the United States* published by the U.S. Department of Justice.

2. To take just two examples from opposite ends of the political spectrum, see Gary Kleck, *Point Blank: Guns and Violence in America* (New York: Aldine deGruyter, 1991), and James Gilligan, *Violence: Reflections on a National Epidemic* (New York: Random House, 1996).

3. Rush H. Limbaugh III, *The Way Things Ought to Be* (New York: Pocket Books, 1992), 169–84; Newt Gingrich, *To Renew America* (New York: HarperCollins, 1995), 201–7; Jeffrey

R. Snyder, "A Nation of Cowards," and William J. Bennett, "The Moral Origins of the Urban Crisis," in David Brooks, ed., *Backward and Upward: The New Conservative Writing* (New York: Vintage, 1996), 247–63, 272–76.

4. Charles Derber, *The Wilding of America: How Greed and Violence Are Eroding Our Nation's Character* (New York: St. Martin's Press, 1996).

5. Richard Maxwell Brown, *Strain of Violence: Historical Studies of American Violence and Vigilantism* (New York: Oxford University Press, 1975); Richard Slotkin, *Regeneration through Violence: The Mythology of the American Frontier, 1600–1860* (Middletown, Conn.: Wesleyan University Press, 1973); Arnold Madison, *Vigilantism in America* (New York: Seabury Press, 1973); Richard E. Nisbett and Dov Cohen, *Culture of Honor: The Psychology of Violence in the South* (Boulder: Westview Press, 1996). For the frontier heritage of violence in an adjacent country, see Judy M. Torrance, *Public Violence in Canada, 1867–1982* (Kingston, Ont.: McGill-Queen's University Press, 1986).

6. Francis Jennings, *The Invasion of America: Indians, Colonialism, and the Cant of Conquest* (Chapel Hill: University of North Carolina Press, 1975); Charles Royster, *The Destructive War: William Tecumseh Sherman, Stonewall Jackson, and the Americans* (New York: Knopf, 1991); Patrick M. Malone, *The Skulking Way of War: Technology and Tactics among the New England Indians* (Lanham, Md.: Madison Books, 1991); Jill Lepore, *The Name of War: King Philip's War and the Origins of American Identity* (New York: Knopf, 1998).

7. Michael N. Nagler, *American without Violence: Why Violence Persists and How You Can Stop It* (Covelo, Calif.: Island Press, 1982); Seymour Feshbach and Robert D. Singer, *Television and Aggression* (San Francisco: Jossey-Bass, 1971); Victoria Sherrow, *Violence and the Media: The Question of Cause and Effect* (Brookfield, Conn.: Millbrook Press, 1996); Barbara Ehrenreich, *Blood Rites: Origins and History of the Passions of War* (New York: Holt, 1996); Donald Kagan, *On the Origins of War and the Preservation of Peace* (New York: Doubleday, 1995).

8. Richard Hofstadter, *Social Darwinism and American Thought*, rev. ed. (Boston: Beacon Press, 1953), 4–5.

9. *New York Times*, 19 January 1995.

10. *The Education of Henry Adams* (New York: Vintage, 1954), 211–12, 216–17.

11. Herbert Spencer, *Social Statics: Or, The Conditions Essential to Human Happiness Specified, and the First of Them Developed* (New York: Appleton, 1865), 414–15; Hofstadter, *Social Darwinism*, 47.

12. Theodore Roosevelt, "The Strenuous Life" (1900), in Michael A. Bellesiles, ed., *BiblioBase* (Boston: Houghton Mifflin, 1998), 1, 4; and *The Winning of the West*, 6 vols. (New York: Current Literature, 1905).

13. Frederick Jackson Turner, "The Significance of the Frontier in American History" (1893), in Bellesiles, *BiblioBase*, 3, 13; Walter P. Webb, *The Great Frontier* (Boston: Houghton Mifflin, 1952); Arthur K. Moore, *The Frontier Mind: A Cultural Analysis of the Kentucky Frontiersman* (Lexington: University of Kentucky Press, 1957); Margaret Mead, *And Keep Your Powder Dry: An Anthropologist Looks at America* (New York: Morrow, 1965); Roy A. Billington, *America's Frontier Heritage* (New York: Holt, Rinehart and Winston, 1966).

14. One notable exception is the editing work of Eric H. Monkkonen: *Theories and Methods in Criminal Justice History, Policing and Crime Control,* and *Violence and Theft* (all Munich and New York: K. G. Saur, 1972); and Monkkonen, with Eric A. Johnson, eds., *The Civilization of Crime: Violence in Town and Country since the Middle Ages* (Urbana: University of Illinois Press, 1996).

15. Michael Stephen Hindus, *Prison and Plantation: Crime, Justice, and Authority in Massachusetts and South Carolina, 1767–1878* (Chapel Hill: University of North Carolina Press,

1980), 59–84; William E. Nelson, "Emerging Notions of Modern Criminal Law in the Revolutionary Era," *New York University Law Review* 42 (1967): 450–82; Kai T. Erikson, *Wayward Puritans: A Study in the Sociology of Deviance* (New York: Wiley, 1966); Jean-Claude Chesnais, "The History of Violence: Homicide and Suicide Rates Through the Ages," *International Social Science Journal*, 1992, 217–34.

16. Wilbur J. Cash, *The Mind of the South* (New York: Knopf, 1941), 44–45; Grady McWhiney, *Cracker Culture: Celtic Ways in the Old South* (Tuscaloosa: University of Alabama Press, 1988); Bertram Wyatt-Brown, *Southern Honor: Ethics and Behavior in the Old South* (New York: Oxford University Press, 1982); Sheldon Hackney, "Southern Violence," in Hugh D. Graham and Ted R. Gurr, eds., *Violence in America: Historical and Comparative Perspectives* (Beverly Hills: Sage, 1969), 393–410.

17. Andrew A. Lipscomb and Albert Ellery Bergh, eds., *The Writings of Thomas Jefferson* (Washington, D.C.: Thomas Jefferson Memorial Association, 1904), 2:191–201, 225–28.

18. John Hope Franklin, *The Militant South, 1800–1861* (Cambridge: Harvard University Press, 1956), viii; Edward L. Ayers, *Vengeance and Justice: Crime and Punishment in the Nineteenth Century South* (New York: Oxford University Press, 1984), 235. See also Jane Dailey, "Deference and Violence in the Postbellum South: Manners and Massacres in Danville, Virginia," *Journal of Southern History* 63 (1997): 553–90; Kenneth S. Greenberg, *Honor and Slavery* (Princeton: Princeton University Press, 1996).

19. Alexander MacKay, *The Western World: Or Travels in the United States in 1846–47*, 3 vols. (London: R. Bentley, 1849), 1:104. See an even earlier commentary in Alexander Hewatt, *An Historical Account of the Rise and Progress of the Colonies of South Carolina and Georgia*, 2 vols. (London: Alexander Donaldson, 1779), 2:298.

20. Nisbett and Cohen, *Culture of Honor*, 21, 53. On modern southern violence as distinctive, see Raymond D. Gastil et al., "Violence," in Charles Reagan Wilson and William Ferris, eds., *Encyclopedia of Southern Culture* (New York: Anchor Books, 1989), 4: 343–417.

21. Wyatt-Brown, *Southern Honor*; John Hope Franklin, *Militant South*.

22. George Rude, *Paris and London in the Eighteenth Century: Studies in Popular Protest* (New York: Viking Press, 1970); George Rude, *Hanoverian London, 1714–1808* (Berkeley: University of California Press, 1971), 185–227; V. A. C. Gatrell and T. B. Hadden, "Criminal Statistics and Their Interpretation," in E. A. Wrigley, ed., *Nineteenth Century Society: Essays in the Quantitative Methods for the Study of Social Data* (Cambridge: Cambridge University Press, 1972), 336–96; J. J. Tobias, *Urban Crime in Victorian England* (New York: Schocken, 1972); John M. Beattie, *Crimes and Courts in England, 1660–1800* (Princeton: Princeton University Press, 1986); Roger Lane, *Policing the City: Boston, 1822–1885* (Cambridge: Harvard University Press, 1967); Paul A. Gilje, *The Road to Mobocracy: Popular Disorder in New York City, 1763–1834* (Chapel Hill: University of North Carolina Press, 1987).

23. Robert R. Dykstra, "Field Notes: Overdosing on Dodge City," *Western Historical Quarterly* 27 (1996): 505–14. See also John Philip Reid, *Policing the Elephant: Crime, Punishment, and Social Behavior on the Overland Trail* (San Marino, Calif.: Henry E. Huntington Library, 1996).

24. Charles Royster, *Light-Horse Harry Lee and the Legacy of the American Revolution* (Cambridge: Cambridge University Press, 1986), 115–68; Ida B. Wells, *A Red Record* (Chicago: Donohue and Henneberry, 1895)

25. Hindus, *Prison and Plantation*, 129–61; Edmund S. Morgan, *American Slavery, American Freedom: The Ordeal of Colonial Virginia* (New York: Norton, 1975), 363–87.

26. William D. Carrigan and Clive Webb, "The Lynching of Hispanics in the United

States, 1848–1928," as yet unpublished paper, courtesy of the authors; David Grimsted, "Ne d'Hier: American Vigilantism, Communal Rebirth and Political Traditions," in Loretta Valtz Mannucci, ed., *People and Power: Rights, Citizenship and Violence* (Milan: Grafiche Vadacca,1992), 75–113; Hubert Howe Bancroft, *Popular Tribunals*, 2 vols. (San Francisco: History Company, 1887).

27. H. V. Redfield, *Homicide, North and South* (Philadelphia: Lippincott, 1880).

28. George Orwell, *Decline of the English Murder, and Other Essays* (Harmondsworth, Eng.: Penguin, 1965), 9–13.

29. Madeline Levine, *Viewing Violence: How Media Violence Affects Your Child's and Adolescent's Development* (New York: Doubleday, 1996); Martha Grace Duncan, *Romantic Outlaws, Beloved Prisons: The Unconscious Meanings of Crime and Punishment* (New York: New York University Press, 1996); Daniel Bell, "Crime as an American Way of Life," in *The End of Ideology: On the Exhaustion of Political Ideas in the Fifties* (Glencoe, Ill.: Free Press, 1960).

30. Frantz Fanon, *The Wretched of the Earth* (New York: Grove Weidenfeld, 1991), 148; Ronald T. Takaki, *Violence in the Black Imagination* (New York: Putnam's Sons, 1972); Ralph Ellison, *Invisible Man* (New York: Random House, 1952); James Baldwin, *Collected Essays* (New York: Library of America, 1998).

31. Edmund Wilson, *Patriotic Gore: Studies in the Literature of the American Civil War* (New York: Oxford University Press, 1962).

32. Graham and Gurr, *Violence in America*, 9–10; Ulrich B. Phillips, *Life and Labor in the Old South* (Boston: Little, Brown, 1963), 211; Samuel E. Morison and Henry S. Commager, *The Growth of the American Republic*, 2 vols. (New York: Oxford University Press, 1960), 1: 537–39.

33. Richard Maxwell Brown, "Historical Patterns of American Violence," in Graham and Gurr, *Violence in America*, 19. For other views of a bloodthirsty America, see Richard Maxwell Brown, *No Duty to Retreat: Violence and Values in American History and Society* (New York: Oxford University Press, 1991); Dee Brown, *Bury My Heart at Wounded Knee: An Indian History of the American West* (New York: Holt, Rinehart and Winston, 1971); Ovid Demaris, *America the Violent* (New York: Cowles Book, 1970).

34. See Richard Hofstadter's introduction to Hofstadter and Michael Wallace, eds., *American Violence: A Documentary History* (New York: Vintage, 1970). Hofstadter wrote as though the dissent of the 1960s would become a permanent routine of American life.

35. American Psychological Association, *Violence and Youth: Psychology's Response* (Washington, D.C.: APA, 1993). See also Brandon S. Centerwall, "Television and Violent Crime," *Public Interest*, Spring 1993; Levine, *Viewing Violence*; Children's Express, *Voices from the Future: Our Children Tell Us about Violence in America*, ed. Susan Goodwillie (New York: Crown, 1993); Geoffrey Canada, *Fist Stick Knife Gun: A Personal History of Violence in America* (Boston: Beacon Press, 1995); J. Alleyne Johnson, "Life After Death: Critical Pedagogy in an Urban Classroom," *Harvard Educational Review* 65 (1995): 213–30; John Devine, *Maximum Security: The Culture of Violence in Inner-City Schools* (Chicago: University of Chicago Press, 1996). There are those who diminish the impact of media violence: Sherrow, Violence and the Media; James Bowman, "The Use and Abuse of Violence," in Brooks, *Backward and Upward*, 107–13.

36. *USA Today*, 9 Jan. 1998.

37. David Grossman, *On Killing: The Psychological Cost of Learning to Kill in War and Society* (Boston: Little, Brown, 1995), 13.

38. Howard Mumford Jones, *O Strange New World* (New York: Viking Press, 1967), 289–90.

39. John W. Shy, *Toward Lexington: The Role of the British Army in the Coming of the American Revolution* (Princeton: Princeton University Press, 1965), 303–20; Ian Gilmour, *Riot, Risings and Revolution: Governance and Violence in Eighteenth-Century England* (London: Pimlico, 1992), 342–70.

40. Ted Tunnell, *Crucible of Reconstruction: War, Radicalism, and Race in Louisiana, 1862–1877* (Baton Rouge: Louisiana University Press, 1982); David Barnes, *The Draft Riots in New York, July, 1863* (New York: Baker and Godwin, 1863); *United States v. Cruikshank*, 92 U.S. 542 (1876).

41. Gilje, *Road to Mobocracy*; Michael Feldberg, *The Philadelphia Riots of 1844: A Study of Ethnic Conflict* (Westport, Conn.: Greenwood Press, 1975); Michael Feldberg, *The Turbulent Era: Riot and Disorder in Jacksonian America* (New York: Oxford University Press, 1980); Sean Wilentz, *Chants Democratic: New York City and the Rise of the American Working Class, 1788–1850* (New York: Oxford University Press, 1984); William Ivy Hair, *Carnival of Fury: Robert Charles and the New Orleans Race Riot of 1900* (Baton Rouge: Louisiana University Press, 1976).

42. Robert V. Bruce, *1877: Year of Violence* (Indianapolis: Bobbs-Merrill, 1959); William M. Tuttle, Jr., *Race Riot: Chicago in the Red Summer of 1919* (New York: Atheneum, 1984).

43. Carl Bakal, *The Right to Bear Arms* (New York: McGraw-Hill, 1966), 354–55.

44. *Atlanta Constitution*, 18 June 1992.

45. Sharon Block, "Where Have All the Women Gone? Presentations of Rape in Early America" (paper delivered at the Berkshire Conference on the History of Women, 1996; courtesy of the author); Elizabeth Pleck, *Domestic Tyranny: The Making of American Social Policy against Family Violence from Colonial Times to the Present* (New York: Oxford University Press, 1987); Mary E. Odem and Jody Clay-Warner, eds., *Confronting Rape and Sexual Assault* (Wilmington, Del.: Scholarly Resources, 1998).

46. Herbert Aptheker, *American Negro Slave Revolts* (New York: International, 1993); Douglas R. Egerton, *Gabriel's Rebellion: The Virginia Slave Conspiracies of 1800 and 1802* (Chapel Hill: University of North Carolina Press, 1993); W. M. Frohock, *The Novel of Violence in America* (Dallas: SMU Press, 1950); Louise Y. Gossett, *Violence in Recent Southern Fiction* (Durham: Duke University Press, 1965); Richard Slotkin, *Gunfighter Nation: The Myth of the Frontier in Twentieth-Century America* (New York: Atheneum, 1992).

John Underhill brought the tactics of surrounding and destroying an enemy Indian village, first used against the Pequots, to Kieft's War. But, without the help of Indian allies, Dutch efforts to intimidate their enemies into submission by massacre failed. Used by permission of Grenville Kane Collection, Department of Rare Books and Special Collections, Princeton University Library.

Chapter One

Kieft's War and the Cultures of Violence in Colonial America

Evan Haefeli

Kieft's War (1640–1645) is one of the most notorious colonial American Indian Wars. It is not as famous as others, like the Pequot War or King Philip's War, because it involved the Dutch rather than the English. It was not the first nor the bloodiest of the colonial Indian wars. The English in Virginia had been fighting the Powhatans for decades, New Englanders won the Pequot War three years before trouble began at New Amsterdam, and King Philip's War was more destructive than Kieft's.[1] However, the very "Dutchness" of Kieft's War has ensured that it is remembered as particularly violent. Dutch politics made Kieft's War the only Indian war in colonial American history that a number of colonists openly opposed. Several of them wrote extremely graphic accounts of the war's violence. Their accounts provide a rare opportunity to explore how Indians and European colonists used and interpreted acts of violence, and to rethink the significance of violence in the history of colonial America.

Willem Kieft was the son of a Dutch merchant with important ties to the West India Company. New Netherland was a small part of the West India Company's commercial empire, which included Brazil, West Africa, and parts of the Caribbean, all of them more valuable colonies than New Netherland. When the English seized the colony in 1664, renaming it New York, the West India Company accepted this transfer of authority in exchange for the more profitable Surinam.[2] Kieft, the fifth director of New Netherland, ruled for nine years (1638–1647). He is remembered mostly for the war against the Indians, which, thanks to the acrimonious politics of New Netherland, has left him with the most unsavory reputation of any governor in colonial North America.[3]

The war's destructiveness made Kieft many enemies among his fellow colonists. He himself died in a shipwreck on his way back to Amsterdam to clear his name. His political enemies survived and published. Most of what we know about the man and the war named after him is colored by their hostile views. This intense political conflict shaped the very nature of the sources available to reconstruct the war. Although there are several narratives of the conflict, none describes it in its entirety. Many of the details have to be pieced together from accusations made in courts during the war and legal suits conducted by the West

India Company in the years after the war. The most complete account is the *Journal of New Netherland*, written if not by Kieft himself, then by one of his allies, for it clearly takes the director's point of view and justifies his controversial actions. It was never published and lay forgotten in a Dutch archive until an American scholar discovered it in the nineteenth century.[4]

Kieft's opponents recorded their dissent in two published accounts. The most important was David de Vries's book, *Short Historical and Journal Notes of various Voyages performed in the Four Quarters of the Globe*.[5] A well-traveled man, De Vries had sailed, traded, and fought in the Mediterranean, Indonesia, India, the Caribbean, and Newfoundland before coming to New Netherland to establish his own plantation. His many varied experiences gave him a sense of perspective that Kieft did not have. De Vries believed all along that political tactfulness, resting on a degree of cultural respect, could have prevented a war. After his property was destroyed in the war's early years, De Vries returned to Holland and so missed most of the war. The last account, a pamphlet, is also of uncertain authorship. The two possible authors are Cornelis Melijn and Joachim Pietersz Kuyter, who both suffered heavy losses in the war.[6] The pamphlet, entitled "Broad Advice, or Dialogue About the Trade of the West India Company," gives a scathing account of the final and bloodiest years of war. Melijn and Kuyter had stayed until the war's end, returning on the same ship as Kieft because Peter Stuyvesant, who replaced Kieft as director-general, had banished them from New Netherland. They survived the shipwreck and "Broad Advice" was published in Antwerp in 1649.[7]

The Dutch accounts contain vivid depictions of violence, but we should not accept their interpretations of its significance at face value. Violence is not just a random or inhuman act. It can also be a vivid expression of cultural values, part of a system that is conditioned by a group's history, culture, and social structure. The violence discussed here is physical, intended to hurt, maim, or kill another person. By assessing violence within its context of meaning and practice, either European or Native American, the gripping details provided by the Dutch can offer new insights on the complex meeting of Europe and the Americas.

Native American Violence

Violence began in July 1640, Kieft's second year in the colony. Economics was the proximate cause of this conflict. Trade, whether in furs, maize, or wampum, was the crucial tie that bound together the Indians and colonists around New Amsterdam. With Kieft's arrival in 1638, several trends began that would transform Indian-Dutch relations. Most pressing of all was a wave of immigration that brought in hundreds of colonists, nearly doubling the Dutch population in the first five years of Kieft's rule. The colonists spread out from New Amsterdam, establishing farms in what is now New Jersey, the Bronx, Westchester, Long Island, and Staten Island. Then in 1639, the West India Company ended its monopoly of the fur trade and threw it open to all colonists. At the same time, the coastal fur trade slowed to a trickle as Indian hunters depleted the local beaver populations. Without furs, the Indians had only maize and land to trade with the colonists. As the farms spread, taking over Indian farmland, they threatened to displace the maize trade. All of these tensions lay behind the war; they did not, in and of themselves, cause it. It was the effort by both sides to resolve the growing problems through the use of violence, and the resulting clash of cultures of violence, that turned a tense situation into an explosive one.[8]

Indian anger over the decline of the fur trade sparked the first confrontation. A group of Raritans, who lived in what is now northern New Jersey, boarded a Dutch yacht sent to trade with them and one angrily slapped its skipper in the face with a bunch of squirrel skins. The Dutch feared for their lives but, thanks to a sudden hailstorm, were able to escape before anyone was hurt. Then word reached Kieft that Raritans had killed some pigs on Staten Island. He determined to assert his authority with a display of power. He sent the colony's secretary, Cornelis van Tienhoven, who spoke the local Indian language,[9] with a company of soldiers and sailors to "attack them, to cut down their corn and to make as many prisoners as they can, unless they willingly come to an agreement and make reparation." When Van Tienhoven failed to get the necessary satisfaction, the soldiers, who "wished to kill and plunder" attacked the Raritans, killing three or four and capturing their sachem's brother.[10]

In the boat on the way back to New Amsterdam, a Dutch colonist tortured the captive "in his private parts with a piece of split wood." De Vries was outraged by this deed, which for him carried a political message. He called it an act of "tyranny" such as "were perpetrated by the servants of the Company" and which "were far from making friends with the inhabitants." The torture was an excessive use of violence in his eyes, and he feared it would cause even more trouble than the actual murders. The man survived, however, and Van Tienhoven ransomed him for a substantial amount of wampum in the hopes that he would persuade his sachem brother to make an official peace with the Dutch.[11]

For almost a year there was no more violence. Then, in June 1641, Raritans killed four of De Vries's servants at his new farm on Staten Island. They burned the farm and another as well. After the attack, an Indian who worked for the Dutch passed on a message from the Raritans that "we [the Dutch] would now come to fight them on account of our men; that we had before come and treated them badly on account of the swine." The Raritans asserted that West India Company men had killed the pigs and falsely accused them of the crime. It seems that the Raritans disagreed with De Vries's interpretation of the torture's significance. It was not the torture but the message that a pig's life was as significant as a Raritan's that angered them. The Raritans had now set things right by killing one Dutch man for every Raritan the Dutch had killed.[12]

Kieft abandoned his initial tactic of direct intimidation and turned to his Indian allies for help. He put out a bounty on the Raritans: ten fathoms of wampum for a head, twenty if they brought in alive "any of the Indians who have most barbarously murdered our people." Stating his reasons for the act, Kieft betrayed an appreciation of the vulnerable Dutch position. He noted that the "planters and farmers and other remote settlers stand in great danger of life and property, which we under the circumstances, on account of the density of the forest and the small number of men, cannot prevent." Given this situation, he concluded that "it was most expedient and advisable to induce the Indians, our allies hereabout, to take up arms, in order thus to cut off stray parties who must pass through their territory, so that they cannot reach our farms and plantations without peril or at least without being discovered." The bounties were designed "to encourage them" to fight the Raritans.[13]

Kieft's strategy worked. No further attacks on colonists were reported. Instead, the allies responded and quelled the conflict in their own manner. In November, De Vries watched as Pacham, a sachem of the Tankitekes who had good relations with Kieft, walked into Fort Amsterdam "in great triumph, bringing a dead hand hanging on a stick, and saying that it was the hand of the chief who had killed or shot with arrows our men on Staten Island, and that he had taken revenge for our sake, because he loved the Swannekens (as they call the Dutch), who were his best friends." That summer Indians from Long Island had also "voluntary killed some of the Raritans." Later that year the Raritans made peace with the Dutch. Though the Raritans had ended their battle with the Dutch, the war soon continued with new enemies.[14]

Kieft has gained the reputation in American history of beginning the practice of offering scalp bounties. The idea that by paying for enemy scalps Europeans had not only encouraged Indians to scalp but had even taught them to scalp in the first place goes back at least to around 1800. But in fact, scalping has ancient roots in Native America.[15] Kieft's bounty was probably inspired by the Pequot War, when New England's Indian allies had offered the English settlers Pequot scalps, heads, and hands as proof of their allegiance. By offering the bounty, Kieft was not distorting the Indians' value system, only trying to direct it in his own interest.[16]

When Pacham walked into New Amsterdam with the Raritan hand dangling on a pole, he was acting in accordance with customs at whose antiquity we can only guess. Throughout colonial America, colonists observed Indians hanging scalps on poles "in the form of Guidons" and carrying them back from the battlefield to their village "like trophies," in the words of one Jesuit missionary. The poles were used to carry the scalps, or in this case the hand, of their enemies back to the village. There the poles were planted in front of their homes or in the center of the village—like "standards," in the words of another Jesuit missionary.[17]

Pacham had not killed the Raritan for the bounty. As his speech makes clear, he did it to keep the peace and to affirm his alliance with the Dutch. He brought in the hand to stop the cycle of vengeance between the Dutch and Raritans. The bounty Kieft gave him can easily be seen as a gift, an essential token of alliance in Native American diplomacy. However Kieft may have understood the bounties, the Indians accepted them as their due. Without some sort of gift as a concrete sign of appreciation, Pacham would have felt snubbed. Indeed, only an enemy did not offer gifts. Thus the Raritan conflict had been resolved largely on

Native American terms, not Kieft's. The scalp bounty allowed Indian sachems to resolve the conflict within their own culture of violence while reinforcing their troubled alliance with the Dutch.[18]

The politics of Amerindian wars were inseparable from Amerindian domestic politics. Behind the killing by men lay the pleas of grieving women. When someone died, Native Americans expected the mourners, especially the female relatives, to fall into a deep depression. Something had to replace their loss. Gifts sometimes sufficed. At other times only revenge on their people's enemies, and there was always someone somewhere who counted as an enemy, would do. Women would urge their male relatives, especially young men, to attack their enemies and bring back either a captive or a scalp to fill the void they were experiencing. Anthropologists and historians have called this system of warfare "mourning wars," because they were at least ostensibly fought to avenge the death of a relative. Bringing back a live captive was a more heroic, because more difficult, deed than bringing back a scalp, but to bring back a scalp (or, at times, a head or hand) was a tremendous achievement. It would be proudly displayed in the village, a visible sign of justice done.[19]

Captives provided an immediate sense of justice. The women who had urged their men to go to war decided the fate of captives. There were two basic options. A captive could be instantly adopted into the woman's family to fill the place of the one who had died, being treated as part of the family and, it was expected, assimilating himself or herself to the ways and loyalties of the newfound family. Adoption was most often the fate of captive women and children. Captured warriors, on the other hand, were rarer and offered a chance for the entire village, and especially the family of mourners, personally to avenge themselves and soothe their grief by torturing the man to death. Occasionally women, and even children, met a similar fate. Not all warriors were killed; some were adopted. But in general, torturing an enemy warrior to death, and then sometimes even cannibalizing parts of the body, was a vital privilege of community life. Warriors knew that such a fate awaited them if captured. They were expected to die heroically, singing, dancing, and defying their tormentors.[20]

Only certain captives, apparently those who had died a virtuous death, were cannibalized, and then only certain parts were eaten. Native Americans did not go to war to feed themselves on the bodies of their enemies.[21] They did, however, talk about "eating" their enemies. One Jesuit complained of his Montagnais protégés' inclination to "speak with us of the flesh of an Iroquois, and praise its good qualities in the same terms as they would praise the flesh of a deer or a moose."[22] Eating was a metaphor for victory—consumption as the ultimate form of conquest and assimilation. The symbolic nature of cannibalism is reinforced by the fact that the parts of the body that were eaten were those with the least meat—especially the feet and hands.

Scholarly discussions of Native American warfare have yet to explore the importance of taking hands. Europeans were struck by the scalps, which they likened to guidons and standards, and scalps became the object of colonial bounties and scholarly study. But in the eastern woodlands at least, hands clearly had a special significance. If one looks at accounts from New France and New England as well, it is striking how regularly they crop up. New Netherlanders were not the only ones to have hands presented to them. Up in Canada, some Hurons tossed the hand of an Iroquois captive they had just tortured to death into the cabin where Jesuit missionaries sat, doing their best to stay away from the ritual violence of the Hurons. The Jesuits took the act as a deliberate affront to their sensibilities because the Hurons knew "the displeasure we feel at these cruelties, and particularly at their inhumanity in eating the bodies of these poor victims at their death." However, they may have been more on the mark when they speculated that the hand was thrown to them "as if giving us our share of the feast." The gesture was probably an effort on the part of the Hurons to get the Jesuits to do what all good Hurons did—feast on the flesh of their enemies. Europeans were horrified that torturing and feasting involved the whole community. After witnessing a village of Montagnais torture an Iroquois captive to death, one Frenchman watched with disgust as some Montagnais children sucked on the Iroquois's finger.[23]

The Dutch personally experienced the eastern woodlands' traditions regarding hands early on. During the Mahican-Mohawk war of the 1620s, several Dutchmen from Fort Orange joined a Mahican war party. Mohawks ambushed the party and killed several of the Dutch. They then "carried a [Dutch] leg and an arm home to be divided among their families, as a sign that they had conquered their enemies." How ancient the practice of taking hands was is unknown, though it may well be as old as scalping. Some of the most compelling artifacts from the precolonial era are Hopewellian (c. 100 B.C.–A.D. 400) ornaments in the shape of hands with long, slim fingers, indicating that hands had held a special ritual significance in the eastern woodlands for many centuries. After Kieft's War, hands rarely emerge again in historical records, though Indians evidently continued to take them. At the end of the seventeenth century, an English officer was shocked to see a French hand surface in a pot of broth some Mohawk warriors offered to share with him.[24]

Gruesome as the Native American culture of violence seemed to most colonists, and to us today, it was far less bloody than the European system, as the colonists themselves recognized. Captain John Mason, who, along with Captain John Underhill, led the slaughter of hundreds of Pequot men, women, and children in 1637, scoffed that "their feeble Manner . . . did hardly deserve the name of fighting." When, toward the end of Kieft's War, some Indians tried to defend their village by scattering in small groups rather than standing up and fighting the Dutch head on, Kieft thought that they "demeaned themselves as soldiers" by doing so. The minister Roger Williams, on the other hand, admired that "their Warres are farre lesse bloudy, and devouring then the cruel Warres of Europe."[25] The conflict with the Raritans bears him out. Some Raritans were killed, but only some. The killing of an individual, friend or foe, was a very significant event in the Native American culture of violence. The few Raritan deaths at the hands of other Indians restored peace. Pacham and his allies were acting according to the rules of a very old, and very effective, system. The problems came when Kieft abandoned his policy of offering bounties, which fit so well into this system, and tried to enforce justice himself, with a display of force he meant to be overwhelming.

Murder and Justice

The war's worst killing began with a clash of methods for dealing with murder. North of New Amsterdam, in the area of present-day Bronx and Westchester Counties, lived the Wecquaesgeeks. A road led from their lands, running the length of Manhattan Island to New Amsterdam at its tip. An elderly Dutch man named Claes Swits, living along that road, took advantage of his location to trade occasionally with the Indians. In August 1641, an unnamed Wecquaesgeek came to him and asked to trade. When Swits bent over his chest to take out some goods, the Wecquaesgeek killed him with a quick ax blow, plundered his house, and (possibly) made off with his scalp. The Dutch were shocked, especially because the two had known each other; the Wecquaesgeek had worked a while for Swits's son. Kieft sent an envoy to demand that the killer be turned over. The Wecquaesgeeks refused. One sachem said "he was sorry that twenty Christians had not been murdered" and explained that the man had taken legitimate and necessary revenge for his uncle, who had been killed twenty-one years earlier by three Dutch servants.[26]

Kieft immediately called a council of the colony's twelve leading citizens. Asking "whether it is not just to punish the barbarous murder," he sought their consent to "destroy the entire village to which he belongs" if he was not turned over for Dutch justice.[27] He then asked who should go after the Indians and when. The council agreed that the Wecquaesgeek should be punished but was divided over the advisability of attacking the village right away. The consensus was to wait, at least until the maize trading season was over. De Vries strongly opposed violent retribution and insisted (correctly) that the West India Company did not want an Indian war started in New Netherland. Kieft waited, reluctantly.[28]

Kieft called another council in the fall and yet another in January. The January council finally agreed that it was time for an expedition, insisting that Kieft lead it.[29] But Kieft notoriously never left the safety of New Amsterdam, and when the expedition set out in March 1642, he stayed behind in the fort. An ensign assisted by a guide led eighty men through the night toward the village. Dutch spies declared that the Wecquaesgeeks suspected nothing. The stage seemed set for a decisive Dutch blow. But the Dutchmen lost their way. Fuming and frustrated after a night of wandering about the woods, they returned to New Amsterdam without having seen or killed a single Wecquaesgeek. Diplomatically, however, the expedition was a success. The Wecquaesgeeks saw by the tracks how close the danger had come to them. They asked the Dutch for peace, which Van Tienhoven negotiated with them on March 28, "on condition that they should either deliver up the murderer or inflict justice themselves." The Wecquaesgeeks agreed but, according to Kieft, "without any result." The killer was not delivered up. For Kieft and several of the prominent colonists, the Wecquaesgeeks' failure to submit to Dutch law invalidated the peace. The Wecquaesgeeks, however, were quite satisfied with it. Their trust in the Dutch would soon have tragic consequences.[30]

The rest of 1642 proved peaceful, almost. A Hackensack killed a Dutchman as he worked on the roof of a farm at Newark Bay. Both the Hackensacks and Kieft had warned colonists not to settle there. De Vries reported he had met a drunk Hackensack only shortly before the murder. The man had complained to De Vries that the Dutchman who had given him the brandy had stolen his beaver coat when he was drunk. He told De Vries that "he would go home and get his bow and arrows, and would kill the villainous Swannekens Dutch who had stolen his goods." De Vries told him "he must not do so," but did nothing to stop him. Soon thereafter some Hackensack sachems came to tell him of the murder.[31]

De Vries set the murder within the context of the worsening trade relations between the colonists and the Indians to emphasize his point that the Indians were only reacting to mistreatment by the Dutch. Kuyter offered another version of the story, saying that a colonist had taunted the drunken Indian, who "was not considered very sensible by the Indians themselves," into shooting his bow. The Indian aimed at the man on the roof and killed him. For his part, Kieft detected a vast conspiracy against the Dutch. He noted that only a little while before the Hackensack murder, Miantonimo, the sachem of the Narragansetts, "came here with one hundred men, passing through all the Indian villages soliciting them to a general war against both the English and the Dutch." As a result "some of the neighboring Indians attempted to set our powder on fire and to poison the Director or to inchant him by their devilry, as their ill will was afterwards made manifest as well in fact as by report." Around the same time, some Hackensacks killed an English servant "who was in their village." Kieft's account is the only one to note this murder, and there is no further discussion of how it was handled, though it clearly fed his growing feeling of paranoia.[32]

The Hackensack sachems were willing to resolve the murder of the Dutchman. Unlike the Wecquaesgeek killing, the Hackensack murder was not justified as an act of vengeance and, according to Native American justice, satisfaction had to be given or the victim's relatives could legitimately take revenge on the Hackensacks. The Hackensack sachems had immediately informed De Vries of the killing and offered to "give one or two hundred fathom of zeewan [wampum] to the widow if thereby they would be at peace." De Vries persuaded them to accompany him to Kieft, whom they did not trust enough to visit on their own. Kieft's response was to demand that the killer "be brought to him." The Hackensacks replied they could not, since he had run away to another tribe, and again insisted on recompensing the dead man's kin for the loss. As De Vries put it, "[T]hey desired in a friendly way to make the widow contented, and to pay for the man's death with zeewan, which is their money; it being a custom with them, if any misfortune befell them, to reconcile the parties with money."[33]

The sachems blamed the murder on alcohol and on the Dutch who sold it to them. They reminded Kieft that Dutchmen got into deadly knife fights when drunk.[34] Believing alcohol was the real cause of the trouble, they asked that the liquor trade be stopped. Kieft persisted in demanding that the killer be turned over. De Vries noted that the sachems "had some fear that the governor would detain them" in the fort and so eventually answered that "they would do their best" to get the killer and bring him to the governor. Kieft let them go. On their way back, the sachems informed De Vries that they could not deliver up the killer because he was a sachem's son.[35]

For several months afterward, a delicate peace prevailed. The sachems were willing to consider the awkward balance of power a friendly peace, and so were most of the Dutch. As De Vries noted after the conference with the Hackensack sachems, "[T]hus the matter passed off." But Kieft rankled at the outstanding affronts to his authority. When fate gave him an opportunity to strike, he did not hesitate to seize it.[36]

Honor and Authority

Perhaps the most tragic aspect of the war was the sachems' effort to preserve both their and Kieft's honor in the midst of all the misunderstandings. Kieft complained that the Indians always laughed at him. His account notes that the "murderers were frequently demanded, either living or dead, even with a promise of reward," but the sachems "always returned a scoffing answer laughing at us." The Dutch, like all Europeans of the time, were extremely sensitive about their honor. Slights and insults were part of community politics and were recognized as being potentially damaging enough to the welfare of the person attacked that slander cases took up a considerable amount of seventeenth-century court business. Throughout his rule, but especially with the advent of war, Kieft was surrounded by a torrent of slander suits, rumors, and insulting insinuations. The insults had powerful political implications for Kieft because, as historian Willem Frijhoff points out, they "touched on his honor—and without honor it was impossible to exercise authority in public life."[37]

Fiercely determined to assert an authoritative presence in the colony, Kieft could not abide the apparent mockery of his authority expressed in the Indians' laughter. The "commonalty [was] very much displeased with the Director," according to Kieft, "upbraided him for conniving with the Indians, and declared that an attempt was making to sell Christian blood."[38] Kieft felt that his honor in the Dutch community and his reputation among the Indians were at stake. Eager to demonstrate that his demands were not to be thwarted or brushed aside, he took advantage of the first possible opportunity to wreak vengeance on those who had insulted him. And so the war can be said to have begun as a laughing matter.

Why did American Indians laugh when there was nothing funny going on? Colonists occasionally noted that Indians laughed at odd times. Generally, they assumed Indians had a strange sense of humor or, as Kieft did, that they were particularly arrogant people. Only rarely did colonists demonstrate an awareness that laughter and smiles could be an expression of something other than humor. An English evangelist trying to convert Indians in South Carolina wrote in frustration that they were "wholy addicted to their own barbarous and Sloathful Customs and will only give a laugh w[he]n pleased or a grin w[he]n displeas'd for an Answer."[39] In her research on the Ojibwa, Mary Black-Rogers has noted, "Occasions for Ojibwa laughter are not always humorous ones, though usually charged." Laughter "could mean, among other things, that everything had gone wrong, that a particularly gruesome scene in a cannibal story has been told, or that elders are reacting to children's trial-and-error education (they teach by laughing at errors)." The sachems' laughter was not defiance. It was an effort to show Kieft that he was behaving badly.[40]

Kieft's demands that the sachems turn over one of their own people to Dutch justice could never be met. Unlike Kieft, the sachems did not have coercive power over their people. Turning a member of their village over to certain death would have brought the vengeance of the killer's family on the sachems' heads. It would be akin to betraying them to the enemy. By refusing to accept gifts as atonement for the killings, or to even offer gifts in exchange for the man they requested, Kieft was acting as an enemy. The sachems were in a truly awkward position. Unable to get Kieft to stop behaving as an enemy but unwilling to stop being allies of the Dutch, the sachems laughed, hoping the conflicting demands could be shrugged off before they became dangerous. Perhaps, like children, the Dutch would realize that they were doing the wrong thing.

Massacre

The equilibrium around New Amsterdam was suddenly broken in February 1643. Mahicans, who lived near the Dutch post of Fort Orange (now Albany), armed with guns obtained in trade, attacked a Wecquaesgeek village, killing some men and capturing a number of women and children.[41] Outfought by the gun-toting Mahicans, the Wecquaesgeeks fled to the Dutch for sanctuary. Putting themselves under Dutch protection, they established two camps, one across the Hudson from New Amsterdam at Pavonia (present Jersey City) and another just above New Amsterdam at Curler's Hook (now the lower East Side of Manhattan). To the Wecquaesgeeks' sorrow, the Dutch would prove to be far more treacherous than the Mahicans.

The Dutch of New Amsterdam gathered in their homes and taverns, debating what to do about the sudden refugee problem. On February 24, 1643, three colonists, Marijn Adriaensen, Jan Jansen Damen, and Abraham Planck, presented Kieft with a petition "to attack the Indians as enemies" because God had "delivered them into our hands." The petition protested that action was necessary because "the reputation which our nation hath in other countries" had been diminished by the sachems' refusal to "deliver the murderer into our hands, (either dead or alive)." De Vries, who believed Kieft had instigated the petition, declared that Kieft boasted "he had a mind to wipe the mouths of the savages" and that the petition urged him "to begin this work."[42]

The next day Kieft sent Van Tienhoven and a corporal over to Pavonia to scout out the Indian camp. Kieft authorized a group of colonists under Marijn Adriaensen to attack the camp at Curler's Hook and ordered a company of soldiers under Sergeant Rodolff to attack the Indians at Pavonia that night. The attacks were murderously successful: approximately eighty Indians at Pavonia and some forty at Curler's Hook were killed, another thirty were taken prisoner. The Indians did not resist. Instead, thinking they had been ambushed by the Mahicans again, they scattered. Some even ran to the Dutch for help. De Vries, waiting out the night inside Fort Amsterdam, saw two Indian neighbors of his, a man and his wife, arrive. They had fled in a small boat from Pavonia, where, they thought, the "Indians from Fort Orange had surprised them." De Vries painfully explained that it was not the Mahicans but the Dutch who had attacked them. With his help, the couple immediately fled "to the woods." With bitter sarcasm, De Vries watched the soldiers return the next day, acting as if "they had done a deed of Roman valor, in murdering so many in their sleep." The only Dutch casualties were a man and woman killed when they went with a group of Englishmen to plunder the Indians' camp that morning.[43]

European Violence

In Europe, violence had long been the prerogative of soldiers and rulers. Since the late Middle Ages, European governments had worked to take the power to enforce law, order, and vengeance away from families and locate it within courts. Popular culture, the church, and governments placed limits on the use of violence through codes of conduct and rules of law, but it was not easy to enforce these standards of behavior, and even when they were respected they permitted a great deal of violence and destruction. The restraints on violence did little to prevent the increase in the size and impact of war in the sixteenth and seventeenth centuries.[44] Because the growing power of states was most palpable in their increasing control over and use of violence, writings about violence were often linked to political propaganda. The Dutch pioneered the art of wartime propaganda during their revolt against Spain. In words and pictures they highlighted and exaggerated Spanish outrages, stressing that the Spanish abuse of violence revealed the injustice of their rule over the Dutch. Kieft's enemies applied this experience to their accounts of Kieft's War.[45]

The attack on Pavonia provided anti-Kieft writers with their greatest propaganda coup. Kuyter worked to discredit Kieft's directorship by portraying, in lurid and poignant detail, the soldiers under Kieft's command as violating all the norms of legitimate violence, and doing so with Kieft's approval. De Vries reproduced Kuyter's lurid and poignant description of the massacre in his *Short History*, making it the only eyewitness account available. Instead of attacking adult warriors, the Dutch soldiers went after women, children, and the elderly; and instead of just killing them, they mutilated them horribly, causing terrible suffering. The soldiers took "young children . . . from their mothers' breasts," then cut them "to pieces in sight of the parents." The pieces they threw "into the fire and into the water." Suckling babes they "bound to wooden boards, and cut, stuck, or bored through, and miserably massacred, so that a heart of stone would have been softened." Some children "were thrown into the river, and when the fathers and mothers endeavored to rescue them, the soldiers would not let them come ashore again, but caused both old and young to be drowned." The horrors of the mutilation were perhaps even worse than the outright killing. With shock and outrage, Kuyter reports that Indians "came running past our people living on the farms, with their hands cut off; others had their legs cut off. Some carried their bowels in their arms; others had such horrible cuts, hacks, and wounds, that the like can never have happened elsewhere." Finally, the soldiers showed no mercy, even after the battle. When the survivors, children and "old, decrepid people . . . came forth in the morning to beg a piece of bread and to warm themselves against the cold, . . . [they] were murdered in cold blood, and pushed to the water or into the fire."[46]

Kuyter noted that the colonists had surprised the Indians at Curler's Hook "in their sleep in the same manner," and "massacred" them "in the same way," but his real outrage was directed at the soldiers. The soldiers were certainly a violent lot, but their status as employees of the West India Company made them the preferred target of propaganda. The West India Company would not have to answer for the actions of the colonists in the same way as those of the soldiers. Kuyter recounted an incident after the massacre, when a skipper tried to save an Indian boy by wrapping him in a sailcloth to hide him from the soldiers he was ferrying back to New Amsterdam. There he planned to turn the "little boy" over to Cornelis Melijn. But "the child, through cold and hunger, made himself heard by the soldiers" and the "German tigers"—for many of the soldiers were German and not Dutch—"dragged him from under the sail in spite of the skipper, who could not, alone, save him against eighteen, cut him in two, and threw the pieces overboard." Kieft was aware of the standards of conduct that should be observed in even the most ruthless engagements. Sergeant Rodolff's orders had been "to destroy all the Indians encamped behind Jan Evertsen's, but to spare the women and children as much as possible, endeavoring to capture the same." However Adriaensen and the other colonists had merely been empowered "to act towards" the Indians "as they shall deem proper according to the circumstances." Evidently Kieft, like Kuyter, was more concerned with the soldiers' savagery than the colonists'. Nonetheless, in both instances the Dutch killed far more Indians than they captured, hoping, it seems, to annihilate Indian resistance to Dutch expansion.[47]

Ruthless as the attacks were, they were not random. Two days after the massacre, some colonists on Long Island presented Kieft with another warlike petition. Writing that the Indians were preparing "for hostilities," the colonists requested permission to "ruin and conquer" the Indians "from time to time, unto the establishment of our common peace and welfare, so that at once the previous much wished for peace of this place, may be and remain permanent." Kieft rejected the petition, saying the Long Island Indians "have not given us hitherto any provocation, and . . . it would draw down an unrighteous war on our heads." Despite Kieft's ruling, some of the colonists snuck into an Indian village to steal their corn. The Indians caught them and drove them away, but three Indians were shot and killed by the colonists. In retaliation, the Indians burned two farms.[48] The war now spread to Long Island as well.

Kieft had genuinely expected that his nighttime ambush would encourage the obstinate Wecquaesgeeks and Hackensacks to submit to his authority and recognize the supremacy of Dutch justice. In the days afterward, as Dutch farms went up in flames and colonists were ambushed by his vengeful victims, he wondered aloud to De Vries "that no Indians came to the fort." De Vries, who had predicted the conflagration and had now lost his other farmstead to an Indian attack, angrily replied, "[W]hy should the Indians come here where you have so treated them?" Roger Williams was in New Amsterdam waiting for a ship to England when Kieft launched his double ambush. Williams wrote of witnessing the "breaking forth of that Indian war, which the Dutch begun, upon the slaughter of some Dutch by the Indians." He noted that they expected "to finish it in a few days" but were wrong. Before he left "their boweries were in flames; Dutch and English were slain. Mine eyes saw their flames at their towns, and their flights and hurries of men, women and children, the present removal of all that could for Holland." In Kieft's words the rest of the winter was "passed away" in "confusion mingled with great terror."[49]

Kieft's authority crumbled. The destruction his ambush had caused almost cost him his life. A Long Island colonist who had lost his house angrily railed against Marijn Adriaensen, blaming him for the chaos. Adriaensen, one of the three petition signers who had encouraged Kieft's midnight massacre, and the leader of the attack on Curler's Hook and two subsequent expeditions against the Indians, believed Kieft had singled him out as a scapegoat for the colony's woes. In a fury, he burst into Kieft's quarters in the fort with his pistol and sword. Only the fast action of another colonist prevented Kieft's assassination. Adriaensen was seized and imprisoned. Shortly afterward his servant shot at Kieft, who barely managed to duck back into his quarters in time. The sentry on duty shot the servant dead. Adriaensen was sent back to Holland as a prisoner. His servant's head was displayed on the gallows as a warning against future assassination attempts. The war's devastation had turned Dutch against Dutch.[50]

Indian Peace

It was the sachems who brought the violence to a halt. In March 1643, only weeks after they had been attacked by the corn thieves, the Canarsees on Long Island contacted the Dutch under "a small white flag." With De Vries's mediation, their sachem Penhawitz concluded a peace with the Dutch. A month later, toward the end of April, with Penhawitz's mediation, the Hackensack sachem Oratamin concluded a peace on behalf of his people, the Tappans, and the Wecquaesgeeks. The peace was celebrated in New Amsterdam with gun salutes. Ominously, one of the cannon exploded, severely wounding the gunner. Kieft was dubious about the peace's durability. The colonists had grown restless, he noted, because the spring was the season for "driving out the cattle; this obliged many to desire peace. On the other hand the Indians, seeing that it was time to plant maize, were not less solicitous for peace." The peace, he felt, was the result more "of the importunity of some than because it was generally expected that it would be durable."[51]

The sachems had their own interpretation of the fragility of the peace. They blamed Kieft's failure to repair properly the damage his killing had done to Indian social life. At the signing of the peace treaties, Kieft made a gesture to indigenous diplomacy and gave the sachems some presents, but not enough. De Vries noted right away that the sachems "were not well content with them." They explained to De Vries that Kieft "could have made it, by his presents, that as long as he lived the massacre would never again be spoken of; but now it might fall out that the infant upon the small board would remember it."[52]

Too many people had been killed in the massacres for Kieft's meager presents to satisfy the sachems. A few months after the peace conference a worried sachem explained to De Vries that "many of the Indian youths . . . were constantly wishing for a war against us, as one had lost his father, another his mother, a third his uncle, and also their friends, and that the presents or recompense were not worth taking up." The man pointed out that "he would much rather have made presents out of his own purse to quiet" the angry young men "but he could no longer keep them still." The sachems wanted to keep the peace, but their authority rested on their ability to supply their people with gifts. Without them, those who had lost kin to the violence could turn to their only other option: revenge.[53]

Kieft, who could arrest Adriaensen and have his servant executed for trying to kill him, could not understand the nature of the sachems' authority. He presumed that authority entitled its bearer to the power of life and death over one's people. After a sachem explained to him the crucial role of gifts in preventing young men from seeking vengeance, Kieft retorted that "he was a chief of the Indians and must kill these young madcaps who wished to engage in a war." Kieft, misunderstanding how his bounties against the Raritans had fit into the Native American culture of violence, offered the sachem "two hundred fathoms of zeewan" to execute the untractable warriors. De Vries "laughed within myself," at Kieft's stupidity in thinking "that the Indian should kill his friends for two hundred fathoms of *zeewan*—that is eight hundred guilders—to gratify us." He knew that they did not hesitate to kill one another "when they are at enmity with each other, but not at the will of foreigners." The sachem replied that he could not kill the malcontents; there were too many. He repeated that had Kieft "paid richly for the murder, it would have been entirely forgotten." Though he promised to "do his best" to keep the young men quiet, he doubted it would work, "for they were continually calling for vengeance." Several months later they began taking it.[54]

Total War

The deadliest phase of the war began in August 1643 when the previously uninvolved Wappingers, who lived along the Hudson River, attacked a Dutch trading boat coming downriver from Fort Orange. They killed the two men in it and made off with four hundred beaverskins. Exactly why the Wappingers launched the attack is unclear. Pacham, Kieft's ally in the Raritan War, had been going "through all the villages urging the Indians to a general massacre," according to Kieft. Probably they, like the Raritans, were upset with their loss of power as the fur trade declined. The Wappingers' actions were probably linked to some sort of growing alliance, for "others" soon joined them in attacks on two more boats. A fourth boat drove off the Indian attackers, killing six. In all, nine colonists, including two women, were killed. Another woman and two children were taken prisoner.[55]

Then, in September, the young men who had been disappointed by Kieft's meager presents began to take the vengeance due them. English settlers on Wecquaesgeek and Tankiteke lands, including Anne Hutchinson and other religious refugees from Massachusetts, were killed by Indians who carried a few of the women and children away as prisoners. More farms were attacked and destroyed. Indians still allied to the Dutch informed Kieft that those who now fought him were "in no way to be pacified . . . until the Director is removed."[56]

New Netherland could not fight the war Kieft had begun. In September 1643, Kieft called a meeting of leading colonists. All resolved that "if any of the Long Island savages can be prevailed upon to secure the heads of the savages, to take steps to that effect," and set about looking for more soldiers. Their savior came in the person of Captain John Underhill, veteran of the Pequot War and before that of the wars in Holland. Underhill had come to settle in New Netherland with his Dutch wife. Taking advantage of his presence, Kieft and the colonists voted to enlist as many Englishmen as possible under his command, and to mortgage the entire colony to pay them.[57]

By October, all of the settlements around New Amsterdam had been burned and abandoned. Only one on Long Island, several on Manhattan and the few on Staten Island remained intact. The miserable refugees cowered in Fort Amsterdam and waited apprehensively for a final assault by an Indian army that the colonists believed represented "alliances with more than seven different tribes" and consisted of "about 1500 men." Many colonists, including De Vries, left the colony and returned to the Netherlands.[58]

After the harvest season ended, in October 1643, Kieft, with a mixed force of English soldiers, Dutch militiamen, and West India Company soldiers, began sending out expeditions to attack Indian villages and plunder their corn harvest. The first troops marched all night across Staten Island, finding nothing but abandoned homes. The soldiers grabbed whatever bushels of corn they could find, burned the dwellings, and returned to New Amsterdam. When word arrived that the English village of Greenwich had been attacked, Kieft sent an expedition against the Tankitekes. These troops marched all night without finding any Indians. However, on their way back to New Amsterdam, some of the English villagers offered to lead them to another Indian village. When the Dutch arrived at the village, twenty-five "of the bravest men" attacked it, killing about twenty Indians, and capturing an old man, two women, and some children, whom they hoped to exchange for the many colonists the Indians now held captive. Then the Dutch somehow persuaded the old man to lead them to the main Wecquaesgeek village. It was abandoned but, looking further, the Dutch discovered some huts with people in them. The Wecquaesgeeks saw them first and fled. The Dutch managed to kill one or two men and to take a few women and children prisoners. They then burned the homes and the corn, and returned with their prisoners.[59]

Meanwhile, word reached Kieft that Penhawitz on Long Island had begun to take up arms against the colonists. An expedition of soldiers and English settlers under Captain John Underhill was sent against two separate villages in Penhawitz's lands. The expeditions "were very successful," Kieft proclaimed, "killing about one hundred and twenty men" and capturing a few. The Dutch suffered only one dead and three wounded.[60] The huge disparity in losses suggests that the Indians were not expecting to be attacked, calling into question the source of the rumors about Pennhawitz, who otherwise proved the most loyal of all sachems to the Dutch. Perhaps the colonists on Long Island, looking to legitimize an expedition against the Indians who owned most of the land around them circulated these stories.

Underhill next led 130 men against a gathering of several Indian groups for a festival near Stamford, Connecticut. When the Indians saw the Dutch coming, they "deployed in small bands," inflicting with their arrows most of the few casualties the Dutch suffered, but they could not stop the Dutch from surrounding the village and setting fire to it. The attack was brutally one-sided, a ruthless surprise reminiscent of the Pequot massacre. The colonists' muskets and tactics overwhelmed the Indians' defenses and trapped the Indians in their burning village. Between five and seven hundred Indians died in the flames. Only eight men, three of them severely wounded, escaped. Only fifteen of the Dutch force were wounded, and one killed. In March 1644, shortly after this devastating attack, a number of sachems, representing the tribes living north of New Amsterdam, including the Wecquaesgeeks and Wappingers, made peace. Others remained at war.[61]

The soldiers and colonists who did the dirty work of violence benefited in several ways. Plunder was certainly the primary motivation for the soldiers. It was one of the reasons they had attacked the Raritans back in 1640. Legitimate opportunities for soldiers to earn money were scarce in New Netherland. Throughout the years of Kieft's rule, the court convicted a number of them on various charges of thievery and illicit trading. Soldiers who took part in expeditions against the Indians got a share in the booty, "belts of zeewan, bows and arrows, sometimes beaver skins," all prized items that soldiers usually did not have the capital to acquire through commerce. Their guides, local colonists who knew the way to Indian villages (more or less), were also granted a share of the booty. Finally, at least one colonist is known to have turned in an Indian head to the governor for a bounty.[62]

Colonists had additional reasons for wanting to attack Indians, most pressing was food. The Dutch man and woman killed the day after the Pavonia massacre had been looking for maize; the Long Island colonists attacked the local Indians to steal their food. Despite the growing number of farms, New Netherland was still dependent on trade with the local Indians and New Englanders for its sustenance. Kieft had waited until the corn-trading season was over before attacking the Wecquaesgeeks in March 1642. Indeed, the war had taken on a seasonal quality. Both Indians and Dutch agreed on the need for the Indians to plant and harvest their corn and were eager to maintain peace at those crucial times. If the Indians were killed or driven off, the colonists could seize their land and cultivate it for themselves.[63]

The desire for food and other plunder accounts for Dutch hostility to the Indians around New Amsterdam. It is more difficult to explain the Dutch acts of cruelty. Fear, hatred, and mistrust of Indians and their culture of violence undoubtedly motivated Dutch cruelty. However, the brutality of the soldiers in Kieft's War was not unprecedented. During the 1620s, a Dutch trader at Fort Orange had held a Mohawk sachem hostage. He then emasculated him, even after the ransom had been paid, killing the sachem. Evidently, Dutch ambivalence about their colonial dependence on the Indians could compel some colonists to deeds that others considered barbaric.[64]

In April 1644, some English colonists on Long Island captured seven Indians, probably Rockaways or Canarsees, accusing them of having killed some hogs. According to Kuyter, Kieft quickly sent Underhill and a squad of soldiers to bring the prisoners to New Amsterdam. Of the seven prisoners, the soldiers killed three right away. The other four they took "with them in the sail-boat, two of whom, with ropes tied around their necks, were thrown overboard and fastened to the boat, and in that manner were towed after it and drowned." The two survivors were taken to Fort Amsterdam, and kept in the guardhouse for a while. Kuyter claimed Kieft "tired of providing" the Indians "with food any longer" and "gave these poor naked prisoners over to" the soldiers "in order to cool off their insolence" in demanding more booty. The soldiers "immediately dragged them out of the guard-house by the arms and legs, and attacked them with knives . . . which Director Kieft had caused to be made expressly" for close combat in Indian villages. Apparently, the soldiers' normal "swords were too long to be used in the huts of the Indians when they wanted to surprise them." Kuyter sarcastically pointed out that the advantage of the knives was that they "could be more handily plunged into their bowels."[65]

Using their special knives, then, the soldiers cut at the Indians, mortally wounding one. The man wanted the soldiers to let him perform his death dance, which would allow him to transform his bloody murder into a death with ritual meaning, such as a captured Indian could expect to receive from his enemies. Unfortunately, he had "received so many wounds, one upon another, that he . . . dropped down dead upon the spot." Meanwhile, the "soldiers cut strips from the live body of the other, from the hams, up the back and shoulders, and down to the knees." According to Kuyter, Kieft stood by, laughing "right heartily, rubbing his right arm and laughing out loud, such delight had he in the work." He ordered the Indian taken out of the fort. The man performed his death dance on the way. Outside the fort, the soldiers took him, "threw him down, and stuck his private parts, which they had cut off, into his mouth while he was still alive, and after that placed him on a mill-stone and beat his head off."[66]

A group of about twenty-five Indian women prisoners in the fort saw what happened to the two men. According to Kuyter, they "threw up their hands, beat their mouths, and said in their language, 'Shame,—what foul and unspeakable villainy this is; such was never heard of, or seen, or happened among us.' " Kuyter claims that the Indians had been critical of Dutch cruelty throughout the war. They would call out "from a distance, 'What scoundrels you Swannekens are! You war not against us, but against our innocent women and children, whom you murdered; while we do your women and children no harm, but give them to eat and drink, yea, treat them well and send them back to you.' " Kuyter emphasized that the Dutch "children, who were taken prisoners by the Indians, on being returned to their parents would hang round the necks of the Indians, if they had been with them any length of time." Indeed, the Indians' ability to absorb captive children into their communities would prove a bone of contention in many colonial American peace treaties to come.[67]

The killing of the Canarsee or Rockaway prisoners was one of the few recorded hostile incidents of 1644. Though no major confrontations took place, the situation remained tense and uncertain. In April, the Mattinecocks on Long Island petitioned to be allowed to plant in peace, saying they would avoid all contact with the Canarsees and Rockaways. In June, a company of West India Company soldiers en route to the West Indies arrived. Kieft and his council promptly decided to keep them in New Amsterdam to shore up their defenses, which would allow dismissal of the hired English soldiers. A sort of uneasy truce prevailed until the end of harvest. The Dutch took on a defensive stance and sent out only one expedition, killing eight Indians. Elsewhere tension and uncertainty prevailed. A group of leading colonists wrote to the West India Company, complaining that the Indians, able to pull in a full harvest unmolested, roved around "in parties, night and day, on the Island of Manhattans, killing our people not a thousand paces from the Fort." The Dutch lived in fear and uncertainty. No one dared "move a foot to fetch a stick of fire wood without an escort."[68]

While the Dutch cowered in fear, their Indian allies began to restore peace. In May 1645, a Long Island sachem offered to go to war against the colonists' enemies. The Dutch accepted this offer. Several days later, the sachem returned with "a head and hands of the enemy" and declared that many Long Island villages had put themselves under his protection. Over the course of the summer, the Mahicans and Mohawks intervened, and in August 1645, the final peace treaty of the war was concluded. Kieft proclaimed a general day of Thanksgiving and actually left Manhattan to sign the treaty.[69]

Once again, sachems had brought the peace that Kieft was unable to secure for himself. Roger Williams certainly felt that the Indians were more in control than the Dutch in New Netherland. In his view, "[A]fter vast expenses, and mutual slaughters of Dutch, English, and Indians, about four years, the Dutch were forced, to save their plantation from ruin, to make up a most unworthy and dishonorable peace with the Indians."[70]

Looking closely at Kieft's War, it becomes clear that it was not violence itself that marred relations between Indians and colonists. The real clash was between the European and Native American cultures of violence, between their ways of interpreting and coming to terms with violent acts. As Pacham's use of the scalp bounty indicates, European and Indian demands for justice could be reconciled. However, this reconciliation required a degree of flexibility and generosity. Kieft misunderstood the role of violence in Native American society and thought that more violence would bring more submission. Instead, it caused more problems. By resorting to raw force, he unleashed a chain reaction of retribution and demands for justice from both the Dutch and the Indians that neither side could easily fulfill. To Kieft's chagrin, the Indians turned out to be not weak and submissive but powerful and determined. In fact, it was their insistence that the values of their system of violence be respected that kept the war going. Kieft may have started the war, but it was the Indians who ended it. The final treaty was not concluded until Native American values, in a mixture of diplomacy and discreet acts of violence, were satisfied enough for the sachems to reestablish peace in their villages. Then the Dutch had their treaty, the Indians their satisfaction, and both cultures of violence could finally be put to rest.

NOTES

Evan Haefeli is a graduate student in the Department of History at Princeton University. For their helpful comments and suggestions, he would like to thank Robert Boyajian, Willem Frijhoff, Ignacio Gallup-Diaz, Charles Gehring, Francine Hirsch, Jaap Jacobs, Jessica Meyerson, Nathaniel Sheidley, the Princeton Society of Fellows of the Woodrow Wilson Foundation, and the editor.

1. Frederic W. Gleach, *Powhatan's World and Colonial Virginia: A Conflict of Cultures* (Lincoln: University of Nebraska Press, 1997); Alfred A. Cave, *The Pequot War* (Amherst: University of Massachusetts Press, 1996); Douglas Edward Leach, *Flintlock and Tomahawk: New England in King Philip's War* (East Orleans, Mass.: Parnassus Imprints, 1992 [1958]).

2. For the West India Company [hereafter WIC] and Dutch merchant imperialism, see Henk den Heijer, *De geschiedenis van de WIC* (Zutphen: Walburg Pers, 1994); Jonathan I. Israel, *Dutch Primacy in World Trade, 1585–1740* (Oxford: Clarendon Press, 1991); C. R. Boxer, The Dutch Seaborne Empire, 1600–1800 (London: Penguin Books, 1990 [1965]), 256.

3. The best current narrative in English of the war and Kieft's rule is Allen W. Trelease, *Indian Affairs in Colonial New York: The Seventeenth Century* (Ithaca: Cornell University

Press, 1960), 60–84. Most histories of his regime have been decidedly unsympathetic; see John Romeyn Brodhead, *History of the State of New York* (New York: Harper & Brothers, 1853), 275–433, and Michael Kammen, *Colonial New York: A History* (New York: Oxford University Press, 1996 [1975]), 44–47. For more sympathetic versions that do not entirely condemn him for the war, see Edmund B. O'Callaghan, *History of New Netherland; or New York under the Dutch*, 2 vols. (New York: D. Appleton, 1846), 1:180–396, and Oliver A. Rink, *Holland on the Hudson: An Economic and Social History of Dutch New York* (Ithaca: Cornell University Press, 1986), 131–37.

4. The exact authorship of the extant journal is uncertain. It is evidently not in Kieft's own hand but clearly does represent his views. J. Franklin Jameson, ed, *Narratives of New Netherland, 1609–1664* (New York: Charles Scribner's Sons, 1990), 267–68 (hereafter *NNN*). Most likely it is a surviving copy of an account he had composed in his own defense but which, like him, was lost at sea on the way back to the Netherlands. Willem Frijhoff, *Wegen van Evert Willemsz.: Een Hollands weeskind op zoek naar zichzelf, 1607–1647* (Nijmegen: SUN, 1995), 721.

5. *NNN*, 267–68; 183–85.

6. Melijn has long been considered the author, but recently the Dutch historian Willem Frijhoff has suggested that it was more probably Kuyter. Frijhoff, *Wegen van Evert Willemsz.*, 583.

7. *New York Historical Manuscripts: Dutch* (Baltimore: Genealogical Publishing, 1974), trans. Arnold J. F. Van Laer, vol. 4, *Council Minutes, 1638–1649*, 370–75; "Broad Advice, or Dialogue about the Trade of the West India Company," trans. Henry Murphy, in *Collections of the New York Historical Society*, 2d ser., 3 (1856): 240, 282–83.

8. J. W. Schulte-Nordholt, "Nederlanders in Nieuw Nederland, de oorlog van Kieft," *Bijdragen en Mededelingen van het Historisch Genootschap* 80 (1966): 38–94; Trelease, *Indian Affairs*, 62–65; Laurence M. Hauptman and Ronald G. Knapp, "Dutch-Aboriginal Interaction in New Netherland and Formosa: An Historical Geography of Empire," *Proceedings of the American Philosophical Society* 121 (1977): 171–73; Lieve Verbeeck, "Van Partner tot Horige: De Relatie tussen Indianen en Nederlanders in Nieuw Nederland, 1609–1673," in Peter Mason, ed., *Indianen en Nederlanders, 1492–1992* (Leiden: Wapmum, 1992); James Homer Williams, "Great Doggs and Mischievous Cattle: Domesticated Animals and Indian-European Relations in New Netherland and New York," *New York History* 76 (1995): 245–64; Frijhoff, *Wegen van Evert Willemsz.*, 713–30; Paul Andrew Otto, "New Netherland Frontier: Europeans and Native Americans along the Lower Hudson River, 1524–1664" (Ph.D. diss., Indiana University, 1995).

9. Or, more likely, the trade pidgin used for Dutch-Indian communication in New Netherland. See Ives Goddard "The Delaware Jargon," in Carol E. Hoffecker, Richard Waldron, Lorraine E. Williams, and Barbara E. Benson, eds., *New Sweden in America* (Newark: University of Delaware Press, 1995), 137–49.

10. *Documents Relative to the Colonial History of the State of New York*, ed. Edmund B. O'Callaghan, 15 vols. (Albany: Weed, Parson, 1853–1887), 13:22–23, 150 (hereafter *DRCNY*); *Council Minutes*, 87; *NNN*, 208.

11. *NNN*, 208–9, 227; *Council Minutes*, 115–16.

12. *NNN*, 208, 211; *Council Minutes*, 116.

13. *Council Minutes*, 115–16.

14. *NNN*, 211, 277; *DRCNY*, 1:199, 410.

15. Peter Farb, *Man's Rise to Civilization: As Shown by the Indians of North America from Primeval Times to the Coming of the Industrial State* (New York: Dutton, 1968), 123–24; Schulte-Nordholt, "Nederlanders in Nieuw Nederland," 60. James Axtell, "The Unkindest

Cut, or Who Invented Scalping? A Case Study," in his *The European and the Indian: Essays in the Ethnohistory of Colonial North America* (Oxford: Oxford University Press, 1981), 16–35, discusses the belief that Europeans introduced scalping to the Indians and argues for its Native American origins. Axtell traces the European-origins theory back to the Seneca leader Cornplanter in 1820 (17–18). I have traced it back to Massachusetts clergymen at the turn of the century, see Rev. John Taylor, *Century Sermon, Preached at Deerfield, February 29, 1804: In Commemoration of the Destruction of the Town by the French and Indians* (Greenfield, Mass.: John Denio, 1804), 27, who blames it on the French. See also Axtell, "Scalping: The Ethnohistory of a Moral Question," in his *European and the Indian*, 207–44.

16. John Winthrop, *Winthrop's Journal "History of New England," 1630–1649*, ed. James K. Hosmer, 2 vols. (New York: Charles Scribner's Sons, 1908), 1:230–31.

17. Reuben Gold Thwaites, ed., *The Jesuit Relations and Allied Documents*, 73 vols. (Cleveland, 1896–1901), 9:253, 27:235 (hereafter *JR*).

18. For the importance of gifts in Native American diplomacy, see Richard White, *The Middle Ground: Indians, Empires, and Republics in the Great Lakes Region, 1650–1815* (Cambridge: Cambridge University Press, 1991), 94–119, which also differentiates gifts from bribes and wages.

19. For a concise summary of mourning wars, see Daniel K. Richter, *The Ordeal of the Longhouse: The Peoples of the Iroquois League in the Era of European Colonization* (Chapel Hill: University of North Carolina Press, 1992), 32–38, 66–74. See also Daniel Richter, "War and Culture: The Iroquois Experience," *William and Mary Quarterly* 40 (1983): 528–59; Alvin H. Morrison, "Dawnland Dog-Feast: Wabanaki Warfare, c. 1600–1760," in William Cowan, ed., *Papers of the Twenty-First Algonquian Conference* (Ottawa: Carleton University, 1990), 258–78; Leory V. Eid, " 'National' War among Indians of Northeastern North America," *Canadian Review of American Studies* 16 (1985): 125–54.

20. Nathaniel Knowles, "The Torture of Captives by the Indians of Eastern North America," *Proceedings of the American Philosophical Society* 82 (1940): 151–220, presumes that where there is no documentary evidence, no torture was practiced. I believe torture had ancient and distinct Native American roots, regardless of how well it happened to be documented.

21. This argument has been advanced for Mesoamerican warfare. See Michael Harner, "The Ecological Basis for Aztec Sacrifice," *American Ethnologist* 4 (1977): 117–35; Marvin Harris, *Cannibals and Kings: The Origins of Cultures* (New York: Random House, 1977). Their argument is dismissed by Inga Clendinnen, *Aztec: An Interpretation* (Cambridge: Cambridge University Press, 1991), 3.

22. *JR*, 10:225.

23. *JR*, 17:65–77, 9: 253.

24. *NNN*, 84–85; Cadwallader Colden, *A History of the Five Indian Nations Depending on the Province of New York in America* (Ithaca: Cornell University Press, 1958), 132, cited in Thomas S. Abler, "Iroquois Cannibalism: Fact Not Fiction," *Ethnohistory* 27 (1980): 314. See Jesse D. Jennings, *Prehistory of North America* (Mountain View, Calif.: Mayfield, 1989), 240; Stuart J. Fiedel, *Prehistory of the Americas* (Cambridge: Cambridge University Press, 1987), 235–39.

25. John Mason, "A History of the Pequot War," in Charles Orr, ed., *History of the Pequot War: The Contemporary Accounts of Mason, Underhill, Vincent and Gardener* (Cleveland: Helman-Taylor, 1897), 41; *NNN*, 283; Roger Williams, "A Key into the Language of America," in James Hammond Trumbull, ed., The Complete Writings of Roger Williams, 7 vols. (New York: Russell & Russell, 1963), 1:204.

26. *NNN*, 213, 274–75; *DRCNY*, 1:410, 414–15. John Philip Reid argues that vengeance

was part of what can be considered a Native American legal system, and that frontiersmen learned to recognize and work within it. See *A Law of Blood: The Primitive Law of the Cherokee Nation* (New York: New York University Press, 1970); Reid, "Principles of Vengeance: Fur Trappers, Indians, and Retaliation for Homicide in the Transboundary North American West," *Western Historical Quarterly* 24 (1993): 21–43.

27. *Council Minutes*, 124; *DRCNY*, 1:414. A similar event took place in 1649 on eastern Long Island, when some Shinnecocks revenged an earlier murder by killing an English woman. The Shinnecock sachem felt that justice was done and would not turn in the killer. The English tried and hanged three Shinnecocks, and the Shinnecocks became Montauk tributaries. This outcome met the strategy of Wyandanch, the Montauk sachem, who used his English allies to gain a unique preeminence over the Indians of eastern Long Island. See John A. Strong, "Wyandanch: Sachem of the Montauks," in Robert S. Grumet, ed., *Northeastern Indian Lives, 1632–1816* (Amherst: University of Massachusetts Press, 1996), 57–58.

28. *DRCNY*, 1:415; *Council Minutes*, 124–26; *NNN*, 214. The WIC's opposition to the war can be traced through the extensive litigation it prepared against Kieft.

29. Council Minutes, 124–26; *DRCNY*, 1:415–16. The documents are a little unclear about these meetings. O'Callaghan, *History of New Netherland*, 1:243–44; Brodhead, *History of the State of New York*, 1:318–19, 325–26; Trelease, *Indian Affairs*, 67–69.

30. *NNN*, 275, 213; *DRCNY*, 1:199, 410–11; Frijhoff, *Wegen van Evert Willemsz.*, 719.

31. *NNN*, 215, 276; *DRCNY*, 1:150, 13:11.

32. "Broad Advice," 254; *DRCNY*, 13:11; *NNN*, 276; *Council Minutes*, 187.

33. *NNN*, 215–16. On the difficulty of negotiating justice in cases of intercultural murder, see James H. Merrell, " 'The Customes of Our Country': Indians and Colonists in Early America," in Bernard Bailyn and Philip D. Morgan, eds., *Strangers within the Realm: Cultural Margins of the First British Empire* (Chapel Hill: University of North Carolina Press, 1991), 117–56; Reid, "Principles of Vengeance," 21–43, White, *Middle Ground*, 75–93.

34. Kieft knew this charge was true, for he had been passing ordinances against disorderly drinking and fighting since he first arrived in the colony; see *Council Minutes*, 3–4, 8. Stuyvesant was shocked at the extent of drinking and fighting even on the Sabbath, and passed an "ordinance against selling liquor during divine service on the Sabbath and against drawing knives" shortly after he took over from Kieft, *Council Minutes*, 366–68. Colonial Native Americans claimed that drunken people were not responsible for their actions, including murders, to the great bafflement of Europeans. In their eyes culpability lay with those who supplied the liquor, not those who consumed it. Peter C. Mancall, *Deadly Medicine: Indians and Alcohol in Early America* (Ithaca: Cornell University Press, 1995), 79–82.

35. *NNN*, 215–16.

36. Ibid., 216.

37. Ibid., 276; Frijhoff, *Wegen van Evert Willemsz.*, 699; Peter N. Moogk, " 'Thieving Buggers' and 'Stupid Sluts': Insults and Popular Culture in New France," *William and Mary Quarterly* 36 (1979): 524–47; Cornelia Hughes Dayton, *Women before the Bar: Gender, Law, and Society in Connecticut, 1639–1789* (Chapel Hill: University of North Carolina Press, 1995), 285–328.

38. *NNN*, 276.

39. Quoted in Merrell, " 'The Customes of Our Country,' " 149–50.

40. Mary Black-Rogers, "Varieties of 'Starving': Semantics and Survival in the Subarctic Fur Trade, 1750–1850," *Ethnohistory* 33 (1986): 370, 379.

41. The identity of the attackers is confused. Most Dutch accounts report them as Mahicans, but occasionally they are described as Mohawks. Some of the rumors in New England even stated that the Dutch were behind the attack. *Winthrop's Journal,* 2:95.

42. *DRCNY,* 1:193; "Broad Advice," 254; *NNN,* 226.

43. *DRCNY,* 1:199–200, 345, 411–12, 416; 13:10–11, 14; *Council Minutes,* 185; "Broad Advice," 255–56; *NNN,* 227–28, 277.

44. Guido Ruggiero, *Violence in Early Renaissance Venice* (New Brunswick: Rutgers University Press, 1980); Edward Muir, *Mad Blood Stirring: Vendetta and Factions in Friuli during the Renaissance* (Baltimore: Johns Hopkins University Press, 1993); Michael Howard, George J. Andreopoulos, and Mark R. Shulman, eds., *The Laws of War: Constraints on Warfare in the Western World* (New Haven: Yale University Press, 1994); James Drake, "Restraining Atrocity: The Conduct of King Philip's War," *New England Quarterly* 70 (1997): 33–56; Frank Tallett, *War and Society in Early Modern Europe, 1495–1715* (London: Routledge, 1992), 232–45.

45. J. S. Fishman, *Boerenverdreit: Violence between Peasants and Soldiers in Early Modern Netherlands Art* (Ann Arbor: University of Michigan Press, 1982); Tallett, *War and Society,* 232–36.

46. "Broad Advice," 255–56.

47. Ibid., 257; *DRCNY,* 13:10.

48. *DRCNY,* 1:416–17; *NNN,* 277.

49. *NNN,* 229, 278; Trelease, *Indian Affairs,* 73; *Records of the Colony of Rhode Island and Providence Plantations in New England,* ed. John R. Bartlett, 10 vols. (New York: AMS Press, 1968 [1856]), 1:294–95.

50. Trelease, *Indian Affairs,* 74; *NNN,* 278; *Winthrop's Journal,* 95.

51. *NNN,* 229–32, 278–79; *DRCNY,* 13:14, 14:44–45; *Council Minutes,* 189, 192, 263.

52. *NNN,* 232.

53. Ibid. For an excellent discussion of the political tension between sachems' need for presents to keep young men from war and young men's imperative to avenge wrongs, see Nathaniel Sheidley, "Hunters and the Politics of Masculinity in Cherokee Treaty-Making, 1763–1775," in Martin Daunton and Rick Halpern, eds., *Empire and Others: British Encounters with Indigenous Peoples, 1600–1850* (London: University College London Press, forthcoming).

54. *NNN,* 232–33.

55. Ibid., 279.

56. *Winthrop's Journal,* 2:137–38, 276–77; *NNN,* 233–34, 279; *DRCNY,* 1:151, 13:16–17.

57. *NNN,* 280; *Council Minutes,* 203; *DRCNY,* 13:16.

58. *DRCNY,* 1:190–91; *Winthrop's Journal,* 2:138; *NNN,* 233–34.

59. *NNN,* 280–82; Trelease, *Indian Affairs,* 78; *Council Minutes,* 207.

60. *NNN,* 282.

61. Ibid., 282–84. *Council Minutes,* 216–17; *DRCNY,* 13:17–18; 14:56. For an analysis of the bloodiness of similar confrontations in New England, see Patrick M. Malone, *The Skulking Way of War: Technology and Tactics among the New England Indians* (Lanham, Md.: Madison Books, 1991); Adam J. Hirsch, "The Collision of Military Cultures in Seventeenth-Century New England," *Journal of American History* 74 (1988): 1187–212.

62. *Council Minutes,* passim; "Broad Advice," 256, 259; *NNN,* 208, 281.

63. Trelease, *Indian Affairs,* 75, takes the seasonal flow of the war as a sign of Indian treachery. He hints that the Indians planned all along to resume the war after the harvest and that the peace was just a stalling mechanism.

64. A. J. F. van Laer, ed. and trans., *Van Reensselaer Bowier Manuscripts: Being the Letters of Kiliaen Van Rensselaer, 1630–1643, and Other Documents Relating to the Colony of Rensselaerswyck* (Albany: University of the State of New York, 1908), 302. Frijhoff, *Wegen van Evert Willemsz*, 789–91, suggests the Dutch emasculators felt threatened by the Indians' more open sexuality. Michael Taussig, "Culture of Terror—Space of Death: Roger Casement's Putamayo Report and the Explanation of Torture," *Comparative Studies in Society and History*, 26 (1986):467–97, suggests how colonists' fear of Indian violence could have motivated their acts of terror.

65. "Broad Advice," 257–58.

66. Ibid., 258.

67. Ibid., 258–59; James Axtell, *The Invasion Within: The Contest of Cultures in Colonial North America* (Oxford: Oxford University Press, 1985), 302–28.

68. *Council Minutes*, 217, 228–29; Trelease, *Indian Affairs*, 80; DRCNY, 1:209–13.

69. *Council Minutes*, 265–66, 279–81; DRCNY, 13:18–19, 14:60.

70. *Records of Rhode Island*, 1:294–95.

A man beaten by his wife often received little sympathy. His community was more likely to blame the man for failing to maintain his masculine authority. Here a distraught husband pouts outside his cabin in an early nineteenth-century amateur woodcut. F. D. Srygley, *Sixty Years in Dixie* (Nashville, Tenn.: Gospel Advocate, 1893), 363.

Chapter Two

"Shee Would Bump His Mouldy Britch"

Authority, Masculinity, and the Harried Husbands of New Haven Colony, 1638–1670

Ann M. Little

There is little doubt that Anne Eaton was a troubled woman.[1] Those who lived in her house—her stepdaughter, her mother-in-law, and various servants—testified that they had been subjected to her damaging lies, verbal abuse, and even physical assault. Her husband, Theophilus, was forced to intervene one evening at supper when Anne reached across the table to strike her mother-in-law "twice on the face with the back of her hand," blows that the older woman felt for three days after the attack. Theophilus leaped up to restrain his wife, "and whilst Mr. Eaton held his wife's hands, she cried out with great vehemency of spirit, " 'I am afflicted, I am afflicted!' " His attempts to correct his wife, either by physical restraint or moral suasion, were ineffective, and moreover thoroughly resented by her. When he would not punish a manservant as she saw fit, she accused him of taking the servant's side against her. "[W]ith much heat of Spirit . . . [she] said to Mr. Eaton, you and this man may go together, for the man well out of the house I can get my bread and cost you nothing!" Anne's words were apparently not just idle threats this time. The recorder of this testimony notes that "this desire of getting from her husband she has prosecuted importunately," a sin "against the Covenant of Marriage, contrary to 1 Cor 7, 10." Any man in New Haven Colony would have been shamed by his inability to restrain his wife's behavior, or indeed to be the object of her wrath, but pity poor Theophilus. He was the governor of the colony.[2]

Theophilus Eaton's household, while greatly roiled by his wife's behavior, was by no means the most disorderly household of New Haven. In terms of the verbal and physical assaults directed at her husband, Anne Eaton was less troublesome than some other wives. Just going by the town and colony court records of New Haven, the harried husband was something of a stock character. Although not widespread, husband abuse was a much more commonly reported phenomenon in early New Haven than the more familiar variant of domestic violence, wife abuse.

Perhaps Anne Eaton's troubles seem especially dramatic in the context of early New England, which has been portrayed as a notably secure and stable region of North America compared to the instability of other English and European colonial ventures. Yet the English settlers saw themselves at the edge of a menacing wilderness and enclosed their towns within defensive fortifications and had men walking the watch every night accounts in part for their emphasis on order. Most of the truly spectacular violence in seventeenth-century New England was not between English or Anglo-American people in their orderly towns and colonies but was used against Indians in the conquest of New England. English men in New England were not reluctant to use violence in their advance on the frontier in the Pequot War, or in their defense of their homes and land in King Philip's War.[3] Nevertheless, deadly violence was almost never seen on the inside of the English garrisons. In New Haven Colony, aside from a few neighbors who came to blows, or drunken fistfights among the colony's youths or visiting seamen, beatings were rare and murder was nonexistent.[4] After Indian warfare, most violence in New England was probably one variant or another of family violence within English-led households, and most of it was probably directed against wives, children, servants, and slaves.

Anne Eaton's behavior was shocking not only because it seemed out of place in orderly New England. Sins "against the Covenant of Marriage" were taken very seriously in New Haven, for orderly marriages were central to the smooth functioning of both private and public spaces. In Puritan New England, marriage was a powerful legal contract that created and reproduced social and gender roles: men were to rule their wives, and their wives were to live in obedient subjection to their husbands. In other words, marriage sustained and helped reproduce patriarchal order.[5] This system of male superiority was not just an amorphous collection of religious ideals or cultural traditions; it was encoded in a large number of enforceable laws.[6] The central legal fiction of marriage was that in marriage, the husband and the wife were one entity represented publicly by the husband. This system of coverture, derived from English common law, erased the independent legal identity of women as wives, daughters, or other dependents, an identity they could claim only in widowhood.[7] Accordingly, wives could not legally own property, not even wealth they brought to the marriage or had created with their own hands. As people who, in the eyes of the law, did not exist, they could not bring cases to court without their husbands' assistance. And of course they had no political identity, and thus no vote in the town meeting. The one aspect of a married woman's identity that remained untouched by marital status or a husband's identity was her standing as a church member. Visible sainthood was something a woman could claim with or without a husband, and regardless of a husband's standing in the church. In Puritan New England, women, in particular, were justified by faith alone.

Although marriage erased women as public actors, it was the central event in a young man's life—indeed, marriage is what made a man a man. Because of the system of coverture, a legally defined and enforced position of male superiority, a man gained great advantages when he married: he claimed his wife's productive labor and skills in running a household, and all of the profits that her labor might generate, as well as his wife's marriage portions from his in-laws. Besides the great economic prerogatives, marriage for men also meant assuming a variety of positions of authority, both as "governors" of their own households and as participants in local government. This common use of the word "governor" to stand for both a civil office and a household role is not accidental, for this eliding of civil and domestic authority is the essence of a corporate, patriarchal society. In marriage, a man became the head of his household, and only in becoming a householder could he also become a "free burgess," or a participant in town meetings with full voting rights.[8] Of course, being a husband in early New England was not just about rights but about responsibilities, too. Men freed themselves of their fathers' authority by assuming governorship over—and responsibility for—wives, and eventually, over their children, servants, and slaves.[9] By effecting this transformation from son to husband and father, from governed to governor, by setting a young man atop a domestic hierarchy, marriage created manhood in early New England.[10]

Because marriage was the primary means of claiming adult male status, understanding marriage is therefore central to defining and understanding the construction of masculinity in early New England.[11] Masculinity can be understood to mean the collection of ideas and practices that people associate with men that legitimate them in claiming their identities as men and thus as "governors," inside and outside the home. *Masculinity* is not a value-free term, nor is it merely the opposite of *femininity*; it is a term freighted with great political as well as personal significance.[12] In a place like seventeenth-century New England, in which duties and privileges were assigned to people according to their gender, masculinity helped men define their position and influence in their towns, their colonies, and in the wider Atlantic world.[13]

This legally and religiously sanctioned dominion of households by husbands and fathers meant that any challenge to their authority not only was perceived as a threat to household order but was understood as an attack on the general social order. According to New Haven's laws, breaches of the Fifth Commandment were considered treason, and children above sixteen found guilty of dishonoring their parents were subject to the death penalty. Although this law was never invoked to its fullest extent, it underscores New England's emphasis on household authority as the basis for order in its commonwealths.[14] A wife who argued with her husband or challenged his authority was guilty of the same violation of the household hierarchy, but a wife who attacked her husband and even subjected him to a semipublic beating produced the most dramatic example of an attack on the social order.[15]

The problem of husband abuse entered New Haven courtrooms because the magistrates saw a profound interest in helping individual men reclaim their masculinity and thus their rightful positions as governors of their households and rulers of their wives. The judges' motives in this intervention were not entirely altruistic, for they understood that households under proper government, their members soundly and firmly governed by men as husbands and fathers, were in the best interests of the community.[16] Even just a few cases of husband abuse demonstrate that in early New England, rule of law was especially important inside as well as outside the household. When it was not enforced by husbands, or when it was brazenly flouted or subverted by unruly wives, the courts found it imperative to cross the threshold to restore patriarchal order.

Domestic Violence and the Invisible Woman

The relatively small number of cases of husband abuse in New Haven is more impressive when set against the colony's record of prosecuting wife abuse: Not a single case of wife abuse was prosecuted in the courts in New Haven Colony, and only two cases came to light in the seventeenth century after the colony became part of Connecticut in 1665.[17] The almost complete absence of prosecutions for wife beating speaks powerfully to the possibility that a husband's abuse of his wife was not considered a crime; however, we can only speculate as to the actual number of women whose husbands abused them. Similarly, New Haven heard no cases of child abuse or excessive correction of servants. Problems of evidence—especially quantity, but also quality—seem unavoidable in the study of domestic violence.[18] Even so, the very limited evidence here suggests a correlation between the effects of coverture—the erasing of women as legal entities—and the invisibility of abused wives in the court records. Because wife beating was an acceptable expression of the traditional hierarchy of marriage, it was not seen as problematic, nor were women seen as creatures with rights to protest their husbands' exercise of domestic statecraft.[19]

Other historians have suggested that in early modern England and New England, domestic violence against wives was recognized as permissible within limits. Extreme cruelty was unacceptable, and neighbors and justices of the peace intervened when women were severely injured or in hazard of their lives.[20] However, none of the few cases on record indicates either limits on the abuse of women or effective neighborly intervention in New Haven. Why neighborly intervention would be nonexistent in the closed, corporate, Christian communities of New Haven might seem anomalous—after, all this was widely considered the colony most fanatically devoted to the Puritan errand. But the question is not one of neighborliness but of patriarchal order, something that was considered a defining virtue in New Haven Colony. Like corporal punishment for children, servants, and slaves, wife beating could be an element of a husband's proper household government, and thus it was not understood as a crime. It should be no surprise, then, that at the same time wife abuse was made invisible in New Haven's courts, there were no complaints of abusive masters by aggrieved servants, or prosecutions of parents for beating their children. Again, this was probably due not to a total absence of servant beating or child abuse but, rather, to New Haven's concern for proper, patriarchal order.[21] Two glimpses of abused wives in the court records may hold clues as to why wife beating was not understood as a crime in the eyes of the community and of the law.

The allegations of wife abuse in the Langden household in 1653—the only hint of wife beating that appears in the town or colony court records before the union with Connecticut—came to light in the investigation of another crime, and the abuse remained ancillary to the focus of the investigation. Accordingly, the Langden case demonstrates the selectivity of both New Haven's neighbors and courts of law in intervening in household affairs. An investigation of Thomas Langden and his wife, Isabell, was initiated in Milford because their neighbors were suspicious about the provenance of some hog parts they had been served at the Langdens' house for supper.[22] After their dinner guests testified and Thomas confessed that he had butchered hogs that belonged to the town minister, the court asked Isabell why she had hidden her husband's crime and abetted it by dressing and cooking the purloined pork. She did not answer the question directly, but "it was answered by some that she had said she durst not [tell] for feare of her husband." One witness, Edward Granest, told the court that Isabell told him that she would be in grave danger if Thomas were convicted because of her testimony: "if her husband was whipt by her meanes, if [Thomas] came to her againe, she must not look to live." In other words, Thomas extorted her silence by threatening her with desertion on the one hand, and murder on the other. Granest further testified that Thomas might be the kind of man to make good on a threat like that because he had seen Thomas "beat his wife because she did not goe to weede corne." This testimony was validated by another neighbor.[23]

The Langdens were not strangers to the magistrates of New Haven. In fact, their household affairs had come under intense scrutiny by the town court two years earlier, when Thomas Langden had been accused and convicted of disorderly conduct for providing wine, hard liquor, and tobacco to other young men in his home. The court found the rude songs Thomas sang for his guests especially shocking, though "he saw no harmes in such songs." Thomas went on to complain about the court's interference, saying that "if they were in old England they could sing and be merry." A year later, Isabell was accused of a similar crime: "for inviteing other mens servants to her house in the night." The court charged her with flouting community standards of household government by "disorderly inviteing Mr Cranes maide in the night to her house to eate a sacke posset (a wine punch), wth an intent to have her meete a young man there, wth a purpose to drawe on a treaty of marriage, wthout parrents or masters consent."[24] By using their home to entertain other young people and to provide a meeting place for trysts, the Langdens challenged Puritan notions of orderly conduct and defined themselves apart from their community and the courts that policed it. In these cases the courts were not willing to relinquish their control of what went on in the Langdens' household. Why then did the court make an exception when evidence came to light that Thomas had beaten Isabell and threatened her life?

It is possible that Thomas Langden's abuse of his wife was never previously reported to the court, neither by her nor by their neighbors. If her neighbors are to be believed about her husband's violent nature, Isabell Langden probably lived with the abuse for a number of reasons. First, economic reality left Isabell few choices. Thomas threatened to abandon her unless she kept quiet about his affairs, and she might have decided that making a living without a husband was too uncertain or daunting. Second, Thomas also threatened to kill Isabell if his hog-stealing came to light, an even more persuasive argument for her silence. And effective—recall that she never opened her mouth in her examination at the trial; neighbors stepped in to explain her fearful silence. Third, Isabell may have despaired of receiving justice from a court that had previously convicted and fined her, especially because she would have had to confess her own part in the hog stealing.

Still, none of these reasons fully explains why the Langdens' neighbors never came forward about the abuse. Although they showed little reluctance to report Thomas's theft and to testify about his disorderly entertaining, they apparently remained mute on the subject of his beating and threatening his wife. Interestingly, Thomas himself knew he was being watched closely and complained of the scrutiny in his first court appearance when he called one witness a "tattelling woman," and blamed her for his troubles with the court because he believed "her tattelling made this stir."[25] Although Isabell's neighbors knew of her husband's violent tendencies, that she had suffered his blows in the past, and even that he had threatened her life, they did not intervene personally or through the courts. Although one incident alone cannot provide conclusive evidence, the Langden case indicates that wife beating was not seen as a crime in New Haven Colony, nor even as something that required neighborly intervention. While many compelling reasons prevented Isabell Langden from reporting her husband's behavior to the town magistrates, chief among them must have been that she couldn't have expected any assistance from them. Based on the reactions of her neighbors, that would have been a reasonable judgment.[26]

The court's handling of the Langden case gives further credibility to the fears of the abused wife because the court did not pursue the allegations of abuse when they came to light in the theft trial. The court accepted Thomas's apology for his behavior toward his wife, concluding that "he had spoken such words, but said he now sees the evil of it." The court ordered him to make restitution of eighteen pounds for the stolen hogs, and to be whipped for lying about the theft and for threatening his wife—a standard sentence for theft and dissembling in court without the additional allegations of wife abuse.[27]

The Langden case illustrates two points about domestic violence against women in early New Haven. First, it wasn't necessarily seen as a crime; neighbors didn't intervene, nor did they take it upon themselves to report wife abuse the way they reported suspected witchcraft, fornication, theft, and most other crimes. Second, a corollary to the first point, is that even if a woman's plight was common knowledge among her neighbors, as in the Langden case, she might not feel confident enough to take her case to court. This may have been due to her reasonable fears that she would not get a fair hearing in court. An abused wife might also conclude that even if she procured a judgment against her husband, his conviction might not be in the economic best interests of their household. Taken together, these points indicate that there was a consensus among the people of New Haven that a man's decision to beat his wife was his prerogative as the governor of his household.[28]

Another case illustrates just how negligible a woman's safety was when compared to the compelling need to uphold patriarchal household government. Shortly after New Haven joined with Connecticut, Ebenezer Browne was prosecuted for beating his wife, and in that case his wife's pregnancy seems to have spurred the court's intervention more than her own safety. With the aid of her mother, Rebecca Vincent, Hannah Vincent Browne brought her husband, Ebenezer, to court in June of 1668 for various "sinfull carriages towards [them]." Married for just over a year, Hannah was pregnant with their second child, but Ebenezer, "in a most barbarous, & in humane manner, both in ffowle, prophane & provokeing language [made] threats to ye sd Hannah his wife, & with rude behavior & actions with neglect of due care in pvideing for ye necessary comfort of her liveing (contrary to ye bounden duty of a husband)." Apparently, Ebenezer did more than just threaten his wife, for their testimony makes it clear that she felt she was in imminent danger. His mother-in-law alleged that he "br[oke] open ye doores & locke of her house, & yt in ye night time to ye great disturbance of ye peace."

The fact that Hannah was pregnant seems to have been crucial in the disposition of the Browne case. The court took action on Ebenezer's offenses and found him guilty of "ye sd crimes, misdemeanors & enormities as a man voyd of ye feare of god, to ye great scandall of a christian people, & offence of many." Even so, the sentence of the court was not terribly harsh: Ebenezer was ordered to give security to the court for his good behavior and was sentenced to be whipped. As with Thomas Langden, a husband's apology to the magistrates carried great weight, because after expressing his great sorrow to the court the following morning the magistrates suspended Ebenezer's whipping. That Hannah's pregnancy was the court's chief concern is illustrated in its provisions for her immediate security. She was given permission to live apart from her husband, either with her mother or "in some good family, under the carefull inspection of the head or heads of such family," only until she gave birth to her child. Ebenezer was to maintain her until the delivery at his own expense, and on the condition that he behave himself he was granted liberal visiting privileges.[29] Once her child was born, Hannah was expected to live under her husband's household government, however it might manifest itself. When faced with a conflict between a wife's safety and a husband's right to rule his household as he saw fit, New Haven's courts demurred to cross the threshold to interfere with the latter.

Perhaps it is not surprising, then, that the vast majority of the cases of domestic discord that came to the attention of the New Haven courts are incidents of wives harassing or even beating their husbands. In these cases, there was no conflict between the safety of one spouse and the authority of another—the court's duty was clear: to restore the proper (patriarchal) ordering of the disordered households.

"Pressing Ye Rule upon His Wife": The Responsibilities of Household Government

Because of their status as household governors, husbands whose wives were hailed before the court were often held partially or equally culpable for the alleged crimes.[30] The same legal fiction that made wife beating not a crime—that husband and wife were one entity represented publicly by the husband—made the husband responsible for his wife's criminal behavior. A survey of these cases reveals that the magistrates believed that a wife's criminality was a sign not only of her personal sinfulness but also of her husband's weak or ineffective moral authority. When Francis Newman's wife, Mary, was accused of defaming Hannah Fuller, their husbands represented both of them in court: Mr. Fuller was the official plaintiff on his wife's behalf, and Francis was named a codefendant for his wife's loose tongue. The court told him that "he fell short of his duty, both in not pressing ye rule upon his wife" and in provoking Hannah Fuller when she would not drop her suit. Because he "should rather have aplyed himselfe to make up what was defective in his wives satisfaction," the court ordered him to pay five pounds to the Fullers. His dereliction of his household duties did not hurt his public reputation permanently, however, for he went on to become the colony's second governor eight years later.[31]

Sometimes a husband was held accountable not just for his wife's crimes but for not reporting crimes against her. When it came to light that William Fancy's wife had been sexually attacked by her former master and two other men in New Haven Town, not only was she sentenced to be "severly whipped" for not reporting their crimes but William Fancy was too. The court lectured him "for his being as it were a panderer to his wife & neglecting the timely revealing of these forementioned attempts to have defyled his wife, who should have bin her p[ro]tector."[32]

Despite the town and colony courts' regular censure of husbands whose wives ran afoul of the law, not all men willingly accepted responsibility for their wives' behavior. When John Morris appeared in court to answer for the charge that his wife, Elizabeth, sold gunpowder to the Indians, he complained to the magistrates that "yt [what] was done by his wife was unknowne to him, & against his will, & he thought it was ignorantly done by his wife, he desired to leave himselfe with yt court &c." Nevertheless, the court fined him five pounds.[33] When Richard Crabb was held responsible for his wife's unorthodox religious beliefs, he resisted and asserted that his wife's strong convictions were quite beyond his control. Although both he and his wife were called to court to answer for their Quaker leanings, only Richard showed up, despite the fact that most of the court's concern was directed at her behavior, not his. She was accused of several public and private speeches "railing o[n] the ministers & said they were preists

& preached for hire, & called them Baalls preists, & she would not heare them, & said we was shedders of bloud, ye bloud of the s[ain]ts of God." Richard, by means of explanation, said that his wife was "a well bred woman in England, a zealous pfessour from her childhood," but admitted that "she hath not power to restraine her passions."[34]

The court's censure of Richard Crabb is indicative of the degree to which husbands were held responsible for their wives' transgressions. The governor of New Haven Colony himself, Francis Newman (who, as described above, had been found guilty thirteen years earlier of "not pressing ye rule upon his wife"), reminded Crabb that restraining his wife's passions was one of his obligations as a husband and as governor of his household. Governor Newman admonished Crabb, saying that "if she had beene a great professour it was certaine she had beene an ill practiser, in wch you have countenanced her & borne her up." For this dereliction of duty, and for his wife's railery, he was fined thirty pounds—a potentially devastating sum. Interestingly, the court focused on Richard himself for further punishment "yt he enter an engagement of a £100 standing security for his good behavior; furthermore, yt he make a publique acknowledgmt at Stamford, to the satisfaction of Francis Bell & those other wch he hath wronged," despite the fact that his wife was alleged to have made the insults.[35] In the punishment of John Morris and especially of Richard Crabb, it is clear that the courts took very seriously the notion that good government began at home.

Masculinity Threatened and Reclaimed: Husband Abuse in the New Haven Courts

There are three trends in the cases of New Haven's abused husbands that help explain why these cases came to court—albeit in small numbers—while cases of abused wives did not. First of all, it should be noted that the victims in these cases have some role in bringing the story of their troubled marriage under the consideration of the court. Like abused wives, the husbands involved do not bring their wives to court, and suggestions of domestic violence come to light only in the course of testimony on other charges. However, in most instances the actual case being investigated was initiated by the wronged husband. As described above, a man's identity as a householder was both public and private, so that any challenge to his stature within his household could affect his stature in the town and colony at large. Typically, a case of slander against a neighbor who had overheard a heated exchange between the husband and wife, and who spread reports that the husband had allowed his wife to usurp his role elevated gossip to a legal proceeding. Thus while men did not find it convenient to avenge their masculinity by taking their wives to court, they believed (correctly) that they would get favorable consideration by taking neighbors to court for questioning their masculinity.[36]

Second, although abused wives fit comfortably (according to the courts) into the patriarchal hierarchy of the household, in the cases of the abused husbands the root cause of their distress was that the hierarchy of the household had been disrupted or entirely subverted. The proper order of household government had broken down because wives had superseded their "natural" roles and were verbally or physically abusive of their husbands, and also because husbands had failed to perform their role as the "natural" governors of the household. The evidence presented in the court cases might seem to point more to one spouse's guilt, but recall that the stereotypes of the shrewish, violent wife and her weak, ineffective husband serve as foils one to the other. They are dependent upon each other, mutually defining and reinforcing one against the other. As the old song goes about a more optimistic view of love and marriage, "you (still) can't have one without the other."[37]

Third, the purpose of these official investigations into troubled marriages seems to have been to help the harried husbands reclaim their proper roles as governors of their households. Perhaps because they feared damage to their reputation as effective husbands and householders, men who suffered insults and violence from their wives did not themselves bring their wives to court. Rather, the courts attempted to rescue men's reputations by making gossip about their marriages a matter of official inquiry, and putting it into an official discourse about gender and power that could be more effectively directed and controlled. Although this process might seem to compromise a man's masculinity further by taking control of a story about a marriage, the courts could perhaps influence how that story was heard and understood by the people of the town. And with men like Newman and Eaton as presiding magistrates, courts did not censure the abused husbands for dereliction of household government, as they did in cases of wifely criminality; perhaps reprimanding an abused husband was considered adding insult to injury. Instead of punishing these husbands, the courts served to reinforce patriarchy within the household by assisting men in reasserting their masculinity and in reclaiming their position as household patriarchs.

The humiliation suffered by abused husbands, if not remedied, could be acute. Disorder within marriage was a common theme in sixteenth- and seventeenth-century English drama and popular verse, which mocked such stock marriage players as the shrew, the fishwife, and the cuckold. Samuel Rowlands's 1609 ballad "A Whole Crew of Kind Gossips," relates the tale of a wife who overspent her husband's purse. When he presumed to discipline her with a knock on the head, she boasted:

> I valiantly took up a faggot-stick
> For he had given me a blow or twain
> But as he likes it, let him strike again
> The blood ran down about his ears apace
> I brake his head and all bescratch't his face
> Then got him down and with my very fist
> I did bepommell him until he pissed.[38]

The tone of this wife's tale is comic; the injuries she inflicts on her husband are crippling. Such a violent subversion of domestic order was not considered a laughing matter in New England.

In many ways, the hearing of husband-abuse cases in the New Haven court-rooms functioned in the way that skimmingtons served in early modern English villages. These popular rituals shamed couples in disorderly marriages by rousting them out of bed and parading them around the village while their neighbors created a commotion of "rough music" by beating pots and pans. With the weak husband often decorated by the cuckold's horns and his shrewish wife facing backward on an ass, their violation of traditional gender roles and the hierarchy of marriage was made very clear. Recent analyses of these village rituals have demonstrated that their purpose was to restore and enforce proper gender roles for weak husbands and shrewish wives.[39] Why did New England Puritans haul harried husbands into court, instead of relying on community ritual? In point of fact, there is no evidence of any skimmingtons or similar community rituals in seventeenth-century New England. This absence of community ritual may have been due in part to the strange quiescence of neighbors when it came to abusive marriages. In the absence of independent community intervention, charivari rituals would have been unlikely. Another possible reason for the absence of skimmingtons is that those rituals were associated with England's West country, whereas early New England was populated most heavily by East Anglians and Londoners; very few West country men and women settled in New Haven.[40] Finally, the scale of court procedures was so small that they were used for all sorts of business that in England had been dealt with by custom rather than by law.[41]

There is a notable clustering of these cases within a single decade, from 1655 to 1665.[42] It was perhaps not coincidental that men in New Haven in those years felt particularly attuned to challenges to their masculinity. In that decade the colony was undergoing social and political changes that had profound effects upon households and families. First, families were themselves the cause of the major social transformation, the maturing of the first generation of native-born New Haveners, who created a youth culture that itself tested the limits of patriarchal household and civil government. From 1655 to 1665, the courts were full of young men and women who, adult (or nearly so) but unable to marry, amused themselves in drinking parties, illegal nighttime gatherings, fornication, thievery, and vandalism. This epidemic of adolescent and young-adult disorderliness may have made both household patriarchs and the magistracy more sensitive to all manner of challenges to their authority, and more determined to reestablish effective patriarchal control. Second, a political crisis within the colony was brought on by the death of Lord Protector Oliver Cromwell and the Restoration of the Stuart king Charles II. This ultra-Puritan colony, which had harbored Charles I's regicides, had no royal charter and little hope of gaining the new king's favor, and so was pressured to join with Connecticut. The 1665 union with Connecticut rent the colony politically. When an outraged defendant could tell the New Haven Town court that "he knew no authority they had since the King was proclaimed, nor would he obey any lawes untill they came thence," the world of Puritan New Haven had certainly turned upside down.[43] The confluence of these social and political upheavals in this decade may have made both the courts and male heads of household jealous of their authority and eager to protect it.

Although these husband-abuse cases were clustered around a time of general crisis in the colony, the couples involved had little else in common with one another. Violent wives and their husbands were of all different ages and stages in life except old age, so husband abuse was not correlated with any particular point in the life cycle or in the life of a marriage. One couple were newlyweds; others had small children or even teenagers under foot. Two couples were second-generation New Haveners; two couples were first-generation settlers. And in the end, three of the marriages lasted to death. These marriages can be considered successful, though, not just in their endurance but in that they seemed to achieve what marriage was supposed to achieve: an orderly basis for the rearing of children and for the support of the family. The people with small children went on to have several more children together after their appearance in court, and there is no evidence of further strife among the surviving three marriages. By intervening on behalf of the harried husbands, the courts seem to have achieved their goals.[44]

In demonstrating the cooperation between the courts and male heads of households on the issue of husband abuse, I do not mean to suggest that patriarchal authority was either monolithic or entirely successful. The unruly women in the following cases (as in the case of Mrs. Crabb above) are strong characters who practically leap out of the court records—indomitable, irascible, and fully fleshed. The existence of these women and their willingness to engage in such vigorous verbal and physical jousts with men give the lie to the efficiency of patriarchy as a system of total social organization. The town and colony courts that disciplined these women understood their subversive potential and knew just how dangerous they could be.

In the New Haven courts, the most common tale of the harried husband began with a wife who reached inappropriately beyond her station and attempted to rule her husband. One of the more dramatic examples is the case of twenty-year-old Mary Dickerman and her husband, Abraham. Abraham sued Thomas Wheadon for slandering him by telling people that one evening he "heard a great noise in Abraham Dickermans house, & thought that there was some body in the house, & that he heard [Abraham's] wife say, I think you are madd, & what aile you, & I thinke the divell is in you." Wheadon affirmed that he had witnessed this, and further said that he saw Abraham come out of his house and "apprehended [Abraham] did cry." Another witness, Mary Kimberly, told the court she had heard Wheadon say that "Goodwife Dickerman beat her husband, & made him goe out crying."[45]

The Dickerman case illustrates the court's expressed interest in taking control of the public discourse about harried husbands, and in helping men reassert their patriarchal right within their households. Despite this dramatic testimony, the court was not interested in establishing the truth of the charge. It did not call Abraham or Mary to testify about their conduct, which was the standard procedure for proving a charge of slander. Although Wheadon continued to insist that he had seen Abraham beaten and weeping outside his house, the court told him that he "should not have reported [the story] but have told them of it." The court implied that the abuse charge might have been enough to warrant a limited official investigation, which it preferred to an indiscreet colonist spreading gossip about a young man who could not control his wife. In the end, the court upheld Abraham's masculinity and his lawsuit by reprimanding Wheadon and requiring him to pay Abraham twenty shillings in damages as well as court costs.[46] Accordingly, like Governor Newman before him, Dickerman's public role was not compromised. The next time he appeared in court, it was as a juror on several slander cases. He served New Haven in many other capacities on various committees and as sergeant of the militia. These were not high offices, but they demonstrate his status as a householder in good standing with the other men of his town.[47]

Another case illustrates that the mere assertion that a man's wife ruled his roost—even without vivid testimony of beatings or verbal invective, as in the previous incident—was damaging enough to warrant a slander suit. It also demonstrates that men under attack for letting their wives take charge could turn the charge of gender-inappropriate behavior against their accusers. When Richard Beckley sued Francis Hitchcock, a widow, much trouble had already transpired between the neighbors. Most vexing from Beckley's point of view was his claim that Hitchcock had made several statements that accused Beckley of letting his wife run their household. Interestingly, this 1659 case was not the first time the Beckleys' marriage had come under the scrutiny of the court. Five years before, Beckley had sued Henry Boutle for claiming that "hee is unkinde to his wife," for he saw her "sitt two howers at ye ferry crying, because she could not get him from ye Ordinary." No physical or verbal abuse was alleged or reported about either spouse.[48] Beckley was not afraid to go to court to vindicate his management of his wife and household.

Whereas managing her household was her responsibility alone as a widow, Hitchcock apparently believed—or found it convenient to imply—that the married Goodwife Beckley should not have the authority in domestic affairs more appropriate to her husband. The specific charges of slander, therefore, involve things that Hitchcock, a formidable woman, supposedly said about both Beckleys. Hitchcock allegedly said that Goodwife Beckley was "pratling, & that shee went about the worke of the divell," as well as "a liar & a backbiter, & that shee made difference amongst neighbours." When Beckley confronted Hitchcock about her opinions of his wife, he said "shee returned very bad language," and threatened him "that shee was told such things concerning them that if he had knowledg of it would make him tremble." After continuing on in like heated manner for some time, he said that Hitchcock "tooke a wisp (of straw) & put it to his nose 2 or 3 times & said, go on scold, go on scold, & wisht them all hangd, & that his nose was in his wives brich & her self a hammer to drive it in."[49]

Hitchcock's choice of insult to Beckley, with its final vulgar flourish, was no accident; the term "brich," or "breeches" in the sixteenth and seventeenth centuries was a garment that only men wore. Moreover, accusing a man of allowing his wife to "wear the breeches" was a common means of impugning his masculinity in Tudor-Stuart England.[50] Thus there could be no misunderstanding exactly what Hitchcock meant—according to her, Goodwife Beckley wore the pants in that family.

Hitchcock's colorful invective, delivered while she taunted him with a wisp of straw, humiliated Beckley as a man unable to properly govern his household and painted a picture of a family out of control. Hitchcock further implied Beckley's ineffectiveness when she said that his children were allowed to break the Sabbath and engage in petty thievery. Beckley protested this portrayal of his family, but did not disagree with Hitchcock's ideas as to the proper, gendered order of the household hierarchy. He said that his family was not so disordered but owned that if Hitchcock's charges were true, "they were not fitt to live in ye woods nor in ye Commonwealth."[51]

Perhaps to deflect attention from his supposedly disorderly household and to focus the court's attention on Hitchcock's inappropriate behavior, Beckley told the court of another man who had been severely insulted by Hitchcock, the brother to her late husband. Accordingly to Beckley, Matthias Hitchcock expressed some displeasure with her carriage in the Beckley affair. This was a gesture proper to a male relative, who although not her legal governor could still be expected to exert some moral influence over her. The widow Hitchcock was incensed at his presumption, and "challenged him into the high way, saying she desired noe better law against him, & yt if she had him abroad, shee would bump his mouldy brich." In supposedly inviting Matthias into such a masculine arena for competition, and in threatening to literally kick his ass, Hitchcock had clearly transgressed the bounds of womanly conduct. Moreover, Beckley charged "she afterwards related some of these evill carriages of hers to some young person or persons, speaking of it in a glorying way," much as the victor in a street fight might relish the tale of his triumph over a pint with the boys in the ordinary.[52] In relating this tale to the court, Beckley turned the tables on Hitchcock by noting that her behavior was inappropriate for a woman, even for a widow.

In the end, the court sided with Beckley, ruling that Hitchcock represented the real trouble in the town. The court agreed that Beckley had been grievously wronged, and that he had not provoked Hitchcock's attack. Although most of her attention had been paid to the behavior of his wife and children, in sentencing Hitchcock the court spoke only of "the wrong done to him." The court harangued Hitchcock about her quarrelsome bearing and her unruly tongue, and warned her that "the poyson of asps is under her lipps." The insults she had leveled at Beckley through his wife and children were things "not to be named amongst Christians," and bespoke a "rotten & corrupt heart." For her sins, she was ordered to make restitution to Beckley and fined forty shillings plus court costs.[53] Thus once again, the New Haven courtroom proved a friendly place for a man seeking to reclaim his good reputation and his rightful place as the governor of his household.

A curious coda to this case gives further proof that the court's goal in these cases of harried husbands was to restore proper, patriarchal order in the troubled homes. Two and a half years later John Cooper, who had testified on Hitchcock's behalf in the Beckley affray, came to court to ask for an abatement of Hitchcock's forty shilling fine because "she did to him express her self sensible of her miscariages, for wch she was fined." More important, perhaps, was his assurance to the court that "her cariage is satisfying in ye family where she liveth." Because Cooper could vouch for her reformed life under good family government, the court remitted her forty shillings.[54]

Abraham Dickerman and Richard Beckley protested when tales of their abusive or breech-wearing wives came to light, but Ralph Lines may have had a compelling reason for failing to protest the picture of his troubles presented to the New Haven Town court. The Lineses' marital troubles found their way into the courtroom because Alice was on trial for various thefts of household items over the course of several years. More seriously, in the course of her examination for these crimes, she was accused of beating and intimidating the young son of one of her accusers, telling him "he was a lyar, and so were all the family, and they will be hanged for their lying."[55]

Because Alice was a married woman, her husband, Ralph, was ultimately responsible for her behavior; he had apparently not governed her appropriately, given the charges against her. This may explain why Ralph Lines did not object to testimony about the Lineses' marriage. The final charge against Alice—perhaps the most serious—was that besides stealing from and beating up her neighbors, Edward Camp said that "to her husband her cariage hath bine verey gross and insufferable." Camp testified that when Alice disagreed with the manner in which Ralph corrected their son, she "fell into a rage and called him very bad names, and up wth a stick and struck him on the head." Alarmed by the commotion, Camp and his wife ran to the scene. Camp said that Ralph's "wife abused him so as never man was abused, not only in words, calling him devill, but in striking him also." When Camp confronted Alice, asking her, "[W]ill you never leave these courses?" she replied furiously, "[H]e is a devill, he is a devill," gesturing at her husband. Lest Ralph had missed the point, she continued, "Goodman Camp is a man, but he is a devill." She confessed that the story Camp told was true but that "she remembers not that she repeated the word devill so often." Ralph's strategy may have worked because he escaped personal censure and punishment completely. The situation in his household may have broken down so thoroughly that the court's punishment of his wife was his last resort.

Of course, his wife's sentence of double restitution to the victims of her thievery came out of the shared wealth of their household, so in effect he paid for her crimes as well.[56]

Another unruly wife not only was verbally and physically violent with her husband but was also accused of being sexually unfaithful. This case started out much like the previous defamation suits in which the harried husband brought his complaint to court to restore his reputation as head of his household, but the charges in the civil suit were so serious that the magistrates chose to prosecute some of the interested parties. Peter Briggs entered an action against Benjamin Graves for all manner of inappropriate conduct with his wife, Ruth, both before and after her marriage to Briggs. The court eventually charged Graves with "Lascivious Carriage by kissing & embraceing" her before she married Briggs and frequenting her company "in a suspicious & offensive manner" after her marriage, once running off with her "neare all ye way to Say Brook." Graves explained his behavior by making the shocking countercharge that he and Ruth had agreed to marry, and that they had even been "published one Lecture day at Boston." (That is, they had published their banns, or publicly announced their betrothal, a step toward marriage that had near-contractual significance.) When asked by the court "if there were noe promise of marriage betweene them?" Ruth said that "there may be such a thing at Boston, but shee was not to answer for that here."[57] Such impudence turned the court against her, and she became the object of its most dogged inquiry. Ruth Briggs had exposed herself as a woman who did not take marriage as seriously as did the colony's authorities, so they examined her married life with Peter Briggs in even greater detail. Ruth confessed to the charge that she had had many suitors, but the court found evidence of other behavior that was even more unsettling to patriarchal notions of household government. She admitted that, as the court put it, she "whilest a widdow, ensnared & deluded sundry young men upon prtence & promise of marriage to countenance & cover unlawfull familiarity with them." A young widow needed to shop around to find a suitable husband, but the court found her entertainment of multiple fiancés not only promiscuous but also threatening to the social and moral order.

More troubling were the charges that she assumed the same liberties after her marriage to Peter Briggs. She allegedly "wilfully depart[ed] from her husband against his mind," while pretending "she had liberty from her husband to come away . . . [but it] appeared otherwise w[he]n enquired into." When Peter came after her to bring her home to New Haven, the court alleged that she regarded him as an object of scorn rather than as her rightful governor. "[S]he contrary to ye duty of a wife refused [to return with Peter] & as herselfe Confest yt in a rage she perumptorily sd severall times yt she would not goe with him, casting contempt upon Authority whoe had enjoined her returne to him." Besides verbal abuse, she threatened physical harm as well, "offring violence to him & by force haleing him from supper at goodw: Roses." In this instance, she made her rejection of patriarchal authority clear, "saying she would keepe him downe while he was young, that soe he might [submit to her] hereafter." By announcing her intention to train him into submission, Ruth's threat to the patriarchal order was clear. The magistrates levied a stiff four-pound fine (plus court costs) against her, and threatened her with whipping and banishment if she did not pay. Like Ralph Lines, Peter Briggs was not personally punished for his wife's crimes against him or against the social order, but her fines came out of their shared wealth. She was returned to his custody, and the court hoped they both had sufficient incentive to reform their conduct and live in peace, and, for Ruth, in proper submission.[58]

When a man was accused of being an inadequate husband and household governor in early New Haven, it was understood as a direct assault on his masculinity. Because marriage was the foundational institution of households, and because being the head of a household brought such privileges to men, marriage was the crucible of masculine identity in seventeenth-century New England. The control of a wife and family, and of their household resources, was central to the ongoing performance of masculinity, a performance that earned social and political benefits outside the household as well. Accordingly, a man's abuse of his wife, children, or servants was not a challenge to the godly order of a household but an expression of it. On the other hand, abused men required the courts' assistance, especially in the socially and politically volatile decade from 1655 to 1665 when these cases appeared. When men could not control their wives, or even their conjugal relationships, the New Haven town and colony courts stepped in to discipline unruly wives and to restore the authority of the husbands. There was more than just marital or family harmony at stake in this uncertain new world, when the future of a rising generation and even the colony itself was in jeopardy.

The pathetic abused husband in Rowlands's "A Whole Crewe of Kind Gossips" took his wife's violence in stride, claiming to acquiesce when she "bends her fist as if she meant to strike." However, he acknowledged that just as his wife was not quite the "gentlewoman" she aspired to be, he did not live up to the manly ideal of ensuring orderly household government. But then, he insists, neither did his neighbors:

> . . . 'tis an honest care
> To have command only by manly carriage
> For I do know the civil wars of marriage
> Too well, by divers of my neighbours lives,
> That are outmatched in combat with their wives.[59]

New England men did not take abusive wives in stride. This kind of assault on the public order could not be tolerated in commonwealths devoted to the proper exercise of godly authority within households and outside them. But like the men in Rowlands's ballad, they knew they were not alone in their distress. Suitably supported by the town and colony courts, any man could climb back to the top of the household hierarchy.

NOTES

1. A draft of this paper was presented at "Early America Examined and Distilled, or Pure Richard's Almanack," a conference in honor of Richard S. Dunn, May 18, 1996, at the University of Pennsylvania. I am grateful to the audience for many helpful comments and suggestions, most especially to Karin Wulf, Dallett Hemphill, Michael Zuckerman, and John Murrin. Sharon Block reviewed an early draft and made useful suggestions.

2. Rev. Newman Smyth, "Mrs. Eaton's Trial in 1644," *Papers of the New Haven Colony Historical Society* (New Haven: New Haven Colony Historical Society, 1894), 5:133–48; quotations from 138, 143. Anne Eaton's case was heard in a rare church trial, no doubt because her husband was the presiding magistrate of the colony. 1 Cor. 7:10 (King James Version) reads: "And unto the married I command, yet not I, but the Lord, Let not the wife depart from her husband." Mary Beth Norton, *Founding Mothers and Fathers: Gendered Power and the Forming of American Society* (New York: Knopf, 1996), also uses the Anne Eaton case to demonstrate the difficult position of elite women, who were empowered by their status but bound to submit to male domestic and civil authorities (165–74).

3. See Francis Jennings, *The Invasion of America: Indians, Colonialism, and the Cant of Conquest* (Chapel Hill: University of North Carolina Press, 1975); Neal Salisbury, *Manitou and Providence: Indians, Europeans, and the Making of New England* (New York: Oxford University Press, 1982); Richard Slotkin, *Regeneration through Violence: The Mythology of the American Frontier* (Middletown, Conn.: Wesleyan University Press, 1973), chs. 1–6.

4. Five cases of assault were prosecuted in the colony during its independent existence (1638–1665); allegations of violence among neighbors were also occasionally reported in civil suits. There were three murder prosecutions in the colony, but all the defendants were Indians accused of "murdering" English men in wartime. See *Records of the Colony and Plantation of New Haven, 1638–1649* (hereafter referred to as *NHCR I*), ed. Charles J. Hoadly (Hartford, Conn.: Case, Tiffany, 1857), 22, 135, 146; *Records of the Colony or Jurisdiction of New Haven from May 1653 to the Union* (hereafter referred to as *NHCR II*), ed. Charles J. Hoadly (Hartford, Conn.: Case, Lockwood, 1858), 458–63.

5. On the arbitrary nature of sex and gender identities, see Judith Butler, *Gender Trouble: Feminism and the Subversion of Identity* (New York: Routledge, 1990); Thomas Laqueur, *Making Sex: Body and Gender from the Greeks to Freud* (Cambridge: Harvard University Press, 1990); Michel Foucault, *The History of Sexuality*, 1, first English ed. (New York: Vintage Books, 1978).

6. "New-Haven's Settling in New-England, And some Lawes for Government, &c," *NHCR II*, 586–87 (on divorce and dower rights), 599–600 (on marriage), 607 (on vital records), 612–13 (on wills, inventories, and probate). That women were not included in the poll tax furnishes further evidence that women were not full political subjects, *NHCR II*, 581.

7. Although unmarried adult women not living in their fathers' households would be considered *femes soles*, this status was exceptional in early New England, where most women married at least once.

8. "Lawes for Government," *NHCR II*, 567–72. Voting rights for New England men were also contingent upon land ownership, and in New Haven, on church membership. Although I do not mean to slight these other very important factors that determined a man's social status, marriage has been overlooked in its contributions to men's status. I have explored these ideas more fully in "Men on Top? The Farmer, the Minister, and Marriage in Early New England," *Pennsylvania History* 64 (1997): 123–50.

9. On patriarchy and gendered notions of order, see Marilyn J. Westercamp, "Puritan

Patriarchy and the Problem of Revelation," *Journal of Interdisciplinary History* 23 (1993); Susan D. Amussen, "Gender, Family, and the Social Order, 1560–1725," and David E. Underdown, "The Taming of the Scold: The Enforcement of Patriarchal Authority in Early Modern England," both in *Order and Disorder in Early Modern England*, ed. Anthony Fletcher and John Stevenson (Cambridge and New York: Cambridge University Press, 1985).

10. Other historians have discounted hierarchy in marriage and have chosen to focus on the affective, companionate aspects of Puritan marriage. See Richard Godbeer, " 'Love Raptures': Marital, Romantic, and Erotic Images of Jesus Christ in Puritan New England, 1670–1730," *New England Quarterly* 68 (1995): 355–84; Edmund Leites, "The Duty to Desire: Love, Friendship, and Sexuality in Some Puritan Theories of Marriage," *Journal of Social History* 15 (1981–1982): 383–408. However, primary sources outside the prescriptive literature and sermons have little to say about the actual emotional content of people's relationships.

11. Elizabeth H. Pleck and Joseph H. Pleck, eds., *The American Man* (Englewood Cliffs, N.J.: Prentice-Hall, 1980), argue that there are four phases of manhood in America: agrarian patriarchy (1630–1820), the commercial age (1820–1860), the strenuous life (1861–1919), and companionate providing (1920–1965). Under agrarian patriarchy, the Plecks note the legal disparity of men and women in marriage, and argue that the institution is central to understanding manhood. They also note that patriarchy was a unifying domestic and political principal (8–12). See also Toby Ditz, "Shipwrecked; or, Masculinity Imperiled: Mercantile Representations of Failure and the Gendered Self in Eighteenth-Century Philadelphia," *Journal of American History* 81 (1994): 51–80; E. Anthony Rotundo, *American Manhood: Transformations in Masculinity from the Revolution to the Modern Era* (New York: Basic Books, 1993); Mark C. Carnes, *Secret Ritual and Manhood in Victorian America* (New Haven: Yale University Press, 1989); and Mark C. Carnes and Clyde Griffen, eds., *Meanings for Manhood: Constructions of Masculinity in Victorian America* (Chicago: University of Chicago Press, 1990).

12. For an analysis of the intersection of gender identities and power, see Catharine A. MacKinnon, *Toward a Feminist Theory of the State* (Cambridge: Harvard University Press, 1989).

13. Amussen, "Gender, Family, and the Social Order," and Underdown, "Taming of the Scold"; Jane Kamensky, "Talk Like a Man: Speech, Power, and Masculinity in Early New England," *Gender and History* 8 (1996): 22–47; Merry Wiesner, "Wandervogels and Women: Journeymen's Concepts of Masculinity in Early Modern German," *Journal of Social History* 24 (1991): 767–82.

14. *NHCR II*, 578; Norton, *Founding Mothers and Fathers*, cites Rhode Island's 1647 definition of treason, which was applicable to servants who murdered their masters, children their parents, and wives their husbands.

15. Ann Kibbey, *The Interpretation of Material Shapes in Puritanism: A Study of Rhetoric, Prejudice, and Violence* (Cambridge and New York: Cambridge University Press, 1986), argues that the close timing of the Pequot War and the Antinomian Crisis in Boston was not coincidental. She analyzes the means by which Puritan men dehumanized the Pequots as unchristian, uncivilized "others" in their efforts to justify the Pequot War, and connects this "othering" to the misogyny employed to dehumanize Puritan women accused of heresy or witchcraft. Perhaps wives accused of violence against their husbands can be interpreted as New England women fighting back. (I am indebted to Michael Bellesiles for helping me see this connection.)

16. Although the courts supported men on these points, I do not mean to suggest that

the relationship between the New Haven courts and individual householders was always so cooperative. In fact, householders greatly resented the courts' intrusions even while affirming their belief that family, town, and colony government were necessarily intertwined. For more on this point, see Ann M. Little, "A 'Wel Ordered Commonwealth': New Haven Colony, 1635–1690" (Ph.D. diss., University of Pennsylvania, 1996), chs. 2–3, 5.

17. *Rex v. Ebenezer Browne* (November 11, 1668), in *New Haven County Court Records* (hereafter referred to as *NHCCR*), 1:18–19; *Rex v. William Roberts* (November 1700), *NHCCR*, 2:40, 51, Connecticut State Library, Hartford. In *Women before the Bar: Gender, Law, and Society in Connecticut, 1639–1789* (Chapel Hill: University of North Carolina Press, 1995), Cornelia Hughes Dayton suggests that New Haven Colony and seventeenth-century New Haven County seems to have been particularly blind to wife abuse; men in Connecticut were fined and whipped for such behavior (136). She also notes that New Haven seems to have persisted in its blindness to wife abuse in the eighteenth century; only nine complaints were heard from 1710 to 1790, "and in all nine instances the husband was discharged once the initial term of his bond was up, since no witnesses (including his wife) appeared to testify that his miscarriage had persisted" (136–37). New Haven's peculiarity in this respect is borne out by C. Dallett Hemphill's findings in "Women in Court: Sex-Role Differentiation in Salem, Massachusetts, 1636 to 1683," *William and Mary Quarterly*, 3d ser., 39 (1982): 164–75. Hemphill found both women and men were prosecuted for spousal abuse in Essex County, Massachusetts, but notes that the prosecutions of women dropped off by the 1650s. Throughout the seventeenth century, wife beating was seen in court almost twice as often as husband beating. Hemphill cites six cases of women brought to court for husband abuse through 1668: *Records and Files of the Quarterly Courts of Essex County, Massachusetts* (Salem, Mass.: Essex Institute), 1911–1921, 1:6, 9, 25, 59, 230; 4:90. There were eleven husband abuse cases through 1671: ibid., 1:49, 57, 58, 133, 136, 138, 158, 258, 414, 423; 4:441.

18. In *Religion and Domestic Violence in Early New England: The Memoirs of Abigail Abbot Bailey* (Bloomington and Indianapolis: Indiana University Press, 1989), Ann Taves presents a singular primary source in the memoirs of an eighteenth- and early-nineteenth-century abused New England wife. Taves argues that Bailey's grounding in evangelical Congregationalism was central to her ability to suffer her husband's abuse in a time when mere abuse was not sufficient grounds for divorce. Bailey casts her memoir as an alternative captivity narrative and eventually secures a divorce on the grounds of incestuous adultery (with their daughter) after twenty-six years of marriage. On the subject of child abuse and its all-but-invisibility, see Norton, *Founding Mothers and Fathers*, 115, 118–19.

19. Dayton, *Women before the Bar*, says that eighteenth-century Connecticut was no better for abused wives as a result of the economic and social hardships women faced if they separated from their husbands, and the continued reluctance of courts to consider abuse in divorce petitions (137–47, 329–35). Norton, *Founding Mothers and Fathers*, asserts that one-third of all spousal-abuse cases in the English colonies before 1670 involved wives as defendants, a fact that she supposes is due to the challenge to male authority implied by husband abuse (78–79).

20. Susan Dwyer Amussen, " 'Being Stirred to Much Unquietness': Violence and Domestic Violence in Early Modern England," *Journal of Women's History* 6 (1994): 70–89. Amussen notes the frequent intervention of neighbors into violent marriages. She makes a convincing argument that domestic violence against women was understood in context with other forms of punitive violence: it had to be limited, and it had to be administered to punish a specific wrong. Similarly, in "Wife Beating, Domesticity, and Women's Inde-

pendence in Eighteenth-Century London," *Gender and History* 4 (1992), Margaret Hunt finds that community intervention was the crucial factor in a woman's ability to escape a brutal husband, although the intervention of others did not challenge the dominion of husbands over wives; it merely challenged the means and extremes of their power. L. R. Poos, "The Heavy-Handed Marriage Counsellor: Regulating Marriage in Some Later-Medieval English Local Ecclesiastical-Court Jurisdictions," *American Journal of Legal History* 34 (1995): 291–309, has found limited but significant intervention of church courts into cases of wife abuse. Elizabeth Pleck, in *Domestic Tyranny: The Making of Social Policy against Family Violence from Colonial Times to the Present* (New York: Oxford University Press, 1987), ch. 1, is somewhat less willing than Amussen to concede that limited violence against wives was acceptable, perhaps because her chapter is broadly "colonial" rather than specific to the seventeenth century. The appearance in the eighteenth and early nineteenth centuries of the "domesticated sentimental family" served to problematize wife beating. See also A. James Hammerton, *Cruelty and Companionship: Conflict in Nineteenth-Century Married Life* (London and New York: Routledge, 1992), ch. 3, "Companionate Marriage and the Challenge to Patriarchy." On the other hand, in "Wife Beating, Domesticity, and Women's Independence," Hunt argues that the shift from domestic violence against women as a publicly acknowledged and acceptable (to a point) means of correction in the seventeenth century to an impermissible abomination of family life in the eighteenth century was merely a rhetorical shift that rendered wife beating literally *unspeakable*: disguising the real abuse that women suffered (25–26).

21. Linda Gordon, in *Heroes of Their Own Lives: The Politics and History of Family Violence: Boston, 1880–1960* (New York: Viking, 1988), demonstrates that "family violence has been historically and politically constructed," and notes that the emergence of family violence as a social problem is correlated to political movements (3–6). *NHCR I* and *NHCR II*; *Ancient Town Records, Vol. I: New Haven Town Records, 1649–1662* (hereafter referred to as *NHTR I*), ed. Franklin Bowditch Dexter (New Haven: New Haven Colony Historical Society, 1917), and *Ancient Town Records, Vol. II: New Haven Town Records, 1649–1684* (hereafter referred to as *NHTR II*), ed. Franklin Bowditch Dexter (New Haven: New Haven Colony Historical Society, 1919); *Guilford Records*, vol. A, *1645–1716*, Town Clerk's Office, Guilford, Connecticut; *Branford Town Records*, vol. 1A, *1645–1679*, Town Clerk's Office, Branford, Connecticut; J. Wickham Case, *Southold Town Records* (Southold, N.Y.: S. W. Green's Son, 1882). Beyond the absence of wife abuse in official records, there are no ministerial pronouncements on the subject, nor are there any records to indicate that ministers counseled or intervened in abusive relationships.

22. *NHTR I*, 169–74. The name Isabell is conjectural, based on the appearance as a witness of an Isabell Langden who testified with Thomas Langden in a 1657 colony court case (*NHCR II*, 209, May 25).

23. *NHTR I*, 172.

24. Ibid., 55–56 (January 7, 1651); ibid., 111, 125–26 (March 2, 1652, May 4, 1652). Providing a place for secret negotiations toward marriage without the knowledge or consent of parents or masters was explicitly forbidden by New Haven's law on marriage (*NHCR II*, 599–600). In addition to the disorderly entertaining charge, Thomas had also been convicted of failing to maintain his fence (*NHTR I*, 52, December 3, 1650). Both Langdens were charged with contempt of court (*NHTR I*, 120, April 6, 1652), but the charges were dismissed the following month. In an unrelated action, Langden's wife was sued for slander and lost (*NHTR I*, 120, April 6, 1652), but the plaintiff accepted her apology.

25. *NHTR I*, 56.

26. Norton, *Founding Mothers and Fathers*, ch. 5, demonstrates the importance of neighborhood gossip in determining which criminal cases could be prosecuted. Pleck, *Domestic Tyranny*, notes the great reluctance of seventeenth-century New Englanders to interfere in wife-abuse cases, even when the woman felt in mortal danger (29–31, 33).

27. *NHTR I*, 174. Whipping plus paying the wronged property owner double the value of the stolen goods was standard punishment for convicted thieves who were not indentured servants. See, for example, *NHCR I*, 77.

28. Dayton, *Women before the Bar*, 106–7. Two historians of domestic violence have demonstrated the importance of community and state recognition and condemnation of wife abuse to the safety of victims and their willingness to report their husbands' abuse. Although his time period covers the late nineteenth through the late twentieth centuries, David Peterson makes the connection between the acuteness of domestic violence for women and the increasingly privatized family. He argues that community oversight was much greater in the nineteenth century, and thus victims of domestic violence had more assistance than women in twentieth-century nuclear households. On a similar tack, Alan Williams argues that when the state made redress available to women in the forms of responsive police and *lettres de cachet*, women used them vigorously against errant husbands. See David Peterson, "Wife Beating: An American Tradition," *Journal of Interdisciplinary History* 23, no. 1 (summer 1992): 97–118; Alan Williams, "Patterns of Conflict in Eighteenth-Century Parisian Families," *Journal of Family History* 18, no. 1 (1993): 39–52.

29. *NHCCR I*, 18–19 (November 11, 1668); family relationships determined in Donald Lines Jacobus, *Families of Ancient New Haven* (Rome, N.Y.: author, 1923), 1:346–47.

30. See for example, *NHCR I*, 233–39 (April 7, 1646), 473–76 (July 3, 1649), *NHCR II*, 242–47 (May 31, 1658); *NHTR I*, 245–46 (July 3, 1655), 460–61 (September 4, 1660); *NHCCR I*, 8 (November 14, 1666). In all of these cases it is clear that the husbands were not involved in the original crimes but were still called to court to answer for their wives' behavior. Wives occasionally appeared in court on their husbands' behalf, but only when the men were out of town, as when Hannah Browne appeared to answer for the charge of disorderly entertaining for her husband, John *NHTR II*, 26–31 (February 3, 1663).

31. *NHCR I*, 476 (July 3, 1649). Mary Newman's name taken from Jacobus, *Families of Ancient New Haven*, 1313. The same source also notes that this disorderly woman, after Francis Newman died, married first the town minister and then the governor of Connecticut. Francis Newman was named as a codefendant and was accused of personally harassing Mrs. Fuller, but he did so only after the troubles between her and his wife had advanced to judicial proceedings. He himself had a troubled history with Hannah Marsh Fuller; four years before he had been rebuked by the colony court for calling her a "Billingsgate slutt" when she was a newly arrived servant, *NHCR I*, 180 (December 3, 1645).

Francis Newman was a well-connected man who by 1649 had served New Haven Town and Colony in a variety of capacities, including stints as an ensign, the surveyor of roads and bridges, lieutenant of the artillery, and court recorder. At the time of the trouble with the Fullers, he was the colony secretary and town deputy (magistrate). *NHCR I*, 76, 148, 156, 158, 171, 274, 304, 325, 354, 381, 456, 457, 481. He was elected governor on May 26, 1658 (*NHCR II*, 231).

32. *NHCR I*, 233–39 (April 7, 1646); quotation from 239. Norton also uses this case to make the same point; *Founding Mothers and Fathers*, 52–54. Dayton, *Women before the Bar*, uses this case to suggest that the inquiry into the sexual attacks and the punishment meted out to her attackers was remarkably proactive compared to Connecticut courts in the eighteenth century (234–37).

33. *NHCCR I,* 8 (Nov. 14, 1666). Elizabeth Morris's name taken from Jacobus, *Families of Ancient New Haven,* 1212.

34. *NHCR II,* 242–46 (May 31, 1658). The name of Richard Crabb's wife is unknown.

35. Ibid., 247 (May 31, 1658); emphasis added.

36. Dayton, *Women before the Bar,* 285–300. She notes the tendency of New Haven's courts to neutralize condemning speech by women: "By focusing on 'the rule' of godly speech that was to guide all inhabitants and by not encouraging the naming of scolds, colony leaders employed the comforting strategy of denying the potential existence of the most telling portent of hierarchical inversion—unruly women"(300). Robert St. George has demonstrated the cultural importance of "speech crimes" and their importance in defining gender roles in " 'Heated' Speech and Literacy in Seventeenth-Century New England," in *Seventeenth-Century New England: Publications of the Colonial Society of Massachusetts* 63 (Boston: Massachusetts Historical Society, 1984): 275–322.

37. Butler, *Gender Trouble,* chs. 1–2. For more on the interdependence of even parodies of gender roles, see Sue-Ellen Case, "Toward a Butch-Femme Aesthetic," in *Making a Spectacle: Feminist Essays on Contemporary Women's Theatre,* ed. Lynda Hart (Ann Arbor: University of Michigan Press, 1989).

38. Quoted in Anthony Fletcher, *Gender, Sex, and Subordination in England, 1500–1800* (New Haven: Yale University Press, 1995), 20–21.

39. See, for example, Underdown, "The Taming of the Scold"; Susan Dwyer Amussen, *An Ordered Society: Gender and Class in Early Modern England* (Oxford: Oxford University Press, 1988), 49–50, 69, 118.

40. On the English origins of early colonists, see David Hackett Fisher, *Albion's Seed: Four British Folkways in America* (New York: Oxford University Press, 1989); on skimmingtons' regional character, see David E. Underdown, *Revel, Riot, and Rebellion: Popular Politics and Culture in England, 1603–1660* (Oxford: Oxford University Press, 1985), ch. 4.

41. Dayton, *Women before the Bar,* ch. 1.

42. In addition to the New Haven Town and Colony records, which are published, this survey of court records included the published town records of Southold and the manuscript town records of Guilford and Branford, but those towns had no similar cases.

43. Little, *A 'Wel Ordered Commonwealth,'* chs. 4, 5; *NHTR I,* 490 (October 21, 1661).

44. All of the following page numbers are from Jacobus, *Families of Ancient New Haven.* Of the couples who stayed married: the Dickermans, 536; Beckleys, 162; and Lineses, 1090–92. Jacobus, *Families of Ancient New Haven,* states that Ruth Briggs deserted her husband shortly after her trial (1449). Both of these couples remained childless. The Briggses and Dickermans were second-generation New Englanders, but the Beckleys and the Lineses were older. (Both couples were married and bearing children in the 1640s). At the time their travails were discussed in court, the Briggses were newlyweds, and the Dickermans already had one baby and another on the way.

45. *NHTR I,* 485–86 (August 6, 1661); Mary Cooper Dickerman's and Mary Kimberly's names taken from Jacobus, *Families of Ancient New Haven,* 536, 1070. At the time of his suit against Wheadon, Abraham Dickerman was about twenty-seven.

46. Interestingly, Thomas Wheadon had troubles with another married couple five years later. He was sued by Richard Newman for calling Mrs. Newman a "rayler," and for complaining that she had spread nasty rumors that implied he was a thief. Once again, the court found for the plaintiff and fined Wheadon forty shillings plus court costs, *NHTR II,* 157–58 (December 5, 1665).

47. *NHTR II,* 253 (January 5, 1670); ibid., 259 (April 5, 1670); ibid., 268 (December 6, 1670).

48. *NHTR I*, 209–10 (May 2, 1654). Although superficially this case might look more like a wife-abuse case, it also seems to indicate that Goodwife Beckley was willing to track her husband down at the ordinary and try to drag him out. This would give weight to Hitchcock's charge, then, that Goodwife Beckley was not afraid to assert herself to achieve her desired ends.

49. *NHTR I*, 413–14 (September 6, 1659).

50. *Oxford English Dictionary*, 2d ed. (Oxford: Oxford University Press, 1989), 2:525. Some of the examples of that exact usage of ''breech'' or ''breeches'': ''He is a cokes: and worthy strokes, whose wife the Breeches beare'' (T. Howell, Newe Sonn., 1568); ''That you might still have worn the Petticoat, And ne'er have stolne the Breech from Lancaster'' (Shakespeare, Henry VI, 5.5.24, 1593); ''She that is master of her husband must weare the breetches'' (*Choice, Chance & C*, 1606); ''The female rules, and our Affections wear the breeches'' (Glanvill, *Sceps. Sci.* xvi. 100, 1665).

51. *NHTR I*, 414–15. Jacobus, *Families of Ancient New Haven*, 162, reports that Richard Beckley eventually moved his family to Wethersfield, Connecticut.

52. *NHTR I*, 415.

53. Ibid., 416.

54. Ibid., 514 (March 4, 1662). There are no clues as to which family she lived with.

55. Ibid., 246–47 (July 3, 1655); Alice Lines's name taken from Jacobus, *Families of Ancient New Haven*, 1090. She was accused of stealing a cap, a purse, a pin cushion, some venison as it was being cured, eighteen pence worth of wampum, and some wool, among other things.

56. *NHTR I*, 246–47 (July 3, 1655); Jacobus, *Families of Ancient New Haven*, 1090–91. Alice Lines, for all of her thievery and assault charges, was sentenced somewhat ambiguously to be ''seveerly corrected,'' which presumably meant a public whipping because she was pregnant at her trial and the execution of her punishment was deferred until after she gave birth. Additionally, she was ordered to provide double restitution for her thefts immediately, and to sit in the stocks for an hour.

57. *NHTR II*, 159–61 (December 14, 1665). Benjamin Graves was found guilty of the charges against him regarding Ruth Briggs, and fined forty shillings plus court charges and prison fees of ten shillings; if he did not pay, he was to be whipped and banished from the colony.

58. Ibid., 161–62 (December 14, 1665). Ruth Pinion Moore Briggs was a daughter of the disorderly Pinion family Norton documents at the beginning of *Founding Mothers and Fathers*, 27–38. Ruth herself was eventually executed for infanticide in 1668.

59. Rowlands, *A Whole Crew of Kind Gossips*, quoted in Anthony Fletcher, *Gender, Sex, and Subordination in England, 1500–1800* (New Haven: Yale University Press, 1995), 21.

Patrols worked in all Southern states before and after the Revolutionary War and even during the Civil War. *The Plantation Police or Home-Guard Examining Negro Passes on the Levee Road below New Orleans*, Francis H. Schell (1834–1909) [incorrectly credited to F. B. Schell]. Engraving appeared in *Frank Leslie's Illiustrated Newspaper*, July 11, 1863.

Chapter Three

Colonial and Revolutionary Era Slave Patrols of Virginia

Sally E. Hadden

The initial thoughts of most people, when considering white-on-black violence in the colonial world, naturally gravitate toward masters and slaves. Scholarship about colonial bondmen has grown exponentially in the past thirty years, breaking new ground concerning labor practices, slave family size and structure, slave fugitives, the Caribbean connection and importation rates, relations between slaves and Native Americans, and much more.[1] This recent research has refined the traditional story of slavery in America, which in the twentieth century had previously focused far too much on slavery in the antebellum period.

Colonial or antebellum, at the root of slavery lay violence, the compulsion to serve under duress—yet what we know regarding white violence toward bondmen in the colonial era has changed very little in the past quarter century compared with other aspects of early American slavery. Perhaps this is because there seem to be few elements of white violence left to explain or clarify beyond the obvious: masters used torture, whippings, deprivation, and any other form of coercion available to get their reluctant "property" to work and obey. Although all this is true, it only partly describes the violence done by whites against blacks in colonial America. Surrounding the bipolar world of master and slave were agents appointed by the community who could also use force against blacks. These agents were called slave patrollers, and their work in Virginia began in 1727 and continued well beyond the American Revolution.[2]

Slave patrols in Virginia developed as weaknesses in other areas of slave control became evident. If masters had had perfect command of their bondmen, there would have been no need for patrols. Threats or actual punishments inflicted by the master would have been enough to keep disobedient slaves in check. Similarly, other civil authorities, such as the sheriff, could not stop slaves from running away, selling stolen goods for whiskey, or doing any other act that undermined the mastery of whites over blacks. One man alone—neither master nor sheriff—could not stop them. When communities in England experienced thefts or other crimes, they invoked the *posse comitatus*, a call for all able-bodied men to pursue the felon until he or she was captured. In America, this "hue and cry" system might have succeeded, but the solution poorly suited many parts of thinly settled colonial Virginia and was quickly abandoned. Profit-minded individuals might attempt to curb slaves' illicit behavior, as some Dutch slave catchers did in the mid-seventeenth century, but Virginians wanted more vigorous controls put into place. The colonial assembly experimented with various incentives to capture runaway slaves, offering rewards in tobacco or money to urge whites to be more vigilant about bondmen, but these offers still did not do enough in the late seventeenth and early eighteenth centuries.[3]

Disturbing events in the 1720s caused white Virginians to create slave patrols. A slave revolt in 1721 and prodding from colonial lieutenant-governor Hugh Drysdale about the militia's inadequacies in terminating the revolt finally persuaded the Virginia House of Burgesses to take decisive action. Instead of simply reacting to slave revolts after they were already happening, why not prevent them from starting in the first place? If slaves plotted insurrections when they gathered during holidays, then a portion of the militia should prevent those meetings. The legislators instructed militia captains in 1727 to call out patrols during the holidays of Christmas, Easter, and Whitsuntide to break up slave meetings and disperse slaves who congregated during the festive celebrations. Initially, patrollers could not whip slaves; captured slaves had to be taken to a constable or justice of the peace, who might order that they be whipped. In 1738, the assembly considered slave patrols such a valuable deterrent that it expanded patrol duties to make them year-round, and enjoined patrollers not only to scatter slave meetings but also to visit slave quarters and take up slaves found "strolling about" without passes. A few years later, the assembly permitted patrollers themselves to whip slaves.[4]

Slave patrols also had the authority to go onto land owned by other white men and search their slaves' cabins. No warrant was needed, save the appointment slip given a patroller when his term of service began (which varied from three months to one year). Even after the Revolution and the creation of both state and national Bills of Rights, white Virginians did not question the legitimacy of slave patrols' entry into their lands and their slaves' cabins without duly issued search warrants. If patrollers encountered a slave away from the master's home, the slave had to present them a proper pass from the master, giving permission to be absent from the plantation, listing the slave's destination, and noting the time and date. Without the pass, the slave was particularly vulnerable to the patrols' violent form of summary justice—a whipping, followed by being tied up and returned to the master's home. Patroller activities in Virginia paralleled those of patrols that South Carolina's assembly had instituted in 1704, with an important exception: Virginians who served in a patrol were exempted from public, county, and parish levies during their term of service. This financial incentive provided by the colony was augmented by some Virginia counties, which chose to pay additional sums to their patrollers, fees that can be traced in annual county tax reports. As counties grew, their slave populations also expanded, and those populations required more diligent oversight.[5]

Three Virginia counties—Southampton, Sussex, and Chesterfield—saw their populations increase rapidly and the need for slave patrols increase likewise. In the half century preceding the Revolutionary War, each of these counties gained so much in population that it was subdivided from a larger "parent" county and given independent existence as a legal entity. The three counties lie south of the James River, in an area roughly known as "Southside" Virginia. Southampton's story is the same one shared by more than ten other Virginia counties in the years preceding the Revolution: extensive population growth resulting in county subdivision and further subdivision, coupled with increasingly large slave communities. Sprawling settlement of Isle of Wight County meant that some residents traveled five days to reach the county courthouse. The legislature divided Isle of Wight in 1749 and created Southampton County, which lies along the southeastern border of Sussex County.

Settlers flooded into Sussex County between 1715 and 1735, many of them drawn by the colony's sale of lands designated for the use of the College of William and Mary. Bridges had replaced ferries, and the Nottoway Indians had retreated to the western edges of the county by the 1750s. Between 1740 and 1776, more than 350 residents patented new land claims in Sussex, carving out plots between Seacock Swamp and Blackwater River. Sussex received so many settlers that in 1754 the colonial assembly made it a separate county, subdivided from Surry County. By 1787, more than 1,200 white residents made their home in Sussex County.[6]

Chesterfield County had an earlier development, different from either Southampton's or Sussex's. It began as part of Henrico County, on the James River, and was one the earliest settled parts of Virginia. By 1650, its eastern quadrant had been heavily settled, although the more remote western reaches were still home to Native Americans. Around 1700, the colony's assembly encouraged the settlement of Huguenot refugees, and by 1730, many of them had settled in the central region of Chesterfield County—their French names in the deed books (Du Puy, Faure, Michaux) are plentiful. In 1749, enough settlers had filled Henrico that the General Assembly created Chesterfield County as a separate entity.[7]

Precise population figures for all three counties are difficult to calculate because no elaborate statewide population tallies exist before 1787. Prior to that time, the best information about county settlement sizes is derived from extant tithe lists, taken by county officials as a means of allocating county expenses on a proportional basis. However, tithe lists included only adult white men and slave men and women over the age of sixteen, omitting white women and all children from their calculus. Tithe lists for Southampton in 1755 indicate a probable population of about 4,000 whites and approximately 2,000 slaves.[8] The 1787 tax lists for Sussex and Chesterfield suggest that both counties had the reverse situation: slaves outnumbered whites by nearly 2 to 1. After the Revolution, Chesterfield's white population hovered near 3,000. With a black majority in these two counties, white officials may have authorized the use of greater force against slaves by paying slave patrols and ordering out greater numbers of patrols in the pre-Revolutionary period. Certainly, all three counties had sizable slave populations by the mid-1750s, which very likely prompted greater concern about their control. And the steadily rising white population may have made it reasonable for county courts to consider paying the slave patrollers because their work required more and more visits to slave quarters and suspected gathering places.[9]

The policy of payment or financial abatement led to the creation of detailed records by patrols, who justified their violent nocturnal activities to courts in order to collect their fees. Itemized patrol journals exist for Southampton County in the 1750s and 1760s, and for Sussex and Chesterfield Counties in the 1760s and 1770s. There are additional sources about patrols, though not nightly patrol reports, in Amelia, Loudoun, Norfolk, and Surry Counties for the same period. These patrol records, or journals, are unique historical resources from which we can learn more about how Virginia communities enforced limits on slave movement and created barriers to illicit slave meetings. Patrol records, even in the period after the Revolution, are rarely so detailed as these itemized journals that list specific plantations visited and the exact evenings that slave patrols went on duty.[10]

Although an argument premised upon the absence, then appearance, of a certain type of document is vulnerable to contradiction (the missing documents might have been destroyed or lost in the intervening years), the existence of extremely detailed patrol records in the 1750s, 1760s, and 1770s when none can be found in earlier periods strongly suggests that a new policy prompted the creation of a new document type. Virginia counties had the option to pay slave patrollers in this era, and these patrol journals were notarized by militia captains or court clerks and then preserved among the county court papers. The existence of slave patrol records among court papers (when patrollers served under the authority of the local militia) indicates that patrollers presented these journals as evidence of patrol work completed for payment due. In 1769, court clerk J. Grant of Southampton noted that "Ben Griffin master of the patroll" had presented his patrol journal "in order to be accounted in the county levy." County clerks preserved the slave patrol reports among other court documents that indicated to whom county funds had been paid and for what purposes.[11]

The appearance and then subsequent disappearance of these extremely detailed records after a few years in each county, coupled with the continuing payment of patrollers year after year, has further implications. Slave patrols continued to receive modest fees for their work even in later years for which detailed patrol journals do not exist. Annual reckonings of county bills and taxes levied can be found in court minute books, which list the obligations owing and the money to be collected for each county; slave patrollers routinely appear in the county levy lists, although the names change from year to year. But the journals of their nightly work simply disappear, after a brief period in each county. Apparently, county court justices stopped requiring patrols to document their nightly rounds prior to payment by the court. Whether their work seemed onerous enough not to demand written confirmation or justices saw the patrollers at work firsthand (as they must have done, when slave patrols visited the slave quarters of local JPs), after the first few years in each county, court justices no longer needed documentation before they paid slave patrols for their work corralling wayward slaves. Thus, the extant patrol journals we have form a rare source base from which to examine the work that community members performed disciplining the slaves of their neighbors.[12]

From these patrol-created files we can learn much about the pattern of violence that slaves experienced in colonial Virginia at the hands of whites who were not necessarily their owners. The earliest extant notes recording patrol activity come from Southampton County in 1754. Three patrol groups submitted extensive accounts in that year, listing the days and times they rode and giving details of the slaves they captured. A comparison of the names of patrollers with the names of the plantations visited suggests that the three patrol groups worked as distinct units in different parts of the county and submitted separate reports of their activities. Multiple patrol groups would have been a necessity in the large and growing counties of Virginia. Even though Southampton had more white residents than slaves by the mid-1750s, the fact that whites outnumbered blacks did not ease the fears of many Virginia colonists; attempted slave revolts in 1729 and 1730, and rumors of insurrections later in the 1730s must have frightened many whites. The knowledge that runaway slaves had repeatedly tried, and failed, to establish maroon communities along the northern, western, and southern margins of Virginia must have been unsettling, and that knowledge provided a strong rationale for the activities and payment of county slave patrols.[13]

The details in patrolling journals vary dramatically, depending upon the individual recordkeeper, but broad similarities can be found in all. Colonial Virginia slave patrols typically rode in groups of four or five, and their journals commence by listing the individuals' names. "John Brantly & Philip Bran[t]ly & Will[ia]m Grimmer & William Joyner Junr have Rode in the patrole servis the 28th of Septem[ber]" runs a standard patrol entry.[14]

Virtually every patrol report gives specifics about the number of hours worked, with a few presenting precise information about the exact number of hours worked by each man in the group. In Southampton, John Seuter, Jacob Turner, Simon Harris, Robert Bittle, and William Kirby worked precisely 50, 32, 126, 108, and 126 hours, respectively, in an eight-month span. The patrol reports usually carry the signature of the militia captain, justice of the peace, or court clerk who vouched that the work had been completed faithfully. Patrols most often worked from sundown to sunup, during the "Negro's day"—when slaves left their cabins to attend meetings or to travel after their workday ended. As they patrolled, they encountered both slave men and women. After an evening's work in October 1754, patroller Bennet Hilsman wrote, "We Patrolers did ketch a negroe man slave belonging to Joshua Barnes & a Negro woman slave and Childe . . . and she was a Runaway she said." By examining the ads placed about runaway slaves in newspapers, historians have determined that young men were more likely than any other kind of slave to flee their masters, and patroller records confirm that they more frequently encountered male slaves on their rounds. Each of the Southampton reports for 1754-1755, and another detailed Southampton journal for 1769, mentions the capture of men; only one indicates the apprehension of a female slave.[15]

When caught by patrols, slaves might be turned over to the county sheriff or returned directly to their owners or overseers. In either case, they risked multiple beatings, one at the hands of the patrol and another when turned over to the next authority. On October 5, 1754, Southampton patrols caught two slaves without passes, whipped them both, and then returned them to their owners. Some patrols simply returned a captured bondman without administering any punishment, as one group did when it found a slave "belonging to William Cooper." Whether the temperament of the master or the slave's circumstances at the time of capture made any difference to the patrol is hard to gauge (and undoubtedly varied from case to case), but perhaps Cooper's slave was thought to have a master who would inflict a punishment that would have rendered a whipping by patrollers unnecessary.

One thing would not save a slave from a beating, however: the social status of his owner. Contrary to what we might expect about social deference in the colonial world, an owner's economic or political status would not deter the whips of patrollers. When patrollers caught a "Negro Man belonging to Etheldred Taylor," they whipped him and then took him back to Taylor's plantation. The slave's punishment was administered despite the patrollers' knowledge that Taylor was part of the Southampton elite (he served as a member of the House of Burgesses). Likewise, Sussex patrollers caught and whipped slaves belonging to William Lightfoot, Nicholas Massenburg, and John Cargill despite their high social status as justices of the peace and officers in the county militia.[16]

Slaves who traveled great distances before capture merited special mention in patrol records, such as the slave caught in Southampton County whose owner lived "over Blackwater," a swampy river separating Southampton from nearby Isle of Wight and Nansemond Counties. Slaves who belonged on plantations beyond Southampton's boundaries were surrendered to the Southampton sheriff for a whipping, as were those owned by "Matthew Holland living in Nansemond county." Runaways being transported back to their owners would be whipped by the sheriff of each county passed through; the further the journey, the more the beatings.

Some slaves fled to nearby cities or to swampy areas. Both destinations held promise: a city could provide anonymity among the abundant urban slave population, and a swamp might mask human presence as well as discourage hunters from entering. The proximity of towns like Richmond and Petersburg at the edges of Chesterfield County must have been a lure, as were Harry's Swamp, Joseph Swamp, and marshes along the Nottoway River in Sussex County. Several Virginia patrols attempted to interdict these "attractive nuisances" by means of vigilant reconnaissance of their perimeters, in a vain effort to prevent runaways from ever reaching sanctuary within them. Every so often, patrols would have to enter towns and swamps to search for slaves who had managed to slip through the cordon. When found, such bondmen could expect a vicious beating.

Patrollers carried no special equipment on their rounds, although they relied upon the tools of intimidation available to slave owners. Colonial slave patrols worked almost exclusively on horseback, which gave them great mobility. They could scour large areas in a few hours and visit as many as six slave quarters in a single evening, even though the plantations might be widely separated. Relying upon horses increased range of movement but decreased the element of surprise. Runaway slaves might conceal themselves from a group of galloping horsemen they could hear from a distance, if there were places to hide. Mounted patrollers could cow frightened slaves, especially in the late evening; figures looming in the darkness on animals five and six feet tall could appear like giants or monsters of black folklore. Patrollers played upon these fears and myths by dressing in dark clothing to conceal their appearance and, on occasion, by costuming themselves as ghosts. For some slaves recently arrived from Africa, the patrols may have been reminiscent of the slave catchers who had carried them off into bondage. If horses and dark clothing could make patrols appear supernatural, the whips patrollers wielded must have seemed all too familiar. Most slave owners had whips at their disposal, and these scourges could cut a slave until blood ran and bones showed.[17]

Although patrollers had the authority to punish runaways and truants, they had to keep some of their violent urges in check. Slaves beaten by patrols too severely at night were of little use to their masters as laborers the next day. Even though masters recognized the volition of their slaves as independent beings, in the end, slaves were still property, pieces of merchandise. Slave "property" flogged to excess was less valuable to the master. The actions of patrollers were exempt from prosecution because colonial law empowered them to catch and whip slaves, but the law could not prevent irritated slave owners from finding ways to take subtle revenge on a too-brutal patroller. A patroller who "excessively corrected" the bondman of a neighbor could be refused a loan, omitted from a party, snubbed at church, or passed over for selection to a county office like sheriff or constable. That patroller might find his own slaves given extreme beatings as retaliation the next time they ventured off his plantation, too. The interdependence of colonial Virginia communities meant that white citizens had a variety of opportunities to register their dislike of a patroller who beat a neighbor's slave too harshly. In this sense, community norms placed limits on a patroller's discretion; unless he was oblivious to community censure, no patroller could afford (literally or figuratively) to discipline another man's slave too cruelly.

The men who served as patrollers came from most ranks of society in Sussex, Southampton, and Chesterfield, and slaveholders could be found among them. Of the Sussex patrollers in 1763, John Sturdivant owned three slaves in 1777 and John Wynne owned eleven slaves in 1787. And the men chosen for work as patrollers sometimes experienced great increases in the number of slaves they owned; patrols included men whose fortunes were on the rise, like William Hatcher, who owned one slave in 1762, later became constable, and owned seven slaves in 1787. Patrolling could provide an introduction for young men to the practice of slave discipline and to acting as a community authority figure. Brothers William and Matthew Turner lived with their father, who owned no slaves in 1762; they served together as patrollers in Chesterfield County in 1777, and by 1787 had between them a total of eight slaves.[18]

Patrol duty did not fall exclusively upon slaveholders, however; at least half the whites who lived in Southside Virginia did not own slaves in the period before the Revolution. In colonial Virginia, owners and nonowners rode together on patrol in roughly fifty-fifty proportions. Counties like Chesterfield, Sussex, and Southampton repeatedly chose patrols along the same patterns as had Amelia and Norfolk Counties in previous decades. A longtitudinal study of patrols appointed between 1750 and 1780 found that slightly more than half of all Amelia County and Norfolk County patrollers owned slaves, usually one to five. "The men appointed in both counties appear to fit into the middle status groups of their respective counties as well, and included some of the biggest land owners and slave owners in the county." The choice of slave owners to work on patrols with men who did not own slaves makes sense when considered in the context of violence against slaves. Bondmen were too valuable to be left solely to the violent urges of the latter; slave owners would make sure that slaves as property did not suffer excessively at the hands of patrollers who might not care if a victim could not work in the fields the next day.[19]

A balanced patrol could ensure other important elements. Owners might be more keen on making certain that a patrol did its duty; after all, a runaway slave meant one less set of productive hands on an owner's farm, a circumstance that a nonowner might dismiss as trivial. Owners might also be more aware of relationships between slaves on different plantations: whose bondmen might attend a religious service at a central plantation on a given night, or which slave men might be courting slave women on farms distant from their own. The intimate knowledge that proceeded from actually owning slaves (gained from overheard conversations or changes in slave behavior from day to day) could be valuable for a patrol group to be effective. Slave owner patrollers could also pressure the patrol group to avoid becoming predictable in its outings, that is, to vary the times of operations.

Many patrols deliberately varied the nights of their work, so as to be less predictable in their movements. Southampton patrols in 1755 recorded that they worked on two Thursdays and a Wednesday in March, April, and May. Location as well as frequency varied not only by day of the week but also by time of day. If patrols became too predictable, slaves could slip through the vigilance of white Virginians. Patrols might work during the daytime, although that was less common than nightly rounds. Records for Southampton, Chesterfield, and Sussex all indicate that patrols could work an entire evening and sometimes continue until the following afternoon. Simon Harris, John Seuter, and William Kirby rode for more than twelve hours, returning home "about two o clocke in the afternoone." But despite attempts to mislead slaves about when they might be operating, patrols still worked repeatedly on Saturday and Sunday evenings, as the patrollers of one Southampton district did in 1754: they worked, successively, on a

Saturday, Sunday, Sunday, Saturday, and Saturday during one two-month period. The repetitive patrolling on some weekends was not by chance. After all, more slaves had permission to travel on weekends than at any other time. But virtually every set of patrol records extant for Virginia demonstrates that patrols had no set pattern.[20]

The locations patrollers searched also had to be not easily guessed at or slaves might avoid capture. Patrols could not go only to slave quarters or their discipline would be ineffective; they had to search out the hidden gathering spots and meeting places slaves used after dark. Truants as well as runaways used these secret locations to congregate with other slaves, away from the prying eyes of their masters and other whites. Scholars who have studied slave truancy disagree about whether it revealed political consciousness among bondmen or was a form of direct slave resistance comparable to arson and rebellion. In any case, truancy, or "lying out," became a capital offense in colonial Virginia—an indication of how slaves had frustratingly remained beyond the total control of white masters. Patrols had to search not just slave cabins but also wooded areas, riverbanks, deserted buildings, and woodland paths—wherever they thought slaves might be likely to congregate.[21]

If patrollers intended to accomplish much work on their farms during the day and end their nightly travels in their own beds, they would work in the areas nearest their homes. Indeed, they could not help doing so, for patrollers were drawn from each captain's district of the county militia, each district representing a different county area. Like Sussex and Chesterfield patrollers, in 1754 Southampton patrollers worked in the areas of the county nearest their homes. For Robert Bittle, Simon Harris, Jacob Turner, and William Kirby, this meant the eastern area, roughly one-quarter of the county. Sussex County patrollers in 1763 went to the lands of their near neighbors, for their names are intermixed with those of the slave owners they watched in the tax lists of the period.

Although regulations in South Carolina prohibited a patrol's "beat" from being larger than a few square miles, no such regulations limited the Virginia militia or its patrols. In the eastern portion of Southampton County, Bittle, Harris, Turner, and Kirby had responsibility for the area between the towns of Jerusalem and Franklin (stretching from the county's center to the southeast and the North Carolina border, a distance of some five miles) and then running some fifteen miles north along the Blackwater River toward Vicksville and Seacock Swamp. Indeed, just as the Blackwater River defines the eastern boundary of Southampton County, the swamp dominates the county's eastern landscape. Characterizing the swamp are numerous streams and marshlands like Jack's Branch and Black Creek, Burk and Cypress Swamps. The Blackwater could be crossed only at selected bridges and fords, and the area patrolled by the four men was crisscrossed by little roads connecting farms tucked among the moors. Riding the four miles from Judkin's Mill to the town of Franklin, they would pass at least fifteen farms, certainly an efficient means to search numerous slave quarters. But slave quarters were not the only place patrollers hunted their human quarry. Venturing into swamps and along rivers was also part of the job. How else could they find the slaves who avoided main roads and trails? The patrols of Chester-field in 1760 worked north, along the James River in the region known as Bermuda, visiting various plantations (Howlett, Parker, Markham) as they neared the northeast corner of the county. Matthew Branch presented his report of the patrol's work to the militia captain John Howlett, whose house they visited last and who notarized their journal. Given that their patrolling had ended at daybreak, Howlett may have signed the document as he ate his breakfast.

The roads of a county could define much of the repetitive quality of patrol work. As they plied their rounds, patrollers would go to plantations in a se-quence dictated by the road. The Sussex County patrol journal of 1763 indicates this pattern most clearly. Almost every evening they went on duty between April 30 and November 6, 1763, slave patrols went to four homes in succession: those of Benjamin Cocke, John Chambliss, Heartwell Marrable, and "Colonel" Massen-burg. The four slave owners lived on adjacent holdings connected by either trails or roads that made it convenient for patrollers to go from farm to farm in a set sequence. The pattern can be confirmed from tax lists made in 1782; the Massen-burg and Marrable homes on the list are separated by only a few other names. This same patrolling pattern can be discerned almost a century later in North Carolina. Wake County patrols of 1857 went to slave quarters in a set order each night, and roads determined the order. Patrollers could not alter a county's geography, nor the proximity of one farm to the next. Logically, then, they took advantage of the roads that led from one plantation to another.[22]

Because patrollers worked in or near their homes, it is not surprising that they sometimes worked in family groups. In an area thickly latticed by family rela-tionships, patrolling did not have to be carried out in the presence of strangers. Although the slaves captured might not know the white men who held them captive and beat them so deliberately, the white men almost always knew one another, and were not infrequently related. The 1763 Sussex patrollers Charles and John Sturdivant were brothers and members of the numerous Sturdivant clan resident in the county. The 1769 Southampton patrollers were Benjamin, Thomas, and Micajah Griffin. Tax lists suggest that Thomas and Micajah were brothers or near cousins because their lands lay so close together. The same pattern prevailed in Chesterfield, when William Turner and Blackman Turner rode side by side in the 1770s, as did the two William Hatchers. Fathers and sons, cousins, uncles, and nephews joined in patrols, enforcing the regulations on slave behavior. The only family members not clearly required to participate were women. Unlike South Carolina, Virginia did not obligate females who owned slaves to provide a substitute to serve on patrol duty.[23]

Just as patrols worked in family groups, the farms they visited were often connected by family ties, among both owners and slaves. When the Chesterfield patrols rode in 1777, they worked the central portion of the county, from the base of Newby Bridge Road up to the Hundred Road and then east toward the courthouse. On March 29, patrols went to the plantations of Henry Winfree, Harry Winfree, and Major Winfree. They began at the home of Francis Farmer, a likely relation of patroller "B. Farmer" and concluded at the home of James

Farmer, probably another relation of his. Likewise, the 1763 Sussex county pa-trollers, Stith and John Wynne, and John and Charles Sturdivant regularly began their rounds at William Wynne's farm or concluded their rounds at William Sturdivant's home. The Sturdivant brothers, when on patrol at the home of Stith Parham on May 18, 1763, would have been visiting their future brother-in-law; Stith later married their sister Lucretia. Patrolling typically began or ended at the home of a patroller's relatives, who provided food and a comfortable resting place at the beginning or end of a long night. After ten, twelve, or more hours in the saddle, a warm fire and refreshing drink might be especially welcome, partic-ularly if the patrollers' quarry had eluded them.[24]

When patrols knew of a slave who refused to curb his wandering ways, they could make special efforts to restrain him. In 1769, patrols in Southampton captured the same slave twice within six weeks. Arthur Washington's boatman, Jim, repeatedly went off his owner's plantation without a pass. Slaves who worked as boatmen enjoyed greater autonomy than many other bondmen; their knowledge of rivers enhanced their responsibilities, rendering them both more valuable and more difficult to control. Their quasi freedom made them much more likely to rebel against their masters, as they did in the abortive 1802 Easter rebellion that flourished in the network of rivers and creeks of eastern Virginia and northeastern North Carolina. Perhaps his work gave Washington's Jim a taste for freedom that he could not resist, and the patrollers knew it. But when he was captured the second time in July 1769, Jim surely received a beating for his renewed challenge to the mastery of whites.[25]

Certain plantations and specific slave gathering places received greater scru-tiny by patrols. Planters who owned many slaves could expect repeated visits, in contrast to small slaveholders. For example, in Sussex, patrols went again and again to the plantations of Heartwell Marrable, Benjamin Cocke, and "Colonel" Massenburg in 1763. During a year that included twenty patrol outings, the slave quarters on those plantations were examined thirteen, fifteen, and fifteen times, respectively. Marrable owned twenty-three slaves in 1782; even if he had owned fewer in 1763, he was still among the largest slave owners of Sussex County. Information about Cocke's slaveholdings is elusive. Massenburg had to be fairly wealthy; he was a justice of the county court several times in the 1750s and 1760s, a strong indicator of high economic status in that era. His two sons, William and John, paid taxes after the Revolution on thirteen and twenty-one adult slaves, respectively. Few other residents in Sussex County owned comparable numbers of slaves. It is possible that large slave owners demanded more patrolling on or near their plantations as a return on the monies they paid in county taxes for their slaves.[26]

Chesterfield County patrollers' accounts for 1776 and 1777 give the names of the plantations visited. In May 1777 patrollers went to the plantations of Nicholas Shearer, Thomas Bridgewater, John Fowler, and Thomas Branch. Possibly the patrols started with Shearer and Bridgewater because they owned five and seven slaves, respectively, and then proceeded to Branch's home because he owned sixteen slaves; such a sequence would be based on the theory that a larger slave community might be a better place to look for illegal gatherings and contraband materials. Whatever their motivation, the last stop turned out to be the "jackpot": the patrollers "took up and whipt 35." With so many slaves apprehended by so few men, there may have been even more slaves at Branch's plantation who successfully eluded capture.[27]

The presence of thirty-five slaves, well beyond the sixteen normally present in Branch's slave quarters, suggests either a secret religious meeting or the massing of slaves for some other reason, such as flight to the British. An evangelical revival spirit inflamed Southside Virginia in the 1770s. Religious groups, such as Baptists and Methodists, regularly attracted patrollers' attentions because their meetings drew large crowds of slaves for prayer and conversion.[28]

Ministers intent on the saving of souls, white or black, could do nothing to prevent patrollers from attacking their black parishioners. And whites themselves were not always safe from patrols. Shortly after the Revolutionary War, the captain of a patrol group in King William County wrote the governor asking for authority to punish slaves gathering with Methodists and Baptists and additional power to prosecute the whites who led the evening prayer meetings. Such meetings made the slaves unfit for work, and the whites who led the prayer groups undermined the authority of masters in the neighborhood. "[T]hey preten[d] to preach & pray with a sett of the greatest Rog[u]es of Negroes in this County & they never break up Till about two or three o'clock in the morning & those Negroes who stay with them goes through the neighborhood and steels everything they can lay there hands on & our Negroes are not to be found when we are in want of them, but are at such meetings. . . ." Some whites made bold to threaten patrols with physical violence if they interfered with either the slaves or the religious meetings. When a patrol group entered a religious meeting "Mr. Charles Neal [threw] one of them out of the doore & said that they should not take up one Negroe that was there, upon which the Paterolers finding themselves over Powered [were] obliged to leave the place & went home. . . ." Obviously, not every white Virginian shared the belief that patrols operated for the good of the community when they attacked slaves in religious gatherings. Not even the slaves of dutiful Anglicans were exempt from the watchful gaze of patrollers; patrol groups visited the plantation of John Cargill, son of the rector of Southwark parish in Sussex, six times in 1763. No matter what their religious persuasion, slaves and their masters became accustomed to patroller intrusions onto plantations in the years before the Revolution.[29]

Breaking up evening religious meetings held by slaves was routine for patrols, but slave escapes to the British during the Revolutionary War appeared to be a far greater hazard. Following the proclamation of Lord Dunmore, who offered safe haven and freedom to any slaves belonging to rebel sympathizers in 1775, male and female slaves made their way to liberty behind the British lines. Virginia's new governor Patrick Henry warned every county militia commander in the state about this possibility in November 1775, declaring that "[c]onstant, and well directed Patrols, seem indispensably necessary" to stop slaves from absconding. His words may have spurred some counties, such as Chesterfield, to greater efforts. Chesterfield patrol journals for 1776 and 1777 describe much more activity, which cost the county far more than had been the case in the years preceding the war. However, the number of men assigned to patrol duty dropped during the year because the army and militia were making increasing demands upon the manpower of the county. On February 22, March 29, April 20, and May 4, 1777, the patrol in the Chesterfield's central region was composed of only two men.[30]

Repetitive patrolling became common during the Revolution, although political allegiance seems to have had little effect on whose slave quarters were visited more frequently. The records reveal no systematic surveillance of the homes of British sympathizers—in fact, a quite different pattern is described: men on the side of independence had their plantations visited just as often as the loyalists. William Ashbrook and Jeremiah Franklyn's slave cabins were searched over and over, even though the two men gave supplies to the rebel militia and Continental Army forces many times during the Revolutionary War. John Fowler, Henry Winfree, and Thomas Branch served in the Chesterfield militia, but patrollers regularly came to their slaves' quarters in 1777. Given that active military duty could call militia men from their homes, the patrollers may have actually increased their scrutiny of patriots' plantations to substitute for the loss of direct supervision by a white master fighting at the front.[31]

Although the Chesterfield County patrol records are the only ones that give direct clues about patrol work done during the Revolution, a clear pattern emerges from those pages. Chesterfield's patrollers made more visits, indeed many more, than patrollers did in the 1790s in the same part of the county. In the 1770s, groups of individual patrols visited a minimum of five plantations in a single night; more frequently, six, and sometimes seven or eight. In the 1790s, patrols rarely went to as many as six; more commonly, three or four. The routes had not become longer in the intervening years; if anything, the county was more thickly settled with whites and slaves. What prompted the Revolutionary era patrollers to such vigilance? Anxieties about the war and Dunmore's message to the slaves, compounded by the absence of men away fighting in the war, resulted in more recurrent surveillance by patrols. Perhaps patrolling came to be viewed as a home-front activity that would bolster the morale of noncombatants and give assurance to the men whose duties had called them from home that their families and properties were being protected.

In the end, slave patrols used the same weapons of violence against slaves as slave masters did: whips and threats. Yet the actions of (and even the existence of) patrols reveal much more about the values of colonial Virginians. The white community prized discipline and control over slaves to such an extent that it was willing to require patrollers to spend nights in the saddle looking for slaves. And it stood ready to pay for having that work done.

Further, the white community permitted slave patrols to invade the private property of any county resident as they searched for runaways and hidden contraband. At the very time when revolutionaries would soon protest the warrantless searches of British customs officers, the same kind of behavior by patrollers was not seen as anomalous by Virginia slave owners. The disciplining of slaves was so highly valued that masters promoted the use of violence against their own slaves by non-slave-owning patrollers, men who otherwise would have had no right to interfere in the relations between masters and slaves. Although the presence of slave owners in patrol groups and indirect pressure from the community might place invisible limits on how much violence could be inflicted, patrollers who did not own slaves knew that, as whites, their maltreatment and abuse of slaves could not be challenged by the slaves themselves. Any study of violence directed at slaves must therefore encompass not only slave masters and white patrollers but the collective will of white Southern communities that promoted the systematic use of violence against African Americans. Patrolling sustained the environment of brutality for slaves that extended far beyond the boundaries of individual plantations. Whether threatened or applied, patrollers' violence helped sustain a society that dominated slaves through fear and the lash.

NOTES

1. Ira Berlin and Philip D. Morgan, eds., *Cultivation and Culture: Labor and the Shaping of Black Life in the Americas* (Charlottesville: University Press of Virginia, 1993); Philip D. Morgan, "Slave Life in Piedmont Virginia, 1720–1800," in Lois Carr, Philip D. Morgan, and Jean B. Russo, eds., *Colonial Chesapeake Society* (Chapel Hill: University of North Carolina Press, 1988); Gerald W. Mullin, *Flight and Rebellion: Slave Resistance in Eighteenth–Century Virginia* (London: Oxford University Press, 1972); Sylvia Frey, *Water from the Rock: Black Resistance in a Revolutionary Age* (Princeton: Princeton University Press, 1991); Peter Wood, *Black Majority: Negroes in Colonial South Carolina from 1670 through the Stono Rebellion* (New York: Norton, 1974); Jack P. Greene, "Colonial South Carolina and the Caribbean Connection," *South Carolina Historical Magazine* 88 (1987): 192–210; Daniel Usner, *Indians, Settlers, and Slaves in a Frontier Exchange Economy: The Lower Mississippi Valley before 1783* (Chapel Hill: University of North Carolina Press, 1992). For an overview of the growing literature on colonial slavery, see the bibliographic essay in Peter Kolchin, American Slavery, 1619–1877 (New York: Knopf, 1993), 266–73.

2. Patrols continued to be used until the close of the Civil War, when many of their violent ways were adopted by the Ku Klux Klan and other white aggressors. See Sally E. Hadden, *Law Enforcement in a New Nation: Slave Patrols and Public Authority in the Old South, 1700–1865* (Cambridge: Harvard University Press, forthcoming), ch. 6 and epilogue.

3. William Waller Hening, ed., *The Statutes at Large; Being a collection of all the Laws of Virginia from the First Session of the Legislature, in the Year 1619*, 13 vols. (New York: R. & W. & G. Barton, 1809–1823), 1:539 (1659); 2:187 (1663); 3:12 (1684).

4. Ibid., 5:19 (1738).

5. Original tithable lists and county court minute books stored at the Library of Virginia (LV). Transcribed copies of several Amelia, Chesterfield, and Sussex tithe lists can be found in *The Southside Virginian*, vols. 1982–1988; Norfolk tithable lists for 1730–1765 have been published in three volumes by Elizabeth and W. Bruce Wingo, *Norfolk County, Virginia, Tithables* (Norfolk, Va.: n.p., 1979, 1985).

6. Michael Nicholls, "Origins of the Virginia Southside, 1703–1753: A Social and Eco-nomic Study" (Ph.D. diss., College of William and Mary, 1972), 4, 6; Writers Program of the Works Project Administration, *Sussex County: A Tale of Three Centuries* (n.p.: n.p., 1942), 24–30.

7. Francis E. Lutz, *Chesterfield: An Old Virginia County* (Richmond: William Byrd Press, 1954), 83–85; Bettie W. Weaver, *Chesterfield County, Virginia: A History 1970* (n.p.: Chester-field County Board of Supervisors, [1970]), 13–17.

8. Thomas Parramore, *Southampton County, Virginia* (Charlottesville: University Press of Virginia, 1978), 30. In 1787, the Virginia assembly created a tax structure that required local commissioners to list all men of twenty-one years of age and older, and slaves both above and below age sixteen. The tax lists excluded women, the old and infirm, and certain exempt persons (clergymen, governor). The tax lists extant for every county have been published by Netti Schreiner-Yantis and Florene Love as *The Personal Property Tax Lists for the Year 1787* (Springfield, Va.: Genealogical Books in Print, various years). For more on the settlement of Southside counties, see Richard L. Morton, *Colonial Virginia*, vol. 2, *Westward Expansion and Prelude to Revolution, 1710–1763* (Chapel Hill: University of North Carolina Press, 1960), 552–64.

9. Calculations based on the Schreiner-Yantis and Love 1787 tax lists reveal 6,070 slaves and 1,092 white males taxed in Chesterfield County. Correcting for white women and children (multiplying by 2.5, which is a minimum figure) slaves still outnumbered whites more than 2 to 1. In Sussex County, 5,200 slaves and 1,265 white males were taxed. Again, correcting for the missing white women and children by a multiplication factor of 2.5, slaves barely outnumbered whites 1.6 to 1. Original calculations drawn from Schreiner-Yantis and Love, *The Personal Property Tax Lists for the Year 1787 for Sussex County, Virginia* (Springfield, Va.: Genealogical Books in Print, 1987), 1098–1113, and Schreiner-Yantis and Love, *The Personal Property Tax Lists for the Year 1787 for Chesterfield County, Virginia* (Springfield, Va.: Genealogical Books in Print, 1987), 1375–91.

10. Originals of Amelia, Norfolk, Loudoun, and Surry tithable lists, LV. Among the post-Revolutionary patrol records that are similarly detailed, those from Wake County, North Carolina, in 1857 are comparable in vivid particulars given about patrols and the slaves they encountered. For an analysis of these documents, see Hadden, *Law Enforcement in a New Nation*, ch. 4.

11. Patrol returns and lists, 1754–1861, Free Negroes, Slaves and Indians records, Southampton County, LV.

12. An alternative explanation is possible for Southampton's patrol records in 1754. The initial stages of the French and Indian War may have exposed parts of that county to violence at the hands of Native Americans, and patrols may have been initiated to prevent slaves from running away to join the Indians. The first patrol journal in Southampton County may thus owe its existence to conflict with an external enemy; the court wished to document the work of patrols who restricted an internal threat.

13. Population estimate based on "A List of Tithables in the Dominion of Virginia, 1755," Southampton Historical Society, *Bulletin*, no. 3 (Winter 1967): 22, cited in Parra-more, *Southampton County, Virginia*, 30. Runaway communities: on the Maryland fron-tier, Allan Kulikoff, *Tobacco and Slaves: The Development of Southern Cultures in the Chesa-peake, 1680–1800* (Chapel Hill: University of North Carolina Press, 1986), 328–29; in the western mountains, William Gooch to the Commissioners for Trade and Plantations, PRO C.O. 5/1322 ff.10–13, Virginia Colonial Records Project, reel 42; southern community in the Great Dismal Swamp, Tommy Bogger, "Maroons and Laborers in the Great Dismal Swamp," in Jane H. Kobelski, ed., *Readings in Black and White: Lower Tidewater Virginia*

(Portsmouth: Portsmouth Public Library, 1982), 1–8; Hugo Leaming, "Hidden Americans: Maroons of Virginia and the Carolinas" (Ph.D. diss., University of Illinois at Chicago Circle, 1979).

14. Patrol returns and lists, 1754–1861, Free Negroes, Slaves and Indians records, Southampton County, LV.

15. Ibid. The gender of two slaves captured was not recorded in the reports. For an analysis based upon collected runaway advertisements, see Lathan A. Windley, *Runaway Slave Advertisements* (Westport, Conn.: Greenwood Press, 1983).

16. Parramore, *Southampton County, Virginia*, 31; Sussex County court papers, 1763–64, positive reel 49, LV.

17. For more on the connnection between slave patrols and figures of myth or folklore, see Gladys-Marie Fry, *Night Riders in Black Folk History* (Athens: University of Georgia Press, 1991). The proportion of slaves born in Africa relative to slaves born in Virginia was gradually shifting during the eighteenth century. For an excellent discussion of the decline of imported African slaves in the years following 1740 and the impact that had on slave life, see Kulikoff, *Tobacco and Slaves*, 335–39.

18. Sussex and Chesterfield County tithable lists, 1762, 1777, LV, transcribed in *Southside Virginian* 3 (1985): 79, 5 (1987): 88, 113; Schreiner-Yantis and Love, *Personal Property Tax Lists for the Year 1787 for Sussex County*, 1104; Schreiner-Yantis and Love, *Personal Property Tax Lists for the Year 1788 for Chesterfield County*, 1389, 1392.

19. Hadden, "Law Enforcement in a New Nation: Slave Patrols and Public Authority in the Old South, 1700–1865" (Ph.D. diss., Harvard University, 1993), 190. The statistics and analysis of the longtitudinal study can be found at 179–91.

20. Patrol returns and lists, 1754–1861, Free Negroes, Slaves and Indians records, Southampton County, LV.

21. See Stephanie Camp's synopsis of the historiographic disagreement on this point in her paper " 'I Could Not Stay There': Slave Women and the Somatics of Everyday Resistance in the Old South" (paper presented at the 1997 Southern Historical Association annual meeting). Her work on this topic will ultimately be presented as a dissertation in the Department of History of the University of Pennsylvania.

22. Sussex County, Virginia Personal Property Tax Lists of 1782 taken by John Mason, LV, trans. Pollyanna Creekmore, *Southside Virginian* 6 (1988): 114–16; Hadden, *Law Enforcement in a New Nation*, chs. 3–4.

23. Claiborne T. Smith, Jr., "The Mathew Sturdivant Line," *Southside Virginian* 6 (1988): 79; Schreiner-Yantis and Love, *Personal Property Tax Lists for the Year 1787 for Southampton County*.

24. Patrollers' Accounts, Free Negro and Slave Records, Chesterfield County, LV; "A Journal of Patrolling," 1763, Sussex County court papers, 1763–1764, positive reel 49, LV; Smith, "The Mathew Sturdivant Line," 79.

25. Patrol returns and lists, 1754–1861, Free Negroes, Slaves and Indians records, Southampton County, LV. On the 1800 and 1802 revolts, see Douglas Egerton, *Gabriel's Rebellion: The Virginia Slave Conspiracies of 1800 and 1802* (Chapel Hill: University of North Carolina Press, 1993).

26. "A Journal of Patrolling," 1763; Sussex County tax list of 1782, trans. Creekmore, 114–16; Works Project Administration, *Sussex County*, 244; Janice Abercrombie, comp., *Virginia Publick Claims: Sussex County* (Athens, Ga.: Iberian, n.d.), 9; Schreiner-Yantis and Love, *Personal Property Tax Lists for the Year 1787 for Sussex County*, 1098, 1102.

27. Chesterfield County tithable lists, 1762, LV; 1786 property tax list, transcribed in

Schreiner-Yantis and Love, *Personal Property Tax Lists for the Year 1787 for Chesterfield County*, 1377, 1394.

28. Works Project Administration, *Sussex County*, 40. For more on how patrols attacked slaves' religious gatherings in the early nineteenth century, see Mechal Sobel, *Trabelin' On: The Slave Journey to an Afro-Baptist Faith* (Westport, Conn.: Greenwood Press, 1979), 169–72.

29. Holt Richardson to the governor, September 5, 1789, Executive Papers, Letters received, LV, cited in James Johnston, *Race Relations in Virginia and Miscegenation in the South, 1776–1860* (Amherst: University of Massachusetts Press, 1970), 97–98; Works Project Administration, *Sussex County*, 38.

30. Broadside, 1775, sent to 'The County Lieutenant of Westmoreland,' William Augustine Washington papers, Duke University; Patrollers' Accounts, Free Negro and Slave Records, 1776–1777, Chesterfield County, LV.

31. Janice Abercrombie and Richard Slatten, comps., *Virginia Publick Claims: Chesterfield County* (Athens, Ga.: Iberian, 1991), 1, 17–18; Chesterfield County order book 6, October 1777, 147, described by Marshall Bosher, comp., *Chesterfield County Virginia: A Collection of Notes Pertaining to Its Early History* (Chesterfield: n.p., 1989), 8–9.

The late nineteenth century romanticized dueling. The reality was a slightly different, and usually less deadly, matter. Woodrow Wilson, *A History of the American People* (New York: Harper & Brothers, 1901), 3: 179.

Chapter Four

The Social Origins of Dueling in Virginia

Bruce C. Baird

The image of the duel—two men, accompanied by their seconds, taking to the field of honor to settle some question of personal integrity—resonates through-out the history of the early American republic. A roll call of some of the more celebrated duels would include many of the new nation's political elite—Andrew Jackson, Alexander Hamilton, John Randolph, Aaron Burr, Henry Clay, William Crawford—along with a whole host of lesser-known congressmen, senators, governors, and other government officials. Political differences sent Federalists, Republicans, Democrats, and Whigs willy-nilly to the field of honor. Indeed, the Civil War is often pictured as one grand duel between North and South.

But for all the importance of the code of honor to the early republic, historians have failed to explain adequately the origins of this passion for dueling. In colonial Virginia dueling was effectively suppressed by an upper-class consensus that condemned all forms of "honor violence" (violence employed in defense of one's honor). Between the late 1760s and the late 1790s, however, a shift occurred. During the decade preceding the Revolution, as aristocratic rivalries and democratic challenges eroded the unity and control of the upper classes, dueling became more acceptable. By 1800, republican rhetoric and romantic ideals of chivalric honor provided a rationale for the upsurge in dueling, but the foundations for this phenomenon were laid in the social changes of the pre-Revolutionary era.

The outlines of this development were anticipated in 1767 in a duel that was not actually fought but nonetheless provoked a substantial public controversy, indeed the first and only major public debate in Virginia on the pros and cons of dueling and honor before the celebrated Hamilton-Burr duel of 1804.[1] The participants in the affair were members of two of Virginia's most prominent families: the Mercers and the Lees. When seen in its full historical context, the Lee-Mercer affair provides an excellent window into the social complexities that underlay the changing notions about dueling in Virginia in the late 1760s. We see democratic forces at play in the pressure on members of the upper class to prove through displays of toughness that they—and not their political enemies—were men of the people. At the same time some of the Virginia elite appealed to an admittedly aristocratic code of honor in the face of ubiquitous public condemnation of anything that smacked of aristocracy. The intertwining of these democratic and aristocratic influences throughout the late eighteenth century would eventually work a revolution in public opinion, promoting a widespread acceptance of dueling among the elite in the early republic as a means of simultaneously avoiding charges of cowardice from below and setting oneself off from the masses.

The Lee-Mercer Affair

Well before sunrise on the morning of April 28, 1767, Dr. Arthur Lee and his second, Corbin Griffin, set out on foot from Lee's house in Williamsburg. They had two sets of dueling pistols, one for themselves and the other for James Mercer, a Williamsburg attorney. They were headed across a field toward a green level spot in a valley on the left side of the road to Yorktown across from the race ground. They were on the spot when they heard the town clock strike five, the time they had informed Mercer they would be there to settle accounts.[2]

The affair was all part of an ongoing war between the Mercer and Lee clans being carried out on the pages of the *Virginia Gazette*, in "the publick coffee room," and on the streets of Williamsburg. The sons of Thomas Lee (Richard Henry, Francis Lightfoot, William, and Arthur) had long resented how the Mercers had taken control of the Ohio Company, a speculative land company, after their father's death in 1750. When he learned in 1765 that George Mercer, then residing in England, had been given the stamp distributorship, Richard Henry Lee took on the role of patriot leader inciting the mobs that first burnt Mercer in effigy and then, after Mercer's arrival from England, drove him to resign as stamp distributor and immediately take passage back to England, never to return again to Virginia. The next year the Mercers got their revenge when John and James Mercer, father and brother of the would-be stamp distributor, reported in the *Virginia Gazette* that Richard Henry Lee had himself applied for the stamp distributorship, to which Lee could only admit that he had at first not realized the serious moral and constitutional principles involved in the Stamp Act. Arthur Lee, a brash young man just returned from England after fifteen years of schooling at Eton and Edinburgh, took up the pen in defense of his brother, causing John and James Mercer to reply in kind. In a series of slanderous diatribes in the pages of the *Virginia Gazette*, the two clans viciously attacked each other throughout the summer and fall of 1766. Over the winter of 1766–1767 the quarrel seems to have hibernated only to erupt in late April 1767, when Arthur Lee felt himself obliged to send Griffin to call James Mercer to an account because, as Lee claimed, Mercer "had used him ill."

As the clock struck five, Mercer's manservant entered his room to wake him as instructed the night before. Mercer got up and dressed quickly. Although

Griffin the day before had promised to bring an extra set of dueling pistols, Mercer grabbed his pair of pocket pistols. Pocket pistols would not be as accurate as a pair of dueling pistols, but at least they would be better than nothing if Griffin had forgotten his promise. After rousing his landlord to witness some deeds that he had drafted the previous night—in order to secure his estate from a forfeiture in the event he killed Lee—Mercer was out the door by twenty minutes past five, just as the sun was beginning to rise. He walked briskly through town toward the race ground, stick in hand, and arrived at the agreed-upon spot about five-thirty.

Anyway, that is the way that Griffin and Mercer independently recalled the events of that early morning later that spring and summer in accounts in the *Virginia Gazette*. But while we would have no trouble reconciling the two accounts in their description of events before 5:30, reconciling them on what took place between 5:30 and 6:00 is indeed difficult. If we are to believe both sets of accounts, both parties were at the green from 5:30 to 6:00, but neither saw the other.

Griffin reported that he and Lee "walked up and down the fence which leads almost directly from [Mr.] Mercer's lodgings to the place appointed, and upon the plain that commands the road leading directly from the town until near 6 o'clock; when, not having seen or heard any thing of [Mr.] Mercer, we returned to Doctor Lee's lodgings slowly, stopping and looking round us several times, to no purpose." Mercer called out three times but heard no answer, sat down for three or four minutes on a dead stump at a spot where he would be sure to see them, walked through the field leading to Dr. Lee's house, asked two people hanging around the race ground whether they had seen a couple of gentlemen walking in the field that morning—to which they replied in the negative—and then walked back to his lodgings.

As they were walking back, Lee reportedly told Griffin "that a person who could act in such a manner he should not think worthy his notice for the future." But upon hearing that Mercer was telling everyone that Lee had failed to meet him, Lee sent Griffin to explain the affair by his testimony in the public coffeehouse. When Mercer persisted in his stories, Lee went to the coffeehouse himself, intent on giving Mercer a caning. Instead, Mercer thrashed Lee. A pseudonymous "Essay on Pride" published in the *Virginia Gazette* later described the scene:

> Canes and pistols are removed, by the resistless command of the surrounding croud, to fisty-cuffs go the exalted duellists. O sad, sad! the Doctor [Arthur Lee], instead of being handsomely run or fired through the body, which would have given him infinite satisfaction, is bled at the nose, and has his eyes closed, as if he had been no better than a clown or a peasant. The poor, abused, unfortunate Doctor, lifts his discomposed, tumefied, bloody, and sightless head; and, notwithstanding the inconvenience of such a situation for a display of oratory, makes a very fine harangue on the most grossly and shamefully violated laws of honour; for which, as a mischief to society, with a truly disinterested spirit, he expresses more concern than for any

injury done to his own person. The Coffee-House world manifest their esteem by laughing.[3]

Biographers of Arthur Lee, the only historians who have taken a close look at the Lee-Mercer affair, have assumed that no one was really lying about the events of the early morning hours of April 28, 1767, that the participants were simply a little off in their times, Lee and Griffin slightly earlier and Mercer slightly later than they asserted. Yet by all modern standards of evidence, one has to believe that James Mercer was telling the truth and Arthur Lee and Corbin Griffin were lying. While Lee and Griffin rested their case on their word as gentlemen, Mercer set about amassing and then having published an impressive collection of sworn affidavits from every individual who knew something of the events, as well as his own highly detailed, five-page sworn deposition vouching for everything he had said earlier in the public coffee room. Several independent witnesses who had been up and about in those early hours had seen Mercer; not one had seen Lee or Griffin, even the two who had been told by Mercer's landlord at about five-thirty to watch the comings and goings from the doctor's house.

This rather farcical affair offers more than just another unsolved historical puzzle, for it provides an excellent window into the complex tensions in the attitudes of white Virginians toward honor, violence, and dueling in the eighteenth century. When compared to the later antebellum era, the late 1760s seem remarkably free from honor violence. Yet by the standards of the earlier colonial era, the late 1760s saw a veritable rash of challenges and, even more remarkably, acceptances of challenges—at least three—by members of the elite, at least one of which culminated in an actual duel. Before the late 1760s no member of the Virginia elite had ever accepted a challenge let alone fought in a duel in Virginia since the spring of 1624 when George Harrison, planter, challenged and fought Richard Stephens, merchant, somewhere near James City.[4] What was happening in the late 1760s to cause such a change? Before we can begin to address this question, we need to understand better the historical context out of which the Lee-Mercer affair and these other affairs of honor emerged.

The Seventeenth-Century Background

When Englishmen settled in Virginia in the seventeenth century, they brought with them from England two competing ideals of honor, one that encouraged honor violence and one that thoroughly condemned such violence as a threat to the social order. Although forever anxious about their reputations, Virginians' concern for the social order won the day. Furthermore, the elite of colonial Virginia were quite successful in checking not only dueling among themselves but all forms of honor violence.

If a chivalric warrior ethic proved the dominant notion of honor among the English nobility in the medieval era, the sense of what honor meant underwent a sea change in the sixteenth century as honor was "increasingly required to adapt itself to the demands of religion, and to those of the state." The reign of the Tudors marked the rise of a state-centered honor system under which the realm and the community of honor became identical with the crown, "the fount of honour."[5]

This transformation was aided greatly by Sir Thomas Elyot's classic *The Boke named the Governor*, which restated "the honour code in terms of the popularized humanism of the age." Elyot's Stoic-Christian ethic of gentility fundamentally challenged the chivalric warrior ethic. The Renaissance ideal of the gentleman governor was by definition a defender and servant of the common good within "a remodelled and unified community of honour" under the crown. Elyot's ideas were echoed by a legion of later writers in the sixteenth, seventeenth, and eighteenth centuries.[6]

Nevertheless, the chivalric warrior ethic did not entirely disappear in England. Indeed, the sixteenth century saw the introduction of the private duel. Some gentlemen found ways of defending dueling and honor violence as basic to the common good; some accepted the inevitability of the practice as a "genteel vice." Still others forsook rationalizations and simply proclaimed themselves subject to a higher law above the common good when matters of honor were at stake.[7] Furthermore, advocates and critics alike noted the power of public opinion to force even men opposed to dueling to engage in duels. Writers in England from Shakespeare to Locke to Mandeville to Boswell lamented the practice but also believed that men were not free to ignore a challenge or redress personal affronts in courts out of fear of being labeled a coward. Yet the dominance of gentility in seventeenth- and eighteenth-century England checked the prevalence of dueling despite its popularity among certain aristocratic and military circles. The defenders of a state-centered honor system condemned honor violence as leading to public disorder and anarchy, as totally contrary to the common good.[8]

Englishmen carried this same tension between "honor-as-virtue" and "honor-as-valor" to seventeenth-century Virginia. However, far more than in the mother country, valor took a back seat to virtue in Virginia. Seventeenth-century Virginia and Maryland—far from being the violent and chaotic frontier so often depicted in history textbooks—were "intensely governed societies" remarkable for "the primacy of law" and their social and political stability. Elyot's image of the gentleman governor was, if anything, a more dominant normative expression in seventeenth-century Virginia than in the mother country. Quite consistently, these Virginians universally condemned and effectively suppressed the practice of dueling.[9]

Colonial Virginians had their genteel vices—sexual misconduct, drunkenness, gambling, and certainly the smoking of tobacco—all behaviors traditionally associated with dueling in Europe. But the colonial Virginia elite drew the line at the vice of dueling. After the Harrison-Stephens affair of 1624, the few challenges sent always ended in the challenger's being dragged into court for disturbing the peace or contempt of authority. Occasionally, one notes an individual who, because of some combination of personality, education, and experience, had absorbed aristocratic notions of honor and dueling, but the other colonists soon put the upstart in his place.[10]

As for more primitive forms of honor violence, there is only sketchy evidence and that restricted almost totally to the lower classes after the mid-eighteenth century. One cannot even say that the lower classes in Virginia were particularly violent. The number of trials of free persons for homicide in Virginia never amounted to more than two or three a year and for manslaughter to no more than one or two a year over the colonial era. What violence there was in colonial Virginia—that directed at Native Americans, felons, servants, and slaves—was strictly controlled by the elite in order to maintain the hierarchical order.[11]

Although they were opposed to honor violence, Virginians were very much concerned about their reputations. Modern scholars who have studied court records have been astonished at the proportion of time consumed by the early county courts in settling cases of slander and defamation, treated as both a civil and criminal offense, brought by individuals from all walks of life. Courts awarded damages, commanded offenders to pay a fine for the public use or to perform a public service, and imposed humiliating public penances on offenders, such as placing them in stocks, towing them over creeks, ducking, whipping, and ordering them to apologize in public. In an era when most members of the Virginia elite served in some public capacity, they were "all quick to take offense at any word or action which indicated the least lack of respect for their official dignity."[12]

Early Virginians found "a means of channeling social friction through the courts . . . and potentially bloody contests over honor, rank, and status were for the most part avoided." But honor violence did not raise its head even after the courts—overloaded by personal defamation suits—adopted procedural and substantive barriers against litigation in the late seventeenth century, a move that led to "a marked decrease in the number of private defamation actions, civil and criminal." And at other times the colonial elite seemed quite content to ignore personal affronts. Politics in seventeenth- and early-eighteenth-century Virginia could be anything but genteel. In this rough-and-tumble politics, "public oaths and remarks such as 'scurrilous,' 'Dogg,' 'bitch,' 'Fifth Monarchist,' 'notorious liar,' 'Beelzebub,' 'mutinous,' 'treasonous,' 'son of whore,' which would be considered by later generations as libelous and justifications for a defense of honor, were hurled with relative abandon." Yet colonial Virginians could agree that whether one chose to ignore or prosecute an insult, these were proper matters for the courts or one's conscience, not for the field of honor or the streets.[13]

The Scotch-Irish Arrive

The societal consensus began to fall apart sometime in the mid-eighteenth century and Virginia took a turn for the violent. Numerous influences played a role in this shift toward greater violence. One obvious influence was the arrival in the Virginia backcountry in the mid-eighteenth century of large numbers of Scotch-Irish.[14]

If medieval notions of honor violence had begun to fade in England, the same could not be said of England's neighbor to the north, Scotland. The Scots seem to have maintained their traditional "addiction . . . to fighting and violence." By the early sixteenth century, "the pride and touchiness of the Scot had already become proverbial. There was something in his character like 'quills upon the fretful porpentine.' " With *lex talionis* (an eye for an eye, a tooth for a tooth) the law of the land, the national emblem the thistle, and "its motto *Nemo me impune lacessit*—no one attacks me with impunity," "the Scot was quick to take offense, lest any man consider him a weakling."[15]

However influenced by institutional and environmental factors, the Scotch-Irish carried similar cultural attitudes toward honor violence to Ulster and eventually to America. The early reputation of the Ulstermen in the American colonies for being a pugnacious people was one rooted in fact. Although dueling was a fairly rare form of honor violence in Ulster, the no-holds-barred fighting that disgusted so many visitors to the South was clearly imported by Ulstermen. The Scotch-Irish shocked Bostonians in the 1720s with their barbarous fighting style, revealed "most graphically in the practice of biting off ears in the course of fights."[16] In Pennsylvania in the early 1740s, the Scotch-Irish, besides spontaneous brawls, engaged in scheduled, deliberate "riots" at fairs and other public places involving rival groups of men. By midcentury, Virginians began to hear of gouged eyes and chewed-off ears in vicious rough-and-tumble contests, moving the assembly in 1752 "to re-enact the 22 and 23 Charles II, chapter I, preamble and all, with practically no changes" making it "a felony to put out an eye, slit a nose, bite or cut off the nose or lip, or to cut off or disable any limb or member."[17]

The Scotch-Irish in Virginia provided the inspiration in the early 1760s for Robert Bolling's poem *Neanthe*, "the first appearance in American literature of the brutal 'fight' story that eventually became a staple of Southern frontier humor." The poem highlights a vicious fight between Euphenor and Dolon on the Eastern Shore in which the opponents bite, squeeze testicles, gouge, and knee-in-the-face, until finally Euphenor kicks Dolon to death. At one point in the poem, "Bolling interrupts the narrative to find an Irish (rather than English) origin for 'our good Planters fisticuff' ":

> You English wou'd abhor that Plight,
> Who strain no Tackling, gouge, nor bite.
> Unknown to Britain are our Modes
> Of Fight, or, if she knows, explodes.
> Upright, her Bruisers ply their Fists
> And all is Peace, when one desists.
>   Tho we from Britons are descended;
> Hibernians have our Manners mended.
> When our good Planters fisticuff,

They never think, they hurt enough:
A toute Outrance they Combat wage;
Submissions scarce their Wrath assuage.[18]

As Bolling shows, by the time he was writing in the early 1760s, many Anglo-Virginians had adopted Scotch-Irish modes of fighting.

Indeed, when Reverend Charles Woodmason wrote his famous "Burlesque Sermon" in the late 1760s condemning equally the litigiousness and no-holds-barred "fisty Cuffs" of the backcountry South Carolina settlers, he singled out not the Scotch-Irish but "Virginians." He warned his parishioners to avoid getting entangled with "the Virginian Crackers—for they'l bluster and make a Noise about a Turd—And they'll think they have a Right because they are American born to do as they please and what they please and say what they please to any Body." Woodmason advised that "when You do fight Not to act like Tygers and Bears as these Virginians do—Biting one anothers Lips and Noses off, and gowging one another—that is, thrusting out one anothers Eyes, and kicking one another on the Cods, to the Great damage of many a Poor Woman."[19]

Woodmason was undoubtedly poking fun at the pretentiousness of the Virginian-born Scotch-Irish like the Chesnuts to whom the sermon was addressed.[20] Nevertheless, prosecutions for maiming and gouging suggest that by the late 1760s rough-and-tumble fighting in Virginia was no longer strictly a Scotch-Irish phenomenon and hardly just a frontier phenomenon. Just how pervasive the Scotch-Irish influence over Virginia society had become is well shown in Philip Vickers Fithian's classic account of a planned riot in Westmoreland County in the Northern Neck in 1774:

> By appointment is to be fought this Day near Mr *Lanes* two fist Battles between four young Fellows. The Cause of the battles I have not yet known; I suppose either that they are lovers, and one has in Jest or reality some way supplanted the other; or has in a merry hour call'd him a *Lubber*, or a *thick-Skull*, or a *Buckskin*, or a *Scotchman*, or perhaps one has mislaid the other's hat, or knocked a peach out of his Hand, or offered him a dram without wiping the mouth of the Bottle; all these, and ten thousand more quite as triffling and ridiculous, are thought and accepted as just Causes of immediate Quarrels, in which every diabolical Strategem for Mastery is allowed and practised, of Bruising, Kicking, Scratching, Pinching, Biting, Butting, Tripping, Throtling, Gouging, Cursing, Dismembring, Howling, etc. This spectacle, (so loathsome and horrible!) generally is attended with a crowd of People!

Although Fithian looked upon "animals which seek after and relish such odious and filthy amusements [as] not of the human species," his description captures the growing support of a large segment of Virginia society for displays of honor violence in the pre-Revolutionary years.[21]

Today the sheer brutality of such modes of fighting might blind us to the more important historical question of why Anglo-Virginians so readily abandoned taboos against honor violence. Such a ready abandonment suggests how very tenuous the balance really was between honor-as-valor and honor-as-virtue in colonial Virginia. For some Anglo-Virginians, all it took to shift the balance in favor of honor as valor was the introduction of a new factor, the Scotch-Irish, to which the elite of Virginia were either unwilling or unable to adjust in order to maintain the ban against honor violence. But this raises the greater question of why there might have been a breakdown in traditional hierarchical control.

Breakdown of Deference

Other factors contributed to the increased levels of violence in mid-eighteenth-century Virginia. A second major influence tending both to undermine societal consensus and to spur violence was the fragmentation of the elite in the increasingly contested politics of the era. The political and press battles of the late 1760s unleashed an unprecented level of personal invective that led some Virginia gentlemen to believe a formal challenge their only recourse to salvage their honor.

In the 1730s and 1740s, about the same time that the Scotch-Irish were arriving in the backcountry, politics in some Virginia counties was getting quite heated. County elections became "boisterous affairs with liquor flowing freely, with jeering, fighting, and riots." For the most part, however, Virginia as a whole remained fairly calm. Although short-lived factions had arisen from time to time in the ninety years following the collapse of Bacon's Rebellion, nothing major had occurred "to ruffle the surface calm of political life in the Old Dominion." Among the elite there were no differences in political philosophies, no long-lasting political feuds, and no attempt on the part of any faction "to appeal to the small planter for support in creating a permanent party. Such a thought would have been alien to the whole philosophy of these men."[22]

But in the peculiar political climate following the Stamp Act crisis—when as Governor Fauquier reported, "Every Thing is become a Matter of heat and Party Faction"—political violence became common throughout the colony. From the mob "led by some of the city's most respectable merchants" that chased George Mercer through the streets of Williamsburg in fall 1766, through the Norfolk smallpox innoculation riots of 1768–1769 led by borough sergeant Joseph Calvert, the gentry played a key role in stirring up the mob violence of the late 1760s. Virginians on the wrong side of the political fence sometimes found themselves tarred and feathered or severely beaten with elite approval or contrivance.[23]

The first major fault line emerged over how aggressive a response Virginia should take to the Stamp Act. This conflict pitted the Tidewater Establishment—led by John Robinson, the man who as joint treasurer of the colony and speaker of the House of Burgesses had thoroughly dominated colonial government for nearly a quarter of a century and kept the Virginia gentry in line—against "the young hot and giddy members" led by Patrick Henry, Richard Henry Lee, and George Mason, generally identified with the Northern Neck, piedmont, and frontier counties. It is quite possible that the factions might have smoothed over their differences as they had in the past but for the death of John Robinson in

May 1766. Following his death, the gentry fractured to a degree that consensus seemed no longer possible.[24]

This fundamental fracture led directly to Virginia's first all-out newspaper war, which further spurred faction by giving Virginians an open forum for expressing all their pent-up grievances. From the establishment of the *Virginia Gazette* in 1736 until May 1766 Virginia was served by only one newspaper, its editors avoiding "Scandal and Detraction." Following the Stamp Act crisis and the death of the old printer Joseph Royle, some of the burgesses decided to bring in their own printer, William Rind, to establish a more independent *Gazette*. At the same time Royle's old foreman, Alexander Purdie, and his partner John Dixon, in an attempt to win the support of other burgesses for the public printing contract, resumed publication of the original *Gazette*.[25]

With the rivalry between the two *Virginia Gazette*s, "the excited inhabitants of the Old Dominion [had] what they had never before experienced, the sensations and sensationalism of a free press." And in 1766 there was much to cover: the issue of whether, with the death of John Robinson, the burgesses should split the positions of speaker and treasurer; allegations of Robinson's embezzlement of funds funneled to his friends and relations; the murder of Robert Routledge by John Chiswell (Robinson's father-in-law) and the furor over Chiswell's bailment by Robinson cronies; and, last but not least, the feud between the Lee and Mercer clans.[26]

In such a heated political atmosphere, once the dike of deference had been breached, the walls came a-tumbling down. "Our writers," as one anonymous Virginian put it, "are generally such as have been very little used to Contradiction, and know not how to bear it from one another; and when they find their Writings not treated with that Respect they have been accustomed to in their private Characters, they grow angry, and sometimes abuse one another." Thus the free press gave rise to "a vastly different, more openly combative style of politics."[27]

Members of the Virginia gentry responded to newspaper attacks in many different ways. Some complained that freedom of the press was being too easily turned into license. At the same time they often answered in kind with their own anonymous and pseudonymous calumny. Still others appealed to the public by publishing signed statements refuting the charges against them.[28]

A few Virginians decided to sue their critics. William Byrd III sued Robert Bolling for libel after somehow finding out that Bolling was responsible for the anonymous insinuations in the *Gazette* about Byrd's role in the bailment of Chiswell. John Wayles—unable to identify his pseudonymous critic "R. M."—filed a suit against both Purdie and Dixon, and Rind for libel. But, in the spirit of the times, few "Friends of Liberty" would even consider such an indictment of libel against authors or newspapers publishing pieces aimed at "correcting the haughty Spirits of some of our great Men, who, from their Fortunes, Connections, and Stations, had conceived very high Ideas of Self Importance." The grand jury returned the indictments against Bolling, Purdie and Dixon, and Rind, "not true bills."[29]

When traditional methods of resolving their disputes failed to achieve their purposes, some Virginia gentlemen turned to physical violence or the threat of physical violence. Invoking *lex talionis*, James Mercer attacked Richard Henry Lee's libels against Mercer's brother by threatening that "had the same facts been sworn to before a tribunal having jurisdiction, I could legally have got the author's ears condemned; indeed, had I known him in due time, I would have attempted it by force of arms." When in Williamsburg, Mercer had begun to carry around a pair of pocket pistols that he said were "sufficient to protect me from Dr. Lee's attacks in the streets, or in company."[30]

Other gentry appealed to the code of honor. Political battles fought in the press lay behind the three challenges of record in the late 1760s. When justice failed Byrd, he challenged Bolling to a duel the following day. Similarly frustrated, Dr. Arthur Lee challenged James Mercer in April 1767, and Joseph Calvert challenged Thomas Burke in the summer of 1769. The would-be duelists (Byrd excepted) had regularly engaged in libelous attacks on their opponents in the pages of the *Gazette*.[31]

The Problem of Honor

Despite this rash of challenges, dueling still faced an uphill battle before gaining general social acceptance. On top of the traditional opposition to honor violence as a threat to the social order, Virginians in the late 1760s steadfastly condemned the aristocratic pretensions of dueling. Yet one can definitely see the origins of a fundamental shift in public opinion in the novel pressure on Virginians to accept duels and the failure of the authorities to take would-be duelists as seriously as they had in the past.

Although we rarely hear what went on in the taverns, inns, and coffee rooms of Williamsburg and the rest of Virginia, what we do hear leaves no doubt that what Rhys Isaac calls "extravagant ways of talking" were quite characteristic of such places. Honor comes alive when we listen to Morgan Edwards's description from 1772 of "a prolonged battle of wits between himself and 'a number of colone[l]s, captains, esquires etc., who had met [at an inn in Goochland County] for public business." The locals clearly took great pleasure in the verbal repartee, "their skill in pressing provocation beyond permitted limits, and then seeming to step back half a pace, to within acceptable bounds." One gentleman might say, "You lie, Sir; I mean on the bed"; to which the butt of the humor would respond, "And you lie, Sir; I mean under a mistake," all accompanied by loud guffaws and applause.[32]

Such an environment undoubtedly led to scuffles at times, as the coffeehouse wrangle between Lee and Mercer demonstrates. But more impressive are the severe restraints placed on honor violence in the colonial era. However much they spoke of their honor, the elite of colonial Virginia almost always seemed to know where to draw the line. And the line was most clearly drawn in the overwhelming consensus against dueling.

Although dueling may have been extremely rare in colonial Virginia and Virginians may have been a bit rusty on some of the fine particulars of the code of honor, they certainly knew what dueling was all about. When Griffin offered Mercer his choice of weapons, Mercer opted for pistols since he "was totally ignorant of the small sword, and pistols were thought equally genteel." After all, these Virginians were still very much Englishmen and knew well what was going on in England from constant commerce, communication, and traveling back and forth. Throughout the colonial era the *Virginia Gazettes* were filled with stories about dueling in England, the Continent, and around the world.[33]

Furthermore, dueling even had its sophisticated proponents in pre-Revolutionary Virginia, most notably Arthur Lee. In defending dueling in 1767, Lee and the anonymous author of the "Essay on Honor" (which most Virginians assumed was written by Arthur Lee) employed all of the arguments that defenders of dueling were using in England and would later use in the antebellum South. In particular, these defenders of dueling celebrated the principles of what eighteenth-century Englishmen called "modern honour" (in contrast to the "ancient honour" of classical Greece and Rome) that they associated with chivalrous knights, principles that "perpetually dictate a fairness, justice, and nobleness of conduct," the protector of one's most valuable possession—one's reputation—which only the law of honor could protect, either through the fear of "the shame of contempt" at being posted as a coward or the ultimate sanction of the threat of death in a duel. "I mean, Sir," Lee wrote to the *Virginia Gazette* six months after his nonduel with Mercer, "that honour which the illustrious *Montesquieu* defines to be the *prevailing principle in monarchies, where it gives life to the whole body politic, and even to virtues themselves.*" Lee went on to proclaim honor "that principle which the British constitution considers in the highest degree, sacred and inviolable . . . in fine, that principle, which Montesquieu deems the parent of virtues in the best constituted form of society."[34]

The law of honor, Lee argued, operated even on those gentleman who opposed dueling in principle because "the opinion of mankind, which is as forcible as a law, calls upon a man to resent an affront, and fixes the contempt of a coward upon him if he refuse." Lee recognized that both common and statute law stood firmly opposed to dueling but seconded Cesare Beccaria, the leading European authority on penal reform, that "[i]n vain have the laws endeavoured to abolish this custom (duelling) by punishing the offenders with death. A man of honour, deprived of the esteem of others, foresees that he must be reduced, either to a solitary existence, insupportable to a social creature, or become the object of perpetual insult; considerations sufficient to overcome the fear of death." Honor rose above all other standards, a law of nature that might prove contrary to the laws of God and man.[35]

But far from earning support for Lee's case, these essays only aggravated Lee's reputation. Denizens of the coffeehouse world laughed at Arthur Lee not because they supposed him a coward for challenging Mercer to a duel and then failing to show up. Certainly Mercer himself felt he had to go to great lengths even after the coffeehouse wrangle to prove by sworn affidavits that he had been at the right place at the right time, for he had no second to vouch for him and Lee did. Rather, they laughed at Arthur Lee as they laughed at Landon Carter and all Virginians who went on and on about their honor. When Lee continued to press the point, a few of Mercer's supporters gathered together and burned Lee in effigy before his own door. As John Mercer summarized general opinion: "In short he has lost his credit (if he had any to lose) and, what I dare say he values much more, his [medical] practice is much hurt, as will very probably dwindle to nothing as his immoderate pride and self-conceit will not suffer him to open his eyes and see how much, how very much, he is fallen into contempt."[36]

Aristocratic notions of honor like Lee's had no place in pre-Revolutionary Virginia. Public opinion before the Revolution did not tolerate challenging someone to a duel or making fine speeches about honor. Arthur Lee was simply out of touch with his native Virginia. Thoroughly discredited, Lee abandoned Virginia the following year for England, but even there he could not escape the taunts. He ever after had bitter feelings toward the people of Williamsburg—a place he called that "sink of idleness and vice"—for the way he had been treated.[37]

For most Englishmen, whether in the colonies or the mother country, the honor that Arthur Lee espoused was a false honor of unrestrained passion and mere vainglory, a fashionable vice, Gothic barbarism. Lee himself lamented sometime after the coffeehouse wrangle, "that honour is become now a subject of ridicule, is either prostituted to infamous purposes, or treated as a chimera." Opponents of dueling were not unconcerned with reputation but believed the true fountain of honor was virtue and character, not opinion. Virginian critics condemned the barbarous practice of dueling in a civilized age, criticizing the order of chivalry as an age in which a group of "hectors"—no more than "professed bullies" or "licensed lunatics"—"strolled about from one kingdom to another, destroying their fellow creatures with impunity." They mimicked the exchanges between duelists as "the ravings of insanity":

> Sir, you have injured me in the most outrageous manner, and I demand reparation. The reparation I demand is that you should meet me with a case of pistols, and endeavour to blow my brains out. If you do, there will be an end of the matter. If you lose your life in the attempt, I shall die with pleasure on a gibbet, having thus vindicated my honour by trespassing on the laws of my country.[38]

Friends, relatives, and concerned citizens went out of their way to prevent duels. At two o'clock the night before their scheduled duel, Byrd and Bolling were both arrested and sworn over to keep the peace, apparently turned in to authorities by the storekeeper from whom Byrd purchased the pistols. Mercer, with all of his many coffeehouse comrades, could not get anyone to serve as his second. He tried to get his friend Dr. William Pasteur to attend him as a witness and surgeon in case he were injured. At first Pasteur refused to be concerned at all. Then "at his [Mercer's] earnest request," he promised to go with him but only "to be in hearing of the pistols, so as to be ready, if necessary; but he positively refused to be an eye witness of Dr. Lee's or my throwing away our lives, as he termed it." Mercer's friends later insisted that he ignore any implied challenge in Griffin's published account of the duel and simply "publish a true account of the affair." Mercer's cousin, Thomson Mason, had a pair of pistols that, as he put it, could "hit the bigness of a dollar many yards," but he refused to lend them to Mercer because they would surely kill Lee and then Mercer "shou'd be guilty of murder." Instead, Mason, like Byrd's storekeeper, informed the authorities to prevent the duel.[39]

The Virginia gentry also found more primitive modes of honor violence unacceptable. Despite his blustering about cutting Richard Henry Lee's ears off, James Mercer understood the need for, as he put it, "a more eligible reprisal, and such as is agreeable to the laws of God and man. *Lex talionis* is of higher authority than human law, and the vengeance denounced against whomsoever should slay Cain, whome the Almighty preserved from death to perpetuate his torments, determines me not to attempt to shorten this Proteus's life." Members of the elite like Benjamin Grymes, who resorted to bullying tactics, were regularly ridiculed just like Arthur Lee.[40]

Fresh in the minds of all Virginians in the late 1760s was the notorious affray—not a duel—of the summer of 1766 in which John Chiswell stabbed and killed Robert Routledge in a tavern quarrel over some debts. Despite the fact that after being thoroughly abused by Chiswell, an intoxicated Routledge had thrown wine out of his glass into Chiswell's face—an indignity which even Chiswell's most severe critics acknowledged any man of honor might react to violently—no Virginian was willing to excuse Chiswell's stabbing to death an unarmed Routledge or declare in print that this was an affair of honor. Chiswell was roundly condemned as a murderer and, luckily for him, died before he could be tried and hanged. Fearful of the same fate, both Lee and Mercer made plans for escape in the event that either happened to kill the other.[41]

In spite of expressed opinion so set against dueling and the great efforts of individuals to prevent duels, other evidence suggests that by the late 1760s the general community had become quite complacent about dueling. In the Lee-Mercer affair, the local justice, Thomas Everard, was out taking sworn affidavits to vouch for the honor of one of the would-be duelists rather than arresting Lee and Griffin for sending and carrying challenges, as local authorities had done previously and were obliged to do under English common law. Apparently, the sending and carrying of challenges was no longer seen as a threat to public order. The Chiswell affair, ironically, may very well have encouraged a greater (if still unspoken) acceptance of dueling and the formality of the code of honor as necessary to avoid even greater disorder, the lesser of two evils.[42]

This shifting consensus also appears reflected in a greater pressure on the Virginia gentry to accept a challenge. This is not to say that challenges always led to acceptance. Despite a general understanding by the Mercers that Griffin's published account of the duel was a second challenge and Mercer's "giving the lie" to Griffin and Lee in print, no duel ever took place between Lee and Mercer, or Griffin. Mercer observed in his sworn statement that if Lee had really wanted to duel, he could have easily come and found Mercer that morning. Likewise neither Byrd nor Bolling felt any need to take up their thwarted duel. But Bolling, Mercer, and Burke, despite their apparent aversion to dueling, did feel pressure to accept the challenges made by Byrd, Lee, and Calvert. Mercer was afraid that if he declined Lee's challenge, then Lee would have plumed himself at Mercer's expense. Thus Mercer was quite upset with his cousin for informing the authorities, out of fear that people would think that he had put Mason up to it in order to avoid the duel.[43]

The pressure to accept a challenge is quite striking in the case of Thomas Burke who, in the aftermath of the Lee-Mercer affair, published in the *Gazette* a signed essay condemning dueling as "destructive of every moral, christian and generous sentiment, dangerous to the peace of society, to liberty and justice," encouraging "men to *fly in the face of our most sacred laws, and subversive of magnanimity and christian heroism.*" Burke furthermore denied that public opinion supported duelists, asserting that it was "the common *practice for mankind to look with contempt upon him who gives an affront, not on him who tamely suffers it.*" Yet in 1769, less than two years after he wrote that essay, Burke fought a duel with Calvert, indeed the only affair of honor in the late 1760s to culminate in an actual duel, although apparently neither was injured.[44]

The Revolution in Public Opinion

If the shift in public opinion in support of dueling began in the late 1760s, the revolution was complete by 1800. This transformation came about through the continuing evolution of democratic influences, spurred especially by the heated national politics of the 1790s. But there is much evidence that the rise of dueling also reflects aristocratic and monarchical influences, an attempt on the part of at least a few of the Revolutionary generation to find some sort of replacement for the state-centered honor system whose head had been cut off with the break from England.

Contemporaries had no trouble laying the root of the problem at the door of public opinion. In sermons, essays, and private letters, critics and advocates alike in the early national period noted the power of public opinion to force even men opposed to dueling to engage in duels. What is amazing, however, in this era when newspapers supposedly played such an important role in shaping the public sphere, is how public opinion could have come to stand so staunchly behind dueling when one can find practically no positive defense of dueling in print.[45]

Some northern opponents of dueling, like Thomas Burke earlier, argued that the public opinion in support of dueling was the opinion only of duelists, in direct opposition to the view of the masses. To the question "Who then is this public?" Timothy Dwight answered, "It is the little collection of duellists, magnified by its own voice, as every other little party is, into the splendid character of the public."[46]

There are several explanations of why the elite might have turned indepen-

dently to honor violence at this time. Numerous scholars associate the rise of the
duel in various nations with an elite threatened by the lower orders and/or
outsiders. The duel set the bounds of the circle of honor while the code of honor
provided the strong inner bond to an aristocratic class pervaded by tension and
antipathy as well as fraternity. Perhaps, then, the numerous political duels between Federalists and Republicans in the early republic were all part of a general
caste response to the democratic changes accompanying the Revolution. For
ambitious young men, appeals to honor may also have proven attractive as a
means of asserting one's right to membership in the post-Revolutionary elite.[47]

Most observers at the time, nevertheless, believed the public opinion in support of dueling far more pervasive than the small band of actual duelists. Some
noted a passive acceptance among the general public in not speaking out for
enforcement of laws and in the election of politicians who had fought duels.
However, observers disagreed on whether this seeming public acceptance of
dueling was more the result of the top-down spread of elite culture or the
bottom-up expansion of the lower orders' social values. If northern and Federalist critics tended to see elite opinion trickling down to the masses, southern and
Republican critics tended to see widespread (if corrupt) public opinion sanctioned by the entire community working its way up to the elite.[48]

Elites generally play an important role in shaping public opinion. However,
much evidence suggests that in Virginia as in the rest of the early republic, the
transformation in public opinion behind dueling combined elements from both
ends of the social spectrum. The American Revolution worked a fundamental
transformation in public opinion, greatly expanding the "public" and democra-
tizing the "opinion." Even before the Revolution—in Virginia at least since the
1740s—some politicians attempted to maintain their independence of the electorate, but others were quite willing to follow the will of their constituents, and
their numbers grew after the Revolution. And there is evidence to suggest that
after the Revolution, Americans across regional and class lines increasingly accepted many forms of "justifiable" violence they had previously rejected. But
these democratic sources should not blind us to the inherently aristocratic nature
of dueling, as developments in Virginia made clear.[49]

John Randolph and the Romantic Revolution

By the end of the 1790s, the last link in the transformation of public opinion in
Virginia behind dueling would be complete with the fruition of Arthur Lee's
aristocratic notions of honor and dueling that Virginians had so staunchly condemned in the pre-Revolutionary era. No one epitomized these changes better
than John Randolph of Roanoke.

Arthur Lee died in 1792, back home in Virginia and—as far as we know—
never having engaged in an actual duel (although as quarrelsome as he was, he
was challenged a few times).[50] That same year John Randolph (not yet of Roanoke) fled Williamsburg after engaging in the first of his many duels as a first-

year student at the College of William and Mary. And, like Lee, Randolph ever after had bitter feelings toward the people of Williamsburg for the way he had been treated. Williamsburg had not changed that much in twenty-five years.

Yet the times were a-changing. Randolph did not fight his first duel out of frustration following some vicious political feud, as did all the participants in the affairs of the late 1760s, but as a result of a dispute in his debating society with another student, Robert Barraud Taylor (afterward a leading Virginia Federalist), over the pronunciation of some word. As Lemuel Sawyer, one of Randolph's biographers and a member of Congress with him for sixteen years, described the affair, "[T]hey had taken opposite sides in politics and were both fiery spirits and full of Virginia pride of chivalry." Neither was hurt in the duel, and they later became the best of friends, although to their dying days they continued to argue over how the word was pronounced. Randolph's aristocratic view of honor might have been out of place in colonial America but not among certain elements of Virginia society in the early republic. In retrospect, we can see Randolph as a harbinger of the chivalric romanticism that would sweep the South and the rest of the United States in the nineteenth century.[51]

For the origins of this chivalric revival one might not have to look any farther than the American Revolution. Administrators bemoaned the way the youth on college campuses across the nation appealed to revolutionary principles to justify a rash of riots in the years 1798–1815. Heroic wars have always had a tendency to put chivalric ideas in the heads of idealistic youth who come of age hearing tales of the courageous deeds of "our illustrious Heroes and patriots," reflected most strongly in the veneration bestowed on the great American warrior George Washington in the early American republic.[52] "The generation which grew to manhood in this interval [the twenty-five years following the Revolution]," recalled John Pendleton Kennedy in the 1840s,

> were educated in all the reminiscences of the war of Seventy-six, which, fresh in the narratives of every fireside, flamed the imagination of the young with its thousand marvels of soldierlike adventure. These were told with the amplification and the unction characteristic of the veteran, and were heard by his youthful listener, with many a secret sign, that such days of heroic hazard were not to return for him.[53]

But the chivalric revival led by John Randolph was in many ways more a rebellion against than a fulfillment of parental values. There is no better proof of this rejection of older social norms than the passion with which the second generation of Virginia patriots took to dueling. The period of intense campus rebellions also saw a dueling craze sweep the College of William and Mary, although students knew that involvement in a duel in any way brought immediate expulsion.

The post-Revolutionary revival shares many parallels with other chivalric revivals, such as the Elizabethan, in which dueling also played an important role. Like "the aspiring mind of the Elizabethan younger generation," the second generation of Virginia patriots believed new circumstances demanded new principles. Reacting against the rationalism of their parents' generation, they sought solutions in romanticism. While critics condemned dueling as "passion run amok," this generation would come to assert that "passion, in its noblest form, was the major force leading men to resent aspersions on their characters, as well it should."[54]

But the rise of chivalric romanticism and dueling in Virginia cannot be explained by strictly local factors. The early nineteenth century also saw the introduction or revival of dueling in many parts of the English-speaking world, including England, Upper Canada, the West Indies, and other English colonies, as well as in post-Revolutionary France. Bourgeois German university students in the early nineteenth century created for themselves a world bound by a code of honor and regulated by the duel, much as did William and Mary students.[55]

Although the timing of the rise of dueling in America can hardly be explained, as some historians are wont to do, by the direct influence of Sir Walter Scott— "the Sir Walter disease" as Mark Twain put it—which came much later, one cannot deny that European opinions and fashions had a significant impact on notions of honor and dueling in America. The romanticism of Virginia youth was part of the romantic movement that swept Europe and America. These young Virginians' volte-face on the French Revolution paralleled those of the European romantics like Wordsworth, Blake, Coleridge, and Hölderin, who were swinging from the prorevolutionary "millenarian excitement" to Burkean conservatism.[56]

Again John Randolph captures perfectly this tremendous swing in opinion. In 1793, the year after being expelled from William and Mary for dueling, he wrote to his stepfather, St. George Tucker, asking permission "to go immediately to France, and to enter into the army of the Republic. . . . My wish is to serve the noblest cause in the world. . . . What life can be so glorious what death so honorable?" Randolph feared the middle-class alternative: "the pursuits of a miserable attorney who stoops to a thousand petty villainies in order to earn the sum of fifteen shillings." The law bored him, but "I feel the most ardent enthusiasm for the cause. I dream of nothing else. I think of nothing else; what [word blotted] do you suppose, then, I should make of old Coke, when my thoughts are dwelling on the plains of Flanders?"[57]

Yet by the second administration of Thomas Jefferson, Randolph had converted "from a partisan to an enemy of the French Revolution and of all revolution," and his rereading of Edmund Burke's *Reflections on the French Revolution* had led him "to suspect that there may be something in the enjoyment of liberty which soon disqualifies a people for self-government, which is but another name for freedom."[58]

Southern romanticism was hardly a simple spreading out of ideas from Europe to America; rather, both involved independent intellectual developments emerging out of "specific social and political crises." But the parallels with European romanticism are indeed striking, such as the increased emphasis on emotion, passion, and introspection; a focus on provincial self-justification; and a shared melancholy emerging at first out of reaction to the French Revolution but sustained by "the permanent crisis of modern industrial society."[59]

Conclusion

Few if any Virginians in the early republic seemed aware of how dramatically views about honor, violence, and dueling, as well as the actual levels of honor violence, had changed since the colonial era. Or, at the very least, they never commented on any such changes. Yet there can be no doubt that such a transformation did occur, and that it has attracted insufficient attention from early American historians. More difficult to assess, though, is why the transformation occurred.

Perhaps, at the risk of oversimplification, we might see the transformation in America and elsewhere as part of a working out of competing democratic and aristocratic tendencies in many parts of the world in the late eighteenth and early nineteenth centuries. In pre-Revolutionary Virginia, the increased levels of honor violence among the lower classes suggest a breakdown in traditional hierarchical control among people who took honor very seriously. Such a breakdown was fostered by divisions among the Virginia elite that opened the door to an increasingly open and more violent politics. Whether—as one anonymous Virginian critic of dueling in the early republic put it—politicians in turning to dueling consciously succumbed to the "general prejudice" in order "to obtain the applause, or avert the contempt of the giddy multitude" or whether they simply succumbed to an increasingly democratized public opinion, democratic factors played an important role in increasing elite acceptance and adoption of the violent means of the lower classes. Such trends continued even more strongly after the American Revolution and reached something of a climax in the heated politics of the early republic.[60]

At the same time the gentry were attempting to redefine the hierarchical order along aristocratic lines. For these would-be aristocrats, ideas of chivalric honor and dueling could provide a means of simultaneously avoiding charges of cowardice from below and setting oneself off from the more barbarous modes of honor violence of the masses.[61] In the pre-Revolutionary era, the arguments of Arthur Lee were ill received; only in the early republic did such appeals seem to resonate with a substantial number of the Virginia elite, reinforced by the crosscurrents of the romantic movement. The net result of these changes was a dramatic transformation in Virginian precept and practice, from a colonial world where Virginians could ridicule those who would employ violence to defend their honor, to an antebellum world where honor violence was no longer a laughing matter and, indeed, for many, would come to define the very essence of what it meant to be a Virginian.

NOTES

1. In August 1780, a meeting of the Phi Beta Kappa Society debated "Ye Question, Whether Duelling ought to have toleration in this or any other free state," although we do not know what arguments were made. See "Original Records of the Phi Beta Kappa Society," *William and Mary Quarterly*, 1st ser., 4 (1896): 238.

2. This account of the Lee-Mercer affair draws primarily upon the following sources: Corbin Griffin, letter to editor, Purdie and Dixon's *Virginia Gazette*, May 28, 1767; James Mercer, letter to editor, Rind's *Virginia Gazette*, July 23, 1767; Amicus Superbiae, "An Essay on Pride," Purdie and Dixon's *Virginia Gazette*, July 30, 1767; Lois Mulkearn, ed., George Mercer Papers relating to the Ohio Company of Virginia (Pittsburgh: University of Pittsburgh Press, 1954), 203–4. For secondary accounts, see Louis W. Potts, *Arthur Lee: A Virtuous Revolutionary* (Baton Rouge: Louisiana State University Press, 1981), 38–42; A. R. Riggs, *The Nine Lives of Arthur Lee*, Virginia Patriot (Williamsburg: Virginia Independence Bicentennial Commission, 1976), 18–19.

3. Purdie and Dixon's *Virginia Gazette*, July 30, 1767.

4. Alexander Brown, *The First Republic in America* (Boston: Houghton Mifflin, 1898), 582.

5. Mervyn James, *Society, Politics and Culture: Studies in Early Modern England* (Cambridge: Cambridge University Press, 1986), 12, 309, 320, 328–38, 381; Arthur B. Ferguson, *The Chivalric Tradition in Renaissance England* (Washington, D.C.: Folger Shakespeare Library, 1986), 17–18.

6. Sir Thomas Elyot, *The Book named the Governor*, ed. S. E. Lehmberg (London: Dent, 1962); James, *Society, Politics and Culture*, 322, 338, 379; Ruth Kelso, *The Doctrine of the English Gentleman in the Sixteenth Century* (Urbana: University of Illinois Press, 1929); W. Lee Ustick, "Changing Ideals of Aristocratic Character and Conduct in Seventeenth-Century England," *Modern Philology* 30 (1932): 147–66; Richard B. Schlatter, *The Social Ideas of Religious Leaders, 1660–1688* (London: Oxford University Press, 1940), 106–23; George C. Brauer, Jr., *The Education of a Gentleman: Theories of Gentlemanly Education in England, 1660–1775* (New York: Bookman, 1959); John M. Major, *Sir Thomas Elyot and Renaissance Humanism* (Lincoln: University of Nebraska Press, 1964); Bertram Wyatt-Brown, *Southern Honor: Ethics and Behavior in the Old South* (Oxford: Oxford University Press, 1982), 26, 34, 59; James, *Society, Politics and Culture*, 358–62, 377–78, 393–94; Ferguson, *Chivalric Tradition*, 63–64; V. G. Kiernan, *The Duel in European History: Honour and the Reign of Aristocracy* (Oxford: Oxford University Press, 1988), 86.

7. Research to date indicates minimal levels of dueling in late-sixteenth and seventeenth-century England. Lawrence Stone, *The Crisis of the Aristocracy, 1558–1641* (Oxford: Clarendon Press, 1979), 242–50; J. A. Sharpe, *Crime in Seventeenth-Century England: A County Study* (Cambridge: Cambridge University Press, 1983), 129, 253 n. 87; Kiernan, *Duel in European History*, 53, 80–83, 100–105, 153. On the late-eighteenth and nineteenth centuries, see Antony E. Simpson, "Dandelions on the Field of Honor: Dueling, the Middle Classes, and the Law in Nineteenth-Century England," *Criminal Justice History* 9 (1988): 99–155; Brauer, *Education of a Gentleman*, 16–18; James, *Society, Politics and Culture*, 313–14, 322; Kelso, *Doctrine of the English Gentleman*, 99–100, 103; Franois Billacois, *The Duel: Its Rise and Fall in Early Modern France*, ed. and trans. Trista Selous (New Haven: Yale University Press, 1990), 127–28, 206–7.

8. *The Works of John Locke*, 10 vols. (London: Thomas Tegg, 1823), 2:106; Kelso, *Doctrine of the English Gentleman*, 104; Kiernan, *Duel in European History*, 11, 102; Donna T. Andrew, "The Code of Honour and Its Critics: The Opposition to Duelling in England, 1700–1850," *Social History* 5 (1980): 409–34; James, *Society, Politics and Culture*, 322, 338, 379 394, 410; Kiernan, *Duel in European History*, 89; Billacois, *Duel*, 30–33.

9. Wyatt-Brown, *Southern Honor*, 78–87; James, *Society, Politics and Culture*, 342–48, 356; David Hackett Fischer, *Albion's Seed: Four British Folkways in America* (New York: Oxford University Press, 1989), 396–97; James Horn, *Adapting to a New World: English Society in the Seventeenth-Century Chesapeake* (Chapel Hill: University of North Carolina Press, 1994),

334–80, quote at 380; James R. Perry, *The Formation of a Society on Virginia's Eastern Shore, 1615–1655* (Chapel Hill: University of North Carolina Press, 1990), 237; Bruce C. Baird, "Ideology, Behavior, and Necessity in Seventeenth-Century England and Virginia" (Ph.D. diss., University of Florida, 1995).

10. Kelso, *Doctrine of the English Gentleman*, 105; Brauer, *Education of a Gentleman*, 16–18; Dickson D. Bruce, Jr., *Violence and Culture in the Antebellum South* (Austin: University of Texas Press, 1979), 31; Kiernan, *Duel in European History*, 8, 81–82, 87, 120–21, 153–55; Thomas J. Wertenbaker, *Patrician and Plebeian in Virginia: The Shaping of Colonial Virginia* (1910; New York: Russell and Russell, 1958), 75–80; Arthur P. Scott, *Criminal Law in Colonial Virginia* (Chicago: University of Chicago Press, 1930), 178–79; "Virginia Gleanings in England," *Virginia Magazine of History and Biography* 20 (1912): 372–81; "The Case of Giles Bland, 1676," ibid., 21 (1913): 126–35; Fischer, *Albion's Seed*, 318–19.

11. Scott, *Criminal Law in Colonial Virginia*, 200–205; Hugh F. Rankin, *Criminal Trial Proceedings in the General Court of Colonial Virginia* (Williamsburg: Colonial Williamsburg, 1965), 204–15; Timothy E. Morgan, "Turmoil in an Orderly Society: Colonial Virginia, 1607–1754; A History and Analysis" (Ph.D. diss., College of William and Mary, 1976); Fischer, *Albion's Seed*, 398–405.

12. Scott, *Criminal Law in Colonial Virginia*, 164–74, 181–83, quote at 171; Bradley Chapin, *Criminal Justice in Colonial America, 1606–1660* (Athens: University of Georgia Press, 1983), 51–52, 76–77, 85–89, 131–34; Mary Beth Norton, "Gender and Defamation in Seventeenth-Century Maryland," *William and Mary Quarterly*, 3d ser., 44 (1987): 3–39; Fischer, *Albion's Seed*, 396–97; Perry, *Formation of a Society*, 113–14, 201–2; Horn, *Adapting to a New World*, 363–68; Norman L. Rosenberg, *Protecting the Best Men: An Interpretive History of the Law of Libel* (Chapel Hill: University of North Carolina Press, 1986), 16–19, 28–30; David A. Williams, *Political Alignments in Colonial Virginia Politics, 1698–1750* (New York: Garland, 1989), 325–26.

13. Horn, *Adapting to a New World*, 367; Scott, *Criminal Law in Colonial Virginia*, 185; Rosenberg, *Protecting the Best Men*, 26–27; Williams, *Political Alignments*, 3, 47, 56, 364–66. Larry D. Eldridge notes a similar evolving leniency toward seditious speech; see Eldridge, *A Distant Heritage: The Growth of Free Speech in Early America* (New York: New York University Press, 1994).

14. Grady McWhiney, *Cracker Culture: Celtic Ways in the Old South* (Tuscaloosa: University of Alabama Press, 1988), 146–70; Fischer, *Albion's Seed*, 689–90, 735–38, 764–71; Fox Butterfield, *All God's Children: The Bosket Family and the American Tradition of Violence* (New York: Knopf, 1995), 3–18; Richard E. Nisbett and Dov Cohen, *Culture of Honor: The Psychology of Violence in the South* (Boulder: Westview Press, 1996), 4–9. This view has received sharp criticism from students of Appalachia. See "Culture Wars: David Hackett Fischer's *Albion's Seed*," *Appalachian Journal* 19 (1992): 161–200; Altina L. Waller, "Feuding in Appalachia: Evolution of a Cultural Stereotype," in *Appalachia in the Making: The Mountain South in the Nineteenth Century*, ed. Mary Beth Pudup et al. (Chapel Hill: University of North Carolina Press, 1995), 347–76.

15. James G. Leyburn, *The Scotch-Irish: A Social History* (Chapel Hill: University of North Carolina Press, 1962), 6–7, 9, 68–70. See also Keith M. Brown, *Bloodfeud in Scotland, 1573–1625: Violence, Justice and Politics in an Early Modern Society* (Edinburgh: John Donald, 1986); Fischer, *Albion's Seed*, 623–29.

16. Maldwyn A. Jones, "Scotch-Irish," *Harvard Encyclopedia of American Ethnic Groups*, ed. Stephen Thernstrom (Cambridge: Harvard University Press, Belknap Press, 1980), 899; J. A. Leo Lemay, "Southern Colonial Grotesque: Robert Bolling's 'Neanthe,' *Mississippi Quarterly* 35 (1982): 109; James C. Klotter, "Feuds in Appalachia: An Overview," *Filson*

Club Historical Quarterly 56 (1982): 307–10; Leroy V. Eid, "Irish, Scotch and Scotch-Irish, A Reconsideration," *American Presbyterians* 64 (1986): 220–21; Fischer, *Albion's Seed*, 735–38. On dueling in Ulster, see James Kelly, *"That Damn'd Thing Called Honour": Duelling in Ireland, 1570–1860* (Cork: Cork University Press, 1995), 63, 80.

17. Carlton Jackson, *A Social History of the Scotch-Irish* (Lanham, Md.: Madison Books, 1993), 70–71; Scott, *Criminal Law in Colonial Virginia*, 205; Rankin, *Criminal Trial Proceedings*, 200.

18. Lemay, "Southern Colonial Grotesque," 109, 121. Robert D. Arner, "The Muse of History: Robert Bolling's Verses on the Norfolk Inoculation Riots of 1768–1769," *Early American Literature and Culture: Essays Honoring Harrison T. Meserole*, ed. Kathryn Zabelle Derounian-Stodola (Newark: University of Delaware Press, 1992), 165.

19. Richard J. Hooker, ed., *The Carolina Backcountry on the Eve of the Revolution: The Journal and Other Writings of Charles Woodmason, Anglican Itinerant* (Chapel Hill: University of North Carolina Press, 1953), 154–59.

20. Woodmason's journal abounds with criticisms of "these Northern Scotch Irish," whom he thought "the worst Vermin on Earth," without any reference to Virginians. See Hooker, *Carolina Backcountry*, xxiv, 13–14, 50, 60–61, 142; Robert L. Meriwether, *The Expansion of South Carolina, 1729–1765* (Kingsport, Tenn.: Southern Publishers, 1940), 134–46, 160. In contrast, Richard Maxwell Brown believes Woodmason's references to violent Virginians refer principally to "British stock from the older sections of the Old Dominion." See Brown, *The South Carolina Regulators* (Cambridge: Harvard University Press, Belknap Press, 1963), 2, 27, 179 n. 2.

21. *Journal and Letters of Philip Vickers Fithian, 1773–1774: A Plantation Tutor of the Old Dominion*, ed. Hunter Dickinson Farish (Williamsburg: Colonial Williamsburg, 1943), 240–41. Purdie and Dixon's *Virginia Gazette*, October 25, November 8, 1770; October 17, November 7, 1771; April 23, May 7, 1772; Scott, *Criminal Law in Colonial Virginia*, 205–7; Jane Carson, *Colonial Virginians at Play* (Williamsburg: Colonial Williamsburg, 1965), 164–67; Rankin, *Criminal Trial Proceedings*, 199–202.

22. Williams, *Political Alignments*, 122, 280–82 (quote), 308, 317–20, 325–37, 357–58 (quote); Carl Bridenbaugh, "Violence and Virtue in Virginia, 1766; or, The Importance of the Trivial," *Early Americans* (New York: Oxford University Press, 1981), 192–93 (quote); Charles S. Sydnor, *American Revolutionaries in the Making: Political Practices in Washington's Virginia* (New York: Free Press, 1952), 24–26; Richard R. Beeman, "Robert Munford and the Political Culture of Frontier Virginia," *Journal of American Studies* 12 (1978): 181; Morgan, "Turmoil in an Orderly Society," 282–86.

23. Patrick Henderson, "Smallpox and Patriotism: The Norfolk Riots, 1768–1769," *Virginia Magazine of History and Biography* 73 (1965): 412–24; J. E. Morpurgo, *Their Majesties' Royall Colledge: William and Mary in the Seventeenth and Eighteenth Centuries* (Williamsburg: College of William and Mary of Virginia, 1976), 145; Warren M. Billings et al., *Colonial Virginia: A History* (White Plains, N.Y.: KTO Press, 1986), 304–6.

24. On the heated political atmosphere of the later 1760s, see Bridenbaugh, "Violence and Virtue," 192–94, 206 (quote); David John Mays, *Edmund Pendleton, 1721–1803: A Biography*, 2 vols. (Cambridge: Harvard University Press, 1952), 1:156–208; Carl Bridenbaugh, *Seat of Empire: The Political Role of Eighteenth-Century Williamsburg* (Williamsburg: Colonial Williamsburg, 1958), 67–71; Williams, *Political Alignments*, 308, 318–20, 327–37, 357–58; Joseph Albert Ernst, "The Robinson Scandal Redivivus: Money, Debts, and Politics in Revolutionary Virginia," *Virginia Magazine of History and Biography* 77 (1969): 146–73; J. A. Leo Lemay, "Robert Bolling and the Bailment of Colonel Chiswell," *Early American Literature* 6 (1971): 101–3; John Sayle Watterson, *Thomas Burke, Restless Revolutionary*

(Washington, D.C.: University Press of America, 1980), 6; Billings et al., *Colonial Virginia,* 285–335.

25. William H. Castles, Jr., "The Virginia Gazette, 1736–1766: Its Editors, Editorial Policies, and Literary Content" (Ph.D. diss., University of Tennessee, 1962), 26–28, 70–73; Lemay, "Robert Bolling," 102, 115, 119–20 n. 7; J. A. Leo Lemay, "The Rev. Samuel Davies' Essay Series: The Virginia Centinel, 1756–1757," *Essays in Early Virginia Literature Honoring Richard Beale Davis* (New York: Burt Franklin, 1977), 131–32, 160 n .15. For earlier and later paper wars in Virginia, see Castles, "*Virginia Gazette,*" 89–92, 170–73, 273–78; Morpurgo, *Their Majesties' Royall Colledge,* 150–53, 162–65; Lemay, "Rev. Samuel Davies," 130–35.

26. Bridenbaugh, "Violence and Virtue," 199–200; J. A. Leo Lemay, "John Mercer and the Stamp Act in Virginia, 1764–1765," *Virginia Magazine of History and Biography* 91 (1983): 24–25; Lemay, "Robert Bolling," 99–102, 116, 126 n. 42; Ernst, "Robinson Scandal Redivivus," 162; Billings et al., *Colonial Virginia,* 309–14.

27. Letter from Virginia, *New York Journal or General Advertiser,* November 27, 1766; Billings et al., *Colonial Virginia,* 313; Bridenbaugh, "Violence and Virtue," 206. For a similar rise in partisanship and decline in deference in other colonies, see Rosenberg, *Protecting the Best Men,* 45–47.

28. Letters to the editor and "On Calumny," Purdie and Dixon's *Virginia Gazette,* July 4, September 26, October 3, November 6, 1766, March 5, May 21, 28, August 6, November 19, 1767; Mulkearn, *George Mercer Papers,* 204; Rind's *Virginia Gazette,* August 8, 1766; July 23, 1767. On popular attitudes toward "the present Freedom of the Press," see Rind's *Virginia Gazette,* August 15, 1766, March 24, 1768; Purdie and Dixon's *Virginia Gazette,* August 22, November 6, 1766; *New York Journal or General Advertiser,* November 27, 1766; Bridenbaugh, "Violence and Virtue," 206, 209–10; Leonard W. Levy, *Emergence of a Free Press* (New York: Oxford University Press, 1985); Rosenberg, *Protecting the Best Men,* 29–55.

29. Letters to editor, Purdie and Dixon's *Virginia Gazette,* July 25, August 22, October 17, November 6, 1766 (quote); *New York Journal or General Advertiser,* November 27, 1766 (quote); *Maryland Gazette,* October 30, 1766; Lemay, "Robert Bolling," 115–16, 126 n. 43; Lemay, "Robert Bolling," 99–142; Rosenberg, *Protecting the Best Men,* 34–35, 45–48, 286 n. 45.

30. James Mercer, letter to editor, Purdie and Dixon's *Virginia Gazette,* October 3, 1766, and to editor, Rind's *Virginia Gazette,* July 23, 1767. John Mercer made a similar threat against an enemy just a week earlier than did his son James. Purdie and Dixon's *Virginia Gazette,* September 26, 1766.

31. Lemay, "Robert Bolling," 105, 109, 116, 142 n. 141. Byrd's son, Thomas Taylor Byrd, acted in a similar fashion when accused of riotous behavior at William and Mary College in April 1769, even threatening the president of the College with violence in denying the charge of disruptive conduct. See "Journal of the Meetings of the President and Masters of William and Mary College," *William and Mary Quarterly,* 1st ser., 13 (1904): 134; Marion Tinling, ed., *The Correspondence of the Three William Byrds of Westover, Virginia, 1684–1776,* 2 vols. (Charlottesville: University Press of Virginia, 1977), 2:778 n.

32. Rhys Isaac, *The Transformation of Virginia, 1740–1790* (Chapel Hill: University of North Carolina Press, 1982), 95.

33. James Mercer to editor, Rind's *Virginia Gazette,* July 23, 1767. See the numerous references under "duels" in Lester J. Cappon and Stella F. Duff, eds., *Virginia Gazette Index, 1736–1780,* 2 vols. (Williamsburg, Va.: Institute of Early American History and Culture, 1950), 1:325–26.

34. Rind's *Virginia Gazette*, December 24, 1767; Purdie and Dixon's *Virginia Gazette*, August 13, November 5, 1767, April 7, 1768. On contemporaneous references to "modern honour" and protection of reputation, see *Virginia Gazette*, August 3, 1739; Rind's *Virginia Gazette*, December 24, 1772; August 19, November 18, 1773.

35. Rind's *Virginia Gazette*, December 24, 1767 (quotations), December 24, 1772; William Blackstone, *Commentaries on the Laws of England*, 2 vols. (New York: Collins and Hannay, 1832), 2:152; Kelso, *Doctrine of the English Gentleman*, 99–105; Kiernan, *Duel in European History*, 53, 100–105, 153; Billacois, *The Duel*, 127–28, 206–7; Joanne B. Freeman, "Dueling as Politics: Reinterpreting the Burr-Hamilton Duel," *William and Mary Quarterly*, 3d ser., 53 (1996): 315.

36. Mulkearn, ed., *George Mercer Papers*, 203–4; Purdie and Dixon's *Virginia Gazette*, April 7, 1768. For poetical attacks on Landon Carter and his response, see Watterson, *Thomas Burke*, 5–8; Lemay, "Robert Bolling," 114, 117; Rind's *Virginia Gazette*, July 23, 1767.

37. Purdie and Dixon's *Virginia Gazette*, October 31, 1771.

38. Letter to editor, Rind's *Virginia Gazette*, December 24, 1767; "An Essay on Duelling," Purdie and Dixon's *Virginia Gazette*, August 27, 1767. See also Purdie and Dixon's*Virginia Gazette*, July 30, 1767, January 28, 1773, December 1, 1774; Rind's *Virginia Gazette*, March 7, 1771, November 18, 1773.

39. James Mercer, letter to editor, Rind's *Virginia Gazette*, July 23, 1767; Mulkearn, ed., *George Mercer Papers*, 203–4; Lemay, "Robert Bolling," 116, 142 n.

40. Letters to editor, Purdie and Dixon's *Virginia Gazette*, August 29, October 3, 1766; Lemay, "Robert Bolling," 110, 124 n.

41. James Mercer, letters to editor, Purdie and Dixon's *Virginia Gazette*, July 18, 1766, July 23, 1767; Bridenbaugh, "Violence and Virtue," 188–212; Lemay, "Robert Bolling," 114–15, 125–26 n.

42. St. George Tucker, ed., *Blackstone's Commentaries*, 5 vols. (Philadelphia, 1803), 5:149, 149 n. Apologists for dueling in the early republic argued that the code of honor actually reduced undisciplined forms of violence. See "Reflections on Duelling," Richmond *Enquirer*, January 18, 1805; [George Tucker], *Essays on Various Subjects of Taste, Morals, and National Policy . . . By a Citizen of Virginia* (Georgetown, D.C.: J. Milligan, 1822), 264–65.

43. James Mercer to editor, Rind's *Virginia Gazette*, July 23, 1767; Mulkearn, ed., *George Mercer Papers*, 203–4.

44. L. O. [Arthur Lee] to editor, Rind's *Virginia Gazette*, December 24, 1767; Watterson, *Thomas Burke*, 7–10; Arner, "Muse of History," 165–83.

45. See, e.g., Timothy Dwight, *The Folly, Guilt, and Mischiefs of Duelling: A Sermon, Preached in the College Chapel at New Haven, on the Sabbath preceding the Annual Commencement, September, 1804* (Hartford: Hudson and Company, 1805), 7, 15; essays on dueling in the *Richmond Enquirer*, January 5, 18, March 30, 1805; Lyman Beecher, *The Remedy for Duelling* (New York: J. Seymour for Williams and Whiting, 1809) 11–12, 21–23, 43; [Tucker], *Essays*, 249–50, 257–58, 262, 265–67; Lorenzo Sabine, *Notes on Duels and Duelling* (Boston, 1856), 42–43; Dickson D. Bruce, Jr., *Violence and Culture in the Antebellum South* (Austin: University of Texas Press, 1979), 28, 42; Edward L. Ayers, *Vengeance and Justice: Crime and Punishment in the 19th-Century American South* (New York: Oxford University Press, 1984), 13–14; Freeman, "Dueling as Politics," 292–93, 315–16.

46. Dwight, *Folly, Guilt, and Mischiefs of Duelling*, 14–15; Beecher, *Remedy for Duelling*, 7, 19, 21, 44.

47. Paul Eidelberg, *The Philosophy of the American Constitution: A Reinterpretation of the Intentions of the Founding Fathers* (New York: Free Press, 1968), 97–99, 196–97; Robert H. Wiebe, *The Opening of American Society: From the Adoption of the Constitution to the Eve of*

Disunion (New York: Knopf, 1984), 37–41; Kelso, *Doctrine of the English Gentleman*, 19, 96–97, 319; Kiernan, *Duel in European History*, vii, 1–5, 7, 49–54, 82, 91, 152–53, 159–60; Robert J. Brugger, *Beverley Tucker: Heart over Head in the Old South* (Baltimore: Johns Hopkins University Press, 1978), 35–41; Ayers, *Vengeance and Justice*, 16–17.

48. "Reflections on Duelling," *Richmond Enquirer*, January 18, 1805; Beecher, *Remedy for Duelling*, 4, 10, 21–23, 25; Samuel Low, *A Discourse on Duelling* (Richmond: John O'Lynch, 1811), 7; Sabine, *Notes on Duels*, 41–44, 343–45, 352–55; Ayers, *Vengeance and Justice*, 30–31.

49. Richard Buel, Jr., *Securing the Revolution: Ideology in American Politics, 1789–1815* (Ithaca: Cornell University Press, 1972), 91–112; Gordon S. Wood, *The Radicalism of the American Revolution* (New York: Vintage Books, 1991), 360–64; Freeman, "Dueling as Politics," 295–97; Billings et al., *Colonial Virginia*, 266–71, 311, 313–14; Sydnor, *American Revolutionaries*, 44–59; Beeman, "Robert Munford," 169–83; David Brion Davis, *Homicide in American Fiction, 1798–1860: A Study in Social Values* (Ithaca: Cornell University Press, 1957), 266–90; Jack Kenny Williams, *Vogues in Villainy: Crime and Retribution in Ante-Bellum South Carolina* (Columbia: University of South Carolina Press, 1959), 31–39.

50. Potts, *Arthur Lee*, 4, 44, 258.

51. William Cabell Bruce, *John Randolph of Roanoke, 1773–1833*, 2 vols. (New York: Octagon Books, 1970) 1:123–26; Bruce, *Violence and Culture*, 41; Daniel P. Jordan, *Political Leadership in Jefferson's Virginia* (Charlottesville: University Press of Virginia, 1983), 166; Fischer, *Albion's Seed*, 412; Vernon Louis Parrington, *The Romantic Revolution in America, 1800–1860* (New York: Harcourt, Brace, 1927), iii–ix; Marcus Cunliffe, *Soldiers and Civilians: The Martial Spirit in America, 1775–1865* (Boston: Little, Brown, 1968), 399–412; Brugger, *Beverley Tucker*, 123–26, 163–66, 172; Michael O'Brien, *Rethinking the South: Essays in Intellectual History* (Baltimore: Johns Hopkins University Press, 1988), 5, 38–56; Jean V. Matthews, *Toward a New Society: American Thought and Culture, 1800–1830* (Boston: Twayne, 1991), 118–23.

52. Edgar W. Knight, ed., *A Documentary History of Education in the South before 1860*, 5 vols. (Chapel Hill: University of North Carolina Press, 1953), 4:274–77; Howard Miller, *The Revolutionary College: American Presbyterian Higher Education, 1707–1837* (New York: New York University Press, 1976), 259–68; Brugger, *Beverley Tucker*, 41–43; Mark A. Noll, *Princeton and the Republic, 1768–1822: The Search for a Christian Enlightenment in the Era of Samuel Stanhope Smith* (Princeton: Princeton University Press, 1989), 150–53, 214–43; Lorraine Smith Pangle and Thomas L. Pangle, *The Learning of Liberty: The Educational Ideas of the American Founders* (Lawrence: University Press of Kansas, 1993), 163–66, 231–49; Kiernan, *Duel in European History*, 80–81; Forrest McDonald, *Novus Ordo Seclorum: The Intellectual Origins of the Constitution* (Lawrence: University Press of Kansas, 1985), 191–95; Barry Schwartz, *George Washington: The Making of an American Symbol* (New York: Free Press, 1987), 162–70.

53. John Pendleton Kennedy, *Memoirs of the Life of William Wirt*, quoted in Jordan, *Political Leadership*, 30.

54. Bruce, *Violence and Culture*, 31; Bruce, *John Randolph of Roanoke*, 2:379–83; Robert Colin McLean, *George Tucker: Moral Philosopher and Man of Letters* (Chapel Hill: University of North Carolina Press, 1961), 212–16; Dickson D. Bruce, Jr., *The Rhetoric of Conservatism: The Virginia Convention of 1829–30 and the Conservative Tradition in the South* (San Marino, Calif.: Huntington Library, 1982), 166–69; Charles T. Cullen, *St. George Tucker and Law in Virginia, 1772–1804* (New York: Garland, 1987); Brugger, *Beverley Tucker*, 18–19, 41–43, 126, 204–9; Phillip Forrest Hamilton, "The Tucker Family and the Dynamics of Generational Change in Jeffersonian Virginia, 1775–1830" (Ph.D. diss., Washington University, 1995), 450–59.

55. Simpson, "Dandelions on the Field of Honor"; Kiernan, *Duel in European History*, 185–203, 293–314; Billacois, *The Duel*, 187–88; Cecilia Morgan, " 'In Search of the Phantom Misnamed Honour': Duelling in Upper Canada," *Canadian Historical Review* 76 (1995): 529–62; Rollin G. Osterweis, *Romanticism and Nationalism in the Old South* (New Haven: Yale University Press, 1949), 96; Ute Frevert, "Bourgeois Honour: Middle-Class Duellists in Germany from the Late Eighteenth to the Early Twentieth Century," in *The German Bourgeoisie: Essays on the Social History of the German Middle Class from the Late Eighteenth to the Early Twentieth Century*, ed. David Blackbourn and Richard J. Evans (London: Routledge, 1991), 277–82; Shearer Davis Bowman, "Honor and Martialism in the U.S. South and Prussian East Elbia during the Mid-Nineteenth Century," in *What Made the South Different?* ed. Kees Gispen (Jackson: University of Mississippi Press, 1990), 19–40.

56. [Tucker], *Essays*, 266–67; Hamilton J. Eckenrode, "Sir Walter Scott and the South," *North American Review* 206 (1917): 595–603; Kiernan, *Duel in European History*, 223–57, 312; Henry F. May, *The Enlightenment in America* (New York: Oxford University Press, 1976), 245–47, 332–33. On the shift to Burkean conservatism, see William R. Taylor, *Cavalier and Yankee: The Old South and American National Character* (New York: Harper Torchbooks, 1961), 23, 156; Robert P. Sutton, "Nostalgia, Pessimism, and Malaise: The Doomed Aristocrat in Late-Jeffersonian Virginia," *Virginia Magazine of History and Biography* 76 (1968): 46–55; Bruce, *Rhetoric*, 87–89, 166–69; O'Brien, *Rethinking the South*, 44, 54; Elizabeth Fox-Genovese and Eugene D. Genovese, "Political Virtue and the Lessons of the French Revolution: The View from the Slaveholding South," in *Virtue, Corruption, and Self-Interest: Political Values in the Eighteenth Century*, ed. Richard K. Matthews (Bethlehem, Pa.: Lehigh University Press, 1994), 202–17; Hamilton, "Tucker Family," 456–58.

57. Randolph to Tucker, May 25, 1793, quoted in May, *Enlightenment in America*, 246; Russell Kirk, *John Randolph of Roanoke: A Study in American Politics* (Chicago: Regnery, 1964), 12–13; Robert Dawidoff, *The Education of John Randolph* (New York: Norton, 1979).

58. Beverley Tucker quoted in Dawidoff, *Education of John Randolph*, 158, 217–20, 322–23. See also May, *Enlightenment in America*, 329.

59. O'Brien, *Rethinking the South*, 42–43, 49–52; Michael O'Brien, *The Idea of the American South, 1920–1941* (Baltimore: Johns Hopkins University Press, 1979), 4–5.

60. "On Duelling," *Richmond Enquirer*, January 5, 1805. For an example of such a bottom-up working of public opinion among upland southerners in the Old Northwest, see Nicole Etcheson, "Manliness and the Political Culture of the Old Northwest, 1790–1860," *Journal of the Early Republic* 15 (1995): 59–77.

61. Dickson D. Bruce has ably demonstrated the general post-Revolutionary acceptance across all classes in the South of the inevitability of violence, so firmly rooted in the passions, while gentleman proved themselves distinct from the lower orders by "an ability, carefully cultivated, to control one's own passions," a self-control epitomized by the duel. See Bruce, *Violence and Culture*, 6–20, 31–41, quote at 40. See also *The Southern Essays of Richard M. Weaver*, ed. George M. Curtis III and James J. Thompson, Jr. (Indianapolis: Liberty Press, 1987), 162–64; Charles S. Sydnor, "The Southerner and the Laws," *Journal of Southern History* 6 (1940): 15; Buel, *Securing the Revolution*, 80–81.

Knocked to the ground. The result of a drunken fight. Edward Winslow Martin, *The Secrets of the Great City* (Atlanta: Jones Brothers, 1868), 371.

Chapter Five

Women and Domestic Violence in Nineteenth-Century North Carolina

Laura F. Edwards

Elizabeth Rhodes was angry. Her husband, Benjamin, had struck her three hard blows with a narrow stick. According to one witness, she had given him no provocation "except some words uttered by her." Evidently, Benjamin found those words more provocative than did the witness. But if he intended to silence Elizabeth with his blows, he failed. Instead of submitting, she filed criminal charges against him. After the county superior court decided against her, Elizabeth appealed to the North Carolina State Supreme Court.[1]

This case has a peculiarly modern ring to it. In fact, many people think of domestic violence as a recent problem, brought on by all the wrenching economic, social, and cultural changes of the late twentieth century. Even those aware of the historical presence of such violence tend to see battered wives in the past as isolated, silent victims without social support or legal recourse. Only recently, we assume, did women begin to speak out. And only after that did others begin to listen. Elizabeth Rhodes's case shatters all these assumptions. She filed charges not in 1967 but in 1867. The circumstances of her life make her case that much more improbable by current standards. At the time, she and her neighbors in rural western North Carolina were just beginning to piece together their lives after the Civil War. For Rhodes, the twenty-five-year-old wife of a landless white man and mother of two young daughters, daily chores, such as putting food on the table, must have been a struggle. Young, poor, and rural, Rhodes seems a most unlikely candidate to question her husband's authority, let alone initiate an important, precedent-setting case.

Yet, Elizabeth Rhodes was exactly the kind of woman to file such charges. Her case was the first of its kind to reach the North Carolina State Supreme Court. But free black and poor white women had been making domestic disputes public and bringing them to local courts long before Rhodes appealed her case in 1868. One study of antebellum North Carolina found that in three counties, at least thirty-nine free black and white women swore out peace warrants against their husbands between 1850 and 1860. Enslaved women could neither marry legally nor file criminal charges against physical abuse of any kind. But once freed, they too began to use the courts against their husbands. The Freedmen's Bureau regularly dealt with family disputes, including domestic violence. So did the local courts. There are records of thirty-three domestic violence cases in Granville, Orange, and Edgecombe Counties in the twenty-five years following the war. Many more complaints never made their way into the written record because minor violence lay within the jurisdiction of local magistrates, who were notoriously bad record keepers. Even if a magistrate made note of a complaint, county authorities generally saved only those cases that moved into the jurisdiction of the superior court.[2]

This essay explores these North Carolina domestic violence cases and the women who brought them. First, it will focus on the women themselves, looking at the local conditions that allowed poor women to challenge violent expressions of their husbands' authority, the specific kinds of claims they made, and the difficulties they had articulating their concerns within the legal system. But there are larger implications of these cases, as they made their way past local jurisdictions to the State Supreme Court after the Civil War, and then results affected not just the position of wives but social and political relations generally.

The tension between law and culture is particularly striking in domestic violence. Before the Civil War, the law in North Carolina and the South as a whole was clear on the subordination of wives to their husbands. Not only did the law give husbands control over their wives' property, labor, and children, it also gave them sweeping authority over every aspect of their wives' lives. Assuming that husbands represented their wives' economic and political interests, the law blocked wives' direct access to public space. It locked them firmly into domestic privacy by allowing husbands wide latitude in governing their own households—including the right to "correct" their wives, when necessary. Women like Elizabeth Rhodes, however, did not necessarily accept the law's definition of the relation between husbands and wives. Although stepping outside the law, poor women remained within the cultural boundaries of their own communities when they made domestic disputes public. Poor people of both races saw the domestic sphere's boundaries as more permeable than did the law. Where the law refused to meddle in household governance, poor people expected neighbors and kin to play active roles in domestic life. Such cultural assumptions made poor women's legal actions against their husbands' violence conceivable, if not always welcome. Widespread acceptance of this view also explains women's success at the lower levels of the judicial system, where community involvement shaped the reception and outcome of their cases. In this way, domestic violence cases became debates over the rights of husbands and wives, for if neighbors and kin agreed that domestic relations were public matters, they did not always agree about the relative distribution of power between husbands and wives. In this arena, wives, even battered wives, spoke with distinct voices, articulating their own ideas about their rights and pushing their kin, neighbors, and local officials to acknowledge their concerns.

Before emancipation, domestic violence cases remained at the local level, where they proliferated despite the law's refusal to acknowledge their legitimacy. Afterward, the North Carolina State Supreme Court began to take an interest in these cases. Beginning with Elizabeth Rhodes's case in 1868, the justices altered the court's position on domestic violence and brought it within the law's purview in ways that favored wives' claims against their husbands. Or so it seemed. But the court's response actually had more to do with changing race and class relationships in the years following emancipation than it did with women. Not only did judges ignore women's specific claims but the social implications were not what the women who brought the cases intended. Ultimately, these decisions expanded the state government's power to oversee the domestic lives of all African Americans and poor whites without enhancing the position of women at all. The results reached into the twentieth century, anchoring the principle of government intervention in family life and the continued exclusion of poor women's voices in formulating these measures.

In the scales of justice, generations of legal practice weighed heavily against Elizabeth Rhodes. Previously, the North Carolina State Supreme Court had heard such charges only in relation to civil suits, primarily divorce. It had never considered wife beating as a criminal offense for the same reasons that the county superior court decided for Benjamin Rhodes. In his order to the jury, the superior court judge ruled that Benjamin Rhodes's violence again his wife could not be criminal because the traditional "rule of thumb" allowed a husband to whip his wife as long as the switch was no larger in diameter than an average man's thumb. On appeal to the state supreme court, Justice Edwin Reade questioned this logic, giving Elizabeth Rhodes a partial but ultimately empty victory. Reversing the lower court and two centuries of legal practice, Reade declared that North Carolina no longer "recognize[d] the right of the husband to whip his wife." He also specifically revised the "rule of thumb," announcing that the court would now judge domestic conflicts by the injuries resulting from the assault, not the size of the instrument that had been used. But the limits placed on the customary powers of husbands remained largely theoretical for Elizabeth Rhodes and other women at this time. In practice, Reade thought it unwise to lift "the curtain" of domestic life and expose "to public curiosity and criticism the nursery and the bed chamber." "Family government," Justice Reade stated, "being in its nature as complete in itself as the State government is in itself, the Courts will not attempt to control, or interfere with it, in favor of either party." Although rebuked, Benjamin Rhodes still retained his right to govern his family as he saw fit.[3]

Justice Reade's legal "curtain" was not new. Before emancipation, higher courts in the South generally kept their distance from domestic disputes of all kinds because of the way southern law continued to link marriage, slavery, and other domestic relationships together. Courts elsewhere in the United States moved away from this view, toward a more companionate, contractual definition of marriage that limited husbands' absolute authority over their wives and allowed for the termination of the relationship when the contracting parties did not fulfill its terms. Not so in the South, where the connection between marriage and slavery was particularly important. White women, according to court rulings, belonged within households as wives, just as African Americans belonged within households as slaves. Wives and husbands, slaves and masters were bound together through reciprocal obligations that were defined as "natural" and divinely sanctioned. The possibility that any domestic relation could be altered or severed at will introduced contingency into this web of relations. More to the point, contingency defied the logic of "natural" subordination by making domestic relations purely the product of human will and thus legitimate subjects for critique and change. And that would be completely unacceptable, for to question any one part was to question the whole.[4]

This logic drew a thick, impenetrable legal drape around the domestic sphere, leaving governance of all domestic dependents to household heads and labeling conflicts there as "private" matters outside the state's purview. By extension, this legal boundary also shaped social and political relations within the household's borders. The domestic authority of white male heads of household translated directly into the public right to represent their own and their dependents' interests in the political arena. By contrast, law and social convention denied power to those who were supposed to be subsumed within the domestic sphere: wives, slaves, and children. Of course, these groups occupied distinctly different positions. Equating the subordination of slaves, which was absolute, with the subordination of free white women and children would constitute a serious misrepresentation of southern society. But all these people were similarly situated in the sense that they lived as dependents within the domestic sphere. Subject to the governance of a household head, they could not claim the requisite civil and political rights that would allow them to move freely in public space.[5]

Georgia and Tennessee passed statutes criminalizing wife beating in the 1850s. These laws reflected widespread concern in the country as a whole about abusive husbands and battered wives. But in the context of the slave South, occasionally lifting the "curtain" surrounding the domestic sphere affirmed its essential privacy. By punishing the most violent excesses of patriarchs, the courts preserved the integrity of the system as a whole. Other southern states, moreover, did not follow the lead of Georgia and Tennessee. Most passed no new legislation, and most state supreme courts refused to consider either wife or child beating as criminal matters until after the Civil War.[6] Domestic violence did figure in antebellum divorce cases, but it did not rank high on the list of marital abuses. Abandonment and extreme cruelty were the only grounds for a divorce from bed and board during the antebellum period. The marital tie could be completely dissolved only in a few circumstances: adultery combined with abandonment on the part of either party, adultery on the part of the wife, and impotence. Even then, women had difficulty proving extreme cruelty because the court granted husbands such wide latitude in family governance and insisted that the integrity of the institution of marriage outweighed the happiness of the individual parties.[7]

The legal construction of marriage and domestic space, however, did not describe the actual domestic relations of many North Carolina residents either before or after the Civil War.[8] For slaves, marriage was a relationship governed by custom and the community, not the law. The community recognized a couple as husband and wife when they took on certain responsibilities for each other: the woman washed, cleaned, cooked, and tended the house; the man contributed to her and her children's maintenance. Both men and women could sever the marital bonds if their partners abandoned their responsibilities or otherwise mistreated them. After emancipation, African Americans blended these cultural practices with legal marriage. Irvin Thompson, for instance, married his first wife in a legal ceremony soon after the war and lived with her about a year. "Then," he told a pension examiner, "she associated with other men and left me." "No I did not get any divorce," he continued, "She just went off a whoring and I lost track of her." Soon afterward, he married another woman in a legal ceremony that his neighbors also accepted as a valid marriage. Mary J. Moore ended her marriage in a similar way. Her husband beat her and ran around with other women on the sly, but when he began to live openly with another woman, she considered the marriage over and her neighbors concurred. She went on to live with several other men in a series of monogamous relationships recognized as valid marriages in her neighborhood.[9]

Most antebellum yeoman and propertyless whites accepted the concept of legal marriage enough to formalize their unions and separations. Even so, community recognition still played a significant role in determining marital status. North Carolina did not recognize common-law marriage in the antebellum period. But the absence of other forms of state supervision, such as marriage-registration laws, forced the courts to accept the word of witnesses as proof of marriages. After the war, the federal Pension Bureau had to do the same when examining the claims of white Union soldiers' widows. Over and over, neighbors testified that the couple in question "were recognized by everybody to be man and wife." As the phrase suggests, it was not so much the legal ceremony as people's acceptance of it that validated the union. In determining validity, common whites looked to the substance of the relationship just as African Americans did. They specifically looked for evidence that a couple lived as husband and wife—that he took economic responsibility for her and their children's welfare and that she worked keeping house for him.[10]

Failure to fulfill these duties could also invalidate a marriage. Such was the argument of Eliza Bell, who charged that her husband, John, left her in 1862 to "take up and cohabit with one Emily Tillotson." John Bell eventually moved on to other women and out of the state altogether. But promiscuity was not the only way he had failed as a husband. He also made no "provision for the maintenance and support of herself or for her child." Unlike her John, Eliza moved more clearly within the culture of legal marriage and used this evidence to establish adultery and abandonment in the formulaic language of her divorce petition. But she also understood the signs of her husband's informal separation—openly "taking up" with another woman and rejecting any responsibility for her economic support.[11]

Neighbors and kin were well positioned to judge the substance of marital relationships because the rhythms of domestic life were so public. Black and

white southerners of poor and even modest means did not think of their dwellings as private havens from the public sphere but as functional components in
an integrated world of work. Productive labor took place inside and out.[12] Just
as work patterns defied the separation between private and public space, so did
the terrain of domestic lives. With doors and windows open, houses mingled
physically with the world outside. Even inside, houses were not neatly divided
into private and public living areas. Most contained only one or two rooms,
where family members slept, ate, visited, and entertained. During North Carolina's sweltering summer nights, poor people abandoned their stuffy interiors
altogether and turned their neighborhoods into parlors.[13]

Family borders were also flexible, expanding and contracting to include kin
and unrelated friends who stayed and worked with the family for extended
periods of time. At special events, such as births, deaths, and illnesses, the
boundary between the family and community disappeared almost entirely as
neighbors gathered to celebrate or to grieve, to offer advice and assistance, or
just to observe. Privacy of any kind was virtually impossible, as the unmarried
Henrietta World discovered. The neighbors all inquired when Henrietta's belly
grew big, only to be told by her mother that Henrietta had a tumor. Unconvin-
ced, their suspicions were confirmed when they found a dead infant nearby in
the woods. This time, the neighbor women came to inspect Henrietta physically.
Among them was one woman who walked into the World house, eyed Henrietta,
then unceremoniously reached out and "felt of Dft's breast." Under the circumstances, this woman felt justified in taking the liberty. But then, walking into a
relative's or neighbor's house unannounced was not that unusual.[14]

In this context, domestic conflicts were rarely secret. Quarrels between husbands and wives, parents and children, sisters, brothers, cousins, and unrelated
housemates all spilled out into streets, yards, and fields. The noise of Gray and
Louisa Thigpen's argument attracted two neighbors, one who was in her house
and another who was working in a nearby field. Both dropped what they were
doing to go to the Thigpens but did not reach them in time to avert a fight that
resulted in Louisa's filing charges against Gray. Even when conflicts were contained within the four walls of individual houses, close living quarters drew in
all the dwelling's occupants. An upstairs neighbor, for instance, knew that David
Burwell had been sick because she could hear his groans through the floor. She
divulged this information while testifying to a fight between David and his wife
Dicey, which she had monitored with great interest from her window. The very
nature of the testimony in domestic violence cases suggests the absence of privacy in domestic life. Those who testified generally knew a great deal, offering
up both detailed information and strong opinions about the domestic lives of the
couples in question.[15]

For Louisa Thigpen and Dicey Burwell, public knowledge translated into
public involvement. For other women, it did not, because both African Americans and poor whites respected men's authority over their households. Unlike
the law, however, they did not consider such authority absolute or an end in
itself. To them, men's power over their households served a larger social good:

well-governed households were central to a well-governed community. Because men ruled at the behest of other community members and in the interests of them all, neighbors and kin felt justified in intervening when they thought husbands were abusing their power. Publicity thus provided women a measure of protection, giving them the opportunity to mobilize others on their behalf and subject their husbands to the scrutiny of neighbors and kin, who could and did reprimand individual male household heads. Of course, women were not always successful in bringing community members to their side. Depending on the circumstances surrounding the conflict and the individual reputations of those involved, neighbors and kin could just as easily throw their weight behind the husband.[16]

When other people did become involved in a domestic dispute, it was generally because the wife had actively enlisted their aid. Kin usually proved the most sympathetic, as Westley Rhodes discovered. Rhodes, who had long "indulged himself in the habits of intemperance and abuse to his wife," beat her "in a most cruel manner" one night in 1823. Mrs. Rhodes "fled to her father's house" for protection. After hearing the story, her mother immediately marched back to Westley, "reprimanded him for his conduct," and "struck him with a tobacco stem which she had picked up on the road." By this time, Mrs. Rhodes's grandfather had also appeared at the house. Infuriated and outnumbered, Westley lunged at the old man with a knife. In so doing, he only widened the scope of community involvement in his domestic affairs and undermined whatever sympathy he might have claimed.[17]

Familial support of female relations took many forms. In addition to housing women and their children who had fled their husbands, family members acted as mediators and assisted in women's legal suits when all else failed. They had strong incentives to do so. If mediation failed, they could gain permanent, perhaps unwelcome additions to their households. After Cynthia Oliver left her husband, for instance, she and her child lived with her parents for several years until her divorce. Cynthia probably remained with her parents afterward, considering that she had custody of a small child, no means of support, and no property except her bedding, linen, and clothes.[18]

Perhaps the most telling example of the importance of women's kin ties are their husbands' objections to them. Richard Oliver threatened to cut his wife, Cynthia, "to pieces" with a switch if "she talked with her people." Later, he drove her out of the house, declaring that "she and her damned mother had aggravated him near to death." David Taylor insisted that his wife, Sarah, "would have been as tolerable and happy" as other women "had it not been for the meddlesome interference of her mother and brothers and father." At one point, he became so angry that he got out his gun and threatened to shoot Sarah's brother. Martha White's husband flew into a rage simply because he suspected her of using all the flour to bake for her relatives.[19]

Women also drew in reluctant neighbors. Martha White, who described her husband as "quarrelsome," "very frequently in the habit of applying abusive epithets to her," and of "striking and attempting to strike her," was particularly ingenious in this regard. Martha was not shy about defending herself against her husband's violence, but when she found herself on the losing side of one particularly brutal battle, she "immediately . . . started to Mr. Grimsley's, a neighbor, for protection." One year later, after she suffered a severe blow to her head, White "immediately left" the house again and sought shelter with another neighbor. Neither neighbor was particularly inclined toward Martha White. As Matthew Grimsley later testified, her husband "provided well for his family." Besides, Grimsley had never actually seen White's husband abuse her. But he could not deny the abuse either, because White had shown him her injuries. In this way, she successfully drew him to her side whether he wanted to be there or not.[20]

Matthew Grimsley sheltered Martha White a few days and testified at her divorce. The neighbors and kin of other women became more directly involved. Mrs. Hedding and her children stayed with three different neighbors for extended periods during her tumultuous marriage. Others provided food and clothes, for Mr. Hedding not only beat his wife and children but refused to support them as well. According to A. J. Yancey, "Mrs. Hedding came to my house one day and said Mr. Hedding had taken every thing from her" and left her "without anything to eat or wear." Mrs. Hedding expected that Yancey and the other neighbors would provide what her husband did not. They did, although their patience ultimately wore thin. In 1883, six neighbors filed charges against Mr. Hedding for abandonment. Admitting no wrongdoing and arguing that he had never technically left his family, Mr. Hedding fought back and won. No doubt the neighbors soon found Mrs. Hedding and her children at their doorsteps once again.[21]

But neighbors and kin intervened in domestic violence only in certain circumstances. They were more likely to take the wife's side when they thought her husband had failed in his duties, while she had remained faithful to hers. It is no coincidence that wives who charged their husbands with violence also accused them of other faults, such as drinking, gambling, and philandering. Husbands countered by pointing out their wives' flaws, arguing that unfaithfulness, laziness, and lack of attention to household chores had either provoked them to violence or forced them to discipline their wives physically. Of course, their claims were constructed to meet legal standards that gave men property rights to their wives' labor and exclusive access to their bodies and construed any dereliction of duty on the wife's part a sufficient provocation for the husband's violence.[22] Still, husbands' and wives' testimony suggests what husbands and wives considered inappropriate behavior in their spouses.

On the day Cynthia Oliver filed charges against her husband, for instance, he had come "home intoxicated in the morning after breakfast was over, got some raw bacon, said it had skippers and his old wife . . . would not clean it, sat down [and ate] a little, threw the coffee cup and coffee pot to the corner of the house, went out [and] cut two switches." Then he whipped her. While leaving the principle of male authority in place, Cynthia Oliver used this situation to argue that her husband had abused his power. Not only had Richard Oliver stayed out all night, returned home drunk, and then made unreasonable demands on this one day but he had appeared frequently in court for his drinking and carousing. It was this string of misdeeds that negated the legitimacy of his actions. Richard Oliver did boast that "he would have worn [Cynthia] out" with his beating if witnesses had not stopped him. Still, in defending himself, he did not necessarily claim a husband's universal right to "discipline" his wife as construed by law. He also carefully emphasized Cynthia's bad cooking and sloppy housekeeping by way of explaining his violence against her. In short, Cynthia's and Richard's assertions fit squarely within their community's cultural construction of marital relations. Both justified themselves by showing how the other neglected the duties of husband and wife, as understood by their friends and neighbors.[23]

People also stepped in at moments of crisis to protect women's lives. A small crowd gathered to watch a fight between Ridley and Mary Ann Mabry. But it was only after Ridley drew a knife and slashed at Mary Ann that one of the bystanders stepped in and pulled her out of harm's way. Those who witnessed the fight between Cynthia and Richard Oliver reacted similarly. They watched Richard strike Cynthia four times before they stopped him, explaining that they considered this sufficient because Richard "struck as hard as he could." Although they did intervene, onlookers in both cases considered the two men's authority to use violence against their wives to be legitimate, at least to some extent.[24]

Sometimes neighbors hesitated too long. Frances Henderson's neighbors, for instance, acted only after her death. As Frances lay moaning in her bed, her husband, Robert, sat visiting with friends just a few yards away. When they asked what was wrong with her, he told them to ignore her, that she was sick. The next morning, Frances was dead. The entire neighborhood turned out to pay their last respects, but this was not the only reason they gathered at the Henderson household. They were also suspicious about the cause of her death. Virtually everyone who testified at the inquest knew that Robert habitually beat Frances. Based on this knowledge and what they gathered as they prepared her badly bruised body for burial, they called in the local authorities. None of these witnesses approved of his behavior, but neither did they stop him before his abuse resulted in death.[25]

Neighbors and kin hesitated to intervene in domestic violence out of an unwillingness to undercut a husband's authority without cause. But they held back for other reasons as well. Errant husbands could threaten outsiders who challenged their domestic prerogatives with the same violence they used against household members. Robert Henderson, for instance, opposed his neighbors' call for an inquest. His position is not particularly surprising, considering the growing suspicions about his guilt. Far more striking is the way he expressed himself, asserting a proprietary right to her body with a belligerence that probably explains both Frances Henderson's bruises and the delay in her neighbors' response: "she was mine before she died and she is mine now." Samuel Lawrence understood his relationship with his wife in similar terms. Accused of beating her in 1882, he responded "that she was his wife and he would prank with her as much as he pleased." Like Robert Henderson, Samuel Lawrence drew a veil around his relationship with his wife, claiming the privilege to act "as he pleased" without interference from either the community or the court. When the justice of the peace announced his intention to protect Mrs. Lawrence "so far as the law was concerned," Samuel Lawrence flew into a rage. After showering the justice with verbal threats, he fought off the deputy charged with arresting him. Declaring that "there were not enough damned negros or poor white men on the ground to arrest him," he also denied the community's authority to act as mediator and judge.[26]

Intervening in domestic disputes could also stretch the social bonds to the point where it created more conflict than it resolved. Neighbors noted Eli Jacobs's abusive behavior toward his wife, Elizabeth, long before she died in November 1879. Afterward, the community was awash in gossip as neighbors held forth on the incident and debated the cause of her death. A group of women who examined the body before the burial concluded that she died of natural causes. But others maintained that Eli was responsible. As Joseph Jacobs later declared, Eli "was verry [sic] unkind to her, and he had threatened to kill her." By January Eli's detractors persuaded the coroner to exhume her body and call an inquest to investigate her death. The jury, however, found the evidence against Eli inconclusive, thus freeing him from further legal charges, but not from the doubts of suspicious neighbors.[27]

Superior court juries also divided in their response to domestic violence cases. The jury that tried Benjamin Rhodes found him guilty of striking his wife "three licks with a small size switch not as large as a man's thumb without any provocation," which by law did not constitute a crime at that time. Nonetheless, it claimed to be "undecided how to find as matter of law upon the guilt or innocence of the defendant" and gave the decision over to the judge, who ruled against Elizabeth Rhodes. Unlike the judge, however, the jury members were not so sure. As their decision indicates, they either failed to agree that Benjamin Rhodes's actions were criminal or disagreed with the law's interpretation of them. The juries that judged Ridley Mabry and Joseph Huntley reached similar verdicts. Because Mary Ann Mabry had sustained no physical injuries, she could not prove excessive physical force under either the traditional rule of thumb or Justice Reade's revision of it, which emphasized the seriousness of the injuries suffered. Rachel Huntley had a better case. Her husband, Joseph, had whipped her with "such violence as to break the skin and raise whelks [welts] upon her person and to draw the blood so that . . . it came through the clothing." But, as Rachel admitted, her injuries were not so severe as to incapacitate her, a fact that could excuse her husband's actions as appropriate chastisement. Yet both juries claimed uncertainty as to the legal meaning of these incidents. "If upon these facts," the superior court jury in Joseph Huntley's case declared, "the defendant is in law guilty we find him guilty and if upon these facts the defendant is in law not guilty we find him not guilty." Ridley Mabry's jury stated its conclusion with virtually the same words. These jury members, like those who tried Benjamin Rhodes, could not dismiss the idea that Ridley Mabry's and Joseph Hunt-ley's transgressions might be sufficiently serious to qualify as criminal acts.[28]

Only men who were not just failed husbands but also perceived troublemakers endured such sustained community action. Neighbors and local officials had run out of patience with Benjamin Rhodes, Richard Oliver, and Joseph Huntley long before their wives even thought of filing charges against them. All three were brawlers, drinkers, and womanizers who appeared regularly in the court records and left a trail of aggrieved victims and angry witnesses in their wake: Benjamin Rhodes had been charged with beating a neighbor woman and for fighting publicly with two other men; Richard Oliver said that one man had assaulted him with a knife and was accused of threatening to kill another; and Joseph Huntley had been arrested four times for selling liquor without a license, twice for fornication and adultery, and once for a public fight. Not surprisingly, their wives had no difficulty convincing others that these men needed disciplining.[29]

If neighbors, kin, and local officials sometimes needed prodding, women themselves were far less ambivalent about the extent of their husbands' prerog-atives. They complained to their neighbors. They filed charges in court. Some even fought back physically. Martha White, took offense when her husband found it necessary to "advise" her "on her duties." As he explained, "[S]he would get into a passion, abuse him, sometimes assault him." One witness saw them rolling around on the floor, pulling out each other's hair. Martha, this witness maintained, seemed to have the upper hand. Although trying to strike the proper pose of wifely submission and domestic competence, Martha admitted defending herself when she felt physically threatened but denied ever instigating an attack. Dicey Burwell reacted similarly when her husband, David, knocked both her and their sixteen-year-old daughter to the ground several times with a maul. Wresting the weapon from David's control, Dicey hit him so hard that he was unconscious for almost an hour.[30]

Given such behavior, it is tempting to view women who challenged domestic violence as valiant protofeminists, rejecting the paternal doctrine of coverture and demanding full recognition of their individual rights. Yet these women were actually making more subtle claims. They questioned the actions of particular husbands and the relative distribution of power between husbands and wives. But even if they did not completely reject the authority of their husbands or demand recognition of their status as autonomous individuals, they did question the legal construction of their husbands' authority. As such, their claims repre-sented a significant departure from the law and its positioning of married women, for these women challenged the notion that men could exercise broad disciplinary rights over them without being subject to public scrutiny. They also questioned the notion that they, as wives, were without direct public recourse.

In some ways, women were simply continuing an already public discussion when they filed charges against their husbands. The lower levels of the court system could function as an extension of community authority, just like church disciplinary hearings. Inquests and magistrates' hearings took place in the front yards and on the porches of residences and country stores. They were attended by neighbors and overseen by officials who were known in the community. The courts were particularly accessible to poor people when Republicans held power during Reconstruction and were elected to key positions within the legal system as magistrates, sheriffs, and judges. Robert Henderson's formal inquest, for instance, bore a remarkable resemblance to the earlier, informal hearing conducted by the community. Neighbors gathered once again to give their recollections of the day Frances died and their impressions of her relationship with Robert. Although the coroner, an outsider, inspected the body and presided over the hearing, the jury, composed of people in the community, rendered the decision. To some extent, the coroner derived his authority from the community, which had already concluded that Robert Henderson had a hand in his wife's death. Eli Jacobs's case proceeded in a similar fashion, with the community acting as a chorus, interpreting and judging the incident from personal knowledge of those involved.[31]

Familiar faces and surroundings, however, could be misleading. The courts were not an extension of the neighborhood but a distinct arena with its own guidelines and discourse. Given the legal presumption of domestic privacy and male governance within the home, it was not a particularly friendly arena for any woman, regardless of whether Republicans or Democrats were in charge. It was that much less hospitable for women who were black, poor, or both. Mrs. Lawrence's experience is particularly telling. After she made her complaint, public attention focused on the conflict between the Democratic magistrate and her husband. In fact, the magistrate's testimony suggests that he was not really concerned with Mrs. Lawrence's well-being at all. Earlier that day, Samuel Lawrence had disrupted the courtroom during a trial and had repeatedly ignored the magistrate's orders to settle down. By the time Mrs. Lawrence walked into his office, the magistrate was already more than willing to make life difficult for her husband and probably agreed to arrest Lawrence for this reason. Then, when Lawrence threatened the magistrate and lashed out at the deputy, even better options presented themselves. Charging Lawrence with resisting arrest, the magistrate dropped all reference to Mrs. Lawrence and her complaint.[32]

Many complaints never made it into the records at all because magistrates deemed them unworthy of legal action. Little information remains for those that they did act on. Usually, only the formal complaint survives, giving just the names of the parties involved. Such transcripts provide no information on the events leading up to the charges, let alone any insight into the woman's perspective on them. Ironically, then, the legal system tended to erase women at the very moment they demanded public recognition.

When court officials did take notice, they imposed legal categories on domestic violence cases that further obscured women's voices. For the court even to consider intervention, women had to cast themselves as blameless victims who helplessly bore their husbands' blows. This construction described few of the domestic violence cases involving poor women of either race. Like so many similar cases, the fight between Dicey Burwell and her husband, David, was not an isolated incident but one of many in a very turbulent relationship. Dicey Burwell testified that her husband had "been kind to me since he professed religion but was cruel before." If David was "cruel," Dicey did not suffer in silence. In the fight that landed the couple in court, it was Dicey, not her husband David, who was officially charged as the assailant. Her position as such was purely a matter of chance. Had it been one of David's blows that had knocked Dicey unconscious, instead of the other way around, she would have become the victim. Other poor women fought back as well—with their fists, handy kitchen utensils, community pressure, and warrants. In all these ways, poor women refused to become victims. But that is how they had to represent themselves if they hoped to gain any hearing at all.[33]

It was not an easy role for poor white women or any African American woman to assume. The very act of filing public charges undercut their credibility in the eyes of elite white court officials. Wealthy white women measured and maintained their respectability through their distance from the immorality and violence associated with public space. Elite white women rarely appeared in court even as witnesses, let alone as complainants.[34] These gender conventions buttressed older assumptions that the "lower classes" were less sensitive and more prone to violent outbursts than those from the "higher ranks" of society. Such distinctions were deeply embedded in the law. As Justice Reade explained in the *Rhodes* decision: "Suppose a case coming up to us from a hovel, where neither delicacy of sentiment nor refinement of manners is appreciated or known. The parties themselves would be amazed, if they were to be held responsible for rudeness or trifling violence. What do they care for insults and indignities?" Reade then contrasted the sensibilities of the poor with those of "the higher ranks, where education and culture have so refined nature, that a look cuts like a knife, and a word strikes like a hammer; where the most delicate attention gives pleasure, and the slightest neglect pain; where an indignity is disgrace and exposure is ruin." By this logic, a poor woman, white or black, had great difficulty proving that any violence against her was particularly unusual or egregious.[35]

But women, even poor women, could still mobilize the law on their behalf. In some respects, the North Carolina State Supreme Court's postemancipation decisions on domestic violence made it easier for women to bring suit against their husbands. Beginning with *Rhodes*, the court affirmed a highly privatized conception of domestic space. But in this same decision, the court also reserved to itself the right to intervene in domestic government "where permanent or malicious injury is inflicted or threatened, or the condition of the party is intolerable." Over time, justices found more reasons to circumvent the authority of household heads and intervene in domestic government. After pronouncing the traditional "rule of thumb" to be inconsistent "with our present civilization" in 1874, the court then lifted the domestic curtain to side with Cynthia Oliver against her husband. In 1879, it gave itself the power to determine the severity of punishment meted out to offending husbands, for "the protection of the wife, and, through it, for the protection and good order of society." Five years later, the court lowered the standards of evidence required of the prosecution to upgrade domestic violence to serious assaults in those cases that could be heard by superior courts instead of the local magistrates. These openings legitimized women's use of the courts in disputes with their husbands and enabled them to enlist the state in their efforts to place limits on men's power within their own households and communities. In this way, the courts became reluctant partners in the efforts of wives to act in defense of their rights.[36]

But the North Carolina State Supreme Court had its own reasons for altering the rules. After emancipation released black men from their role as dependent slaves, postwar legal and political changes set them up as household heads in their own right. White yeomen and propertyless white men who had been politically marginalized in North Carolina benefited as well, although to a lesser degree. Historians of Reconstruction have documented how profoundly disturbing elite white southerners found these changes and how they tried to overturn them in desperate battles over economic independence, civil rights, and universal manhood suffrage. But the legal principle of domestic privacy also buttressed the independence of all poor and politically marginalized people, with its protective "curtain" shielding large portions of their lives from state interference. After the war, African Americans and some whites wielded this legal weapon with great success, using it to protect their families from the intrusion of meddling outsiders. They also mobilized key components of the ideology of domestic privacy to justify demands for a more equitable distribution of economic resources and political power. As they argued, women and children could not perform their role as dependents unless their menfolk could protect and provide for them; men could not meet these duties without the necessary economic and political power; and families—the cornerstone of society—would disintegrate unless men and women could fulfill their proper roles.[37]

The domestic autonomy of African Americans and poor whites came under attack at the same time that their public rights did. As Peter Bardaglio has argued, southern courts and other state institutions increased their power to oversee and regulate the domestic sphere throughout the late nineteenth century. Even as many whites increasingly relied on vigilante violence to "regulate" the behavior of African Americans, southern lawmakers began transferring other key elements of patriarchal power from the hands of individual men to the state. This process, which continued into the twentieth century, gave agents of the state the latitude to pass judgment on a wide range of family issues affecting poor white as well as black families. To this end, judges delved into the characters of litigants to ferret out the "worthy" husbands, wives, and children from among the "unworthy" ones.

The 1877 divorce case *Taylor v. Taylor* illuminates the court's role. Citing frequent evidence of abuse, Sarah Taylor maintained that the abuse from her husband, David, had made her life intolerable and, therefore, constituted grounds for divorce. In response, Justice Bynum reiterated the court's long-standing position that no universal measure of "intolerable" conditions could ever apply in all cases: "The station in life, the temperament, state of health, habits and feelings of different persons are so unlike, that treatment which would send the broken heart of one to the grave, would make no sensible impression upon another." But instead of throwing out the case, as an earlier judge might have, Bynum insisted on the court's right to judge the matter.[38]

As long as poor whites and African Americans retained a democratic stake in public power, they could use their access to the system and their clout with Republican officials to include themselves among those considered "suitable" and "worthy." But these decisions acquired far more ominous meanings as the tide of Republican influence ebbed and conservatives flooded back into the judicial system in the mid-1870s. The legal curtain surrounding the domestic sphere began lifting at the same time poor whites and African Americans lost power within governmental institutions, exposing them to unprecedented state regulation at the moment of their greatest vulnerability. Justice Bynum's 1877 decision in *Taylor v. Taylor* is suggestive. Reiterating the same racial and class distinctions as Justice Reade did in *Rhodes*, he noted that "[a]mong the lower clases [*sic*], blows sometimes pass between married couples who in the main are very happy and have no desire to part; amidst very coarse habits such incidents occur almost as freely as rude or reproachful words." In this particular case, however, the court could not overlook such behavior because both the husband and wife belonged to "respectable walks of life." Although the logic of this decision would seem to remove the households of poor whites and African Americans from public scrutiny, it did not. While obstructing "unrespectable" women's claims to protection from their husbands, it labeled "lower classes" as coarse, rude, violent, and uncivilized people in need of state supervision.[39]

In 1913, progressive reformer Judge Walter Clark addressed the Federation of Women's Clubs in New Bern on the legal status of women. After discussing the laws relating to married women's property rights, domestic violence, and suffrage, Clark attributed the recent changes to "progress." "Among savage tribes," he argued, "the club of the husband was logical. And under the common law so was the lash, because women being kept in ignorance and deprived of property rights could be thus governed. But when they were educated and given the right to own property these things became illogical and impossible." If "progress" made such change inevitable, it was a circle of enlightened men and women who carried out its designs. This assumption, widespread among Progressive reformers in the South, positioned the poor and dispossessed as passive recipients of reforms they never could have conceived of themselves. In his talk in New Bern, for instance, Clark made no mention of the women who actually brought domestic violence cases. If anything, he left the impression that the lash and club were still common where ignorance and poverty reigned. In other forums, he advocated governmental programs to bring civilization to these impoverished, violent people.[40]

Judge Clark's analysis still carries a great deal of power today. Historians look to the Progressive Era, its women's clubs' members, and outspoken male advocates to find evidence of reform. Restoring the voices of poor women in the nineteenth century recasts our understanding of this later period. Judges did transform the laws governing domestic life, but they did not do so in a cultural vacuum. It was poor women who challenged their husbands' power and insisted on making their domestic disputes public. In this way, they claimed public space for themselves and politicized their own domestic concerns long before middle-class women reformers ever thought to do so. Of course, the results were not what the women who brought the cases had intended. The court intervened in private life to promote "good order" and to uphold the rules governing "our present civilization," expanding its own power to oversee the lives of all poor people, while also maintaining the line around domestic space that proved so problematic for women.[41] Ultimately, poor women could appeal only to the patriarchal protection of male judges. These constraints effectively silenced them because they found it so difficult to express the complexities of their lives in those terms. The legacy of these legal decisions continues to shape scholarship today. Like reformers of the Progressive Era, historians assume poor women's passivity and even presume to speak for them without ever stopping to consider the political reasons for their silence.

NOTES

Michael Bellesiles, Giovanna Benadusi, Kirsten Fischer, John McAllister, Don Nieman, and Chris Waldrep all read drafts of this essay and their comments have improved it enormously. Helpful, too, were the thoughts of Ed Baptist, who read an early version. I also owe a great deal to the insightful questions and comments of Stephanie McCurry, Steven Hahn, Rachel Klein, and a group of wonderful graduate students at the University of California at San Diego, where I presented this work. A postdoctoral fellowship from the Smithsonian Institution at the National Museum of American History provided research funds and the time to write the first draft. The Newberry Library graciously opened its doors and provided me intellectual stimulation and work space during the time I worked on revisions.

1. *State v. Rhodes*, #9368, Supreme Court Original Cases, 1800–1900, North Carolina Division of Archives and History (cited hereafter as NCDAH); *State v. Rhodes*, 61 N.C. 453 (1868).

2. For antebellum cases, see Victoria Bynum, *Unruly Women: The Politics of Social and Sexual Control in the Old South* (Chapel Hill: University of North Carolina Press, 1992), 81, 74. For postwar cases, see *State v. Jones*, 1866; *State v. Taylor*, 1867; *State v. Bryant*, 1868; *State v. Phillips*, 1868; *State v. Thigpen*, 1869; *State v. Williams*, 1869; *State v. Robbins*, 1872; *State v. Thorn*, 1874; *State v. Harrell*, 1875; *State v. Dawson*, 1877; *State v. Daniel*, 1877; *State v. Lloyd*, 1878; *State v. Sugg*, 1879; *State v. Lawrence*, 1886; all in Criminal Action Papers, Edgecombe County, NCDAH. *State v. Lyon*, 1866; *State v. Ray*, 1867[?]; *State v. Harris*, 1868[?]; *State v. Mayo*, 1869[?]; *State v. Riley*, 1875; *State v. Doherty*, 1885; all in Criminal Action Papers, Orange County, NCDAH. *State v. Estes*, 1866; *State v. Newton*, 1867; *State v. Clay*; *State v. Wortham*, 1870; *State v. Hunt*, 1871; *State v. Webb*, 1875; *State v. Snit*, 1875; *State v. Frazier*, 1875; *State v. Thorp*, 1878; *State v. Gipsom*, 1880; *State v. Lewis*, 1881; *State v. Hall*, 1882; *State v. Hedding*, 1885; all in Criminal Action Papers, Granville County, NCDAH. For family disputes in the Freedmen's Bureau, see Nancy Bercaw, "The Politics of Household: Domestic Battlegrounds in the Transition from Slavery to Freedom in the Yazoo-

Mississippi Delta, 1850–1860" (Ph.D. diss., University of Pennsylvania), ch. 5; Ira Berlin, Stephen F. Miller, Leslie S. Rowland, eds. "Afro-American Families in the Transition from Slavery to Freedom," *Radical History Review* 42 (1988): 89–121; Eric Foner, *Reconstruction: America's Unfinished Revolution* (New York: Harper and Row, 1988), 88; Noralee Frankel, *Freedom's Women: Black Women and Families in Civil War Era Mississippi* (Bloomington: Indiana University Press, 1999); Leslie Ann Schwalm, "The Meaning of Freedom: African-American Women and Their Transition from Slavery to Freedom in Lowcountry South Carolina" (Ph.D. diss., University of Wisconsin, 1991), 344–48. For the presumption that domestic violence was always "minor," regardless of the injuries sustained, see *State v. Huntley*, 91 N.C. 617 (1884).

3. *State v. Rhodes*, 61 N.C. 453 (1868).

4. For changes in the legal treatment of marriage in the North, see Michael Grossberg, *Governing the Hearth: Law and the Family in Nineteenth-Century America* (Chapel Hill: University of North Carolina Press, 1985). For the South, see Victoria Bynum, "Reshaping the Bonds of Womanhood: Divorce in Reconstruction North Carolina," in *Divided Houses: Gender and the Civil War*, ed. Catherine Clinton and Nina Silbert (New York: Oxford University Press, 1992); also see Bertram Wyatt-Brown, *Southern Honor: Ethics and Behavior in the Old South* (New York: Oxford University Press, 1982), 244–47, 283–91, 300–306. For the connection between the subordination of women in marriage and that of African Americans in slavery, also see Bynum, *Unruly Women*; Peter Bardaglio, *Reconstructing the Household: Families, Sex, and the Law in the Nineteenth-Century South* (Chapel Hill: University of North Carolina Press, 1995); Stephanie McCurry, *Masters of Small Worlds: Yeoman Households, Gender Relations, and the Political Culture of the Antebellum South Carolina Low Country* (New York: Oxford University Press, 1995), and "The Two Faces of Republicanism: Gender and Proslavery Politics in Antebellum South Carolina," *Journal of American History* 78 (March 1992): 1245–64; Elizabeth Fox-Genovese, *Within the Plantation Household: Women in the Old South* (Chapel Hill: University of North Carolina Press, 1988), 334–71; Eugene Genovese, *Roll, Jordan, Roll: The World the Slaves Made* (New York: Vintage Books, 1976), 3–112.

5. McCurry, *Masters of Small Worlds* and "The Two Faces of Republicanism."

6. The Puritans had criminalized wife beating in the colonial period as part of their mission to revise the laws and social governance, and to create a harmonious society. But these and other legal measures that limited husbands' authority over wives fell into disuse as religious enthusiasm weakened, the colonies grew, and the courts began to follow English common law more closely. See Cornelia Hughes Dayton, *Women before the Bar: Gender, Law, and Society in Connecticut, 1639–1789* (Chapel Hill: University of North Carolina Press, 1995). Georgia and Tennessee were actually the first states in the nation to criminalize wife beating after the Revolution. Although northern courts and legislatures were slow to deal with this particular issue, they did begin intervening in other domestic matters long before southern courts. For the North, see Grossberg, *Governing the Hearth*. For the treatment of domestic violence generally in the nineteenth century, see Bardaglio, *Reconstructing the Household*, 33–34, 103–5, 157–65; Bynum, *Unruly Women*, 70–72; Linda Gordon, *Heroes of Their Own Lives: The Politics and History of Family Violence* (New York: Viking, 1988); McCurry, *Masters of Small Worlds*, 85–91; Jerome Nadelhaft, "Wife Torture: A Known Phenomenon in Nineteenth-Century America," *Journal of American Culture* 10 (fall 1987): 39–59; Elizabeth Pleck, *Domestic Tyranny: The Making of Social Policy against Family Violence from Colonial Times to the Present* (New York: Oxford University Press, 1987), and "Wife Beating in Nineteenth-Century America," *Victimology* 4, no. 1 (1979): 60–74; Christine Stansell, *City of Women: Sex and Class in New York, 1789–*

1860 (Urbana: University of Illinois Press, 1987), 78–83; Wyatt-Brown, *Southern Honor*, 281–83.

7. For the legal changes in divorce in nineteenth-century North Carolina, see Bynum, "Reshaping the Bonds of Womanhood," and *Unruly Women*, 68–77. According to Bynum, decisions in county superior courts often ran counter to the state's strict statutes and the edicts issued by the state supreme court. With greater personal knowledge of the couples, judges and juries at the local level were also far more sympathetic to their difficulties and thus more willing to bend the abstractions of the law to fit the complex reality of individual cases. The state supreme court's position on divorce relaxed somewhat after 1848 when Richmond M. Pearson joined the bench. Pearson felt little sympathy for the paternalistic ethic promoted by Justice Ruffin. Where Ruffin emphasized the organic nature of marriage and the mutual obligations of husbands and wives, Pearson took a more contractual view, focusing on wives' obligations and husbands' privileges. Consequently, he was more willing to sever the marriage tie, particularly in the interests of aggrieved husbands. After the Civil War, the courts and the legislature liberalized divorce even more, although they did so gradually and in the interests of husbands. Also see Bardaglio, *Reconstructing the Household*, 32–34, 134; Jane Turner Censer, " 'Smiling through Her Tears': Ante-Bellum Southern Women and Divorce," *American Journal of Legal History* 25 (January 1982): 114–34; Catherine Clinton, *The Plantation Mistress: Woman's World in the Old South* (New York: Pantheon Books, 1982), 79–85; Wyatt-Brown, *Southern Honor*, 242–47, 283–91, 300–307.

8. For an expanded discussion of these issues, see Laura F. Edwards, " 'The Marriage Covenant Is at the Foundation of All Our Rights': The Politics of Slave Marriages in North Carolina after Emancipation," *Law and History Review*, 14 (spring 1996): 82–124, and *Gendered Strife and Confusion: The Political Culture of Reconstruction* (Urbana: University of Illinois Press, 1997), ch. 1.

9. Quotes from Jacob Moore, 14th Reg., Co. A, U.S. Colored Troops, Heavy Artillery; Irvin Thompson alias Cherry Thompson, 37th Reg., Co. K, U.S. Colored Troops, Infantry; both in Pension Records, RG 15, National Archives (cited hereafter as NA). My analysis is based on hundreds of Civil War pension files, which provide an excellent source for the construction of marriage because soldiers' widows had to establish the legitimacy of their relationships to claim a pension. In North Carolina, most of the testimony comes from the eastern counties, which were occupied early by Union troops and where many black and white Union veterans continued to live after the war. But pension records from other parts of the South suggest similar attitudes. Divorce cases and other local court records dealing with marital relations elsewhere in North Carolina confirm that this view of marriage was not confined to the state's eastern shore or even just to African Americans. My reading of these records relies heavily on Noralee Frankel's conceptualization of African American marital relations in "Freedom's Women." Also see Bercaw, "The Politics of Household." Although she does not draw the same conclusions, Schwalm's discussion of African American families in "The Meaning of Freedom" is suggestive on this point; see especially 87–90, 335–49. Also see Leon Litwack, *Been in the Storm So Long: The Aftermath of Slavery* (New York: Knopf, 1979), 243–44. For parallels between African Americans and nineteenth-century attitudes as a whole, see Hendrik Hartog, "Marital Exits and Marital Expectations in Nineteenth Century America," *Georgetown Law Journal* 80 (October 1991): 95–129.

10. Quote from the pension file of Benjamin Braddy; also see the pension file of Ford Howell, both in Reg. 1, Co. F, North Carolina Infantry; Pension Records, RG 15, NA. For a discussion of state regulation of marriages in the South, see Grossberg, *Governing the*

Hearth, 75–81. The court recognized common-law marriages after the war, see *Jones v. Reddick* 79 N.C. 290 (1878).

11. *Bell v. Bell*, 1871, Divorce Records, Granville County, NCDAH. Divorce Petitions from the antebellum period confirm that poor white men and women regularly took up and separated from each other without legal sanction; see General Assembly Records, NCDAH. Also see McCurry, *Masters of Small Worlds*, 89–90, 183; J. Wayne Flynt, "Folks like Us: The Southern Poor White Family, 1865–1935," in *The Web of Southern Social Relations: Women, Family and Education*, ed. Walter J. Fraser, Jr., R. Frank Saunders, Jr., and Jon L. Wakelyn (Athens: University of Georgia Press, 1985), 225–44. For the tension between legal and customary forms of marriage and separation see Hartog, "Marital Exits and Marital Expectations."

12. For the lack of distinction between "home" and "work" in the lives of the yeoman, poor white, and African American women as well as the commonality of field work and wage labor for them, see Margaret Jarmon Hagood, *Mothers of the South: Portraiture of the White Tenant Farm Woman* (Chapel Hill: University of North Carolina Press, 1939; reprint, New York: Greenwood Press, 1969); Tera Hunter, *To 'Joy My Freedom: Southern Black Women's Lives and Labor after the Civil War* (Cambridge: Harvard University Press, 1997); McCurry, *Masters of Small Worlds*, esp. 73–84; Bercaw, "The Politics of Household," ch. 5; Charles C. Bolton, *Poor Whites of the Antebellum South: Tenants and Laborers in Central North Carolina and Northeast Mississippi* (Durham: Duke University Press, 1994), 38–39; Frances Sage Bradley and Margetta A. Williamson, *Rural Children in Selected Counties of North Carolina* (Washington, D.C.: U.S. Children's Bureau, 1918; reprint, New York: Negro Universities Press, 1969), 34–35, 72–73; Frankel, "Freedom's Women"; Dolores E. Janiewski, *Sisterhood Denied: Race, Gender, and Class in a New South Community* (Philadelphia: Temple University Press, 1985), 28–38; Jacqueline Jones, *Labor of Love, Labor of Sorrow: Black Women, Work, and the Family from Slavery to the Present* (New York: Basic Books, 1985), 58–66, 74–75, 81–99; Schwalm, "The Meaning of Freedom"; Deborah Gray White, *Ar'n't I a Woman?: Female Slaves in the Plantation South* (New York: Norton, 1985), 119–41.

13. In contrast to the housing of the elite, most North Carolina houses contained only a few rooms, where the residents lived without making elaborate distinctions between public and private space. See Catherine W. Bishir, *North Carolina Architecture* (Chapel Hill: University of North Carolina Press, 1990), 287–99; John Michael Vlach, *Back of the Big House: The Architecture of Plantation Slavery* (Chapel Hill: University of North Carolina Press, 1993), 153–82; Michael Ann Williams, *Homeplace: The Social Use and Meaning of the Folk Dwelling in Southwestern North Carolina* (Athens: University of Georgia Press, 1991). In *To 'Joy My Freedom*, Hunter notes a lack of distinction between "family" and "community" in Atlanta's black community. Historians have made similar arguments for antebellum common whites; see Bill Cecil-Fronsman, *Common Whites: Class and Culture in Antebellum North Carolina* (Lexington: University Press of Kentucky, 1992), 150–68; Robert C. Kenzer, *Kinship and Neighborhood in a Southern Community: Orange County, North Carolina, 1849–1881* (Knoxville: University of Tennessee Press, 1987).

14. *State v. World*, 1883, Criminal Action Papers, Edgecombe County, NCDAH. For the flexibility of family structures among black southerners and the importance of extended family ties, see Berlin, Miller, and Rowland, "Afro-American Families"; Orville Vernon Burton, *In My Father's House Are Many Mansions: Family and Community in Edgefield, South Carolina* (Chapel Hill: University of North Carolina Press, 1985), 237–38, 263–64, 274–79; Barbara J. Fields, *Slavery and Freedom on the Middle Ground: Maryland during the Nineteenth Century* (New Haven: Yale University Press, 1985), 156; Hunter, *To 'Joy My Freedom*; Jones, *Labor of Love, Labor of Sorrow*; Charles Joyner, *Down by the Riverside: A South Carolina Slave*

Community (Urbana: University of Illinois Press, 1984); Schwalm, "The Meaning of Free-dom," 87–90, 335–49. By contrast, studies of poor and common whites in the South have largely ignored these questions because they have generally assumed the presence of individuated nuclear families and focused on households in relative isolation from one another. Recent work, however, suggests both the importance of community ties and the fluidity of individual families. See Bolton, *Poor Whites of the Antebellum South*; Cecil-Fronsman, *Common Whites*; Kenzer, *Kinship and Neighborhood in a Southern Community*.

15. *State v. Thigpen*, 1869, Criminal Action Papers, Edgecombe County; *State v. Burwell*, 1880, Criminal Action Papers, Granville County; both in NCDAH. In both poor white and African American communities, family and neighbors (who were often kin), as well as local church congregations, also mediated family conflicts.

16. The dynamics are not unlike those associated with colonial New England. See Laurel Thatcher Ulrich, *Good Wives: Image and Reality in the Lives of Women in Northern New England, 1650–1750* (New York: Oxford University Press, 1983); Dayton, *Women before the Bar*.

17. The account of Westley Rhodes appears in Cecil-Fronsman, *Common Whites*, 133; also see 156–64. Kenzer, *Kinship and Neighborhood in a Southern Community*, 20–22, makes a similar point.

18. *Oliver v. Oliver*, Divorce Records, Alexander County; *State v. Oliver*, 1873, Criminal Action Papers, Alexander County; *State v. Oliver*, #10,815, Supreme Court Original Cases, 1880–1900.

19. *State v. Oliver*, 1873, Criminal Action Papers, Alexander County and #10,815, Supreme Court Original Cases, 1800–1900; *Taylor v. Taylor*, #11,767, Supreme Court Original Cases, 1800–1900; *White v. White*, Divorce Records, Lenoir County; all in NCDAH. Unlike the other couples discussed in this article, the Taylors were not poor or even of moderate means. But like poor women, wealthier women also relied on the protection of family ties because they could summon so few resources in their own names.

20. *White v. White*, Divorce Records, Lenoir County, NCDAH.

21. *State v. Hedding*, 1883, Criminal Action Papers, Granville County, NCDAH.

22. These legal standards are stated in *Tapping Reeve, The Law of Baron and Femme*, 3d ed. (Albany: William Gould, 1862; reprint, New York: South Book Press, 1870). Reeve insists, without proof, that civilization in the United States had advanced to the point where husbands no longer exercise their right to "discipline" their wives physically. See Dayton, *Women before the Bar*, 105–56.

23. *State v. Oliver*, 70 N.C. 60 (1874); *State v. Oliver*, #10,815, Supreme Court Original Cases, NCDAH.

24. *State v. Mabrey*, 64 N.C. 592 (1870); *State v. Oliver*, 70 N.C. 60 (1874). Also see *State v. Mabrey*, #9,616; *State v. Oliver*, #10,815; both in Supreme Court Original Cases, NCDAH.

25. *State v. Henderson*, 1883, Criminal Action Papers, Granville County, NCDAH. For similar cases, see Cecil-Fronsman, *Common Whites*, 133; McCurry, *Masters of Small Worlds*, 130–35.

26. *State v. Henderson*, 1883; *State v. Lawrence*, 1882; Criminal Action Papers, Granville County, NCDAH.

27. *State v. Jacobs*, 1880, Criminal Action Papers, Orange County, NCDAH.

28. *State v. Rhodes*, #9368, Supreme Court Original Cases, 1800–1900; *State v. Mabrey*, #9,616, Supreme Court Original Cases, 1800–1900; *State v. Huntley*, 1884, Criminal Action Papers, Haywood County and #14,130, Supreme Court Original Cases, 1800–1900; all in NCDAH.

29. *State v. Rhodes et al.*, 1864, 1867, Criminal Action Papers, Wilkes County. *State v. Teague*, 1873; *State v. Oliver*, 1874; Criminal Action Papers, Alexander County. *State v. Huntley*, 1883, 1884, Criminal Action Papers, Haywood County; all in NCDAH.

30. *State v. Burwell*, 1880, Criminal Action Papers, Granville County, NCDAH. *White v. White*, Divorce Records, Lenoir County, NCDAH. Also see Frankel, "Freedom's Women."

31. *State v. Henderson*, 1883, Criminal Action Papers, Granville County; *State v. Jacobs*, 1880, Criminal Action Papers, Orange County; both in NCDAH.

32. *State v. Lawrence*, 1882, Criminal Action Papers, Granville County, NCDAH. For discussions of the gendered meanings embedded within the law, see Grossberg, *Governing the Hearth*, and *A Judgment for Solomon: The d'Hauteville Case and Legal Experience in Antebellum America* (New York: Cambridge University Press, 1996); Linda K. Kerber, "The Paradox of Women's Citizenship in the Early Republic: The Case of Martin vs. Massachusetts, 1805," *American Historical Review* 97 (April 1992): 349–78; Martha Minow, *Making All the Difference: Inclusion, Exclusion, and American Law* (Ithaca: Cornell University Press, 1990); Carole Pateman, *The Sexual Contract* (Stanford: Stanford University Press, 1988); Joan Hoff Wilson, *Law, Gender, and Injustice: A Legal History of U.S. Women* (New York: New York University Press, 1991).

33. *State v. Dicey Burwell*, 1880, Criminal Action Papers, Granville County, NCDAH. In " 'Smiling Through Her Tears,' " Censer argues that antebellum women also had to conform to the court's vision of victimized womanhood to obtain divorces. Also see Bardaglio, *Reconstructing the Household*, 32–34. This gender construction hardly fit those held by poor white and African American women. See Bercaw, "The Politics of Household"; Bynum, *Unruly Women*; Laura F. Edwards, *Gendered Strife and Confusion: The Political Culture of Reconstruction* (Urbana: University of Illinois Press, 1997), ch. 4; Frankel, "Freedom's Women"; Hunter, *To 'Joy My Freedom*; Schwalm, "The Meaning of Freedom"; Jacquelyn Hall, "Private Eyes, Public Women: Images of Class and Sex in the Urban South, Atlanta, Georgia, 1913–1915," in *Work Engendered: Toward a New History of American Labor*, ed. Ava Baron (Ithaca: Cornell University Press, 1991), 243–72, and "O. Delight Smith's Progressive Era: Labor, Feminism, and Reform in the Urban South," in *Visible Women: New Essays on American Activism*, ed. Nancy A. Hewitt and Suzanne Lebsock (Urbana: University of Illinois Press, 1993), 166–98; Nancy A. Hewitt, "In Pursuit of Power: The Political Economy of Women's Activism in Twentieth-Century Tampa," in Hewitt and Lebsock, *Visible Women*, 199–222, and "Politicizing Domesticity: Anglo, Black, and Latin Women in Tampa's Progressive Movements," in *Gender, Class, Race and Reform in the Progressive Era*, ed. Noralee Frankel and Nancy S. Dye (Lexington: University of Kentucky Press, 1991).

34. *Torchlight* (Oxford, N.C.), 25 January 1876; also see *Torchlight*, 23 September 1879. Also see Edwards, *Gendered Strife and Confusion*, ch. 3; Glenda Elizabeth Gilmore, *Gender and Jim Crow: Women and the Politics of White Supremacy in North Carolina, 1896–1920* (Chapel Hill: University of North Carolina Press, 1996); George C. Rable, *Civil Wars: Women and the Crisis of Southern Nationalism* (Urbana: University of Illinois Press, 1989); LeeAnn Whites, *The Civil War as a Crisis in Gender: Augusta, Georgia, 1860–1890* (Athens: University of Georgia Press, 1995). As these works point out, elite white women in the late nineteenth century did take steps into the public sphere, but small and tentative ones. Also see Nell Irvin Painter, "The Journal of Gertrude Clanton Thomas: An Educated White Woman in the Eras of Slavery, War, and Reconstruction," introduction to *The Secret Eye: The Journal of Gertrude Clanton Thomas, 1848–1889*, ed. Virginia Ingraham Burr (Chapel Hill: University of North Carolina Press, 1990), 1–67.

35. *State v. Rhodes*, 61 N.C. 453 (1868).

36. Ibid.; *State v. Oliver*, 70 N.C. 60 (1874); *State v. Pettie*, 80 N.C. 367 (1879); *State v. Huntley*, 91 N.C. 617 (1884).

37. For an expanded discussion of these issues, see Edwards, " 'The Marriage Covenant Is at the Foundation of All Our Rights' " and *Gendered Strife and Confusion*.

38. *Taylor v. Taylor*, 76 N.C. 433 (1877). As Grossberg's *Governing the Hearth* has argued, northern courts during the antebellum period had taken on broad discretionary powers in issues of family law. What emerged was, in his words, a judicial patriarchy. While North Carolina courts continued to uphold the patriarchal power of male household heads, they also expanded their own power to oversee family relations. Peter Bardaglio makes a similar case for Southern state governments as a whole in *Reconstructing the Household*. The cases dealing with domestic issues are too lengthy to list here; for representative cases that extended the court's control over the private sphere, see, for instance, *Beard v. Hudson*, 61 N.C. 180 (1867); *State v. Rhodes*, 61 N.C. 453 (1868); *State v. Harris*, 63 N.C. 1 (1868); *Stout v. Woody*, 63 N.C. 37 (1868); *State v. Hairston and Williams*, 63 N.C. 451 (1869); *State v. Reinhardt and Love*, 63 N.C. 547 (1869); *Biggs v. Harris*, 64 N.C. 413 (1870); *State v. Mabrey*, 64 N.C. 592 (1870); *State v. Adams and Reeves*, 65 N.C. 537 (1871); *State v. Brown*, 67 N.C. 470 (1872); *Mitchell v. Mitchell*, 67 N.C. 307 (1872); *State v. Alford*, 68 N.C. 322 (1873); *Horne v. Horne*, 72 N.C. 530 (1875); *Thompson v. Thompson*, 72 N.C. 32 (1874); *Long v. Long*, 77 N.C. 304 (1877); *State v. Shaft*, 78 N.C. 464 (1878); *State v. Keesler*, 78 N.C. 469 (1879); *Miller v. Miller*, 78 N.C. 102 (1878); *Webber v. Webber*, 79 N.C. 572 (1878); *Scoggins v. Scoggins*, 80 N.C. 319 (1879); *Muse v. Muse*, 84 N.C. 35 (1881); *White v. White*, 84 N.C. 340 (1881); *State v. Edens* 95 N.C. 693 (1886); *Johnson v. Allen*, 100 N.C. 131 (1888). The court, however, avoided the issue of child abuse; *State v. Jones*, 95 N.C. 588 (1886).

39. *Taylor v. Taylor*, 76 N.C. 433 (1877).

40. Walter Clark, "The Legal Status of Women in North Carolina: Past, Present, and Prospective," New Bern, North Carolina, 8 May 1913, in the North Carolina Collection, University of North Carolina at Chapel Hill.

41. Quotes from *State v. Oliver*, 70 N.C. 60 (1874); *State v. Pettie*, 80 N.C. 367 (1879). For this process, see Bardaglio, *Reconstructing the Household*.

The slave-owners' greatest fear: an armed slave. Harriet Beecher Stowe, *Dred: A Tale of the Great Dismal Swamp* (Cambridge, Mass.: Riverside Press, 1896), frontispiece.

Chapter Six

Complicity and Deceit
Lewis Cheney's Plot and Its Bloody Consequences

Junius P. Rodriguez

"History," the antebellum historian James Louis Petigru once asserted, "is to the human family what experience is to the individual." The simple act of considering certain historic dates generally conjures significant affective memories that we associate with these chronological markers. The date 1837, for example, suggests severe economic distress as we recall the panic that swept the nation during the first year of Martin Van Buren's presidency. More astute scholars of the antebellum era might also recognize 1837 as the date marking Elijah P. Lovejoy's martyrdom to the abolitionist cause as mobs attacked his antislavery press in Alton, Illinois.[1] Yet an alternative history, but one that is nonetheless essential, is that which chronicles the ebb and flow of human existence among ordinary individuals in a more localized setting. For example, among the residents of west-central Louisiana, 1837 was the year that the unthinkable almost happened as details of a sophisticated slave conspiracy emerged, and white inhabitants imposed swift vigilante justice to crush the plot. The individual experiences of all whom this savage episode of frontier violence and retributive justice touched constitute a powerful example of corporate remembrance.

Rapides Parish, Louisiana, was a growing frontier outpost in the late 1830s. Situated along the Red River 175 miles northwest of New Orleans, the region boasted a population of 7,575 in 1830, and the Sixth Census, taken in 1840, reflected a near doubling of residents to 14,132. Cotton was king in Rapides, and slavery was the primary mode of agricultural labor used in the region. Figures from both the Fifth and Sixth Censuses show that slaves formed 70 percent of the populace of Rapides Parish as the 1830s began and ended. Isolated from the population center of the state and distinguished by their region's substantial black majority, white residents of Rapides Parish regularly maintained community vigilance to impede formation of any servile disturbances.[2]

Despite the region's historic seclusion from other population centers, Rapides Parish began to feel the initial pangs of modern economic development in the 1830s and the associated ills of social dislocation had become apparent to all social classes by 1837. In April 1833, Captain Henry M. Shreve had begun the arduous process of clearing the Great Raft of timber that had long blocked navigation along a two-hundred-mile stretch of the Red River to points well beyond Alexandria. Somewhat prophetically, this event coincided with a tremendous meteor shower remembered in the local folklore as "the year the stars fell," but it did not take a celestial sign to portend the commercial changes that free and open navigation on the Red River (eventually accomplished by 1836) would hold for developing expanded plantation agriculture in northwestern Louisiana. The year 1837 marked the founding of Shreveport, which soon became the largest city in the northern part of the state; and that same year also saw the establishment of the first railroad built west of the Mississippi River, which began operating within Rapides Parish. Although hardly sinister, the rather modest forty miles of the Red River Railroad that linked the town of Alexandria to Bayou Hauffpauer near Cheneyville symbolized accessibility, denoting the decline of the region's semi-isolation. The unprecedented opportunity to transport locally produced sugar and cotton more efficiently had the unanticipated consequence of tying heretofore distant plantation districts into the ever expanding vortex of world markets, and local residents soon found themselves reeling from the capricious nature of market economics. Still, many planters along Bayous Boeuf and Rapides invested in railroad development, served as project directors, and seemingly welcomed the greater contact and more numerous opportunities that the rails provided.[3]

Other economic forces also heightened existing distress in Louisiana in 1837. Lower tariff rates placed upon foreign sugar caused domestic prices to plummet, and many Louisiana planters turned increasingly to cotton farming as a hedge against what they perceived to be potential economic ruin. This intense speculation caused short-term cotton prices to rise to twenty cents per pound, and many farmers responded to the favorable economic news by expanding their cotton acreage and bringing marginal lands into cultivation. Certainly, this structural adjustment placed increased demands upon slave laborers who cleared new fields and planted additional cotton. When the anticipated higher prices never appeared in the global cotton market, many plantation bankruptcies resulted in Louisiana, especially in those areas that had attempted the transition from sugar to cotton. As Louisiana residents coped with this economic crisis and the entire nation struggled through the Panic of 1837, the common spectacle of property auctions, including chattel property from defunct cotton plantations, occurred often in parishes like Rapides as economic woes prompted societal dislocations.[4] This crisis embittered many who felt the frustration of failing during an era of rising economic expectations, as the popular enthusiasm of Jacksonian Democracy suddenly gave way to more sobering realities.[5]

Proximity to the Republic of Texas was another concern among Rapides residents because much of the unfinished business in Texan-Mexican relations occasionally threatened the peace and security of west-central Louisiana. Sam Houston, president of the Republic of Texas, repeatedly voiced concern that "the Mexicans with their abolition policy . . . will invite the slaves of the South to revolt."[6] Houston maintained regular contact with U.S. military officers stationed at Fort Jesup in northwestern Louisiana, and these officers, in turn, frequently reported news to War Department officials regarding the Texas situation. In January 1837, Colonel J. B. Many reported that "nothing has occured [sic] in Texas, (within my knowledge), . . . calculated to disturb our inhabitants on this frontier."[7]

Established in 1822, Fort Jesup, which was about sixty miles northwest of Alexandria, served the dual mission of protecting frontier settlers against domestic disturbances (i.e., slave revolts) and guarding against foreign (i.e., Mexican, and later Texan) incursions. Soldiers charged with this mission found themselves responsible for protecting a vast territory that was difficult to patrol because of the logistical problem of negotiating land transportation in a region that remained veritably unsettled. In summer 1837, while the slaves in Rapides Parish were planning their rebellion, the War Department seriously considered abandoning the site of Fort Jesup and creating a new fortification farther west along the Sabine River. Colonel Many defended the merits of maintaining Fort Jesup, arguing, "[Y]ou can always have an efficient force at it . . . ready to move in any direction" depending upon the exigencies faced at the time. He noted specifically that the fort was "well calculated to protect the planters and others on the Red River against their slaves," and that the fort was centrally located to defend most of the settlements in west-central Louisiana.[8]

Alarmed by the dangers posed by threats both external and internal, and cognizant of their woeful defensive posture, residents of Rapides Parish often petitioned the financially strapped state legislature to provide increased support for their defense. As expected, state officials could do little, but they regularly forwarded calls to bolster inadequate defenses to the federal government. As early as November 1831, in the immediate aftermath of Virginia's Nat Turner insurrection, Rapides Parish residents petitioned Secretary of War Lewis Cass in the hope that he might provide additional federal troops to protect settlers due to "the exposed situation of Alexandria and its vicinity." But federal authorities did not provide the additional soldiers, citing their inability to satisfy the multitude of demands for increased troop strength coming from communities that had significant slave populations. Cass did inform officers at Fort Jesup that "in case of any application from the authorities or citizens of Alexandria . . . [they were] to detach an adequate force for that place, to preserve order, if . . . circumstances should justify it."[9]

National authorities did not ignore the persistent requests of Louisiana's officials for more assistance, but there was little that federal troops could do to make the isolated frontier communities more secure from slave unrest. Because the army's role was to defend against enemies both foreign and domestic, strategic positioning within Louisiana amounted to a compromise that could not adequately address either problem. An officer stationed at Fort Jesup recognized what he perceived as the pointless nature of his mission and advised Missouri Senator Lewis F. Linn that "we are too far from the former [Texas border] to protect the frontier inhabitants . . . and also to protect the master from the violence of his slaves."[10]

Another reason for refusing to increase federal troop support was the relative calm that endured in Louisiana despite a flurry of insurrection scares. Every time authorities detected a plot, local patrols and militia units adequately handled the crisis, thus preventing modest rebellions from spreading. This record of success prompted one visitor to assert that "there is no reason to apprehend serious insurrection" because even "the voice of a white ... would make a whole regiment of rebellious slaves throw down their arms and flee." Yet, even this enthusiastic report included a cautious comment that rebellion could occur if free persons of color ever decided to lead slaves into battle.[11] Apparently, cracks in the armor of white public self-perception were unacceptable in an environment where slaves formed a numerical majority, for slaves might perceive any sign of hesitancy or potential vulnerability among whites as an invitation to rise in rebellion. In an 1833 report that evaluated troop strength within Louisiana, the inspector general of the army observed that "there cannot exist a just cause to apprehend anything like a continued rising" among Louisiana's vast slave population. His optimistic report concluded with the reassuring declaration "Negroes no more than whites can effect much without arms and ammunition, and until they do procure them, be assured that their feelings as hostile as they may [be], they will attempt nothing."[12]

White self-assurance overlay a deeper nightmare of a concerted slave uprising. In fall 1837, that terror seemingly developed into reality. In early October, Lewis Cheney, the slave of David Cheney, exposed an insurrection "better planned and managed than any before" to the authorities of Rapides Parish."[13] The sophisticated plot involved a few whites, some free blacks, and nearly fifty slaves on six plantations located along Bayous Rapides and Boeuf near Alexandria.[14] Because local authorities had detected a similar conspiracy two years earlier, the news alarmed Rapides residents, who had theretofore maintained exuberant confidence in the loyalty and trustworthiness of their slaves.[15] Solomon Northup, a slave who labored in the affected region, noted the plot's significance in local black folk culture by remarking that it would be the "chief tradition" in the narratives of future progeny. Yet, this conspiracy's remarkable legacy appears neither in its formation nor its exposure but, rather, in its highhanded duplicity. Lewis Cheney, the slave who revealed the planned insurrection, was also the plot's organizer.[16]

Northup stated that Cheney's original plan had not contemplated wholesale murder but an insurrection that would expedite an organized escape to Mexico. The Mexican government had abolished slavery in 1829, and Mexican nationals within Texas could probably help the rebels' cause, hence the plan seemed sound to many and conspirators joined the plot. Cheney traveled from one plantation to another under cover of darkness recruiting accomplices and pilfering provisions needed for the difficult journey to freedom in Mexico. Northup describes Cheney as an avenging angel "more intelligent than the generality of his race" but also as "shrewd, cunning, ... unscrupulous and full of treachery." The relative ease with which he gathered mules and wagons for this purpose suggests his followers' loyalty and belief that their goal was attainable. Only when authorities discovered a cache of supplies hidden in the swamp behind the Hawkins plantation did Lewis Cheney decide that his plans needed immediate revision. Placing self-preservation before any sense of community solidarity, Cheney alerted his own master that slaves in the vicinity had planned an uprising that would wreak great bloodshed. The news that blacks planned to massacre the white residents of Rapides Parish initiated a frenzied reaction among the populace.[17]

Community leaders held an emergency meeting at the parish courthouse in Alexandria on October 6, establishing the Committee of Vigilance and issuing an emergency request that officers at Fort Jesup send two companies of U.S. troops into the affected area immediately. The leaders of the committee professed to have "the most ample proofs" of the planned insurrection, and the tone of their urgent dispatch reflects the great anxiety felt throughout the region among residents "much exhausted with watching and patroling [*sic*]." On October 6, the Committee of Vigilance executed two alleged conspirators by hanging, and the group planned to hold "trials" for twenty additional suspects.[18]

Lewis Cheney, "a shrewd, cunning negro," combined a brilliant strategy with the means of support to craft a plot that could have produced initial success. Cheney won the confidence of other slaves by telling them he hated his master for having removed him from service as a house servant and making him labor instead as a common field hand. He timed the event to coincide with the annual exodus of white residents caused by fever conditions around Alexandria. He induced local whites with abolitionist sympathies and an unidentified Spaniard to champion the cause and support the plot. Local authorities understood the degree of external support only when they reportedly discovered a letter from abolitionist Arthur Tappan in the possession of one of the captured slave conspirators. This evidence persuaded local authorities to eliminate any trace of insurrectionary thought in the region by organizing extralegal courts to administer swift and certain justice. Upon hearing information that plot participants quarreled among themselves whether they should spare women and children or murder all whites, the planters believed that a public display of retribution was necessary. Conspirators confessed "on the gallows" as "a committee of the citizens" condemned nine slaves and three free persons of color to death by hanging.

An observer remarked that they held the trials "not in a legal manner," and that the proceedings were generally "without the form and contrary to law." The very sketchy pattern that emerged from Rapides Parish was that residents held a series of extralegal trials, each generally followed by a quick community-sanctioned public execution. This pattern suggests that the suspects accused of conspiracy to revolt did not receive the legal benefits of due process or the right to cross-examine witnesses, nor did they live to enjoy the right to an appeal. And the great likelihood that white planters made up the jury of peers that assented to these verdicts is more indicative of a cathartic community bloodletting than an impartial judicial proceeding.[19]

Because state legislation prohibited the acceptance of black testimony against white conspirators, the Rapides Parish planters employed means beyond the law to root out these suspected race traitors. Mr. Fuzilin, a local plantation owner, reportedly shot a white man suspected of "completing [*sic*] with the negroes."[20]

Lewis Cheney's treachery proved that a slave could beat white society in a dangerous social game, but his individual victory carried a steep price for others. Future generations of blacks "despised and execrated" the name of the turncoat who transformed a popular revolutionary movement into a self-serving charade for personal emancipation. Although Cheney's chicanery in betraying his comrades might seem atrocious to the modern observer, his creative actions to gain freedom do entail an incipient realization of his personal rebellion by other means, or in Jean-Paul Sartre's words, "The rebel's weapon is the proof of his humanity."[21] Cheney was willing to pursue two extremely dangerous courses of action simultaneously: first, by being the messianic rebel leader who structured a wide-ranging slave conspiracy; and second, by being the loyal slave who informed his master of the nefarious plot that was afoot. And he could act effectively in each role. Oblivious to any deception, the Louisiana state legislature manumitted Lewis Cheney and provided $500 to finance his removal from the state while compensating his master, David Cheney, $1,500—the former's original purchase price. Surprisingly, the legislature also compensated five other slave owners for seven slaves executed in an extralegal fashion by vigilantes.[22] The expenditure of state tax dollars for this purpose suggests that the legislature indirectly condoned the type of primitive vigilante justice that had occurred at Alexandria.

The Cheney conspiracy heightened tension throughout Louisiana. Statements made by slaves during gallows confessions that were surely spoken under duress suggested that plans had been made to extend the revolt to both Natchitoches and New Orleans once it proved successful near Alexandria. In late December 1837, authorities dispatched troops from Fort Jesup to Natchitoches when authorities in that community received word of a slave conspiracy in the area.[23] Additionally, many white inhabitants viewed the willingness of some free blacks to aid Cheney and the other slaves as sufficient reason "to drive away all free persons of color" from the region.[24]

One should not underestimate the public impact of the discovery of Lewis Cheney's conspiracy. The usually guarded Louisiana state legislature, which did not want to lend credibility to idle rumors of revolt, broke its self-imposed ban and called the 1837 incident an insurrection, a term previously used only when referring to the 1811 German Coast Rebellion. The spirit of public anarchy that followed the plot's discovery disturbed many area residents because violent reactions "without the form and contrary to law" established "a bad example and . . . will always injure any country." Local vigilante gangs captured slaves suspected of complicity in the plot and marched them in chains to Alexandria, where they hanged many as part of a public spectacle. On October 10, four days after the violence began at Alexandria, two companies of federal troops (one hundred soldiers) stationed at Fort Jesup moved into Rapides Parish to protect public property, not in response to threatened slave violence but to the terror caused by vigilante enforcers. Upon arrival, the troops restored order by destroying the recently constructed gallows and liberating many prisoners from the Alexandria jail. Authorities did continue to hold thirty slave conspirators in jail for their suspected role in the plot. These actions astonished some inhabitants favoring vigilante justice, who argued that "when laws can not be made to preserve society, give it up and let each preserve himself." Events at Alexandria proved that the imposition of law and order by an enraged public upon a community can assume a spirit of lawlessness in its own right, especially when the innate tension of racism defines one's understanding of justice.[25]

Perhaps the violence that occurred at Alexandria was merely symptomatic of an antebellum culture that was essentially savage in its public manifestations of power relationships. Officials reported one death by drowning and eight desertions among the one hundred troops who formed Companies D and K of the Third Infantry (from Fort Jesup) that quelled the 1837 disturbances in Rapides Parish. The desertion rate was rather high for a generally localized foray of sixteen days in the field. The army eventually captured three of the soldiers who had escaped, and all were court-martialed at Fort Jesup. Punishments imposed upon each deserter included "fifty lashes on his bare back with rawhide" and being forced to perform "hard labor with a ball and chain attached to his leg until the expiration of his term of enlistment." Apparently, even among the defenders of civil society there existed a code whereby soldiers understood judicially imposed brutality to be an effective agent of social order.[26]

Public perception of the events in Rapides Parish and community remembrance of the outcome are also significant indicators of societal distress and perceptions of historical validity. Psychologist Edmund Blair Bolles's studies suggest that memory is an act of imagination and that remembering is a "creative, constructive process" rather than the mere retrieval of information. So too, community memory is not a passive depository of isolated facts but an active creation of public meaning.[27] Solomon Northup's assertions that Lewis Cheney's actions became "a subject of general and unfailing interest in every slave-hut on the bayou" before his treachery and that his name became "despised and execrated" after the fact reveal the existence of well-established community sanctions. That Northup heard these stories nearly five years after the events occurred also suggests the lasting influence of this episode upon the communal mentality of Rapides Parish slaves.[28]

The story of Lewis Cheney is not a typical trickster tale, though it does share certain attributes of that motif. Cheney undeniably used intrigue and cunning to achieve a desired outcome, unbeknownst to those whom he duped. His was also a tale that, in Lawrence W. Levine's words, "taught the art of surviving and even triumphing in the face of a hostile environment," as Cheney beat the odds and gained his freedom.[29] Yet similarities end there, for the slave community of Rapides Parish experienced no vicarious pleasure from the duplicitous emancipation of Cheney at the expense of broken dreams and shattered lives. Perhaps Cheney was a nihilistic hero who found value only in actions that placed self ahead of community, but future generations of Louisiana's black residents continued to vilify his name.

This episode in Rapides Parish history is also noteworthy for revealing one panic-stricken community's resolve when faced with the ultimate crime within its value system. The harsh vigilante justice imposed at Alexandria was swift, but it was neither impartial nor fair. It is indeed ironic that only one individual, Lewis Cheney, gained freedom from the experience. Cheney's accomplices, while guilty of lesser offenses, faced more severe punishment because of his testimony against them. Fears of white residents demanded immediate, albeit irrational, justice, and a mob mentality prevailed. It is difficult to sort through the details of this episode without sensing a bizarre morality play in which no one was blameless. Unusual as it might seem, all were complicit, all were deceived, and in the end, Lewis Cheney went free.

NOTES

1. South Carolina Historical Society, http://historic.com/schs/; Gorton Carruth, *What Happened When: A Chronology of Life and Events in America* (New York: Harper and Row, 1989), 118–19.

2. Census Manuscripts of the Fifth Census and the Sixth Census, National Archives, Washington, D.C.

3. James Calhoun, ed., *Louisiana Almanac, 1984–85* (Gretna, La.: Pelican Publishing, 1984), 108, 217; and James H. Workman Papers MSS, Louisiana and Lower Mississippi Valley Collections, Louisiana State University Libraries, Baton Rouge.

4. Francois-Xavier Martin, *The History of Louisiana, from the Earliest Period* (Gretna, La.: Pelican Publishing, 1975), 439–40; Edwin Adams Davis, *Louisiana: The Pelican State* (Baton Rouge: Louisiana State University Press, 1959), 178; Bennett H. Wall, ed., *Louisiana: A History*, 3d ed. (Wheeling, Ill.: Harlan Davidson, 1997), 139.

5. Crane Brinton, *The Anatomy of Revolution*, rev. ed. (New York: Knopf, 1965), 250.

6. Sam Houston to Col. J. B. Many, 28 August 1838, cited in Harry F. Middleton, Jr., "Frontier Outpost: A History of Fort Jesup, Louisiana, 1822–1846" (master's thesis, Louisiana State University, 1973), 167.

7. J. B. Many to Arbuckle, 13 January 1837, RG 393 Records of the United States Army Continental Commands, 1821–1920, NA 61 Letters Received in the Second Military District, 1834–38 MSS, National Archives.

8. Inspector General's Report for 1833, RG 159 Records of the Office of the Inspector General, M624, Inspection Reports of the Office of the Inspector General, 1814–1842 MSS; and J. B. Many to Alexander Macomb, 25 July 1837, RG 94 Records of the Adjutant General's Office, 1780s–1917, M567 Letters Received by the Office of the Adjutant General (Main Series), 1822–1860 MSS, National Archives.

9. Alexander Macomb to Lewis Cass, 19 February 1833, and Lewis Cass to Alexander Macomb, 29 February 1836, in Benjamin Franklin Cooling, ed., *The New American State Papers: Military Affairs*, vol. 10, *Combat Operations* (Wilmington, Del.: Scholarly Resources, 1979), 142–44.

10. Bennett Riley to Lewis F. Linn, 28 August 1837, in Cooling, *American State Papers: Military Affairs*, 7:957; "Fort Jesup, Fort Selden, Camp Sabine, Camp Salubrity: Four For-

gotten Frontier Army Posts of Western Louisiana," *Louisiana Historical Quarterly* 16 (1933): 674–75.

11. Harriet Martineau, *Society in America* (London: Saunders and Otley, 1837), 330–31.

12. Inspector General's Report for 1833.

13. In 1830, the Cheney family owned thirty-seven slaves. James H. Workman Papers MSS, Louisiana and Lower Mississippi Valley Collections.

14. These were the plantations of David Cheney, Samuel Cakford, John Pettway, Carter Beaman, John Compton, and Vincent Page. G. P. Whittington, *Rapides Parish Louisiana: A History* (Alexandria: National Society of the Colonial Dames in the State of Louisiana, 1935), 90.

15. Ulrich B. Phillips, *American Negro Slavery* (Baton Rouge: Louisiana State University Press, 1987), 486.

16. *Clinton Louisianian*, 8 November 1837; *Boston Liberator*, 3 November 1837; Niles' *National Register* (Baltimore), 28 October 1837; Solomon Northup, *Twelve Years a Slave*, ed. Sue Eakin and Joseph Logsdon (Baton Rouge: Louisiana State University Press, 1975), 188–89; James W. Jones, Jr. MSS, Cammie G. Henry Research Center, Watson Library, Northwestern State University of Louisiana, Natchitoches.

17. Northup, *Twelve Years a Slave*, 188–89; Sue Eakin, *Rapides Parish: An Illustrated History* (Alexandria, La.: Windsor Publications, 1987), 26–27.

18. Committee of Vigilance to J. B. Many, 8 October 1837, RG 94 Records of the Adjutant General's Office, 1780s–1917, M567 Letters Received by the Office of the Adjutant General (Main Series), 1822–1860 MSS, National Archives.

19. Dr. R. F. McGuire Diary, 1818–1852 MSS, entry for August 1837, Louisiana and Lower Mississippi Valley Collections.

20. *Clinton Louisianian*, 8 November 1837; Dr. R. F. McGuire Diary, 1818–1852 MSS, entry for August 1837, Louisiana and Lower Mississippi Valley Collections.

21. Jean-Paul Sartre, preface to Frantz Fanon, *The Wretched of the Earth* (New York: Grove Press, 1968), 22.

22. *Acts Passed at the Second Session of the Thirteenth Legislature of the State of Louisiana, 1837–1838* (New Orleans: Jerome Bayon, 1838), 118.

23. H. Barnbridge to M. Arbuckle, 9 January 1838, RG 393 Records of the United States Army Continental Commands, 1821–1920, NA 61 Letters Received in the Second Military District MSS, National Archives.

24. Eakin, *Rapides Parish*, 26–27.

25. *Clinton Louisianian*, 8 November 1837; Dr. R. F. McGuire Diary, 1818–1852 MSS, entry for August 1837, Louisiana and Lower Mississippi Valley Collections.

26. Third Infantry Reports, November 1837, RG 94 Records of the Adjutant General's Office, 1780s–1917, M665 Returns from Regular Army Infantry Regiments, June 1821–December 1916 MSS; and Court Martial Records, November 1837, RG 393 Records of the United States Army Continental Commands, 1821–1920, NA 61 Letters Received in the Second Military District, 1834–38 MSS, National Archives.

27. Edmund Blair Bolles, *Remembering and Forgetting: An Inquiry into the Nature of Memory* (New York: Walker, 1988), xi; Alexandro Portelli, *The Death of Luigi Trastulli, and Other Stories: Form and Meaning in Oral History* (Albany: State University of New York Press, 1991), 52.

28. Northup, *Twelve Years a Slave*, 188–89.

29. Lawrence W. Levine, *Black Culture and Black Consciousness: Afro-American Folk Thought from Slavery to Freedom* (New York: Oxford University Press, 1977), 115.

A battle between rival vigilante gangs. Frank Soule et al., *The Annals of San Francisco* (New York: D. Appleton, 1854), 553.

Chapter Seven

Good Men and Notorious Rogues
Vigilantism in Massac County, Illinois, 1846–1850

Nicole Etcheson

On a November night in 1846, twenty men visited the house of an elderly man named Mathis in rural Massac County, Illinois. Although some of his neighbors described Mathis as a man of "honest, industrious character," many suspected him of knowing more than he chose to tell of the criminal activities then rampant in this southern Illinois county. His visitors that night were Regulators, a body of vigilantes who hoped to elicit some of that information. They "arrested" him, although they had no warrant and no legal authority. When he and his wife resisted, the Regulators brutally struck them. One of the Regulators shot Mrs. Mathis accidentally when she grappled with him for the gun he held to her chest. The Regulators took Mathis away and his wife, who survived, never saw him again.[1]

Regulator violence claimed many victims other than Mathis in 1846. If he suffered a fate similar to the others, which his wife certainly believed and there is little reason to doubt, then his captors took him to the Ohio River. There Regulators probably tortured him as they sought to elicit information about his neighbors. Regulator methods included holding a captive's head under water or tying a rope around his midriff and arms, twisting the rope with a stick, until the victim sputtered a confession or the stubborn were drowned or crushed. Upon occasion, Regulators took prisoners across the river into Paducah, Kentucky. Their Kentucky allies sent letters saying that these men had "gone to Arkansas," meaning they had been drowned in the Ohio River and the bodies left to drift southward.[2]

The Regulators who murdered Mathis and shot his wife presented themselves as honest men who sought to eliminate the "notorious rogues" who infested their region of southern Illinois. In this, the Regulators unknowingly emulated the model that later historians would create of the classic vigilante: an honest citizen frustrated with lawlessness who takes the law into his own hands. Violence became the recourse of the law-abiding when there was no law. The Massac Regulators fit that description, up to a point. Many Regulators were men of substance, such as Elijah Smith, or prominent local professionals, such as Judge

Wesley Sloan or Angus M. L. McBane, a relative of the founder of Massac County's only town. These men, and their followers, struck against a local criminal gang called the Flatheads. The Flatheads appear to have taken their name from the species of catfish found in the Ohio River. By the nineteenth century, the term was also being used to mean a poor white settler on river bottomlands or "a member of any of several gangs of southern Illinois riverbank bandits in the early and mid-nineteenth century." The Mathis name, and that of the even more infamous Linn clan, made frequent appearances on the court records of Massac and Pope Counties in southern Illinois. Cheatem Linn, his sons, and a wide circle of neighbors formed a criminal network involved in horse theft, counterfeiting, and robbery.[3]

That only a small number of men formed the nucleus of both the Flatheads and Regulators appears evident from the recurrence of a handful of names in the records. But each side drew on a network of kin and neighbors in other counties and in Kentucky when they required larger forces—often more than a hundred men—to form posses, defy posses, rescue prisoners, or intimidate neighbors. Reliable reports do not exist recording the numbers of people who suffered Mathis's fate, but the melodramatic accounts that appeared in newspapers and pleas to the governor spoke of hundreds driven from their homes and more than two dozen killed by Regulators. Even if Regulator violence did not reach quite those levels, one should not underestimate the fear that only one death, disappearance, or midnight visit could create.

The Regulator-Flathead war was not, however, a simple case of vigilantism, despite the apparently clear lines between the honest and the criminal. The Flatheads did not merely prey on the community; they were the community. Flatheads served as sheriff, representative to the state legislature, and county clerk. And long after the "war" had ended, Flatheads such as the Linns could still be found in Massac County. The Regulators formed, then, not because there was no law in Massac but, rather, because there was no law that they respected. The Regulators declared that the legal system had been captured by the criminals. The county owed its very existence to Flathead political influence. Flatheads had pushed for the creation of Massac County in 1843 in order to strengthen their political base.[4]

The new county was small in population, isolated, and lacking in economic prosperity. Illinois had been a state for thirty-five years by the time the county of Massac was formed out of parts of Pope and Johnson Counties. When the Regulator-Flathead war broke out in 1846, Massac County had existed for only three years. It lay almost two hundred miles from the state capital at Springfield. Situated along the Ohio River, with its town, Metropolis, on a bluff overlooking the river, Massac had been a military post off and on since the 1750s. Although Fort Massac was defunct by the 1840s, William A. McBane founded Metropolis as a likely site for a railroad bridge spanning the river. These hopes were not realized until the twentieth century, and Massac depended on the trade along the river rather than across it.[5]

The river trade does not appear to have stimulated the county's growth.

According to the 1850 census, only 4,092 people lived in Massac, 427 of them in Metropolis, the county's only town. Massac, like neighboring Pope and Johnson Counties, fell in the bottom quarter of Illinois counties by population. Its chief product was tobacco, but its level of production, while respectable, lagged far behind that of the chief tobacco-producing counties in Illinois. In the 1840s, Massac County was sparsely populated and isolated from the center of Illinois politics.[6]

It is tempting to find in these conditions, common to a frontier area, explanations for the Regulator-Flathead war, but Massac's youth and underdevelopment had little to do with the cycle of violence that continued there into the 1850s. Lawlessness plagued the county because its legal institutions possessed little if any commonly accepted legitimacy. Again, this disorder was similar to many frontier areas where newness undermined the efficacy and the community's support of the law, and vigilantes, such as those in Gold Rush San Francisco, superseded a legal system that they argued had failed to function. In Massac County, however, the Regulators refused to accept the legitimacy of a functioning police and court system because they held it to have been co-opted by the criminals themselves. The Flatheads, and many others who grew disenchanted with the Regulators' methods, naturally refused to accept the legitimacy of the extralegal institutions, such as posses and trial by committee, that the Regulators created. Each side asserted that the other acted lawlessly, and both sides used violence in the name of the law.

Even before the events that provoked the Regulators to organize, residents of southern Illinois complained of the region's lawlessness. The locals first blamed westward migrants, but by the mid-1840s suspicion came to focus on certain prosperous Massac farmers. Chief among the suspects were Cheatem Linn and his sons, these "well-to-do farmers" were believed to be running a criminal gang. Joe Linn was among those accused of being an accomplice in the kidnapping of local free black children, who were then sold as slaves in St. Louis. According to local legend, the Flatheads were open and egregious in their activities. "In those days it wasn't safe to leave a boy plowing alone in the field, for some of the Flatheads would come along and drive the team off. No one dared to go after his stock because he would never come back alive."[7]

As this story indicates, by the 1840s "an ancient colony of horse-thieves, counterfeiters, and robbers, had long infested the counties of Massac and Pope. They were so strong and so well combined together, as to insure impunity from punishment by legal means."[8] Crimes remained unsolved and convictions went unobtained as barns burned, witnesses were intimidated or killed, and gang members served as jurors. One criminal docket contained thirty-two cases, mostly for counterfeiting, but only one conviction resulted. Previous vigilante efforts had produced incomplete victories. In 1831, a Pope County gang of counterfeiters, horse thieves, and robbers led by a man named Sturdevant had built a fort and defied the local government. "Honest" citizens retaliated by attacking the fort with small arms and artillery. They took the fortification by storm, killing three of the criminals and losing one of their own number. The result was, however, not altogether satisfactory. Although the rest of the criminals were taken prisoner, none were convicted.[9]

The most serious crime involved an attack on farmer Henry Sides. Sides, a former slaveholder, had settled north of Golconda, in Pope County, in the 1830s. He had also settled his freed slaves there. Another slaveholder, a Tennessean named Dobbs, had brought his freed slaves to Illinois. When Dobbs died, he left his estate to the freedmen with Sides as executor. Sides stored the money, two boxes with more than $2,000 in silver half-dollars, in his barn in a bag of seed cotton. In 1846, Sides, his wife, and servant girl were attacked, robbed of the money, and left for dead. Their attackers set the house on fire but a rainstorm saved the building and the evidence. The leading men of Pope County, including a local doctor and a judge, formed a committee to investigate the crime. They traced a homemade butcher knife found on the scene to William Slankard. Slankard was imprisoned, and "tortured" according to some accounts, until he named the members of his band. This confession led to more arrests, perhaps more torture, and the naming of more accomplices. Among the leaders was Hiram (or Hite) Green, whose father, a "man of excellent character," owned a "valuable water mill." Gang members attempted to avoid arrest by giving back the money. Hite Green waded into a swamp and recovered the silver. Green's efforts failed. The attackers received eight years in the penitentiary, where several of them died.[10]

The Pope County Regulators acted with scrupulous attention to detail. They arrested and guarded the prisoners, gave orders to the sheriff, and foiled a rescue conspiracy. When legal authorities succeeded in transferring the trial to the county seat of Johnson County, an army of three hundred Regulators escorted their chained prisoners from Pope. After extralegal action in Pope solved the crime against Henry Sides, some Massac County men asked their neighbors in Pope to join them in a "campaign against crime." Seventy-five Pope County men joined in a sympathy march in Massac County.[11] But the Regulator movement in Massac proved less successful than that of Pope. Pope County Regulators used many of the same tactics, including arresting, whipping, and exiling gang members, later used in Massac. But although Regulators in Pope possessed evidence that allowed them to strike against perpetrators of a single crime, Massac Regulators attacked what they saw as a widespread criminal presence corrupting local politics.

Local elections in August 1846 for sheriff of Massac County came just after the resolution of the Sides case and triggered more Regulator activity. Major John W. Read, the victorious candidate, had long served as county sheriff. Twice before Read had defeated Elijah Smith, a wealthy man with little popularity or political support. In 1846, Read beat Smith again by more than three hundred votes out of five hundred. Smith and his supporters attributed Read's popularity to his Flathead connections and even brought charges of counterfeiting against him. Read's well-publicized arrest preceded but did not prevent his reelection, and a jury acquitted Read of the charges shortly thereafter. However, Smith, leading a body of Regulators, continued to torture suspects and extract confessions. Regulators tied ropes around the waists of four men, including Young Linn, and used a handspike to twist the ropes until the victims fainted. Still, they refused to implicate Read.[12]

The Regulators asserted that the "rogues" involved in the attack on Sides had elected Read and the other county officers. When Sheriff Read succeeded in jailing some Regulators, others forced him and the county clerk and state representative out of the area temporarily. The jailed men were freed.[13]

It is difficult to know how to interpret the election results. If the Regulator candidates were indeed unpopular men, the two hundred votes Smith received might indicate surprising support for the Regulators—support that might have been stronger if a more popular man had been the candidate. On the other hand, Read won by a sizable majority while under the cloud of serious allegations, suggesting that the anti-Regulator strength was substantial in Massac. And, in one account, the Regulators had ordered 150 families out of the county before the election, cutting into the Flathead electorate. Two things seem clear. First, Read may or may not have been a counterfeiter, but he had Flathead support. His acquittal meant little in a county with a history of letting criminals go free, and the refusal of Young Linn and others to implicate Read even under duress can be a testament to either Read's innocence or the loyalty of his friends. But even the Regulators acknowledged that the majority of Massac residents were Flatheads and that Flatheads formed the bulk of Read's political base—an accusation Read never denied. Second, the election results and Smith's role as both losing candidate and Regulator captain gave credence to the Flatheads' later charges that the Regulators were merely disappointed office seekers.[14]

Petitioned to send in the militia but ignorant of events in Massac County, Illinois governor Thomas Ford turned to General John T. Davis of Williamson County in August 1846. Ford ordered Davis to investigate recent events in Massac and Pope Counties, where it seemed that the people were "arrayed against each other" in such force "as to render life and property insecure and to put down the regular administration of the law." Ford requested Davis's recommendation on whether the militia should be sent into Massac to restore order.[15]

Davis had trouble raising a company of men to accompany him, but whether the men he turned to feared retaliation or inconvenience he did not say. In Massac, the sudden appearance of an emissary from the state government provoked the Regulators to abruptly adopt a conciliatory posture. They made overtures to the Flatheads, and representatives from the warring parties met at the house in Massac where Davis was staying. Each side presented proof of the other's wrongdoing. The Regulators pled that they wanted "to bring the guilty to justice and to see that the laws was justly and properly administered." Frustrated in this effort, they had resolved to drive the Flatheads from the county. The Flatheads insisted on their innocence but lacked a convincing reply to Regulator evidence against them. Davis warned the Regulators against the use of violence and the temptation to seek revenge for individual grudges. The Regulators declared that they were careful to avoid being used to settle private grievances and acted only on the agreement of four or five of their number, not on one man's urging. At a public meeting a few days later in Metropolis, Smith, the Regulator captain and defeated candidate for sheriff, made a favorable impression on Davis. Davis reported that Smith "spoke very mild and good sense."

Under Davis's mediation, both sides agreed on a committee of twelve, each side choosing six, to investigate crime over the next two months. The committee, meeting the next day, selected four men (three from the Linn family) to leave the state immediately, granted twenty days to others ordered to leave, and provided a referendum on the expulsion of others. Davis reported that the committee's work seemed popular in Massac and Johnson Counties.[16]

This extraordinary meeting proves that few were in doubt of the leadership of each group. Amazingly, the Flatheads largely confessed to their criminality and acceded to the expulsion of their more notorious figures. The flatheads no doubt agreed so quickly because they had little intention of actually leaving Massac. If Regulator violence had failed to drive them out, Davis's meetings could hardly be expected to intimidate them. And all this was done in an extralegal proceeding that drew its legitimacy from the acquiescence of both sides and the presence of state-sanctioned authority in the person of General Davis presiding over the parley.

Davis thought he had reconciled the two sides, and even attended a barbecue held in Metropolis to celebrate his successful mediation, but war broke out again when Davis left. In fact, the fighting widened. More people were drawn in by "family connections" and their views on "maintaining the supremacy of the law." If the Linns and others ordered out of the county actually left, they quickly returned.[17]

Davis had clearly recognized one source of the widening conflict when he lectured the Regulators on avenging old grudges. In arresting one reputed Flathead in late 1846 in the Metropolis Hotel, the Regulators fired on him twice, missed, but persuaded him to surrender. As they led him downstairs, a Regulator stabbed him from behind. When the victim screamed, a Methodist minister captaining the Regulators exclaimed, "Now they are using them as they should be." The governor's informants described the wounded man as a respectable, honest, industrious youth whose only crime was being related to counterfeiters. The victim and the man who stabbed him were reported to have "previously" had "some personal difference." Others maintained that personal animosities grew when some in the community refused to countenance Regulators or serve on their posses. In another case, Regulators arrested and tried the brother-in-law of Regulator Charles Shelby. Although the vigilante committee acquitted the man, they whipped and ordered him out of the county. Many neighbors charged that an old grudge existed between Shelby and his kinsman.[18]

In addition to these known instances of personal attacks, the sheer ingenuity of Regulator torture bespeaks a deep animosity and frustration on their part. Beatings, tar and feathering, and warnings to leave the neighborhood were common vigilante tactics. However, the frequently mentioned torture included strapping alleged Flatheads across logs and beating their bare backs with hickory switches. Sometimes Flatheads were tied to trees and weights hung from their arms.[19] Regulators sought confessions or demanded that their victims name accomplices. Flathead resistance may have required the Regulators to refine and perfect their techniques of interrogation. Or it may have been that the Regulators' personal dislike of men they had known as neighbors and long suspected of criminal activity provoked them to create more elaborate punishments.

The Regulators made clear their disaffection with Davis's peace agreement when the fall term of the circuit court met. The court, Judge Walter B. Scates presiding, found indictments against several Regulators, who were arrested and jailed. The Regulators' friends rallied, threatening to lynch Scates. The sheriff summoned a posse, but only sixty men responded. The Regulators outnumbered the posse in Metropolis and forced its surrender.[20]

The sheriff, state legislative representative, and others appealed to the governor for help. Governor Ford proved reluctant to act. He was about to leave office and hesitated to embark on a policy that would bind his successor. Feeling it would be useless to call out the militia to protect those whose criminality was equal to, if not greater than, that of the Regulators, Ford instead ordered Dr. William J. Gibbs of Johnson County to call on militia officers in neighboring counties for a force to protect the county officers, jurors and witnesses, and citizens of Massac. On November 11, 1846, Gibbs met county residents at the hotel in Metropolis. The meeting cobbled together another legalistic solution. Gibbs proposed, and the meeting resolved, that he should select five justices of the peace as a panel to hear accusations of wrongdoing.[21]

But Gibbs's meeting quickly proved as ineffective as Davis's. Local residents had until November 21 to bring charges to the panel. When no one came forward, Gibbs summoned the militia from neighboring Union County, but it refused to come. Both Governor Ford and his successor lamented Gibbs's inability to identify "the notorious rogues and horse thieves . . . against whom the People had become exasperated," and his subsequent declaration that because he could not find the criminals, they did not exist.[22] Some accounts suggest that Gibbs worsened an already bad situation. The Regulators, now unopposed, tried suspects by committee, beating and torturing the convicted. As the numbers of accused counterfeiters rose, the Flathead strength grew as previously neutral residents of Massac became disenchanted with Regulator justice. Gibbs's failure to resolve the dispute made it apparent that the legitimate legal processes were defunct in Massac.[23]

In November 1846, while Gibbs was in Massac, twenty Regulators attempted to arrest Mathis. Because Mathis was a common Flathead name, the elderly Mathis may have known quite a bit about Flathead activities, thus provoking the visit from the Regulator party. The "arrest" quickly turned into the brawl described earlier. Mrs. Mathis, believing her husband dead, swore out an affidavit against the Regulators. Judge Scates charged a grand jury to investigate this encounter, and it returned indictments that led to the arrest of ten Regulators. Rumor spread that the Flatheads would kill the ten men if the courts failed to convict them. The Regulators, some evidently from other parts of Illinois and Kentucky, threatened the judge, jury, and citizens. The sheriff attempted to raise

a posse and mustered sixty or seventy men, many of dubious honesty themselves. A Regulator force marched on Metropolis and met the sheriff and his
men. The sheriff hesitated and then—to avoid bloodshed—gave the prisoners to
the Regulators. The Regulators then arrested some of the posse, several of whom
were believed to have been drowned in the Ohio River.[24] On December 23, 1846,
a convention of Regulators from Massac, Pope, and Johnson Counties met at
Golconda. They once again ordered the sheriff, clerk of the county court, and
others out of the region for thirty days. The sheriff and others left for the winter.
Judge Scates succumbed to Regulator intimidation and resigned his office on
January 11, 1847. William A. Denning, who seemed neutral, replaced him a week
later.[25]

By the beginning of 1847, the governor's agents in southern Illinois had concluded that although most of the county had tired of the controversy, "there are
but few responsible men [who] take an open part in favor of the Regulators at
this time, but there are some influential men behind the curtain, and stimulating
others to act; some very abandoned, and some very honest men, who are acting
with the best intentions; and the same may be said of the Flatheads."[26] The war
had begun as an effort by honest men to rid the county of its criminal element;
by early 1847, the lines dividing the groups had grown increasingly indistinct.
Honest men now recoiled from Regulator tactics, and the dishonest often sought
to ally themselves with the Regulators in order to escape their attacks.

Again and again, the state of Illinois proved itself unequal to the task of
restoring order. Governor Ford had a much more widely publicized problem of
attacks on Mormons in northwestern Illinois. Preoccupied with the Mormons, a
powerful voting bloc in Illinois and much closer geographically to Springfield,
Ford looked forward to leaving office and passing the troubles in Massac County
on to his successor, Augustus C. French. French also hesitated. Writing Captain
George W. Akin of Franklin County in late December 1846, French confided that
he had heard so many different versions of events in Massac, none of which he
had reason to trust above any other, that he felt unable to act forcefully. French
asked Akin, to visit Massac and provide a "full and correct statement of facts."
He stressed both Akin's impartiality and his military credentials as reasons for
assigning him this task, and warned that Akin might be required to lead a
military force into the county.[27]

The state legislature also considered how best to restore order throughout the
state. Much of the debate revolved around the best use of violence to put down
violence. The representative from Macoupin thought the militia should suppress
the "mobocrats" and restore the "supremacy of the law." Others proposed establishing martial law and suspending the writ of habeas corpus. One House member explained that the legislature hesitated because the Regulators were respectable men but urged that it was now time to reassert "the preeminence of the
laws," no matter how honorable the offenders.[28]

The state felt increasing pressure to use force. Local citizens appealed to the
state government to stop the violence and chaos in southern Illinois. Darius
Phillips warned Governor French that state laws were being "trampled under-

foot by a mob in this county." Phillips had been threatened and told to leave his home of thirty years. If French intervened, he wrote, "I may hope for a few days safety of life."[29] A public meeting, held in late January in Franklin County, sent resolutions to the state government testifying that the

> unfortunate difficulties in Massac county continue unabated; the party called "Regulators," not only killing, whipping and torturing, in every way possible men, but are engaged in tearing down houses, over the head of defenceless women and children, turning them adrift in the inclemency of the weather, unprotected; insulting and abusing them; trampling under their feet all law and order, and the dearest and best rights of American citizens.

The meeting resolved: "That we have lost all confidence in the legislature passing any law to restore order, and punish the guilty," and that the legislature had wasted time "making 'buncomb' speeches," despite "the cries of innocent women and children." Because the legislature had failed to act, the meeting called upon the governor "to act *immediately* and *promptly*." The meeting further resolved that "as lovers of justice, humanity, and the maintenance of the supremacy of the laws, we cannot longer look on with indifference, while such scenes of violence are being perpetrated." Unless the state authorities acted quickly, the signatories would "take the responsibility into our hands, . . . let the consequences be what they may." Franklin County had not itself experienced Flathead or Regulator violence, so its citizens' concern provides further evidence of how severe the disruption of Massac's civic order had become. No doubt the petitioners' language struck a melodramatic note to gain the governor's and legislature's attention. Nonetheless, by the winter of 1847, large bands of armed men had roamed the region for several months, forcing more than one hundred families out of Massac County. The state capital's newspaper recorded thirty lynchings in Massac by January of 1847. Although the figures are imprecise, the problem was clearly serious.[30]

In the end, the legislature stopped short of sanctioning the use of force. Instead, on February 20, 1847, it established a district court system that would supersede the regular circuit court and remove trials from the immediate neighborhood of their occurrence, where local jurors might be influenced by intimidation from or friendship with the accused. To "preserve law and order, and put down rebellion or mobs, or combinations to prevent the execution of law," the governor could order the district court judge to call the court into session within thirty days. The legislature hoped the new system would render the more extreme alternative of calling out the militia unnecessary.[31]

Within two weeks of the law's passage, French received a petition signed by, among others, Enoch Enloe and John W. Read, asking for a district court and the militia to enforce its decisions. Enloe was Massac County's state representative and Read its sheriff. Regulators considered both men to be Flathead "tools." French's use of the law stopped short of the overt use of force but hinted at the state's coercive powers. French sent a marshal and a posse to Massac with the announced power to try offenders in a district court. French offered arms to

Denning and stressed the need for the marshal to act with "coolness, firmness, and steady energy" in identifying and rounding up Regulators from "their secret haunts."[32] If the governor had hoped that a new law would faze the Regulators, he was quickly disillusioned. The violence in Pope County subsided, but Johnson and Massac Counties remained troublesome enough that local observers insisted that more rigorous enforcement would be necessary.[33]

Judge Denning reported in February that the Regulators still held meetings and received support from Kentucky. He estimated that one hundred men would be needed to enforce the acts of the district court, and he anticipated that the Regulators would make countercharges against the criminal activities of the Flatheads. Wesley Sloan, a judge and one of the original Pope County Regulators, reported that he had told an assembly of Regulators in January that they had accomplished what they had set out to do and should quit now that the state government was against them. The Regulators not only disagreed but condemned Sloan as a tool of the "proscribed." Sloan called the Regulators "irresponsible men, many of whom are without character and respectability," unlike the Pope County men Sloan had helped organize. Emboldened by their new "power" and "self importance," they would not defer to the state. Sloan warned that Sheriff Read and others would be killed if they returned to Massac.[34] Read reported "that the Regulators are assembled nearly all the time and doing and carrying on the same as before the law was passed." Denning cautioned that since passage of the district court law, travelers in Massac had been stopped and searched to ascertain if they were agents of the governor. Two unlucky travelers had been whipped, and another tarred and feathered. Although the Regulators had promised to stop, Denning did not trust their promises. When Marshal Akin's posse conveyed more than a dozen Regulators to Benton, Franklin County, for trial on charges of breaking the peace, assaulting Mrs. Mathis, and assault to commit murder, neither the Regulators nor their attorney, Henderson P. Boyakin, expected convictions. In March 1847, some residents wrote Governor French that lawlessness in Massac was spreading.[35]

Nonetheless, there were indications that the district court law was getting off to a reasonably good start. Although many Regulators escaped Akin's posse, other turned themselves in to the district court, seventy-five miles away. According to Denning, they appeared "quite cowed." He believed that the grand jury would be able to restore order. "But if [the Regulators] are still encouraged to go on by men of influence . . . there is no telling where or when regulating will end."[36]

Denning's forebodings proved correct. Many leading Regulators avowed their honesty and attacked the district court law. Their continued defiance of the state's authority was rooted in their firm belief that they were honest men who could not possibly be subject to punishments reserved for criminals and in their experience with the ineffectiveness of the state authority that Davis and Gibbs had wielded. James A. Middleton reviewed for Governor French the history of regulating in Massac. The "honest community," finding itself without legal means of stopping the criminals and losing faith in the state government, faced either "compulsion" or being "troden down under the foot of dishonesty." It was only because the Regulators had acted that criminals had been sent to the state prison. (This was an apparent reference to the successful Pope County action in the Sides case, for there is no evidence that the Massac Regulators acted through the regular courts or sent anyone to prison. Massac's Regulators sent men out of the county or floating down the Ohio River instead, but when under attack they rallied behind the comparatively successful and less socially disruptive action that had worked so well in the neighboring county.) Regulators, denying they had done anything wrong, resisted the district court on the grounds that although willing to stand trial, they wanted the court in their own county. The district court, they asserted, was too far away and too expensive. They would allow such a court to be held in Massac because they wanted "truth and honesty and good morals" and because they thought it would "be a sin" for the honest people to fight among themselves. The new law, however, would prevent Regulator action and "therefore we despair of ever bringing those to justice or getting rid of their [criminal] associates."[37]

A resident of southern Illinois sympathetic to the Regulators described how, on the morning of April 10, 1847, seventeen or eighteen Regulators had been seized from their homes by ninety armed militiamen. They were denied bail until they reached Benton. These men, and those who had turned themselves in, were confined in crowded rooms for several days, their quarters soon becoming "disagreeable." The court forbade visits to the accused and required those discharged to pay for the expenses of their captivity. In court, Denning treated the Regulators with prejudice. They had incurred this ill treatment "for rioting and disturbing the peace and harmony of a band of *horse thieves and counterfeiters*."[38]

In response, Regulators, led by Judge Scates, attacked the constitutionality of the law. Denning credited Scates not only with encouraging the Regulators in the first place but with keeping the movement alive in the spring of 1847. Scates, with the aid of John A. McClernand, a rising Illinois politician, argued that the district court law conflicted with Article 8, section 9 of the state's constitution, which said that a trial should take place in the accused's "vicinage." Denning denied requests for a change of venue on the grounds that it would defeat the legislature's purpose in passing the law. The Regulator attorneys also argued that the district court law violated the prohibition against ex post facto laws because men were being tried for crimes committed before the district court was created. Some feared that the district court law would become a way for the state to "entitle itself to a change of venue in criminal cases, against the will of the prisoner."[39]

Sources do not make it clear why Scates, driven off the bench by Regulator threats, would defend these same men. One possible explanation is that Scates, although having no love for criminals, objected to the subversion of the law by an unconstitutional district court law. Judge Scates's ambiguous role may thus indicate just how difficult it was to ascertain the legitimate legal authority in Massac County. Like other citizens of Massac, Scates could neither entirely trust the Regulators, whose tactics included violence and extralegal activity, nor actively condemn them; the Regulators were struggling, after all, against a genuine criminal problem and now faced a state government prepared to bend the rules in order to suppress them. But this explanation for the judge's behavior may be overly complex. The Regulators, everyone acknowledged, were men of substance. Perhaps they simply had the money to buy the best possible legal talent, including that of their former victim, Judge Scates.[40]

Denning reported to French that the district court had adjourned on June 1 after an eight-day session, having obtained twenty convictions for assault, riot, and other offenses. He believed that the court had effectively ended "Regulating" and the political sentiment that had supported extralegal action. Denning argued that even if the court's decisions were overturned, "the object of the Legislation is now consummated."[41]

Although the Regulators lost the battle over the district court law's implementation, they appear to have won the war over its constitutionality. In 1847, a new state constitution included the right to a speedy public trial by an impartial jury in the "county or district" where the offense was committed. The wording of "county or district" meant that the accused could no longer be removed from local jurisdiction to a district court, as had been done to the Regulators. Delegate Thomas G. C. Davis of Massac County had proposed this language.[42]

The district court's success was short-lived. In August 1849, John W. Read was reelected for a third term as sheriff. But Read quickly found himself unable to enforce the law because of continued Regulator activity, including the intimidation of potential posse members. As one county officer reported that month, a "state of rebellion and confusion Rains throughout said County."[43] Once again, reports of a "lawless band," acting with "impunity," crossed the governor's desk. The district court law, these reports averred, had failed to end the disorder, and the state should act immediately to restore peace. Citizens of Massac still complained of the lack of "disinterested" county officers, without whom law became a "scourge" and the efforts of good citizens were "neutralized." Judge Denning was at a loss: he could not raise a posse without the governor's order, and there would be no peace until a dozen or so men were punished. He asked the governor to intervene and call a new district court.[44]

The resurgent troubles had their source in the return of the Flatheads, especially the Linn clan. One who had known the Linns for years labeled "their character one of the blacker dye." In addition to their previous crimes of counterfeiting and of stealing and selling free blacks, the Linns were now accused of murdering a man who had prosecuted the patriarch of the clan, Cheatem Linn, for stealing his slave. Some of the Linns were believed to belong to the Pennington gang, a notorious criminal ring that operated in several states. When the barn of Flathead Henry Tolson burned in 1849, two men were tried and acquitted. Several Flatheads had "coerced by threats of corporal punishment" one of the acquitted men, Andrew Douglass, into accusing Regulators Isaiah Baccus and Charles Shelby of the arson. Before either Baccus or Shelby could be tried, they became victims of Flathead beatings. Reports to the governor specifically mentioned the Linns as among those leading the attack on Shelby.[45]

The acting constable for Massac County, David Edwards, had writs for the arrest of Daniel Linn and others for the attack on Shelby. Making the arrest, however, did not prove simple. Regulators and Flatheads each had mustered forces of about one hundred men. To avoid a pitched battle, Edwards reached an agreement with State Representative Enoch Enloe and the Flathead captain. Edwards and one of the Flathead leaders selected a group of twelve, six of them Flatheads, to guard the suspects. Enloe agreed to turn over Linn and the others to Edwards at Cheatem Linn's place on July 28, 1849. When Edwards, apparently with only two men, arrived at Linn's, he found a party of at least twenty armed Flatheads who told him he would have to fight to get his suspects. Edwards retreated temporarily but returned with a force of sixty to seventy men. The Flatheads formed a line in front of the Linn house, saying they could whip five-to-one odds. When Edwards marched his men to within a hundred yards of the line, the defending Flatheads fired. The posse returned fire and charged, forcing the defenders to flee. Two Flatheads were killed and four wounded; the posse lost one dead and two wounded. Among those killed was Daniel Enloe, son of Enoch Enloe.[46]

The fight at the Linn farm further demonstrated the confusion over legal authority in the county. While Edwards's posse possessed legal writs for the arrest of the men suspected in the attack on Charles Shelby, the Flatheads had summoned some of the defenders on the pretext that they, the Flatheads, would be making a legal arrest. The Flatheads still possessed sufficient political connections to give credence to that claim. In addition, after the battle, some of the Flatheads went to Judge Denning and asked him to urge the governor to call out the militia.[47]

By August 1849, residents of southern Illinois were expecting another civil war in Massac County. According to some accounts, Flatheads had killed a Regulator informer by tying him naked to a tree in a mosquito-infested swamp. Determined to arrest the murderers, the Regulators sent to Kentucky, where many of them had family, for cannon and aid. The Flatheads barricaded themselves in a house with ammunition and two cannon taken from the Regulators.[48]

A climactic battle did not occur. There is some evidence that another district court was held in September 1849. In one account, a mob of 120 persons surrounded the courthouse and threatened to remove Denning from the bench if he impaneled a jury that they disliked. The legislature's continued interest in refining the district court law as a tool against the violence in Massac and later political rivalries in the county proved that the Regulator and Flathead conflict had not entirely disappeared, but it seems to have gone largely underground after 1849.[49]

The troubles in Massac County corresponded with a call for a special session of the legislature to deal with a number of issues, including internal improvements and electing a new senator. In his message to the special session, Governor French spoke of "difficulties of an unpleasant and embarrassing character" that had been occurring in Massac County since the legislature's adjournment. Because the sheriff had failed again to maintain order, the governor had been asked for military force; the existing law had proved "inadequate," chiefly because the 1847 constitution invalidated the district court law. French preferred civil to military force, the latter being not only expensive but ineffective. "A military force sent into the county might, indeed, preserve the peace, so far as to repress lawless outrage, but it could do little more. It could not bring a single offender to justice nor redress existing grievances. Offenders might be overawed by it, but not quelled. By the withdrawal of such force from the county, the same scenes of violence and outrage might be again renewed." He called on the legislature to act "for the vindication of the supremacy of the law."[50]

In November 1849, the legislature passed a bill to extend the jurisdiction of the circuit court. The bill resembled the district court law in its creation of a special term for the circuit court; in its requirement that jurors had to be residents only of the district, not of the county, in which rioting occurred; and in its provision that the governor, when necessary to suppress mob rule, could call a special term of the circuit court. The bill reflected the legislature's long-standing discomfort with the constitutionality of the district court bill of 1847. Still, complaints continued. In 1850, "A Deeply Injured Citizen of Massac" attributed a local murder to Regulator activity and complained that the law was still not being enforced—a condition favorable to a resurgence of the Regulators. There are no records indicating that these new circuit courts ever met to handle cases arising from the Flathead-Regulator war.[51]

In 1850, yet another political dispute in Massac County threatened trouble. Having been elected county judge in November 1849, John B. Hicks received his commission and began to hold court. However, his opponent, Angus M. L. McBane, successfully appealed the election to a three-member justice of the peace court. Hicks turned to the circuit court, now reestablished with expanded powers by the legislature's act of November 1849, to protest the decision of the justice of the peace court in McBane's favor. Hicks's faction maintained that the majority of the justices of the peace on the court were Regulators, as was McBane. McBane asserted that the Flatheads had declared they must defeat him or lose control of Massac County altogether. By 1850, Hicks had been a county official of long standing in the county. He had been appointed circuit clerk by Judge Scates in 1843, when Massac County was first organized (and would serve often in that capacity until 1864). Hicks and McBane once again demonstrate the deep roots of both Flatheads and Regulators in the county's political community. Hicks possessed an extended political career as did other presumed Flatheads. McBane was related to Metropolis's founder, William McBane. Although the worst of the violent outbreaks were evidently over before 1850, neither the Regulators nor the Flatheads disappeared as factions in Massac society.[52]

Many accounts of the occurrences in Massac County discuss the lasting effects of the violence. One declared that Massac continued to have a "lawless spirit." One man recalled that the "enmities aroused by that conflict lasted for several generations."[53] Although by the 1850s some stated that "disturbances died away and law assumed sway," the Flatheads remained in the county. In 1866, a man named Linn harbored horse thieves and stolen horses from other counties.

Clearly, the state succeeded in breaking the organized Regulator movement. Although McBane's challenge to Hicks's election indicates the Regulators remained as a political faction, the Linns' continued presence and outlawry in Massac County indicates that the Regulators had learned to tolerate a certain amount of criminal activity. Conflict on the scale of the 1840s had dissipated, but neither side had completely disappeared.[54]

What made the Massac County disturbances unusual was the "nearly equal" split between the two sides in the community. Governor John Reynolds noted this division when he compared the disturbance with others in Illinois at that time. But this phenomenon is not without precedent in United States history, as one can see from Robert Utley's discussion of the Lincoln County War or Richard Maxwell Brown's of the activities of the South Carolina Regulators, events in which the forces arrayed on each side were relatively equal in numbers and power. However, Massac County seems not to fit the pattern of violence arising from the struggle for control of economic resources, as occurred in such famous vigilante outbreaks as those of San Francisco, Revolutionary-era North Carolina, or Gilded Age Lincoln, New Mexico. The Flatheads were a criminal gang, many of whose economic activities were genuinely illegal. Their power arose not merely from their use of violence but also from the numbers that gave them political power.[55]

Massac County also distinguished itself by the elasticity of the definitions for each side. "Flathead" quickly came to mean not just the criminals but all who disagreed with the Regulators' methods. The fuzziness of group boundaries further impeded honest members of the community from finding the best way to uphold legitimate legal authority. Like many cases of vigilantism, that of Massac County followed a common pattern: Acting from the highest motives, "[s]ome of the best men of the county," who, "had they stopped at the right time, their conduct would have been generally approbated by the best men in the south of the State," instead "finally became a greater problem to the governor and authorities than the criminal class itself."[56]

The Regulators, one commentator noted, began with "the moderate and honest intention of exterminating notorious rogues only." However, they quickly incurred the opposition of citizens who firmly believed "that the laws of the country are amply sufficient for the punishment and prevention of crime." To maintain their assumed authority in the face of increasing opposition, the Regulators became increasingly lawless, and "in this mode, that which at first was merely a war between honest men and rogues, is converted into a war between honest men alone, one party contending for the supremacy of the laws, and the other maintaining its own assumed authority." The Regulators' defense attorney in the 1847 district court, Henderson P. Boyakin, wrote Governor French:

> Good men have taken the administration of what they call Justice into their own hands; and I fear they have to some extent been encouraged in it by those of whom we might have hoped for better things. They have assured me time and again that in the first instance their intentions were good, and they were even no more than an association of men engaged in arresting and bringing to Justice felons thieves &c

pursuant to Law. That to avoid them many bad men gained their ranks and commenced to violate the Laws. Hence many of them abandoned the association entirely.[57]

Written at a time when state authorities attacked regulating, some of this pleading that criminals had infiltrated their ranks was doubtless self-serving. Nonetheless, the difficulty of identifying Flatheads and Regulators arose from the deep roots each party had in the community. Family connections linked genuine criminals to honest men, who were then tainted by those connections.

Many studies of vigilantes have rooted their violence in political and economic conditions.[58] The violence in Massac County had such links. It would be a mistake, however, to ignore the vital role of legal institutions relative to incidents of Regulator violence. "Law and order" depends as much on what the community agrees to be permissible or impermissible behavior as it does on the letter of the law. A recent study of the Hatfield and McCoy feud argues that the court system possessed legitimacy in that Appalachian region, and that the Hatfields and McCoys had a long history of resolving their disputes through that system. Only when the courts became the arenas for outside forces, those of late nineteenth-century capitalism, did they lose their legitimacy with the local people, who then turned to extralegal means. Violence is not necessarily the opposite of law and order but often an attempt to preserve the social order against the alleged subversive threat of those who seem to endanger it.[59]

The Massac Regulators certainly attempted to use violence to achieve law-and-order, but because they failed to create or sustain a local consensus that legitimized their activities, they made it possible for the Flatheads, the alleged criminals, to turn the law-and-order argument against them. Ironically, in seeking various legal solutions to end the violence in Massac County, the state of Illinois pursued a course that could prove effective only by relying on the state-sanctioned use of coercion and the potential use of violence—namely, the threat of militia, and of marshal and posse. The Massac County war thus demonstrated not only the importance of legitimate legal authority in preventing violence but also the intimate connection of that authority to the legitimate wielding of official force.

Massac County vigilantism differs from the classic cases of vigilantism that emphasize the "extralegal" nature of this type of violence.[60] Nothing about Massac vigilantism was extralegal; instead, all the controversy revolved around the functioning, or malfunctioning, of legal authority. The violence was rooted less in the frontier experience than in the lack of a commonly agreed-upon legal authority in the county. The two may indeed be linked, as some authors have suggested.[61] Legal systems are weaker and more prone to break down on a frontier where those institutions are newer and more fragile. But it is the inability of the legal system to function, regardless of whether the location is a frontier or a long-settled region, that leads to conflict. In Massac County, local courts never possessed legitimacy. The legal system could not function in Massac because the county was so evenly divided between Flatheads and Regulators: both sides claimed legitimate legal authority and both sides committed crimes. The state of Illinois possessed the authority to restore order but either hesitated to act or acted ineffectively by passing a district court law that temporarily suppressed the Regulators but that remained open to challenges to its constitutionality. The contested election of 1849, and the complaints of illegal activity that continued into the 1850s, indicate that the tensions that gave rise to the Regulator-Flathead war were not fully ended. At best, residents of Massac County had found that extralegal violence did little to restore the civic order they desired.

NOTES

1. George W. May, *History of Massac County, Illinois* (Galesburg: Wagoner Print, 1955) 86; James A. Rose, "The Regulators and Flatheads in Southern Illinois," *Transactions of the Illinois State Historical Society for the Year 1906* (Springfield: Illinois State Historical Society, 1906), 108–21, esp. 114–16.

2. Thomas Ford, *A History of Illinois, from Its Commencement as a State in 1818 to 1847* (Chicago: S. C. Griggs, 1854), 438, 442–44; Theodore Calvin Pease, *The Frontier State, 1818–1848* (Chicago: A. C. McClurg, 1922), 428–29.

3. Jens Lund, *Flatheads and Spooneys: Fishing for a Living in the Ohio River Valley* (Lexington: University Press of Kentucky, 1995), 176–77.

4. Clare V. McKanna, Jr., "Alcohol, Handguns, and Homicide in the American West: A Tale of Three Counties, 1880–1920," *Western Historical Quarterly* 26 (winter 1995): 455–82; [James A. Rose], *Papers Relating to the Regulator and Flathead Trouble in Southern Illinois* (Springfield, Ill.: n.p., n.d.), 2–3; May, *History of Massac County*, 81; Rose, "Regulators and Flatheads," 113–14.

5. [Rose], *Papers Relating to the Regulator and Flathead Trouble*, 2–3; Federal Writers' Project, Work Projects Administration, *Illinois: A Descriptive and Historical Guide* (Chicago: A. C. McClurg, 1939), 433–34.

6. *The Seventh Census of the United States: 1850* (Washington: R. Armstrong, 1853), 701–2, 713, 731–32.

7. Charles S. Neely, *Tales and Songs of Southern Illinois* (Menasha, Wis.: George Bants, 1938), 35; Gen. Green B. Raum, in [Rose], *Papers Relating to the Regulator and Flathead Trouble*; May, *History of Massac County*, 78–79.

8. Ford, *History of Illinois*, 437–38.

9. Ibid., 232–33; O. J. Page, *History of Massac County, Illinois* (Metropolis, Ill.: n.p., 1900), 78–79. Alice Louise Brumbaugh, "The Regulator Movement in Illinois" (master's thesis, University of Illinois, Urbana, 1927), 29–30, says the Sturdevant gang members all escaped.

10. Statement of Mrs. C. P. Boazman and Raum, in [Rose], *Papers Relating to the Regulator and Flathead Trouble*; Rose, "Regulators and Flatheads," 108–13; Page, *History of Massac County*, 77–79; May, *History of Massac County*, 78–79, 81; Ford, *History of Illinois*, 437–38; *Illinois State Register* (Springfield), January 22, 1847; *Sangamo Journal*, August 21, 1845.

11. Rose, "Regulators and Flatheads," 111–13; Raum in [Rose], *Papers Relating to the Regulator and Flathead Trouble*.

12. *Illinois State Register* (Springfield), January 22, 1847; *Sangamo Journal*, January 28, 1847; Newton Bateman and Paul Selby, *Historical Encyclopedia of Illinois* (Chicago: Munsell, 1904), 355; Ford, *History of Illinois*, 438.

13. Ford, *History of Illinois*, 438; Bateman and Selby, *Historical Encyclopedia*, 355; May, *History of Massac County*, 82–83.

14. Rose, "Regulators and Flatheads," 114–16; "Communication from the Governor Relative to the Difficulties in the County of Massac," in [Rose], *Papers Relating to the Regulator and Flathead Trouble*.

15. Gov. Ford to Brigadier General John T. Davis, September 1846, Governors' Correspondence, 1816–1852 (Illinois State Archives, Springfield); cited hereafter as Governors' Correspondence. Ford, *History of Illinois*, 439.

16. John T. Davis to Ford, October 6, 1846, Governors' Correspondence.

17. John Moses, *Illinois: Historical and Statistical*, 2 vols. (Chicago: Fergus Print, 1895), 513–14; Brumbaugh, "Regulator Movement," 39; Bateman and Selby, *Historical Encyclopedia*, 355; May, *History of Massac County*, 84.

18. Ford, *History of Illinois*, 442–44; "Communication from the Governor Relative to the Difficulties in the County of Massac," and Boazman, in [Rose], *Papers Relating to the Regulator and Flathead Trouble*, n.p.; *Sangamo Journal*, January 28, 1847.

19. Rose, "Regulators and Flatheads," 114–16.

20. Moses, *Illinois*, 513–14.

21. Ford, *History of Illinois*, 441–42; *Illinois State Register* (Springfield), November 27, 1846.

22. August C. French to Doct. W. J. Gibbs, December 21, 1846, in Evarts Boutell Greene and Charles Manfred Thompson, eds., *Governors' Letter-Books, 1840–1853* (Springfield: Trustees of the Illinois State Historical Library, 1911), 135; May, *History of Massac County*, 85–86; Ford, *History of Illinois*, 441–42; Rose, "Regulators and Flatheads," 115–16.

23. Rose, "Regulators and Flatheads," 114–16; Ford, *History of Illinois*, 441–42; Moses, *Illinois*, 513–14.

24. May, *History of Massac County*, 86; Rose, "Regulators and Flatheads," 114–16; Andrew Douglass Affidavit, July 30, 1849, Governors' Correspondence; Ford, *History of Illinois*, 442–44; "Communication from the Governor Relative to the Difficulties in the County of Massac," in [Rose], *Papers Relating to the Regulator and Flathead Trouble*; James A. Middleton to Gov. French, May 21, 1847, box 1, Augustus C. French Papers (Illinois State Historical Society, Springfield).

25. Bateman and Selby, *Historical Encyclopedia*, 355; May, *History of Massac County*, 87; Ford, *History of Illinois*, 440–41, 444; Rose, "Regulators and Flatheads," 116; Brumbaugh, "Regulator Movement," 44, 49; May, *History of Massac County*, 84; Executive Record of Illinois, in [Rose], *Papers Relating to the Regulator and Flathead Trouble*.

26. "Communication from the Governor Relative to the Difficulties in the County of Massac," in [Rose], *Papers Relating to the Regulator and Flathead Trouble*.

27. Aug. C. French to Capt. Aiken, December 21, 1846, in Greene and Thompson, *Governors' Letter-Books*, 133–35; Rose, "Regulators and Flatheads," 117. August C. French to Doct. W. J. Gibbs, December 21, 1846, in Greene and Thompson, *Governors' Letter-Books*, 135; Ford, *History of Illinois*, 441–42.

28. *Sangamo Journal*, January 14, 1847; *Illinois State Register*, January 8, 15, 1847.

29. Darius Phillips to Gov. French, n.d., box 1, French Papers.

30. Communication from the Governor, February 19, 1847, Reports Made to the House of Representatives of the State of Illinois (Springfield: State of Illinois, 1846), 299–300; *Sangamo Journal*, January 28, 1847.

31. "An Act to Establish District Courts in the State of Illinois," *Laws of the State of Illinois, 15th General Assembly session begun Dec. 1846* (Springfield, 1847), 44–46; *Journal of*

the Senate of the Fifteenth General Assembly of the State of Illinois (Springfield: State of Illinois, 1846), 63, 83, 99, 131–40, 153–54, 238, 281; *Journal of the House of Representatives of the Fifteenth General Assembly of the State of Illinois* (Springfield: State of Illinois, 1846), 91, 95, 102–3, 108, 115, 150, 152, 160, 198, 207, 229–30, 279, 343, 401, 470, 484, 496; *Reports Made to the Senate and House of Representatives of the State of Illinois* (Springfield: State of Illinois, 1846), 171; Greene and Thompson, *Governors' Letter-Books*, 133 n. 2; Ford, *History of Illinois*, 444–45; Rose, "Regulators and Flatheads," 118.

32. Enoch Enloe et al. to Gov. French, March 8, 1847, box 1, French Papers; A.C.F. to Wm. A. Denning, March 27, 1847, in Greene and Thompson, *Governors' Letter-Books*, 141–42; "Executive Record of Illinois," March 27, 1847, in [Rose], *Papers Relating to the Regulator and Flathead Trouble*; Rose, "Regulators and Flatheads," 118.

33. Thomas C. Davis to French, March 19, 1847, box 1, French Papers.

34. W. A. Denning to French, February 28, 1847; Wesley Sloan to French, March 5, 1847; and H. P. Boyakin to Gov. French, March 16, 1847, all in box 1, French Papers.

35. George W. Akin to Gov. French, March 23, 1847; W. A. Denning to French, March 16, 1847; H. P. Boyakin to Gov. French, April 17, 1847; M. C. Cunningham to Gov. French, March 5, 1847, all in box 1, French Papers.

36. W. A. Denning to French, April 24, 1847, box 1, French Papers; Rose, "Regulators and Flatheads," 118.

37. James A. Middleton to Gov. French, May 21, 1847, box 1, French Papers.

38. *Sangamo Journal*, July 23, 1847.

39. Ford, *History of Illinois*, 444–45; *Sangamo Journal*, July 28, 1847; W. A. Denning to French, April 24, 1847; John Daugherty to A. C. French, June 1, 1847, both in box 1, French Papers.

40. Switching sides was not unheard of in Massac County. Richard S. Nelson, a Regulator supporter who had left them when their illegalities and violence became apparent, was so disaffected that he became a lawyer for the Flatheads. *Sangamo Journal*, January 7, 1847; Brumbaugh, "Regulator Movement," 38.

41. W. A. Denning to French, June 2, 1847; Richard S. Nelson to Gov. French, June 3, 1847, both in box 1, French Papers.

42. *Journal of the Convention . . . Altering, Amending, or Revising the Constitution of the State of Illinois* (Springfield: Lanphier & Walker, 1847), sec. 9.

43. Affidavits of William W. Clark, John W. Read, David Leach, John McDonald, Reuben King, and Samuel Musselman in [Rose], *Papers Relating to the Regulator and Flathead Trouble*; Greene and Thompson, *Governors' Letter-Books*, 133 n. 2; May, *History of Massac County*, 88.

44. Francis M. Rawlings to A. C. French, August 9, 1849, in [Rose], *Papers Relating to the Regulator and Flathead Trouble*; John W. Carmichael to Denning, [August 8, 1849]; Wm. McLean to French, August 11, 1849; W. A. Denning to French, August 8, 1849, all in Governors' Correspondence.

45. Affidavits of G. M. Gray and Andrew Douglass; John W. Carmichael to Denning, [August 8, 1849]; Lt. Richard Peters to Gov. French, August 12, 1849, all in Governors' Correspondence; *Sangamo Journal*, January 28, 1847; Brumbaugh, "The Regulator Movement," 30–32; Jno. H. Wood, Sr., to Augustus C. French, October 20, 1849, box 1, French Papers.

46. David Edwards et al. Affidavit, August 10, 1849; Lt. Richard Peters to Gov. French, August 12, 1849, both in Governors' Correspondence; Jno. H. Wood, Sr., to Augustus C. French, October 20, 1849, box 1, French Papers; Brumbaugh, "Regulator Movement," 55–56.

47. Lt. Richard Peters to Gov. French, August 12, 1849, Governors' Correspondence.

48. Theodore Calvin Pease, *The Frontier State, 1818–1848* (Chicago, 1922), 429.

49. Act for the Relief of William J. Stephenson, *Private Laws of the State of Illinois*, 17th General Assembly, 1st sess. (Springfield: State of Illinois , 1851), 176; Brumbaugh, ''Regulator Movement,'' 63.

50. F. D. Preston to French, April 12, 1849; P. C. Morris to French, June 28, 1849; A. Wentworth to French, June 23, 1849, all in box 1, French Papers; Message to the Special Session, October 23, 1849, *Journal of the Senate of the Sixteenth General Assembly of the State of Illinois at Its Second Session* (Springfield: State of Illinois, 1849), 12–13. The auditor's office recorded a total of $7,809.19 spent in 1847 and 1848 on the district court, particularly in fees to Marshall Akin and his posse and witnesses. Auditor's Ledger, in [Rose], *Papers Relating to the Regulator and Flathead Trouble*.

51. ''Act to Extend the Jurisdiction of the Circuit Courts of the State of Illinois,'' *Laws of the State of Illinois*, 16th General Assembly, 2d sess. (Springfield: State of Illinois , 1849), 8–10; [Rose], *Papers Relating to the Regulator and Flathead Trouble*; Rose, ''Regulators and Flatheads,'' 120; May, *History of Massac County*, 89; Journal of the House of Representative of the Sixteenth General Assembly of the State of Illinois (Springfield: State of Illinois, 1849), 3, 56–57, 60, 77–78, 172; Journal of the Senate of the Sixteenth General Assembly of the State of Illinois (Springfield: State of Illinois, 1849), 85, 120, 147, 157; Journal of the House of Representatives of the Sixteenth General Assembly of the State of Illinois at Its Second Session (Springfield: State of Illinois, 1849), 18, 23, 39, 44–46, 61; Journal of the Senate of the Sixteenth General Assembly of the State of Illinois at Its Second Session (Springfield: State of Illinois, 1849), 50; ''A Deeply Injured Citizen of Massac'' to Augustus C. French, January 28, 1850, box 2, French Papers.

52. J. W. Bailey, February 4, 1850; William J. Allen to Gov. French, February 5, 1850; Affidavit of John W. Read, February 6, 1850; Richard S. Nelson to Gov. French, February 8, 1850, A. M. S. McBane to Augustus C. French, February 13, 1850, all in box 2, French Papers; Page, *History of Massac County*, 56.

53. Moses, *Illinois*, 513–14; Neely, *Tales and Songs of Southern Illinois*, 35. See also Bateman and Selby, *Historical Encyclopedia*, 355.

54. May, *History of Massac County*, 89–90.

55. John Reynolds, *My Own Times: Embracing Also the History of My Life* (Chicago: B. H. Perryman, 1879), 114; Robert M. Utley, *High Noon in Lincoln: Violence on the Western Frontier* (Albuquerque: University of New Mexico Press, 1987); Robert M. Senkewicz, *Vigilantes in Gold Rush San Francisco* (Stanford: Stanford University Press, 1985); Richard Maxwell Brown, *The South Carolina Regulators* (Cambridge: Harvard University Press, Belknap Press, 1963); John S. Bassett, ''The Regulators of North Carolina (1765–1771),'' *Annual Report of the American Historical Association for the Year 1894* (Washington, D.C.: American Historical Association, 1895), 141–212.

56. Boazman, in [Rose], *Papers Relating to the Regulator and Flathead Trouble*; *Illinois State Register* (Springfield), January 22, 1847; Henry Clyde Hubbart, *The Older Middle West, 1840–1880: Its Social, Economic and Political Life and Sectional Tendencies before, during and after the Civil War* (New York: D. Appleton-Century, 1936), 41.

57. Ford, *History of Illinois*, 439–40; H. P. Boyakin to Gov. French, April 25, 1847, box 1, French Papers.

58. Senkewicz, *Vigilantes in Gold Rush San Francisco*; Brown, South Carolina Regulators.

59. Philip S. Paludan, ''The American Civil War Considered as a Crisis in Law and Order,'' *American Historical Review* 77 (October 1972): 1013–34; Altina L. Waller, *Feud:*

Hatfields, McCoys, and Social Change in Appalachia, 1860–1900 (Chapel Hill: University of North Carolina Press, 1988).

60. Richard Maxwell Brown, "The American Vigilante Tradition," in *The History of Violence in America: Historical and Comparative Perspectives*, ed. Hugh Davis Graham and Ted Robert Gurr (New York: Praeger, 1969), 154–226, esp. 154–213; Roger D. McGrath, *Gunfighters, Highwaymen, and Vigilantes: Violence on the Frontier* (Berkeley: University of California Press, 1984), 225, 245.

61. Joe B. Frantz, "The Frontier Tradition: An Invitation to Violence," in Graham and Gurr, *History of Violence in America*, 127–54; Richard Maxwell Brown, "Historical Patterns of Violence in America," in Graham and Gurr, *History of Violence in America*, 45–84; Mabel A. Elliott, "Crime and the Frontier Mores," *American Sociological Review* 9 (April 1944): 185–92.

Women could defend themselves, but men should enact vengeance. W. Gilmore Simms, *Guy Rivers: A Tale of Georgia* (New York: A. C. Armstrong, 1882), 255.

Chapter Eight

Armed and "More or Less Dangerous"
Women and Violence in American Frontier Literature, 1820–1860

Laura McCall

"The vote means nothing to women. We should be armed."

—Edna O'Brien, in Robert Byrne,
The Woman's Calendar, 1993

Studies of women in frontier literature commonly feature reluctant pioneers who hated wilderness and feared Indians. Taken west against their wills, women were isolated and lonely, toiled in endless drudgery, and received little recognition for their efforts. Women have been described as conquests or prizes to be won in a region where they were rare or, in their capacity as civilizers, have been blamed for destroying wild country.[1] Regarded as intruders, they have been targeted as the chief cause of historic racism in the United States.[2]

Although countless monographs document violence against women and thereby highlight their role as passive victims, studies that analyze them as aggressors are virtually nonexistent.[3] This gap undoubtedly reflects certain realities—only 10 percent of present-day violent crimes are committed by women, and only 15 percent of American women own a handgun, compared with 50 percent of the men—but it also reflects a sentiment deeply rooted in our culture. Because women are seen as the nurturers and civilizers of society who have been trained to be less aggressive, many Americans do not wish to accept the possibility they might be capable of, or even know how to commit, acts of brutality.[4]

This essay examines a long-neglected aspect of frontier literature: women who were familiar with the use of firearms or other weapons, and women who committed violent acts. Current scholarship emphasizes the passivity and submissiveness of antebellum American women, which apparently was reinforced by novels in the genteel tradition. A systematic analysis of 104 best-selling novels and 304 female characters, however, reveals that, at least fictionally, women were capable of ferocious behavior.[5] They fought in wars, defended themselves against

Indian attack, and shielded their honor. Whether violent or not, the over-whelming majority of women in this sample were not docile or submissive responders, and their repeated presence in four decades of antebellum literature challenges several notions about the alleged "true womanhood" ideal.[6]

In eighty-eight of the stories studied, frontier or rural America was the chief setting; in the remaining sixteen, it was a secondary setting. The physical land-scape figured prominently in ninety-three of these tales; Native Americans were extremely or somewhat important in forty-two; and violence was central to twenty-four of the stories and of some importance in thirty-six. Twenty-three of the stories featured organized warfare; thirty-four described battles with Native Americans; sixteen discussed "violence born of sexual dishonor"; thirty-nine included "violence born of wealth and power"; seventeen described violence arising out of family disputes; and fifteen touched upon vigilantism.[7]

Despite the critical emphasis placed on women's "civilizing mission," only twenty-nine of the stories expressed the notion of woman as a "civilizing force (usually identified with the East) in a Western, uncivilized environment."[8] The character codebook elicited more specific information about individual women and tested the hypotheses of scholars who have designated images of pioneer women. Only 12.2 percent of the characters, however, were classified as "refined ladies," 22.7 percent as helpmates, and a mere 0.7 percent as mannish or promis-cuous.[9]

Slightly more than 15 percent of the women in this sample were familiar with the use of firearms and other weapons. In Mrs. W. H. Corning's *Western Border Life* (1856), Madame Granby, who manages the farm in Kansas after her hus-band's death, is asked by Nanny Catlett if her isolated existence arouses fear: " 'What should I be afraid of, child? Why, bless you, I keep a loaded gun at the head of the bed, and I'd shoot down the first person that entered my premises just as quick as I'd shoot a squirrel.' " The protagonist of Ann Stephens's *Sybil Chase* (1861), a novel set in the California goldfields, owns a delicately worked Colt revolver she carries for protection: "But, small and fanciful as it was, the weapon would have been a dangerous instrument in the hands of that woman had interest or self-preservation rendered it necessary for her to use it. She loaded the several barrels with dexterity and quickness, which betrayed a perfect knowledge of her task . . . and hid the pistol in her pocket." *Mary Derwent*, Ste-phens's 1858 novel of Revolutionary turmoil set in the Wyoming Valley of Penn-sylvania, describes a frontier matriarch thoroughly familiar with the use of a musket. While her granddaughters are frozen with fright in the face of impend-ing attack, "Mother Derwent was affected differently, and bringing down the old rusty rifle that had belonged to her son, set to work and scoured out the lock, and wiped the muzzle with a piece of oiled deer-skin, which she afterwards wrapped around her bullets when she was ready to load."[10]

In James Fenimore Cooper's *The Deerslayer* (1841), Chingachgook and Natty Bumppo discover a cache of rifles and decide to have a shooting match: "On the present occasion, it only remained to freshen the primings, and each piece was in a state for service. This was soon done, as all assisted in it, the females being as expert in this part of the system of defense as their male companions." Yet earlier in this novel, Cooper expressed a mild ambivalence about women's knowledge of firearms, which may explain why other critics, many of whom rely heavily on Cooper, conclude that women were timid and afraid. This scene more likely reflects Cooper's ambivalence toward the major female character, Judith Hutter, whom he described in his preface as an "admirable" and stoic but fallen woman who deserved the reader's guarded respect:

> Judith, in the main, was a girl of great personal spirit, and her habits prevented her from feeling any of the terror that is apt to come over her sex at the report of firearms. She had discharged many a rifle, and had even been known to kill a deer, under circumstances that were favorable to the effect.[11]

William Gilmore Simms, the enormously popular southern novelist and biographer, invoked a similar reaction in his description of heroine Margaret Cooper, another fallen woman, who inspects the pistols of her late father.

> She had often, with a boldness not common to the sex, examined these pistols. . . . Often and again had she handled these weapons, poising them and addressing them at objects as she had seen her father do. On one occasion she had been made to discharge them, under his own instructions; she had done so without terror.[12]

These instances prove that some women displayed a familiarity with firearms and were unflinchingly capable of using them. In fact, 10.5 percent of the women in this sample did. The majority of these committed violence in response to Indian attack, followed by violence within the family, violence born of wealth or power, in organized warfare, or in defending their sexual honor. Two characters engaged in extralegal or vigilante activities. A notable number of women were hunters.

Despite Dawn Lander's assertion that one of the main themes of American wilderness literature was "hunting as a sacred and exclusively masculine activity," which reinforced the image of wilderness as "an exclusively masculine domain," antebellum fiction depicted women who were Dianas of the chase.[13] Judith Hutter had been known to bring down a deer, and Capitola Black, the heroine of E. D. E. N. Southworth's *The Hidden Hand* (1859), owns a "game-bag, powder-flask, shot-horn and fowling-piece." Calling "her favorite pointer," she goes birding and returns with a brace of partridges. Gleefully, she tells her cousin: "Oh, you should have been out with me and Sweetlips! we've had *such* sport!" In Cooper's The Pioneers (1823), Elizabeth Temple, feeling "inclined to try my chance for a bird," wants to join the Christmas Day turkey shoot. When Oliver Edwards exclaims: "Is this a sport for a lady!" Elizabeth retorts: "Why not, sir? If it be inhuman, the sin is not confined to one sex only."[14]

Frontier women were often called upon to assist the men in their defense against Indian attack. In James Kirke Paulding's *The Puritan and His Daughter* (1849), the Tyringham and Habingdon households prepare for Indian combat. The men position themselves at strategic loopholes, and the women, "having refused to retire to an inner apartment, were to supply ammunition as it might be wanted."[15] In Paulding's *Westward Ho!* (1832), heroine Virginia Dangerfield recalls the early days in Kentucky when "I and my dear mother, have more than once stood by our husband and father, when the savages were approaching to set fire to our house, loading the guns that he and his people were discharging at the painted warriors."[16] In the same tale, backwoodsman Bushfield describes the Indian attack that killed his mother and sister but not until "[t]hey barred the doors and windows, and my little sister loaded the gun, which my mother fired as fast as she loaded. They killed two of the varmints, the others set fire to the house."[17] In David Belisle's *The American Family Robinson* (1854), the Duncan family discover they are surrounded by hostile tribes and, with the exception of two children, the entire party is armed. "Mrs. Duncan and Jane [age fifteen] could handle a rifle with as much precision as was necessary to protect themselves in an emergency." Later, when the Crows descend upon their encampment, Martin Duncan fires upon the first Indian and Mrs. Duncan "raised her rifle and another fell beneath her aim; at the same moment Jane's rifle disabled another."[18]

Women also engaged in colonial and Revolutionary War skirmishes. In Cooper's *Wyandotte* (1843), the inhabitants of the Hutted Knoll prepare for a siege from rebel irregulars and their Indian allies. The valley could muster at least thirty-three able-bodied men, and there could also "be added some ten or fifteen women, who had occasionally brought down a deer, and who might be thought more or less dangerous, stationed at a loop with a rifle or musket." Nevertheless, when the knoll is actually besieged, Cooper reveals his typical ambivalence toward women and warfare when he writes that "the women and children were up also; many of the former repairing to the loops, while the least resolute, or the less experienced of their number, administered to the wants of the young, or busied themselves with the concerns of the household."[19]

In *The Yemassee* [sic] (1835), a fictional account of the Yamassee War of 1715–1716, William Gilmore Simms skillfully portrays Mary Granger, who is set up as a foil to illustrate men's rashness and imprudence. Described as "a tall, fine looking woman, of much masculine beauty," with her hair "cut short like that of a man," Mary was usually "gentle and even humble in her usual speech [but] there were moments when her tone was that of reckless defiance." As a result, Mary "preserved her own and commanded the respect of others."[20] Mary is both braver and smarter than her trader husband. Marriage had "carried her into dangers, to which he could oppose with far less ability than his wife. Her genius soared infinitely above his own, and to her teachings he was indebted for many of those successes which brought him wealth in after years."[21]

Mary Granger's heroism throughout the novel contrasts sharply with the indecision and confusion of the men. When the men of the settlement refuse to relinquish the peace treaty and wampum to Chief Sanutee, Mary seizes the documents and throws them to the tribe. Her action buys the settlement time because, without the treaty, Sanutee and his warriors would have razed the village. Later, Mary, "who had been something more observant than her husband," notes that the Indians are trading with a Spanish vessel that is supplying them with arms that may be used against the colonists. The Grangers inform commander Gabriel Harrison, who urges the trader to spy on the Indian camp and determine their designs. Richard Granger balks at this suggestion, but his wife insists they will go together. Harrison praises Mary's "noble, strong, and manly soul, such as would shame thousands of the more presumptuous sex."[22]

Mary is also the only person who remains composed during preparations against the Indian siege. She successfully counsels the hero, Walter Grayson, against sending men out of the fort, insisting that their best tactic is to plan for the defense of the stockade. And, as author Simms sarcastically interjects, she succeeds without offending "the *amour propre* of the nobler animal." Simms becomes so carried away describing her fortitude that he mistakenly substitutes "himself" for "herself" (an error he failed to correct in the 1853 edition) while describing her participation in this debate and her cool deliberation "when all was confusion among the councils of men."[23]

Finally, Mary Granger is capable of violence. When an Indian tries to enter the blockhouse apartment containing the women and children, Mary, who is keeping watch, prepares to attack him with a hatchet. Upon discovering that his adversary is a woman, the Indian responds "with something of a chuckle." "But it was a woman with a man's spirit with whom he contended," and when he tries to pull her out of the second-story window, she eludes his grasp. When he again attempts to crawl through the window, she grabs his arm and "pressed the arm across the window until her ears heard the distinct, clear crack of the bone—until she heard the groan, and felt the awful struggles of the suffering wretch." Mary releases the Indian only after he faints in pain; then "a crashing fall of the heavy body among the branches of the tree at the foot of the window" is heard.[24]

Additionally, women assertively defended their family names or sexual honor. In Mary Jane Holmes's *Lena Rivers* (1856), the protagonist and her aged friend Mrs. Nichols are insulted by John Livingstone because they are Yankees newly arrived in Kentucky. "Lena darted forward hitting him a blow in the face, which he returned by puffing smoke into hers, whereupon she snatched the cigar from his mouth and hurled it into the street bidding him 'touch her again if he dared.'" Lena's actions win John's respect, and he later tells his friend Durward Bellmont, "[w]hen she dealt me that blow in my face, my admiration was complete."[25]

On rare occasions, women also defended themselves against sexual innuendo or in the wake of seduction. Literary critic Daryl Jones has argued that "in the sentimental novel, sex and death were inextricably related." According to his analysis, heroines in the sentimental tradition were typically caught between two suitors, one motivated "by lust and greed" and the other offering "pure romantic love." The sentimental novel "established the villain as a specifically sexual symbol of universal evil who, by attempting to seduce the heroine, was striving to overcome the power of good in the world. It was necessary, then, that the villain be destroyed." Jones, however, furnishes no evidence that fictional women engaged in such destruction until the emergence of the dime novel in the late nineteenth century. In women, "the desire for vengeance is born of sexual dishonor. The dime novel western abounds with aggressive women who thirst for the blood of the men who ruined them."[26]

Despite allegations that the content of antebellum novels reflected "the appalling popularity of the seduction motif,"[27] only twelve of the women in this sample (4 percent) fell from virtue in the strictest sense of the word. More interesting is the manner in which they were portrayed. Contrary to previous assessments that "American literature seemed to express an increasing consciousness of the evil in women" by depicting them as "coldhearted, dishonest and morally seductive" or that women were "drugged, tricked, coerced, mesmerized, hypnotized or otherwise ensnared," these women fell for other reasons. Commonly, they were tragic figures who were victims of a careless upbringing, a profligate male, or their own innocence. Despite assertions that "to be guilty of such a crime ... brought madness or death" or that "seduction meant homicide" or that "the only truly honorable alternative for fallen women in Victorian society was suicide," the fates of these women were far more diverse and usually less horrifying.[28] Only four died; four others were shunned by their communities; and two married and settled down. None ended their days in a lunatic asylum or as prostitutes, although one story concluded with the suggestion that the woman would continue her dissolute life.

Very few men or women sought vengeance in the aftermath of sexual disgrace. Antebellum authors preferred to seal the fate of the sexual transgressor in other, more indirect ways. In Simms's "The Giant's Coffin" (1845), the villain drowns in a large stone formation during a flash flood. In Charles Fenno Hoffman's *Greyslaer* (1840), the evil Walter Bradshawe is killed and scalped by Indians.[29]

Some women characters did, however, carry out acts of vengeance. In Catherine Sedgwick's *Hope Leslie* (1827), the lecherous Sir Philip Gardiner is blown up when his discarded mistress hurls a lantern into a barrel of gunpowder—an act of passion rather than premeditation.[30] More commonly, women and men who actually plotted against sexual transgressors often found their plans thwarted by true love or Christian charity, an interesting twist on the limitations of their violence.

William Gilmore Simms's *Beauchampe, or, The Kentucky Tragedy* (1842), based upon an incident that occurred in western Kentucky during the 1820s, chronicles the fate of Margaret Cooper. Simms paints a very ambitious and complex portrait of his heroine, a country maiden who is seduced by the profligate Warham P. Sharpe, a lawyer from Frankfort, Kentucky, who moves to Charlemont village for the sole purpose of compromising Margaret. Sharpe changes his name to Alfred Stevens and poses as a divinity student. Being worldly and educated, he fulfills her desires for intellectual companionship and promises her artistic fame in the city. After Margaret is seduced and abandoned, she moves to the outskirts of Frankfort, changes her name to Anna Cooke, and meets Orville Beauchampe while practicing with the pistols she plans to use against Stevens. Anna confesses the entire history of her dishonor, but the avid young Beauchampe loves her despite her past. Before pledging their troth, Beauchampe swears to avenge Anna and either kill her paramour or die in the process.

The ceaseless devotion of her husband softens Anna's heart, and she begins to regret ever having extracted a promise of vengeance. Living on their isolated farmstead, she trusts she will never meet her paramour and thus believes the oath will never be acted upon. Ironically, Beauchampe pays a visit to his mentor, none other than Warham P. Sharpe, who promises to visit the young couple in the near future.

Sharpe arrives at their country home, and when Anna recognizes her seducer it nearly prostrates her. The attachment to her husband has become so strong that she fears he may be killed if the men fight a duel. Thus she determines to act as if Sharpe is a stranger and not arouse any suspicions in Beauchampe's mind. At the first opportunity, she intends to tell Sharpe to quit their home and break off all contacts with her husband.

Such measures might have succeeded if Sharpe had been an honorable man, but his ego is so colossal that he thinks he can reestablish the affair. He refuses to believe Anna when she tells him Beauchampe knows every detail of her past, and he thinks she is bluffing when she tells him about the oath of vengeance. Rather than leaving the house, Sharpe remains the week, and when he proposes to extend his visit, Anna finally confesses to her husband Sharpe's true relationship. Sharpe escapes to Frankfurt, pursued by Beauchampe, who insists on a duel. When Sharpe viciously insults Anna, Beauchampe plunges a dagger into the villain's heart. Sentenced to death for murder, Beauchampe passes his final days in prison, where he is joined by his wife. As the executioners are about to carry Beauchampe to the gallows, Anna produces a dagger, which she stabs into her breast and dies instantly. Her husband, however, merely wounds himself with his dagger and is carried to the scaffold where the sentence is carried out.

Simms is clearly ambivalent about human vengeance, often suggesting that retribution is the province of God alone. He quotes the Biblical passage "Vengeance is mine, saith the Lord," and adds, "Wo, then, for the guilty soul that usurps this sublime privilege of Deity!" At another point, Simms muses: "Strange that human being[s] in a Christian land should really fancy for a moment that God's sanction should hallow the purposes of a bloody vengeance." Elsewhere, however, Simms justifies the vendetta sworn against Sharpe, calling it a "virtuous vengeance." Vowing to requite Anna's disgrace, Beauchampe adds that "it shall sound as an ominous voice of terror, speaking doom and sudden judgment to the cold-blooded profligates who pride themselves on the serpent conquest over all that is blessed and beautiful in the world's Eden!" Simms also suggests that despite the dictates of hospitality, Beauchampe should "have chosen the most direct mode of vengeance—such as the social sense everywhere would have justified—and put the offender to death upon the very hearth which he had striven to dishonor."[31]

But for Simms, it is clear that vengeance is the duty of men, not women.

Give us, say I, Kentucky practice, like that of Beauchampe, as a social law, rather than that which prevails in some of our pattern cities, where women are, in three fourths the number of instances, the victims—violated, mangled, murdered—where men are the criminals—and where (Heaven kindly having withdrawn the sense of shame) there is no one guilty—at least none brave enough or manly enough to bring the guilty to punishment! What is said is not meant to defend or encourage the shedding of blood. We may not defend the taking of life, even by the laws. We regard life as an express trust from Heaven . . . but there is a crime beyond it, in the shedding of that vital soul-blood, . . . the untainted reputation; and the one offence . . . should be placed in the opposing balance, as an offset, in some degree, to the crime by which it is avenged.[32]

Yet, when Margaret Cooper—then not yet Anna Cooke—decides to kill her seducer, Simms not only defends her decision but describes her experience as a catharsis.

Why should she not seek to avenge her wrong? Was he to escape without penalty? was she destined to be a quiescent victim? True, she was a woman, destined it would seem to suffer—perhaps with more than ordinary share of that suffering which falls to her sex. But she had also a peculiar strength—the strength of a man in some respects; and in her bosom she now felt the sudden glow of one in his fiercest passions. Revenge might be in her power. She might redress her wrong by her own hand. It was a weapon of death which she grasped [a pistol]. In her grasp it might be made a weapon of power. The suggestion seemed to be that of justice only. It was one that filled her whole soul with a triumphant and wild enthusiasm.[33]

In another tale of feminine revenge, Hoffman's *Greyslaer*, heroine Alida de Roos believes that while in Indian captivity and unconscious, she had been forced into marriage to the wicked Walter Bradshawe. As in *Beauchampe*, Alida is practicing with pistols when she meets Max Greyslaer, whose offer to exact retribution is refused. "No, Max Greyslaer; my hand, as well as my heart, hath been schooled for years to the accomplishment of one only end, and they will neither of them fail me at my purpose. . . . Alida's own hand shall alone avenge Alida!"[34] Nevertheless, as her feelings for Greyslaer deepen into love, "her woman's heart awoke for the first time to the graces of woman's tenderness, and her spirit grew more and more feminine as it learned to lean upon another, she even shuddered at remembering the strange fantasy of revenge that was the darling dream of her girlhood." Although Greyslaer fleetingly considers a design of vengeance, which the author describes as "the brief but bitter punishment of a single lapse from virtue," the story favors legitimate channels of justice, stating that "Bradshawe was rather a subject for the punishment of the criminal laws than for the chastisement of a gentleman's sword." After her name is cleared in a courtroom and Bradshawe dies in an ambush, Alida and Max marry and thereafter "the current of their days was as calm as it had hitherto been clouded."[35]

One heroine truly extracts vengeance and, in so doing, illustrates that women can rightfully take the law into their own hands when men are unwilling. In E. D. E. N. Southworth's *The Hidden Hand*, villain Craven Le Noir lusts after both the money and virtue of the heroine. When Capitola Black unremittingly rejects his suit, Le Noir embarks upon a campaign to besmirch her name, and Capitola's irresolute cousins will not defend her. During a night of anguish, when Capitola must decide whether to challenge and perhaps kill Le Noir, her Christian principles prevail. She shoots him with a pistol loaded with dried peas, but not before Le Noir, who believes he is dying, retracts his damaging rumors.[36]

Because so few analyses concerning women who commit violent acts exist, accounting for the incidence of ferocious women in antebellum literature is difficult. The few studies available focus on contemporary women confronting child batterers or extremely vicious men. These investigations suggest that women who commit violent acts feel trapped in unsuccessful and unsatisfying lives or are out of control and over the edge. Most warn that feminine brutality is imprudent and dangerous to the social fabric because women are the nurturers and caretakers whose pacific behavior acts as an antidote to a culture of violence.[37] These analyses do not apply to the women portrayed in the most popular novels of the early nineteenth century.

Given that most of these stories are set chiefly on America's frontier, traditionally regarded as the nation's most convulsive region, one might suspect that violence would be more pervasive, but this is not the case. The frequency of contentious behavior and the importance of violence to the overall tone of each story were relatively low and suggest that the emphasis on violence in early American literature has been overdrawn.

Second, despite the relatively low incidence of violence, fictional women were capable of committing violent acts and, with the exception of violence born of sexual dishonor, the authors discussed this issue casually and rarely felt the need to defend their female characters. On rare occasions, writers pointed out that a woman's familiarity with firearms was exceptional, but, for the most part, women protecting themselves or their families were described matter-of-factly. In addition, authors freely accepted the propriety of women's hunting.

The greatest amount of discussion in these books was generated when women felt compelled to defend their sexual honor. Clearly, a woman's reputation was her power, and to malign it in any way could provoke dangerous wrath; but authors set limits to how far a woman and her male champions could properly go to exonerate her. These novels debated the choices of vigilantism, justice through legitimate channels, and reliance upon divine intervention. Authors solved the dilemma of vengeance-seeking women through the discovery of love or reminders of Christian charity. Men were similarly encouraged to rely upon due process or holy retribution. Dueling or other extralegal activities were sanctioned only when all other options had been spent.

The presence of brave-hearted women contradicts notions of feminine passivity during the supposed height of the "cult of true womanhood." Whether violent or not, the women in antebellum literature were overwhelmingly assertive, and obedience and dependency were not cherished ideals for either male or female authors. When the content analysis tested a woman character's submission to all forms of authority, 68.4 percent of the women described by male authors and 73.1 percent of those created by women were depicted as not submissive. This consensus is further supported by other questions that touched upon feminine dependence. When asked whether the woman character was depicted as independent or self-reliant, writers of both sexes were deemed to have created women of temerity with resounding frequency (72.7 percent and 74.2 percent, respectively). In addition, 81.1 percent of the women crafted by men and 82.3 percent of those created by women were depicted as emotionally strong or strong willed. Antebellum authors did not cast weak women as characters in their novels, but strong and resourceful ones. Violence tested their character; their strength generally led them to avoid its use.

NOTES

Laura McCall is a professor of history at Metropolitan State College of Denver. She wishes to acknowledge the support of the University of Michigan's Department of History for computer funds and Mary Vinovskis's programming assistance. She is grateful to Julie Roy Jeffrey, Stephen Leonard, and Merritt Roe Smith for their comments and corrections on an earlier draft, and to Deborah Jennings Mahoney and Sandra Dempsey for their valuable time testing the preliminary coding sheets.

1. Studies of American frontier literature invariably describe white women who hate rugged wilderness, who were taken West against their wills, and who either languished or died. Sylvia Grider, for example, writes that "fictional women are literary symbols of all those other unnamed but very real women who suffered and were broken by the West." Susan Armitage, who examines letters, diaries, and novels, asserts that image and reality merge and that women in frontier fiction parallel real women in terms of loneliness and homesickness. Annette Kolodny, in her analysis of Margaret Fuller's *Summer on the Lakes*, equates the experiences of farm wives in Wisconsin and Illinois with those of the colonial captivity heroines, who were "taken there against their will." Even worse, the home "now stood as a place of imprisonment, with the small, dark, often windowless cabins isolating women from the fields without." Sylvia Grider, "Madness and Personification in *Giants in the Earth*," in *Women, Women Writers and the West*, ed. L. L. Lee and Merrill Lewis (Troy, N.Y.: Whitson, 1979), 111–17; Susan Armitage, "Reluctant Pioneers," in *Women and Western American Literature*, ed. Helen Winter Stauffer and Susan J. Rosowski (Troy, N.Y.: Whitson, 1982), 40–51; Barbara Meldrum, "Women in Western American Fiction: Images or Real Women?" in Stauffer and Rosowski, *Women and Western American Literature*, 57; Annette Kolodny, *The Land before Her: Fantasy and Experience of the American Frontiers, 1630–1860* (Chapel Hill: University of North Carolina Press, 1984), 123. See also Barbara Meldrum, "Images of Women in Western American Literature," *Midwest Quarterly* 17 (1976): 252–67; Annette McElhiney, "The Image of the Pioneer Woman in the American Novel" (Ph.D. diss., University of Denver, 1978); Robert L. Griswold, "Anglo Women and Domestic Ideology in the American West in the Nineteenth and Early Twentieth Centuries," in *Western Women: Their Land, Their Lives*, ed. Lillian Schlissel, Vicki L. Ruiz, and Janice Monk (Albuquerque: University of New Mexico Press, 1988), 15–33.

2. Women have been described as the unfortunate and passive victims of Indian rapine, murder, or captivity who, in an interesting twist, were also responsible for gener-

ating frontier violence. Richard Slotkin argues that the wilderness must "be destroyed so that it can be made safe for the white woman and the civilization she represents." The hunter, who escapes to savage environs in order to test his primal masculinity, is placed in a fatal predicament when white women intrude. He must rescue the captive woman, whom Slotkin describes as weak, emotional, and prone to frenzy, and make the frontier safe for settlement. The hunter uses his savage "powers, not to sustain the wilderness world, but to destroy it in the name of something higher." Richard Slotkin, *Regeneration Through Violence: The Mythology of the American Frontier, 1600–1860* (Middletown, Conn.: Wesleyan University Press, 1973), 552–54, and Slotkin, *The Fatal Environment: The Myth of the Frontier in the Age of Industrialization, 1800–1890* (Middletown, Conn.: Wesleyan University Press, 1985), 64, 140, 343. See also David Brion Davis, *Homicide in American Fiction, 1789–1860: A Study of Social Values* (Ithaca: Cornell University Press, 1957); Dawn Lander, "Women and the Wilderness: Tabus in American Literature," *University of Michigan Papers in Women's Studies* 2 (1977): 62–83; Henry Nash Smith, *Virgin Land: The American West as Symbol and Myth* (Cambridge: Harvard University Press, 1950), 112–13.

3. Jane Totman asserts, "[T]he literature suggests that a woman doesn't do others in because she is trained to be less aggressive, because she has other outlets (sex), because she has fewer opportunities and temptations, since she is at home most of the time, because she is punier, because she is of a different biological nature, and because she can probably get a man to do it for her if she wants the foul deed done." Jane Totman, *The Murderess: A Psychosocial Study of Criminal Homicide* (San Francisco: R and E Research Associates, 1978), 4. Dawn Lander, on the other hand, suggests that the spell of wilderness might compromise a woman's restraint and make her lustful, mannish, or violent; see "Women and the Wilderness," 66. See also June Stephenson, *Men Are Not Cost Effective: Male Crime in America* (New York: Harper Perennial, 1995).

4. Anne Campbell, *Men, Women, and Aggression* (New York: Basic Books, 1993), 2, 82. As Jane Totman explains: "It is woman's duty to promote the humanitarian ideals.... Woman is an emotional, rather fragile, creature who civilizes and humanizes, or tries to, the male beast." Totman, *Murderess*, 8.

5. This study is based upon a content analysis of literature set on the American frontier, traditionally regarded as the most violent and contentious region in the United States. The "tales" codebook contained 145 questions and examined the larger issues of form, content, and meaning. It enumerated fundamental aspects of the story's setting and tone, and examined the interpretations put forward by other scholars. The "character" codebook, containing 130 questions, measured the pervasiveness of stereotypes attributed to nineteenth-century women. A full discussion of the methodology and codebooks can be found in my dissertation, "Symmetrical Minds: Literary Men and Women in Antebellum America" (Ph.D. diss., University of Michigan, 1988). Those interested in the nature and uses of content analysis should consult Klaus Krippendorf, *Content Analysis: An Introduction to Its Methodology* (Beverly Hills and London: Sage, 1980); William C. Schutz, "On Categorizing Qualitative Data in Content Analysis," *Public Opinion Quarterly* 22 (winter 1958–59), 501–15; and O. R. Holsti, *Content Analysis for the Social Sciences and Humanities* (Reading, Mass.: Addison-Wesley, 1969).

6. Barbara Welter, "The Cult of True Womanhood: 1820–1860," *American Quarterly* 18 (1966): 151–74. The "true womanhood" and "separate spheres" ideals are deeply embedded in the scholarship, and virtually every historian and literary critic feels compelled to address these concepts. A small number of scholars, however, are beginning to question their pervasiveness and even their existence. See Lisa Wilson Waciega, "A 'Man of Business': The Widow of Means in Southeastern Pennsylvania, 1750–1850," *William and Mary*

Quarterly 44 (1987): 40–64; Susan Juster, " 'In a Different Voice': Male and Female Narratives of Religious Conversion in Post-Revolutionary America," *American Quarterly* 41 (1989): 34–62; E. Anthony Rotundo, "Romantic Friendship: Male Intimacy and Middle Class Youth in the Northern United States, 1800–1900," *Journal of Social History* 23 (1989): 1–25; Karen Lystra, *Searching the Heart: Women, Men, and Romantic Love in Nineteenth-Century America* (New York: Oxford University Press, 1989), 55, 20; Nina Baym, *Novels, Readers, Reviewers: Responses to Fiction in Antebellum America* (Ithaca: Cornell University Press, 1984), 21; Laura McCall " 'The Reign of Brute Force Is Now Over': A Content Analysis of *Godey's Lady's Book*, 1830–1860," *Journal of the Early Republic* 9 (1989): 217–36.

7. "Violence born of sexual dishonor" and "violence born of wealth and power" are categories suggested by Daryl Jones, "Blood 'n Thunder: Virgins, Villains and Violence in the Dime Novel Western," *Journal of Popular Culture* 4 (1970): 507–17.

8. Glenda Riley, *Women and Indians on the Frontier, 1825–1915* (Albuquerque: University of New Mexico Press, 1984), 24; Meldrum, "Images of Women in Western American Literature," 252.

9. Beverly Stoeltje categorizes frontierswomen as refined ladies, helpmates, or bad women. Stoeltje, " 'A Helpmate for Man Indeed': The Image of the Frontier Woman," *Journal of American Folklore* 88 (1975): 25–41. See also Meldrum, "Images of Women in Western American Literature," 252–67.

10. [Mrs. W. H. Corning?], *Western Border Life; or What Fanny Hunter Saw and Heard in Kanzas* [sic] *and Missouri* (New York: Derby, 1856), 55–56; Ann S. Stephens, *Sybil Chase; Or, The Valley Ranche: A Tale of California Life* (New York: Beadle, 1861), 32; Stephens, *Mary Derwent* (Philadelphia: T. B. Peterson and Brothers, 1858), 356.

11. James Fenimore Cooper, *The Works of James Fenimore Cooper*, vol. 1, *The Deerslayer* (1841) (New York: P. F. Collier, 1892), 98, 115, 236.

12. [William Gilmore Simms], *Charlemont; or, The Pride of the Village. A Tale of Kentucky* (New York: Redfield, 1856), 408.

13. Lander, "Women and the Wilderness," 68.

14. E. D. E. N. Southworth, *The Hidden Hand or, Capitola the Madcap* (New Brunswick: Rutgers University Press, 1988), 361–62 (The Hidden Hand was first serialized in 1859 in the *New York Ledger*); James Fenimore Cooper, *The Pioneers; or, The Sources of the Susquehanna*, 2 vols. (1823; Albany: State University of New York Press, 1980), 186–87.

15. James Kirke Paulding, *The Puritan and His Daughter* (New York: Baker and Scribner, 1849), 2:31.

16. [James Kirke Paulding], *Westward Ho! A Tale* (New York: J. J. Harper, 1832), 2:188.

17. Ibid., 107.

18. David W. Belisle, *The American Family Robinson; or, the Adventures of a Family Lost in the Great Desert of the West* (Philadelphia: W. P. Hazard, 1854), 69, 74.

19. James Fenimore Cooper, *Wyandotte; Or, The Hutted Knoll* (1843), vol. 21 of *The Complete Works of J. Fenimore Cooper* (New York: G. P. Putnam's Sons, n.d.), 181, 235.

20. William Gilmore Simms, *The Yemassee: A Romance of Carolina* (1835; New York: American Book Company, 1937), 102, 141.

21. Ibid., 329–30.

22. Ibid., 102, 222, 227.

23. Ibid., 329–30.

24. Ibid., 351–52.

25. Mary Jane Holmes, *'Lena Rivers* (1856; New York: Hurst, n.d.), 27, 112.

26. Jones, "Blood 'n Thunder," 508–10.

27. Herbert Ross Brown, *The Sentimental Novel in America, 1789–1860* (Durham: Duke University Press, 1940), 44.

28. Davis, *Homicide in American Fiction*, 156, 201–2; Welter, "The Cult of True Womanhood," 315; Victoria E. Bynum, *Unruly Women: The Politics of Social and Sexual Control in the Old South* (Chapel Hill: University of North Carolina Press, 1992), 119–20.

29. William Gilmore Simms, "The Giant's Coffin, Or The Feud of Holt and Houston. A Tale of Reedy River," in *The Wigwam and the Cabin*, 2d ser. (New York: Wiley and Putnam, 1845), 276; Charles Fenno Hoffman, *Greyslaer: A Romance of the Mohawk* (New York: Harper & Brothers, 1840), 2:253.

30. [Catharine Maria Sedgwick], *Hope Leslie: Or, Early Times in The Massachusetts*, vol. 2, (1827; New York: Harper & Brothers, 1842), 221.

31. William Gilmore Simms, *Beauchampe: A Tale of Passion* (1842; New York: n.p., 1970), 148–49, 321, 334.

32. Ibid., 342–43.

33. [Simms], *Charlemont*, 428–29.

34. Hoffman, *Greyslaer*, 1:159.

35. Ibid., 2:124–25, 257.

36. Southworth, *Hidden Hand*, 360–77.

37. Campbell, *Men, Women, and Aggression*, 1, 18, 141–60; Totman, *Murderess*, 92.

Mary Harris at the time of her trial. *Harper's Weekly*, March 4, 1865, 140.

Chapter Nine

Seduced, Betrayed, and Revenged
The Murder Trial of Mary Harris

Lee Chambers-Schiller

From July 3 to July 19, 1865, the city of Washington, D.C., and, indeed, much of the northern United States, were riveted by the trial of Mary Harris of Burlington, Iowa, for the murder of Adoniram Judson Burroughs, late of Chicago. Burroughs, a thirty-three-year-old clerk in the Treasury Department, had been shot down in the hall outside his office on January 31 that year by a nineteen-year-old daughter of Irish immigrants. After seeing the announcement of Burroughs's marriage to socialite Amelia Boggs in the Chicago newspapers, Harris had traveled to Washington, D.C., by train to confront with his perfidy the man she believed to be her fiancé. She signed into a respectable boardinghouse, where she fell ill.

Rising from her sickbed after three weeks of contemplating love letters and other documents intended for a Washington attorney she meant to engage in her suit for civil damages, Harris went to the Treasury building and inquired after Burroughs. Denied admittance, she asked the guard if she might wait at his post for her friend. Impressed by her soft voice and ladylike demeanor, he allowed her to remain. But he lost track of Mary Harris, and she entered the building, seeking additional help in locating her target. There being two Burroughses who worked for the Treasury, she followed the directions of a friendly receptionist and stepped inside the large office that housed the clerks of the comptroller of the currency to check on the identity and presence of her prey. Finding Adoniram there, Mary secreted herself across the hall in a recess created by a doorway and a hanging clock. There she waited.

When Burroughs left the office, she retrieved a hidden gun and fired at him. The bullet crossed the path of his companion, Alfred Everett, and struck Burroughs in the back. It lodged two inches from his spine between the fourth and fifth ribs. Everett fell back as Burroughs fell forward, flinging up his hands and crying out. Burroughs turned, looked upon his attacker and ran in an attempt to escape. The young woman, dressed in a brown cloak and black hat, with a green or blue veil covering her face and a scarf softly wrapping her head and neck, stepped calmly out into the middle of the hall, cocked her gun, held it out at arm's length, raised her veil and fired a second shot. Burroughs had almost reached the stairwell at the end of the hall when he fell dead, clutching the corner of the wall at the head of the stairs. The second bullet plowed into the wall behind him at about the height of a man's head. "Cool" and "self-possessed," the assassin turned and walked "deliberately" away, her face "perfectly colorless."[1]

Historians of domestic violence would recognize in this case both continuity and change in a frightening trend. Mary S. Hartman, in studying nineteenth-century domestic murder, has argued that married women in France took up "crimes of passion" (the revenge murder of a spouse in criminal protest over infidelity) in ever increasing numbers after 1870.[2] In so doing, these women turned on its head the legalized violence of sexual revenge traditionally reserved for men. Under the Napoleonic Code, legal execution of an adulterous lover in a crime of passion was restricted to men alone. A husband undertaking the *crime passionel* could not be tried for premeditated murder (although he could be indicted and tried on a lesser charge) if he killed either his wife or her lover in circumstances of *flagrant delit* (Article 324 of the Penal Code).[3] Closely aligned to the *crime passionel* was the "revenge of the soiled maiden" in which unmarried women revenged themselves upon lovers and fiancés for infidelity, ravishment, or abandonment.

Not only did crimes of passion by women increase in France after 1870, so too did the use of firearms in such crimes.[4] One criminalist argued that the revolver replaced acid as the weapon of "disfigurement" used by women to gain their revenge and regain their honor.[5] The first widely discussed revolver case involving a bourgeois woman in France occurred in 1880, when Marie Briere killed the lover who fathered her child but refused to marry her.[6]

Similarly, before the Civil War, most murders committed by women in the United States were domestic in nature, and the tide rose over the course of the nineteenth century.[7] Most domestic murders by American women were accomplished with poison.[8] Far less frequently, and more often in cases of sexual revenge, women used a knife. Poison, of course, was the weapon of choice because it was easily obtained and dispensed with little physical threat to the murderer. So too, it was not always apparent in such cases that murder had been done. A knife was a more chancy affair, both as to discovery and success, when wielded by a woman likely to be both shorter and weaker than her opponent.[9] From the 1840s through the Civil War, guns became more widely available in the United States. Beginning in the 1870s, women more frequently used them in cases of domestic murder and sexual revenge.[10] In this context, the Mary Harris case offers an early instance of an old motive combined with a new and more deadly means—a woman scorned who stalked the man who betrayed her and ensured his demise by use of a concealed and deadly weapon.

Although the scholarship on domestic violence and crimes of passion provides one vantage point within which to understand the murder of Adoniram J. Burroughs, there is another valuable historiography that must be taken into account, given the timing of the murder and, more important, its reportage in the national press: the historiography on women and war. Women's historians have focused on the importance of social change in war-time society as markers in the progress of women toward social, economic, and political equality with men. Their attention has largely addressed the world wars and, to a lesser extent, the American Revolution.[11] Recently, the Civil War has become a subject of much interest as historians have looked at the impact of war on women's lives; the ways in which women's presence in the hospitals and camps altered the course of the war; the effect of women's war work on popular attitudes toward women's social role; the value of home-front production to the prosecution of the war; and the impact of war work on women's occupational opportunities, sense of achievement, and professionalism.[12]

Although much of this work has been done by social historians, cultural historians have focused attention on wartime society discussions of gender and the significance of such discussions for issues of identity as men and women attempt to construct new selves in the aftermath of war.[13] These studies have demonstrated that when society talks about gender and redefines cultural notions of male and femaleness, it is also talking about the realignment of power relations, concerns about moral order, and attitudes toward change. As Mary Louise Roberts has written of France, "[G]ender was central to how change was understood in the postwar decade. . . . Debate concerning gender identity became a primary way to embrace, resist, or reconcile oneself to changes associated with the war."[14]

Much has been written about the political, economic, racial, and other social changes that took place during and after the Civil War, but less has been said about how Americans understood these changes as they were taking place. The debate about gender that accompanied the Civil War helps focus our attention on the narratives that emerged at the time and the hopes and fears with which that society was grappling. This chapter will address the complex and compelling gender narratives offered by the murder trial of Mary Harris. The trial expressed critical concerns roiling the northern public at the end of the Civil War, concerns having to do with what was perceived to be a dramatic and dangerous upturn in both sexual and gender disorder during the war. The arguments of attorneys at trial and the attempts of contemporary newspaper reporters and editors to interpret the trial's meaning crafted vivid images foreboding dire consequences for the well-being of the republic. In this way, the trial helped to shape the political perceptions of those following the case, contributed to northern unease about the remaking of the Union, and emphasized the importance of restoring marital, sexual, and gender order in so doing.[15]

Burroughs had met Harris, the child of Irish Catholic parents who had put her out to work and live with the owner of a fancy-goods shop in Burlington, Iowa, Mrs. Alexander. Harris was but nine or ten years old when the twenty-four-year-old Burroughs, who had a shop in the same block, began to drop into the store to provide instruction of both an intellectual and social nature. He apparently advised her as to what books she should read, how she should dress, and how she should speak in public. He became very fond of her and was seen to hold her on his lap, fondle, and caress her. After losing his own establishment, Burroughs took a position as Mrs. Alexander's bookkeeper. Thereafter, he was able to see Mary daily. Her father became sufficiently concerned about Burroughs's attitude and behavior toward Mary to warn him away. Harris was but thirteen in 1858 when Burroughs, apparently following her father's advice, returned to Chicago.

Although Burroughs left town, he nevertheless wrote to Mary frequently between 1858 and 1863, a series of love letters that were admitted into court as evidence of the nature of their relationship. Periodically, he returned to Iowa, persuading Mary to visit him secretly. Mrs. Alexander may have facilitated these meetings but chose not to inform the Harris family of Burroughs's activities. Finally, Burroughs succeeded in persuading Mary to leave Burlington and follow him to Chicago in the expectation that they would be wed immediately. However, the marriage set for June of 1863 was postponed. First Burroughs injured his leg and then he lost his job. He asked Mary to wait until he could set himself up in such a state as to take proper care of a wife.

Unable to find appropriate work in Chicago, Burroughs sought employment in Washington, D.C. Again he sent for Mary to join him. She refused, perhaps losing faith in Burroughs's marital intentions. She became convinced that he had lured her to a Chicago brothel with a false letter in an effort to ruin her reputation so that he might be released from his engagement. She feared what he might do in a city where she had neither friends nor family to protect and support her. Whatever her doubts and fears, Mary nevertheless was shocked to read in the newspapers of Burroughs's marriage to another woman in September, only three short months after their own nuptials had been scheduled.

Following the marriage, Harris grew highly agitated and deeply depressed. Her two roommates described her behavior as becoming increasingly erratic and violent. She attacked one roommate with a brush and ran at her with a carving knife. She purchased a gun. Her friends took her out of the city in an effort to cut painful associations and begin a new life in Wisconsin. But Harris was obsessed with Burroughs's betrayal. She made two trips to Washington in an attempt to instigate a civil action for breach of promise. She missed seeing him the first time because he had apparently returned to Chicago on business. On her second visit, Harris located and killed him.

Making no effort to escape the consequences of her actions, Harris was apprehended quietly at the scene of the murder. During her incarceration, she garnered a modest celebrity because of the renown of the lawyers and doctors drawn to her case; the attentions paid her by the widowed first lady, who sent flowers; the considerable speculation over details of Harris's relationship with Burroughs; and the prominence of Burroughs's family. The brother who had presided over his wedding was the Rev. Dr. J. C. Burroughs, president of the University of Chicago. Dr. Burroughs worked so closely with prosecutors to bring their case that the defense accused him of paying off witnesses and interfering with the investigation. Throughout the five months she awaited trial, Harris received a number of visitors and spoke freely with them about her situation. They in turn spoke to the press, keeping alive public interest in the case.

Harris's defense rested upon a plea of insanity: that "under an impulse she could not resist," Harris drew her pistol and killed Burroughs.[16] Hers was only the second case of temporary insanity heard in the United States. The first established the "irresistible impulse" defense in a crime of passion. In 1859, the flamboyant (some said blackguard and profligate) New York congressman and friend of President James Buchanan, Daniel Edgar Sickles of New York, aged forty, had pled temporary insanity in the murder of Philip Barton Key, the forty-year-old district attorney of the District of Columbia. Key was a handsome and popular man-about-town, a married father of four children and the lover of the beautiful and young (some said naive and others disingenuous) Teresa Bagioli Sickles, aged twenty-three. John Graham, one of Sickles's eight lawyers (among whom were Senator Stephen A. Douglas and future secretary of war Edwin M. Stanton), argued that in murdering Key, Sickles was acting in accordance with biblical "law" providing that a husband had a right to kill an adulterer caught in bed with his wife. Given "the heinousness of the crime" committed by Keys, Sickles was within his rights under the "principle of the old rule that palliates the act committed by a husband." Sickles pled temporary insanity, saying that his mind had been "affected" by his wife's infidelity and that there had not been "sufficient time" for "his passion to cool."

Insanity had long been a defense before the law. After the McNaughton case of 1843, insanity was defined in Anglo-American practice as a state of mind in which the defendant could not differentiate between right and wrong nor understand the consequences of his or her actions. However, the idea of temporary insanity was a new one. No one asserted that Sickles was mentally deranged, only that he had a sudden, temporary lapse from reason when, still reeling from his wife's late-night confession of adultery, he saw Key signaling her for an assignation the following afternoon from a position across Lafayette Square from his house. Attorney Graham insisted that Sickles was "at the time of the homicide, such a mere creature of instinct, of impulse, that he could not resist, but was carried forward, like a mere machine, to the consummation of that so-called tragedy." His client had acted in "a transport of frenzy," Graham argued, for there could be "no cooling off after such an offense." Graham also asserted that the prosecution must "prove that the prisoner was at the time in sound mind and memory." There was no precedent for such an assertion—the law presumed everyone to be of sound mind and that the burden of proving otherwise rested with the defendant.[17]

The key to the defense case was the idea that knowledge of Teresa's offending behavior was equivalent to Daniel's having seen the adulterers in the sex act itself. Defense counsel Philip Phillips argued that the key question was not when the adultery took place but, rather, when the adultery first came to the defendant's knowledge: "This is the time it took place, when the husband first heard of it. It then took place before his eyes." Such knowledge, "places the deceased in *flagrante delicto* at the time of his death," said Phillips. In accepting this point and allowing the defense to submit evidence of his wife's affair to the jury, Judge Thomas Hartley Crawford altered the nature of Sickles's trial from one of murder to one of adultery. Sickles never took the stand to defend his behavior, but his counsel produced forty-three witnesses to some aspect of the affair between Key and his wife. In closing argument, Edwin Stanton said:

> The theory of our case is, that there was a man living in a constant state of adultery with the prisoner's wife, a man who was daily by a moral—no, by an immoral power—enormous, monstrous and altogether unparalleled in the history of American society, or in the history of the family of man, a power over the being of this woman—calling her from her husband's house, drawing her from the side of her child, and dragging her, day by day, through the streets in order that he might gratify his lust. The husband beholds him in the very act of withdrawing his wife from his roof, from his presence, from his arm, from his wing, from his nest, meets him in that act and slays him, and we say that the right to slay him stands on the firmest principles of self defense.

District Attorney Robert Ould (later in charge of the Confederate Secret Service) argued that the case was not about adultery and tried to focus the jury upon the charge of homicide. If Sickles had found his wife and Key in the act, said Ould, the law might have reduced the charge to manslaughter; but if the husband pursued the adulterer and slew him out of revenge, the act was clearly one of murder.[18]

However, Judge Crawford instructed the members of the jury that they were to determine "the state of Mr. Sickles' mind as [to] the capacity to decide upon the criminality of the homicide." He further stated, "If the jury have any doubt as to the case either in reference to the homicide or the question of sanity, Mr. Sickles should be acquitted. . . . The humane, and I will add, just doctrine, that a reasonable doubt should avail a prisoner, belongs to a defense of insanity, as much, in my opinion, as to any other matter of fact." The jury deliberated for an hour and ten minutes before unanimously acquitting Sickles of murder. The case was the first of a series that established the principle enunciated by the judge, that if a jury has a reasonable doubt as to the sanity of a defendant at the moment that a crime is committed, the defendant is entitled to the benefit of that doubt.[19]

American law accepted insanity as a defect of reason such that an individual was unable to tell right from wrong and unable to understand the nature and consequences of his or her act. Based in large part on the Sickles case, the law also accepted that sometimes an "irresistible impulse" might so impair an individual's will that the individual could not help doing what reason told him or her to be wrong. But in terms of human faculties, psychology recognized the power of emotion as well as those of reason and will. Isaac Ray, a leading psychiatrist, proposed a condition that he called moral mania, or moral insanity, in which reason was intact but emotional propensities were distorted. Indeed, some experts believed that "irresistible impulse" sprang from deranged passions rather than from a defect of the will. However, women were deemed to be less rational and more emotional than men. Despite having a finer, more sensitive, and receptive moral nature, they were believed to be more susceptible to derangement of both the will and the emotions (there being some disagreement among psychologists as to which faculty housed "the moral nature"), while lacking the true capacity to make moral choices, which required the exercise of reason.[20]

Experts agreed on the need to look for the underlying condition that predisposed the person to insanity and the precipitating event that brought it on. Among the causes that might predispose a woman to insanity were nervous diseases such as uterine irritation, excessive excitement, including grief, and disorderly or abnormal menstruation. Counsel's theory of Harris's condition was that she suffered from a case of "moral insanity" stemming from her "disappointed affection," aggravated by "moral shock" due to Burroughs's efforts to ruin her reputation, and immediately precipitated by an attack of "paroxysmal insanity" caused by severe dysmenorrhea (the latter explaining the two-year gap between the broken engagement and the murder). In other words, Mary Harris, having despaired for months over her broken engagement and the loss of her proper place in the world as a good man's wife had been in a susceptible frame of mind such that the shock caused by the belief that her fiancé had not only abandoned her but also tried either to kidnap her into white slavery or to ruin her reputation by associating her with a house of prostitution had driven her to the edge. Because she experienced painful menstrual flow, she was especially at risk. During one such period, she went mad and became temporarily homicidal. "She was insane from moral causes, aggravated by disease of the body. . . . A pure, virtuous, chaste, delicate little girl, not more than twenty years of age at this time, whose frame is wasting and whose spirits are gone, whose heart is broken, in a paroxysm of insanity has slain the man who has brought upon her all this suffering."[21]

Furious at the sympathy Harris provoked from spectators in the courtroom, District Attorney E. C. Carrington appealed to the jury: "You know this woman is not insane. If you acquit her upon the ground of insanity, it will be a pretext only." Nevertheless, the jury took just five minutes to pronounce her not guilty, a popular verdict that produced a noisy demonstration of approval in court.[22]

To interpret the meanings of the verdict, it is important to recollect the traumatic political context in which the trial took place. News of Lee's surrender at Appomattox Courthouse was received on the morning of April 10, 1865. A mere four days later President Lincoln was assassinated, inspiring a degree of panic and uncertainty on the part of many northerners who feared that the South was perhaps not prepared to surrender after all but, rather, to continue the conflict by other means. Did the conspiracy to assassinate the president involve the southern leadership? Unionists feared that winning the peace might prove to be as difficult and long-lasting a process as winning the war.[23]

Lincoln's assassins were quickly caught and brought before a military tribunal for judgment. The trial began on May 15, 1865, and continued to July 7, when four of the conspirators, including Mary Surratt, were hanged. The trial was fully covered by the press, which provided detailed descriptions of other southern conspiracies and recounted reports of wartime brutalities practiced by southerners on enslaved and freed blacks, captured Northern soldiers and Union sympathizers.[24]

Coverage of the Lincoln assassination tribunal and the trial of Mary Harris overlapped in the nation's newspapers. Editors published front-page stories on both, with word-for-word testimony and detailed descriptions of the atmosphere, actors, and activities in the courtrooms.[25] Several journalists explicitly linked the two Marys, Surratt and Harris. *Frank Leslie's Illustrated Newspaper* attacked the Harris verdict and suggested that it was a good thing that the conspirators in the assassination of the president were tried under martial law, for "[i]t is now clear that one certainly, perhaps most of these conspirators, would have escaped the penalty of their crimes, had they been handed over to the judicial Dogberrys and the morally-perverted juries of the national capital." The editor decried public sentiment in favor of Harris's vindication, believing it due to "an unhealthy sentimentality, or an imperfect concession to the repugnance to capital punishment" caused by Surratt's hanging.[26]

The *National Republican* also linked the two trials. A commentator called the verdict of the court against Mary Surratt "a vindication of woman's right to be hung for murder; that of the jury in favor of Miss Harris is a tribute to the purity of woman." The first, he argued, was a warning to infamous women and the second to sneaky men.

> All honor to the jury which tells the world that the honor of its daughters must be defended—that to invade the sanctity of the weaker is to dare the manhood of the stronger sex, and that man's refusal to meet the emergency is cowardice! All honor to the gallant jury which says that it is woman's virtue which makes home influence; that home influence is the beginning of patriotism, and that patriotism is a nation's life.

As the "nation's life" hung in the balance, many northerners focused on the proper regulation of domestic affairs and the sexual order as the basis for its salvation. To these observers, the Harris case served as an example of the need for stricter sexual morality and better regulation of courtship and marital relations between women and men.[27]

Shaping this perspective was a widespread sense of the disorderliness of gender roles at the time, a disorder linked causally to the war. The *Chicago Times*, for example, deplored the state of public morals:

> Never before in the history of this country was there so much cause for public apprehension and alarm. On every side, turn where you will, are seen evidences of vice, corruption and moral deformity, existing in the highest stations in life, as well as the humble homes of the poor and unpretending. . . . War is not more exhaustive of the material and physical power of a nation than of its virtue and its morals. The unsettled condition of social relations opens wide the door for the entrance of the tempter and seducer; the inordinate greed for gain stifles the voice of honor; power defies justice; profligacy is the result of sudden wealth in the hands of the few, and poverty in many paves the way for crime.

The history of the Civil War, exclaimed the editorial, said far more about treachery, misery, want, and crime than about the deeds of its "most infamous participants." A true history of the war would tell of the "moral pestilence [that] is brooding over us."[28]

The columns of the North's newspapers during the period from the commission of the Burroughs murder to the rendering of the verdict in the Harris trial illustrated and decried the social, sexual, and gender disorder caused by war.[29] Among the commonly addressed concerns were those of cross-dressing and gender role-playing by women serving in the army as men. Reporters detailed the stories of Georgiana Peterman, who served for two years as a drummer in the 7th Wisconsin; of Ida Bruce, who made her way north from Atlanta after the death of her parents by serving in the 7th Ohio cavalry; of Mary A. Wright of Crosby's scouts and Margaret Henry of Jenkin's scouts.[30] So too, considerable coverage was given to Dr. Mary E. Walker, who made an "unseemly display" by "clothing herself in men's clothes," as did Dr. Ellen Beard Harman, who was arrested by a policeman who did not know that it was not against the law for a woman to wear trousers in the street.[31]

Soldiering women particularly seemed to alarm the folks back home. They were deemed dangerous because of their potential for acting like men of violence in peace as in war. Manliness depended upon men's refinement of their sexual and violent natures through great discipline and mental exertion. The war shaped manly men by training them to direct their innate violence "purposefully toward a licensed enemy."[32] Because of women's very nature, their greater emotional and less rational nature, they could not develop the discipline or exert sufficient intellect to curb such violent feelings as their unnatural wartime experience may have evoked. Ellen Forehand provided a case in point. Discharged from her Indiana regiment, she married another soldier, who had her arrested on the complaint that she followed him for several days armed with a pistol and threatening to take his life. Her husband said that he had no wish to prosecute her, only "to be safe," and Justice Handy assisted by ordering her to leave Washington, D.C., on the first train.[33]

Causing less alarm but equally salacious was news of men dressing as women in pursuit of wartime goals. The southern cases of Jerome Clark, alias Sue Mundy, a member of John Morgan's command, and of Charlie, alias Charlotte, Anderson, who donned women's clothing in order to spy for the South, were widely covered in the press. One disconcerting case involved a northern deserter disguised as a woman to evade military authorities. He was arrested while living with a teenaged girl in a Cleveland hotel. But if cross-dressing and role reversals among military men and women undermined distinctions between the sexes, additional alarm arose from a perceived rise in marital disorder due to the war.[34]

Increases in marital disorder—bigamy, adultery, abandonment, and divorce— were frequently cited by the press as evidence of both moral and social crisis.

> Not the least among the pernicious effects of this "cruel war," is the frequent disruptions which it causes in the best regulated families. A high-souled patriot goes forth to fight the battles of his country, leaving a loving wife and a small family behind him. After a two year absence, he returns, covered with glory, anticipating a

fond and admiring welcome from his disconsolate partner, only to find, like Ben Battle, "that his wife has got another Ben, whose christian name was John."

For the first time, editors published divorce proceedings, noting the high percentage of soldier husbands abandoned by their unfaithful (and unpatriotic) wives and the numerous husbands who deserted their wives and children.[35]

The stories of Enoch Arden, George Pearson, James A. Keirnan, Henry Morse, and T. M. Lang were virtually interchangeable. Each involved a man returning from war to find his wife living with or married to another man, and having born that man's child. The story of one Mr. La Grave of St. Paul is illustrative. He returned from three years' service with the 5th Wisconsin to find that his wife had eloped with one Henry Baldwin, and that his two children had been sent to Dubuque in order to distract him. The newspaper detailed his successful search for his children.[36] The *Chicago Times* editorialized on the "innumerable cases of divorce, brought by returned soldiers against their wives," and specifically of that of Theodore S. against Martha E. Couch:

> What must be the feelings of a veteran, who has fought bravely for his country, to return to his house after a long absence, and find the wife of his bosom guilty of such monstrous crimes? It proves the frailty of woman, more forcibly than it was ever proven before. By glancing at the daily court reports in *The Times*, an astonishing record of adultery will be found, in nearly every case of which the complainant is a returned soldier.

Similar cases appeared of husbands abandoning their wives. For example, Catherine Ellison's husband, Thomas, a soldier with the 8th Iowa Infantry for three years, returned home only to elope with a mistress. He left four children to be supported by their disabled mother.[37]

Sexual disorder—rape, seduction, and prostitution—also claimed attention from social commentators and editorial pundits. Newspapers throughout the North denounced the growth of prostitution on the home front along with the official recognition and regulation of prostitution at the front lines. In a story entitled "The Trials of a Soldier's Wife," a reporter regretted:

> One painful consequence of the war has been that the patriotism of many of the gallant spirits who have gone to the front has led them, in too many cases, to forget their homes and leave their families unprotected. It is very pitiable to see at times some of these neglected females carrying their babies in their arms up before the Police court on such charges as theft and prostitution.

The *Chicago Times* deplored the "importation of French morals in Memphis," where an act to register prostitutes and certify their medical condition for use of soldiers was seen as the "Fruit of the War."[38]

Newspapers decried what they perceived to be a rise of sexual crimes such as seduction and rape. The story of Captain Alfred De Costa and Matilda James, an orphan looking for work and but newly arrived in Chicago from Delavan, Wisconsin, filled newspapers for a week in July 1865. De Costa seduced James, who was taken in by his promises of protection and marriage. Editors noted the popular delusion that the "illustrious Don Juan had long since trod the path to that spirit land which has received so many heroes of his caliber. . . ." Then, "Here, under our very eyes, the amorous young Spaniard, not a whit the worse for wear, turns up in the guise of a gallant Frenchman, disguised as an officer and a gentleman, lately of the army of the United States."[39]

The most dramatic of the rape cases detailed in newspapers during the spring of 1865 involved two couples: Mr. Smith and Miss Fanny L. Storme, and Mr. Colman and Miss Elvira Sieger. The two recently returned soldiers and their fiancées had gone to visit relatives on the eve of their nuptials and were attacked on the road by ruffians who left the men for dead and raped the women. A shocked and horrified media sympathized with these military heroes, "who had faced death on many a battle-field" and had returned home "to enjoy the peace for which they fought, and the company of those they loved," only to experience the violation of their women.[40]

For much of the sexual disorderliness they reported, northern newspapers blamed men. In criticizing the sentence in a case of infanticide involving a seventeen-year-old who killed the child she bore to an unnamed married man, the editors averred, he "deserves hanging, instead of the girl."[41] Editorials attacked male jurors for not taking sexual crimes seriously, accusing them of prurience and a lack of integrity in addressing the problems embedded in the cases before them. And in bemoaning the unhappiness of so many married couples, the editors of the *Chicago Evening Journal* held that it was the husband who "holds in his hands the happiness of all his household—his own, his wife's, their children. There is scarcely one woman in a thousand who will not at length become just, conciliatory, and kind, if her husband is firm, just, and tender. When a man has attained self-control," affirmed the journalist, "he has acquired a supremacy over all who are still the slaves of caprice and ill-temper."[42]

There were many interpretations of the verdict in the Harris case. Some pundits believed that the jurors were swayed by pity, taken in by her vulnerability or the tragedy of her story; others, that they were reluctant to hang a woman, or that they accepted the insanity plea as a chivalrous means of letting a woman escape responsibility for her all-too-understandable actions, or that they approved of murder as a solution to sexual wrongs. It is difficult to know what was in the minds of the jurors, but the verdict was read by many northern editors as a stand for social and sexual order.[43]

In their arguments to the Harris jury, both prosecution and defense harped upon the dangers attending postwar society. District Attorney Carrington in particular urged the jury to take a stand for law and order. "Unfortunately for us," he said,

> the city of Washington has acquired the reputation abroad of being the city of licentiousness, violence, and crime. . . . I repudiate this slander. . . . The citizens of Washington are a law-loving, law-abiding, religious people; and we are indebted to eminent criminals, who come from a distance, for this unenviable reputation. It is

the rendezvous for thieves, garrotes, murders, and adventurers. The city swarms with wicked men and women; and public safety depends upon the firmness and integrity of the judiciary.

He demanded that the jury send a message saying that the capital would no longer be "a sewer for all the vices and immoralities of the age in which we live." Said Carrington, "This is a central and a radiating point. We exert an influence in all sections of this great confederacy." The capital city must reassert appropriate values and behavior for the rest of the country so as to lead society out of wartime chaos.[44]

Order in the state required orderliness in the family and in male/female relations. Victorian Americans who read the newspapers may well have feared what they believed to be the wartime breakdown of the North's sex-gender system, threatened daily with becoming more like that of the licentious South. Beaten at arms, would the enemy nevertheless win the peace by spreading its libertine ways and undercutting the disciplined and orderly social ties that had enabled the North to conquer the South? Like their readers, many editors believed that the key to peace lay in spreading the northern ideal of manly self-regulation and discipline.[45]

The Harris trial offered rich fodder for sectional politics precisely because in their arguments to the jury, the defense and the prosecution attributed to the protagonists in this battle of the sexes their own version of which character represented the greatest danger to home and country. Carrington for the prosecution figured Harris as an unwomanly woman, a danger to men and a traitor to her sex and her country:

> We each have seen the noblest exhibition of true female character during the unhappy strife which has existed in our country for the last four years. Did you ever go to yonder hospital? See that young man. He is pale, attenuated, and emaciated. He has received some terrible wound, while fighting in his country's cause. He is far away from family and friends. . . . No kind mother stands by his bedside to cool the fevered brow. But hark! He hears woman's gentle voice. . . . It falls upon his ear like the name of home in some distant land. . . . She administers to his wants and whispers words of comfort and of consolation. He revives; he shoulders his musket and strikes another blow for his Government and his flag. Perhaps his last hour has come. Ever faithful, gentle woman, points him to a Saviour's dying love. . . .

And "when the noble daughters of America were kneeling by the bedside of the dying soldier, where was Mary Harris?" Carrington asked. At a "time when an appeal was made to every woman who had a heart to love her country and her race,"

> where then was Mary Harris, the model of female excellence? Arming herself with this instrument of death, practicing the use of deadly weapons, going in company . . . to a house of assignation without a protector, and at last imbruing her hands in the blood of one who had drawn his sword in his country's cause. . . .

Carrington drew for his image upon a mixture of prewar and wartime views of true womanhood.[46]

The devoted mother consoling her child in times of grief and illness, and the wife selflessly ministering to her husband when his work was done were traditional images. So too was woman's piety, her religious responsibility in bringing her husband to Christ. New was the emphasis upon nursing wounded men. Carrington's ideal of women who shepherded men to their redeemer in dying moments when necessary, or strengthened them and returned them to battle when possible, stemmed from the experience of war and women's new wartime roles and responsibilities. In particular, Carrington drew upon revised ideals of female sacrifice: "Women's self-sacrifice for personally significant others—husbands, brothers, sons, or family—was transformed into sacrifice of those individuals to an abstract and intangible cause."[47]

Mary Harris, insisted the district attorney, did not sacrifice in any sense of the word. She did not sacrifice because she did not love. "True love, gentlemen," he averred, "is a noble, pure, and generous passion. It refines the manners, purifies the heart, elevates the thoughts, gives zest and delight to every energy and to every aspiration." Neither pure nor good, Harris was instead a "proud, cruel, ambitious woman." Her motive for murder was jealousy, inflamed by greed.

> The lady discards her true-hearted, honorable lover; and he, like a man of honor, offers to return her letters and her portrait and try his fortune in another quarter. The lady, exercising a woman's right, in a spirit of coquetish-ness, discards the man she loves, and then, fired by the demon of jealousy, murders him for marrying another, her superior in all respects.

According to the prosecution, Burroughs did not wrong and abandon Harris; she wronged and abandoned him.[48]

Unlike Harris, Burroughs was honorable. Carrington represented him as a manly man and a patriot who had "drawn his sword in his country's cause." As the district attorney reiterated in closing argument, "[I]t is in my judgment, a fearful aggravation of her guilt that she slew a public servant while at his post of duty, and who drew his sword in his country's cause in that hour of national danger and distress, when loyal, patriotic men constituted the great wealth and chief hope of the republic." Burroughs did raise two companies of fighting men for the Union army, but he never actually served with either of them. In any case, neither the jury nor the press seems to have accepted Carrington's effort to attach to Burroughs the label of manly man and patriot and to Harris that of unnatural woman and traitor.[49]

Harris was instead, "that little girl" with "that little hand" that could barely hold that little pistol. According to one of her lawyers, Judge James Hughes, Harris was but a child with a toy:

> That little girl, (pointing to the prisoner,) with that little hand posed the pistol which might, upon ordinary occasions, have been discharged a hundred times, or rather snapped, (for they will not discharge one time in fifty) without any serious consequence, but with that toy of a pistol she was the instrument of punishment in the hands of God. . . .

But just as Harris was no "little girl," the gun was no "toy." Based on the testimony of Edwin G. Handy, the officer in charge of the Treasury watch, the murder weapon was probably a Sharps four-barrel, breach-loading pistol.[50] These were small guns, manufactured in three calibers. By far the most common, the .22 caliber pistol, had a barrel length of only two and a half inches and weighed only eight and a half ounces. But although small and lightweight, the Sharps was recommended for its "simplicity of construction, compactness and durability." And it was deadly. Advertised as having "more penetration than any other Firearm of its size," the Sharps was able to force a ball through a one-inch soft-pine board at the distance of three hundred feet. Not only did this "pepperbox" pistol have more firepower than the small, single-shot derringer, it carried four cartridges and could be repeatedly fired before reloading.[51]

Harris had purchased the gun in Chicago at least a year before the murder. Her roommate, Louisa Devlin, swore that Harris showed her the pistol and a box of cartridges in the fall of 1864 and said that she had purchased it for purposes of self-defense, believing that Burroughs and his brother were plotting to kidnap her off the street. She defended her purchase in the face of Devlin's dismay by saying that "she was not the only lady who carried a pistol."[52]

Her lawyers ensured that the jury did not view Harris as a gun-packing moll. They presented her as the frail, vulnerable, modest young woman who came into court surrounded by female friends and sat there, day after day, demure, submissive, passive, and delicate; swathed in veils and leaning upon the arm of her lawyers. In the iconography of the day, her very weakness made Harris the truest of women. As Kristin Hoganson has said, presenting women as gentle, weak victims "generated more than sympathy; it generated recognition that womanhood was at stake." Harris's lawyers stressed her weakness because gender identity based on helplessness conferred power—the right to demand honor and protection.[53]

An innocent young thing, her counsel insisted, Harris desired only what all good women wanted—to devote themselves to their husbands. Like Ruth of the Bible, Mary Harris held faithfully to "the object of her love."

> She did no more than what the proudest, the purest, and the best have done in all countries and at all times. She endowed him upon whose arm she leaned with the principles of justice and honor; she crowned his brow with a constellation of all the virtues and then trusted him. She turned her back on home, kindred, and friends and with him faced the world alone.

It was calumny, argued the defense, to accuse Harris of wrongdoing, and not only against Harris. The defense reconfigured Mary as everywoman: "Not only do I pronounce [the charges] a slander upon Mary Harris, but it is equally a slander upon the truth, fidelity, and virtue of womanhood," roared counsel.[54]

Northern newspapers seized upon this construction of Harris and contrasted the image counsel sculpted of her with that of the rebellious viragoes of the South, including Mary Surratt, whose deeds peppered their pages in the summer of 1865.[55] Mary McLain of Washington, D.C., became infamous for pulling down a Union flag and the mourning bunting that bedecked her boardinghouse in the wake of the president's assassination, proclaiming that "she had always been a friend of Jeff Davis and would not permit anything in her room to triumph over his defeat." Four women were hauled before Washington's second police ward in a single night in April, charged with "exulting over the murder of the President and trying to prevent loyal citizens from exhibiting tokens of grief by tearing down the mourning emblems from the windows of their neighbors." Bessie Perrine of Baltimore was widely reported to have flirted with and rendered assistance to rebel train robbers during the war. In sentencing her for these crimes, the judge advocate described her as "displaying malice, hatred, cruelty, a facility to adapt herself to the society of bandits and robbers . . . glorying in the sum of all crime—a party to arson, to larceny, and highway robbery."[56]

In accepting the defense's view of Harris's womanliness, northern reporters and editors also accepted their contention that it was Burroughs who was both unmanly and unpatriotic. As Harris's attorney argued, "[H]ad Burroughs been faithful to his vows, as he was called on to be, by every attribute which ennobles manhood, by every law human and divine, then this unhappy girl would have been to-day his respected wife, and the world would have applauded her sublime devotion to him." But he was false. And at this specific moment, when confusion and fear reigned, as a president lay dead, as armed bands marauded through the countryside, many northern commentators came to see in Burroughs an affront not just to masculinity but to northern masculinity. They reconstructed him as a prototypical southerner—lecherous, undisciplined, depraved and dishonorable—a view of southern manhood that was reinforced by the assassination of the president and the military defeat of the southern armies.[57]

The abolitionist view of southern men and slave society as characterized by lust, rapine, and miscegenation was not the only view to circulate in antebellum, northern culture, but it had been reinforced at the end of the war by the circulation of stories in the news media about southern outrages against the sexual decency of white women. A guerrilla leader named Coulter was reported to have compelled "by force of arms" the deputy clerk of the Hawkesville, Kentucky, County Court into issuing a marriage license, and then to have forced a local minister into uniting him in bigamous marriage with "Mrs. F," the "beautiful young wife of a discharged Union soldier." After living with the woman for three or four days, Coulter paid her five hundred dollars in gold and abandoned her. Following the Lincoln assassination, John Wilkes Booth was widely reputed to have fostered an easy "intimacy" with women—a quality that was equated with his being a "war monger," a "secessionist," and an assassin.[58]

Adoniram J. Burroughs was reconfigured by the Harris defense team into the very symbol of perversion. He was "a man of comparatively mature age, more than twice [Harris's] senior . . . almost old enough to be her father. [Harris] sat upon his knee in the purity of unconscious childhood." Burroughs's exact age was never clearly stated during the trial. His brother testified that he would have been thirty-three or thirty-four in the spring of 1865, making him fourteen or fifteen years older than Harris. However, the representation that he was "old enough to be her father" demonstrated to many northerners Burroughs' degeneracy and suggested his southernness (the differential between men and women in age at marriage was greater in the plantation South than in the North).[59] That he had perhaps seduced a child was bad enough. But to have seduced one young enough to be his own child suggested not only molestation but incest, a crime that abolitionists had particularly associated with slaveholders.[60] Whether or not Burroughs took sexual advantage of Harris (a highly contested issue in the trial), he certainly seduced her emotionally and intended to make her his mistress if not his wife.[61] Then, in cowardly fashion, he attempted to compromise her reputation and dishonor her name before running away and evading responsibility for his actions by avoiding service of a civil writ and hiding behind his brother's stonewalling of Harris's inquiries. Not being a manly man, a self-controlled and courageous man, Burroughs got what he deserved in the eyes of much of the northern public.

In commenting on the verdict, some editors expressed concern that the message sent by the jury might give women a dangerous edge in the war between the sexes.[62] When attorney Bradley kissed Mary Harris following the verdict, a reporter asked "whether, after this demonstration of affection, Miss Harris will be justified in shooting Mr. Bradley, if he refuses to marry her?" Showing a manly bravado and disregard for any real danger to the male sex as a whole, newspapers published such satirical articles as "General Orders, No. 1," by "Shay K. Morals." The fictitious order given to Treasury Department guards urges the disarming of all female guards, the inspection of all female guards for mental, moral, and paroxysmal condition, and the prohibition of communication by female guards with men. "Recent developments," argues Shay K. Morals, "have shown that the males of this corps require additional protection from the wily and (supposed) weaker sex, and this order is made upon earnest and tearful supplications from many deserving and unprotected males of this command." So too, a small paragraph in the *Washington Evening Star* headlined "The Effect of It," testified to the following conversation, ostensibly overheard on the day the Harris verdict was announced: " 'Carrie, dear, will you please lend me your revolver, I fear George will not be true to his promise, to-night?' 'Why Emma! I'm so sorry! I've just lent my revolver to Mary, as she has found a beau with ever so much more money than Alfred; but, dear, I can let you have my ivory handled stiletto, with much pleasure.' "[63]

The Mary Harris trial told of seduction, abandonment, betrayal, and retribution. But it was not simply understood by its audience as a narrative of despoliation and revenge in the sex wars. This was a seduction story writ large on the national scene by virtue of the ways in which gender served as a central metaphor shaping political discourse before and after the Civil War. As Kristin Hoganson has said of abolitionist literature, "The rhetoric of gender . . . politicized the self by using individuals to embody social and political issues. That it was contested so hotly only underlines the importance of gender as a leading ideological language in mid-nineteenth-century political debate, a language capable of creating and dissolving a unified national political culture." According to abolitionists, the seduction and rape of black women by white men and the disruption of proper gender roles of slaves by slaveholders were among the primary reasons for ending slavery. Slavery threatened a social order regulated and structured by rigidly prescribed gender roles. But while slavery was destroyed by the war, in order for the North to truly restore social and moral order, it must end seduction, rapine, and licentiousness universally; it must restore true gender roles and sexual relations.[64]

The seduction, abandonment, and betrayal of Mary Harris stood analogously to that of the country itself and resonated with the northern public's understanding of relations between the states. The South, like Adoniram J. Burroughs, was disorderly.[65] It had abandoned the manly virtues of discipline, industriousness, and self-control, and in so doing, betrayed itself and the Union. Its evil ways could not be permitted to spread, further undercutting the social values of the North, already weakened by five years of war. The danger was great: a mere month after the Harris verdict came a copycat attempted murder. The *Washington Evening Star* reported a "case of paroxysmal insanity and dysmenorrhea" in which one Margaret Wiener attempted to murder John Lyon, a cavalry officer. He bolted for the street and was wounded in the leg. The pistol used in the attack was a four-barreled Sharps revolver "of precisely the same pattern as that used by Miss Harris," affirmed the newspaper, "and which pattern, from its convenient size and facility of discharging would seem to be coming into general use as an article of lady's wear for retributive purposes."[66]

However, Margaret Wiener was no Mary Harris. An essentially false figure, Wiener lacked Harris's virtue, frailty, and womanliness. Not an engaged woman who might or might not have given sexual expression to her love in the throes of impassioned courtship but a wanton woman enjoying promiscuous sex with a "temporary lover." In another time and place, Wiener's behavior would have offered a familiar and mild challenge to public morality; but in this time and place it posed serious implications for the body politic.

As Nina Silber has suggested, the North in its military victory declared that the manlier men had won the contest at arms and asserted the moral high ground over southern braggarts, bullies, and knaves. Those who followed the Harris trial largely approved a verdict that called for resistance, violent if necessary, to creeping moral decay, marital disorder, sexual license, and gender confusion. As defense counsel Hughes argued: "There are those things, gentlemen, in this world, that are more precious than life, and especially is female honor and female character." Even Prosecutor Carrington agreed: "In this country a thousand swords would leap from their scabbards to avenge a look that threatened with injury or with insult an honest and a virtuous woman."[67] Harris was forgiven for having wielded the sword herself. After all, the North accepted that it, too, had been forced into a deplorable but necessary act of violence in conducting a devastating war. The jury was seen to have taken up the metaphorical sword a second time in approving Harris's course. The popularity of the verdict suggested that the public was willing to hoist it yet again, if need be, to sustain the Harrises of the world and to cut down both the men who attacked their virtue and whatever simulacra appeared whose lack of honor and false character posed a threat of their own. The implications of the verdict and the gender representations that underwrote the trial narrative did not bode well for northern attitudes toward Reconstruction, still fluctuating between retribution and magnanimity.

NOTES

1. *Official Report of the Trial of Mary Harris, Indicted for the Murder of Adoniram J. Burroughs, Before the Supreme Court of the District of Columbia. (Sitting As A Criminal Court.) Monday, July 3, 1865.* Prepared by James O. Clephane, *Official Reporter* (Washington, D.C.: W. H. & O. H. Morrison, 1865), 19–20.

2. Mary S. Hartman found female violence in Britain more individualized, with these domestic murderesses engaged in a more calculated pursuit of personal fulfillment. Her argument for the lack of a pattern of *crime passionel* in England had to do with the slower pace of modernization in France; because Britain modernized more rapidly, English women skipped this cultural stage. Hartman, *Victorian Murderesses: A True History of Thirteen Respectable French and English Women Accused of Unspeakable Crimes* (New York: Schocken Books, 1977), 266–67. Patrick Wilson argues that "the desire for assertion and freedom, a need to sweep away everyone in the home in the hope of some ill-defined, better future" motivated murderous Englishwomen. Wilson, *Murderess* (London: Michael Joseph, 1971), 172.

3. Joel Guillais argues that crimes of passion were essentially working-class crimes in late-nineteenth-century France and that it was only the literature of adultery that made it seem like a middle-class crime in the eyes of the public. Furthermore, he found that of the 1,278 acts of domestic crime in France between 1871 and 1880, 735 were crimes of passion. Of these, some 20 percent stemmed from acts of adultery and 34 percent from acts of debauchery, cohabitation, or jealousy among nonmarried couples. He found that of the 824 individuals charged with domestic crime during this period, 80 percent were male. In crimes where poisoning was involved, however, women outnumbered men. Guillais, *Crimes of Passion* (London: Routledge, 1990), 16, 22.

4. Guillais shows that although guns were used in about one-third of French cases during the 1870s, the proportion rose to two-thirds by 1930. Ibid., 70, 235, n. 13.

5. See Louis Proal, *Le Crime et le suicide passionels* (Paris: Alcan, 1900), 114, noted in Hartman, *Victorian Murderesses*, n. 81, 300. A wave of vitriolage, the crime of throwing sulfuric acid in a person's face, swept France late in the century. Usually, the acid was thrown by a woman in the face of her rival. Guillais, *Crimes of Passion*, 233, translator's note.

6. For the Briere case, see Guillais, *Crimes of Passion*, 189–91.

7. In her study of family murder, Elizabeth Pleck describes the trend of wives killing husbands as rising over time. No figures on murder have been kept for courting couples. Pleck, *Domestic Tyranny: The Making of Social Policy against Family Violence from Colonial Times to the Present* (New York: Oxford University Press, 1987), 217–25.

8. Ann Jones, *Women Who Kill* (New York: Ballantine Books, 1980), 108–11.

9. Jones, for example, describes the case of Amelia Norman, a servant in New York City who, after having born his child and been abandoned in a brothel, took a knife to Henry Ballard in 1843. The blade glanced off a rib and Ballard survived with only a small knife wound in the chest, just above the heart. Ibid., 156–57, 163–64.

10. Michael Bellesiles has studied 685 nineteenth-century murders and found that prior to the Civil War, the gun was not the weapon of choice. Prior to 1846, guns were used in 17.2 percent of murders; from 1846 to 1860, in 32.6 percent; and for the rest of the century, in 47.5 percent. He does not differentiate between male and female murderers. Bellesiles, "The Origins of Gun Culture in the United States, 1760–1865," *Journal of American History* 83, no. 2 (1996): 441. Jones records two cases similar to that of Mary Harris, in which "spoiled maidens" shot the men who dishonored them: Fanny Windley shot George Watson on January 26, 1872, and Elizabeth King shot Charles Goodwich on March 21 of the same year, both in New York. Jones, *Women Who Kill*, 165. Pleck believes that the handgun has been the great equalizer in domestic murder, enabling women to catch up with men. Pleck, *Domestic Tyranny*, 221. Another study doubts the association between handguns and female-accomplished murder, arguing that murderers choose guns because they want to commit homicide, and those who opt for knives are less intent on taking life. See James Wright, Peter Rossi, and Kathleen Daly, *Under the Gun: Weapons, Crime, and Violence in America* (New York: Aldine, 1983), 175–212.

11. Dorothy Schneider and Carl J. Schneider, *Into the Breach: American Women Overseas in World War I* (New York: Viking, 1991); William H. Chafe, "World War II as a Pivotal Experience for American Women," in *Women and War: The Changing Status of American Women from the 1930s to the 1950s*, ed. Maria Diedrich and Dorothea Fischer-Hornung (New York: Berg, 1990); D'Ann Campbell, *Women at War with America: Private Lives in a Patriotic Era* (Cambridge: Harvard University Press, 1984); Susan Hartmann, *The Home Front and Beyond: American Women in the 1940s* (Boston: Twaine, 1982); Mary Beth Norton, *Liberty's Daughters: The Revolutionary Experience of American Women, 1750–1800* (Boston: Little, Brown, 1980); Linda Kerber, *Women of the Republic: Intellect and Ideology in Revolutionary America* (Chapel Hill: University of North Carolina Press, 1980).

12. Mary Elizabeth Massey, *Bonnet Brigades* (New York: Knopf, 1966); George C. Rable, *Civil Wars: Women and the Crisis of Southern Nationalism* (Urbana: University of Illinois Press, 1989); Anne F. Scott, *Natural Allies: Women's Associations in American History* (Urbana: University of Illinois Press, 1991); Wendy Hamand Venet, *Neither Ballots nor Bullets: Women Abolitionists and the Civil War* (Charlottesville: University Press of Virginia, 1991); Catherine Clinton, *Tara Revisited: Women, War, and the Plantation Legend* (New York: Abbeville Press, 1995); Drew Gilpin Faust, *Mothers of Invention: Women of the Slaveholding South in the American Civil War* (Chapel Hill: University of North Carolina Press, 1996).

13. Margaret Randolph Higonnet, Jane Jenson, Sonya Michel, Margaret Collins Weitz, eds., *Behind the Lines: Gender and the Two World Wars* (New Haven: Yale University Press, 1987); Lori D. Ginzberg, *Women and the Work of Benevolence: Morality, Politics, and Class in the Nineteenth-Century United States* (New Haven: Yale University Press, 1990); Anne C. Rose, *Victorian America and the Civil War* (New York: Cambridge University Press, 1992); Catherine Clinton and Nina Silber, eds., *Divided Houses: Gender and the Civil War* (New York: Oxford University Press, 1992); LeeAnn Whites, "The Civil War as a Crisis in Gender," in Clinton and Silber, *Divided Houses*, 3–21; Elizabeth Leonard, *Yankee Women: Gender Battles in the Civil War* (New York: Norton, 1994). For comparative studies that detail the reconfiguration of gender identity after twentieth-century wars, see Susan Kingsley Kent, *Making Peace: The Reconstruction of Gender in Interwar Britain* (Princeton: Princeton University Press, 1993); Mary Louise Roberts, *Civilization without Sexes: Reconstructing Gender in Postwar France, 1917–1927* (Chicago: University of Chicago Press, 1994).

14. Roberts, *Civilization without Sexes*, 5.

15. See Edward Berenson, *The Trial of Madame Caillaux* (Berkeley: University of California Press, 1992), for a model microhistorical study in which a close reading of the docu-

ments in a single trial provides a window into fundamental aspects of contemporary culture. See also Charles E. Rosenberg, *The Trial of the Assassin Guiteau: Psychiatry and the Law in the Gilded Age* (Chicago: University of Chicago Press, 1968); George Cooper, *Lost Love: A True Story of Passion, Murder and Justice in Old New York* (New York: Vintage Books, 1995).

16. *Official Report*, 16.

17. *Opening Speech of John Graham, Esq., to the Jury, on the Part of the Defence, in the Trial of Daniel E. Sickles* (New York: W. A. Townsend, n.d.), quoted in Nat Brandt, *The Congressman Who Got Away with Murder* (Syracuse: Syracuse University Press, 1991), 171–74.

18. *Trial of Hon. Daniel E. Sickles* (Washington, D.C.: Wentworth and Stanley, 1859), 66, 91–93. Ould was elevated from assistant district attorney by President Buchanan, a friend of Sickles's, on Key's death. Sickles's defense team so overwhelmed the mild-mannered Ould that Key's relatives and friends retained attorney John Carlisle to aid the prosecution. Their concern seemed validated when Ould refused to call to the stand Samuel Butterworth, who was with Sickles when he spotted Key across Lafayette Square. Butterworth, believed by many to have held Key in conversation while Sickles retrieved his pistols, stood by and watched the attack. Nor did Ould submit evidence of Sickles's own numerous infidelities, which would have undercut sympathy for him as the victim of his wife's misconduct. W. A. Swanberg, *Sickles the Incredible* (New York: Charles Scribner's Sons, 1956), 58, 63–66.

19. *Trial of Hon. Daniel E. Sickles*, 105–6; Brant, *Congressman Who Got Away with Murder*, 182; Henry Weihofen, *Mental Disorder as a Criminal Defense* (Buffalo: Dennis, 1954), 246. District Attorney Carrington specifically addressed the Sickles case as a precedent for the Harris case in his concluding argument. He saw Sickles ("and I mention his name with respect for he has proved to be a true patriot and a gallant soldier") acting in a "species of paroxysmal insanity," which he did not believe to be the case with Harris. *Official Report*, 178. Sickles was a controversial figure during the war. Swanberg, *Sickles the Incredible*, 199–235.

20. See the discussion of the psychology of the day in Jones, *Women Who Kill*, 169–74.

21. Ibid., 170–71; *Official Report*, 17.

22. *Official Report*, 177. In her brief analysis of this case, Jones assumes that Burroughs seduced Harris, a fact that Harris vehemently denied, and that the jury made new law in releasing her from custody. At the time, the American legal system did not protect female chastity. A father or husband could sue for loss of services due to a wife's or daughter's seduction or rape, but a woman could acquire neither protection from seduction nor restitution for her injury. Society, Jones believes, would not limit male sexual prerogatives by protecting women (or children) from predatory men. She argues that although the jury ratified Burroughs's punishment (his death) by acquitting his killer, the legislature refused to grant women the power in law to defend themselves. The law offered chivalry, not justice, to the victim who took matters into her own hands. Jones, *Women Who Kill*, 149–86.

23. Nina Silber, *The Romance of Reunion: Northerners and the South, 1865–1900* (Chapel Hill: University of North Carolina Press, 1993), 13–17. Mary Harris, for example, was deeply upset by the assassination. Dr. Charles H. Nichols, a visitor to her cell, recalled, "It was the evening of the day of the funeral of the late President; and she expressed great apprehension lest further violence might be committed by his assassins, and particularly to herself." *Official Report*, 76.

24. The sentence of Mary Surratt to hang produced considerable debate in the media because of the tribunal's rejected recommendation for leniency and the fruitless efforts of

Surratt's daughter and priest to win a reprieve. Thomas Reed Turner, *Beware the People Weeping: Public Opinion and the Assassination of Abraham Lincoln* (Baton Rouge: Louisiana State University Press, 1982), ch. 12.

25. The number of daily newspapers increased by 40 percent between 1860 and 1870, and their circulation by 70 percent. Few communities lacked a newspaper by the end of the Civil War. Mark Wahlgren Summers, *The Press Gang: Newspapers and Politics, 1863–1878* (Chapel Hill: University of North Carolina Press, 1994), chs. 1, 5.

26. "Can Women Commit Murder?" *Frank Leslie's Illustrated Newspaper*, 12 August 1865, 322.

27. "The Two Verdicts," *National Republican*, 21 July 1865, 2; Reid Mitchell, *The Vacant Chair: The Northern Soldier Leaves Home* (New York: Oxford University Press, 1993), xi–18.

28. "A Scandalous Case. Alarming Evidences of Demoralization," *Chicago Times*, 3 April 1865, 3. See also the *New York Herald* of 13 October 1865, in which the editor comments on the war's having "brought all corruptions of the body politic to the surface." Quoted in Mary Elizabeth Massey, *Women in the Civil War* (Lincoln: University of Nebraska, 1994), 265.

29. Massey notes the increased attention of the press to scandal, divorce, abortion, illegitimacy, and illicit relations during the war. Massey, "A Grand Convulsion in Society," in *Women in the Civil War*, 260–65. My thanks to Mary Waalkes and Ellen Aiken for their assistance in culling the northern newspapers used in this project.

30. "Female Soldier," *Chicago Evening Journal*, 13 February 1865, 4; "Romance," *Chicago Evening Journal*, 14 June 1865, 1; "Notice" of two female rebel soldiers captured, *Washington Evening Star*, 29 April 1865, 4. Information on women soldiers—those who escaped sexual boundaries to fight as men—is scarce and difficult to analyze. Military leaders and civilian authorities assumed that such women were prostitutes. Some of these women were wives accompanying their husbands and dressing like men to ease their escape from the enemy. More instances were reported of Northern than Southern white women's masquerading as men. Contemporary accounts suggested as many as four hundred, but there are no real studies of the matter. See Clinton, *Tara Revisited*, 98–100; Faust, *Mothers of Invention*, 202–3; Massey, *Women in the Civil War*, 81–84 ; Janet E. Kaufman, " 'Under the Petticoat Flag': Women Soldiers in the Confederate Army," *Southern Studies* 23 (1984): 363–75. The case of a black woman, Emma Edmonds, who briefly impersonated a young black man is discussed in Lyde Cullen Sizer, "Acting Her Part: Narratives of Union Women Spies," in Clinton and Silber, *Divided Houses*, 124.

31. "Miss Major Walker: How She Acted in Church," *Chicago Times*, 26 April 1865, 1; "Will Wear the Trousers," *Chicago Evening Journal*, 10 May 1865, 3. During the war, scores of women were arrested for posing as men—some with women and others with men to whom they were not married. The topic received considerable press coverage by editors worried that women were adopting military styles, weapons of war, and male habits such as smoking, swearing, and drinking in public. Massey, *Women in the Civil War*, 259–60. Faust discusses Southern women's adoption of male dress in *Mothers of Invention*, 220–33.

32. For a discussion of men's coming of age in the war and the value placed upon the curbing of sexuality and violence through self-discipline and civilized morality, see Mitchell, *Vacant Chair*, 11–12.

33. "A Dangerous Wife," *Washington Evening Star*, 4 February 1865, 2.

34. "Sue Mundy," *Chicago Times*, 16 February 1865, 4; "Execution of Sue Mundy," *Chicago Times*, 20 March 1865, 2; "A Rebel Spy in Female Attire," *Washington Evening Star*, 18 February 1865, 1. The last was republished from the *Cleveland Leader* and reprinted in *Chicago Times*, 16 February 1865, 1; *Cleveland Leader*, 13 February 1865, noted in Massey,

Women in the Civil War, 260. For a discussion of the capture of Jefferson Davis in a dress and the ways in which this incident helped shape Northern views of effeminate Southern men, see Nina Silber, "Intemperate Men, Spiteful Women, and Jefferson Davis," in Clinton and Silber, *Divided Houses*, 283–305. For a different interpretation of the meaning of Davis's capture as having to do more with unmasking than effeminacy, see Kenneth S. Greenberg, *Honor and Slavery: Lies, Duels, Noses, Masks, Dressing as a Woman, Gifts, Strangers, Humanitarianism, Death, Slave Rebellions, the Proslavery Argument, Baseball, Hunting, and Gambling in the Old South* (Princeton: Princeton University Press, 1996), 25–31.

35. "The Transgressions of War-Widows," *Chicago Times*, 19 July 1865, 3. A study of the increase in the annual numbers of divorces granted in New York was detailed in the *New York Express* and reprinted in the *Chicago Times*, 31 July 1865, 1.

36. Reprinted from the *Boston Post*, February 15: "Seduction and Child Desertion," *Chicago Times*, 21 February 1865, 1; "Sorrows of a Man of War," *Chicago Times*, 13 February 1865, 3; "Two Husbands," *National Republican*, 1 August 1865, 2; reprinted from *Rock Island Argus*, March 23, "Domestic Infidelity," *Chicago Times*, 25 March 1865, 4; reprinted from the *Coos Republican* (N.H.), "Domestic Tragedy," *Chicago Evening Journal*, 23 February 1865, 1; "The Father Found—The Mother Lost," *Burlington Weekly Hawk-Eye* (Iowa), 27 May 1865, 6.

37. "The Transgressions of War-Widows," *Chicago Times*, 19 July 1865, 3; *Burlington Weekly Hawk-Eye* (Iowa), 25 March 1865, 8.

38. "The Trials of a Soldiers Wife," *Chicago Times*, 7 March 1865, 3; Anna Dickinson, "Woman's Rights and Dangers," *Chicago Evening Journal*, 11 March 1865, 2; *Chicago Times*, 28 March 1865, 3, 29 March 1865, 3, 10 March 1865, 1. Soldiers discussed sexual promiscuity and prostitution in their war journals and correspondence. For instance, Kansas Cavalry Sergeant W. W. Moses detailed the "fall" of sixteen-year-old Mary French, a respectable girl seduced by the "indirect" promises of marriage of Lieutenant William Henry. Henry slept with the girl every night for a month before she was taken away by her father, a Union soldier home on leave. Moses blamed Henry for corrupting the girl, although he did not intervene to warn her that Henry was married. Not surprisingly, soldiers returning from the field brought back with them their experience of sexual adventuring on the battlefront, and the concerns about such behavior on the home front resulted in such coverups as someone literally accomplished with the Moses diary entry, shielding it with a piece of paper. Mitchell, *Vacant Chair*, 6–7; the Diary of W. W. Moses, 24 January 1865, Kansas State Historical Society, quoted in Michael Fellman, "Women and Guerrilla Warfare," in Clinton and Silber, *Divided Houses*, 160; Thomas Lowry, *The Story the Soldiers Wouldn't Tell: Sex and the Civil War* (Harrisburg, Pa.: Stackpole Press, 1994).

39. "An Unprincipled Rake," *Chicago Times*, 21 July 1865, 3. See also "Heartless Seduction," *Chicago Tribune*, 21 July 1865, 4; "The Crime of Seduction," *Chicago Evening Journal*, 22 July 1865, 2; "The Da Costa-James Seduction," *Chicago Tribune*, 24 July, 1865, 4; "The Seduction Case," *Chicago Tribune*, 27 July 1865, 4. Illicit sex was also seen as being on the rise as well and was addressed in the language of "seduction." Martha Hodes, "Wartime Dialogues on Illicit Sex: White Women and Black Men," in Clinton and Silber, *Divided Houses*, 230–46; Fellman, "Women and Guerrilla Warfare," 149–55; Massey, *Women in the Civil War*, 261.

40. The presumed sympathy of the editors with the young women went unspoken, although they gave the full names of the women and only the surnames of these heroes. "Atrocious Rape Case," *Chicago Evening Journal*, 7 March 1865, 3. For other examples, see "Diabolical Outrage," *Chicago Times*, 8 February 1865, 3; *Baltimore National Republican*, 9 August 1865, 1; "A Serious Charge," *Chicago Times*, 13 April 1865, 3.

41. "Sad Case of Infanticide," *Chicago Evening Journal*, 27 February 1865, 2.

42. "Diabolical Outrage," *Chicago Times*, 8 February 1865, 3; "A Plea for Justice," *Chicago Evening Journal*, 17 May 1865, 4; "Unhappy Married People," *Chicago Evening Journal*, 15 April 1865, 2.

43. "The Mary Harris Verdict. Opinions of the Press," *Washington Evening Star*, 22 July 1865, 1; *Chicago Evening Journal*, 18 February 1865, 3.

44. *Official Report*, 9, 181.

45. Silber, *Romance of Reunion*, 25. There is a large literature linking the South as a region with licentious behavior and eroticism, including the antislavery literature that described the South as a brothel. Ronald G. Walters, "The Erotic South: Civilization and Sexuality in American Abolitionist Literature," *American Quarterly* 25, no. 2 (1973): 177–201; Bertram Wyatt-Brown, *Yankee Saints and Southern Sinners* (Baton Rouge: Louisiana State University Press, 1985); Anne Norton, *Alternative Americas: A Reading of Antebellum Political Culture* (Chicago: University of Chicago Press, 1989); Kristin Hoganson, "Garrisonian Abolitionists and the Rhetoric of Gender 1850–1860," *American Quarterly* 45, no. 4 (1993): 558–95; Karen Sanchez-Eppler, *Touching Liberty: Abolition, Feminism, and the Politics of the Body* (Berkeley: University of California Press, 1993). Mitchell discusses the wartime use of the family metaphor for the Union and the body politic; *Vacant Chair*, 14–16.

46. *Official Report*, 163.

47. Faust, *Mothers of Invention*, 17; Nancy Cott, *The Bonds of Womanhood: Woman's Sphere in New England, 1780–1835* (New Haven: Yale University Press, 1977), 78; Lee Chambers-Schiller, *Liberty, A Better Husband: Single Women in America, the Generations 1790–1840* (New Haven: Yale University Press, 1984), 3, 27, 51–52, 158, 207.

48. *Official Report*, 171, 174, 179. Carrington did not accuse Harris herself of seeking money but did argue that her friends the Devlins hoped to profit by her suit for breach of promise. In viciously attacking the character of the Devlins (who, after all, provided the strongest supporting evidence both for Harris's relationship with Burroughs and her erratic behavior after he abandoned her), Carrington roused the ire of Judge Andrew Wylie, who consistently ruled against the district attorney. On Wylie, see *Who Was Who in America*, 1:1387.

49. *Official Report*, 180.

50. Ibid., 22, 125. On Hughes, see Carl W. Mitman, "James Hughes," in *Dictionary of American Biography*, ed. Dumas Malone (New York: Charles Scribner's Sons, 1932), 9:351–52. Defense counsel also referred to the Sharps as a "toy pistol" in opening remarks. See *Official Report*, 15. It is interesting to note by way of contrast that Daniel Sickles's five-shot revolver misfired twice. Brandt, *Congressman*, 121–22. I thank Lawrence Schiller and Cathy Weigley for help locating information on the Sharps pepperbox and Paul Simmons for taking the time to explain the workings of this gun.

51. Frank M. Sellers, *Sharps Firearms* (North Hollywood: Beinfeld, 1978), 134. Sixty-one thousand of the model 1A .22 short, rimfire pistols were manufactured, along with thousands of other models based upon the original 1859 patent. The guns did not often misfire, as the judge suggested. Indeed, next to the Colt percussion revolver, the Sharps four-barrel pistol was the most-copied American gun; it was produced by more than fifty companies in twenty countries. As of 1978, it remained in production. Ibid., 125–67; *Official Report*, 103.

52. *Official Report*, 45. Gun-packing women were a new concern during and after the war, when firearms were so much more available and many women, particularly in the South, had learned how to shoot. Emma Holmes, for example, notes in her diary her pride in learning to load and clean pistols, and then to fire them. John F. Marszalek, ed., *The*

Diary of Miss Emma Holmes, 1861–1866 (Baton Rouge: Louisiana State University Press, 1984), 84, 91. For discussions of Southern women learning to use guns during the war, see Rable, *Civil Wars*, 152–53; Faust, *Mothers of Invention*, 202–4.

53. Hoganson was speaking of slave women in abolitionist discourse. Kristin Hoganson, "Garrisonian Abolitionists and the Rhetoric of Gender 1850–1860," *American Quarterly* 45, no. 4 (December 1993): 581. Carrington recognized the power of the iconography of female frailty and insisted that a true woman, a woman of honor, would have done what Harris did not—she would have depended upon the protection of a father, brother, or friend rather than employ "the assassin's dagger to redress even . . . the foulest wrongs." *Official Report*, 178.

54. *Official Report*, 140, 141. One often wonders if lawyer Judge Charles Mason was not deliberately speaking over the heads of the jury to the press in the way that he crafted his prose and his arguments. He brought to the defense a practical knowledge of newspaper work, having written for the newspapers on many occasions and served temporarily as editor of the *New York Evening Post* in the late 1830s.

55. Much recent historiography on Southern women's role in the war has attempted to undercut this contemporary image and to emphasize the ambivalence or opposition to the war of white slaveholding women. See Rable, *Civil Wars*, and Faust, *Mothers of Invention*. But the diaries of Emma Holmes and Ellen Renshaw House suggest that there was some truth to the picture of fiery, unreconstructed "secesh females" that dominated northern newspapers. See Marszalek, *Diary of Miss Emma Holmes*, and Daniel E. Sutherland, ed., *A Very Violent Rebel: The Civil War Diary of Ellen Renshaw House* (Knoxville: University of Tennessee Press, 1996); William Hanchett, *The Lincoln Murder Conspiracies* (Urbana: University of Illinois Press, 1986), 86–88, 94–99, 103–4, 110–14, 122–23, 170, 180.

56. *Washington Evening Star*, 18 April 1865, 2; *Washington Daily Chronicle*, 11 May 1865, 4, 16 May 1865, 4; *Washington Evening Star*, 17 April 1865, 3.

57. *Official Report*, 140, 141; Silber, *Romance of Reunion*, 9.

58. *Chicago Evening Journal*, 18 February 1865, 3; "Booth and His Intimacy with Ladies," *Chicago Times*, 5 April 1865, 1.

59. *Official Report*, 84, 140. Elizabeth Fox-Genovese, *Within the Plantation Household: Black and White Women of the Old South* (Chapel Hill: University of North Carolina Press, 1988), 113; Suzanne Lebsock, *The Free Women of Petersburg: Status and Culture in a Southern Town, 1784–1860* (New York: Norton, 1984), 33.

60. The theme was stressed throughout the trial. In his opening statement, Harris's defense counsel, Judge Hughes, said—exaggerating Burroughs's age and therefore his degeneracy—that "the deceased first became interested in this young lady when she was about ten years old; took charge of her as it were; he being a man of some thirty-two years, a merchant in the city, and she quite a little girl. . . ." *Official Report*, 28, 127, 139–40.

61. Harris vehemently denied having had sex with Burroughs and asserted her chastity throughout her incarceration and trial. Hugh McCullough, comptroller of the currency, had spoken to her and testified: "I asked her if Mr. Burroughs had done her any other injury than the violation of his engagement. She exclaimed, with a great deal of emphasis, that he had not. I put the question to her, 'Are you a virtuous girl?' 'Yes, as God is my witness,' was her answer." She asserted that Burroughs had attacked her reputation and that that alone caused her grief and was the reason for instituting her suit for breach of promise. However, her lawyer, D. W. Voorhees, acknowledged in closing arguments, "It is true that in this case the additional crime of seduction occurred. . . ." *Official Report*, 24, 144.

62. The Chicago newspapers carried a "shocking" story during the Harris trial about

a middle-class, young schoolteacher, Charlotte Munson, who lured her lover, the married James Kerr into a buggy, where she took out a concealed gun and shot him after he refused to return her love letters. The paper sympathized with Munson's situation while expressing shock about the crime. *Chicago Times*, 30 June 1865, 2; *Chicago Tribune*, 6 July 1865, 2.

63. "A Question," *Washington Evening Star*, 2 August 1865, 2; "The Great Danger in Washington—Wise Defensive Precautions," *National Republican*, 5 August 1865, 1; "The Effect of It," *Washington Evening Star*, 25 July 1865, 4.

64. Hoganson, "Garrisonian Abolitionists and the Rhetoric of Gender," 588.

65. It is perhaps important to note that among Harris's well-known lawyers were vehement antisecessionists. Judge Hughes, a Democrat, became an ardent Republican and unionist after secession. Judge Charles Mason of Burlington, Iowa, a lifelong Democrat, had rendered a decision when serving on the Iowa Supreme Court that a slave going into free territory by the consent of his master was, thereafter, a free man (a precedent that was overturned by the U.S. Supreme Court in the *Dred Scott* decision). Daniel W. Voorhees, another Democrat, was aligned with the proslavery side of his party before the war but, like Mason, became vehemently antisecessionist. He was widely known for his defense of John E. Cook, a participant in the raid on Harpers Ferry.

66. "Case of Paroxysmal Insanity and Dysmenorrhea," *Washington Evening Star*, 7 August 1865, 2.

67. Official Report, 133, 178; Silber, *Romance of Reunion*, 19. Washington, D.C., had been a distinctly southern city before the war but its ambiance was in transition as war profiteers and northern military men swelled its population and southern politicians and their families left. Many jurors could still have been more southern than northern in their cultural background. However, they might have felt the same sense of chivalry in protecting the sexual honor of frail, white womanhood (as Carrington expressed it) and could have voted acquittal on these grounds as well.

Dodge City, Kansas, at the intersection of Bridge and Front streets, the town's busiest intersection, circa 1880. The topmost sign reads: "THE CARRYING OF FIRE ARMS STRICTLY PROHIBITED." Used by permission of the Kansas State Historical Society, Topeka, Kansas.

Chapter Ten

To Live and Die in Dodge City
Body Counts, Law and Order, and the Case of Kansas v. Gill

Robert R. Dykstra

Never mind that during its celebrated decade as a tough cattle town only fifteen persons died violently in Dodge City, 1876–1885, for an average of just 1.5 killings per cowboy season.[1] Today, three decades after the first release of the homicide data, frontier Dodge City remains a universal metaphor for slaughter and civic anarchy.[2]

Professional historians of the American West are, of course, presumed to know better. And yet there have been recent hints of scholarly skepticism about Dodge City's modest body count. In 1994, for instance, a very prominent essay on frontier violence discussed Dodge and the other Kansas cattle towns without so much as noting in passing their low absolute numbers of killings.[3]

This odd disregard is puzzling. One explanation might be that the homicide data are deemed irrelevant to the question of frontier violence. This is simply hard to credit. A second might be that the data do not conform to the New Western History paradigm, which tends to insist that things were always worse than we thought. That notion can be argued either way.[4] A third possibility is that the data are somehow suspect, and thus better left unmentioned until the question can somehow be settled once and for all. This last possibility, more than the persistence of the Dodge City metaphor among those who learned their Western history in darkened theaters, suggests the value of a revisit to the real, if legendary, town in question.

All the Homicide News Fit to Print

Dodge City was indeed a legend in its own time. It was where livestock herded up from Texas to the railroad tracks in Kansas would be sold, shipped east to market, or walked onward to the ranges of the northern Great Plains. The summertime influx of transients—well-heeled drovers and cattle brokers, festive cowboys, predatory gamblers, and sporting women—more than equaled the town's resident population. But a police force of multiple officers, their salaries totaling nearly half of Dodge City's entire municipal budget, closely supervised the behavior of these itinerants by enforcing strict gun-control laws.[5]

The richest man in town, merchant Robert M. Wright, had been present in the bad old days when, in its unorganized first year of existence, Dodge had been the scene of several violent deaths. Wright and his entrepreneurial colleagues had not feared for their lives; they feared for their pocketbooks—that is, their local property values—as the newspapers of eastern Kansas delighted in such energetic headlines as "HOMICIDE AT DODGE CITY. A Notorious Desperado Killed" or "SHOT DEAD. Another Tragedy at Dodge City," or in such sly one-liners as "Only two men killed at Dodge City last week."[6]

But with an expectation of the Texas cattle trade's coming to Dodge, local businessmen foresaw that the influx of new transients would only magnify all problems related to law and order. They therefore established a municipal government late in 1875, levied taxes to pay for it, and criminalized gun toting by private citizens. A photograph taken a few years later shows the town's busiest corner, downtown Front Street at its intersection with Bridge Street, the main thoroughfare in and out of Dodge. In the left background stand R. M. Wright's brick store and the facade of the celebrated Long Branch Saloon. In the middle foreground the superstructure of a town well displays a prominent sign: "The Carrying of Fire Arms Strictly PROHIBITED."[7] As this proximity suggests, hand-gun violence was considered bad for business, an emphatic collective belief of Dodge City's business and professional elite that ultimately explains the low body count.

Scholars' attempts to dilute the significance of such body counts first appeared in the 1980s. "These statistics seem to indicate that the cattle towns were not particularly violent," wrote Roger McGrath. "However, a note of caution is appropriate. Dykstra compiled his statistics exclusively from the local newspapers." The subtext here: How can we be sure that more murders and justifiable homicides than reported did not occur?[8]

There is no known official list of violent deaths at Dodge. Pending discovery of any such compendium, we must depend on a few reasonable assumptions about those reported by the press. The first is the absolute and primal newsworthiness of violent death. However enthusiastically they might conspire in cover-ups and damage control regarding local social conflict, Dodge City's journalists seemed no more able to resist a good homicide story than any circulation-chasing New York or Chicago city editor.

A second assumption involves the substantial array of local weekly newspapers that offer a fairly intimate summary of life in Dodge during the trail-driving era. The *Dodge City Times* began publishing in May 1876, just in time for the town's first cattle-trading season. The *Ford County Globe* joined it in January 1878. The *Dodge City Democrat* appeared in December 1883. And the *Kansas Cowboy* moved to Dodge from Ness County in June 1884. True enough, the first ten months of the *Times*, save for a single issue, are not extant. For 1876, one must extrapolate from the absence of murderous dispatches about Dodge in the press of eastern Kansas; so far, none has been discovered.[9] But certainly from March 1877 to the close of the Texas cattle trade at Dodge City late in 1885, all newspaper runs are virtually complete. Every nineteenth-century village should be so well documented.

A third guiding assumption seems equally reasonable. Cattle-town homicides, when they occasionally occur, are almost always reported in some detail, as the story of Henry Heck's demise will show. This attention lends weight to the notion that news concerning violent death tended to be revealed rather than suppressed.

Deadly Competition: Miami (1980) versus Dodge (1880)

A rather more comprehensive criticism of the cattle-town death statistics also appeared in the 1980s. This critique questioned the significance of the absolute numbers themselves, and argued for replacing them with homicide rates of the type annually devised by the FBI to measure urban violence. For today's metropolitan areas, each case of "murder and non-negligent manslaughter" (excluding justifiable homicides by the police) is calculated as a proportion of every 100,000 of population. The simple formula is

$$hr = (100,000/N_p)\,N_h,$$

where hr equals homicide rate, N_p equals population, and N_h equals number of homicides. Since the 1940s the FBI has used this formula in running a kind of annual negative sweepstakes in which the losing city becomes America's most violent community, the murder capital of the world. In 1980, for example, greater Miami's homicide rate soared to 32.7—the nation's highest that year.[10]

But, as a few scholars began to note, a murder rate of 32.7 is not very high when contrasted with similarly calculated homicide rates back in time. That for late-thirteenth-century London, noted James Given, was about the same as the yearly average for Miami, 1948–1952. Barbara Hanawalt similarly discovered that the rate for London in the early fourteenth century soared even higher, to something between 36.0 and 51.3. Then, uncritically borrowing the two medievalists' methodology, Roger McGrath discovered that the average annual homicide rate at nineteenth-century Bodie, California, a mining camp, was a stratospheric 116.0.[11]

These historians have been compromised by the statistical fallacy of small numbers. In 1980, Miami's absolute number of homicides exceeded 500, while Hanawalt's yearly average for London was only 18 and McGrath's body count for Bodie over several years was a measly 29. It was London's modest population (an estimated 35,000 to 50,000) and Bodie's small population (no more than 5,000 in any year) that caused their homicide rates to surpass modern Miami's.

As to tiny Dodge City—population 1,275 in 1880—its FBI homicide rate calculates out at an enormous 78.4 for that year, compared with Miami's 32.7 exactly a century later. Yet, the absolute numbers of murders on which these ratios are based are these: Dodge, 1; Miami, 515. In other words, if a bullet fired by John ("Concho") Gill had missed Henry C. Heck instead of striking him in the chest, Dodge City's 1880 murder rate would have been zero instead of soaring to more than twice that of the 1980 murder capital of the world.[12]

But one may argue that a single killing in a village like frontier Dodge may have had more traumatic psychological impact on its residents than Miami's 515 homicides must have had on its citizens in 1980. This proposition is supported by such personal testaments as Elizabeth Salamon's account of a double murder in her quiet New Jersey town in 1997 ("a killing has occurred in our midst and we will never be the same"), the emotional agony in awaiting identification of the shooter ("at night, my husband and I try to sleep, but sleep does not come easily"), and her guilty elation when she learns that the killer himself has died violently ("when murder hits this close to home, a dark heart is a regrettable residual").[13] And the general idea accords with what scholars have occasionally noted about the sociological equivalence of small and large places concerning such things as population fertility and rural-urban value conflicts.[14]

But how does the argument fare in any specific contrast between 1980s Miami and 1880s Dodge? The *Miami Herald* for late December of 1980 is studded with allusions to the "record 555 homicides in Dade County this year," as reported by the local medical examiner's office—a figure that evidently includes 40 justifiable homicides by the police that would not be included in the FBI calculation. The newspaper reported that things are much worse in California, where Los Angeles County's homicides had reached a record 2,130 for the year. (Unfortunately for the *Herald*, however, greater Miami's smaller population imposed a 32.7 murder rate as against only 23.3 for Los Angeles.)[15]

In any event, such defensive finger-pointing did not help much. The mood of urgency within Miami's political and economic leadership was palpable. Announcing itself "very concerned about the high incidence of homicides and other acts of violence occurring in certain liquor establishments," Miami's city council urged that they be put out of business, and a special police task force convened to identify these evil influences. "It will help when we get sufficient manpower aboard," complained the chief of Miami's patrol division. As if in anticipation, a federation of local homeowner associations formed a blue-ribbon Citizens Action Council "to pressure state and local legislators to bolster programs to counter Dade's rising crime rate." At the behest of the Citizens Crime Commission of Greater Miami, the Dade County Metro Council endorsed the new group, which planned to meet with judges, state legislators, and Governor Bob Graham. One of the commissioners set the agenda by demanding that Graham convene a special legislative session to appropriate a hundred million dollars for Dade's "war on crime." "For too long," he conceded, "the word 'war' has been over-worked. . . . Nevertheless, our city can quite accurately be described at this moment as a battleground of war." Such was the local response to Miami's 32.7 murder rate for 1980.[16]

In contrast, the public mood of Dodge City in late 1880 in the wake of its 78.4 homicide rate is much less alarmist. True enough, Concho Gill's killing of Henry

Heck on November 17 caused a sensation, especially in view of the fact that nobody had died violently at Dodge in more than a year. Both weekly newspapers expressed considerable indignation. N. B. Klaine, the dour and moralistic editor of the *Times* who moonlighted as Ford County's probate judge, broke the story on Saturday, November 20, complete with sinister overtones:

MURDER IN DODGE CITY.

On Tuesday night a murder was committed in this city, in that part of town south of the railroad track. . . . It has been some time since a murder has been committed in Dodge City, but the shooting Tuesday night offers no parallel to any of the crimes committed here. There was no provocation, and it is hinted that the unfortunate Heck was the victim of a conspiracy, the facts of which may be developed upon the trial of the murderer.

On November 23, in its turn, the *Globe* ran a much more forthcoming account that contained most of what we know of the killing's background. The paper was managed by D. M. Frost, a practicing attorney, and his journalistic associate Lloyd Shinn, who doubled as Dodge Township justice of the peace. From the breezy vernacular tone of the article, we may be almost certain that its author was Shinn rather than the more earnest Frost. The piece opens as follows:

HENRY C. HECK KILLED.
John Gill, Alias Concho, Establishes
Himself as a Killer

On last Wednesday morning the report that a killing had taken place in the city the night previous, was rife on the streets at an early hour. The report was soon confirmed and everybod[y] felt that Dodge had still some of the bloody instinct for which she was so famous in the lawless days of her infancy, when money was as dross and whisky four bits a drink.

But to the locals, as to any reasonably sensitive historian, the death of Henry Heck was much more than just a blemish on Dodge City's 1880 crime-control statistics. A human life had been taken, an industrious citizen was gone, the community diminished.[17]

The Unredeemed Lover

Where does the story begin?

In southwestern Kansas. In the year 1876 or 1877.[18]

Henry C. Heck arrived in Dodge. We know that he was single, the Ohio-born son of German immigrants, twenty-four or twenty-five years old.[19] In fairly short order he became the trusted employee of H. B. ("Ham") Bell, the owner of a popular livery stable, a man not much older than himself. The two evidently become close friends. Heck, according to Lloyd Shinn's account, was often "left in charge of the extensive livery and other business, whenever Mr. Bell was absent from the city." Bell's "other business" increased considerably in June 1878, when he had a local contractor build him a dance hall, the Varieties Theatre, on Locust Street in the "notorious" south side of town. The establishment was a success from the start, and a month after its opening the *Globe* reported that "the Texas boys and visitors generally still continue to throng the Varieties nightly."[20]

Ham Bell placed Heck in charge of this enterprise. In a legal deposition of early 1879, in which he adroitly distanced himself from entrepreneurial proximity, Bell described the place as "kept by Henry Heck." It is, he wrote, "a long frame building with a hall and bar in front and sleeping rooms in the rear." A contemporary photograph shows a low room with dark, wood-paneled ceiling and large side windows. In the foreground a bar extends along the right wall, three gaming tables stand beyond the bar, and a dance floor lies beyond the tables. Presumably the bedrooms are behind the wall in the back.[21]

Management of the Varieties naturally brought Henry into close—not to say intimate—association with several young women (one as young as fourteen) identified by Ham Bell as "prostitutes, who belonged to the house and for the benefit of it solicited the male visitors to dance." And, Bell added, "The rooms in the rear [are] occupied, both during the dancing hours and after, both day and night[,] by the women for the purpose of prostitution."[22]

In short, Heck's was not a particularly savory occupation, although it entailed much responsibility. Overseeing the bar and kitchen; tallying receipts; dispensing payments to liquor and grocery wholesalers, to the cook and bartenders and musicians, and (of course) to the young women. And keeping order, a task that brought him several close acquaintanceships among the police—successive marshals Ed Masterson and Charlie Bassett, the various assistant marshals (Wyatt Earp, for one), and the rank-and-file officers—who kept a watchful eye on the Varieties and its two competitors, the Lady Gay and the Comique, especially during the wee hours when spirits were high and inhibitions low.

There soon arose a complication. One of the young women, a violet-eyed blonde named Caroline ("Callie") Moore, had captured Henry's affections.[23] "Nearly ever since Mr. Heck has resided in this county," wrote Shinn, ". . . this woman has been his faithful companion, according to the approved method of this class of Dodge City lotus eaters." Read: Henry and Callie lived together. And in time they planned a joint future beyond the confines of Dodge south of the tracks. Ham Bell had acquired a ranch twelve miles below town where the Camp Supply trail toward Texas intersected Mulberry Creek. Later, when trying to sell it, Bell laconically described Mulberry Ranch as "good range, good water running by the place, a well of good water at the door, good corral 100 feet square, good house 22 x 35." But better still was its situation: "a No. 1 location for keeping passersby, and cattle or sheep." Heck agreed to lease Mulberry Ranch. In the latter part of 1879 Heck and Callie Moore quit Ham Bell's employ and settled at the ranch.[24] Here, as Lloyd Shinn puts it in words that suggest strong community approval, Heck "was raising a little stock which was being steadily accumulated by his industry and prudence." And "for nearly a year," wrote Shinn, Moore "performed the duties which usually fall to the lot of a rural housewife." Her life seemed a model of common-law domesticity.

But, we may guess, bright prairie flowers and frisky colts and wonderful sunsets and a convivial parade of teamsters stopping for dinner cannot forever compensate for the relative isolation of agricultural pioneering, which had defeated many a woman of stronger psychological construction than Callie Moore. Ranch life may have begun to pall. In any event, in September 1880, while on a shopping trip to town that no doubt included a visit to old friends and old haunts, she met Concho Gill, an unemployed cowboy whom the newspapers refer to as a gambler—a common cattle-town usage for any man who frequents saloons to play cards for money.

Gill, aged twenty-three, was the Texas-born son of an Irish immigrant father and a mother from Mississippi. The father must have died, for the mother was married to James D. Young, a Mississippi-born preacher.[25] Gill's nickname probably refered to an adolescence in frontier Concho County of west-central Texas. Gill stood a half inch short of six feet, had a fair complexion, hazel eyes, and black hair. He could read and write, and "was a quiet man," said Shinn, "and not considered quarrelsome or dangerous." When visited in June 1880 by the Dodge City census taker, Gill was sharing a Front Street building with four other unattached males, each in his own apartment: two sheep raisers, another unemployed cowboy, and the manager of the local stockyard.[26]

On that same day Gill also said he was sick, suffering from scurvy. This is not as unlikely an illness for a cowboy as it might seem today, when the disease is occasionally encountered among infants and the very elderly. But scurvy had been diagnosed as recently as the 1850s among frontier settlers lacking sustained access to foods rich in vitamin C—citrus fruits, tomatoes, vegetables. Adult symptoms include swollen, bleeding gums and loose teeth, bleeding under the skin and into the joints, mental depression, fatigue, and increased susceptibility to infection. Unless treated, the disease is fatal. Yet, as physicians of the time well knew, scurvy is easily cured; since the early sixteenth century lime juice was the infallible remedy, and fresh vegetables—especially potatoes and wild salad greens—were by the 1860s prescribed as effective preventives.[27]

So why was Concho Gill sick in June and again in November? In a community blessed with doctors and druggists and grocery stores? Perhaps he suffered from some more serious malady than just a vitamin C deficiency. It is possible that he had a misdiagnosed case of gonorrhea or secondary-stage syphilis (not uncommon among cowboys), some of whose symptoms—joint pain, skin blotches, depression, lassitude—resemble those of scurvy.[28]

Concho's illness, whatever it was, did not diminish his attractiveness to Callie Moore; in fact, a touch of chronic illness possibly added a certain Byronic allure, prompting some maternal impulse, perhaps. In any event, according to Shinn, Moore was immediately smitten. "His dark brown eyes, classic features, and complexion bronzed by a southern sun, together with [a prospect of] the indolent life of a gambler's paramour, were too dazzling to be resisted, when compared with kitchen drudgery, and the society of her more homely lover." Soon the young woman bid a permanent farewell to Mulberry Ranch, moving back to Dodge and in with Gill.

Moore's betrayal devastated Heck. He turned to drink, but it did no good. He at last resorted to an ultimatum. On Saturday, November 13, Heck told Moore that she had three days to return to him or leave Dodge City forever. Or else.

Late in the evening of November 16 Henry Heck came to Dodge City to separate Callie Moore from Concho Gill. But some things, as John Demos reminds us, we have to imagine. We know nothing of how Heck managed his wait. But wait he did, as an unseasonably early winter gripped the village. Perhaps he had proposed their old workplace, the Varieties Theatre, as a rendezvous, where he now lingered, occasionally greeting friends, but moody, on edge, drinking too much. At last she arrived, accompanied by a companion, Sallie Frazier, a middle-aged woman of color who, we can imagine, hovered protectively as a tearful Moore faced her former lover. The young woman reaffirmed that she would neither get out of Dodge nor leave Gill. She and Frazier turned to go. Heck says that if she does not return to him by midnight he will, as both women later remember his words, kill Concho Gill "before morning."[29]

At midnight, Heck gathered himself into his coat and stepped out into the night, somewhat unsteadily perhaps, his mood as bitter as the weather. He trudged through fallen snow, crossing the railroad track toward Front Street and the intermittent glow of its all-night saloons. He made his way to Gill's apartment and, without announcing himself, began kicking in the front door.

Inside, Gill had been sick for the past ten days.[30] Moore was building a fire in the stove. A friend, one Charlie Milde, was also present in the room. Aroused from bed, Gill grabbed a pistol and went to the door. It flew open and he fired twice.

One bullet struck Henry Heck in the right breast just below the nipple, perforating the lung.

Heck retreated back into the darkness. We do not know how he spent the next half hour—perhaps dazed, bewildered by shock. Probably there was no pain: his neural synapses have shut down. Perhaps he rested, leaning upright in an alleyway, out of the wind, uncontrollably trembling. Perhaps he collapsed unconscious until the snow against his cheek finally brought him around. He roused himself and stumbled toward a lamp-lit saloon. He entered, and after calling for a drink told the night bartender that Gill had shot him. He left the saloon for a moment, returned, dropped to the floor, and expired "without a groan." It had taken him forty-five minutes to die.[31]

This love story from early Dodge City is over. But the consequences were not, and they provide us with an important cultural reading of frontier justice in Dodge City.

The Judgment of Concho Gill

As the dying Henry Heck silently stumbled along Front Street, Assistant Marshal Neil Brown, alerted by the gunshots, arrived at Gill's apartment. He confiscated the fatal pistol, ordered Gill to dress, and escorted him to jail.

Later that morning of November 17, a coroner's inquest convened, as required for any death happening by violence or under suspicious circumstances. The coroner's jury was heavy with law-enforcement types characteristically impatient with troublemakers. The county coroner himself, Col. John W. Straughn, doubled as a deputy sheriff. The six jurors included Ham Bell, now the deputy U.S. marshal in Dodge; blacksmith Pat Sughrue, a former Dodge Township constable and future Ford County sheriff; and merchant A. B. Webster, soon to run for mayor on a law-and-order platform. W. J. Miller, a local cattle raiser; James Mufty, an unemployed carpenter; and Fred Berg, a baker, rounded out the jury.[32] They presumably viewed the body and then took testimony from bartender A. J. Tuttle, Officer Brown, Charlie Milde, and Callie Moore.

Although the victim literally broke into Gill's domicile, he may not have been armed. Tuttle testified that Heck was not carrying a weapon when he took his last drink. The jurors returned a verdict of felonious homicide, thereby asserting that the killing had been done without justification or excuse and signaling that Gill was in very serious trouble indeed. The following day editor N. B. Klaine, in his role as probate judge, appointed Under-Sheriff Fred Singer as administrator of the deceased's estate. As for Callie Moore, she "is still true to her imprisoned lover," noted Lloyd Shinn, "and supplies him daily with tempting viands."[33]

The excitement subsided, life resumed its normal rhythms. Cattle continued loading down at the freight yard, and wagons bearing livestock feed, hay, and millet, arrived daily from outlying farms. U.S. Senator P. B. Plumb was in town several hours on his way home from Colorado. Saloon-owner Chaulk Beeson's sojourning parents departed for Iowa "well pleased with their visit." The respectable "dancing people" of the town announced plans to organize a social club. "Professor" W. H. LyBrand, hotel proprietor and former bandmaster, was recruiting an orchestra "to supply music for the holidays." On Thanksgiving Day churchgoers held interdenominational services and the Methodists hosted an oyster supper. The following afternoon children presented "literary exercises" at the grammar school. A baby was born to businessman A. J. Anthony and his wife. "Mother and son are doing well," it was reported.[34] All of which suggests that frontier Dodge had more in common with fictional Grover's Corners, New Hampshire ("nice town, y'know what I mean?"), than with modern Miami.[35]

And in contrast to Miami's plea for more cash for cops late in 1980, Dodge City's municipal council late in 1880 continued pressing the mayor to cut police expenditures. The reason was liquor prohibition, adopted as a constitutional amendment in November's general election, ending the legal sale of intoxicants in Kansas. With saloon license fees far and away the most important source of municipal income, citizens did not view the loss of revenue with equanimity. By mid-December 1880 the village found itself more than $2,200 in debt, with unpaid bills shortly hiking the total to $3,239. More than a hundred taxpayers panicked, petitioning the council for a referendum on dissolving the municipal corporation entirely. The council scheduled a vote for New Year's Eve. The *Ford County Globe* approved this drastic proposition, warning that saloon closings would leave Dodge City "without resources except such as might be derived from direct taxation. . . . This would swell the total tax upon the property owners of the city to about eight cents on the dollar." But cooler heads prevailed, and on December 31 a low voter turnout doomed this solution to the crisis.[36]

Meanwhile, Concho Gill's fate was being decided. On December 1, Gill appeared at a preliminary examination before Lloyd Shinn, in his role as justice of the peace, to determine if sufficient evidence existed to warrant his trial by a higher court. Col. Thomas S. Jones appeared for the accused, County Attorney Mike Sutton, Dodge City's most prominent attorney, for the people. Owing to the absence of one witness, the defense requested a continuance, which Shinn granted. The hearing resumed on the fourth. We lack details; both newspapers evidently considered the testimony old news. On December 7, Shinn ruled that the evidence merited binding Gill over for trial at the January 1881 term of district court. Shinn set bail at $3,000. The charge was first-degree manslaughter, meaning that Gill allegedly killed Heck, in the words of the law, "without a design to effect death," at a moment when Heck was "engaged in the perpetration or [the] attempt to perpetrate [a] crime or misdemeanor, not amounting to a felony."[37]

Justice Shinn's reasoning is discernible. Heck's death clearly had not been murder: provocating circumstances closely preceding the shooting—the unlawful attack by Heck on the defendant's door—had caused Gill to react on impulse, in the heat of the moment. Yet it also seemed to Shinn not to be a case of justifiable homicide, although Kansas law gave as one definition a killing "committed by any person . . . in resisting any attempt to murder such person, or to commit any felony upon him or her, or in any dwelling house in which such person shall be."[38]

Gill probably assumed that Heck had a gun. But—and this was a major qualifier—whether Heck was or was not armed, Gill had had an obligation to "retreat to the wall," to avail himself of any reasonable avenue of escape, even if that was only a few feet of floor space, before employing deadly force. That Concho may have failed to understand this virtually universal responsibility was simply his bad luck. As it happened, Texas was unlike most other states. Where Gill came from, the law said a man did not have to retreat from an attacker any farther than "the air at his back."[39] Unfortunately for Gill, Kansas was not Texas.

State of Kansas v. John Gill alias Concho opened at the courthouse in Dodge on January 17, 1881—two months to the day after the shooting. Again we lack details, although Judge Samuel R. Peters's summary for the record preserves the essential procedural facts. Again Mike Sutton prosecuted, Colonel Jones defended. As late as December 21 the charge was still first-degree manslaughter, punishable by "confinement and hard labor for a term not less than five years nor more than twenty-one years."[40] But since then Mike Sutton, for some reason, had upped the charge to first-degree murder, punishable by death. The accusation Sutton filed with the court asserted that Gill "feloniously, willfully and of his deliberate and premeditated malice did kill and murder one Henry Heck contrary to law." Gill pleaded not guilty, he and Jones still probably confident that his act could be seen as self-defense.

A jury was empaneled, consisting of twelve men from outside the corporate boundaries of Dodge, the most prominent of them being the prosperous sheep rancher R. W. Tarbox.[41] After hearing the evidence and arguments of counsel and being instructed in writing by the court, the jury retired to deliberate. The next day it rendered its verdict: Gill was guilty not of first-degree murder but of murder in the second degree—a killing "committed purposely and maliciously, but without deliberation and premeditation," and punishable by "confinement and hard labor for not less than ten years."[42]

The jurors evidently concluded that Gill had killed Heck with no set design to take life but that, nevertheless, there was a purpose to kill (or at least a purpose to inflict injury without caring whether it caused death or not) formed instantaneously in Gill's mind. And they must have been unimpressed by testimony suggesting that Gill had been so provoked by Heck's behavior as to reduce the crime to manslaughter.

Colonel Jones immediately moved for a new trial on the ground that the verdict was "contrary to evidence"—that is, the jurors had mistakenly interpreted the weight of the testimony in the case. Judge Peters pondered that for three days, then brought attorneys and defendant together again on January 21. He denied the motion to retry, and sentenced Gill to fifteen years' hard labor in the Kansas State Penitentiary. Concho was taken into custody, and the next day Sheriff George Hinkle and Under-Sheriff Singer took him off to Lansing.[43]

The Rest of the Story

In March 1884, somebody—presumably Mike Sutton, the man who had successfully prosecuted Concho Gill three years earlier—addressed a petition to Governor George W. Glick. "We the undersigned Citizens of Ford County Kansas respectfully ask your excellency to commute the sentence of John Gill now confined in the penitentiary of the State of Kansas, under a sentence for fifteen years," Sutton wrote. "Since his incarceration his health has failed, and there is strong probability that . . . he will not live until the expiration of his term." But, the petition added, "The crime for which said John Gill was convicted was committed by him under a misapprehension . . . that the man he killed was hunting him [in order] to kill him."[44]

This document resulted from a visit to Dodge City by Gill's stepfather, the Reverend Young. Probably after conferring with Callie Moore (now Mrs. C. F. Lane) and Sallie Frazier, he brought them to Sutton. The former county attorney took depositions from the two women, and then had these sworn to before E. D. Swan, a notary public.[45] Incredibly enough, it seems, the knowledge that Heck had specifically threatened Gill's life, and that Gill knew it, had not been presented at the trial; apparently this was the first Sutton learned of it. Thus he drafted the petition, which the Rev. Mr. Young then circulated.

Soon thirty-six names graced the document. The signatories included Dodge City's mayor and its city clerk; *Times* editor and now postmaster N. B. Klaine; W. F. Petillon, Ford County's registrar of deeds; Sheriff Pat Sughrue, who had been a member of the coroner's jury that had initiated the case against Gill; Assistant City Marshal David ("Mysterious Dave") Mather; merchants R. M. Wright, H. M. Beverley, and a scattering of other commercial men; lawyers Sutton, Swan, and T. S. Jones, who had defended Gill; baker Fred Berg, who also had sat on the coroner's jury; plus a butcher, a druggist, two hoteliers, a bookkeeper, and two of the town's more respectable saloon owners. Although admitting that "I was not here at the time," Police Judge R. E. Burns added a note that "from Statements of Responsible citizens I believe this petition should be granted." In addition, Jones and Petillon each wrote supporting letters to Governor Glick.

"Everyone here seems to sympathize with him," said Petillon of the Reverend Young, and journalist Klaine agreed. "Time seems to efface unpleasant memories," he philosophized, "as well as to soften prejudices and produce sympathy." The tendency of cattle-town people to find excuses for leniency in cases of shooting homicides was belatedly asserting itself.[46]

In his letter, Colonel Jones added an interesting interpretation of the trial. Gill "would have been promptly acquitted," he told the governor, "had a it not been for the evidence of a personal enemy." The identity of this enemy is unknown. One may guess that it was Heck's friend Ham Bell, who may have been responsible for the severe stance taken by the coroner's jury, who then had less influence over the more lenient Shinn decision but who later yet may have convinced Mike Sutton to escalate the charge against Gill to first-degree murder. What testimony Bell may have offered is also unknown; perhaps it maintained that Heck's killing was the result of a conspiracy, as suggested in the first news report of the death. In any event, Mike Sutton's implicit repudiation of his role in Gill's conviction included the suggestion that he, as county attorney, had been duped by somebody into wholly discounting Gill's claim of self-defense. For him, the two women's affidavits now proved definitive.

Gill's stepfather evidently hand carried the petition, the two affidavits, and the two supporting letters to Topeka, delivering them to Governor Glick. The governor said that prior to any formal application to commute, Young must give public notice in plenty of time for those with objections to make them known. On April 3 and 10, therefore, the *Dodge City Times* printed the required notice, editor Klaine certified its publication, and lawyer Swan sent copies of both to the governor. Formal application to commute his stepson's sentence would be made by Young on April 16, 1884.[47]

But in the end the governor refused the request for unknown reasons. Concho did not die in prison, but he did stay for another seven years. On August 19, 1891, his sentence at last commuted, he emerged from the Kansas penitentiary after having served ten and one-half years for the murder of Henry Heck.[48]

Body Counts or Murder Rates?

The point of the story of *Kansas v. Gill* is that the people of Dodge City took Heck's death seriously, and instituted deliberate legal action against his slayer according to conventions nurtured through a thousand years of Anglo-American judicial tradition. The judgment of Concho Gill was, as it was meant to be, a series of civic rituals assuring villagers that although situated on the geographic extremity of civilization, theirs was a fully domesticated society, culturally located well within the larger American community.

As for public fear, neither in Miami in December 1980 nor in Dodge in December 1880 did any important number of citizens cower behind locked doors. But Miami's business community clearly had been terrified by how its spiraling homicides would affect property values and tourism; Dodge City's businessmen, although attuned to the need to attract new residents and capital investment, were not. The important cause of these different responses was hardly the contrast between homicide rates of 32.7 and 78.4 but between body counts of 515 (or 555) and 1.

Let anthropologist Lawrence Keeley have the penultimate word on murder rates versus body counts. Keeley's recent book criticizing the "peaceful-savage" myth displays a wealth of evidence on the lethal nature of tribal life. Its relevance to the present discussion is that its author employs death rates somewhat similar to those calculated for the FBI crime reports, leading him to relish a number of absurd comparisons. For example, he judges a chance Blackfoot massacre of a 52-man Assiniboine raiding party more lethal (100.0 percent killed) than the loss of 21,392 British soldiers on the horrifying first day of the Battle of the Somme (only 13.5 percent killed).[49] Obviously, the statistical fallacy of small numbers is in full flower here.

But Keeley has a ready reply. The unsophisticated, he says, are always "more impressed by absolute numbers than ratios." And he asks if, consistent with such views, any reader would rather undergo a critical medical operation at a "small, rural, Third-World clinic"—where the number of inadvertent deaths from surgery is numerically small but the death rate high—than at a large American "university or urban hospital" where such deaths are more frequent but the rate low. According to the same reasoning, would anyone prefer to fly regularly on small planes rather than airliners? And would one prefer to live on an Indian reservation than in a large city, "since the annual absolute number of deaths from homicide, drug abuse, alcoholism, cancer, heart disease, and automobile accidents will always be far fewer on the reservations than in major cities and their suburbs"?[50]

There are, for the sake of argument, answers. Most health insurance would not pay for elective surgery in a jungle hospital, so that point is moot. But yes, those wealthy enough to own airplanes regularly and routinely defy the odds. And yes again, many persons would rather live in Navaho country than in parts of Manhattan.

But more to the point of this essay, a great majority of fully informed time-travelers surely would feel safer cruising the all-night saloons of Dodge City in 1880 than barhopping in Little Havana, Coconut Grove, or downtown Miami a hundred years later. And that is a ratio beyond dispute.

NOTES

1. Robert R. Dykstra, *The Cattle Towns* (New York: Knopf, 1968), 144.

2. See media quotes in Robert R. Dykstra, "Overdosing on Dodge City," *Western Historical Quarterly* 27 (1996): 506. The metaphor was recently employed by an Oregon congressman in explaining cutthroat competition within the fertility-clinic industry. "It's kind of like Dodge City before the marshals show up," he said. "Ethics and Embryos," *Newsweek*, June 12, 1995, 67.

3. Richard Maxwell Brown, "Violence," in *The Oxford History of the American West*, ed. Clyde A. Milner II, Carol A. O'Connor, and Martha A. Sandweiss (New York: Oxford University Press, 1994), 401.

4. See the divergent scholarly viewpoints of Brian Dippie and Thomas Noel quoted in Dykstra, "Overdosing on Dodge City," 511–12.

5. Dykstra, *Cattle Towns*, 119–20, 125. Law-enforcement duties at Dodge were shared by a city marshal, an assistant marshal, and one or two policemen, backed up when necessary by a township constable, a county sheriff, an under-sheriff, one or two deputy sheriffs, and a deputy U.S. marshal. An individual sometimes held two of these jobs simultaneously. See listings in Nyle H. Miller and Joseph W. Snell, eds., *Why the West Was Wild* (Topeka: Kansas State Historical Society, 1963), 642–45.

6. *Kansas Daily Commonwealth* (Topeka), September 8, December 31, 1872; *Ellsworth Reporter*, March 27, 1873.

7. The remainder of the sign's text, which seems to end in the word "fine," may read: "Violators subject to fine." The photograph, known as "the Prickly Ash Bitters photo" because of another sign prominently advertising that product, is in the collections of the Kansas State Historical Society (cited hereafter as KSHS), Topeka. It dates from between 1877 and the early 1880s. Dykstra, *Cattle Towns*, 94, and illustration 25.

8. Roger D. McGrath, *Gunfighters, Highwaymen, and Vigilantes: Violence on the Frontier* (Berkeley: University of California Press, 1984), 268.

9. The only homicide report from in or near Dodge in 1876 concerned the lynching of a suspected horse thief several miles north of town. Miller and Snell, *Why the West Was Wild*, 28–30. Wyatt Earp, who was a Dodge City policeman in 1876, supposedly told his biographer, Stuart Lake, that at Dodge that year "there were some killings in personal quarrels, but none by peace officers." Lake's book, however, is no longer deemed credible about Earp's career in Kansas. Although its preface declares it to be an as-told-to account, Lake privately admitted that "Wyatt never 'dictated' a word to me." Stuart N. Lake, *Wyatt Earp: Frontier Marshal* (Boston: Houghton Mifflin, 1931), 143; Glenn G. Boyer, ed., *I Married Wyatt Earp: The Recollections of Josephine Sarah Marcus Earp* (Tucson: University of Arizona Press, 1976), 249, 251, 258 n.

10. Federal Bureau of Investigation, *Crime in the United States — 1980: Uniform Crime Reports* (Washington, D.C.: FBI, 1981), 74.

11. James Buchanan Given, *Society and Homicide in Thirteenth-Century England* (Stanford: Stanford University Press, 1977), 36, 39; Barbara A. Hanawalt, *Crime and Conflict in English Communities, 1300–1348* (Cambridge: Harvard University Press, 1979), 98–99, 271–72, 301 n; McGrath, *Gunfighters*, 248 n, 253–55.

12. Dykstra, "Overdosing on Dodge City," 508–10.

13. Elizabeth Apone Salamon, "Murder Close to Home," *Newsweek*, May 12, 1997, 18–19.

14. John Modell, "Family and Fertility on the Indiana Frontier, 1820," *American Quarterly* 23 (1971): 627–32; Robert R. Dykstra, "Town-Country Conflict: A Hidden Dimension in American Social History," *Agricultural History* 38 (1964): 195–204.

15. Eston Melton, "State Funds Sought for Crime War," *Miami Herald*, December 24, 1980, 2B; "3 Suspects Charged in Restaurant Killings," ibid., December 23, 1980, 4 A; FBI, Crime in the United States—1980, 73.

16. "Metro Commission Recognizes Anti-Crime Leadership Group," *Miami Herald*, December 21, 1980, "Neighbors" sec., 5; Elizabeth Willson, "Ordinance Pressures Violent Bars," ibid., "Neighbors" sec., 26–27; Melton, "State Funds Sought," 2B.

17. This narrative is inspired by John Demos's poignant saga of Eunice Williams. Demos, *The Unredeemed Captive: A Family Story from Early America* (New York: Knopf, 1994).

18. Except where noted otherwise, this section of the essay is based on the previously quoted news story by Lloyd Shinn in the *Ford County Globe*, November 23, 1880.

19. U.S. Census, 1880, Kansas: Ford County, Dodge Township South of the Arkansas River, 8, dwelling 1.

20. *Ford County Globe*, June 11, July 2, 1878, November 23, 1880: *Dodge City Times*, June 15, 1878.

21. *Ford County Globe*, February 17, 1879; Dykstra, *Cattle Towns*, illustration 22; *Dodge City Times*, July 27, August 3, 1878.

22. *Ford County Globe*, February 17, 1879; *Dodge City Times*, June 22, 1878.

23. Callie Moore is referred to as Caroline Moore and as Mrs. C. F. Lane in M. W. Sutton et al., to George W. Glick, [c. March 20, 1884], Pardon Papers No. 584 (John Gill), Kansas State Penitentiary Records, KSHS.

24. H. M. Bell in *Ford County Globe*, January 25, 1881. That Bell still owned Mulberry Ranch at the time of Heck's death is stated in a report about vandalism at the deserted property. *Ford County Globe*, December 7, 1880.

25. U.S. Census, 1880, Kansas: Ford County, Dodge City, dwelling 94; entry 2395 (John Gill alias Concho), Prison Ledger B, Kansas State Penitentiary Records; James D. Young in *Dodge City Times*, April 3, 10, 1884; U.S. Census, 1880, Texas: Bee County, Precinct No. 1, family [and dwelling] 131.

26. U.S. Census 1880, Dodge City, dwelling 94; affidavit by Mrs. C. F. Lane, March 19, 1884, Pardon Papers No. 584.

27. H. Winter Griffith, *Complete Guide to Symptoms, Illness and Surgery*, 3d ed. (New York: Putnam, 1995), 634; Robert Berkow, Mark H. Beers, and Andrew J. Fletcher, eds., *The Merck Manual of Medical Information: Home Edition* (Whitehouse Station, N.J.: Merck Research Labs, 1997), 661, 1289–90; William A. Hammond, "Scurvy," in Hammond, ed., *Military Medical and Surgical Essays Prepared for the United States Sanitary Commission* (Philadelphia: U.S. Government, 1864), 177, 184, 196, 200–202.

28. Griffith, *Complete Guide*, 317, 575; Berkow, Beers, and Fletcher, *Merck Manual*, 938–42.

29. Affidavit by Lane, March 19, 1884, Pardon Papers No. 584; affidavit by Sallie Frazier, March 19, 1884, ibid. Frazier is identified in U.S. Census, Dodge City, dwelling 23.

30. Affidavit by Lane, Pardon Papers No. 584; *Dodge City Times*, November 20, 1880.

31. *Dodge City Times*, November 20, 1880.

32. *Ford County Globe*, November 23, 1880. For jurors' identities, see U.S. Census, Dodge City, passim., although Webster is to be found in ibid., *Dodge Township North of the Arkansas River*, 1, dwelling 1.

33. *Dodge City Times*, November 27, 1880; *Ford County Globe*, November 23, 1880.

34. These items are from various issues of the *Globe* and *Times* for late November and early December 1880.

35. Thornton Wilder, *Our Town: A Play in Three Acts* (New York: Harper's, 1938). The quotation is from the famous opening monologue of the Stage Manager.

36. *Dodge City Times*, December 11, 18, 25, 1880; *Ford County Globe*, December 21, 1880, January 4, April 12, 1881. Although the original petition had 125 signatories, the referendum proposal attracted only 44 votes.

37. *Dodge City Times*, November 27, December 11, 1880; *Ford County Globe*, December 7, 1880; C. F. W. Dassler, ed., *Compiled Laws of Kansas*, 1879 (St. Louis: W. J. Gilbert, 1879), 329.

38. Dassler, *Compiled Laws*, 328.

39. C. L. Sonnichsen, *I'll Die before I Run: The Story of the Great Feuds of Texas* (New York: Harper's, 1962), 8–9. The Texas Supreme Court specifically upheld the state's "noretreat" doctrine in 1883. Ibid., 328 n.

40. Judge's Journal A (1874–1883), 329–30, Ford County District Court Cases, KSHS; *Ford County Globe*, December 21, 1880; Dassler, *Compiled Laws*, 330.

41. No jurors are listed in the 1880 census as residing in Dodge City.

42. Dassler, *Compiled Laws*, 328.

43. Judge's Journal A, 330; *Ford County Globe*, January 25, 1881.

44. Mike Sutton et al. to Glick, [c. March 20, 1884], Pardon Papers No. 584. That Sutton composed the petition is implied by his having been the first to sign it.

45. The depositions are in the same handwriting as the petition. That Swan did not compose them can be seen in comparing them to a letter from him also in the file. Nor were they written, as might have been expected, by Gill's former attorney, T. S. Jones. See E. D. Swan to George W. Glick, April 12, 1884, Pardon Papers No. 584; Thomas S. Jones to Glick, March 20, 1884, ibid.

46. W. F. Petillon to Glick, March 20, 1884, Pardon Papers No. 584; *Dodge City Times*, March 27, 1884; Dykstra, *Cattle Towns*, 128–30.

47. Affidavit by N. B. Klaine, April 10, 1884, Pardon Papers No. 584; Swan to Glick, April 12, 1884, ibid.

48. The Kansas Board of Pardons received a request for commutation in April 1890. It was approved by Gov. Lyman Underwood Humphrey on July 30, 1891. Records of Pardons and Commutations, December 1887–December 1895, KSHS.

49. Lawrence H. Keeley, *War before Civilization* (New York: Oxford University Press, 1996), 64, 194.

50. Ibid., 214 n.

In the earliest twentieth century, local publishers brought out postcards of lynchings. These cards were sent through the U.S. mails, often with mocking messages on the obverse. This postcard is of two labor organizers, Castenego Ficcarotta and Angelo Albano, who were lynched in Tampa, Florida, in 1910 for attempting to unionize cigar workers. The James Allen Collection, Woodruff Library Special Collections, Emory University. Used by permission of James Allen.

Chapter Eleven

Word and Deed
The Language of Lynching, 1820–1953

Christopher Waldrep

I enjoy crime waves. I made one once.
Lincoln Steffens

In 1894, W. E. B. Du Bois began a career in social science, applying scientific law to society. Laws of science, he thought, ruled the world, directing even human society toward greater accomplishment and civilization. In 1899, he published *The Philadelphia Negro: A Social Study*, a relentlessly objective compilation of facts about Philadelphia's mostly black seventh ward. The same year Du Bois published his social science magnum opus, Atlanta lynchers murdered Sam Hose, subsequently exhibiting his knuckles at the grocery store on Mitchell Street. This murder so outraged Du Bois it shook his faith in social science. Calm, cool, detached science was not the correct response to the problem of racial violence. Du Bois never forgot the value of science as rhetoric, but he chose a more openly polemical approach. Just four years after *The Philadelphia Negro* appeared, DuBois published *The Souls of Black Folk*.[1]

In *Souls of Black Folk*, Du Bois took a "linguistic turn," understanding language as a malleable tool that he could shape to persuade, a tool that never merely neutrally describes.[2] Few students of lynching have pursued Du Bois's insight, choosing instead to finesse language. The best current scholarly analysis of lynching violence now insists that the "historian's task is less to provide a precise definition of lynching than to explain the phenomenon."[3] But, as Clarence Thomas demonstrated, the word *lynching* can be a powerful vehicle in the hands of a skilled polemicist. The relationship between actual extralegal violence and the language describing it was fundamentally arbitrary; the language never exactly reproduced the reality it tried to describe. Scholars' attempts to apply social science methodology to a political tool, one with a fluid definition, misses lynching's fundamental rhetorical reality. This essay presents a history not of lynching violence but of the discursive politics, narrative strategies, and rhetorical devices used to denounce and promote it. Rhetoric implies an awareness of audience.

From the antebellum era into the 1950s the meaning of *lynching* took four sharp turns, always in response to political pressures. In the 1830s, abolitionists learned that many northerners indifferent to slavery could be won over by stories of white southerners' lawless violence. The abolitionist press began charging white southerners with "lynching," murder approved by the neighborhood. By asserting that the corruption of local courts forced the people to enforce the law themselves, Californians rehabilitated *lynching* shortly before the Civil War. After the Civil War white southerners learned that northerners could be persuaded to tolerate lynching violence if the lynchers accused their victims of rape. In the twentieth century, when many white southerners turned against extralegal violence, organizations opposed to southern discrimination broadened the meaning of *lynching* to keep this very effective rhetorical tool alive. Users of lynching language shaped and molded its meaning over time to meet their own needs as well as those of their audiences.

"Lynching" probably began in Virginia, where neighborhood leaders (led by William Lynch or, perhaps, Charles Lynch) sometimes ordered local Tories whipped without proper trial. "Lynching" had nothing to do with racial violence.[4] When racial violence did occur, no one thought to call it "lynching." In one 1797 episode, the *Norfolk Herald and Public Advertiser* reported a Georgia mob had condemned a slave "to the flames" and the "sentence was immediately put in execution." Newspapers in the early national period did not often use the term *lynching* to describe crowd violence. Even in Virginia, the press sometimes reported riots and mobs but not "lynchings." The Virginia *Gazette*, in its various incarnations, did not use the word. In part, this absence must be because newspapers reached for a level of discourse high above the vulgar, reporting crime and violence only rarely.[5]

Nevertheless, the word entered the language. In 1811, diarist Andrew Ellicott described "lynch law [as] so well known and so frequently carried into effect some years ago in the southern states." Ellicott probably meant less-than-lethal punishments, a whipping or a tarred and feathered him. Through the 1820s, *Niles' Register* reported on "club law" and "summary justice" and "regulation" without using the term *lynching*. By the 1820s, the term had penetrated ordinary conversation but not journalism in Kentucky. An 1823 traveler found "Lynch law" there, as did another traveler five years later, though he called it "Linch's law."[6]

Many observers believed that rioting increased in the mid-1830s, perhaps in response to the abolitionists' 1835 pamphlet campaign. In 1835, the American Anti-Slavery Society flooded the mails with tracts, newspapers, and other anti-slavery paraphernalia. According to one historian, this campaign made the South "hysterical" and turned New York City into a "powder keg." The *New York Sun* accused racist rivals of stirring up mob violence against African Americans. Riots in Baltimore and Washington, D.C., in August 1835 prompted political leaders to worry about the prevalent spirit of mob law. Hezekiah Niles agreed that "a spirit

of riot . . . prevails in every quarter." But Niles also thought that white southerners had been driven to mob law by the "disease" of abolitionism.[7]

In the midst of this abolitionist assault on the violence of slavery, a new kind
of newspaper appeared. Cheap newspapers, a product of the steam-powered
printing press, commercialized news coverage. Unlike previous newspapers,
these journals existed primarily to make money, not exhort voters. They recruited
new readers with crime reporting. As Andy Tucher demonstrated, the Helen
Jewett murder case in 1836 stands as the classic example of crime sensationalized
to sell papers. New York's penny press competed to run sensational articles
about the murder, denouncing the witnesses, suspects, the judge ("the tool of the
Aristocracy"), and other editors, publishing evidence that allowed readers to
second-guess the jury. Such papers found New Yorkers in an almost constant
state of riot for prosaic reasons having nothing to do with slavery.[8] This emphasis
on violence attracted many new readers to newspapers. Within six months of its
first issue on September 3, 1833, the *Sun* had built a circulation of 8,000; four
years later it printed 30,000 issues a day. By 1860 the *Sun*'s rival, the *New York
Herald*, published 77,000 copies a day, more than any other paper in the world.
Contrasting themselves with the "party press," penny press journalists proclaimed themselves dedicated to truth and science. In fact, they lied flagrantly,
often favoring the conventions and formulas readers wanted over objective
truth.[9]

Competing for readers, New York's penny press learned to play to its audience, to supply readers with the humbugs and truths they wanted. Other journalists absorbed the insight. The abolitionist press, for example, learned from
papers like the *National Police Gazette* to use the language of its subjects. By
emphasizing thieves' slang and cant, *Gazette* writers situated readers in the world
of police and crime. The *Gazette* briefly ran a column dedicated to translating
criminals' slang, a sort of rogues' lexicon. The paper always laced its articles with
criminal cant, translated in footnotes or parenthetically. The abolitionist press
sold papers for far more than a penny but also hoped to shock readers by
affecting a style designed to open a window on a crudely corrupt world. The
Boston Liberator regularly ran reports of southern murders, cowhidings, duels,
and assaults clipped from southern papers in columns headed "THE SOUTH . . .
VIOLENCE AND BLOOD ITS INHERITANCE" or "THE BLOOD-REEKING
SOUTH" or "SOUTHERN ATROCITIES." Just as the penny press used the
colorful language of urban criminals to attract middle-class readers, abolitionist
journals used the words of southern newspapers to expose the shocking horrors
of slave society—and to recruit new readers.[10]

The *Liberator* made no pretense that every atrocity perpetrated in the "blood-
reeking South" reached its pages. In this era many lynchings never reached print.
The ultimate source for news about extralegal violence was always the small-
town, rural press. Through the nineteenth century, the big city papers often
simply reprinted accounts of lynchings published in local papers. In 1835, the
New York Sun reprinted a story from the *St. Francisville Louisiana Journal* telling of

two "sacrifices . . . to the code Lynch" at Madisonville, Louisiana. The same paper told its readers when it received files of South Carolina newspapers by steam packet that included white southerners' justifications for lynching.[11]

Although the New York papers condemned mob law of all kinds, other media offered five distinct justifications for lynching. Most important was the justification that because law emanated from the people, persons could be executed on behalf of the public good. In 1828, traveler James Hall wrote that "citizens" of a neighborhood carried out lynchings, implying that popular sovereignty vindicated their actions. Another writer explained that when "the people" reach unanimous agreement that someone should be put to death for murder, their decision rendered the act legal "to all intents and purposes." In 1836, a St. Louis judge agreed with this reasoning when he instructed a grand jury that a killing committed by one or two people might constitute murder, but when "congregated thousands" kill, "the case transcends your jurisdiction—it is beyond the reach of human law."[12] Localism lies at the heart of this kind of popular sovereignty. Only a fairly small community or neighborhood can achieve the unity of pupose necessary to sanction murder; broaden the sphere and opponents of such extralegal action can mobilize too effectively. Lynchers have justified themselves with the local-popular-sovereignty argument throughout American history.[13]

Defenders of extralegal violence also asserted that the evil nature of the individuals lynched justified their execution. James Hall assured his readers that "in general" only the "basest and most lawless men" suffered lynchings. In 1842, the *New Orleans Picayune* compared one gang of lynching victims to water rats, "for their depredations are committed in as thoroughly sneaking, sly and despicable a manner as is so characteristic of those vermin." The *Picayune* thought they should not be allowed to mingle among primates, except to be beaten and kicked. When residents of Dubuque, Iowa, hanged an accused murderer named Patrick O'Conner in 1834, the *Galenian* reported that the bad character of the executed villain justified the proceedings against him. For six years, the *Galenian* reported, O'Conner had committed crimes and misconduct "of the blackest hue." "His whole character," the paper implied, made any alternative to lynching impossible.[14]

Inadequate courts could also be used to justify lynching. Popular sovereignty gave the public the right to judge the adequacy of courts, supplementing them when necessary. Writers for the *New Orleans Picayune* did not want "to be understood as being *advocates* either for or *before* Judge Lynch" but observed that "great necessity for the system must exist during early settlements of a new country." Hall stated that "whenever a county became strong enough to enforce the laws," lynching ended. When the Dubuque lynchers executed their victim, the *Galenian* insisted, they did so only because no courts functioned in Iowa. The man they lynched tried to work this fact to his advantage, insisting that "ye have no laws in the country, and cannot try me."[15]

When the people wielded their sovereignty to execute someone, they did not act out of passion or revenge. The populace could be outraged by evil conduct, and mass outrage then became a justification for extralegal violence. More often, though, early lynchers presented themselves as coolly restrained, dignified, civilized citizens who turned to lynching as a moderate solution to a serious problem. The earliest lynchers did not kill their victims, administering whippings instead. In 1823, Indiana vigilantes defined "Lynch law" as "a whipping in the woods." The Iowa mob acted "with the utmost regularity and good order," the *Galenian* assured its readers. All the lynchers agreed to stay sober and "not a drop of spirits was sold until after the execution." The crowd seated a jury, appointed a prosecuting attorney, and even allowed their victim to select defense counsel from their number. Southern newspapers justified brutal executions of slaves with the same rhetoric. In Alabama, the *Huntsville Democrat* wrote, "There was no passionate conduct here. The whole subject was disposed of with the coolest deliberation and with regard only to the interest of the public."[16]

Defenders also justified lynching through the rhetorical device of establishing a rapport with the audience through concession before making the major point. For lynchers, the minor point to be conceded was always the distastefulness of extralegal punishment. The major point was that it worked. James Hall conceded that in principle lynching could not be defended but went on to say that lynchers acted only from necessity and the results were "salutary." The Iowa lynchers reported that their work frightened "the reckless and abandoned outlaws," sending them to the safety of "warmer climes." Lynching's defenders have traditionally expressed a grim determination to carry out their disagreeable task. "We regret . . . the necessity for such scenes," one writer solemnly declared, before making known his pleasure at the "public spirit" that made lynching possible.[17]

The same reform effort that drove state-sanctioned punishments out of public spaces led some to challenge the legitimacy of "lynch law." Critics turned the most salient excuse for lynch law against it. If solid community support justified lynching, it could, from another perspective, implicate the entire neighborhood in a monstrous crime. *Niles' Register* had argued against this logic as early as 1825, but in 1841 and 1855 legislatures in Pennsylvania and New York passed laws allowing the victims of mob violence in those states to recover damages for property lost. New York's supreme court acknowledged that the law would almost certainly force all taxpayers in a community to pay for the damages inflicted by mobs. New York justices found precedent in English common law for making the entire county take responsibility. The justices expected to curb lawlessness and violence by making every person contribute to the cost of repairing mob-inflicted damages to property.[18] In Pennsylvania and New York, popular sovereignty had a price, one resented by *Niles' Register*. Mobs "will happen," the *Register* argued; "it does not become anyone to imprecate a whole society for the sudden and unanticipated actions of an inconsiderate or vicious few."[19]

When the *Register* and other newspapers used the term *lynching* to describe crowd violence, they meant an extralegal whipping. In 1834, when William Lloyd Garrison's abolitionist newspaper, the *Boston Liberator*, first used the term *lynching*, it accepted the traditional, nonlethal, meaning of the word. In 1834, residents of Lancaster, Pennsylvania, called it a lynching when they tarred and feathered a stranger they disliked.[20]

Before 1835, when mobs turned murderous, the press did not think to call their actions lynchings. The *New York Sun*, for example, reported one riot after another without finding a single lynching. Some of these "riots" resembled lynchings, as when rioters tarred and feathered a woman of "doubtful fame," or when rioters in Charlestown, Massachusetts, bludgeoned a man to death, or when a New York crowd attacked a storekeeper after he allegedly abused a woman. The *Sun* used the word *riot* indiscriminately at times. When protesters shouted "you lie" at a minister in church, the *Sun* thought that constituted a riot.[21]

After July 1835, many newspapers began to denounce as lynchings more deadly incidents where there is no evidence the perpetrators considered themselves *lynchers*. The change came from Vicksburg, Mississippi, where professional gamblers apparently terrorized the town, roaming the streets in armed bodies. By one account, "the streets every where resounded with the echoes of their drunken and obscene mirth." The laws and courts proved "wholly ineffectual"— or so apologists for the lynchers later declared. Vicksburg citizens hanged five gamblers on July 4, 1835.[22]

When Vicksburgers killed the gamblers, they did not believe they had *lynched* anyone. A local diarist described the killings as "rash & bloody transactions" but not as lynchings. A letter written from Vicksburg described the killings as an "outrage" carried out by a "mob" but, again, not as lynchings. A contemporary Vicksburg newspaper account did not describe the gamblers as lynched. Published travelers' accounts describe the incident as a "massacre" or an "execution." *Niles' Register* published an anonymous Vicksburger's justification for the executions dated July 9, just days after the incident. And this letter, the most complete account of the affair, described the "lynching" of one gambler in the woods. The "lynchers" tied their victim to a tree, whipped him, and then tarred and feathered him. Ordered to leave the vicinity, he left. The *Natchez Courier* used the same definition in its account of the same incident. When citizens hanged the gamblers, neither the *Register*'s correspondent nor the *Courier* called that a lynching. Those were "executions."[23]

At the same time Vicksburgers carried out their lynching and executions, whites in nearby Madison County asserted that they had uncovered a vast plot to incite a servile insurrection. In the spring of 1835, Virgil Stewart peddled a pamphlet describing how he had disrupted a plot by John A. Murrell to incite a multistate slave uprising. Stewart had testified against Murrell and sought to vindicate himself through the pamphlet, making the scope of Murrell's crimes as gigantic as possible. Murrell, Stewart's pamphlet proclaimed, planned to incite a rebellion among blacks throughout the entire slaveholding South. "I look upon the American people as my common enemy," the pamphlet quoted Murrell as saying.[24]

Stewart's pamphlet found a ready market northeast of Vicksburg in Madison County. Excited by news of Murrell's alleged conspiracy, locals charged two

whites with planning to turn area slaves into an "army of incendiaries" that
would sweep through southwest Mississippi, "burning, sacking, and laying des-
olate the whole country." According to Mississippi newspapers, whites organized extralegal tribunals and carried out inquiries that "would not do discredit
to the most dignified judicial tribunal in the country," before executing the two
whites and their slave accomplices. The vigilantes themselves said they had
carried out their work patiently, with "calm deliberation of their judgments . . .
to shield the innocent from being confounded with the guilty." Local newspapers
and pamphlets published by the vigilantes did not describe these actions as
lynchings.[25]

Before these episodes, few Americans had heard the word *lynching*. Afterward,
national journals published accounts of the Vicksburg "sensation." As one observer commented, "Lynch law" and "lynching became familiar as household
words" only after Vicksburg. The Vicksburg killings, along with the executions
in Madison County, gave *lynching* a national notoriety.[26]

Hezekiah Niles declared that he would not consent to hold up his own country to the censure of Europeans. Therefore, he announced, the *Register* would
"generally suppress" news of riots, "though some cases of peculiar atrocity must
be inserted." The penny press proved less circumspect, in part because of the
"discovery" of the asylum and a trend toward moving state-sanctioned punishment out of public spaces.[27] Making executions private enhanced the appeal of
pain pornography. Titillating representations of pain gained currency precisely
because humanitarian sensibility made public displays of pain revolting, a taboo.
Lynchings themselves represented a refusal by some people to be denied the
actual sight of a guilty criminal's suffering for his or her misdeeds. The steam-
powered printing press allowed many more people to experience such scenes
vicariously. Published accounts of lynchings filled a public need the state had
once supplied through public executions. Newspaper accounts of lynchings
flourished as punishment of criminals became less accessible to the curious.[28]
New York's penny press followed the Vicksburg story closely, and it affected
their reporting. Before July, the *New York Sun* rarely encountered anything it
could call a lynching. In the weeks following the Vicksburg killings, the *Sun*
found lynchings in Tennessee, Maine, New Jersey, and Boston. Hardly anything
had qualified as a lynching before Vicksburg; now the paper described a trial
and execution carried out by an Indian tribe as a "lynching."[29]

Abolitionists recognized the value of violence carried out by proslavery forces
and the language used to describe it. "If the Southern people knew as much
about the North as we do, they would see that by every such act of violence they
strengthen the hands of the Abolitionists," one wrote. This ferocity also made it
easy for abolitionists to accuse lynchers of racism. In 1836, the *Liberator* published
an account of a grisly St. Louis lynching. White lynchers burned to death Francis
J. McIntosh, described as "a yellow fellow." McIntosh had murdered a constable,
but the author of the article charged that McIntosh's "great, unpardonable offence," "was manifestly his color."[30] When a St. Louis judge subsequently used
the popular-sovereignty argument to justify the lynching, he fueled the rhetoric

of abolitionists like Elijah Lovejoy. In 1838, the *Liberator* reproduced an account of the murder of an African American on a steamboat by white passengers, headlining the affair as "A HORRIBLE ENFORCMENT OF LYNCH LAW."[31]

In the 1830s, the abolitionists turned the popular-sovereignty argument against southern lynchers, charging that they did not represent the entire community. They associated community-sanctioned violence with racism, which implied that mobs or crowds represented only an interest group, not the whole community. In the 1830s, opponents of slavery launched a campaign to label episodes of white southerners' most murderous racial violence as lynchings. Abolitionists worked to redefine *lynching* and to shift ordinary northerners' views of white southerners. Mississippi residents did not describe their "executions" in Vicksburg and Madison County as lynchings, but outside observers did. The *Boston Liberator* reprinted an account published by the *Louisiana Advertiser*. Like the *Natchez Courier*, the Louisiana paper did not use the term *lynching* in its article, but the *Liberator* headlined the story as an example of "LYNCH LAW." William Lloyd Garrison's use of the passive voice in his commentary at the foot of the *Advertiser*'s article, "Lynch law, as it is called" implied that white southerners resorted to murderous "summary justice" so often that they had developed a name for it themselves. By 1840, the abolitionist press had succeeded in changing the meaning of *lynching* from a whipping to an action resulting in death.[32]

Increased reports of violence, especially southern violence, proved an effective rhetorical tool for the enemies of slavery. Even northerners supportive of slavery found lynching hard to take, some northerners tempering their support for slavery as a result. In the wake of the Vicksburg execution, the *New York Herald* reaffirmed its support for slavery, but its fear of disorder of any sort led it to join the *Sun* in denouncing southern violence.[33]

By characterizing the South as reflexively homicidal, abolitionists hoped to appeal to those unimpressed by the evils of slavery. Abolitionists hoped some would find anarchic violence threatening even if they did not care about the slaves' plight. This strategy enjoyed some success. The abolitionist press cited the case of Ohioan Samuel Lewis, who had not felt "it my duty to take any active part" in opposing slavery. But although the horrors of slavery did not move Lewis to action, the news that southern mobs had attacked abolitionists did. In 1845, angered that southern communities and leading citizens countenanced mobbing, Lewis began making public demands for an end to lynching.[34]

Despite such condemnations, lynchers all over America imitated their Vicksburg cousins. *Niles' Register* reported that after the Vicksburgers executed the gamblers, "a disposition to take the law in their own hands, prevails in every quarter." An Aiken, South Carolina, newspaper reported that "Judge Lynch" and "Judge Hang" had been active there. Virginia newspapers reported lynchings, as did those in Louisiana and Massachusetts. The *Louisville Journal* printed a warning from "Capt. Slick" threatening to administer "Lynch Law" to gamblers. The paper warned gamblers that "the inexorable 'Judge Lynch' has recently been holding court in our city." For readers curious about the origins of the strange new term, *Niles' Register* traced lynching to the extralegal punishment of a poacher in Pennsylvania, "many years ago." The *Register*'s etymology may be suspect, but the article proved a prototype for many feature stories on the origins of lynching thereafter.[35]

A month after the Vicksburg executions, rioters in Baltimore distributed handbills praising "judge Lynch" as "free and unbiass'd," superior to "designing lawyers." The Baltimore handbill made the popular-sovereignty argument: lynchers acted on behalf of "the people enmasse." When Judge Lynch took the seat of justice, "the people will rise in their majesty and redress their own grievances."[36]

Vicksburg did much to connect *lynching* to narrow factional violence, especially that carried out by racist white southerners, but "lynchers" in California partially rehabilitated the word. To this day, antebellum westerners' extralegal suppression of crime seems justified in the minds of many.[37]

In the late 1840s and through the 1850s, Californians adopted a diverse nomenclature for their various vigilante organizations. California vigilantes called themselves "hounds," "volunteer police," "regulators," and the "vigilance committee." But unlike the Vicksburgers fifteen years earlier, they always understood themselves as "lynchers." According to one contemporary account, "[P]eople . . . began to talk among themselves of . . . adopting Lynch law."[38] Handbills explicitly called on the populace to adopt the "never failing remedy so admirably laid down in the code of Judge Lynch." Newspapers praised "The Spirit of Lynch Law."[39]

The Californians pioneered no new arguments to justify their actions, but by embracing the old popular-sovereignty argument, they legitimated it. "This was not a mob, but the *people*, in the highest sense of the term," Frank Soule, John Gihon, and James Nisbet avowed in 1854. Just as earlier lynchers asserted that the executed deserved their fate, so too did the Californians. The "rogues" they lynched—most famously, James Stuart—were awful men. Such men could never be rehabilitated: for them, misbehavior was instinctive. Just as earlier lynchers justified themselves by saying that no adequate courts existed to punish rampant criminality, the San Francisco vigilance committee insisted that its town's small and insecure prisons could hardly hold the many criminals flocking to California. Handbills soliciting vigilantes declared the law "a nonentity, to be scoffed at." The citizens of San Francisco turned to lynchings only when they had no other alternative, or so they professed.[40]

Earlier lynchers presented themselves as restrained and moderate, civilized in the face of provocation; so too did the Californians. The first wave of California vigilantes, the so-called Hounds, were mostly anti-immigrant drunken toughs, b'hoys from the New York Bowery. But the subsequent vigilance committee pretended to try miscreants fairly, albeit not according to the forms of law. The 1851 Committee of Vigilance formally resolved that its deliberations must be "marked with dignity." No loud demonstrations of approval or disapproval would be allowed.[41]

The Californians also declared that their extralegal justice worked. Thanks to the vigilance committee, "outrages against person and property almost disappeared." The *Alta California* smugly reviewed criticism made of vigilantism when the committee had first formed. Now, the newspaper crowed, the committee had established "such a state of quiet and safety as never could have been accomplished by our courts." One writer asserted that grand juries praised the San Francisco vigilantes for restoring order.[42]

Later writers like the historian H. H. Bancroft praised the San Francisco vigilantes for their "mildness and forbearance," but many Californians developed doubts. Western attitudes toward extralegal justice can be tracked by following the language they used to describe it. As late as 1850, the word *mob* rarely appeared in descriptions of western vigilantism. California newspapers still described extralegal punishments of malefactors as incidents of "lynch law" or "lynch courts." Through the 1850s, though, more pejorative descriptions appeared; and by 1860, vigilantes had become "lynch mobs." As the West commercialized, manufacturing and financial enterprise eclipsed transient and impermanent mining camps in westerners' self-definition. But the nature of lynching also changed as it began to be carried out by secret and disguised parties.[43]

The San Francisco lynchings occurred over a space of several years but otherwise closely resembled the extralegal violence in Vicksburg. In both cities, citizens, after pronouncing the courts ineffective, acted outside the law to execute men they called criminals. In both cities, apologists justified community violence by insisting that crime raged beyond the control of formal law-enforcement mechanisms. The people of Vicksburg could plausibly lay claim to more justification than the San Francisco lynchers. Vicksburg appears to have been a truly violent place, with a portion of the town out of control; San Francisco actually had an effective court system and little crime. The California lynchers may well have been more bigoted than those in Mississippi. There is no evidence that the Vicksburg gamblers belonged to a particular ethnic group, whereas the 1856 San Francisco vigilantes came primarily from the Know-Nothings and lynched Irish Catholics almost exclusively.[44]

What really distinguished Vicksburg from San Francisco were the rival narratives that gained national currency for each, the rhetoric that emerged to denounce one affair and praise the other. The Californians enjoyed a good press. A San Francisco banker at the time of the lynchings, William Tecumseh Sherman wrote, "As they controlled the press, they wrote their own history."[45] There is a logic to Sherman's assertion, but it cannot fully explain what happened. Local journalists could not control the many books published afterward. Bancroft's *Popular Tribunals* of 1887 and other works did more to construct the national myth than local newspapers. And if California's newspapers could so powerfully control popular understandings of doings in that state, why did Mississippi's newspapers fail so completely to control the national understanding of their state's "lynchings"?

More likely the needs of the audience determined which narrative triumphed. Abolitionist readers wanted and expected to see Mississippians as bloodthirsty and lawless. California's vigilante episodes came at precisely the moment when northerners worried about the role of law in the western territories. Northern Republicans feared that white southerners and outsiders, using legal capers like the Lecompton Constitution (Kansas) and the *Dred Scott* decision, would impose slavery on honest nonslaveowning pioneers in the West. Abraham Lincoln made precisely that charge in the Lincoln-Douglas debates. To preserve freedom, abolitionist pioneers had to resist the corruption found in local courts and in law. Some turned to vigilantism. Thus the Free Soil forces in Kansas organized militia units, really vigilante bands, in defiance of their proslavery legislature and governor.[46]

In the Civil War and after, Republicans like Congressman Thaddeus Stevens used white southerners' violence to justify imposing military rule on the South. Stevens insisted that his sole purpose was to protect Union men in the South. Southern barbarians, he told his House colleagues, daily murdered loyal whites and blacks. An ally of Stevens's asserted that fifteen hundred Union men had been "massacred in cold blood," loyalty to the Union their only crime. Failure to pass the bill, another warned, would be a "death-blow" to Unionists in the South. "A mangled corpse," one newspaper in Stevens's district charged after reporting the murders of a pair of northern travelers in Mississippi, shocked northern sensibilities but "hardly startles southern nerves." The paper picked up the same argument made by the antebellum abolitionists: "We want a country—a common land [with] national citizenship." Congress passed the Reconstruction Act in March 1867, placing southern states under the command of Union generals. Though modified in ways Stevens thought abominable, the bill still began by announcing that "no adequate protection for life or property now exists in the rebel states."[47]

Some white southerners responded to such charges with simple denials. Although New Orleans experienced dramatic episodes of racial violence, the *Picayune* still insisted that the white South was conciliatory and patient, not violent and precipitate. The *Athens Post* (Alabama) doubted any people on earth had ever shown more peaceful forbearance than white southerners in the five years after Appomattox. When northerners declared that white southerners had committed 3,500 political murders, the *Picayune* stated that the evidence reached eight "and stuck hopelessly." The paper insisted that it had been statistically established that African Americans made up a majority of the New Orleans law violators. In 1877, when a white mob in DeKalb, Mississippi, murdered local Republicans, the *New Orleans Picayune* hastened to condemn the killings. "Lynching *is* murder," the paper nervously reminded its readers, worrying that vindictive men in Congress would use the incident to defame the entire South. Later the *Picayune* observed that lynching injured "our material interests. Such things make the very name of Louisiana a reproach...." When reports surfaced of a lynching in Amite County, Mississippi, the *Picayune* again editorialized against extralegal violence. In 1880, the paper responded angrily to reports that honest northern businessmen had been lynched solely because of their politics. The *Picayune* was emphatic: carpetbaggers' "profession of plunder and rapine" naturally led them to "the limb of a convenient tree." The *Picayune* repeated its earlier denunciations of "that unjust form of justice known as Lynch law," but an outraged public, the paper warned, could not always be stayed.[48] The *Athens Post* made the same argument: white southerners turned to violence only after they had been "oppressed, outraged, plundered, insulted" by Radical fanatics trampling the Constitution.[49] The *Picayune* understood fully the rhetorical power of lynching discourse, accusing northern papers of operating an "outrage mill." The paper hoped that the fickle public had lost interest in lynching talk by 1880.[50]

At the same time that the *Picayune* and like-minded papers minimized lynching violence, other white southerners openly used the San Francisco lynchings to justify extralegal violence. In 1868, South Carolina's *Griffin Star* followed the lead of the Californians, excusing lynching on the basis of the villainy of those it proposed lynching. The *Star* thought criminal gangs, stealing "at wholesale and retail, and where stealing cannot be effected, *to rob, plunder and murder!*" justified "a California Vigilance Committee." The *Charleston News and Courier* (South Carolina) made the same argument in 1880, publishing a lengthy list of crimes committed by African Americans. The paper asserted, "The offences which are prompted by greed and lust are virtually unknown among white people in this State." The *News and Courier* advocated lynchings. "We have no fear," the paper explained, "that the people of the Eastern or Western States will be shocked." After all, "They know how it is themselves, and do as the South Carolinians have done." Westerners, the paper charged, turned to lynching with less cause than white southerners.[51]

Northerners opposed to this violence often had to rely on newspaper accounts for their information. From the beginning, some doubted newspaper reports could be used to produce truly accurate data. Early in 1867, General Ulysses S. Grant submitted to Secretary of War Edwin M. Stanton a table of nineteen "outrages committed in Southern States" the previous year. Grant did not see himself as a social scientist, but his data nonetheless resemble Gilded Age efforts at empiricism. Grant, disenchanted with President Andrew Johnson's policy of returning antebellum white elites to power, had compiled the list to persuade Congress to impose martial law on the former Confederacy. When Stanton presented Grant's list to the cabinet, Secretary of the Navy Gideon Welles called it "wholly unreliable," an "omnium-gatherum of newspaper gossip" and "rumors." In his diary, Secretary of the Interior Orville Browning expressed his conviction that Grant's list not only exaggerated the facts but was "a mean, malicious thing" done to advance Radical Republicans' Reconstruction plans.[52]

Northern consumers of lynching news shaped southern rhetoric. The *Chicago Tribune* expressed sympathy for blacks, but other newspapers railed against "nigger outrages." Northerners proved vulnerable to these arguments. Through the 1870s the *New York Times* editorialized against lynchings whether in the West or the South, but its news reports revealed periodic sympathy for the lynchers. When Virginia City residents extralegally executed a white murderer, the *Times* complimented the lynchers for carrying out their business in an orderly manner. A *Times* correspondent excused a lynching in Abilene, Kansas, as understandably prompted by the city's overwhelming lawless element. The newspaper came close to endorsing lynching in its own city when it worried that a "fiend in human shape . . . now chuckling over his crime" and being held at the Leonard-Street police station might get away with murder. It warned that if authorities did not act, the people would, asking menacingly, "this Leonard-Street Station House—is it impregnable?" Like many southern newspapers, the *New York Times* acknowledged that lynching was a crime, "but sometimes it is palliated by many circumstances." When authorities would not or could not punish crime, lynch law "may at times be almost forced upon a people." The *New Orleans Picayune* or the *Athens Post* could not have said it better.[53]

The *New York Times* article about the Leonard-Street station shows that northerners could be persuaded to tolerate lynching violence. White southerners needed a persuasive justification for lynching that would impress northerners and doubters in their own region as well. Rape began to appear in the southern press as a justification for lynching blacks at least as early as the 1860s. Southern whites hoped to trump politics with gender.

Southern newspapers sought to convince readers and northern observers that Republican policies incited crimes against white women. In 1871, South Carolina newspapers justified Ku Klux Klan violence as made necessary by blacks' rapes of white women. Newspapers sometimes reported that all-black or black and white crowds administered summary justice to black malefactors.[54] In 1871, crowds in Kentucky lynched black men charged with rape in Morganfield and Frankfort. The following year, a group of Tennesseeans lynched a "desperate character" who had raped a woman, and another man charged with entering a white couple's bedroom. In 1876, black alleged rapists were lynched in Mississippi and Tennessee.

Northerners lynched as well. When lynchers killed a rapist, the *New York Times* reported that "the citizens generally approved of the action." In 1872, Ohio men lynched a black rapist who had attacked a woman on her way home from Sunday school. When Ohioans lynched again the next year, they again charged their victim with rape. The *New York Times* reported that "public opinion is decidedly in favor of the lynchers." The *Times*, in fact, generally softened its own opposition to lynching when lynchers asserted that their victims had "outraged" women. In 1880, when a white mob in South Carolina lynched a black man it charged with rape, the *Times* justified the crime by stating that the victim's reputation was "exceedingly bad." This lynching violated the law, the paper wrote, but "is generally approved by white and colored."[55]

There seemed to be an unwritten law in the United States that had long recognized the right of men to punish adultery or seduction informally when those sex acts involved "their" women. This attitude could just as easily endorse lynching, as when George Lippard wrote in 1844 that the assassin of "an innocent girl's soul . . . is worthy of death by the hands of any man, and in any place."[56] Defense attorneys successfully smuggled the unwritten law before juries by arguing the temporary insanity defense. Several prominent nineteenth-century murder trials involved men charged with enforcement of the unwritten law. In

1867, George Cole killed his wife's lover; in 1869, Daniel McFarland killed his former wife's fiancé; in 1870, Harry Crawford Black shot and killed his sister's seducer; in 1882, Daniel Giddings killed his wife's lover; the next year James Nutt killed his sister's seducer; in the same year "Little Phil" Thompson killed his wife's debaucher; in 1884, Edward Johnson killed his wife's lover. In each case defense counsel won an acquittal after advancing the plea of insanity induced by a rival's sexual misconduct. Many ministers and some religious publications declared that God's law required death for fornicators and adulterers. Henry Watterson's *Louisville Courier-Journal* endorsed the law as "unwritten, but inexorable." Watterson added that he hoped "never to see the day when the unwritten law requiring the life of a man for the honor of a woman shall be relaxed." Some states did not even bother to pass laws against seduction, their legislators being convinced that such matters should be punished outside the law.[57]

The "right" of a community to punish African American males who trespassed with white women emerged from this tradition. Even when white women welcomed black suitors, the white community believed it had the right to act. Some of the earliest lynchings of black sexual transgressors actually involved African Americans who had—according to contemporary newspapers—"seduced" white women. The earliest opponents of lynching virtually conceded the argument that African American rapes of white women contributed to lynching violence.[58]

Northerners' opposition to southern violence wavered when the lynchers cried rape. The earliest apologists of lynch law had said that their victims were wicked beyond redemption because they knew the argument worked. The rape gloss on this argument proved particularly popular because it was especially persuasive to nineteenth-century Americans. Woman irretrievably ruined, hardened into harlots or victimized by male lust and violence, composed the most popular literary cliches of the time.[59] Northern newspapers found that black rapes of white women fit their expectations perfectly. In 1868, the *New York Day Book* denounced rapes of white women by animalistic African Americans. In South Carolina, the *Edgefield Advertiser* happily reprinted the article. Writer L. E. Bleckley reported that "good and fairly sensible people" believed the killing of a ravisher was only technically a crime and not "moral murder" at all.[60]

Just as whites constructed justifications for lynching, the most influential history of San Francisco and California vigilantism appeared, justifying extralegal violence. When H. H. Bancroft published his authoritative and readable *Popular Tribunals* in 1887, he differentiated between "vigilance" and "mob law." He admitted the phenomena looked the same but insisted that differences existed. The doctrine of vigilance, Bancroft explained, held that the people possess the right and the duty to hold perpetual vigil over all matters relating to their governance. Weak law or political corruption justified vigilante government: "A true vigilance committee is [the] expression of power on the part of the people in the absence or impotence of law." "Mob-violence," by contrast, was "the blunt instrument of dull wits." Vigilance punished malefactors based on principle, not passion. Mobs cried for revenge; passion clouded their minds. But Bancroft admitted that when a mob represented the majority, it was no longer a mob.[61]

Bancroft used the term *lynching* less often than *mob* or *vigilance committee*. The original lynchers in colonial Virginia, Bancroft wrote, had been true vigilantes, but by the 1850s the term had come to mean mob law. Bancroft wrote after this change had occurred; he worked to rehabilitate lynch law, though he called it "vigilantism" to avoid the opprobrious word. He and other writers did much to legitimize lynching nationally.[62]

The rape argument made it more difficult to oppose lynching, but not impossible. Even in South Carolina, some objected to lynching.[63] But the most serious attacks came from outside the South. Before the Civil War such attacks on "lynch law" took narrative form, as abolitionists published stories of violence designed to shock and incense northern readers. Not long after the war opponents of extra-legal executions had donned new rhetorical garb, attacking vigilante violence with social science. This social science approach placed demands on lynching language that have little to do with the reality of the actual violence.[64]

The press aspired to reliability and objectivity rather than rumor. In 1882, the *Chicago Tribune* began collecting data on lynching. Editor and owner Joseph Medill made the *Tribune* profoundly Republican, deeply conservative, and fundamentally elitist. Medill hated "boodlers, bummers, and taxeaters," not to mention socialists. For all his elitism, Medill believed in popular democracy and insisted that the masses, properly educated and informed, could move society in a positive direction.[65]

The *Tribune* followed in the steps of the penny press, more commercial than political, serving, in other words, merchants rather than politicians. The journalistic endeavor that ultimately led the *Tribune* to compile its famous list of lynchings began with a combination of commercial boosterism and faith in science. On January 1, 1875, just months after Medill took control, the *Tribune* announced that improvements in business demanded a new style of writing. This "new style" amounted to lots of facts, numbers, and tables: what a later generation called scientism. The *Tribune* at first reported only on business. Prepared by Elias Colbert, the *Tribune*'s 1875 review of business statistics for 1874 launched a long-running tradition. By 1883, the paper boasted of having achieved new levels of truly objective science; "bombast or brag" had been expunged from the annual review. In good social science fashion, Colbert explained that the facts could speak for themselves.[66]

This new interest in objective science led the *Tribune* to expand its annual review beyond commerce. It began including tallies of suicides, train wrecks, shipwrecks, embezzlements, murders, legal executions, and epidemics. Lynchings joined the annual review in 1883.[67] At first the *Tribune* included lynchings with legal executions, a subset of "hangings." But in 1888, it began pointing out that most lynchings occurred in the South. In 1890, the annual report on "Judge Lynch's Work" carried "How the Colored Man Has Suffered" as a subheadline.[68]

Although social science motivated *Tribune* editors to collect lynching statistics, their methods were less than rigorous. The *Tribune* never provided readers with a clue as to what its editors thought constituted a lynching. They probably did not think about it very much. If the papers that supplied them with their information called a homicide a lynching, then it became one. Nor did *Tribune* editors have any way of allowing for papers that chose not to report lynchings. It is quite likely some newspapers did not report all acts of violence against blacks. Roy Wilkins complained that the twentieth-century *Kansas City Star* had a "blind spot" for black news. The *Star* reported bombings in Bulgaria but not in Kansas City. The same may have been true in the nineteenth century, when many newspapers thought crime news too vulgar to report. As late as the 1890s the *New York Post* did not report crimes. When its editors finally dispatched Lincoln Steffens to the Mulberry Street station, they assured him he was "not to report crimes and that sort of thing." The cops on Mulberry Street sneered at Steffens when he arrived, "The *Post* has always despised police news, true police news. . . . We'll see how long he stays here." He stayed. Once Steffens and the *Post* tasted the wine of crime news, they could hardly resist it. By reporting crime news hitherto ignored, the *Post* and other New York papers manufactured "crime waves." In a similar fashion, the *Tribune* created a perception of a lynching wave after 1882.[69]

In 1892, journalist Ida B. Wells used the *Tribune* data to launch a frontal attack on white claims that rape justified lynching. She denounced as a "thread-bare lie" whites' arguments that the African Americans' savage lust justified lynching. Wells asserted that thousands of southern white women preferred black males over whites. When caught, they cried rape, inspiring lynching hysteria. Wells exposed rape as a rhetorical device, the latest of several deployed by whites. In 1895, she deconstructed whites' statements on behalf of lynching, showing how they constantly shifted. Whites first defended lynching as necessary to repress planned insurrections after emancipation. Next, that blacks' political rights "caused" lynchings. When state governments subverted blacks' rights, whites shifted gears again: lynchers defended white women from black rapists.[70]

A brilliant rhetorician, Wells carefully crafted her public persona, presenting herself as a neutral presenter of facts, an objective investigative reporter. She used the same narrative strategies abolitionists had relied on. The story of how she came to crusade against lynching illustrates the continuing power of the old narrative form. Wells said that she had rejected rape as a justification for lynching only when Memphis whites lynched three black grocers in 1892. These lynchings, Wells wrote, "changed the whole course of my life." Wells decided that the three grocers had been lynched because they threatened white competitors economically. "This is what opened my eyes to what lynching really was. An excuse to get rid of Negroes who were acquiring wealth and property."[71]

Wells also appealed to the new science of sociology. Just as the *Tribune* insisted it reported without bombast or brag, giving just the facts, Wells worked hard to suppress emotion, making the facts—as she packaged them—seem to speak for themselves. Using the *Tribune*'s statistics, Wells pointed out that only one-third of lynching victims had even been charged with rape.[72]

Wells and other blacks accepted the lynchers' popular-sovereignty argument, but they transformed it from a justification into a general indictment of white society. Accordingly, in the very case that inspired Wells, Memphis blacks held all whites in the area responsible for the deaths of the three black grocers lynched in 1892. African Americans boycotted Memphis streetcars. When the streetcar operators protested they had nothing to do with the lynching, Wells retorted that Memphis blacks "feel that every white man in Memphis who consented to" the lynchings "is as guilty as those who fired the guns."[73]

One of the earliest scholarly investigations of lynching also accepted the community-responsibility argument. In 1905, James Elbert Cutler published *Lynch-Law: An Investigation into the History of Lynching in the United States*. Cutler doggedly studied nineteenth-century publications, seeking the origins of lynching and the evolution of the word's meaning. Historians still rely on Cutler's work. But his definition of *lynching*, though exactly representative of contemporary thinking, is not widely supported today. Cutler defined *lynching* as "an illegal and summary execution at the hands of a mob . . . who have in some degree the public opinion of the community behind them." Cutler went on to call popular justification the sine qua non of lynching. "It is this fact that distinguished lynching from murder." After Cutler's work appeared, the popular-sovereignty paradigm for lynching collapsed. Social scientists find Cutler's public-opinion requirement too difficult to meet; opponents of racial violence and discrimination generally found lynching too useful a rhetorical device to allow its meaning to be so narrowly constructed.[74]

Pressures for a broader definition came from organizations campaigning against lynching. They found in *lynching* a word that could be an effective tool in their campaigns against many evils, not just group violence. The National Association for the Advancement of Colored People (NAACP) came into existence after the 1908 race riot in Springfield, Illinois. Based outside the South, the organization had a constituency anxious to combat discrimination of all types. Lynching became the symbol of a broader problem, not the problem itself. Their strategy mobilized publicity and propaganda. Knowing they challenged a long-term, deeply rooted enemy, NAACP founders expected their organization to be permanent.

The enormous propaganda value of lynching became clear to the NAACP in 1916, when Boston philanthropist Philip G. Peabody offered the NAACP $10,000 to devise a feasible plan to end lynching. The NAACP proposed gathering and publishing data, preparing model antilynching bills, and organizing local committees to identify and prosecute lynchers. Peabody ultimately decided not to award the NAACP the money because, he said later, he realized such a small sum would hardly make a dent in such an immense problem. Though the NAACP failed to persuade Peabody to make the grant, writing the grant proposal convinced officials they should make lynching their top priority. NAACP leaders recruited Walter White as an investigator to go to the South and get inside information on lynchings. His reports created "a gratifying sensation" that replenished the NAACP's empty treasury with contributions from blacks and whites shocked by the details he provided. The NAACP vigorously battled for a federal law against lynching. By campaigning against lynching, the NAACP could gain a hearing for other issues. As one writer explained, "[L]ynching became the wedge by which the NAACP insinuated itself into the public conscience."[75]

By the time the NAACP came into existence, W. E. B. Du Bois and other leaders had already abandoned sociology as an appropriate vehicle for attacking lynching. After he joined the NAACP, Walter White wrote a novel about an African American doctor who travels to the South and learns that a life devoted to pure science is impossible. Having turned away from objective science, Du Bois and White launched a frankly polemical attack on racial violence, relying on statistics only when rhetorically useful.[76]

The Tuskegee Institute also campaigned against lynching. But, unlike Du Bois, its chief collector of lynching data, Monroe Work, had not lost faith in empiricism and remained true to objective social science. Like Ida B. Wells, Work, a sociologist, presented himself as an objective reporter, expressing controlled outrage. Work believed that unvarnished facts—objective reality—made the most effective propaganda. He thought the NAACP too loose, too openly propagandistic in its collection of statistics. For its part, the NAACP thought Work too conservative. Work's concern with science led him to worry consciously about the problem of definition. Work refused to include riot victims but did include those killed by posses. In some cases he included murder victims when he had little or no information about how the killings occurred. If the victim had been tied up, Work reasoned, the murder must have been the work of a mob because no lone individual could tie up, mutilate, and torture his victim. He discarded Cutler's community-support definition, broadening the meaning of *lynching* to include any racial killing committed by two or more perpetrators outside the environment of a riot. Despite its methodological problems, even white southern newspapers began publishing Work's statistics as authoritative.[77]

Many southern whites welcomed Work's scholarship as they sought to turn public opinion against racial violence. Josephus Daniels of the *Raleigh News and Observer* denounced lynching on the pages of his newspaper in the strongest terms, arguing that such violence disgraced the state.[78] But his strongest attack on lynching violence was less direct. Because lynching connoted community approval, and Daniels wanted to deny murderers community sanction, he called racial killings cold-blooded murder. He wanted to craft a truth that would deny racial murderers the sanction of their neighborhoods. When whites in Salisbury, North Carolina, killed two African American youths in 1902, Daniels condemned the slayings as premeditated murder, which implied a violence perpetrated in defiance of community norms, not as lynchings, which implied community sponsorship. In another incident, Daniels identified a former convict "with a long list of crimes to his credit" as the leader of a mob. Obviously, such an outlaw did not represent his community.[79]

Jessie Daniel Ames followed the same strategy through the Association of Southern Women for the Prevention of Lynching (ASWPL), founded in 1930. For twelve years the ASWPL worked to persuade white southerners that black men did not cause lynching by raping white women. But Ames also opposed efforts to enact a federal law against lynching. Like Daniels, she focused instead on changing the attitudes of white southerners. She did not think outsiders could help in that effort. Ames worked to change southern white public opinion by corresponding with southern newspaper editors.[80]

Ames built the ASWPL campaign against lynching around the goal of a "lynchless year." Some years could be heartbreakers. In 1936, Ames suffered "a spell of depression" when a lynching occurred in Mississippi. "Our hopes had grown so high," Ames wrote, consoling herself that at least Texas had stayed clear. In 1939, the Tuskegee Institute prevented Ames from declaring that year free of lynchings when it counted as a lynching a black man found dead with his hands and feet tied. Ames objected, insisting that a single murderer could have both tied and murdered his victim.[81]

While Ames sweated out each year, hoping for twelve consecutive months free of lynching violence, the NAACP revised its definition of *lynching* to make her goal impossible. In 1916, when the organization applied to Peabody for money to fight lynching, it repeated Cutler's understanding of lynching as murder sanctioned by the community. A successful fight, the NAACP declared, "must start with the recognition that popular justification is the sine qua non of lynching." The difference between ordinary murder and lynching, the NAACP explained, is that lynchers have some degree of community support behind them. Within a few years, though, the NAACP no longer regarded community support as necessary for lynching. The NAACP's count of lynchings for 1927 included a white man beaten to death by prisoners in a Los Angeles jail and two men murdered by posses.[82] Through the 1920s, the NAACP broadened its definition of *lynching* to include any case where "three or more persons conspire to cause the death of or physical injury to another person."[83]

Other organizations picked up the broader definition. In 1940, Anna Damon, secretary of the International Labor Defence, wrote Jessie Daniel Ames to concede that "the exact procedure hitherto defined as lynching has recently changed." As another reformer explained, racial violence "went underground." Southern whites, Damon wrote, had started lynching blacks surreptitiously. She asserted that in Mississippi alone there had been twenty secret or "quiet lynchings." Damon then lectured Ames that a person tortured to death "by persons not strictly definable as a 'mob' who do their murder in secrecy, is no less murdered than one who is 'lynched' in the full sight of a mob in a town square."[84]

The NAACP's "quiet lynching" rhetoric frustrated Ames's expectation of a lynch-free year; she had high hopes that 1940 would be the first. As early as January 8, 1940, she wrote that lynching-prone Mississippi had yet to have a lynching for the year, "This . . . is good news as far as the news goes and as long as it lasts." Just two days later, another ASWPL woman wrote that she gave thanks for every day that passed without a lynching. In the middle of 1940, Tuskegee declared that the first six months of 1940 had passed without a lynching. Ames went even further, saying that there had not been a lynching in the previous twelve months. The NAACP vigorously rejected both assertions. Journalist Oswald Garrison Villard sharply chastised Work. Tuskegee, Villard insisted, had not included as lynchings three Georgia murders: police had found Sarah Rawls and Benton Ford beaten to death in a "lovers' lane," and a few nights later, Ike Gaston, body, similarly flogged to death. The NAACP insisted that the three homicides must be counted as "quiet" lynchings, and Villard accused Tuskegee of giving out a false statement, adding, "If Tuskegee cannot make accurate statements on lynchings it should cease all publications in regard thereto." Thurgood Marshall thought the Tuskegee statement had given the fight against lynching a "tremendous set-back." Ames defended her reckoning by conceding that whites quietly murdered blacks, but it was a practice that had been going on for many years, she complained. It was nothing new. The NAACP repudiated Ames's statement—just as it had Work's—and prevailed upon Will Alexander, director of the Commission on Interracial Cooperation, to do the same.[85]

Each organization worked to end something it called lynching, but each relied on different strategies to do so. These differences in strategy account for the differing definitions of *lynching*. All had agreed to drop the community-sanction or popular-sovereignty portion of the nineteenth-century definition, though all implicitly agreed that a corrupt southern society made lynchings possible. But they disagreed in other ways as each tried to shape the word to meet its own needs.

The public quarrel between Tuskegee and the NAACP led to a summit conference to iron out differences. On December 14, 1940, the NAACP and other antilynching organizations met at the institute to work out a definition of *lynching*. McClellan Van der Veer, a Birmingham journalist, joined Jessie Daniel Ames to argue in favor of a precise and narrow definition. Journalists, Van der Veer insisted, would not accept an overly broad definition, wanting "reality" instead. He argued that accurate information on lynching, carefully defined, would do more to fight racial violence than overt propaganda. Ames also urged a narrow definition. She thought that a corpse and a court record should actually exist before a homicide could be counted as a lynching. In her opinion, misclassifications of murders as lynchings had actually hurt the antilynching effort. Both Van der Veer and Ames calculated that frequent reports of lynchings hardened whites to racial violence. A steady stream of headlines reporting "NEGRO TREADS AIR" or "NEGRO MURDERER GIVEN SHORT SHRIFT" or "DRAGGED FROM JAIL TO DIE BY THE ROPE" encouraged lynchers by making lynching appear a routine and accepted practice. If newspapers were to make lynching seem rare, Van der Veer and Ames anticipated that the practice would become less frequent. Accurate information would "create the feeling that lynchings are not to be expected." Ralph Davis of the Tuskegee Institute proposed a narrow definition along the lines Van der Veer and Ames urged. Davis wanted to restrict lynchings to activities "in which persons, not officers of the law, in open and public defiance of the law, administer punishment by death to an individual for an alleged offense of or to an individual with whom some offense has been associated."[86]

Walter White, Arthur Raper, and Ira Reid of Atlanta University argued for a loose definition of *lynching*. White began by saying that the NAACP used the same definition as in proposed federal antilynching bills but admitted that his organization often counted as lynchings murders that did not fit the federal definition. Raper warned the conference not to "drive lynching out of the picture by definition." Implicit in his warning was concern that such an excellent rhetorical device as the lynching label should not be sacrificed on the altar of science. Raper cautioned that murders organized by officers of the law must be counted as "lynchings." Reid insisted that he did not want lynchings restricted to acts in defiance of the law nor did he want officers of the law excluded. The Tuskegee definition would not count as lynchings the so-called quiet lynchings the NAACP thought must be included.[87]

Seeking to reconcile these competing views, the meeting agreed on four criteria. First, before an incident could be declared a lynching, there had to be a dead body. Second, the corpse had to have met death illegally. Next, the murderers had to be a group. Participants debated the meaning of *group*, some urging the definition used by several states in their antilynching statutes: three or more. Others thought that too limiting. The conference never agreed, so *group* remained undefined. Conferees did agree that the murderers must have acted under pretext of service to justice, race, or tradition.[88]

Jessie Daniel Ames ultimately rejected this compromise, writing that the new definition "could be made to convert into a lynching the death of every Negro at the hands of white persons." For instance, the new definition included two 1941 murders for which authorities promptly and successfully prosecuted the killers. Journalist Jonathan Daniels wrote that including such murders threatened to reduce lynching statistics to silliness. And, in fact, even after the conference, the NAACP and Tuskegee still produced contradictory counts of lynchings. The NAACP remained doggedly determined to maintain the loosest definition of lynching possible. In 1953, Marguerite Cartwright wrote in the NAACP's journal that "lynching has become a symbol and should be so understood." With startling candor, she admitted that reports of declines in lynchings threatened NAACP fund-raising. "I was once refused an NAACP contribution by a wealthy acquaintance as he cited the decline in lynching," Cartwright complained. Instead of a "technical and doctrinaire" definition, lynching should be understood as a "technique of racial exploitation,—economic, cultural and poltical."[89]

Although the NAACP and other antilynching organizations found the 1940 definition inadequate, historians have rallied around it. Scholars writing about lynchings routinely invoke the 1940 definition, even when using data collected before 1940.[90] In fact, there is no way to control the definition of *lynching*. Lynching data come from accounts published by local newspapers, the product of decisions made by editors and their correspondents. The *Chicago Tribune* pointed out in 1890 that the number of "unrecorded victims . . . lynched" in the South "will never be known." A Kentucky newspaper, the Boone County *Recorder*, described an 1894 lynching as the eighth in the county, even though earlier issues of the paper had mentioned only three.[91]

The horror of racial violence and mob law occupied a universe parallel to but distinct from the language used to describe it. Surviving sources make it clear that whites perpetrated an uncountable number of acts of violence against blacks. Failure to understand this critical point has led positivists to "document" statistical peaks and valleys on the basis of newspaper reports. Lynching must be understood as a discourse, a new label attached to particular incidents abstracted from a larger, hidden reality. As journalists and other contemporary observers warned, there is no way to document fully the depth of extralegal violence in America. The history of lynching is a narrative of contested language and discursive politics. A crime that claimed many lives, lynching also become a powerful symbol of American racial politics, and should be understood as such.

NOTES

1. W. E. B. Du Bois, *The Autobiography of W. E. B. Du Bois: A Soliloquy on Viewing My Life from the Last Decade of Its First Century* (New York: International Publishers, 1968), 205, 221–22; W. E. B. Du Bois, *The Philadelphia Negro: A Social Study* (1899; reprint, New York: Schocken Books, 1967), 1–9; W. E. B. Du Bois, *The Souls of Black Folk: Essays and Sketches* (Chicago: A. G. McClurg, 1903). Dominic J. Capeci, Jr., and Jack C. Knight, "Reckoning with Violence: W. E. B. Du Bois and the 1906 Atlanta Race Riot," *Journal of Southern History* 62 (November 1996): 727–66; David Levering Lewis, *W. E. B. Du Bois: Biography of a Race, 1868–1919* (New York: Holt, 1993), 226–29, 333–37; Thomas C. Holt, "The Political Uses of Alienation: W. E. B. Du Bois on Politics, Race, and Culture, 1903–1940," *American Quarterly* 42 (June 1990): 301–23; Cornel West, *The American Evasion of Philosophy: A Genealogy of Pragmatisim* (Madison: University of Wisconsin Press, 1989), 138–50.

2. Peter Novick, *That Noble Dream: The "Objectivity Question" and the American Historical Profession* (Cambridge: Cambridge University Press, 1988), 522–72; John E. Toews, "Intellectual History after the Linguistic Turn: The Autonomy of Meaning and the Irreducibility of Experience," *American Historical Review* 92 (October 1987): 879–907.

3. W. Fitzhugh Brundage, *Lynching in the New South: Georgia and Virginia, 1880–1930* (Urbana: University of Illinois Press, 1993), 291–92. Brundage is hardly unique in sidestepping the definition problem: Stewart E. Tolnay and E. M. Beck, *A Festival of Violence: An Analysis of Southern Lynchings, 1882–1930* (Urbana: University of Illinois Press, 1992), 260, concede a "natural ambiguity" but refuse to allow definitional issues to trouble their text; George Wright, *Racial Violence in Kentucky, 1865–1940: Lynchings, Mob Rule, and "Legal Lynchings"* (Baton Rouge: Louisiana State University Press, 1990), ignores the problem of definition; Richard Maxwell Brown, *Strain of Violence: Studies of American Violence and Vigilantism* (New York: Oxford University Press, 1975), 103, tries to distinguish "organized" vigilantism and "ephemeral" lynch law from "instant vigilantism." But, as David Johnson points out in "Vigilance and the Law: The Moral Authority of Popular Justice in the Far West," *American Quarterly* 33 (1981): 560 n. 6, vigilance committees could be unorganized and ephemeral, and lynch mobs could be highly organized. For the importance of precise definitions in social science research, see Janet Saltzman Chafetz, *A Primer on the Construction and Testing of Theories in Sociology* (Ithaca, N.Y.: F. E. Peacock, 1978), 45–

61; Abraham Kaplan, *The Conduct of Inquiry: Methodology for the Behavioral Sciences* (San Francisco: Chandler, 1964), 46–52; Frank E. Hagan, *Research Methods in Criminal Justice and Criminology* (New York: Macmillan, 1989), 14–16.

4. The most important studies of lynching's origins are James Elbert Cutler, *Lynch-Law: An Investigation into the History of Lynching in the United States* (1905; reprint, New York: Negro Universities Press, 1969), 13–154; John Ross, "At the Bar of Judge Lynch: Lynching and Lynch Mobs in America" (Ph.D. diss., Texas Tech University, 1983), 49–118. Alfred Percy, *Origin of the Lynch Law, 1780* (Madison Heights, Va., 1959), makes an indignant lawyer's brief on behalf of the original lynchers.

5. *Norfolk Herald and Public Advertiser*, March 25, 1797; *Virginia Herald and Fredericksburg Advertiser*, September 29, October 6, 1791. For another instance of informal, neighborhood justice administered on slaves, see Melton A. McLaurin, *Celia: A Slave* (Athens: University of Georgia Press, 1991), 33–39.

6. Catharine Van Cortlandt Mathews, *Andrew Ellicott: His Life and Letters* (New York: Grafton, 1908), 220; *Niles' Register*, January 9, July 24, 1819; June 1, 1822; July 17, 1824; W. Faux, *Memorable Days in America: Being a Journal of a Tour to the United States. . . .* (1823; reprint, New York: AMS Press, 1969), 304–5; James Hall, *Letters from the West. . . .* (1828; reprint, Gainesville: Scholars Facsimiles, 1967), 291.

7. Leonard L. Richards, *"Gentlemen of Property and Standing": Anti-Abolition Mobs in Jacksonian America* (New York: Oxford University Press, 1970), 50–52 (in general, see 6–52); Bertram Wyatt-Brown, *Lewis Tappan and the Evangelical War against Slavery* (Cleveland: Press of Case Western Reserve University, 1969), 149–63; David Grimsted, "Rioting in Its Jacksonian Setting," *American Historical Review* 77 (April 1972): 361–97; *New York Sun*, June 25, 1835; *Niles' Register*, September 19, 1835.

8. See, for example, *Lancaster Examiner and Herald* (Pa.), September 4, 1834; *New York Sun*, December 3, 1833, March 25, June 24, July 9, 24, October 10, 1834, February 2, 27, January 10, April 18, May 9, June 24, 25, 26, 1835. Richard D. Brown, *Knowledge Is Power: The Diffusion of Information in Early America, 1700–1865* (New York: Oxford University Press, 1989), 218–96; Andie Tucher, *Froth and Scum: Truth, Beauty, Goodness, and the Ax Murder in America's First Mass Medium* (Chapel Hill: University of North Carolina Press, 1994), 7–96; Michael Emery and Edwin Emery, *The Press and America: An Interpretative History of the Mass Media* (Englewood Cliffs, N.J.: Prentice-Hall, 1992), 92–117.

9. Edwin Emery, *The Press and America: An Interpretive History of the Mass Media* (Englewood Cliffs, N.J.: Prentice-Hall, 1972), 167, 172. For purported objectivity and science, see "AQUATIC OBJECTS AS SEEN IN A SINGLE DROP OF WATER," *New York Sun*, February 23, 1835. For lying, see "GREAT ASTROLOGICAL DISCOVERIES," *New York Sun*, August 29, 1835. Tucher, *Froth and Scum*, passim, but see esp. 176–209; Dan Schiller, *Objectivity and the News: The Public and the Rise of Commercial Journalism* (Philadelphia: University of Pennsylvania Press, 1981), 1–95; Brown, *Knowledge Is Power*, 218–44; Sean Wilentz, *Chants Democratic: New York City and the Rise of the American Working Class, 1788–1850* (New York: Oxford University Press, 1984), 23–103; Michael Schudson, *Discovering the News* (New York: Basic Books, 1978), 6–60; Helen MacGill Hughes, *News and the Human Interest Story* (1940; reprint, New York: Greenwood Press, 1968), 1–29.

10. See, for example, *Boston Liberator*, October 27, 1848, April 13, May 11, 1849. For the *Boston Liberator*, see Walter M. Merrill, ed., *The Letters of William Lloyd Garrison*, vol. 1, *I Will Be Heard* (Cambridge: Harvard University Press, Belknap Press, 1971), 119, 124; Walter M. Merrill, *Against Wind and Tide: A Biography of William Lloyd Garrison* (Cambridge: Harvard University Press, 1963), 40–55; James Brewer Stewart, *William Lloyd Garrison and the Challenge of Emancipation* (Arlington Heights, Ill.: H. Davidson, 1992), 49–53. Schiller,

Objectivity and the News, 110–13. Brown, *Knowledge Is Power,* 218–44, emphasizes the competition for readers among papers.

11. *New York Sun,* September 2, 24, 1835. On this point, see Tucher, *Froth and Scum,* 88–90. For an excellent discussion of the changing styles of information dissemination, see Brown, *Knowledge Is Power,* 245–67.

12. Hall, *Letters from the West,* 291–92; *Niles' Register,* July 19, 1834; [Henry Tanner], *The Martyrdom of Lovejoy: An Account of the Life, Trials, and Perils of Rev. Elijah P. Lovejoy* (1881; reprint, New York: A. M. Kelley, 1971), 81–82.

13. James Madison addresses similar concerns in Federalist 10. See *The Federalist Papers by Alexander Hamilton, James Madison, and John Jay* (New York: Bantam, 1982), 48.

14. Hall, *Letters from the West,* 291–92; *Picayune* quoted in *Boston Liberator,* October 14, 1842; *Galenian* quoted in *Niles' Register,* July 19, 1834. Johnson, "Vigilance and the Law," 558–86.

15. *Picayune* quoted in *Boston Liberator,* October 14, 1842; Hall, *Letters from the West,* 291–92; *Galenian,* June 16, 1834; Eliphalet Price, "The Trial and Execution of Patrick O'Conner at the Dubuque Mines in the Summer of 1834," *Palimpsest* 1 (1920): 87.

16. Faux, *Memorable Days in America,* 304; *Galenian,* June 16, 1834; Price, "The Execution of O'Conner," 90–91; *Picayune* quoted in *Boston Liberator,* October 14, 1842; Kenneth M. Stampp, *The Peculiar Institution: Slavery in the Antebellum South* (New York: Knopf, 1956), 191.

17. Hall, *Letters from the West,* 291–92; Price, "The Execution of O'Conner," 97; *Niles' Register,* August 1, 1835.

18. Act of May 31, 1841; act of April 13, 1855, c. 428; *Darlington v. City of New York,* 31 New York 185. Courts generally saw riotous behavior as a threat to property, and defined disturbances involving as few as three people as "riots." *State v. John H. Bennett,* 20 North Carolina 170 (1838); *State v. Jesse Allison,* 11 Tennessee 428 (1832); *State v. Joseph Cole, et al.,* 2 McCord 115; *Commonwealth v. Jenkins and others,* in Peter Oxenbridge Thacher, *Reports of Criminal Cases Tried in the Municipal Court of the City of Boston,* ed. Horatio Woodman (Boston: Little and Brown, 1845), 118; *State v. J. L. Brooks, and others,* 1 Hill 232; *Douglas v. State,* 14 South Carolina 525 (1834).

19. *Niles' Register,* May 28, 1825. In 1893, Walter Page warned that a lynching community loses its civic spirit; terrible demoralization follows toleration of mob violence. Page, "The Last Hold of the Southern Bully," *Forum* 16 (November 1893): 303–14.

20. James Lal Penick, Jr., *The Great Western Land Pirate: John A. Murrell in Legend and History* (Columbia: University of Missouri Press, 1981), 59, 64; *Boston Liberator,* September 27, 1834.

21. *New York Sun,* December 3, 1833, July 2, 1834, January 17 and February 27, 1835. At least some courts agreed that disturbing religious worship constituted a riot. See *Commonwealth v. Dupuy, et al.* in John A. Clark, comp., *Pennsylvania Law Journal Reports,* 5 vols. (Philadelphia, 1872), 4:222.

22. *Niles' Register,* August 1, 1835; Christopher Morris, *Becoming Southern: The Evolution of a Way of Life, Warren County and Vicksburg, Mississippi, 1770–1860* (New York: Oxford University Press, 1995), 121–23.

23. James Burns Wallace Diary, January 13, 1836, Louisiana State University Library; Richard Wynkoop to H. S. Wynkoop, October 1, 1836, reprinted in *Vicksburg Herald,* December 27, 1912; *Vicksburg Register,* July 9, 183; Harriet Martineau, *Retrospect of Western Travel* (London, New York: Harper and Brothers, 1838), 17; G. W. Featherstonhaugh, *Excursion through the Slave States* (London: J. Murray, 1844), 250–54; *Niles' Weekly Register,* August 1, 1835; *Natchez Courier* quoted in *Boston Liberator,* August 8, 1835.

24. Augustus Q. Wilson, *A History of the Detection, Conviction, Life and Designs of John A. Murell, the Great Western Land Pirate....* (n.p., 1835), 28–31; Penick, *Great Western Land Pirate*, 32–54.

25. *Clinton Gazette* (Miss.) quoted in the *Boston Liberator*, August 8, 1835; Thomas Shackelford, *Proceedings of the Citizens of Madison County, Mississippi at Livingston, in July, 1835, in Relation to the Trial and Punishment of Several Individuals Implicated in a Contemplated Insurrection in This State* (Jackson, 1836), iii.

26. Cohee, "Lynch Law," *Harper's New Monthly Magazine* 18 (May 1859): 794.

27. Quoted in Richards, "Gentlemen of Property and Standing," 12–13. Richards concludes that Niles actually suppressed very little. David Ray Papke, *Framing the Criminal: Crime, Cultural Work and the Loss of Critical Perspective, 1830–1900* (Hamden, Conn.: Archon Books, 1987), 33–53; Michael Ignatieff, *A Just Measure of Pain: The Penitentiary in the Industrial Revolution, 1750–1850* (New York: Pantheon, 1978); Michael Meranze, *Laboratories of Virtue: Punishment, Revolution, and Authority in Philadelphia, 1760–1835* (Chapel Hill: University of North Carolina Press, 1996), 131–71.

28. Karen Halttunen, "Humanitarianism and the Pornography of Pain in Anglo-American Culture," *American Historical Review* 100 (April 1995): 303–34; Randall McGowen, "Civilizing Punishment: The End of the Public Execution in England," *Journal of British Studies* 33 (July 1994): 257–82.

29. *New York Sun*, July 25, 27, 28, 30, 31, September 3, 14, 21, 29, October 8, 20, 1835. The term became associated with almost any antiabolitionist activity. When the post office refused to deliver abolitionist tracts, that refusal constituted a "lynching" of the mails. *New York Emancipator*, September 17, 1840. When proslavery forces intercepted a petition signed by Cincinnati abolitionists, that petition was "lynched," according to the *Cincinnati Philanthropist*, March 13, 1838.

30. *Boston Liberator*, September 26, 1835, May 21, 1836; [Tanner], *Martyrdom of Lovejoy*, 81–82. In fact, he had committed murder. For a detailed account of this lynching, see Merton L. Dillon, *Elijah P. Lovejoy: Abolitionist Editor* (Urbana: University of Illinois Press, 1961), 81–82.

31. *Boston Liberator*, May 18, 1838; [Tanner], *Martyrdom of Lovejoy*, 81–85.

32. *Boston Liberator*, August 1, 1835.

33. *New York Herald*, September 25, 1835.

34. *Cincinnati Chronicle* reprinted in the *New York Emancipator*, October 21, 1841. Phillip Shaw Paludan and James McPherson have both argued that northern troops saw their enemies as lawless. In part this view reflects Lincoln's argument that secession represented anarchy, but northerners had also come to see southerners as prone to extralegal violence. Phillip Shaw Paludan, *"A People's Contest": The Union and Civil War, 1861–1865* (New York: Harper and Row, 1988), 3–31; James McPherson, *For Cause and Comrades: Why Men Fought in the Civil War* (New York: Oxford University Press, 1997), 18–19.

35. *Niles' Register*, August 8, August 22, October 3, 1835; *Lynchburg Democrat* quoted in ibid., October 3, 1835; *Louisiana Advertiser* and *Franklin Mercury* quoted in ibid., December 5, 1835; *Louisville Journal* quoted in ibid., August 8, 1835.

36. Grimsted, "Rioting in Its Jacksonian Setting," 380–82.

37. See, for example, Bruce L. Benson, "Reciprocal Exchange as the Basis for Recognition of Law: Examples from American History," *Journal of Libertarian Studies* 10 (fall 1991): 64–77. Popular culture regularly endorses vigilantism and lynching. See, for example, Larry McMurtry, *Lonesome Dove* (New York: Simon & Schuster, 1985). McMurtry, like so many writers, uses a trope pioneered by Owen Wister, *The Virginian: A Horseman of the Plains* (New York: Macmillan, 1902).

38. Frank Soule, John H. Gihon, and James Nisbet, *The Annals of San Francisco* (New York: D. Appleton, 1854), 310. For the 1851 vigilantes' debate over what name to adopt for themselves, see Hubert Howe Bancroft, *Popular Tribunals*, 2 vols. (San Francisco: History Co., 1887), 1:207–8.

39. Soule, Gihon, and Nisbet, *Annals of San Franciso*, 316; Robert M. Senkewicz, *Vigilantes in Gold Rush San Francisco* (Stanford: Stanford University Press, 1985), 82.

40. Soule, Gihon, and Nisbet, *Annals of San Francisco*, 315, 318, 320, 352, 566–67; Bancroft, *Popular Tribunals*, 1:185, 267.

41. Soule, Gihon, and Nisbet, *Annals of San Francisco*, 350–51; Bancroft, *Popular Tribunals*, 1:304.

42. Soule, Gihon, and Nisbet, *Annals of San Francisco*, 351; Bancroft, *Popular Tribunals*, 2:402–6.

43. Bancroft, *Popular Tribunals*, 43–44, 135; David A. Johnson, "Vigilance and the Law: The Moral Authority of Popular Justice in the Far West," *American Quarterly* 33 (winter 1981): 561–86.

44. For the state of affairs in San Francisco, see Richard Maxwell Brown, *Strain of Violence*, 134–43, which argues that businessmen used the Vigilance Committee to take control of the city away from professional politicians. Kevin J. Mullen, *Let Justice Be Done: Crime and Politics in Early San Francisco* (Reno, Las Vegas: University of Nevada Press, 1989), 16–34, 72–147. See also Senkewicz, *Vigilantes in Gold Rush San Francisco*, 134–202; [James O'Meara], *The Vigilance Committee of 1856* (San Francisco: Berry, 1887). For Vicksburg, see Morris, *Becoming Southern*, 114–31.

45. William Tecumseh Sherman, *Memoirs of General William T. Sherman* (1875; reprint, New York: Library of America, 1990), 150.

46. Harold Holzer, ed., *The Lincoln-Douglas Debates* (New York: HarperCollins, 1993), 73–77; Stephen B. Oates, *To Purge This Land with Blood: A Biography of John Brown* (New York: Harper and Row, 1970), 114–16. For the importance of the West to northern Republicans, see Eric Foner, *Free Soil, Free Labor, Free Men: The Ideology of the Republican Party before the Civil War* (1970; reprint, New York: Oxford University Press, 1995), 51–58.

47. *Lancaster Daily Evening Express*, November 27, 30, 1866; *Congressional Globe*, 39th Cong., 2d sess., January 3, 1867, 250–51; *An Act to Provide for the More Efficient Government of the Rebel States*, *Statutes at Large*, 14, chap. 153, 428–29 (1867).

48. *Athens Post*, April 14, 1871; *New Orleans Picayune*, May 19, February 6, December 31, 1875, May 3, 1877; *New Orleans Picayune*, May 3, 1877, April 15, May 4, 1880. George C. Rable, *But There Was No Peace: The Role of Violence in the Politics of Reconstruction* (Athens: University of Georgia Press, 1984), 43–58, 122–43.

49. *Athens Post*, April 14, 1871. The *Post* thought the congressional investigation of the Ku Klux Klan "a monstrous humbug" because "no such association exists." *Post*, March 3, 1871.

50. *New Orleans Picayune*, June 28, 1880.

51. *Griffin Star* quoted in the *Edgefield Advertiser*, December 16, 1868; *Charleston News and Courier*, March 5, 8, 1880.

52. Grant to Staunton, February 8, 1867, *The Papers of Ulysses S. Grant*, ed. John Y. Simon (Carbondale, Edwardsville: Southern Illinois University Press, 1967–), 17:50; James G. Randall, ed., *The Diary of Orville Hickman Browning* (Springfield: Illinois State Historical Society, 1933), 2:130; Howard K. Beale, ed., *Diary of Gideon Welles: Secretary of the Navy under Lincoln and Johnson* (New York: Norton, 1960), 3:42–43; John A. Carpenter, *Sword and Olive Branch* (Pittsburgh: University of Pittsburgh Press, 1964), 129–30.

53. *New York Times*, February 1, 1870, March 26, 1871, March 10, 1872. For the pseudo-

scientific justification for the view that an "animal nature" took hold of African Americans' minds as they matured, see N. S. Shaler, "The Negro Problem," *Atlantic Monthly* 54 (November 1884): 696–709. Shaler opposed lynching.

54. *St. Louis Democrat* quoted in the *Edgefield Advertiser*, July 14, 1870; ibid., August 31, September 7, November 9, 1871.

55. *New York Times*, May 18, August 9, 30, 1871, March 10, July 9, August 10, 19, 1872, January 18, June 15, 27, July 22, August 7, 15, September 26, 1876, January 13, 20, February 18, March 3, April 14, 1880. Joel Williamson, *The Crucible of Race: Black-White Relations in the American South since Emancipation* (New York: Oxford University Press, 1984), 117.

56. David Brion Davis, *Homicide in American Fiction, 1798–1860: A Social Values* (Ithaca: Cornell University Press, 1957), 159.

57. *Baltimore American and Commercial Advertiser*, April 18, 1879; Robert M. Ireland, " 'The Libertine Must Die': Sexual Dishonor and the Unwritten Law in the Nineteenth-Century United States," *Journal of Social History* 23 (fall 1989): 25–44; Davis, *Homicide in American Fiction*, 179–236; Hendrik Hartog, "Lawyering, Husbands' Rights, and the 'Unwritten Law' in Nineteenth-Century America," *Journal of American History* 84 (June 1997): 67–96; Winfield H. Collins, *The Truth about Lynching and the Negro in the South: In Which the Author Pleads that the South Be Made Safe for the White Race* (New York: Neale, 1918). As late as 1949 a Mississippi jury took only twenty-eight minutes to acquit a husband who shot and killed a man he caught hugging and kissing his wife. Newspapers report the defendant openly argued "an 'unwritten law' defense." *Greenville Delta Democrat-Times*, January 21, 1949. Ten years later Otto Preminger made *Anatomy of a Murder* (Columbia Pictures, 1959), about a murderer acquitted by the "unwritten law."

58. See, for example, *New York Times*, January 20, 1880. See L. E. Bleckley, "Negro Outrage No Excuse for Lynching," *Forum* 16 (November 1893), 300–302; Frederick Douglass, "Lynch Law in the South," *North American Review* 155 (July 1892): 17–24.

59. Davis, *Homicide in American Fiction*, 56–170; Tucher, *Froth and Scum*, 69; Carroll Smith-Rosenberg, *Disorderly Conduct: Visions of Gender in Victorian America* (New York: Knopf, 1985), 109–28.

60. *Edgefield Advertiser*, October 14, 1868; Bleckley, "Negro Outrage No Excuse for Lynching," 301.

61. Bancroft, *Popular Tribunals*, 1:7–20; Soule, Gihon, and Nisbet, *Annals of San Francisco*; Franklin Tuthill, *The History of California* (San Francisco: Bancroft, 1866); John S. Hittell, *A History of the City of San Francisco* (San Francisco: Bancroft, 1878). But see also E. S. Capron, *History of California from Its Discovery to the Present Time* (Boston and Cleveland: Jewett, 1854), 159; [O'Meara], *The Vigilance Committee of 1856*, 3–11.

62. Bancroft, *Popular Tribunals*, 1:7–14. Thomas J. Dimsdale describes lynching after lynching in almost pornographic detail, but never describes these instances of "popular justice" as lynchings. Dimsdale, *The Vigilantes of Montana or Popular Justice in the Rocky Mountains* (1866; reprint, Norman: University of Oklahoma Press, 1955). See Ann Waybright Childs, "A Hoosier Goes West: The Diaries and Letters of David Wallace Springer," *Wyoming Annals* 7 (spring 1993): 11.

63. The *Charleston News and Courier* sneered at such people as preferring Grant to Judge Lynch. See *News and Courier*, March 5, 1880.

64. Ross, for example, argues in "At the Bar of Judge Lynch," 8, that lynching cannot be defined as murder by a community because of the difficulty of determining community support for particular murders. On post–Civil War objectivism and scientism, and the belief that objectivity could serve reform goals, see George H. Daniels, *American Science in the Age of Jackson* (New York: Columbia University Press, 1968); Luther Lee Bernard and

Jessie Bernard, *Origins of American Sociology: The Social Science Movement in the United States* (New York: Crowell, 1943), 530–31; Mary O. Furner, *Advocacy and Objectivity: A Crisis in the Professionalization of American Social Science, 1865–1905* (Lexington: University Press of Kentucky, 1975), 14–23. For the assertion that crime could be eliminated through science, see *Chicago Tribune*, January 2, 1898.

65. David Paul Nord, "The Paradox of Municipal Reform in the Late Nineteenth-Century," *Wisconsin Magazine of History* 66 (winter 1982–83): 128–42; Lloyd Wendt, *Chicago Tribune: The Rise of a Great American Newspaper* (Chicago: Rand McNally, 1979), 247–81.

66. *Chicago Tribune*, January 1, 1875, January 1, 1883; Gerald J. Baldasty, *The Commercialization of News in the Nineteenth Century* (Madison: University of Wisconsin Press, 1992), 36–58. For the *Tribune* see Wendt, *Chicago Tribune*; Philip Kinsley, *The Chicago Tribune: Its First Hundred Years*, 3 vols. (New York: Knopf, 1943). In recent years, it has been almost de rigueur for historians of lynching to compile their own lists and not depend on the *Tribune*'s tabulation. Oddly, they always begin in 1882 or 1880. See Brundage, *Lynching in the New South*; Tolnay and Beck, *Festival of Violence*; Terence Finnegan, " 'At the Hands of Parties Unknown': Lynching in Mississippi and South Carolina, 1881–1940" (Ph.D. diss., University of Illinois, 1993).

67. *Chicago Tribune*, January 1, 1880, January 1, 1883, January 1, 1884, January 1, 1886. Students of lynching have been enormously influenced by the *Tribune*'s decision. Tolnay and Beck, in *Festival of Violence*, 3, 17, for example, write that a lynching "frenzy" that started in the 1880s "peaked" in the 1890s. Joel Williamson has written that the "lynching phenomenon" appeared suddenly after 1889. Williamson, *Crucible of Race*, 184. Had the *Tribune* started counting earlier, Tolnay and Beck, Williamson, and many other writers might well have written that the "frenzy" started in 1870 or 1860 or 1850. George Wright starts his analysis in 1865 and finds more lynchings immediately after the Civil War than at any time in the 1890s. George C. Wright, *Racial Violence in Kentucky, 1865–1940: Lynchings, Mob Rule, and "Legal Lynchings"* (Baton Rouge: Louisiana State University Press, 1990).

68. *Chicago Tribune*, January 1, 1890. The *Tribune* carried similar subheadlines January 1, 1891, January 1, 1892, January 1, 1895.

69. Roy Wilkins with Tom Mathews, *Standing Fast: The Autobiography of Roy Wilkins* (New York: Viking, 1982), 64–65; Lincoln Steffens, *The Autobiography of Lincoln Steffens* (New York: Harcourt, Brace, 1931), 195–200, 285–91.

70. Ida B. Wells, *Southern Horrors and Other Writings: The Anti-Lynching Campaign of Ida B. Wells, 1892–1900*, ed. Jacqueline Jones Royster (Boston and New York: Bedford, 1997), 75–79. *Southern Horrors and Other Writings* conveniently reprints *Southern Horrors: Lynch Law in All Its Phases, A Red Record*, and *Mob Rule in New Orleans*.

71. Alfred M. Duster, ed., *Crusade for Justice: The Autobiography of Ida B. Wells* (Chicago: University of Chicago Press, 1970), 35–66.

72. Wells, *Southern Horrors*, 52, 55.

73. Shirley W. Logan, "Rhetorical Strategies in Ida B. Wells' 'Southern Horrors': Lynch Law in All Its Phases," *Sage* 8 (summer 1991): 3–9; Hazel V. Carby, " 'On the Threshold of Woman's Era': Lynching, Empire, and Sexuality in Black Feminist Theory," *Critical Inquiry* 12 (autumn 1985): 262–77; Gail Bederman, " 'Civilization,' the Decline of Middle-Class Manliness, and Ida B. Wells's Antilynching Campaign (1892–94)," *Radical History Review* 52 (1992): 5–30. Frederick Douglass defined *lynching* as the mob killing of a prisoner seized from jail. "Lynch Law in the South," 17–24.

74. Cutler, *Lynch Law*, 1, 276. A recent dissertation still relies on the community defi-

nition of *lynching*. See Robin Bernice Balthrope, "Lawlessness and the New Deal: Congress and Antilynching Legislation, 1934–1938" (Ph.D. diss., Ohio State University, 1995), 7, 17.

75. Robert L. Zangrando, *The NAACP Crusade against Lynching: 1909–1950* (Philadelphia: Temple University Press, 1980), 18–22, 28–29, 210–16; Walter White, *A Man Called White: The Autobiography of Walter White* (1948; reprint, Athens: University of Georgia Press, 1995), 52. For the NAACP's campaign for a federal antilynching law, see Walter White, "The Costigan-Wagner Bill," *Crisis* 42 (January 1935): 10–11; George S. Schuyler, "Scripture for Lynchers," ibid., 12; "Can the States Stop Lynching?" ibid., 43 (January 1936): 6–7; "The New Federal Anti-Lynching Bill," ibid., 44 (March 1937): 72; Balthrope, "Lawlessness and the New Deal," 133–201.

76. Herbert Shapiro, *White Violence and Black Response from Reconstruction to Montgomery* (Amherst: University of Massachusetts Press, 1988), 63; White, *Man Called White*, 67.

77. Linda O. McMurry, *Recorder of the Black Experience: A Biography of Monroe Nathan Work* (Baton Rouge: Louisiana State University Press, 1985), 19–127.

78. This argument ultimately worked on many chambers of commerce. See Taylor Branch, *Parting the Waters: America in the King Years, 1954–63* (New York: Simon & Schuster, 1988), 425–26.

79. Josephus Daniels, *Editor in Politics* (Chapel Hill: University of North Carolina Press, 1941), 389, 401, 493–94. Hodding Carter made the same argument. See Ann Waldron, *Hodding Carter: The Reconstruction of a Racist* (Chapel Hill: Algonquin, 1993), 206, 223–24.

80. Jacquelyn Dowd Hall, *Revolt against Chivalry: Jessie Daniel Ames and the Women's Campaign against Lynching*, rev. ed. (New York: Columbia University Press, 1993), 159–91; Ames to Hatton Summers, July 9, 1937; Ames to Hatton Summers, March 29, 1937; microfilm reel 6, ASWPL Papers (Atlanta University).

81. Ames to Mrs. Alex Spence, December 9, 1936; Ames to Bessie C. Alford, July 6, 1939, microfilm, reel 6, ASWPL Papers (Atlanta University).

82. Roy Nash, "Memorandum for Mr. Philip G. Peabody on Lynch-Law and the Practicability of a Successful Attack Thereon," May 22, 1916, part 7, series A, reel 1, NAACP Papers (Library of Congress); "The Week's Editorial: White Press (From the Greensboro, N.C. News, Jan. 10. 1928," part 7, series A, reel 3, NAACP Papers.

83. Walter White to J. E. Dowd, November 2, 1938, part 7, series A, reel 5, NAACP Papers.

84. Anna Damon to Jessie Daniel Ames, May 14, 1940, ASWPL Papers; anonymous, *Lynchings Goes Underground: A Report on a New Technique* (n.p.: n.p., 1940), ASWPL Papers; White, *A Man Called White*, 102.

85. Ames to Alford, January 8, 1940; Alford to Ames, January 10, 1940; Ames to Lillian Smith, June 4, 1940, microfilm reel 6, ASWPL Papers; *New York Times*, May 10, 12, 17, 1940; *Richmond Times-Dispatch*, May 18, 1940; Villard to F. D. Patterson, July 8, 1940; Marshall to Harry T. Moore, August 9, 1940, part 7, reel 28, NAACP Papers; Press Release, May 17, 1940, NAACP, reel 5, ASWPL Papers.

86. "Summary of the Conference on Lynchings and Reports on Lynchings, Tuskegee Institute, Alabama," December 14, 1940, microfilm reel 8, ASWPL Papers; *Raleigh News and Observer*, August 1, 24, November 14, 21, 1902.

87. "Summary of the Conference on Lynchings and Reports on Lynchings," December 14, 1940, microfilm reel 8, ASWPL Papers.

88. Ibid.

89. Jessie Daniel Ames, *The Changing Character of Lynching* (Atlanta: Commission on Interracial Cooperation, 1942), 30; Virginius Dabney to Walter White, June 26, 1941, series

A, part 7, reel 28, NAACP Papers; Marguerite Cartwright, "The Mob Still Rides—Tuskegee Notwithstanding," *Crisis* 60 (April 1953): 222–23.

90. See, for example, Tolnay and Beck, *Festival of Violence*, 260; Brundage, *Lynching in the New South*, 291; Finnegan, " 'At the Hands of Parties Unknown,' " 1 n. 1; Oliver Cox, *Caste, Class, and Race: A Study in Social Dynamics* (1948; reprint, New York: Modern Reader, 1970), 549. Stephen Whitfield deals with this question with subtle precision in *A Death in the Delta: The Story of Emmett Till* (New York: Free Press, 1988), 24–31. Roberta Senechal de la Roche has made a sophisticated attempt to distinguish lynching from other forms of collective violence. See "The Sociogensis of Lynching," in *Under Penalty of Death: Essays on Lynching in the South*, ed. W. Fitzhugh Brundage (Chapel Hill: University of North Carolina Press, 1997), 48–76.

91. *Chicago Tribune*, January 1, 1890; Wright, *Racial Violence*, 6 n. 8.

Lizzie Borden, at approximately thirty years of age, shortly before the Borden Family murders. Used by permission of The Fall River Historical Society, Fall River, Massachusetts.

Chapter Twelve

"The Deftness of Her Sex"
Innocence, Guilt, and Gender in the Trial of Lizzie Borden

Catherine Ross Nickerson

Something terrible and mysterious happened one August morning in Fall River, Massachusetts, in 1892. Andrew Borden, one of the wealthiest men in town, was found murdered in the sitting room of his own home, and minutes later the body of his wife was found upstairs in the spare bedroom. Both had been killed by multiple blows to the head, face, and neck with an axe. The only others known to be in and around the house that morning were Lizzie Borden, Andrew's thirty-two-year-old unmarried daughter, and Bridget Sullivan, the family's Irish housemaid. The people of Fall River were horrified and fascinated by the news of the murders; their excitement only increased when Lizzie was arrested one week later. The story of the murder of the respectable, elderly couple in the middle of day in their own home quickly became national news.

What exactly happened in that house on that day has been a matter of speculation and debate since the discovery of the bodies. Though Lizzie was acquitted of all charges at her trial, she was never fully exonerated in the public imagination, and she remains, to most people, the most famous murderess in American history. There is a voluminous literature about the Borden murders; much of it is the work of people who become fascinated with the case as an intricate puzzle of opportunity, motive, and physical evidence and who attempt to settle the question of Lizzie's guilt or innocence by reconstructing the crime in minute, even obsessive detail.[1] There are also more imaginative treatments of the Borden case in fiction, poetry, drama, dance, opera, and film; Lizzie has been used as a symbol of Victorian repression, of female madness, of rebellion against patriarchy, and even of mystery or uncertainty itself.[2]

We can trace much of this collective compulsion to retell and reconstruct the crime to the fact that Lizzie did not testify at her trial and that a jury acquitted her in the face of strong evidence of guilt; both the absence of the defendant's own testimony and the irresolution of a "not guilty" verdict invite alternate versions of the story and speculation about what "really happened." However, the verdict itself is, for a student of history, as interesting as the question of whether she actually committed murder. How and why she escaped conviction is a matter of culture more than of simple logic, and her acquittal reveals a good deal about the tensions surrounding changing expectations of middle-class women's behavior at the turn into the twentieth century. To contemplate the trial of Lizzie Borden, then, is to encounter both a fascinating legal case and a vivid, concentrated picture of the complexity of gender ideology in the past. This essay argues that Lizzie Borden, who seemed to present a perfect image of genteel Christian womanhood, could not have been convicted in that place and at that moment in time. The first section will sketch the known facts of the case, including Lizzie's own explanation of what happened that day in interviews and in testimony she provided at the coroner's inquest. The second section analyzes the arguments of the defense and the prosecution at the trial and the way in which their rhetoric resonated with the most powerful and pervasive ideas about men, women, and morality at the end of the nineteenth century. But before turning to the particularities of the crime, the investigation, and the trial, it is appropriate to consider the study of criminal trials as historical events.

Trials that excite a high level of popular interest are always rich sources for understanding the history of a culture and its sense of itself. While popular trials are, of course, an arena for the exercise of the law, they also allow performances of other kinds of authoritative discourse or drama. Both the arguments and strategies of the lawyers, on the one hand, and the commentary by newspaper reporters and by ordinary folks, on the other, draw on and make visible what Robert Hariman, a communications scholar, calls the "fund of social knowledge constituting a society."[3] Such crucial matters as what it means when the defendant refuses to look at autopsy photos, why one witness is more trustworthy than another, or whether inconsistencies in two versions of an alibi are evidence of deceit or of unrehearsed honesty are all interpreted and resolved by the jury and by spectators in light of what they know from lived experience in their cultural and historical moment. This social knowledge is far more complex than what we call "common sense," though it incorporates common sense. Social knowledge includes a dense array of stereotypes, labels, and expectations; even elements that an individual rejects as untrue are ideas that he or she knows to be in circulation within the culture and to be held in esteem by certain groups.

In a trial, the structure of accusation and advocacy produces a contest of narratives, one of which offers a story of guilt and one of which offers either a story of innocence or a strategic series of attacks on the prosecution's narrative of guilt. The jury, in the end, must decide which narrative is more persuasive: more coherent, more logical, more true to jury members' experience. The internal consistency of a narrative of guilt or innocence is important to both jury and spectators, but the narrative must also square with their social knowledge in order to be convincing. A scandalous trial can thus shed light on the relative power of different cultural perceptions at a given point in time, since the defense and the prosecution deploy stereotypes and ideologies as tools of persuasion. Because the trial sets up competing narratives, we can see in the strategies and arguments of the prosecution and the defense the actual usages of the ideas and icons that are always in danger of becoming static in our understanding of the past.

Trials involving murder are especially useful in this respect, for one of our responses to criminal violence is the attempt to explain and classify it with great precision. The trial transcript offers the record of a collective effort to contextualize the extraordinary event of murder within the shared structures of social knowledge. Although nothing in the law requires the prosecution to state a motive for any crime, the appetite of the jury for tightly woven narrative obliges both prosecution and defense to spend a great deal of energy establishing or refuting motive in a case of murder. The concentration of storytelling in a murder trial has to be understood as something more than a chronicling of past events; its purposes are bound up in our desire to prevent future crimes by identifying murderers, punishing them, and offering a cautionary example to all. The trial has to be understood as an arena of argument and intervention, a site where cultural codes are reiterated and contested. This process works to reabsorb the unaccountable into the logic of a culture, to give a murder a place both in the official record and, in some cases, the folklore of the culture. The trial is both an instrument of the historical moment and a product of it. As George Lipsitz, a theorist of popular culture, has written about the O. J. Simpson case, a big-time trial "reflect[s] the ambiguities, uncertainties, and contradictions of everyday life and its complex social relations."[4]

In the 1893 trial of Lizzie Borden, the main cultural ideas in dispute were those having to do with definitions and interpretations of male and female nature and behavior. Lizzie Borden was accused, tried, and acquitted in light of one of the largest social questions of the day: What is a woman capable of? Indeed, both the prosecution and the defense presented arguments about the possibility of a genteel woman slaughtering her parents and about the responsibilities of the all-male jury in determining her fate that reiterated and drew upon the conflicts over gender roles that shaped the culture of the decades surrounding the turn of the century. In politics, the struggle for female suffrage continued to meet active resistance to the idea that women could be rational, responsible voters; in the realm of business, reformers worked to open the doors of all occupations and professions to women and split over the question of whether women workers required special treatment such as shorter hours; in medicine, newly prominent theories of women's health argued that almost any disease of the mind or body might be attributed to problems of the reproductive system or the failure to marry and bear children.[5]

The crimes in Fall River obviously and urgently needed explanation not only because they were so violent, but also because that violence was itself so stunningly at odds with the ideal of protective and dutiful tenderness that was supposed to govern women's behavior within the family circle. The trial, then, was animated and intensified by the ways in which the crimes resonated with the most widespread social problems and fears of its time. The idea that the defendant was a genuine lady was central to the prosecutor's case and to the defense's arguments, and it was surely important to the process by which the jury weighed the evidence and declared the accused "not guilty." To say that Lizzie Borden got off because she was a woman is both to miss the point entirely and to hit the nail right on the head.

Lizzie Borden offered contradictory and sometimes cryptic testimony about the events of the day of the murders, though she always maintained that she was entirely innocent. In response to police questions at the scene and at the coroner's inquest (in those days a formal procedure to rule a death a homicide), she told of a rather desultory round of activities at home that morning. She awoke and came downstairs after her father, stepmother, and a visiting uncle had eaten their breakfasts. Her uncle and father left to go about their separate business errands; her stepmother assigned the maid, Bridget, to wash the outsides of the windows and began herself to dust and straighten the house.

In the hours between about 8:45 and 10:45, Lizzie put away some clean laundry, did a little mending, read an old magazine, and prepared to iron a few handkerchiefs on the dining room table, according to her testimony. Her father returned home shortly after 10:30, and she described helping him settle in for a nap on the sitting room sofa, removing his shoes and suit jacket and offering to adjust the window for his comfort. Then, while waiting for her irons to reheat on the stove, she said she went out to the barn behind the house to look for a piece of screen to repair a door, or a piece of tin to wedge her bedroom window screen more tightly into the frame, or some lead to make sinkers for a fishing trip in the future—the details varied from telling to telling. In the barn she paused to eat three pears from the tree in the yard and to look out the window. On one occasion she said that she had heard a groan or a scraping noise coming from the house; later she swore that she had heard nothing.

When she returned to the house after some period of time (maybe ten minutes, maybe thirty), she discovered the kitchen door wide open and her father where she had left him, bleeding profusely from ten gashes in his skull and face. She ran to the back staircase, called Bridget down from her attic room, and sent her to fetch Dr. Bowen, who lived across the street. The woman who lived next door heard the commotion and came over, saw Andrew's body, and asked someone at the livery stable on their block to call the police (that call came in at 11:15), then returned to the house to sit with Lizzie. The doctor arrived shortly thereafter and pronounced Andrew Borden dead.

People began to ask after Abby Borden; Lizzie said that her stepmother had received a note from a sick friend and had gone to call on her, though, on second thought, she was sure she had heard her stepmother return home. The next-door neighbor and Bridget went upstairs to look for her. They found Abby Borden's body on the floor of the guest bedroom, where she had been changing the pillowcases. She had been dead, the coroner later concluded, for approximately ninety minutes before her husband was killed. She had, like her husband, been murdered by multiple blows to the head and neck, though all nineteen of them had come from behind.

One of the first questions anyone asked Lizzie was "Where were you when it happened?"[6] Her failure to provide a satisfactory answer was the main reason that she became a suspect in the case. To believe Lizzie's tale of ignorance and innocence, one needed to allow an intruder to slip into the house undetected, to murder Abby so quietly that neither Lizzie nor Bridget heard a sound (not even the sound of Abby's two-hundred-pound body falling on the second floor). The intruder would then have had to hide for at least an hour in the house or on the grounds, to murder Andrew Borden in the same remarkably silent manner, and finally to escape unnoticed before any alarm was raised. This series of events seemed particularly implausible, given the peculiar design of the Borden house and the customs of its inhabitants. The Borden house was unexpectedly small and comfortless for the family of a man of Andrew Borden's great wealth; it did not have running water above the first floor and was not connected to the city gas line. The house was long and narrow and divided into small rooms that opened onto one another, without connecting hallways. With three women (and then two women) moving about doing housework, where would there be a safe place to hide in those walk-through rooms, or a safe place to wield an axe without hallways to muffle sounds?

The plan for the second floor was especially awkward. Lizzie's bedroom could be entered from off the front staircase landing, but it also opened onto her elder sister Emma's bedroom and her parents' bedroom. For as long as anyone could remember, the door that communicated between the parents' bedroom and Lizzie's had been kept locked on both sides, an arrangement that split the second floor front, with the guest room and the daughters' rooms, from the second floor rear, with the elder Bordens' room. Andrew and Abby Borden's bedroom could be entered only by the back staircase (which continued up to the maid's attic room), and they further insured their privacy by keeping the door to that room locked at all times.

Locked doors were something of a point in the daily life of the Borden household. Not only did Andrew keep his bedroom locked, he also had installed three locks on the front door. From the testimony of Bridget and Lizzie, it is clear that all the inmates of the house were also careful to keep the cellar and kitchen doors locked when not in use. Despite their diligence, someone broke into the elder Bordens' bedroom about a year before the murders and stole jewelry and cash stored there; the custom of keeping the master bedroom key on the mantelpiece may have been a typically tight-lipped way for the parents to let Lizzie know that they suspected her of the theft.[7] With all this locking of exterior and interior doors, a stranger would not only have had difficulty getting into the house, he or she would have had trouble moving about once inside, and would have faced obstacles in fleeing the scene.

The case against Lizzie Borden was entirely circumstantial, built on the fact that she was at home, and driven by police suspicions about the way she answered questions and the way she behaved in the days following the discovery of the crimes. There were immediate problems with her stories. Though she declared that she had last seen her stepmother when Abby received that note calling her to someone's sickbed, no such note was ever found, and no one came forward to say that he or she had sent a message to the house. Police also wondered why Lizzie would want to go into, let alone linger in, the loft of a barn at midday during an August heat wave. One of the most suggestive actions Lizzie took was to destroy one of her dresses three days after the murders. She tore up the dress and burned it in the kitchen stove in the presence of her sister Emma and their friend Alice Russell.

Russell was troubled enough by the incident to approach the authorities with the information a few months after the murders; her last-minute testimony persuaded a previously indecisive grand jury to indict Lizzie Borden for the murders of her parents. Lizzie asserted that the dress had been ruined the previous spring when she brushed against wet brown paint inside the house, that she had worn it for some weeks after to do housework, and that she had burned the dress that morning because her sister complained that it was dirty and taking up space in their closet. At trial, the defense offered the observations of a dressmaker and Emma Borden to corroborate Lizzie's story. Lizzie's wardrobe was an important issue throughout the case. When the police asked her, days after the murders, to give them the clothes she had been wearing that morning, she furnished a blouse and skirt of blue silk and linen fabric. The dress she burned was also blue; there is contradictory testimony about what she was wearing when the first witnesses came on the scene, but it seems likely that she was not wearing the same dress that she furnished to the police.

Then there was the matter of the poisonings. In the two days before the murders, the Bordens and their maid had suffered from an acute intestinal illness; there was something about the circumstances that drove Abby across the street to Dr. Bowen's house, stating that the family was being poisoned. Lizzie had also said the family was under attack; the night before the murders, she visited Alice Russell and told of a "something hanging over me that I cannot throw off" and her fear that her father had enemies who might burn the house down around them. "I am afraid sometimes that somebody will do something to [Father]; he is so discourteous to people," she said. She made rather wild assertions that the milk was being poisoned, or perhaps the bread from the baker. She related an anecdote about overhearing an argument between a prospective tenant and her father, a story she later told at the coroner's inquest.[8] The authorities were extremely skeptical about these presentiments of disaster, especially after their investigation revealed that Lizzie had attempted to buy prussic acid, a highly concentrated poison, the day before the murders (though that evidence was excluded at her trial).[9]

Apart from her circumstantial position and the improbability of her stories, there was little hard evidence against Lizzie Borden. Bridget Sullivan insisted she had neither heard nor seen anything that suggested Lizzie's guilt. She testified that she had been washing the outside of the windows for much of the morning, and that she was taking a nap on the third floor between the time that Andrew Borden arrived and the time that Lizzie called her downstairs with the words "Come down quick; Father's dead; somebody came in and killed him."[10]

One witness, passing by the house, testified that he saw Lizzie walking from the barn to the house at around the time she said she had been doing so, and a few people testified to seeing various suspicious strangers near the Borden house that morning or in the environs of the city soon after the murders. Though there were several hatchets in the house, none was positively proven to be the murder weapon (one that looked suspicious tested negative for blood residue in a forensic laboratory). The witnesses who had seen her immediately after the bodies were discovered all said that they had seen no blood on her clothing, skin, or hair. Police, friends, and neighbors who had seen her at that time concurred that she appeared calm and self-possessed, though one person said she saw tears in Lizzie's eyes.[11] The questions of how Lizzie might have washed the blood off her body, concealed any bloodstained clothing, and hidden or thoroughly washed an axe in the very short period of time she had while Bridget was taking her nap—about ten or fifteen minutes[12]—raise substantial doubts about her guilt, or her exclusive guilt. One reason for the enduring fascination of the case is the way in which the implausibility of her tale of an intruder is so evenly matched by the implausibility of the prosecutor's tale of a daughter who murders her parents suddenly and violently and appears fifteen minutes later looking normal in every way.

Lizzie was arrested one week after the crimes, and imprisoned in the jail in nearby Taunton, Massachusetts. As early as the day of the murders, the press began to point the finger of suspicion toward her; the *Boston Advertiser* reported in its evening edition that the police were focusing their investigations on "persons within the family circle," specifically Lizzie and her uncle John Morse (who was eliminated as a suspect in the first twenty-four hours). The more circumspect *Fall River Herald* waited thirty-six hours before gently suggesting that since "Mr. Borden's daughters were ladies who had always conducted themselves so that the breath of scandal could never reach them," the pattern of evidence at the Borden home would soon bring the police "face to face with embarrassing difficulties."[13] That tension between the obvious need to consider Lizzie a suspect on the strength of the evidence and the impossibility of considering a woman of her social stature as an axe murderer made the story especially fascinating, since it interwove questions of logic with questions of culture and lived experience. In general, papers in and close to Fall River tended to highlight the suspicion against Lizzie; the more distant New York papers tended to underline carefully the indeterminacy of the case against her, perhaps because the locally delectable irony of a Borden being arrested for a violent crime was less germane to the interest of the story elsewhere. Upon Lizzie's arrest, some newspapers expressed surprise and even outrage. One editorialized that given the brutality, depravity, and "devilish malignity" of the murders, "to believe that it could have been committed by a physically weak woman, whose entire life has been one of refined influences, of Christian profession and work, of filial devotion, of modesty and self-abnegation, is to set aside as of no value all that experience and observation have taught us."[14]

The coverage of the case quickly proved to be in and of itself a contentious matter, especially when it came to gender politics. Two days after the murders, one woman reporter for the *Boston Herald* began an article about Lizzie's good character by asserting that "it is the men who have, since the murder, been accorded the space" to present Lizzie's character and personality; "a woman's opinion of a woman is a consideration Lizzie Borden has not yet been allowed."[15] While Lizzie was in jail awaiting trial, she received a public vote of confidence from her fellow members of the local chapter of the national alcohol reform movement, the Women's Christian Temperance Union (WCTU), and had her case presented sympathetically in the journal of the American Woman Suffrage Association by famous women's rights advocates Mary Livermore and Lucy Stone.[16] Livermore, suffragist and author of a book arguing for women's employment entitled *What Shall We Do with Our Daughters?*, interviewed Lizzie in jail and came away impressed with her innocence. She stressed Lizzie's sensitivity, declaring that the press's negative depictions of her unfeeling "stolidity" were "absurd. You can see that she feels her position very keenly." Livermore reinterpreted Lizzie's cool manner for her readers, suggesting that it was actually the outward show of gentility and good breeding: her Lizzie exclaims, "[W]hat would they have me do? Howl? Go into hysterics? . . . I am trying hard to keep calm and self-controlled until I shall be proved innocent."[17]

Another jailhouse interview by a female reporter came to similar conclusions: it presented a sentimental vignette about Lizzie kissing her father's corpse after it was carefully prepared by the undertaker and allowed Lizzie to respond to specific allegations in the press, particularly the mistrust of her detached, inexpressive demeanor. Her Lizzie explains, "I have tried very hard to be brave and womanly through it all."[18] This last article provoked a condescending response from the *Fall River Globe*, one of the newspapers most certain of Lizzie's guilt. In an editorial, the *Globe* mocked the "flap-doodle, gush, idiotic drivel, misrepresentations, and in some instances, anarchic nonsense, which is being promulgated by women newspaper correspondents, WCTU conventions, and other female agencies."[19] Although it is not true that support for Lizzie split on simple gender lines, with men accusing and women defending, it is clear that the question of Lizzie's guilt or innocence was very much caught up in the rhetoric about women's distinctive moral style that surrounded the suffrage and temperance movements.

Overall, Lizzie did not suffer too badly at the hands of the press and seemed to learn that reporters would be reassured of her innocence if they saw overt signs of conventional upper-middle-class femininity in her attitude and behavior. The press, in other words, rewarded her for performing (deliberately or unconsciously) the role of the beset maiden in a style it could understand. She fainted at several strategic moments in the trial, leaned visibly on the arm of the minister who escorted her into the courtroom each day, and reverted to wearing deep mourning for the trial. She was beseiged by the press after the murders, but she rarely gave interviews before or during her trial, and never afterward. She showed what we might now call "media savvy" when she employed a private detective from the Pinkerton agency only days after the murders. His charge seems to have been more in the area of public relations than forensic investigation, for the *New York Herald* reported that "Mr. Hanscom's time is chiefly spent about the Mellen house [presumably a tavern] in affable conversation with the newspaper men in whose affections he has made great progress" and suggested that he is the source of at least one of the rumors of strange men lurking about the Borden property on the day of the murders.[20]

Given the public thirst for information about the Borden murders, it is not surprising that the *Boston Globe* was hoodwinked by an enterprising writer into printing a highly sensational account of life in the Borden household later that fall. The utterly groundless tale had Lizzie pregnant and described a violent row between Lizzie and Andrew the night before the murders, in which Andrew threatened to disown her if she did not name the man who had got her "in trouble"—a man who the article's author indicated was none other than Lizzie's uncle John Morse.[21] This story reads like the seediest type of late-Victorian melodrama, and is interesting only for the way it plays out in sensational terms the period's concerns with paternal authority and daughterly dependence in the threat of disinheritance and banishment. In a cynical inversion, it also twists the ideals of domestic intimacy and intensity into a plot of incest.[22] Ultimately, even this story did not damage Lizzie too greatly; the *Boston Globe* was embarrassed into the position of thereafter defending the woman it had so blatantly abused, and the incident on the whole bolstered arguments that she was being mistreated. During the trial , press accounts were almost uniformly straightforward and, as time wore on, convinced that Lizzie would be acquitted (especially after her damaging inquest testimony was excluded). We can trace, over time, a general movement from quick accusation to belief that conviction was unjustified or impossible as reporters considered the tension between Lizzie's social status (well-bred lady) and her forensic status (prime suspect).

However, the trial itself was vigorously argued, and demonstrated, even more clearly than the newspapers, how deeply the mystery of the Borden murders resonated with cultural questions about women's nature. At the trial, which began ten months after the murders, there was much to say, of course, about the physical condition of the crime scenes, the timetable of events, the results of the autopsies of the victims, and other details of the murder, but the real focus of attention was on the character of the defendant—in both senses of the term. Both the prosecution and the defense offered interpretations of her moral character, and they wanted to present her as a knowable type or character in familiar cultural narratives. As we might expect, the two versions of Lizzie's character were diametrically opposed, but each was drafted from the "fund of social knowledge" that constituted Victorian culture's view of women. This focus on character is not unusual in a popular trial. Hariman calls it a "generic constraint" of the phenomenon, one that "amplifies both the dramatic nature of the trial . . . and [the trial's] rhetorical disposition, for character (in the classical vocabulary, *ethos*) is one of the three basic modes of proof."[23] Hariman argues that characters serve to focus the abstractions of the ideas and social issues being adjudicated in a trial, so that, for example, "communism became the Rosenbergs" in the popular imagination. That association works in both directions; in the Lizzie Borden case, as Kathryn Jacob puts it, "not only a particular woman, but the entire Victorian conception of womanhood, was on trial for its life."[24]

Because Lizzie was accused of murdering her father and stepmother, it is perhaps not surprising that the most consistent element in the various characterizations was her status as a daughter, despite her fully adult age of thirty-two years. Alexander Woollcott, a professional wag of the time, dubbed her a "self-made orphan," a joke that cuts right to the heart of the matter.[25] Now fatherless and motherless in any case, the question was whether Lizzie had entered that state by chance or by design, and whether she was deserving of public sympathy or of the death penalty.

Her lead defense attorney, Andrew Jennings, made much of her vulnerable position as an unmarried, unparented woman. He made her out to be the pitiable victim of a police force unable to solve the crime, and he made it clear that she was undeserving of their suspicion. Her past life made that task easy. Lizzie was the real thing, a lady by virtue of her old New England name and Anglo-Saxon ancestry, her father's wealth, and her own personal style. Lizzie's public life before the trial was a long list of good works and worthy undertakings: she was a member of the most fashionable and influential Congregational church in Fall River and taught Sunday school there to Chinese immigrant children. She served as secretary and treasurer of the church's Christian Endeavour Society, and helped serve holiday dinners for the impoverished newsboys of the city. She joined the Fruit and Flower Mission to the city hospital and eventually had a place on its board, and she was elected secretary of the Fall River chapter of the WCTU. She lived a model life for a single woman of her day; she seemed to know her place in the social hierarchy and seemed to want to make herself "useful," in the terminology of her class. Because genteel women did not work unless they fell on hard times—and only then at a few professions, like teaching—a slate of church-associated charity work was the fitting occupation for an unmarried gentlewoman like Lizzie Borden.

She had, as part and parcel of this ladylike style, lived her life as a dependent of her father. In his opening argument, Jennings cast himself and the jury as the protectors of this young woman in distress, the enforcers of the sheltering "circle of the presumption of . . . her innocence" that the law inscribes around a defendant, the replacements for the father she had lost. In his closing argument, her other attorney, George Robinson, also lingered on this idea, pointing out that in the special oath reserved for capital cases, the jurors had accepted responsibility for the defendant as being in their "charge."[26]

Robinson painted a picture of the relationship between father and daughter meant to make the accusation of patricide seem not just cynical, but unspeakable. He focused the jury's attention on a ring Lizzie had given to Andrew, "a man that wore nothing in the way of ornament, of jewelry, but one ring, and that ring was Lizzie's." The ring, even at that moment on Andrew's hand as he lay in his casket, "stands as the pledge of plighted faith and love, that typifies and symbolizes the dearest relation that is ever created in life . . . the bond of union between the father and the daughter." In a deft rhetorical move, Robinson offered this proof of Andrew's devotion to his daughter as an argument for Lizzie's innocence, declaring, "No man should be heard to say that she murdered the man that so loved her.[27] Though, as historian Ann Jones points out, this portrait of father-daughter devotion takes on a troubling tint in our post-Freudian age, it drew forcefully from the mainstream emotional vocabulary of the Victorian era.[28] The culture of the middle and upper classes of the nineteenth century was in many ways defined by its intense longing for tender, harmonious, and demonstrative relationships within the family circle. As life in the world of advancing industrialization and accelerating capitalism came to seem more rough, competitive, amoral, and alienating, the domestic sphere became increasingly the province of women, who were charged with making the home a serene refuge, redolent of beauty and goodness, for their husbands, fathers, brothers, and sons. The symbolic reading of the ring may sound forced to our ears, but it would have sounded more natural, even reassuring, to the all-male jury, most of whom were property-owning, middle-class fathers more than fifty years of age.

Although the wearing of the ring proved nothing in a legal sense, it gave the jury something to count as physical evidence of the tenderness they were already educated to expect of a woman and of the charming displays of enduring affection that they might have wished from their own daughters.[29] Robinson wanted the jurors to juxtapose this portrait of Lizzie's tender expressiveness with the brutality of the murders:

> The terror of those scenes no language can portray. The horrors of the moment we can all fail to describe. And so we are challenged at once, at the outset, to find someone that is equal to the enormity, whose heart is blackened with depravity, whose whole life is a tissue of crime, whose past is a prophecy of the present. A maniac or a fiend, we say. Not a man in his senses and with his heart right, but one of those abnormal productions that the Deity creates or suffers, a lunatic or a devil.[30]

Robinson's fundamental argument for her innocence was that "such acts as those are morally and physically impossible for this young woman defendant," and he demanded that jurors call on their Victorian common sense about the strength of family ties: "To foully murder her stepmother and then go straight away and slay her own father is a wreck of human morals."[31] By expressing outrage at the accusation of patricide, Jennings and Robinson not only reassured the jurors that all was right with their view of the world, they also allowed the jurors to cast themselves in the pleasant role of a manly guardian of womanly honor.

The prosecution also focused on Lizzie's career as a dependent daughter, but to very different effect. In District Attorney Hosea Knowlton's version of the crimes, the motive for the murders lay in exactly those family relationships that Jennings and Robinson presented in such hushed tones. They offered, through the testimony of neighbors, servants, and even a reluctant Emma Borden, a starkly different picture of life in the Borden household.

Knowlton's theory was that Lizzie was driven to murder by a combination of greed and a deep hatred of her stepmother. Andrew Borden was a very wealthy man, but a notorious miser. He was born into the poorer branch of the successful Bordens in the Fall River area, and began his working life as an undertaker. He was known as a shrewd businessman, and he was disliked for it. In Fall River, the story circulated that Andrew Borden had, in those early years, bought a batch of undersized coffins at a cut rate, then severed the legs of his corpses to make them fit. Borden also owned a good deal of real estate, which he managed for a profit. Later, as Fall River reached the peak of its industrial boom, water rights that he had inherited brought him great wealth. He built a large building in the business district, which he named for himself, and he sat on the boards of several local banks and textile mills. His estate, at his death, was worth about $300,000, several million in today's money.

Yet, the Borden home was not on the fashionable hill where others of Andrew Borden's wealth and standing lived, nor did it boast the standard comforts of the urban middle-class home of the period. One of the few light notes in this grisly case is the revelation of the habits of frugality in the Borden kitchen and dining room: in the days before they died, the elder Bordens had interrupted a steady progress of leftovers through a leg of mutton (so steady that they even served mutton broth for breakfast on the day of the murders) only to consume reheated swordfish, suggesting that they had iron wills if not iron stomachs.[32] Andrew Borden did not believe in waste and he did not, it seems fair to speculate, believe in comfort or pleasure either.

The defense, in trying to minimize the portrait of Andrew Borden as a despot who might provoke murderous rebellion, spoke to the jury of middle-aged men in the language of the older generation: Andrew Borden was an admirably old-fashioned man resisting the general trend toward spending instead of saving, of indulging in conspicuous consumption instead of building a solid financial foundation.[33] In any case, how fully Borden's parsimony extended to his relationships with his daughters is unclear. Some people reported that Lizzie was deeply distressed by her inability to buy the sort of clothes that she wanted or to entertain her social peers at her home. Others said that she had her father wrapped around her little finger and that, to the chagrin of his second wife, he gave her whatever she wanted. In any case, her desire to participate in the capitalist elite's patterns of consumption seems to have been a source of friction within the Borden household.

As in many families, in the Borden household disputes over money were conflated with struggles for power; long-standing resentments between the two generations had come to a crisis point in the five years preceding the murder. Lizzie's sister Emma, though ten years older, was a close ally in a divided household. Their mother had died when Emma was twelve and Lizzie was two years old, their father remarried two years later, and the girls never accepted

Abby in the role of mother nor, it seems, brought her to any place in their affections. At the trial, the prosecution made much of Lizzie's "unkindly feeling"[34] toward her stepmother. A policeman testified that while interviewing Lizzie only hours after the murders, he was corrected sharply when he referred to Abby as "your mother."[35] A seamstress testified that about five months before the murders, her use of the term "Mother" for Abby had likewise provoked an angry rebuke; Lizzie said that her stepmother was a "mean, good-for-nothing thing. . . . I don't have much to do with her; I stay in my room most of the time. . . . [W]e don't eat with them if we can help it."[36] Both Bridget Sullivan and Emma Borden also testified that the daughters avoided eating meals with their parents, and that they had understood the front part of the upstairs, including their bedrooms and the guest room, to be their portion of the house. Even though Emma was testifying in her sister's defense, she could not completely gloss over the frigidity in the relations between stepmother and stepdaughters. To the question "Were relations between you and Mrs. Borden cordial?" she answered, "I don't know what you mean by cordial. We always spoke." Emma had always addressed her stepmother as "Abby"; Lizzie, who had called Abby "Mother" in her childhood, took up addressing her as "Mrs. Borden" after a serious family quarrel that occurred five years before the murder.[37]

That dispute, which brought simmering resentments to a rolling boil, centered on Andrew's real estate holdings. Emma and Lizzie Borden became highly agitated when they learned that Andrew helped Abby's half sister, Sarah Whitehead, by buying up a piece of property in which she had held a partial share, and giving Abby the deed.[38] Emma and Lizzie demanded an equal consideration, and as a result their father deeded to them a rental property, formerly their grandfather's house, in Fall River. The defense tried to argue that Lizzie had such personal wealth (about $5,000) that she would never have thought of killing her father for his money. The prosecution suggested that the attacks might have been precipitated by talk about making a will.[39] No will was ever found. There has been some rather imaginative speculation, at the time of the murders and in more recent accounts, that Lizzie burned a will that named Abby Borden as chief beneficiary. It is important, legally, that Abby Borden was killed before her husband; had she survived him even briefly, at least a third of his estate would have gone to *her* heirs.[40] In the end, Emma and Lizzie (after the latter was acquitted) inherited their father's entire fortune.

The conflicts and anxieties of this family connected in many ways to larger historical conflicts and anxieties in the New England of the late nineteenth century. The daughters' worry over the dispersal of their father's fortune echoes, on a smaller scale, the general distress over the decline of Fall River's cotton textile industry after the Civil War, and the narrowing prospect of family fortunes made at midcentury enduring through future generations. Their apparent greed was also connected to their social status and experience in more gender-specific ways. Emma and Lizzie were New England spinsters at a time of growing concern over spinsterhood and the problem of women with "nothing to do." As middle-class women, their main chance at social standing was married motherhood, but their father's refusal to take his rightful residential place in the stratified society of Fall River, with its attendant refusal to fund the courtship rituals of dinner parties and dances, must have undermined their marriageability. Had Emma and Lizzie been sons, they would have been able to enter their father's businesses, taking some corner of his empire to make their own fortunes. As it was, the only way their father's money could come to them was in the form of gifts, including the ultimate gift of inheritance. As daughters, they had no way to earn the family money or the freedom it stood for; as the daughters of a miser, they could not enjoy the wealth that he had accrued.

Knowlton saw in this pressurized family situation a motive for murder, and he thought the jury, cognizant of the social problem of the "superfluous" woman, would see it, too. Like the defense attorneys, the prosecutors focused on Lizzie's character as the key to understanding the truth of the murders. But if Jennings and Robinson relied on the ideological, socially constructed category of womanliness as an a priori argument for Lizzie Borden's virtue and innocence, the prosecutors in the case exposed the cultural double of female virtue, which is secret and irrational vice. As Nina Auerbach has explained, Victorian culture understood the "lunatic or devil," "fiend or maniac" (Robinson's description of the murderer) to be not entirely the opposite of virtuous womenhood but something more like a shadow or even a corollary of it.[41]

Robinson, in his closing argument for the defense, argued for the reliability of appearance. He pointed out that "to find her guilty you must believe her to be a fiend! Does she look it?" And he insisted that the jurors could believe their own eyes: "As she sat here these long weary days and moved in and out before you, have you seen anything that shows the lack of human feeling and womanly bearing?"[42] Robinson, in effect, contended that social knowledge is simple and straightforward: we know what we know because people and things are as they appear.

District Attorney Knowlton offered a more complicated reading of Lizzie's demeanor and history in his closing argument. He acknowledged that the prisoner was the social peer of the jurors and judge, calling her "of the rank of lady, the equal of your wife and mine." His goal, however, was to suggest that Lizzie Borden's respectable, Christian appearance was deceptive. Knowlton asserted, drawing on the strongest cultural fears about the female body and female wickedness, that "time and time again have we been grieved to learn, pained to find, that those set up to teach us the correct way of life have been found themselves to be as foul as hell inside."[43]

Knowlton used the principles of trickery, treachery, and unpredictability to articulate a theory of female criminality: "If [women] lack in strength and coarseness and vigor, they make up for it in cunning, in dispatch, in celerity, in ferocity. If their loves are stronger and more enduring than those of men, their hates are more undying, more unyielding, more persistent."[44] And continuing to work his arguments around inversions of the cultural principles that assigned women to the realm of ornament and sentiment, Knowlton offered this way for the jurors to estrange themselves from the accused and to dismiss the evidentiary questions raised by the defense: "How could she have avoided the spattering of her dress with blood if she was the author of these crimes? I cannot answer it. You cannot answer it. You are neither murderers nor women. You have neither the craft of the assassin nor the cunning and deftness of the sex."[45]

Knowlton's rhetoric indicates the ease with which Victorian ideology could be made to produce doubles, inversions, and shadows of its most sacred truths about gender and class. Even as it contradicted the defense portrait of natural feminine docility and devotion, this picture of womanhood was equally expressive of the social knowledge clustered around gender in the late nineteenth century. Although women were, in Knowlton's words, the "sex that all high-minded men revere, that all generous men love, that all wise men acknowledge their indebtedness to," Victorian wisdom had it that when women went bad, they went very bad indeed. Insanity was the usual form and symptom of women's deviance in Victorian literature and art, and one of the most important figures for the period is, as Sandra Gilbert and Susan Gubar have shown, the "madwoman in the attic."[46] Like Bertha Rochester in Charlotte Brontë's *Jane Eyre*, the madwoman rebels against being shut away in the interior of the house and becomes a symbol for the anger that is so utterly unacceptable in the demeanor of the genteel lady.

The prosecution's closing argument drew directly on this cultural mythology. Knowlton focused on Andrew Borden's murder, calling it the "far sadder tragedy" of the two murders, for he hypothesized that Lizzie killed her stepmother first in a rage and killed her father out of the cold realization that he would know the truth about his wife's death no matter what she said in protest. He dramatized for the jury an imagined encounter between father and daughter just before the murder in which Andrew confronts Lizzie about the murder of his wife. In Knowlton's wording, Andrew Borden takes on mythological stature as "Nemesis," the punisher of the proud and the insolent, and historical significance as "that just old man of the stern Puritan stock" (stock, Knowlton reminded the jurors, that they shared with the victim). Lizzie became nothing less than the madwoman escaped from her attic: "[S]he came down those stairs [from the room where she had killed Abby] . . . transformed from the daughter, transformed from the ties of affection, to the most consummate criminal we have read of in all our history or works of fiction."[47]

Knowlton worked to show Lizzie as a woman—or madwoman—of sufficient evil and cunning to plot and commit parricide between visits to hospital wards and the preparation of Sunday school lesson plans. Such a character is difficult to believe in and uncomfortable to contemplate, so Knowlton made sure to include more mundane demonstrations of a bad nature. Unkind to her stepmother, selfish in her desire for luxury, willful in her actions—if Knowlton's murderess were in a novel of the period, she would quickly be brought to grief or to heel. It is an understatement to say that the prosecutor's strategy was complex and that his arguments were contradictory; what is consistent in them is a desire to consign female criminality to a female realm of the irrational, the emotional, the unknowable.

In the end, normative domestic ideology prevailed; jurors rejected the common-wealth's case against this moneyed female defendant. They did not even deliberate but produced a unanimous "not guilty" vote on the first ballot (then, they later revealed, cooled their heels in the jury room for an hour so as not to seem hasty). By continually reminding the members of the all-male jury that they were in a paternal relationship with Lizzie Borden, by depicting her as a young woman bereft of her own father's protection, by allowing them to see her as a grateful and devoted daughter to her father, and by trading on the cultural currency of class types, Jennings and Robinson successfully argued for acquittal. A story of parricide within a wealthy household was, apparently, not a story that the justices and jurors, themselves middle-class fathers and heads of households, wished to hear. They would rather, it seems, see Lizzie as the angel hovering solicitously over the parlor sofa where her father prepared for a nap than as the madwoman descending the staircase with an axe to bash his head in and claim her inheritance. The defense allowed them to feel comfortably masculine and comfortable with their sense of what women are capable of doing.

Lizzie left the courthouse and went back to the family home with her sister. She and her sister soon used part of their inheritance to buy a comfortable, elegantly decorated home in a fashionable neighborhood of Fall River. Until 1905, the two sisters, neither of whom ever married or began a career, lived together there. They had a serious quarrel—the nature of which they kept to themselves— and Emma moved to New Hampshire, leaving Lizzie to live in the new house, attended by four servants, until her death in 1927. Though Lizzie was acquitted, she never lived down the accusations against her, and she was shunned by most of polite Fall River society, even the congregation of the church to which she had belonged before the trial. Anecdotes about her life after the murders include fits of violent rage and shoplifting. Others who knew her said that she was an extremely generous person, who put several young men through college and lent her automobile for the pleasure of shut-ins and the elderly.[48] Upon her death, which preceded Emma's by only days, she left the bulk of her fortune to the Animal Rescue League and made generous provisions for her servants, for im-pecunious friends, and for the perpetual upkeep of the family cemetery plot. She lies there together with her sisters, her mother, her father, and her stepmother.[49] No one else was ever tried for the murders.

For us, looking back from a distance of one hundred years at this case about which so much has been argued, imagined, and interpolated, there is still reason to ponder this notorious parricide and acquittal. A crime that becomes national or even regional news has to present something extraordinary and puzzling— the viciousness of the attack, the extreme innocence of the victim, the hitherto unblemished public life of the person accused of the murder. For the purposes of historical study, however, what seems deviant and exceptional actually sheds light on what is normative and typical. Indeed, for a case of murder to move into the public eye, and from there into the popular imagination, it must resonate with the old and new mythologies, anxieties, and conflicts of the culture.

The Borden murders became important, and remain important, because so many of the things that seem particular to the case were also expressive of larger economic and social questions at issue in that historical period in New England. Moreover, study of the trial reveals the process by which a community collectively struggles over and puts into narrative an act of unexpected violence. In the Borden case, that process revealed the paradoxes and contradictions in Victorian wisdom about woman's nature, and yet reaffirmed the power of appearances, of "common sense," of middle-class platitudes about daughterly devotion and feminine morality. Lizzie beat the charges against her not just because she was a woman but more precisely because she was a lady in all the ways that her historical moment demanded. As many pointed out at the time and in the century since, had Lizzie been a poor woman or a man of almost any class, the murder would have had a different meaning within the culture and the trial might well have had a different outcome.[50] The Borden case tells us that although the power of conventionality is at any time formidable, each era actively negotiates what common sense about violence will consist of and to whom it will offer relief.

NOTES

1. All of these historians have strong theses or opinions about Lizzie Borden's guilt or innocence. A famous early book on the case, which argued for Lizzie's guilt, was Edwin Porter's *The Fall River Tragedy* (1893; reprint, Portland, Me.: King Phillip Publishers, 1985). Legend has it that Lizzie bought up nearly every copy of the book. The authoritative early work on the case was that of the true-crime chronicler Edmund Pearson, who wrote a long essay arguing for Lizzie's guilt: *Studies in Murder* (Garden City, N.Y.: Macmillan, 1924). Pearson also edited (reliably, though with omissions) the transcript of her trial: *The Trial of Lizzie Borden* (New York: Doubleday Doran, 1937). For documents pertaining to the case, see Joyce Williams et al., *Lizzie Borden: A Case Book of Family and Crime in the 1890s* (Bloomington, Ind.: TIS Publications, 1980); David Kent and Robert A. Flynn, *The Lizzie Borden Sourcebook* (Boston: Branden, 1992). One of the more temperate and well-documented books on the subject was written by a judge: Robert Sullivan, *Goodbye Lizzie Borden* (1974; reprint, New York: Penguin, 1989). David Kent's *Forty Whacks: New Evidence in the Life and Legend of Lizzie Borden* (Emmaus, Pa.: Yankee Books, 1992), analyzes the debates and contradictions in the case. Some of the more controversial books take the same basic facts but reconfigure them to "prove" the guilt of Emma Borden—Frank Spiering, *Lizzie* (New York: Random House, 1984)—Bridget Sullivan—Edward Radin, *Lizzie Borden: The Untold Story* (New York: Simon & Schuster, 1961)—or of a secret bastard son of Andrew Borden: Arnold Brown, *Lizzie Borden: The Legend, the Truth, the Final Chapter* (New York: Doubleday, 1991). Another famous account of the crime, which attributes Lizzie's murderous activities to "psycho-motor epilepsy" is Victoria Lincoln's *A Private Disgrace* (New York: G. P. Putnam's Sons, 1967). Ann Jones has an excellent chapter on

the case in her *Women Who Kill: A History of America's Female Murderers* (Boston: Beacon Press, 1996).

2. There are many fictional treatments of the murders. Noteworthy for its dreamlike quality is Angela Carter's short story "The Fall River Axe-Murders" in her *Saints and Strangers* (New York: Penguin, 1985). Notorious for its theory of a sadomasochistic lesbian relationship between Bridget Sullivan and Lizzie Borden is Evan Hunter's *Lizzie* (New York: Arbor House, 1984). Other novels of historical interest include Lily Dougal, *The Summit House Mystery* (New York: Funk and Wagnalls, 1905). Most of the poetry is humorous verse or doggerel, for which see Jonathan Goodman, ed., *Bloody Versicles: The Rhymes of Crime* (London: Newton Abbott, 1971), though there are more literary long poems by Ruth Whitman, *The Passion of Lizzie Borden* (New York: October House, 1973) and Stephen Ronan, *Our Lady of Fall River* (Berkeley: Ammunition Press, 1983). Two of the most important plays include *Nine Pine Street*, which premiered in 1933, starring Lillian Gish (New York: Samuel French, 1934), and Sharon Pollock's *Blood Relations*, 1981, reprinted in Michele Wandor, ed., *Plays by Women*, vol. 3 (London: Methuen, 1984). Agnes DeMille choreographed *Fall River Legend: A Ballet*, which premiered at the Metropolitan Opera Company in 1948. See also her *Lizzie Borden: A Dance of Death* (Boston: Little, Brown, 1968). Jack Beeson composed an opera about the murders that premiered at the New York City Opera Company in 1965. A made-for-TV movie, *The Legend of Lizzie Borden* (Paramount, 1974) features Elizabeth Montgomery committing the murders in the nude to avoid blood spatters. For an analysis of the meaning of some of the more recent appearances of Lizzie Borden in fiction and drama, see Ann Schofield, "Lizzie Borden Took an Axe: History, Feminism, and American Culture," *American Studies* 34 (1993): 91–103.

3. Robert Hariman, "Performing the Laws: Popular Trials and Social Knowledge," in *Popular Trials: Rhetoric, Mass Media, and the Law*, ed. Robert Hariman (Tuscaloosa: University of Alabama Press, 1990), 29.

4. George Lipsitz, "The Greatest Story Ever Sold: Marketing and the OJ Simpson Trial," in *Birth of a Nation'hood: Gaze, Script, and Spectacle in the OJ Simpson Case*, ed. Toni Morrison and Claudia Brodsky LaCour (New York: Random House, 1997), 10.

5. On the suffrage movement, see Ellen Carol Dubois, *Feminism and Suffrage* (Ithaca: Cornell University Press, 1978). On female employment and reform and on the opening of occupations and professions, see Nancy Schrom Dye, *As Sisters and As Equals: Feminism, the Labor Movement and the Women's Trade Union League of New York* (Columbia: University of Missouri Press, 1980); Alice Kessler-Harris, *Out to Work: A History of Wage-Earning Women in the United States* (New York: Oxford University Press, 1982). On medicine and psychiatry, see Cynthia Russett, *Sexual Science: The Victorian Construction of Womanhood* (Cambridge: Harvard University Press, 1989).

6. Adelaide Churchill, the neighbor who first came to Lizzie's aid, testified that she asked Lizzie this question as she walked into the house. Pearson, *Trial*, 153.

7. Virginia Lincoln offers this interpretation in *Private Disgrace*, 51–52. After reporting the incident to the police, Andrew abruptly asked them to drop the matter, suggesting that he suspected a friend or family member. Whoever committed the burglary stole Abby's jewelry (of very little monetary value), cash from Andrew Borden's desk, and a book of horsecar tickets, a haul neatly symbolic of Lizzie's resentments about attention, money, and confinement for those who believe in her guilt.

8. Testimony of Alice Russell; Pearson, *Trial*, 157–59.

9. The testimony was excluded on the grounds that because the commonwealth was

attempting to prove murder by axe, the question of whether Lizzie Borden tried to poison her parents was irrelevant.

10. Testimony of Bridget Sullivan; Pearson, *Trial*, 137.

11. Dr. Bowen attended her in the early afternoon and gave her a mild preparation called bromo-caffeine for "nervous excitement and headache," a prescription he changed to morphine (a drug commonly prescribed for emotional distress in this period) the next day. He gave her what he called a "double dose" (one quarter grain) for the next week, and the defense's argument that her memory and judgment were impaired by the opiate was one of the reasons that her evasive and incriminating inquest testimony was excluded from the trial proper.

12. Testimony of Bridget Sullivan; Pearson, *Trial*, 139. The time between the actual attack on Andrew and Lizzie's report of it was so short that Dr. Bowen testified that Andrew's blood was still flowing when he initially examined the body.

13. *Boston Advertiser*, 4 August 1892; *Fall River Herald*, 5 August 1892.

14. From the *Concord Patriot*, in Kent, *Lizzie Borden Sourcebook*, 101.

15. The *Boston Herald*, 6 August 1892.

16. Votes of confidence by the Fall River WCTU on August 15 and by the Christian Endeavour Society were reported in the *Woman's Journal* 23 (20 August 1892): 270; the resolutions accompanying them included a declaration of "our unshaken faith in her as a fellow-worker and a sister tenderly beloved." Lucy Stone suggested that all-male juries were inherently unfair: "a woman especially should have a jury of her peers, not her sovereigns, as in the case of Lizzie Borden." Ibid., 24 (17 June 1893): 188.

17. The Livermore piece was originally written for the *Boston Post*, and was reprinted in *The Woman's Journal* 24 (27 May 1893): 162–63.

18. *New York Recorder*, 20 September 1892.

19. *Fall River Globe*, 21 September 1892.

20. *New York Herald*, 7 August 1892.

21. *Boston Globe*, 10 October 1892. The *Globe* printed a retraction and "abject apology" to Lizzie and John Morse on 12 October 1892.

22. I am often asked, when I speak formally or informally about the Borden murders, whether Lizzie Borden was sexually abused by her father. There is no evidence of incest or physical abuse in the family, and the question itself probably says more about our present conceptions of female criminality and domestic violence than it does about these murders.

23. Hariman, "Performing the Laws," 27–28.

24. Kathryn Allamong Jacob, in what is surely the best-titled piece on the case ever written; "She Couldn't Have Done It, Even If She Did: Why Lizzie Borden Went Free," *American Heritage* 29 (February/March, 1978): 42–53.

25. Quoted in Jones, *Women Who Kill*, 222.

26. From the official transcript: *Trial of Lizzie Andrew Borden: upon an indictment charging her with the murder of Abby Durfee Borden and Andrew Jackson Borden; before the Superior Court for the County of Bristol*, Frank Burt, stenographer: 1, 620. Microfilm of the full transcript is available only at the Boston Public Library and at the University of Massachusetts, Amherst, so I have referred to Pearson's edited version throughout. His is a fair edition except that he heavily edits Robinson's closing, diminishing its force considerably and making the jury's verdict more puzzling than it should be.

27. Defense closing; Pearson, *Trial*, 306.

28. Jones, *Women Who Kill*, 218.

29. Jacob makes a similar point about the psychology of the jurors: "If they could believe that a gentlewoman could pick up a hatchet such as surely lay in their own basements, and by murdering her parents become an heiress, what could they think the next time they looked into their own girls' eyes?" ("She Couldn't Have," 52), as does Jones, *Women Who Kill*, 218–19.

30. Defense closing; Pearson, *Trial*, 285.

31. Ibid., 286.

32. The mysterious intestinal affliction that Abby and Lizzie attributed to malicious poisoning may well have come from the stoic insistence on eating leftovers, especially in the summertime in the days before reliable refrigeration.

33. Official transcript, 1689.

34. Opening argument of District Attorney William Moody, in Pearson, *Trial*, 105.

35. Testimony of Assistant City Marshall John Fleet, ibid., 166.

36. Testimony of Hannah Gifford, ibid., 232.

37. Testimony of Emma Borden, ibid., 276.

38. Although this transaction is widely reported in histories of the case, it is somewhat unclear whether Andrew Borden put the property in Abby's name or in that of her half sister. Regardless, he had in effect bought a house for Sarah Whitehead to live in, and it was the transfer of Borden money to Abby's family that would have angered the daughters.

39. Defense closing, in Pearson, *Trial*, 305; commonwealth closing, ibid., 344.

40. The prosecution never stated this point directly, but it was made in the press even before Lizzie was arrested. See the *Fall River Herald*, 7 August 1892 and the *Fall River Globe*, 8 August 1892.

41. Nina Auerbach, *The Woman and the Demon: The Life of a Victorian Myth* (Cambridge: Harvard University Press, 1982). See chapter 3, esp. 63–65.

42. Commonwealth closing, in Pearson, *Trial*, 324.

43. Ibid., 326. In the immediate context of this remark, Knowlton is referring to ministers who have betrayed their flocks as one in a string of examples of deceptive appearances. However, I think my reading of the gendered resonances of his words is accurate, given the larger context of his arguments about women.

44. Ibid., 327.

45. Ibid., 357.

46. Sandra Gilbert and Susan Gubar, *The Madwoman in the Attic: The Woman Writer and the Nineteenth-Century Literary Imagination* (New Haven: Yale University Press, 1979). See also Bram Djikstra, *Idols of Perversity: Fantasies of Feminine Evil in Turn-of-the-Century Culture* (New York, Oxford University Press, 1986).

47. Commonwealth closing, in Pearson, *Trial*, 344–45.

48. For a lively collection of the folklore of aberrant behavior on Lizzie's part, see DeMille, *Lizzie Borden*. For the portrait of her as a more gentle recluse, see a letter to the editor of the *Fall River Herald* from Helen Leighton, founder of the Animal Rescue League, 12 June 1927 (ten days after Lizzie's death); interview with Emma Borden, *Boston Sunday Post*, 13 April 1913; letters in Williams et al., *Casebook*, 261–68.

49. "Sisters" because there was a daughter born between Emma and Lizzie who died in early childhood and was the first buried in the family plot.

50. Jones compares Lizzie Borden's arrest and trial to the treatment meted out to Bridget Durgan, an Irish housemaid accused of murdering a doctor's wife. Durgan told of strangers breaking into the house in which she worked one night while the doctor was

away, of her own heroic rescue of her employers' child, and her consequent ignorance of the brutal beating, slashing, murder, and arson that followed; but it seemed quite impossible that events transpired in the way that she asserted. Motive remained entirely obscure, but Bridget Durgan was hanged for the crime. Jones points out that, as in Lizzie's trial, the lawyers reasoned "the murder could only have been committed by a fiend. The difference was that in this case everyone was eager to believe that Bridget Durgan was indeed a fiend. After all, she was Irish" (*Women Who Kill*, 201).

TOMBS, SUNDAY MORNING.

An African American women argues her case before the court. Matthew Hale Smith, *Sunshine and Shadow* (Hartford, Conn.: J. B. Burr, 1870), 164.

Chapter Thirteen

Treat Her Like a Lady

Judicial Paternalism and the Justification for Assaults against Black Women, 1865–1910

Uche Egemonye

Three years after Atlanta erupted into one of the worst racial conflicts in Georgia's history, Lula Brawner, a Black woman, brought a suit for damages in the sum of $5,000 against W. H. Irvin, the White Elberton City chief of police. According to Brawner, Irvin had savagely whipped and verbally abused Brawner in her front yard and then hauled her to the city prison.[1] After two hours, Irvin released Brawner from jail, without formally charging her with any crime or requiring her to post bail for a court appearance. Irvin subjected Brawner to this public and painful humiliation because he believed that she had overstepped her boundaries as a Black woman. Irvin began his assault by accusing Brawner of striking his relative's child. Brawner vehemently denied the charge, contending that Irvin's behavior was wanton, unprovoked, and unjustified.[2]

Before she professed her innocence, she first described herself to the court. Brawner's self-depiction is a telling revelation of Southern mores:

> . . . your petitioner was living in the City of Elberton County, Georgia, with her husband, William Brawner, and her children in her own house, attending to her domestic duties, at peace with all the world and demeaning herself as an orderly and law-abiding woman.[3]

In this short but loaded paragraph, Brawner presents herself as a married woman and a mother who was suddenly attacked and imprisoned for no good reason.[4] Contesting this self-portrait, Irvin justified his behavior by depicting Brawner as unwomanly enough to hit a defenseless child and wanton enough to disrespect the supremacy of White folk.

Several cases brought by Black women in southern courts against their assailants during the late nineteenth and early twentieth centuries follow this pattern.[5] The White or Black attacker usually accused the Black woman of acting in an unfeminine and unladylike manner and justified any actions taken by pointing to the offending Black woman's behavior. Not to be outdone, Black women deflected this attack by positioning themselves as proper ladies and appealing to judicial paternalism. By examining the justifications for assaults against Black women and analyzing the ideological-legal strategy Black women employed to counter these assaults and actually win awards, this essay argues that for a limited time during Reconstruction and again at the turn of the century, a few members of the judiciary allowed Black female plaintiffs to appropriate the language of ladyhood and reap the rewards of being a lady.[6]

This appropriation constituted a shrewd maneuver by Black women who were acutely aware of the nefarious stereotypes regarding their character. They valiantly strove to counter such misrepresentations by putting forth a contrary image of correct female bearing.[7] Black women recognized that judges and even members of grand juries were propertied White men and strong adherents of the belief that ladies deserved protection. To gain the sympathy of these White males, Black women had to represent themselves as respectable women, ladies in spite of their Blackness. Besides being an excellent strategy, Black women's repeated assertions of their ladyhood suggest that they were shocked and hurt that anyone would willfully refuse to recognize and respect their newly won status, one that they had struggled so hard to attain. Although there is a sizable and quite sophisticated corpus of literature on racial violence during Reconstruction and the Progressive Era, most scholars concentrate on the Black male targets of White male racism and ignore the violent treatment meted out to Black women, as well as the ingenious ways Black women enlisted the aid of the courts.[8]

There are several reasons for historians' failure to concentrate on Black women as major actors during the racial conflagration that raged in the Reconstruction South and in the "New South." Primary among them is that lynching represents the most egregious form of racial violence to most scholars of these eras, and most of Judge Lynch's victims were Black men. Another reason is that many scholars consider this an era dominated by men; for example, only men could vote and hold office. Black women, therefore, resided on the periphery of the public imagination, appearing only as sexual pawns. Some historians have even interpreted the sexual abuse of Black women as a warning to Black men. The argument goes that if Black men anticipated any change in status, they had better think again. Just as White males had enjoyed unlimited sexual access to Black women during slavery, they intended to maintain the tradition after slavery's demise.[9]

This male-centered interpretation is flawed in two major respects. It overstates the extent to which White males wielded rape as a tool of oppression against Black males and understates the fact that Black women were the primary physical and psychological victims of rape. No matter what it might have been in the second instance, the sexual abuse of Black women was first and foremost an attack against Black women themselves.

Several mostly Black female scholars have labored intensively to prove that Black women during Reconstruction and after were actors in their own right. Apart from a few early articles, the legal history of Black women has only recently attracted systematic and sustained attention. Whereas most of this new historiography chronicles Black women's aggressive albeit embattled struggle to vindicate their rights, much can also be learned by approaching this topic from a different angle.[10] This work seeks to discern what the pitting of a White or Black defendant against a Black female plaintiff in front of an elite White male judge indicates about the flexibility of Reconstruction and post-Reconstruction laws and the concomitant legal culture. It also explores the willingness of judges to assume the paternal mantle last worn by planters in adjudicating cases involving respectable Black women.[11]

With the signing of the Emancipation Proclamation and the surrender of the Confederate army, slaves abruptly found themselves free. Former slaves could not afford to savor the sweet taste of liberty because southern Whites resented the sudden change of circumstances that catapulted their former chattel into freedpeople, with legal rights that they had to respect.[12]

Freedpeople harbored an intense and abiding respect for education, land, and labor. With the assistance of northern abolitionists, they went about procuring the first two and calling upon the court system to protect their rights. Freedwomen, in particular, were quick to seek legal redress for their grievances. Perhaps Black women, barred from public and political forums and denied real economic independence, turned to the courts with such enthusiasm because it was all they had. White males of a certain class responded to and protected virtuous Black females from riffraff, just as they protected virtuous White females.[13]

Black women usually prevailed in their lawsuits regarding sexual assault and segregated seating if they displayed the accouterments of ladyhood in dress, demeanor, or honest vocation and the defendants were lower class, of dubious origins, and/or proffered unacceptable reasons for their behavior toward the Black female plaintiffs. Several freedwomen successfully litigated cases against White men and even won damages against these exploiters, regardless of the status of these men. A Black lady did not necessarily have to belong to the middle class, but she had to carry herself in a way that showed her respect for middle-class values.

In 1865, two freedwomen brought charges against Andrew B. Payne, "one of the most respectable among men" in Murfreesboro, Tennessee. Tabby Wheatley accused Payne and Miles Ferguson of accosting and then beating her daughter. When Tabby intervened to protect her daughter, Payne attacked Tabby. Payne also attacked Maria Posey, a former slave and mother of a five-year-old girl. When Payne barged into her room, Posey jumped up from her bed. Payne then tried to rip off her clothes. When she screamed, he stopped, and she made it to her door, where she espied Payne's companion. Meanwhile, Payne had grabbed a fire shovel and was just about to strike Posey when his companion wrenched the shovel from him. Persistent to the last, Payne pushed Posey into a fire, scorching her dress. As evidence, Posey presented her burnt garment to the Freedmen's Bureau agent. Although there is no evidence of how the agent resolved this case, his behavior in a case involving two other former slaves, Unity and Minerva, suggests that he tended to view Black women's claims sympathetically. Accordingly, Black women in Murfreesboro may have been emboldened to bring claims against White men, knowing that the Freedmen's Bureau agents were willing to give them at least a hearing.[14]

In 1866, Unity and Minerva brought an action against their former owner, Mr. Beasley, alleging that he had breached an oral agreement with them. According to their testimony, Beasley had initially left them on his plantation in Murfreesboro as he was fleeing from the Yankees. Before he left, he told the women that "they [might] stay and have everything." After the war, he returned and drove them off the land. Surprisingly, Beasley admitted that he "drove off the old woman [Unity] because she could not work and Minerva because she would not submit to his lust." The Murfreesboro Freedmen's Bureau agent levied a fine of nine dollars against Beasley and made him give the women "rent free" occupancy of the disputed land.[15]

By recognizing the claims of two newly emancipated Black women over those of a propertied White male, this agent or judicial officer vindicated the rights of the two Black women, demonstrating that they had the ability to exercise power in the judicial system during Reconstruction. Black women did not flex their litigation muscles only in Murfreesboro, Tennessee.

Three freedwomen's testimony led to the arrest and conviction of two "respectable" White men in Amite City, Louisiana. According to Martha Kemp, these men, like Payne, barged into her home early in the morning. One of the men, Clements, propositioned Kemp, who replied that she "was a woman of the church and did not do such things." Jules Dalyet, the other white man, accused Kemp of trying to report them to an officer. Her tart rejoinder was that he should "go to a white woman and not . . . trouble colored women." The events that transpired next demand complete rendition:

> He said he didn't want me to tell him about white women anymore, he then hit me three times with his fist twice on the head & once on the collar bone. I ran and hollowed murder. He said he would shoot me & ran as if to get a pistol & I ran the other way. He stopped and pulled off his petticoats, he had been dressed in women's clothes.
>
> Dalyet's brutality was not confined to Martha Kemp. He choked Eliza Kemp, who was carrying a child, threw her down, hit her with his fist, and felt her body with his hands. Both men beat and sexually assaulted the third woman, Manerva Moore.

A neighbor, Cecilia, corroborated their testimony and furnished further details. According to Cecilia, the men climbed through a window and into her bed, where they began to hit her. Cecilia shouted for help, threw a chair at her violators, and verbally lambasted them for their shameful behavior.[16]

Like Beasley in Murfreesboro, Tennessee, neither man denied the allegations. They declared that they had been inebriated and could not recall their actions. Bureau officers determined that Clement owned a lot of property and that although propertyless, Dalyet was "a strictly up right young man." Finding that the evidence was "conclusive of insult to females of color," the bureau agent fined the men fifteen dollars each. Their having "always borne a good character" occasioned the paltry fine.[17]

It is not surprising that these White males assumed unlimited and unimpeded sexual access to Black women as one of their prerogatives. Even after emancipation, White men routinely and aggressively propositioned Black women on the street in broad daylight. It is even less astonishing that the White men who committed crimes against Black women were often considered the creme de la creme of their communities. Many former slaves asserted that the "best blood of the South ran in their veins" and that many White men who presented one face to the White public behaved in another fashion amongst Blacks. What is most intriguing about these cases was the way in which Black women presented themselves to the court, regardless of regional or class differences. In Tennessee, Beasley testified that Unity had spurned him. Martha Kemp of Louisiana also had rejected the sexual advances of the two White men who invaded her home. Although Unity and Martha seem to have come from different classes (Unity did not own a home; Martha did), they both appropriated the same ideology of ladyhood and employed it to evoke sympathy from their respective judicial audiences. In both cases, judicial paternalism netted the Black female plaintiffs awards that symbolized Black women's newly acquired legal acumen and strength.[18]

Judicial paternalism was neither limited to bureau agents nor to Reconstruction. Black women who convinced local and state judges that they were worthy recipients of judicial paternalism received it. In 1876, Leathea Harris accused James Stewart, a freedman, of assault in Granville County, North Carolina. When Harris attempted to ward off Stewart's sexual advances, he "struck [her] in the mouth and called for a stick and said that he would beat [her] to death." In his defense, Stewart accused Harris of having provoked the assault with her abusive harangue. One of Stewart's witnesses was the sheriff, who testified that Harris was temperamental, disruptive, and mendacious. By calling the sheriff, Stewart hoped to demonstrate that White power supported him and renounced Harris. His display of White power was in vain, for the court indicted him for assault and battery. Six years later, Clarissa Wortham, a Black woman, charged Jack Allen, a Black man, with attempted rape. Like Stewart, Allen argued that Wortham initiated their contact. Despite his attempt to play on the court's stereotypes of Black women's wantonness, he was found guilty and indicted.[19]

The Black assailants in these two cases seem either to have believed or tried to exploit the negative stereotypes of Black female character. Their attempts to impugn the characters of the Black female plaintiff (even with the support of a White sheriff) failed because the women persuaded the judges that they were damsels in distress. Appealing to judicial paternalism, however successful in the short run, proved untenable for the long term. Even when Black women were victorious in court, their attackers rarely served any prison sentence for their crimes. All they were required to do in most cases was to pay a small fine. The leniency of judges presented with uncontroverted evidence of malfeasance against Black women indicates ambivalence toward Black women and their cases. Relying on judges' acceptance of the sanctity of ladyhood was also tenuous because what behavior was considered ladylike changed over time and because a Black woman's aggressive pursuit of a lawsuit could render her unladylike in the eyes of the judge.

The great antilynching crusader Ida B. Wells-Barnett learned the limitations of White paternalism early in her career. In 1883, as a young schoolteacher, Wells bought a first-class ticket from Memphis to Woodstock, Tennessee, and sat down in the ladies' coach. The White conductor ordered her to move to the forward car, a place Wells described as being filled with "colored people and those who were smoking." When Wells resentfully refused to move, the conductor tried to remove her forcibly and she bit him on his hand. He then called two other White men to his aid, and they dragged the diminutive Wells out of the car. Later that year, Wells sued the Chesapeake, Ohio and Southwestern Railroad Company in the Shelby County Circuit Court. Implicitly accepting Wells's contention that she deserved to be treated like a lady and to sit in the ladies' car (and was therefore a lady), Judge James O. Pierce awarded Wells five hundred dollars in damages. Her victory was short-lived. Four years later, the Tennessee Supreme Court overturned Pierce's ruling and required Wells to pay court costs. Chief Justice Peter Turney lambasted Wells for harassing the railroad company and opined that her "persistence was not in good faith to obtain a comfortable seat for the short ride." The language of this holding explicitly castigates Wells for her unladylike pursuit of justice. This case is especially important not only for its precedential value but for its deliberation of the limits of judicial paternalism.[20]

The cases discussed here show that in a few instances when elite White male judges adjudicated cases involving "virtuous" Black women, they found in their favor, even when White males contradicted the Black women's testimony or when Black males presented evidence designed to impugn Black women's characters. Legal actions by these Black women demonstrate that they understood their rights and shrewdly employed the available legal system to prosecute and punish men who assaulted them. These cases also reveal that sexual stereotypes of Black women were not routinely accepted by the judiciary and could not be bandied about. Seemingly aware of these opportunities for justice, Black women brought suit for pragmatic reasons.

Demands that the executive branch enforce laws designed to protect Blacks would have fallen on deaf ears. President Andrew Johnson was well noted for his vituperative hatred of nonwhites. Johnson consistently vetoed and attacked legislation that recognized Blacks as human beings and accorded them the rights and privileges of American citizens. Johnson's successors were not much better: they either ignored Blacks altogether or paid only lip service to the idea that Blacks had rights. By the turn of the century, both state and national legislatures became increasingly hostile to the needs of Blacks. Prodded and goaded by radical Reconstructionists such as Charles Sumner and Thaddeus Stevens, Congress eventually enacted the Civil Rights Act of 1875 and amended the Constitution three times.[21] Two years after passage of the Civil Rights Act, with the removal of Union troops and the resurgence of the South, the Supreme Court gutted, refused to enforce, and finally overturned these legislative provisions, thus demonstrating the limits of the judiciary's support and usefulness. Before the onset of the period of redemption, Black male delegates to several different state constitutional conventions tried unavailingly to enact laws that protected Black women from White men's lust.[22]

Faced with the realities of a hostile executive and beleaguered legislatures, Black women may have turned to the courts as a last resort. They may have held the judiciary to a higher standard, based on their experiences with bureau courts during Reconstruction. In this respect, Black women differed from Black men, who tried to advance their lot through the political process.[23] Black women's reliance on the judiciary was often misplaced. When judges were convinced that the plaintiff was not a "proper Black woman," they denied her protection under the laws and penalized her for getting out of her place. Notwithstanding this reality, Black women took Black and White men who disrespected them to court and exposed the relationships they had with these men to the public unreservedly. Two modern legacies spring from Black women's willingness to litigate in spite of the considerable odds of their losing.

The first is Black people's seemingly unwavering and heavily criticized predisposition to view the judiciary, especially the Supreme Court, as countermajoritarian. Derrick Bell and Giradeau A. Spann, two renowned legal scholars, decry Blacks' reliance on the law as a transformatory tool because the judiciary is hostile to minority interests.[24] Like those who erroneously located the call to armed self-defense with Malcolm X, Bell and Spann mistakenly trace Blacks' reliance on judicial review to Thurgood Marshall and the NAACP. The roots of this Black tradition of viewing the judicial system as countermajoritarian run much deeper than the civil rights era. The evidence presented here indicates that Black women attempted to mold the judicial system into a supportive institution responsive to their needs in particular and Black peoples' needs in general.

The second implication of this study complicates academics' assertions that Anita Hill received criticism because she charged Clarence Thomas with sexually harassing her in front of White men.[25] Black women have a history of courageously prosecuting their male abusers, Black and White, thus Hill's action was not unprecedented. Unlike Thomas, however, Hill was not able to evoke a racial memory of Black women's continuous mistreatment by both White and Black men because it is a history that the Black community has chosen to forget. As Emma Coleman Jordan points out in her article on the confirmation hearings, Thomas shrewdly resurrected and wielded lynching imagery to his advantage. In contrast to Hill, Thomas was successful because Blacks, like other Americans, place more importance on the harm done to men and the male ego than that visited upon women.[26]

The period from Reconstruction to the Jim Crow era represented a time in flux, when the United States might have been able to reverse its tendency to privilege the man's word over that of the woman. During these decades, certain elite White males were willing to accept and honor Black women's claims to ladyhood. Ambivalence brought on by competing stereotypes that branded Black women as loose, immoral, and degraded tinged judges' acceptance and protection of Black ladies. When the pendulum of judicial opinion swung abruptly in the opposite direction and White judges accepted the negative stereotypes of Black women, they effectively endorsed violence against these women.

Unfortunately for Black women, the clamor of those who propagated negative stereotypes of Black women drowned out the cries of the Black women who suffered the slow but sure erosion of their legal rights, and an escalation of violence against their bodies that continues to this day.[27]

NOTES

Uche Egemonye is a law and history graduate student at Emory University, Atlanta. She thanks Michael Bellesiles, David Garrow, Leslye Obiora, Mary Odem, and Polly Price for reading and commenting on earlier drafts of this essay.

1. *Brawner v. Irvin*, 169 F. 964 (C.C.N.D. Ga. 1909), reprinted in *Civil Rights Legislation: Cases and Materials*, ed. Theodore Eisenberg, 4th ed. (Charlottesville, Va.: Michie, 1996): 65. For more information on the Atlanta race riot of 1906, see David Godshalk, "In the Wake of Riot: Atlanta's Struggle for Order, 1899–1919" (Ph.D. diss., Yale University, 1992); Gregory Lamont Mixon, "The Atlanta Riot of 1906" (Ph.D. diss., University of Cincinnati, 1989); and Charles Crowe, "Racial Massacre in Atlanta, September 22, 1906," *Journal of Negro History* 54 (1969): 150–73.

2. *Brawner v. Irvin*, 66. Writing about lynching in Georgia, W. Fitzhugh Brundage asserts that from 1880 to 1930 more than 150 Blacks and 10 Whites fell victim to lynch law in the state. See W. Fitzhugh Brundage, *Lynching in the New South: Georgia and Virginia, 1880–1930* (Urbana: University of Illinois Press, 1993), 197–207. Given this particularly tumultuous and harrowing period for Blacks in Georgia, Brawner's decision to take a White police chief to court was courageous.

3. *Brawner v. Irvin*, 65.

4. District Judge Newman ruled against Brawner, finding Irvin had not deprived her of any rights, privileges, or immunities secured by the Constitution or federal law. Accordingly, he held that she had no right to bring her case to the federal court because it lacked jurisdiction: "Whatever rights the plaintiff has must be enforced therefore in the courts of the state." See *Brawner v. Irvin*, 66–69. Research in Elbert County courthouse records did not reveal the final disposition of her case on the state or local level.

5. On suits brought by Black women in southern courts during Reconstruction, see Laura F. Edwards, "Sexual Violence, Gender Reconstruction, and the Extension of Patriarchy in Granville County, North Carolina," *North Carolina Historical Review* 68 (1991): 237–60; Sara Rapport, "The Freedmen's Bureau as a Legal Agent for Black Men and Women in Georgia, 1865–1868," *Georgia Historical Quarterly* (1989): 26–53; Victoria Bynum, *Unruly Women: The Politics of Social and Sexual Control in the Old South* (Chapel Hill: University of North Carolina Press, 1992); Suzanne Lebsock, *Free Women of Petersburg: Status and Culture in a Southern Town, 1784–1860* (New York: Norton, 1985); Catherine Clinton, "Bloody Terrain: Freedwomen, Sexuality and Violence during Reconstruction," *Georgia Historical Quarterly* 76 (1992): 310–32; Catherine Clinton, " 'Southern Dishonor': Flesh, Blood, Race, and Bondage," in *In Joy and in Sorrow: Women, Family, and Marriage in the Victorian South, 1830–1900*, ed. Carol Bleser (New York: Oxford University Press, 1991); Barry Crouch, "Black Dreams and White Justice," *Prologue* 6 (1974): 255–65.

6. Patricia Hagler Minter, "The Failure of Freedom: Class, Gender, and the Evolution of Segregated Transit Law in the Nineteenth-Century South," *Chicago-Kent Law Review* 70

(1995): 995. She discusses judicial paternalism in the context of streetcar segregation. My understanding of the ideology of ladyhood relies heavily on Barbara Welter, "The Cult of True Womanhood: 1820–1860," *American Quarterly* 18 (1966): 151–74.

7. For scholarship on how Black women fought to defend their sexual image, see Darlene Clark Hine, "Lifting the Veil, Shattering the Silence: Black Women's History in Slavery and Freedom," in *Black Women in United States History*, vol. 9, ed. Darlene Clark Hine (New York: Carlson, 1990), 235–62. Other works on this topic include Renee Stimson, "The Afro-American Female: The Historical Context of the Construction of Sexual Identity," in *The Powers of Desire: The Politics of Sexuality*, ed. Ann Snitow, Sharon Thompson, and Christine Stansell (New York: Monthly Review Press, 1983), 229–35; Paula Giddings, *When and Where I Enter: The Impact of Black Women on Race and Sex in America* (New York: Morrow, 1984); Evelyn Hammonds, "Black (W)holes and the Geometry of Black Female Sexuality," *Differences: A Journal of Feminist Cultural Studies* 6 (1994): 126–45; Elsa Barkeley Brown, "Negotiating and Transforming the Public Sphere: African American Political Life in the Transition from Slavery to Freedom," *Public Culture* 7 (1994): 107–46; Hazel Carby, "Policing the Black Women's Body in the Urban Context," *Critical Inquiry* 18 (1992): 251–74; Darlene Clark Hine, "Rape and Inner Lives of Black Women in the Middle West: Preliminary Thoughts on the Culture of Dissemblance," *Signs* 14 (1989): 915–20.

8. Peter Bardaglio, *Reconstructing the Household: Families, Sex, and the Law in the Nineteenth-Century South* (Chapel Hill: University of North Carolina Press, 1995), 137–75; Joel Williamson, *The Crucible of Race: Black/White Relations in the American South since Emancipation* (New York: Oxford University Press, 1984); Paul Finkelman, "Exploring Southern Legal History," *North Carolina Law Review* 77 (1985): 101–8; Jacquelyn Dowd Hall, *Revolt against Chivalry: Jessie Daniel Ames and the Women's Campaign against Lynching* (New York: Columbia University Press, 1993); W. Fitzhugh Brundage, ed., *Under Sentence of Death: Lynching in the South* (Chapel Hill: University of North Carolina Press, 1997). For a discussion of Black women's intellectual engagement during this era, see Hazel Carby, " 'On the Threshold of Woman's Era': Lynching, Empire, and Sexuality in Black Feminist Theory," in *"Race," Writing, and Difference*, ed. Henry Louis Gates, Jr. (Chicago: University of Chicago Press, 1986), 301–16.

9. Gerda Lerner, *Black Women in White America: A Documentary History* (New York: Vintage Books, 1972), 172.

10. For an overview of Black women's historiography, see Evelyn Brooks Higginbotham, "Beyond the Sound of Silence: Afro-America Women in History," *Gender and History* 1 (1989): 50–67. Pioneering articles include Maude White Katz, "The Negro Woman and the Law," in Hine, *Black Women in United States History*, 278–86; Maude White Katz, "She Who Would Be Free—Resistance," *Freedomways*, winter 1962, 60–70; Mary Frances Berry, "Judging Morality: Sexual Behavior and Legal Consequences in the Late Nineteenth-Century South," *Journal of American History* 78 (1991): 835–56 (I wish to thank Dr. Clayborne Carson for bringing this reference to my attention); Victoria Bynum, "On the Lowest Rung: Court Control over Poor White and Free Black Women," *Southern Exposure* 12 (1984): 40–44; Paul Finkelman, ed., *Law and Freedom Symposium, Parts I and II*, *Chicago-Kent Law Review* 70 (1994–95); Ann Gordon et al., eds., *African-American Women and the Vote, 1837–1965* (Amherst: University of Massachusetts Press, 1997).

11. On planters' paternalism, see Eugene D. Genovese, *Roll, Jordan, Roll: The World the Slaves Made* (New York: Vintage Books, 1976).

12. For the impact of emancipation on Southern justice, see Edward L. Ayers, *Vengeance and Justice: Crime and Punishment in the Nineteenth Century South* (New York: Oxford University Press, 1984); Eric Foner, *Nothing but Freedom: Emancipation and Its Legacy* (Baton

Rouge: Louisiana State University Press, 1983), 52–53, 58–59; Donald Nieman, "Black Political Power and Criminal Justice: Washington County, Texas, 1868–1884," *Journal of Southern History* 55 (1989): 391–420; John Hope Franklin, *Reconstruction: After the Civil War*, 2d ed. (Chicago: University of Chicago Press, 1994).

13. For the primacy of a woman's class in determining her treatment in the South, see Elizabeth Fox-Genovese, *Within the Plantation Household: Black and White Women in the Old South* (Chapel Hill: University of North Carolina Press, 1988), 192–241.

14. Murfreesboro, Tennessee, complaints enclosed in John Seage, January 1866, to J. D. Alden, T/42-39-3, Tennessee Freedmen's Bureau MSS., Record Group 105, National Archives. On the Freedmen's Bureau, see Donald Nieman, ed., *The Freedmen's Bureau and Black Freedom* (New York: Garland, 1994).

15. Murfreesboro, Tennessee, complaints.

16. Register of Complaints, Amite City, Louisiana, 11 Sept. 1865, Louisiana Freedmen's Bureau MSS., Record Group 105, National Archives, Washington, D. C.

17. Ibid.

18. Herbert G. Gutman, *The Black Family in Slavery and Freedom, 1750–1925* (New York: Vintage Books, 1976), 396–402.

19. Edwards, "Sexual Violence," 246–48. Stewart's strategy is similar to that employed by Clarence Thomas during his confirmation hearings. For an exposition of this idea, see Emma Coleman Jordan, "Race, Gender, and Social Class in the Thomas Sexual Harassment Hearings: The Hidden Fault Lines in Political Discourse," *Harvard Women's Law Journal* 15 (1992): 1–24.

20. *Chesapeake, Ohio & Southwestern R.R. Co. v. Wells*, 85 Tenn. 613, 615 (1883); Paula Giddings, *When and Where I Enter*, 22; Alfreda Duster, ed., *Crusade for Justice: The Autobiography of Ida B. Wells* (Chicago: University of Chicago Press, 1970); Joseph H. Cartwright, *The Triumph of Jim Crow: Tennessee Race Relations in the 1880's* (Knoxville: University of Tennessee Press, 1976), 189–91.

21. Kenneth Milton Stampp, *Era of Reconstruction, 1865–1877* (New York: Knopf, 1965), 111–19, 139–40. For President Johnson's veto of the Civil Rights Act of 1866, see Bernard Schwartz, ed., *Statutory History of the United States: Civil Rights* (2 vols., Washington, D.C.: Chelsea House, 1970), 1:150–55. Congress voted to override Johnson's veto.

22. For several examples of Black male legislators' futile attempts to pass laws punishing White male/Black female concubinage, see Gutman, *Black Family*, 396–402.

23. Rapport, "Freedmen's Bureau," 26–53; Eric Foner, *Reconstruction: America's Unfinished Revolution, 1863–1877* (New York: Harper & Row, 1988), 277–87.

24. Derrick Bell, "Racial Realism," *Connecticut Law Review* 24 (1992): 363–79; Giradeau Spann, "Pure Politics," *Michigan Law Review* 88 (1990): 1971–81.

25. "Anita Hill put her private business in the street and she downgraded a Black man to a room filled with White men who might alter his fate—surely a large enough betrayal for her to be read out of the race." Rosemary Bray, "Taking Sides against Ourselves," *New York Times Magazine*, 17 November 1991, 56.

26. Jordan, *Race*, 19–20.

27. On the images of Black women in the postbellum South, see Patricia Morton, *Disfigured Images: The Historical Assault on Afro-American Women* (Westport, Conn.: Greenwood Press, 1991); Madelin Joan Olds, "The Rape Complex in the Postbellum South" (Ph.D. diss., Carnegie-Mellon University, 1989). For an interpretation of the sexuality of Black female bodies in nineteenth-century Europe, see Sander Gilman, "Black Bodies, White Bodies: Toward an Iconography of Female Sexuality in Late Nineteenth Century Art, Medicine, and Literature," in Gates, *"Race," Writing, and Difference*, 223–61.

The caption reads: "Searching Negroes for arms in police station." The Chicago Commission on Race Relations found that the police routinely stopped and searched black citizens, convinced that they bore responsibility for the majority of crimes. Chicago Commission on Race Relations, *The Negro in Chicago: A Study of Race Relations and a Race Riot* (Chicago: University of Chicago Press, 1922), 34.

Chapter Fourteen

"The Negro Would Be More Than an Angel to Withstand Such Treatment"
African American Homicide in Chicago, 1875–1910

Jeffrey S. Adler

Violence exploded in the African American communities of northern cities during the late nineteenth and early twentieth centuries. In the era of the Great Migration, the formation of the ghetto, and the implementation of Jim Crow–like laws and social conventions, discrimination increased, white-on-black conflict spiraled, and black-on-black violence surged. Historians, sociologists, and criminologists have devoted considerable attention to the relationship between discrimination and violence.[1] Such scholarship touches on two enormously important and complex issues. First, it explores the ways in which external economic and social pressures can generate conflict within minorities' communities. Second, many historians have traced the "roots" of modern inner-city violence to the racial conflict and discrimination of the late nineteenth century and early twentieth. It was in this period, for example, that a wide gap between white and African American homicide rates emerged. The sources of modern rates of homicide for African American men, which are nearly seven times greater than the homicide rates for white men, can at least in part be traced to the racism and discrimination of the turn-of-the-century city.[2]

Two general theoretical perspectives have informed historical studies of African American violence, though most scholars have eschewed monolithic explanations and have blended elements of these frameworks. The most influential model borrows from the criminologist Marvin E. Wolfgang and Franco Ferracuti's idea of a "subculture of violence."[3] Wolfgang and Ferracuti proposed that in particular pockets of society, or subcultures, aggression represents a legitimate, coherent mechanism for attaining or affirming status. Culturally derived rules of conduct encourage violence in certain well-defined contexts. Historians of the American South have relied on such a framework to explain the development of an ethic of honor, the prevalence of dueling, the popularity of rough-and-tumble brawling, the persistence of feuding, and the enduring correlation between regional culture and high rates of homicide.[4] The historian Clare V. McKanna, Jr., has expanded this model in arguing that African Americans brought an honor-based culture in which aggression affirmed status to northern cities during the Great Migration, thus explaining the very high levels of violence that plagued early-twentieth-century ghettoes.[5]

Wolfgang and Ferracuti's model shaped the debate for more than two decades. Sustained efforts to test the subculture of violence model, however, have produced serious challenges and revealed significant shortcomings in the theory.[6] In part, scholars have bristled at the conceptual looseness of the model; even the most subtle studies employing this framework, for example, seldom effectively explain the source or define the boundaries of the subculture. Moreover, sociologists and criminologists have found little direct empirical evidence to support Wolfgang and Ferracuti's idea. Even if violence has been disproportionately concentrated in the South or in the African American community, variables other than region or race correlate more positively with high levels of homicide. Nonetheless, Wolfgang and Ferracuti's model, with its emphasis on the relationship between aggression and rules of social interaction, continues to influence analyses of violence.

The second theoretical perspective focuses on the effects of structural pressures. Discrimination and dislocation, according to this framework, have long been the wellsprings for violence in the African American community. The historian Roger Lane has analyzed this process most persuasively, arguing that increasing levels of discrimination and poverty isolated northern African Americans from the rewards of urban, industrial society. Excluded from unions, shut out of secure employment, forced into deteriorating housing stock, and denied the socializing benefits of the factory and the school, African American city dwellers lived in an unstable, violent world where poverty and vulnerability produced a reliance on self-help solutions and aggressive responses to conflict, generating high rates of homicide.[7]

This structural model can either challenge or complement the subculture of violence theory. Social and economic dislocation, according to many historians, sociologists, and criminologists, accounts for the violence of the inner city. Employing sophisticated methods, proponents of this framework have identified statistical correlations between African American violence and poverty, unemployment, inequality (particularly race-specific stratification), and segregation.[8] Despite the methodological rigor of such studies, they too suffer from conceptual vagueness. For all their efforts to identify the structural sources of violence, these scholars also rely—though implicitly—on cultural arguments. Poverty, after all, does not directly or inevitably produce lethal violence, and most poor people do not commit violent acts. Instead, inequality or poverty may condition or shape behavior, thus producing the frustration, defining the sense of relative deprivation, or forging the oppositional values that, in turn, spark violence. Put differently, despite the important contributions and the sophistication of structural analyses, these studies have identified statistical correlations more effectively than they have explained causation.

Turn-of-the-century Chicago is a useful context for exploring these varying interpretations of the roots of violence in the black community for three reasons. First, as the home of the influential *Defender* and the site of unusual racial conflict, such as the riot of 1919, Chicago played a special and particularly prominent role in the Great Migration and in the making of the first ghetto. Second, scholars have explored the history of race relations in the city with extraordinary care and sophistication.[9] Historians possess an unusually complete understanding of the ways in which discrimination in housing and employment, for example, affected the city's African American community. Third, a remarkable set of late-nineteenth- and early-twentieth-century police records has survived, making it possible to chart homicide in the city during this turbulent period. In 1870, the Chicago Police Department established a log of homicide cases.[10] By the mid-1870s, police officials maintained this log systematically. The police records reveal that African Americans committed (or were believed to have committed) 297 homicides in Chicago between 1875 and 1910, constituting 11 percent of the homicides in the city. These cases, combined into a database and analyzed using quantitative methods, form the heart of this study.[11] Each homicide was traced in leading Chicago newspapers, including the African American *Chicago Broad Ax*, to gain additional information and a more contextualized perspective.[12]

To analyze the character of African American homicide in Chicago between 1875 and 1910, the data were examined from three perspectives. First, black-on-black homicides were compared with black-on-white homicides. In view of the fact that more than 77 percent of the murders occurred within racial lines, the comparison is based on a small sample of interracial cases, though it reveals important differences. Second, the homicides committed by African Americans were compared with homicides committed by whites. Third, changes over time in the nature of African American homicide were examined.

Ironically, exploring murders committed by African American Chicagoans provides a more revealing glimpse into the effects of white racism than would examining murders committed by whites against African Americans. The discrimination that racked the city's African American community spawned violence therein. White Chicagoans belittled, mocked, jeered, threatened, and assaulted African Americans in the city, though they rarely murdered them.[13] Nor was this pattern, where tensions were principally directed inward, unique to turn-of-the-century Chicago. Many scholars, most notably anthropologists, have explored the ways in which discrimination and oppression produce conflict within minority communities.[14] When the racial climate of Chicago deteriorated at the end of the nineteenth century, the African American homicide rate swelled. Just as white Chicagoans began to deny stable jobs to African Americans and to refuse to share neighborhoods, restaurants, or schools with them, the gap between the white and African American homicide rates widened. Moreover, this gap broadened as discrimination in employment, housing, and public accommodations increased. The forced making of the ghetto, in short, coincided with a surge in the African American homicide rate, which ballooned from 13.9 per hundred thousand during the late 1870s to 49.0 during the first decade of the twentieth century, and to 102.8 during the early 1920s, as fire bombings, restrictive real estate covenants, and poverty secured the borders of Chicago's "black belt."[15] Yet, the proportion of murders crossing racial lines remained unchanged; racial discrimination produced tensions that erupted principally within the African American community.[16] This intraracial conflict represents one of the ways in which discrimination was so insidious. Shifts in the character of African American homicide, however, produce telling clues about the process through which white racism spurred African American violence.

The Great Migration and the early stages of the making of the ghetto transformed African American life in Chicago and redefined the nature of African American homicide. Even the initial flow of the southern migrants remade the city's African American community as the African American population of Chicago increased from 6,480 in 1880 to 44,103 in 1910 (see table 14.1).[17] Sex ratios evened in the process, changing from 1.25:1 in 1890 to 1.06:1 in 1910. Homicide was not a random act in turn-of-the-century Chicago. Thus, it did not simply change in step with the population. Moreover, although the formation of the ghetto affected most African American Chicagoans, the overwhelming majority of the city's African American residents neither committed murder nor were victims of murder. Nonetheless, the combination of population growth and racism produced new patterns of lethal violence. After 1890, for example, the character of African American homicide changed dramatically.

The rhythms of working-class life and plebeian culture shaped African American violence before 1890. African American killers were young, single, poor men, and they murdered people remarkably similar to themselves. Like their white counterparts during this period, African American murderers disproportionately killed their peers, and half of such lethal interactions occurred in local barrooms or on the streets of the city, often immediately outside local saloons.[18] Card games, tests of strengths, and drinking rituals often sparked such homicides. On January 22, 1884, according to the *Chicago Times*, " 'Big' Stephen Alexander, the 'emperor of craps,' was shot and killed instantly by 'Mush' Johnson in a gaming establishment frequented by colored gamblers." Alexander, the newspaper reported, "had been 'spoiling' for a fight for some time. He had vowed he would whip the 'mush-and-milk scoundrel' at the first opportunity."[19]

If white killers were young, poor, and likely to murder friends and acquaintances during leisure activities, African American killers were even younger, poorer, and more likely to murder friends and acquaintances in the context of working-class leisure. In fact, African American killers represented the youngest and the poorest group of murderers in the city; 63 percent were in their twenties, compared with 44 percent of white murderers, and 77 percent of African American killers worked in unskilled positions, compared with 27 percent of white killers. Brothels proved to be unusually violent sites for African American Chicagoans. Nearly one-fifth of the homicides committed by African Americans before 1890 occurred in houses of prostitution, compared with 3 percent of the homicides committed by white Chicagoans. Such fights most often reflected patterns of male sociability, involving two poor, young, African American men

TABLE 14.1
African American Population and Total Population of Chicago, 1880–1910

	African American Population	Total Population
1880	6,480	503,185
1890	14,271	1,099,850
1900	30,150	1,698,575
1910	44,103	2,185,283

engaging in drunken brawls or battling over games of chance, bar tabs, and challenges to status within the community.

In many ways, these patterns are not surprising. The city's African American community was very young and concentrated on the bottom tiers of the working class. In addition, single young men formed a larger segment of the African American population of Chicago before 1890 than they did of the overall population of the city. Men between twenty-five and twenty-nine (the prime age for murderers in the city), for example, constituted more than 17 percent of the African American population, compared with 11.6 percent of the total population.[20] Discrimination reinforced the link between age and violence for African American Chicagoans in myriad ways. With the complicity of municipal law enforcers, Chicagoans clustered rough saloons and brothels in African American areas, and African American residents disproportionately worked as porters, waiters, and bartenders in such unstable and often violent "hot spots." The Vice Commission of Chicago concluded in 1911 that "invariably the larger vice districts have been created within or near the settlements of colored people."[21] Furthermore, discrimination in employment often pushed African American city dwellers into dangerous work, such as prostitution and petty crime, contributing to the ways in which African American young men came into sustained contact with the most volatile social contexts in the late-nineteenth-century city.[22] Bagnios—as contemporaries often referred to brothels—concentrated rowdy, intoxicated young men, and drunken rows and knife fights were frequent occurrences in such institutions and, therefore, in African American neighborhoods. In short, the demographic and economic character of the African American community, in combination with the effects of discrimination and informal law-enforcement policies, exaggerated the potential for violence, thus contributing to an African American homicide rate between 1875 and 1890 that was more than six times the white homicide rate (see table 14.2).[23] As the historian Eric H. Monkkonen has noted, other groups with high proportions of young, single, poor, unattached men, particularly Irish immigrants in the middle decades of the nineteenth century, also had very high rates of homicide.[24]

Between one-quarter and one-third of African American killers during this period murdered white victims. These assailants were particularly young and poor, and they often found themselves in settings where avoiding violence was difficult. For example, on August 1, 1881, three white men spilled out of a local bar and "bull-dosed" Jerry Mulligan and an African American prostitute, pursuing the couple along Twelfth Street and pushing Mulligan off the sidewalk.[25]

TABLE 14.2
Chicago Homicide Rates (per 100,000 Residents)

	African American Homicide Rate	Chicago Homicide Rate
1875–1879	13.9	3.19
1880–1889	27.0	4.03
1890–1899	36.5	5.69
1900–1909	49.0	7.89

Unable to flee from the men and fearing—or perhaps recognizing—the intentions of his harassers, Mulligan "whipped out a great navy revolver, and blasted away at the three men," killing thirty-five-year-old Dennis Mahoney.[26] Mulligan's companion reported to the police that she and Mulligan "were crowded off the [side]walk and vilely abused before any shot was fired."[27] Largely as a consequence of such interracial incidents, African Americans killed strangers at double the rate of whites.[28] Put differently, when African Americans murdered white Chicagoans, an event disproportionately sparked by white aggression, their victims were strangers in 70 percent of cases. But when African Americans killed within racial lines, only 11 percent of their victims were strangers. Older African Americans struggled to avoid settings in which such defensive actions might become necessary. Neighbors regarded Giles Hunt, for instance, as "someone frequently known to avoid a quarrel by refusing an insult."[29] Although white, working-class Chicagoans often "abused" and attacked African American residents, the outcome in the Mulligan case was unusual. Most African Americans, like Hunt, probably employed strategies of risk aversion, and thus the overwhelming majority of homicides committed by African Americans before 1890 occurred within racial lines and involved other single young men who killed their peers.

The character of African American homicide, however, changed dramatically after 1890. No longer did homicide disproportionately spring from male, working-class leisure activities. Instead, African Americans in Chicago began to kill their wives and lovers. The proportion of homicides in which African Americans murdered their spouses, for example, nearly doubled after 1890, rising from 7 percent to 13 percent.[30] Before 1890, the rate of spouse homicide among African Americans was among the lowest among major groups in the city; after 1890, it was among the highest. The pattern of lovers' quarrels that resulted in murder followed an even more pronounced trajectory, rising from 0 percent of African American homicides before 1890 to 9 percent after 1890, which represented more than double the figure for the entire city. As a consequence of these shifts, the proportion of homicides in which men were assailants and women were victims also more than doubled between 1890 and 1910. Before 1890, male-on-female murders accounted for 12.5 percent of African American homicides; between 1890 and 1900, 17 percent; and between 1900 and 1910, 26 percent.

As domestic violence surged in the African American community, the locus of homicide changed accordingly. Before 1890, 6 percent of African American homicides occurred in the home, the lowest proportion among major groups in the city. After 1890, 38 percent of African American homicides occurred in the home, a figure above the overall average for the city. Not surprisingly, the proportion of murders occurring in barrooms and brothels contracted after 1890: the former from 19 percent to 15 percent; the latter from 19 percent to 4 percent. Other quantitative changes chart the same shift. The proportion of victims who were acquaintances—as opposed to friends, strangers, relatives, and others—of their killers fell from 43 percent between 1875 and 1890, the highest level in the city, to 28 percent between 1890 and 1910.

This pattern is revealed in a different way in changes in the apparent causes of lethal violence. Throughout the period from 1875 to 1910, jealousy sparked more homicides committed by African American Chicagoans than any other single cause.[31] Furthermore, the proportion of killings triggered by jealousy remained remarkably constant. Before 1890, jealousy was the identified cause of 23 percent of African American homicides; during the 1890s, 20 percent; and between 1900 and 1910, 24 percent. When such figures are disaggregated, however, a very different pattern emerges. Before 1890, 83 percent of these murderers involved male acquaintances. Young, single men killed one another in fights over girlfriends and prostitutes. But after 1890, the figure fell to 58 percent. Nearly one-third of the jealousy-inspired homicides after 1890s resulted in the death of a lover, compared with 0 percent during the earlier period. Instead of suitors battling one another in barroom and brothel rows, African American men increasingly grew jealous of their lovers or enraged when relationships ended, and they murdered their lovers. When Edward Decourcey, a night watchman, and Thomas Buckner, a porter, both "called on" nineteen-year-old Dora Perkins on the afternoon of December 15, 1895, the two suitors forced the woman to choose. Asked, "Whom do you love?" by Decourcey, Perkins responded, "Tom," whereupon Decourcey "drew a revolver from his overcoat pocket" and fired at the woman, instantly killing her.[32] Such episodes contributed to a sharp rise in male-on-female homicides after 1890, as fatal disputes increasingly emerged not from rituals of male competition and bachelor sociability but from tensions linked to courtship and family formation. In short, even while the proportion of murders attributed to jealousy remained unchanged, the social context of homicides resulting from jealousy shifted significantly, following a pattern comparable to the surge in domestic homicides, in murders occurring in the home, and in killings in which women were victims.

In one way, however, the character of African American homicide remained unchanged. The proportion and the nature of interracial murders fluctuated little between 1875 and 1910. Although racial tensions in the workplace soared during this era, as white workers associated African Americans with scab labor, such welling hostilities did not produce either an appreciable surge in homicides in the workplace or an increase in the proportion of interracial killings. Instead, divisive local strikes contributed to the deterioration of race relations in ways that increased violence within the city's African American community. During the teamsters' strike of 1905, for example, white Chicagoans, with the tacit support of local law enforcers, established a "dead line" beyond which African

American residents were "assaulted, spat upon, dragged from street cars and beat [sic] into insensibility by the striking teamsters and their followers," according to the *Chicago Broad Ax*.[33] Both African American and white newspapers reported that African American men increasingly armed themselves for protection. It is impossible to determine if such observations were accurate. Nonetheless, homicide patterns during 1905 provide intriguing clues about the relationship between racial tensions and violence. The proportion of murders in which African Americans killed whites barely fluctuated, though the percentage of homicides committed with firearms surged during 1905, including a sharp increase in the proportion of intraracial homicides and domestic killings committed with guns. The sample size for a single year is too modest to sustain more detailed quantitative analysis, but it seems likely that the guns secured by African Americans for protection during the tumult of 1905 were more often used at home and against spouses and lovers than on the streets, in the workplace, or against coworkers, striking teamsters, and their supporters. Far from altering the locus or the nature of African American homicide, the teamsters' strike and the workplace turmoil of the era reinforced the tensions that erupted within the African American community and thus contributed to broader shifts in the nature of violence; homicide became even more concentrated in the home and directed against family members, particularly women.

Changes in the demographic character of Chicago's African American community contributed to the new patterns of homicide. Although the Great Migration was just beginning during the late nineteenth century, it remade the city's population of African Americans. The flow of newcomers included many women, for example, and their arrival evened sex ratios within the African American community. Between 1890 and 1910, the ratio of male-to-female African Americans in their twenties became balanced, falling from 1.24:1 to 1.01:1. This contributed to two other demographic shifts. First, the proportion of the African American community comprising young men, in their prime for rough behavior, fell, reflecting the more diverse age structure of the newcomers.[34] Second, the proportion of unmarried young African Americans dropped sharply. In 1890, young African American men were married at a rate below the overall rate for the city; twenty years later, at a rate higher than that for the entire population of Chicago.[35]

Such changes should have affected the nature of homicide in turn-of-the-century Chicago. As the population of African American women in the city grew (both absolutely and relatively), the proportion of female homicide victims would be expected to rise. Similarly, in view of the fact that a higher percentage of young men were married, it is not surprising that women killed by their husbands constituted a higher percentage of homicide victims. Such demographic pressures also contributed to the proportion of homicides committed in the home. Moreover, the physical making of the ghetto generated enormous friction. As the African American community grew, became more culturally diverse, and endured increasing resistance and hostility from white residents, neighborhood life became more intense and more important. This process, not unexpectedly, sometimes produced lethal conflict. Although no African American homicides occurred as a result of fights between neighbors between 1875 and 1890, 10 percent of the murders between 1890 and 1910 involved neighborhood rows, 94 percent of which occurred within racial lines.

Demographic shifts, however, fail to explain fully the changing character of homicide in African American Chicago. The nature of murder did not mirror the new demographic composition of the community. The proportion of killers in their twenties exceeded the comparable proportion of the African American population of the city; this group made up 41 percent of assailants and 15 percent of Chicago's African American population.[36] Similarly, the increase in wife murder was far greater than the rise in the proportion of married young men in the African American community. The proportion of homicide victims killed by their spouses increased by 88 percent; the proportion of married men, by 24 percent. Moreover, the demographic transformation occurred gradually; in 1900, sex ratios remained uneven, and the proportion of unmarried African American young men continued to be higher than the overall rate for the city. The character of African American homicide, however, changed abruptly during the early 1890s and modestly between the early 1890s and 1910.[37] Changes in the size and the composition of the African American community during the late 1890s and the 1900s did not alter the basic patterns of lethal violence; the relationships between participants, the times, the locations, and the ages and occupations of assailants and victims barely fluctuated.

Although the nature of African American homicide remained largely unchanged after 1890, the homicide rate surged, nearly doubling between the 1880s and 1910—by 35 percent between the 1880s and 1890s, and by 34 percent between the 1890s and the 1900s (see table 14.2). This curious combination of relative continuity in structure from 1890 until 1910 but dramatic change in the rate is doubly remarkable in view of the social, economic, and institutional pressures that buffeted the city's African American community. The climate of race relations in Chicago deteriorated rapidly and profoundly during this era as African Americans were forced out of stable jobs and schools and forced into particularly poor housing. Welling discrimination, in short, produced an exploding rate of murder but no significant changes in the character of murder after 1890.

Both of the leading theoretical frameworks offer an explanation for this mix of continuity and flux. The unchanging post-1890 structure of conflict may point to the existence of a subculture of violence in turn-of-the-century Chicago. McKanna relies on this model to explain rising levels of African American homicide in Omaha during this period, arguing that the Great Migration increased the number of city dwellers embracing an ethic of southern honor.[38] Quick to anger and culturally disposed to use aggression to establish status and to resolve disputes, these newcomers transported violent, southern folkways to northern African American communities. Because they used aggression in structured (as opposed to random) ways, it is not surprising that the character of violence changed little in Chicago after 1890. The homicide rate, however, rose because the Great Migration increased the proportion of southern migrants in the city's African American community.

Contemporary observers often relied on a similar explanation, linking violence to the volatility of a subset of the newcomers. White newspaper editors and reporters typically viewed young, male African American newcomers as impulsive and dangerous, "walking around with chips on their shoulders and an arsenal on their persons."[39] Moreover, crime-beat reporters frequently characterized rows between African American men not as brawls, the term most often used to describe fights involving white men, but as "duels," a label chosen to evoke ties to southern society.[40] Other white Chicagoans formed similar impressions, associating African American newcomers with violent southern folkways.[41]

Middle-class African Americans and the editors of local African American newspapers also identified a connection between the violence in their community and the rough behavior of the newcomers, particularly unattached young men. In 1897, for example, "prominent" African American Chicagoans recommended the formation of an organization to look after the "young colored strangers" who "drift into channels of crime and wrongdoing."[42] The violence spawned by the teamsters' strike of 1905 elicited an even more conservative reaction from the African American *Broad Ax*, which viewed some among the migrants, specifically those hired to replace union workers, as wild and quick to resort to violence. They "resemble or act like desperadoes," the newspaper lamented, "and judging by the conduct of many of them they are ready to cut and shoot at the drop of a hat." The *Broad Ax* linked aggressive behavior to the character of the migrants "from the remote parts of the South—many of them representing the lowest and the toughest elements of the race, who are armed to the teeth and are ready to shoot at the slightest provocation."[43] As tensions increased during the teamsters' strike, the newspaper moved away from this explanation for the turmoil and placed increasing blame on the incendiary behavior of Marshall Field and other employers who recruited strikebreakers to the city. Moreover, civic leaders often sought to protect their community's reputation either by holding outsiders responsible for problems or by using their influence to restrain newcomers whose behavior was thought to jeopardize the standing of the group.[44] Community-building impulses notwithstanding, many prominent African American Chicagoans expressed concern about the "a bad and lawless element" of young men among newcomers.[45] Such characterizations of violence appear to support Wolfgang and Ferracuti's—or McKanna's—framework.

Although the subculture of violence model is almost as difficult to disprove as it is to prove, the weight of quantitative evidence from turn-of-the-century Chicago homicides challenges its explanatory power. Even if young, unattached "roughens and sluggers," fresh from the South, were hired as scabs, these newcomers were not the principal killers in African American Chicago after 1890.[46] Though not southerners, pre-1890 African American murderers were young, single, and poor, and they employed violence in the social contexts, such as barrooms and brothels, where aggression was often used to affirm status. Their post-1890 counterparts, however, tended to be slightly older and slightly wealthier. The proportion of killers older than thirty, for example, increased from 24 percent before 1890 to 41 percent after 1890. The economic status of murderers also rose slowly. Before 1890, 82 percent of African American killers worked in unskilled positions, and during the 1890s, African American assailants remained similarly clustered in low-blue-collar work. After 1900, however, murderers were slightly less concentrated at the bottom of the occupational structure; 71 percent of the assailants held unskilled jobs. The scale of this change was modest, though in view of the declining economic conditions in the African American community—both as a result of the influx of unskilled newcomers and as a result of the employment discrimination that sharply depressed the fortunes of African American artisans and entrepreneurs—this small shift is significant. In short, killers were not the youngest or the poorest men in the community.

Changes in the locus and in the nature of homicide after 1890 provide powerful evidence to challenge the subculture of violence model. Wolfgang and Ferracuti's work, as well as McKanna's and most other applications of the model, ground the subculture to the oppositional values generated in the bachelor world of barrooms, street-corner socializing, and brothels. Discrimination in turn-of-the-century Chicago should have nurtured and sustained such a subculture. Public policy during this period, after all, concentrated tough saloons, gambling dens, and houses of prostitution in African American neighborhoods, where such institutions operated with virtual impunity. Yet the proportion of murders committed in these centers of the urban underworld plummeted after 1890. Homicide in the African American community left the world of male sociability, moving rapidly into the domestic realm. Moreover, the new locus for African American homicide was not consistent with a subculture of violence. Honor-based violence occurred in the public view because it served to affirm status by establishing or safeguarding the reputations of the participants. But in Chicago after 1890, murderers increasingly killed their victims in private settings, beyond the gaze of peers. Similarly, the sharp increase in the proportion of assailants who murdered their wives and lovers is also at odds with a model emphasizing the inversion of middle-class norms and values. The men who killed their spouses during domestic rows seemed to be struggling to attain middle-class ideals of respectability, which celebrated family life as the linchpin of personal fulfillment. Finally, patterns of African American homicide after 1890 challenge the notion that southern traditions shaped ghetto violence in one additional respect. According to recent scholarship, African Americans in the rural South during the late nineteenth century rarely killed their spouses.[47] Yet, as the number of African American Chicagoans from the rural South increased, the rate of uxoricide (the killing of a woman by her husband) also increased. Thus, the locations and the contexts in which homicides occurred, as well as the character of the participants, were not consistent with the subculture of violence model or with its southern, honor-based variation.

Far from taking the distinctive character associated with a subculture of violence, African American homicide assumed forms and experienced shifts that paralleled white homicide, though the rate of American American homicide was considerably higher. Like their African American counterparts, white killers in Chicago disproportionately struck in bars and alleys until the 1890s, when homicide moved to the home. For African Americans, the patterns of violence were not so much distinctive as exaggerated. Before 1890, white killers tended to be young, poor, single, and engaged in barroom fights; African American killers were younger, poorer, more often single, and more likely than white murderers to engage in lethal rows in saloons and bagnios. Similarly, after 1890, whites increasingly killed relatives and committed homicide in the home. The pattern for African Americans, once again, was more pronounced, with a higher proportion of murderers killing their spouses and a higher proportion of homicides occurring in the home.

But despite these similarities, African American homicide was distinctive in its frequency. During the late 1870s, for example, the African American homicide rate was 4.5 times the white homicide rate for the city. Three decades later, the African American homicide rate had more than tripled and was 6.5 times the white rate for Chicago. Because the character of African American violence did not reflect an alternative culture or an inverted value system, dislocation models provide a more compelling explanation for the homicide patterns. Many scholars have documented the increasing scale of discrimination in employment and housing in Chicago during this period. Thus, at least at a macrocosmic level, dislocation and rates of homicide moved together in turn-of-the-century Chicago. Nor was this relationship lost on contemporaries. In 1907, for example, W. S. Scarbourough concluded that whites assumed responsibility for African American criminality. "Our race is discriminated against and our people are forced out of the best industrial fields," Scarbourough explained to a group assembled at the Bethel A. M. E. Church. "We are burned at the stake, lynched, and hunted, and the negro would be more than an angel to withstand such treatment."[48] But why would social and economic dislocation produce both a sharp rise in rates of homicide and a shift in lethal violence away from the bars, alleys, and brothels, away from the rhythms of male leisure activities, and toward homes and family life?

The specific character of African American homicide yields clues about the ways in which social and economic dislocation generated intragroup conflict. As levels of discrimination surged, some African American Chicagoans lashed out violently more often than did members of other ethnic groups. Put differently, if dislocation generated violence, then it seems likely that the segments of a community with increasing rates of homicide felt the dislocation with particular force.

Although it is impossible to determine the full impact of racism on African American Chicagoans, discrimination simultaneously contributed to violence and directed aggressive behavior within the African American community in two concrete ways. First, discrimination in the workplace disrupted family life and gender roles, particularly for young men. African American men who were slightly older, slightly wealthier, and more often married or involved in romantic relationships than the norm confronted a particularly unsettling combination of social and cultural pressures; the gap between expectation and reality was unusually great for members of this group. Like other African American newcomers, they arrived in Chicago from southern states with high hopes, inflated by newspaper accounts and other reports of conditions in the North, just as social and economic conditions began to deteriorate. Moreover, fragmentary evidence indicates that these men, many of them semiskilled workers, were clustered in the positions hit most immediately by changing racial conventions. Some, for example, worked as cooks at a time when white restaurateurs started to deny such positions to African Americans. Charles Rollins, who murdered his wife and seriously wounded his sister-in-law on July 17, 1904, operated a tailor shop just as such establishments were losing their white patrons. Men like Rollins, perhaps even more than their less-skilled friends and neighbors, felt their economic status slipping.

Age and marital status reinforced such pressures. The African American Chicagoans who contributed disproportionately to the swelling rate of homicide endured widespread discrimination in employment as they tried to establish family lives. Many scholars have argued that the declining or insecure status of working-class men during the nineteenth century produced rising levels of domestic violence.[49] If deskilling could incite Chicago butchers to abuse their wives, it hardly seems surprising that the profound dislocation experienced by semi-skilled African American men, as they tried to marry and form families, resulted in domestic conflict. Rollins, for example, killed his wife after she separated from him and refused to return.[50] By jeopardizing the economic independence of men such as Rollins, racial hostility probably challenged their sense of class status.

At the same time, discrimination also challenged their sense of masculinity. Black male Chicagoans confronted new and rising difficulties in supporting their families and were often compelled to rely on the incomes of their wives. Scraps of evidence from homicide cases indicate that uxoricide often erupted from these tensions. Fifty-one-year-old Henry Russell, an unemployed waiter, stabbed his wife, Carrie, to death after a row triggered by his difficulty in supporting the family. "Mrs. Russell," the *Chicago Record* reported, "had been compelled to take in washing to sustain herself and through this cause frequent quarrels had occurred."[51] Likewise, on October 27, 1905, Daniel Francis, enraged at his wife's refusal to live with him, shot and killed her. Forty-five-year-old Myra Francis had left him in July, she explained to a friend, because he had "failed to support her."[52] Ophelia Williams died under similar circumstances. Angelo Williams murdered her on March 13, 1908, after she "refused to live with her husband any longer," charging that he "failed to properly provide" for her.[53] In short, absolute dearth did not produce the rising rate of homicide in the African American community. Nor did the drunken behavior of wild young newcomers disproportionately account for the surge. Instead, discrimination in the workplace, by disrupting the family economy and thus young married men's sense of authority within the household, contributed to violence in turn-of-the-century Chicago.[54]

Second, discrimination in housing reinforced the tensions welling in the household. African American Chicagoans confronted myriad problems in securing adequate housing. White Chicagoans, relying on legal devices such as restrictive covenants and nonlegal devices such as fire bombings, confined a growing population of African Americans to a shrinking section of the city—the so-called black belt. This process produced high population densities in the emerging ghetto. Moreover, landlords typically charged African Americans higher rents than white tenants, often as much as 50 percent higher.[55] As a result of the combination of low wages and high rents, African American families took in roomers or boarders at a higher rate than did other groups.[56]

Crowding and the presence of roomers generated particular instability in African American life. Such conditions, like economic problems, challenged the authority of male heads of households, particularly young heads of households. The shock of such high-density living was probably unusually unsettling for men who had come from rural—and thus sparsely settled—areas. Just as these men found that discrimination in the workplace undercut their control of the family economy, they jostled with neighbors and lodgers for control over the domestic realm. Such discord often triggered homicides. After 1890, American American homicides occurring within the home involved neighbors 50 percent more often than did white homicides occurring in the home. Poverty and economic insecurity exaggerated the potential for these battles, as neighbors borrowed money and household goods from one another. A dispute "over the ownership of a can of coffee," for example, sparked the murder of thirty-six-year-old Elizabeth Girod. James Pauly awoke from a deep sleep to the sound of his wife quarreling with Girod in the kitchen of the apartment that they shared. Gun in hand, Pauly entered room and "fired a shot that passed through the heart of Mrs. Girod."[57]

The necessity of having boarders generated tensions that occasionally resulted in violence. In some instances, the presence of a roomer interceding in domestic disputes challenged a man's sense of authority in his home. Moreover, boarders were sometimes the focal point for jealousy murders, as husbands responded with violence to the love affairs—or perceived love affairs—between their wives and roomers, or as boarders lashed out at the married women with whom they shared crowded tenements. Thirty-three-year-old John Hampton, a boarder in the home of Mrs. Roselia Evans, for example, murdered his landlady in 1902 because she refused to return his affections.[58] In other cases, the stress of living in densely packed apartments generated lethal violence. Two boarders bludgeoned to death forty-year-old Ellen Randolph with a "big lemon-squeezer." Randolph had overheard the men discussing the unseemly circumstances that had led to their migration to Chicago. She then "warned Kate Davis, a young colored girl, against" one of the men. Shortly thereafter, the two roomers murdered Randolph in her bedroom in the Dearborn Street apartment they shared.[59] The Chicago Commission on Race Relations perceptively observed that "housing must be considered as an important element in the environmental causes of crime."[60]

In sum, for all Chicagoans, poverty, crowding, and uncertainty sparked turmoil and produced frustration. For African American Chicagoans, however, such tensions were exaggerated as a consequence of discrimination in employment and housing. But poverty and crowding did not, by themselves, produce violence. Rather, by disrupting men's role as suitors and as heads of households, these tensions generated friction that dramatically increased the potential for violence. Thus, discrimination in employment and in housing indirectly challenged men's sense of status at a crucial point in the life cycle. Racism, therefore, upset gender roles in ways that sparked the surge in uxoricide, in homicide within the home, and in homicide within the African American community.

A rich and sophisticated scholarly literature has established a strong statistical correlation between dislocation and violence, though the relationship between correlation and causation remains murky. The selective nature of violent behavior and the shifts in the character of Chicago homicide between 1875 and 1910 provide clues about the ways in which dislocation sparked conflict. Most African American Chicagoans did not respond with violence to their deteriorating social and economic circumstances, but the men who disproportionately committed murder experienced the discrimination and dislocation particularly profoundly. Other African American Chicagoans no doubt felt anger and experienced frustration, but the precise cluster of pressures affected them in ways less likely to trigger violence. To men close to the rough-and-tumble world of bachelor life yet ready to make a transition in life cycle and become heads of households, the pressures from racial discrimination in turn-of-the-century Chicago proved to be especially jolting. Arriving in the city with high hopes, facing deteriorating housing and employment prospects, and enduring consequent challenges to their roles in the family and in the household, these newcomers, more than other groups of African American Chicagoans, turned to violence.

The nature of African American violence in turn-of-the-century Chicago was ironic for two reasons. First, despite the distinctive experience born of racism, African American homicide, though occurring at a much higher rate than white homicide, was remarkably similar in character to white homicide. African American Chicagoans were not the reckless and pathological criminals described by conservative observers. Rather, they resorted to violence in the same kinds of social circumstances as did white residents of the city, who also lashed out at loved ones with increasing frequency during this period. Second, the pressures generated by poverty, discrimination, and insecurity exploded principally within the city's black belt. Moreover, as discrimination increased, the rate of intraracial homicide exploded. In short, racism did not spark random acts of violence. Rather, in the age in which the the African American ghetto first took shape in cities, discrimination generated violence by undercutting economic and domestic stability, thus profoundly disrupting the marrow of household life.

NOTES

1. For a few examples of this literature, see Darnell F. Hawkins, ed., *Ethnicity, Race, and Crime* (Albany: State University of New York Press, 1995); Edward S. Shihadeh and Darrell J. Steffensmeier, "Economic Inequality, Family Disruption, and Urban Black Violence," *Social Forces* 73 (1994): 729–51; Robert Nash Parker, "Poverty, Subculture of Violence, and Type of Homicide," *Social Forces* 67 (1989): 983–1007; Steven F. Messner, "Regional and Racial Effects on the Urban Homicide Rate," *American Journal of Sociology* 88 (1983): 997–1007.

2. According to a recent study, based on data from 1987 and 1988, an African American man's lifetime risk of becoming a victim of homicide is 1 chance in 24.1, compared with a white man's risk of 1 chance in 161.3 and a white woman's risk of 1 chance in 384.6. See Albert J. Reiss, Jr., and Jeffrey A. Roth, eds., *Understanding and Preventing Violence* (Washington, D.C.: National Academy Press, 1993), 62–63. Proponents of the view that the roots of modern African American violence can be traced to the turn of the century argue that recent conditions, such as the economic deterioration of the inner city, have exaggerated or contributed to a long-established patterns of poverty and dislocation. See Roger Lane, *Roots of Violence in Black Philadelphia* (Cambridge: Harvard University Press, 1986).

3. Marvin E. Wolfgang and Franco Ferracuti, *The Subculture of Violence* (London: Tavistock, 1967).

4. See, for example, Bertram Wyatt-Brown, *Southern Honor* (New York: Oxford University Press, 1982); Dickson D. Bruce, Jr., *Violence and Culture in the Antebellum South* (Austin: University of Texas Press, 1979); Raymond D. Gastil, "Homicide and a Regional Culture of Violence," *American Sociological Review* 36 (1971): 412–27; Sheldon Hackney, "Southern Violence," *American Historical Review* 74 (1969): 906–25; William Lynwood Montell, *Killings* (Lexington: University Press of Kentucky, 1986).

5. Clare V. McKanna, Jr., "Seeds of Destruction: Homicide, Race, and Justice in Omaha, 1880–1920," *Journal of American Ethnic History* 14 (1994): 65–90.

6. For a few examples of this literature, see Sandra J. Ball-Rokeach, "Values and Violence: A Test of the Subculture of Violence Thesis," *American Sociological Review* 38 (1973): 736–49; Darnell F. Hawkins, "Black and White Homicide Differentials," in *Homicide among Black Americans*, ed. Darnell F. Hawkins (Lanham, Md.: University Press of America, 1986), 119–26; Patricia L. McCall, Kenneth C. Land, and Lawrence E. Cohen, "Violent Criminal Behavior: Is There a General and Continuing Influence of the South?" *Social Science Research* 21 (1992): 286–310.

7. Lane, *Roots of Violence in Black Philadelphia*; Lane, "On the Social Meaning of Homicide Trends in America," in *Violence in America*, ed. Ted Robert Gurr (Newbury Park, Calif.: Sage, 1989), 55–79. Also see Roger Lane, *William Dorsey's Philadelphia and Ours* (New York: Oxford University Press, 1991).

8. For example, see James W. Balkwell, "Ethnic Inequality and the Rate of Homicide," *Social Forces* 69 (1990): 53–70; Miles D. Harer and Darrell Steffensmeier, "The Differing Effects of Economic Inequality on Black and White Rates of Violence," *Social Forces* 70 (1992): 1035–54; Kenneth C. Land, Patricia L. McCall, and Lawrence E. Cohen, "Structural Covariates of Homicide Rates: Are There Any Invariances across Time and Space?" *American Journal of Sociology* 95 (1990): 922–63; Steven F. Messner and Reid M. Golden, "Racial Inequality and Racially Disaggregated Homicide Rates: An Assessment of Alternative Theoretical Explanations," *Criminology* 30 (1992): 421–47; Steven F. Messner, "Economic Discrimination and Societal Homicide Rates: Further Evidence on the Cost of Inequality,"

American Sociological Review 54 (1987): 597–611; Robert J. Sampson, "Urban Black Violence: The Effect of Male Joblessness and Family Disruption," *American Journal of Sociology* 93 (1987): 348–82.

9. See Allan H. Spear, *Black Chicago* (Chicago: University of Chicago Press, 1967); William M. Tuttle, Jr., *Race Riot* (New York: Oxford University Press, 1975); Thomas Lee Philpott, *The Slum and the Ghetto* (New York: Oxford University Press, 1978); James R. Grossman, *Land of Hope* (Chicago: University of Chicago Press, 1989); Nicholas Lemann, *The Promised Land* (New York: Knopf, 1991).

10. *Homicides and Important Events, Chicago Police Department, 1870–1920* (microfilm). Entries in the log are relatively brief, providing the names, often the ages, the races, often the ethnicities, and occasionally the occupations of those involved, as well as the location and the time of the homicide, a short description of the circumstances leading to the homicide, and a summary of the arrests and the legal disposition of the case.

11. By basing my analysis on the police records, rather than on court records, I have reduced the principal biases built into the criminal justice system. The identity of killers and their victims was seldom in question for the police or for reporters. Whether the killers acted justifiably, however, was very much in doubt and was profoundly affected by race-, class-, and gender-based assumptions. Thus, an analysis based on convictions would have been significantly distorted by the cultural perspectives of lawyers, judges, prosecutors, and jurors. My database, therefore, is based on police reports identifying the alleged perpetrators—not on convicted killers. It is indeed possible that the police and local reporters sometimes incorrectly identified the killers, though most Chicago murderers were found, gun or knife in hand, standing over the bodies of their victims.

12. In theory, the ledger included every homicide occurring in the city. Some cases, however, do not appear in the log, though it included the overwhelming majority of homicides, and by the turn of the century the police ledger is virtually complete—when measured against other sources, such as the annual tallies compiled by the coroner and the year-end figures published by city newspapers. I found newspaper accounts of three-fourths of the homicides.

13. Between 1875 and 1909, African Americans killed sixty-five whites in the city, and whites killed forty-six African Americans. It is unlikely that the police records overlooked white-on-black killings. Rather, the police investigated each homicide, and white assailants often would not be indicted or would be acquitted.

14. See, for example, Frantz Fanon, *The Wretched of the Earth* (1961; reprint, New York: Grove Press, 1963); Daniel Touro Linger, *Dangerous Encounters: Meanings of Violence in a Brazilian City* (Stanford: Stanford University Press, 1992).

15. For the 1920s figure, see H. C. Brearley, *Homicide in the United States* (1932; reprint, Montclair, N.J.: Patterson Smith, 1969), 218.

16. During the seven five-year periods between 1875 and 1909, intraracial homicides constituted 75 percent, 56 percent, 75 percent, 80 percent, 79 percent, 80 percent, and 78 percent of the homicides committed by African Americans. Except for the 1880–84 period, the proportion fluctuated between 75 percent and 80 percent in every five-year period.

17. Demographic data were culled from decennial reports of the United State Census Office. See *Compendium of the Eleventh Census: 1890. Part I* (Washington, D.C.: GPO, 1892), 443, 544, 674–75, 814–15; *Report of the Population of the United States at the Eleventh Census: 1890. Part I* (Washington, D.C.: GPO, 1895), 374–75, 884; *Census Reports: Twelfth Census of the United States, Taken in the Year 1900. Population: Part II* (Washington, D.C.: GPO, 1902), 126, 314; *Thirteenth Census of the United States Taken in the Year 1910: Abstract of the Census*

(Washington, D.C.: GPO, 1913), 104, 139, 164, 250; *Thirteenth Census of the United States Taken in the Year 1910. Population: Vol. I* (Washington, D.C.: GPO, 1913), 208, 278, 439, 619, 643.

18. For an analysis of overall patterns of homicide for the city, as well as a discussion of working-class violence, see Jeffrey S. Adler, " 'My Mother-in-Law Is to Blame, But I'll Walk on Her Neck Yet': Homicide in Late Nineteenth-Century Chicago," *Journal of Social History* 31 (winter 1997): 253–76.

19. *Chicago Times*, January 23, 1884.

20. For studies linking race, age, and marital status to rates of homicide, see Robert J. Sampson, "Race and Criminal Violence: A Demographically Disaggregated Analysis of Urban Homicide," *Crime and Delinquency* 31 (1985): 47–82; Steven F. Messner and Robert J. Sampson, "The Sex Ratio, Family Disruption, and Rates of Violent Crime: The Paradox of Demographic Structure," *Social Forces* 69 (1991): 693–713.

21. The Vice Commission of Chicago, *The Social Evil in Chicago* (Chicago: Gunthorp-Warren Printing, 1911), 38–39. Also see Chicago Commission on Race Relations, *The Negro in Chicago* (Chicago: University of Chicago Press, 1922), 343; John Landesco, *Organized Crime in Chicago* (1929; reprint, with an introduction by Mark H. Haller, Chicago: University of Chicago Press, 1968), 32; Herbert Asbury, *Gem of the Prairies* (1940; reprint, with an introduction by Perry R. Duis, DeKalb: Northern Illinois University Press, 1986), 109, 122; Grossman, *Land of Hope*, 170. This pattern was not unique to Chicago. See James Borchert, *Alley Life in Washington* (Urbana: University of Illinois Press, 1980), 188; Kenneth L. Kusmer, *A Ghetto Takes Shape* (Urbana: University of Illinois Press, 1976), 48.

22. Lane, *Roots of Violence in Black Philadelphia*, 95–143. Also see George A. Levesque, "Black Crime and Crime Statistics in Antebellum Boston," *Australian Journal of Politics and History* 25 (1979): 220; McKanna, "Seeds of Destruction," 71, 78; James Oliver Horton and Lois E. Horton, *Black Bostonians* (New York: Holmes and Meier, 1979), 35.

23. The African American homicide rate between 1875 and 1890 was 23.4; the white, 3.58. McKanna found similar rates of 36.5 and 3.8 for Omaha during the 1880s. See McKanna, "Seeds of Destruction," 77.

24. Eric H. Monkkonen, "Murder in Nineteenth-Century New York" (paper presented at the Annual Meeting of the Social Science History Association, Atlanta, October 15, 1994; Monkkonen, "Diverging Homicide Rates: England and the United States, 1850–1875," in Gurr, *Violence in America*, 88–93; Monkkonen, "Racial Factors in New York City Homicides, 1800–1874," in Hawkins, *Ethnicity, Race, and Crime*, 107–8.

25. *Chicago Times*, August 2, 1881.

26. Ibid.

27. *Chicago Daily News*, August 2, 1881.

28. African Americans were killed by strangers before 1890 less than half as often as whites.

29. *Chicago Times*, October 7, 1884.

30. The proportion increased slightly during the early twentieth century. After 1900, 16 percent of African American homicides involved the murder of a spouse.

31. These calculations rely on the categorization and the language of police investigators, checked against newspaper descriptions of the murders. The biases of both Chicago policemen and local reporters no doubt distorted these assessments, though such distortions affected the entire span of the records, thus permitting me to examine change over time in the categorizations.

32. *Chicago Record*, December 16, 1895.

33. *Chicago Broad Ax*, May 27, 1905.

34. In 1890, men between the ages of twenty and twenty-nine made up 17.1 percent of the African American community; in 1910, 12.9 percent. For the entire population of the city, the figure changed little during this period, falling from 11.6 percent in 1890 to 11.5 percent in 1910.

35. Between 1890 and 1910, the proportion of African American men aged twenty to thirty-four who were married—or widowed—rose from 39 percent to 50 percent; for the entire population of Chicago, the proportion rose from 45 percent in 1890 to 46 percent in 1910. For African Americans older than fifteen, the proportion rose from 49 percent in 1890 to 61 percent in 1910. The comparable figure for the entire population of the city increased from 56 percent in 1890 to 58 percent in 1910.

36. Men in their twenties made up 35 percent of all killers in the city between 1890 and 1910. Male residents between twenty and twenty-nine composed 11.6 percent of the population of Chicago in 1890, 9.8 percent in 1900, and 11.5 percent in 1910.

37. Although this transition occurred abruptly, it produced some intriguing short-term patterns, most notably evident in an upsetting of gender relations in Chicago. Before 1890, women committed 6.5 percent of African American homicides. During the 1890s, however, women committed 20 percent of African American homicides.

38. McKanna, "Seeds of Destruction," 80–84.

39. *Chicago Record*, May 24, 1899.

40. See, for example, *Chicago Herald*, February 20, 1893; *Chicago Tribune*, May 31, 1902, and August 17, 1908.

41. Chicago Commission on Race Relations, *Negro in Chicago*, 329.

42. *Chicago Record*, June 19, 1897; *Chicago Tribune*, June 22, 1897.

43. *Chicago Broad Ax*, May 6, 1905.

44. For a speech by the Rev. H. E. Stewart on this issue, see *Chicago Tribune*, April 17, 1908. For a fascinating analysis of a related phenomenon, see Hazel V. Carby, "Policing the Black Woman's Body in an Urban Context," *Critical Inquiry* 18 (1992): 738–55. Immigration history is replete with studies of comparable tensions between different waves of immigrants or different segments of the immigrant community.

45. *Chicago Tribune*, April 17, 1908.

46. For the "roughens and sluggers" description, see *Chicago Broad Ax*, May 20, 1905. Although most African American Chicagoans, particularly after 1900, were newcomers to the city, the men most visible as strikebreakers were probably younger, poorer, and less often married than were the men who committed homicide.

47. Gilles Vandal, "Black Violence in Post–Civil War Louisiana," *Journal of Interdisciplinary History* 25 (1994): 61.

48. *Chicago Tribune*, December 30, 1907. For a similar assessment, see George Edmund Haynes, "Conditions among Negroes in the Cities," *Annals of the American Academy of Political and Social Science* 49 (1913): 115.

49. See, for example, Pamela Haag, " 'The Ill-Use of a Wife': Patterns of Working-Class Violence in Domestic and Public New York City, 1860–1880," *Journal of Social History* 25 (1992): 447–77.

50. *Chicago Tribune*, July 18, 1904.

51. *Chicago Record*, August 8, 1894.

52. *Chicago Tribune*, October 28, 1905.

53. *Chicago Broad Ax*, March 14, 1908. According to the newspaper account, Mrs. Williams objected to the lack of support at the same time that her husband "cruelly" treated her.

54. The criminal justice system reinforced this sense of frustration and loss of control.

Although most homicides in the city resulted from fights between two participants, Chicago policemen responded to African American homicides with massive "sweeps" of the city's black belt. Believing that aggressive African Americans uniquely imperiled public safety, local law enforcers frequently rounded up dozens of young men after murders (particularly after interracial killings), often charging them with disorderly conduct or the illegal possession of a weapon (see, for instance, *Chicago Tribune*, May 8, 1893, and May 23, 1899; *Chicago Record*, May 24, 1899). Discrimination permeated every layer of the legal system, though nowhere more starkly than in the disposition of capital cases. African Americans were 11 percent of killers and 36 percent of those executed. After 1895, African Americans were executed at five times the rate for whites. The gap was most pronounced when homicide crossed racial lines; 3 percent of African Americans charged with intraracial murder were hanged, compared with 19 percent of African Americans charged with interracial murder.

55. Alzada P. Comstock, "Chicago Housing Conditions," *American Journal of Sociology* 18 (1912): 244–55. Also see Philpott, *Slum and the Ghetto*, 146–61.

56. Chicago Commission on Race Relations, *Negro in Chicago*, 341; Comstock, "Chicago Housing Conditions," 245.

57. *Chicago Broad Ax*, February 29, 1908.

58. Ibid., January 18, 1902.

59. *Chicago Tribune*, February 21, 22, 1896, and May 16, 1896.

60. Chicago Commission on Race Relations, *Negro in Chicago*, 341.

Kicking the stranger out of the local bar. Edward Winslow Martin, *The Secrets of the Great City* (Atlanta: Jones Brothers, 1868), 541.

Chapter Fifteen

Homosociality and the Legal Sanction of Male Heterosexual Aggression in the Early Twentieth Century

John C. Pettegrew

In June 1898, Mary Balderson of rural central Wisconsin, sued for a divorce from her husband, charging that his "licentious conduct . . . impair[ed] her health and endanger[ed] her life." Balderson's petition specified that her husband, Frank, required her "to submit to sexual intercourse" three or four times a day and "by reason of his treatment toward her in this regard caused several miscarriages." The petition added that when she tried to resist, he became violent in other ways, on one occasion throwing her "into a chair with such force as to injure her and produce a miscarriage." Mary Balderson's petition for divorce was granted because many civil court judges by the late nineteenth century recognized marital rape and sexual abuse by the husband as legitimate grounds for dissolving a marriage.[1]

Mary Balderson's subjection to Frank Balderson's physical abuse in marriage and her subsequent divorce from him provides a good starting point for considering the legal mediation of masculine heterosexual violence. The ability of a wife to sue successfully for divorce in such occurrences is representative of the slow progress women made in wresting some power from the male-dominated legal system. At the same time, that legal system tended to decriminalize the violence of men when it occurred within the institution of marriage. Legal sanction of heterosexual aggression and violence would be particularly pronounced in the late-nineteenth-century development of the marital-rape exemption and the heat-of-passion defense. These legal doctrines have roots back to the seventeenth and eighteenth centuries in the writings of William Blackstone and Matthew Hale, and earlier in the ancient genesis of patriarchy. But a difference at the turn of the twentieth century is that this legal standard was applied in a new context of heterosexual culture, one in which the ancient laws of the man's having an exclusive right to possess the sexuality of his wife gained new currency in a modern sexual culture that highlighted and privileged the primal expression of male heterosexuality.

Homosociality and Heterosexuality

Perhaps the most valuable finding of the first wave of men's history is that masculine self-understanding, behavior, and the political structures that have organized, supported, and privileged male social experience are all generated not so much out of an essential drive to dominate women but, rather, from an individual man's concern about his place among other men. To be sure, homosociality works from and depends on the routine subordination of women; sexual inequality, though, is something of a given in the perfect homosocial world. If a man can assume the systematic taking of female rights, autonomy, and volition, then women are no longer the subjects of political contestation but, instead, the sexual objects of intramasculine competition.[2]

Although the struggle among men for homosocial status and prestige has taken place on many fronts, all are connected by the mandate of performance and the concomitant fear of being judged less than a "real man." This is where homosociality and masculinity come together. In fact, fear of public emasculation is one of the best definitions of masculinity—a turn of the century *epistemology* of anxiety and potential loss in which the primary motivation becomes avoidance of shame before other men. Homosociality both ensures a seemingly constant specter of failure and humiliation among individual men while also supporting the wholesale empowerment of men as a social group over women.

Masculine empowerment and dominance have never been total or complete; although men have achieved considerable success in separating women out from equal access and social standing. In this regard, homosociety can be understood simply as the opposite of feminism or, more specifically, that which feminism has been designed to oppose. Much of the history of sex-gender relations in modern America can be seen as an elaborate, multifaceted struggle by women against the historical constant of the homosocial perpetuation of male power. Feminists seek not only to open up male institutions to women but also to subvert homosociety by reconstructing the base of all sociosexual relations.

This historical conflict between homosociety and feminism provides a valuable way to get at the sociolegal struggle between women and men in heterosexual relations. On the one hand, U.S. history has seen the rise of female sexual subjectivity and women's slow, incomplete accrual of power both to decide when and if they will enter into sexual relations with a man and to control their person and body throughout that experience. On the other hand, there is a homosocial model of heterosexuality, replete with networks of male-based institutions, laws, and conventions governing access and distribution of women among men. The feminist anthropologist Gayle Rubin has called this series of arrangements "traffic in women," a masculine-orientated "sexual system" that works on the assumption that women are devoid of sexual power or rights. For Rubin, women are subject to the "political economy" of heterosexuality—what she defines as a "systematic social apparatus that takes up females as raw materials and fashions domesticated women as products."[3] Men, as Rubin emphasizes, are the agents and beneficiaries of this heterosexual economy: "If it is women who are being transacted, then it is the men who give and take them who are linked, the woman being the conduit of a relationship rather than a partner to it." Women become, in Michael Kimmel's word, a type of "currency" among men, with heterosexual contact as the most material coin of that exchange.[4]

If the concept of homosocial competition and status seeking is added to Rubin's description of "traffic in women," we move closer to understanding the history of heterosexual relations from a masculinist perspective. Physical power and the threat and use of male-on-male violence is one determinant of heterosexual status within homosociety. This physical determinant also locates itself in more generalized and diffused formulations of homosocial difference, many of which can be found in American society at large. Indeed, the triumvirate of race, class, and gender works quite effectively in locating and analyzing the standards of male heterosexual power and success.

Race would have to be considered one of the most determinative factors in male hierarchy, as white men responding to the perceived sexual threat of free African American men and the competition they embodied for white women attempted to control black male sexuality through lynching and other forms of violent intimidation. The limitation of black male sexuality also happened in the everyday establishment of non-expressly-violent practices and conventions of racial segregation, but it is the lynch mob that best illustrates homosocial power in action. In killing thousands of African American men for rumored sexual transgressions, these cells of white masculine authority effectively policed and controlled access to women and also worked to contain the economic and social power of a race trying to realize some measure of autonomy and freedom.

Class, along with the subsidiary factors of material wealth and social standing, would be a second key homosocial determinant of an individual man's heterosexual capacity. Traditionally, class background and economic well-being have helped establish patterns of courtship and marriage. By the turn of the century, though, economic privilege could lead to different types of leverage over male competitors as powers of spending and consumption became more and more consequential within the burgeoning heterosexual dating cultures of modern urban America.

The ideological formulation of manhood included, in addition to the dichotomy of masculinity and femininity, a new equation of *difference*. By the end of the nineteenth century, a man could no longer distinguish himself solely from women; homosexuality would also have to be negated from his person. A man would not be fully masculine until he displayed explicit heterosexuality in his manner, dress, and demeanor, as well as his sexual behavior. The late-nineteenth-century bifurcation of homo- and heterosexuality and its impact on normative standards of masculinity has been delineated by George Chauncey in his valuable study *Gay New York* (1994). "[A]s queer men began to define their difference from other men on the basis of their homosexuality," Chauncey explained, " 'normal' men began to define their difference from queers on the basis of their renunciation of any sentiments or behavior that might be marked as homosexual." As a result of this homo-heterosexual bifurcation, Chauncey argued, sexuality "emerged as a distinct domain of personhood and an independent basis for the assertion of manliness. Chauncey concluded, "Middle-class men increasingly conceived of their sexuality—their heterosexuality, or exclusive desire for women—as one of the hallmarks of a real man."[5]

"Real men" needed not only to desire a woman but *to express* that desire in ways that made other men supremely aware of it—the more public, exaggerated, and demonstrative the better. Within the context of homosociety, heterosexuality would be not just an identity a man has or does not have; it would also serve as an ideal of manhood, and thus an individual man's ability to meet that standard would be determined in more or less visible *relation* to other men competing for social-sexual contact with women.

That heterosexuality serves as an ideal of manhood becomes clearer when that characteristic is set within the context of the turn-of-the-century emergence of American masculinity and, in particular, the broad-based cultural privileging of *primitivist* expression and behavior. The real man maintained the nineteenth-century Victorian qualities of intellect, self-control, and reason while also routinely shaking off the overlay of civilization and thereby tapping into his primal side of physicality, cunning, and aggression. The late-nineteenth-century rise of college football offers a perfect example of how ever increasing numbers of American men made time to revel in the brutal and animalistic side of the male constitution.

This reflex of de-evolution is key to understanding the modern definition of male sexuality. Led by Dr. William Robinson, perhaps the period's most influential authority on normative standards of male sexuality, who described heterosexuality as "man's most dynamic urge," early-twentieth-century medical literature and marriage and sex manuals rooted male sexual expression in instinct and advised men that rather than trying to overcome that urge, good health and true manhood required its full expression.[6]

Consistent with the definition of masculinity as an epistemology of potential loss and shame, expectations of male heterosexual behavior would be most effectively stated in the negative—that is, in prescriptions against the abnormalcies of homosexuality and, perhaps most telling of all, impotency. "[A]n impotent man," Robinson proclaimed, "is a more pitiable man than a venereally infected one." As other physicians, theorists, and reformers linked impotency to "sexual neurasthenia" and generally described it as a result of modern urban life and overcivilization, advertisers told men they could regain potency through cultivation of "giant strength and power," "enlarged organs," and "sexual power."[7] Of course, these are all relative terms, which leads back to the fact that masculinity became a comparative and public affair as homosociety awarded heterosexual status according to sexual prowess and also to a man's overall physical capacity.

When set within a homosocial framework, this turn-of-the-century prescription of primal heterosexual expression would lead to newfound motivations for aggression between men. Heterosexual prowess could be achieved through sexual potency and a man's physical size, strength, and power in relation to other men. Modern sport became a key institutional determinant of physical capacity. The early twentieth century also witnessed the birth of the muscle-man fable, in which a man of slight build sitting with a woman on the beach loses her after a larger, muscle-bound man kicks sand on him. But through strenuous bodybuilding he wins her back. This before-and-after narrative of realizing heterosexual success after attending to one's body, serves as a founding story of modern American homosocial relations, offering a paradigmatic illustration of the conflation of physical aggression and masculine heterosexuality.[8]

Law and Sexual Violence

Historians of male sexuality have heretofore located the construction of male heterosexual self-identity in medical discourse and in sex and marriage manuals. But the law has also played a vital role in this process. For instance, the separation of homosexuals from the full rights, privileges, and protection of American citizenship illustrates how the legal system helped formulate normative standards of masculinity. The law has also legitimated masculine control of women's sexuality. The criminalization of abortion at different points in American history is a clear example of the law's undermining of women's power and autonomy, as is the law's silence on a myriad of sexual assault cases. Male use of rape as a war tactic has remained largely outside legal purview; perhaps no other instance of male heterosexual violence better reveals the homosocial dynamic at work. "Rape by a conqueror," as Susan Brownmiller has written, "is compelling evidence of the conquered's status of masculine impotence."[9] Wartime rape affirms the male-centeredness of some heterosexual motivation and behavior—in this case, abuse of women becomes an ultimate method of humiliating other men.

If there is a masculine logic of the law that legitimates and excuses excessive and violent male heterosexuality, then one of the best examples of that sanction has been the marital-rape exemption that recognizes the "need" of a man to express himself sexually and allows him to "take" sex within the context of marriage. For many American feminists in the 1960s and 1970s, marital rape and its exemption proved "patriarchy," testifying to the ever-present quality of male sexual aggression and transgression and the perfectly insidious ways that law and society mediate and protect that apparently innate masculine impulse.[10]

As Mary Balderson's successful divorce from her husband, demonstrates, the courts at the turn of the century did not completely condone sexual abuse within marriage. But the husband acted without threat of criminal penalty. This legal compromise decriminalized sexual abuse in marriage while granting divorce for the same behavior. Such an inconsistent balancing act betrays the homosocial nature of the legal justice system's orientation to heterosexuality. Although the husband's transgressions do not go unnoticed (at least not after they are brought successfully to the state's attention by Mary Balderson), the law refuses to attribute guilt to these violent acts, thereby recognizing the masculine need for sexual

expression over moral proscriptions of sexual behavior. But the courts also recognized a woman's right to escape this masculine conduct if it proved excessively
unwelcome.

Generally speaking, the turn-of-the-century law of marital rape betrayed its
homosocial orientation by accommodating an individual man's feeling and response of shame at being unable to express what he and the law would consider
his "natural impulses." One implication is that men who rape and who commit
other acts of physical and sexual violence against women may be motivated, as
sociologist Kathleen Daly has pointed out, by a perceived powerlessness and
failure among other men.[11] The muscle man at the beach forced to "give up" the
woman of his dreams, may displace his anxieties of masculine inferiority by
physically overpowering other women.

Another distinctive and important example of how the concept of shame
underlies the law of heterosexuality can be found in the treatment of a husband's
murderous response to his wife's adultery. In the late nineteenth century, the
"honor defense" or the "unwritten law" that allowed a court to acquit a defendant for killing his wife and/or paramour was joined by the "heat-of-passion"
claim. The last formulation reduced the charge against the defendant from murder to manslaughter when he killed his wife's lover immediately after finding
them in the act of adultery. Again, as with the marital-rape exemption, the heat-
of-passion defense did not ignore the husband's actions, the defendant being
subject to severe criminal sanction and the leveling of moral blame, but the state
reduced the degree of guilt, explicitly recognizing extenuating circumstances and
implicitly acknowledging the presence of shame that the husband, or indeed any
"reasonable man," would feel under the circumstances. In fact, the logical basis
of this defense is that the defendant, jolted out of control of his aggressive
predisposition, could literally take no course other than a violent one.

That the heat-of-passion doctrine constructed itself around the peculiar characteristics of masculine consciousness stands out. Women defendants were generally unsuccessful in arguing provocation after murdering a paramour because
turn-of-the-century courts continued to cultivate a type of strategic ignorance
toward female subjectivity. What is remarkable, though, is the explicit legal
formulation of the primitivist psychology of men and how recognition of that
irrationality is in perfect accordance with the logic of homosociety. Few areas of
turn-of-the-century law focused so closely on the dynamics of male emotion. In
applying the heat-of-passion doctrine, courts assumed and further defined a
bifurcated masculine consciousness, one divided between, in the words of the
standard Texas jury instructions of the time, the powers of reason and "cool
reflection" and a preexisting foundation of "emotions of the mind known as
anger, rage, sudden resentment, or terror."[12] After splitting masculine consciousness in two, the law establishes a certain homosocial sympathy and allowance
for a man's actions occurring outside reason, or at least when the circumstances
show that the crime happened before the defendant had a chance to reintegrate
his behavior with his senses.

Heat-of-passion law is based on the idea that the defendant acted reflexively to finding his wife and paramour in flagrante delicto (in the very act of committing the crime). Indeed, in theory, the peculiarity that allows for a reduction from murder to manslaughter is not hearing rumors about said adultery nor even listening to a wife's confession but the specific experience of *seeing* and *witnessing* his wife with another man and consequently having to endure the implicit physical comparison and sudden dishonor that that scenario entails—a scenario that (within the homosocial world of performance, status, and competition) would seem to necessitate decisive forceful response.

If we scrutinize the way the actual murders of paramours took place, however, it becomes clear that courts followed heat-of-passion doctrine when the defendant did not act on its *premises*. In literal terms, there are few cases whose facts follow the scenario of the husband's catching the adulterous pair in the act. Of the twenty-three cases examined from turn-of-the-century Texas, not one involves flagrante delicto. The Texas Criminal Court of Appeals nevertheless found adequate provocation and reduced the charge to manslaughter for eighteen of the defendants—including such cases when the defendant acted after discovering a letter revealing completed adultery; when the defendant had been informed by various parties that the victim had been intimate with his wife and then killed him seeing him and the defendant's wife walking out of church arm in arm; and when the husband-defendant, wife, and victim had been walking outside together for some time and the murder took place after the paramour confirmed having intercourse with the woman.[13] Clearly, the heat-of-passion defense, as developed by the Texas appellate court, did not require the defendant to witness his wife actually engaged in sexual relations with the victim—the experience that supposedly triggers the uncontrollable passion on which the doctrine is based.

Appellate courts at the turn of the century also accepted the heat-of-passion defense when the defendant proved to be mistaken in believing his wife had been unfaithful. In a 1901 case considered by the Texas Criminal Court of Appeals, the defendant had been told by his wife that the "deceased had offered numerous indignities to her prior to her marriage with him and several insults after her marriage." After going to the deceased's residence, the defendant shot him once and then ran after him and fired five more shots into him. Uncontrovertible evidence came out in the murder trial that the insults to the defendant's wife never occurred. But the appellate court nevertheless reduced the charge to manslaughter under the heat-of-passion doctrine. "The guilt of the accused party," the decision reads, "should not depend upon the existence or nonexistence of the fact itself, but upon the circumstances as they appeared to and were understood by him at the time of his acting upon them."[14] In a very similar murder case on appeal, the Supreme Court of Connecticut followed the same logic, emphasizing that it is the defendant's "belief, so reasonably formed, that excites the uncontrollable passion."[15] These decisions emphasize just how closely heat-of-passion law concerned itself with not so much the factual circumstances precipitating violence but the defendant's subjective state of masculine rage and passion.

Finally, it is also worth noting that courts expanded the heat-of-passion defense at the turn of the century to cover not only husband-defendants but also
men who killed because of a close family relationship with a woman involved
with the deceased. In 1902, a Texas appellate court applied the doctrine in a case
in which the defendant, after finding love letters addressed to his sister and
apparently written by a married man, sought out the man and shot and killed
him "because," as the defendant testified, "he had ruined [my] sister."[16] In
another case the following year, the Texas Criminal Court of Appeals dropped
the charge to manslaughter for a defendant who had killed his sister's husband.
The court paid special attention to what the defendant had learned of the deceased's treatment of his wife. The brutality ranged from compelling "his wife to
his lusts while she was sick with menstruation, against her consent and protes-
tation, from three to four times a night," to one assault in which he poured rat
poison down her throat. "A grievous insult or injury directed toward a cherished
female relative," the appellate court ruled, "would be adequate cause" to incite
uncontrollable passion in a "reasonable man."[17] In these decisions, the court
dropped all pretense that the defense is based on the defendant's acting reflexively to finding his wife and paramour in flagrante delicto; rather, the heat-of-
passion doctrine became a way to uphold a certain male duty to protect women
and also to maintain homsocial order.

In conclusion, successful use of the heat-of-passion defense in Texas or elsewhere
did not depend on true consistency with the premise of the law: that the husband
was so surprised and so shamed that he acted reflexively in a flurry of aggressive
instinct. The idea of overwhelming physical-emotional provocation is a legal
fiction, a metaphor for what is taking place between the two men, allowing the
defendant to correct violently the wrong outside the full sanction of moral blame
and full penalty of the law. In creating the fiction of the man literally transported
beyond the law by passion, the legal system rationalized both the particular act
of violence and the more generalized violence inherent within homosociety. So,
too, with the marital-rape exemption. Here, American law recognized a measure
of shame inherent in the husband's not being able to express his "natural" sexual
desires freely. By the turn of the century, a wife could use the fact of rape to free
herself from marriage, but the homosocial logic of the law refused to condemn
such behavior with moral and criminal sanction.

NOTES

1. *Balderson v. Balderson* (1898), Circuit Court, Marquette County, Wisconsin; Elizabeth
Pleck, *Domestic Tyranny: The Making of American Social Policy against Family Violence from
Colonial Time to the Present* (New York: Oxford University Press, 1987).

2. Michael Kimmel, *Manhood in America: A Cultural History* (New York: Free Press,
1996); David Leverenz, "The Last Real man in America: From Natty Bumpo to Batman,"
American Literary History 3 (1991), and "Manhood, Humiliation and Public Life: Some

Stories," *Southwest Review* 71 (fall 1986). See also Eve Kosofsky Sedgwick, *Between Men: English Literature and Male Homosocial Desire* (New York: Columbia University Press, 1985).

3. Writing in 1975, Rubin doesn't use the word *homosociety*, and she explicitly rejects *patriarchy* (as a term best "confined to the Old Testament–type pastoral nomads"); but she does emphasize the intramasculine dimension of heterosexual relations. Gayle Rubin, "The Traffic in Women: Notes on the 'Political Economy' of Sex," in *Toward an Anthropology of Women*, ed. Rayna Reiter (New York: Monthly Review Press, 1975), 157.

4. Ibid.; Kimmel, *Manhood in America*, 7.

5. George Chauncey, *Gay New York: Gender, Urban Culture, and the Making of the Gay Male World, 1890–1940* (New York: Basic Books, 1995), 117.

6. W. J. Robinson, *Sex Morality* (New York: Critic and Guide, 1919), 26, as cited in Kevin White, *The First Sexual Revolution: The Emergence of Male Heterosexuality in Modern America* (New York: New York University Press, 1993), 70. Kevin Mumford, " 'Lost Manhood' Found: Male Sexual Impotence and Victorian Culture in the United States," in *American Sexual Politics: Sex, Gender, and Race since the Civil War*, ed. John C. Fout and Maura Shaw Tantillo (Chicago: University of Chicago Press, 1993), 75–100.

7. Robinson, *Sex Morality*, 26, as cited in White, *First Sexual Revolution*, 71; Mumford, " 'Lost Manhood Found,' " 90.

8. Muscle-beach stories first appeared in turn-of-the-century Bernarr MacFadden's masculinist physical fitness journal *Physical Culture* (founded 1899).

9. Susan Brownmiller, *Against Our Will: Men, Women, and Rape* (New York: Bantam Books, 1975), 82.

10. Jaye Siton, "Old Wine in New Bottles: The 'Marital' Rape Allowance," University of *North Carolina Law Review* 72 (1993): 261–89; Rebecca M. Ryan, "The Sex Right: A Legal History of the Marital Rape Exemption" (senior honors thesis, Princeton University, 1994).

11. Kathleen Daly, book reviews, *Signs* 20 (spring 1995): 765.

12. *McAnear v. State*, 43 Tex. Crim. 518 (1902); *Finch v. State*, 44 Tex. Crim. 204, 206 (1902).

13. *Pauline v. State*, 21 Tex. Crim. 436 (1886); *Cannister v. State*, 46 Tex. Crim. 221 (1904); *Young v. State*, 54 Tex. Crim. 417 (1908).

14. *Messer v. State*, 43 Tex. Crim. 97 (1901).

15. *State v. Yanz*, 74 Conn. 177 (1901). Emphasis added.

16. *McAnear v. State*, 43 Tex. Crim. 518 (1902).

17. *Willis v. State*, 75 S.W. 790 (1903).

Belle Gunness and three of her children. Used by permission of the LaPorte County (Indiana) Historical Society.

Chapter Sixteen

"The Unspeakable Mrs. Gunness"

The Deviant Woman in Early-Twentieth-Century America

Paula K. Hinton

During the early morning hours of April 28, 1908, thick smoke and the "crakling [*sic*] of fire" awakened Joseph Maxson, a hired hand on the Gunness farm in the small town of LaPorte, Indiana, sixty miles from Chicago. He ran to his bedroom window and saw with horror that the house was ablaze. Maxson attempted to gain access to the area inhabited by Mrs. Belle Gunness and her three children, but he was unsuccessful. Two neighbors, William Clifford and William Humphrey, arrived on the scene and joined Maxson in his attempt to awaken Gunness and the children.[1]

The three threw bricks at windows, and when that failed to rouse anyone, they found a ladder and used it to climb to the bedrooms on the second floor. There was no sign of Gunness or the children. The men were unable to enter through the windows because flames were shooting up through the floor. More neighbors rushed to the scene to offer assistance. Maxson rode off in search of Sheriff Smutzer. When he returned, the house had almost completely collapsed; only part of one wall still stood. At four o'clock that afternoon the bodies were located in the cellar. "The mother was lying on the frame of a bed," Maxson reported. "The children were lying kind of over the mother."[2]

LaPorte had two newspapers at that time—the *LaPorte Argus-Bulletin* and the *LaPorte Daily Herald*. Both papers put the story of the fire on the front page—a position it would occupy for more than a month—and neither registered surprise at news of the fire. In fact, both newspapers reminded readers of past events on the property, and each asserted that Ray Lamphere, Mrs. Gunness's former hired man, had set the fire, knowing full well that Gunness and her children had been inside asleep. The papers speculated that Lamphere had set the fire because Gunness had failed to return his "affection" and had hired a new hand to replace him.[3]

Lamphere and Gunness were no strangers to the newspaper-reading public in LaPorte. The death of Peter Gunness, Belle Gunness's second husband, in 1902 had stolen the attention of the community for several days. Six years later, on March 11, 1908, Smutzer arrested Lamphere and charged him with "annoying"

Belle Gunness. The court found Lamphere guilty of trespassing and fined him one dollar in addition to court costs. A month later Gunness claimed that Lamphere was insane and brought action against him, but a panel of physicians pronounced him "sane." On April 16, 1908, less than two weeks before the fire, the papers reported that Gunness had brought trespass charges against Lamphere for the second time, and that the court had again found him guilty and this time ordered him to pay five dollars plus court costs. Lamphere's and Gunness's fourth run-in took place on April 25, three days before the fire. Authorities "arraigned [Lamphere] for surety of the peace," but he had an alibi this time and was acquitted, leaving Gunness to pay the court costs.[4]

Immediately after the fire, Sheriff Smutzer interviewed Gunness's neighbors and learned that Lamphere had been enamored of Belle Gunness and had threatened her often. The sheriff also discovered that Gunness had paid a visit to her attorney, M. E. Lelliter, just days prior to the fire and had "talked to him of the persecutions to which she was subjected." In addition, the day before the fire, Gunness had acquired a safe deposit box "and there left a bundle of papers. She was somewhat agitated and had tears in her eyes, but she appeared relieved as she walked out."[5] This picture of Gunness as the relentlessly hounded and persecuted woman was very appealing to the papers' readership. Not surprisingly, Sheriff Smutzer focused his investigation on Lamphere's possible involvement in the fire.

Maxson related his escape from the fire in the papers alongside a report that detailed Gunness's financial status at her death—she died with $700 in the bank and with an insurance policy on the farm worth $4,700. The *Daily Herald* also reported that Gunness had an eighteen-year-old daughter who was in California attending school. Authorities were attempting to contact her, but they believed from what Gunness had told neighbors and Maxson, that her daughter was already on her way home.[6]

Smutzer arrested Lamphere on April 30 and charged him with arson and murder. No bail was set. At first Lamphere denied any firsthand knowledge of the fire, but he finally admitted that he had passed the farm that morning on his way to work and had noticed the fire but was afraid to approach the house because it would make him appear to be the one who had set it. He stated, however, that he had alerted another passerby. Later he changed his story and said that he was nowhere near the fire but had seen it from across a field.[7]

That same day, a very gory and detailed description of the remains of Gunness—whose head was never found—and her children appeared in the *Argus-Bulletin*. In an ironic twist only later appreciated, the newspaper also reported that at the time of her death her estate was estimated at "between $12,000 and $15,000, this being represented by the home place, the insurance on the house which was burned, . . . and money on deposit in a LaPorte bank, with the belief that Mrs. Gunness had other interests from which she derived an income."[8]

Men aiding with the cleanup found some watches in the debris of the Gunness place, and authorities sent the internal organs of Gunness and her children to be tested for the presence of poison. Authorities suspected Lamphere had poisoned the four victims before setting fire to the house.[9]

On May 3, the focus of the investigation changed drastically. On that day Asle K. Helgelein came in search of his brother, forty-nine-year-old Andrew K. Helgelein. Both had been farmers in South Dakota and had been very close. Asle began to worry when his brother had not returned from what was supposed to be only a weeklong trip. Asle checked with family and friends, even some family members still in Norway, and no one had heard from Andrew. While going through Andrew's things, Asle discovered letters from Belle Gunness. In them, Gunness had asked Andrew to sell all of his property, "and bring the money on his body, not trusting the banks, to her." Asle had heard about "a rich widow here in Indiana advertising in a Norwegian paper for a Norwegian husband: the hired men on my place and on my brother's place joked with one another about this." Asle had not seen or heard from his brother since January 2, 1908.[10]

Asle wrote to Gunness, and she wrote back, asserting that Andrew had gone to Chicago and might have gone from there to Norway. Asle and Gunness continued to exchange letters—he demanded to know his brother's whereabouts, and she located Andrew in countless different places. Finally, Gunness urged Asle to come and see her in May, and they could look for Andrew together. True *Why?* to form, as the reader shall discover, she suggested that he liquidate Andrew's assets and bring the profits to her. Gunness told him that she would then aid him in his search for his brother.[11] Asle continued to correspond with Gunness, and grew increasingly suspicious of her.

In April, Asle began a complicated correspondence with several banks, in South Dakota and LaPorte, and was finally able to determine that his brother had transferred money from his account in South Dakota to a LaPorte bank. Further investigation revealed that Gunness had accompanied Helgelein to the bank to pick up the funds. The final letter from the First National Bank in LaPorte contained the April 28 issue of the *Daily Herald*, which carried the story of the fire. Helgelein left immediately for LaPorte, concerned that his brother may have perished in the fire.[12]

On May 5, Helgelein arrived at the Gunness farm. Maxson and Hutson were there, digging in the rubble as they had been doing every day since the fire. Still suspicious of the woman who had apparently been the last to see his brother alive, Helgelein asked the men how deep the lake was and whether they had noticed any holes in the ice recently. They said no. He then asked Maxson whether there had been any digging on the grounds during the early part of spring. Maxson knew of one hole that Gunness had helped him fill with rubbish sometime in March. He pointed it out, and the three men began to dig. Asle related what then occurred:

> After we had been digging a little I noticed an awful bad smell. Mr. Maxson told me Mrs. Gunness had put a lot of tomato cans and fish cans there. Maybe it was they [that] made it stink. We struck something hard and covered with a gunny sack. We lifted the oil cloth and the gunny sack. Then we saw the neck of a body and an arm. Then we stopped and I sent Maxson to town to sheriff, telling him [Maxson]

to bring an officer. I covered the place with an old coat and two gunny sacks that I picked up around the yard there. I and the other man, i.e. Hutson, cleaned away the dirt, digging around the hole, until the officer came. When the sheriff came I turned the matter over to him.[13]

The body that was uncovered had been dismembered and decapitated. The torso was in a gunny sack, the head and limbs outside the sack around the body.[14] Incredibly, Asle Helgelein had stumbled upon the remains of his brother.

The grounds of the Gunness place were scoured for more "soft spots" that might indicate where digging had occurred. Investigators found many such areas and some local men, under the direction of Smutzer, set out to uncover what might lie underneath. What they found shocked and excited everyone. In the end, they unearthed eleven bodies on the Gunness farm. Two of the victims were female, one of these Gunness's long-awaited adopted daughter, Jennie, who had not been seen for two years; the identity of the other female victim was never ascertained. Authorities would later assert that Gunness was responsible for these deaths in addition to the deaths of her two husbands, and possibly the deaths of all of her children.

Nine of Gunness's victims were male. As some of these bodies were identified, Gunness's modus operandi slowly came into focus. Authorities interviewed Asle Helgelein and others and learned that Gunness advertised for husbands in Norwegian newspapers. She lured men to her home with promises of wedded bliss, of a wife who worshipped at the altar of domesticity in a home that was truly a palace, located on acres and acres of beautiful and fertile land. Advertised as a dream come true, it was in reality a nightmare for the men who were drawn into her "web." She stole whatever money and belongings they brought with them, and then poisoned, bludgeoned, and dismembered the bodies, disposing of them in pits sprinkled with quicklime and cluttered with rubbish in her yard. As Gunness had written to Helgelein, "My heart beats in wild rapture for you, My Andrew, I love you. Come prepared to stay forever."[15]

Dr. J. H. William Meyer, part of the team formed to perform autopsies on the bodies, informed eager journalists that the legs of all the victims had been cut off above the knee, and the flesh had been cut with a "keen knife and then the bone sawed squarely off." Meyer noted that "the disarticulation of the ball and socket joints of the shoulders" was not the job of "an amateur. . . . Every one of these operations was clean cut. It was done by a strong hand with nothing less sharp than a surgeon's knife."[16] Gunness was strong, and she had experience with slaughtering hogs and making sausage. In short, she had the necessary strength, experience, and instruments. She had carved up her victims as she had carved up animals on her farm.

Though authorities discovered eleven bodies, it is quite possible that there were more, for many men with some connection to Gunness were reported missing. But the authorities tired of their grisly work, and because Gunness was presumed dead and identification of the bodies was almost impossible in most cases, they simply called a halt to the digging. Authorities charged Gunness with only one murder—that of Helgelein—and only because the court wanted to charge Lamphere as an *accomplice* to murder. In order to do so, they had to charge someone else with the homicide.[17]

Belle Gunness was a classic serial killer: "one who kills at least four people in a predatory manner." Although the FBI declared in 1992 that Aileen Wournos was the "USA's first 'textbook' female serial killer," she was in fact the latest in a long line of them, something that even modern-day theorists seem reluctant to admit. Gunness displayed many of the same characteristics that Wournos did: the ability to manipulate people around her; frequent relocation to escape discovery; the lack of conscience; the desire for "keepsakes" or "souvenirs" from the victims, often useless items such as the men's clothes that Gunness kept; and finally the utilization of similar tactics for obtaining and killing victims in that both women took advantage of the way in which society perceives women in order to attract victims—Gunness set herself up as a comely and wealthy widow in need of a husband, and Wournos posed as a stranded motorist and then robbed and killed the men who picked her up.[18]

The "mystery" of Gunness's death was never solved, though theories as to what really happened abounded. It is entirely possible that Gunness knew that her home was going to burn down at least one day before it did. It appears that she had planned the fire in order to escape prosecution for her crimes. Witnesses stated that from the time of Helgelein's disappearance until the fire, Lamphere continually bragged that Gunness owed him a lot of money and that he "had something on her." Two weeks following Helgelein's murder in January 1908, Lamphere quit. He left without his belongings and without money that was owed him. After Gunness refused Lamphere permission to retrieve his things, he hired an attorney. His lawyer urged him to go back one last time and demand his belongings, and this time Gunness had acquiesced.[19] It was then that Gunness began legal proceedings against him. Lamphere was a loose cannon, and Gunness realized that his anger, jealousy, and his drinking problem were a dangerous combination. He was talking too much. She had to get him out of the way. She went after him in the courts, in the hope that it would deter him from causing further trouble, but it only made the situation worse. The final time that the two appeared in court together, on April 15, just two weeks prior to the fire, Lamphere's attorney confronted Gunness on the stand with suspicions that he had about her.

Wirt Worden, Lamphere's attorney, asked Gunness questions that should have been asked of her long before. He asked her how her first two husbands had *really* died; whether she had collected any insurance money; and when her daughter Jennie would finally be returning from her supposed trip to California. Gunness became very "agitated" and refused to answer the questions, which was her right because the trial had nothing to do with the line of questioning— even Worden admitted that. But Gunness became anxious, and the constant stream of letters from Helgelein's brother forced her into a corner.[20]

Gunness devised a plan that would take care of all of her problems. A few days before the fire she visited Bertha Schultz, a store clerk, and told her that she was afraid of Lamphere and that she feared he was going to kill her. Schultz stated that Gunness told her she feared Lamphere "would some day set fire to her home and buildings and that he would murder herself and her children." Gunness returned the next day and again related the same fears. Gunness then proceeded to a jeweler, from whom she bought rings for her children, perhaps as a bizarre farewell present.[21]

The day before the fire, Gunness's actions became even more suspicious. The prosecution used them to prove that Gunness feared for her life so they could successfully prosecute Lamphere, but what the actions really show is her careful planning of the fire. On that day she kept her children home from school and ran several errands in town. She had her will drawn up, acquired a safe deposit box, into which she deposited her will and other papers. She also deposited seven hundred dollars in the bank. She then visited several stores where she purchased "a large quantity of cheap candies," some cakes, and some kerosene. The candies and cakes were used to house the poison with which Gunness killed her children, and the kerosene jugs were found empty in the rubble—they had been used to set the fire.[22] That she made out her will and deposited the money was a ruse utilized to show her "fear" of Lamphere. It is far too coincidental otherwise.

Forensic evidence showed that the children had been dead before the fire. Most observers of the case agree that Gunness killed her children, but there was much debate concerning the adult female body found in the cellar. The corpse's measurements did not fit those that a dressmaker had made of Gunness, nor were people who knew her well able to identify the body as hers; and although some bridgework identified as Gunness's was located in the rubble, many people believed Gunness capable of planting the "evidence" of her demise.[23] So either she planted a body and escaped or she set the fire and then committed suicide. She had asked Lamphere to come out to her home knowing full well that someone would probably see him, put two and two together, and prosecute him for arson and murder.

At the time, however, many LaPorteans did not know what to think of this horrific crime. From the beginning, LaPorteans viewed the case as an additional "chapter" in a very long mystery. Gunness had purchased a home already shrouded in mystery, and the death of her second husband there, the legal battles that Gunness waged with Ray Lamphere and then the fire itself piqued the interest of the community. Following the discovery of Helgelein's body, and the bodies of others, excitement grew to such heights that it became an embarrassment to LaPorte. As many as fifteen thousand people a day (an astonishing number for a town of approximately ten thousand residents) gathered on the Gunness grounds to watch the digging and to view the bodies. Sundays became "Gunness Sundays," the day when the largest number of people ventured to LaPorte. Newspapers all over the country commented on the "morbid curiosity" of the crowds and on the mood, which should have been subdued, but was in fact the same as one might find at a circus or carnival.[24]

On the grounds, revelers could find "souvenir vendors, ice cream cone men and lemonade dispensers." Incredibly, "boys were actually seen peddling alleged bones of the burned and murdered victims." According to a *New York Times* reporter,

> Women clawed at the little red carriage house which has become the repository of the dismembered bodies. They stuck their fingers in the cracks and wrenched in an attempt to pry them apart far enough to see inside. Men boosted each other to the window in the end of the structure and gazed until others behind them pushed them from their places to make room for other gazers. Several times during the day the doors were opened and the spectators filed in line past the door, through which could be seen the bodies.[25]

Visitors' names riddled the Gunness stable wall (part of which is housed in the LaPorte County Historical Museum). Additional railroad cars were needed in order to handle the crowds.[26]

The carnival atmosphere spread far and wide. The Edison Company made "moving pictures" of the Gunness farm and distributed them throughout the country. The chief of police of Ann Arbor, Michigan, found the show so distasteful that he banned it. A restaurant in Chicago advertised a dish called "Gunness Stew," and the residents of that city were privy to a gruesome display—an exhibition that featured a representation of the Gunness burial grounds and the Gunness home. It housed a watchdog and two chickens from the farm.[27]

Toward the end, though, as the "mystery" unfolded in more gruesome ways, excitement about the case gave way to disgust. LaPorteans reacted by calling the case a "blot on LaPorte county," and by suggesting a " 'clean-up' day in La-Porte" in an effort to present a better city image. Both papers attempted to ease the embarrassment created by Gunness and her crimes by pointing out similar cases that had occurred in other towns. The most obvious sign of the city's frustration with its place in the limelight is the fact that stories concerning Gunness dwindled and were retired to the back pages of the town's papers. The language also changed. Letters from people all over the country who asserted they had knowledge of the possibly missing Gunness had initially been greeted enthusiastically, but by the end of May any and all letter writers were dismissed as "kooks."[28]

Gunness arrived in the United States in the early 1880s. A young woman in her early twenties, she emigrated from Trondheim, Norway. An example of chain migration, she had been sponsored by her sister and brother-in-law and lived with them in Chicago until she married Mads "Max" Detler Sorenson in 1883. The couple had four children and an adopted daughter, Jennie Olson.[29]

Gossip about Gunness's possible malevolence began while she lived in Austin, Illinois. Two of her children died with symptoms consistent with poisoning. Mysterious fires destroyed two of her homes and a store that she owned. Gunness collected insurance from all three fires and on the death of both children. After the second fire, authorities and neighbors suspected Gunness of arson but found no evidence. Finally, in 1900, after the death of her husband, Mads, many neighbors and the police suspected her of having poisoned him.[30]

[Handwritten marginalia:] You can compare these times when Public Lynching was considered a Family event or when member of the Community would take pictures next to the corpse Hanging from the trees. These event had a profound effect on people who felt this Type lawlessness would go down in history across the country. Many towns that we live in today For example Va is where the slave Trade originated and many of the most Horrific Crimes of Lynching and beating were recorded in these Towns. Today it is embarrassing for town to be associated w/ Crimes of Blacks or being accused of slavery and could only wonder if the if there was no Freeing of the slaves and no civil rights movement that the same occur atmosphere would after some tragic event such as lynchings would still be taking place.

Suspicions concerning Sorenson's death were well founded. Mads Sorenson died July 30, 1900. His death certificate listed the cause of death as a stomach hemorrhage.[31] Gunness did not send for a doctor until after her husband had died. Furthermore, Sorenson could not have picked a more auspicious moment to breathe his last. On that day, and that day only, two life insurance policies came into effect. He had decided to cancel his older policy and had purchased another one from a different company. The two policies overlapped on July 30. The older one paid out $2,000 to his widow; the new one, $3,000. But even though Gunness avoided a serious run-in with authorities, she found it impossible to remain in Austin.[32]

Gunness moved to LaPorte in November 1901, and tragedy followed her there. She married Peter Gunness in April 1902. He died in December under mysterious circumstances. Belle asserted that her husband had accidentally been hit on the head with a meat grinder. There were many elements of the explanation that did not make sense. Authorities and neighbors grew suspicious, but during the inquest conducted by Dr. Bo Bowell, Belle Gunness played the role of the devoted and loving wife and mother well enough to satisfy the coroner. The little gossip that did exist diminished after the funeral. According to the *Argus-Bulletin*, "Mrs. Gunness displayed considerable grief [and] she wore mourning weeds for a number of months," which was "a sufficient length of time to quiet suspicion." She also netted $3,500 in insurance money.[33]

How could Gunness get away with her crimes for so long? How was she able to avoid detection? The answers are found in the gender dynamics of the early twentieth century. Although the discovery of Gunness's crimes occurred at a time when women were making significant inroads into "man's sphere," the image of the "ideal woman" remained intact and few could believe that a woman could so completely violate that norm. Society's idea of "woman" and what it meant to be "womanly" not only affected the way women acted, it also influenced reactions to "deviant" women.

To escape redefining "woman," late-Victorian American society often rescued her from the clutches of the law by allowing her the chance to prove her "true womanhood." When that failed, the public denied that she was a "true woman" at all. People could reconcile themselves to the fact that a female had committed murder because they could deny that a "woman" had killed, thereby negating the threat to the community, the patriarchy, and the image of women.

The dynamics of the Belle Gunness case illustrate this point. Unlike most women murderers, Gunness was not available to answer for her crimes, so the people of LaPorte, and others across the United States who kept up with the case, set about proving that Gunness was not a "true woman" at all. In fact, as the reader shall discover, Gunness not only was denied her place as a "true woman" but was said by some to be actually a man in disguise.

In the nineteenth and most of the twentieth century the idea of "separate spheres" defined gender roles in order to maintain middle-class gentility. The market economy had taken men away from the home and into the stressful world of business. Woman's place was in the home, taking care of the household and children and maintaining, for the public male, a haven in a heartless world. She oversaw domestic chores and used her moral superiority to fashion her children into moral beings.[34] This is not to say, however, that women were completely "home bound." But in 1908, the majority of middle- and upper-class women restricted their outside activities, for the most part, to work that could be viewed as an extension of their roles within the home: church work, club activities, and charitable endeavors. According to Carroll Smith-Rosenberg, the "male medical model was simple: genitals determined gender, gender determined social role to which economic options were ineluctably associated."[35]

During the 1880s and 1890s a "novel social and political phenomenon—the 'New Woman'—emerged." These women took advantage of the progress their mothers had made in obtaining a degree of freedom for women; they married later, attended college, and trained for professional careers. They were settlement house workers, educational reformers, writers, artists, and physicians. The "New Women" "reject[ed] conventional female roles and assert[ed] their right to a career, to a public voice, [and] to visible power."[36]

Many men felt threatened as women in the twilight of the nineteenth century began pursuing projects outside the home. According to Smith-Rosenberg, "[T]o place a woman outside of a domestic setting, to train a woman to think and feel 'as a man,' to encourage her to succeed at a career, indeed to place a career before marriage, violated virtually every late-Victorian norm." Objections quickly arose. During the 1890s, social critics and male physicians launched "attacks upon the respectability and legitimacy of the New Women." They primarily focused on the "New Woman's" perceived new attitude toward "family"—the fear that she was turning her back on the husband and children that she was supposed to make the center of her world.[37] Many "New Women" favored a change in tactics to minimize their perceived threat to the patriarchy.

Some "New Women," while admitting that "mothering" was a part of being a woman and the path to fulfillment, argued that a woman did not have to give birth—she could be a "public mother" through her work in the settlement houses, women's clubs, the suffrage movement, and other projects.[38] In this way, "New Women" utilized the opposition's insistence on maternal roles while still obtaining what they wanted: a woman's right to participate in the public sphere.

Those critical of women's rights simply modified their arguments. Instead of attacking the "New Woman's" "rejection of motherhood," they focused their attention on the "New Woman's" "rejection of men." Smith-Rosenberg states, "From being 'unnaturally' barren, the autonomous woman, outside of heterosexual marriage, emerged as 'unnaturally' sexual." The enemies of women's equality "insisted that unmarried career women and political activists constituted an 'intermediate sex.' They violated normal gender categories. They fused the female and the male. They were 'Mannish Lesbians,' the embodiment of social disorder."[39]

According to Havelock Ellis, a turn-of-the-century sexologist, "[F]eminism,

[Handwritten margin notes:]

Key

Key

also look for the Time-frame of the womens suffrage movement

You can compare are women to to a different Type of slavery not far off from slavery of the african American slave less the beating.

Women had no 1. Voting Rights 2. Was Literally forced to stay at home 3. no Participation in Public life whatsoever 4 Considered unnaturally Barren because they choose to be an autonomous woman and fight for women rights 5 Considered Lesbean

This could compare to use Southern whites who felt that blacks were inferior to whites. The whites kept us from reading and writing the only thing they felt we were good for was a good field Hand. This why Southern whites lashed out against blacks after they received their freedom because the were afraid of what we may become

6. It was unnatural because it challenged the norms that society has placed on women and marriage and bearing children

lesbianism, and equality for women" were "unnatural, [and] related in disturbing and unclear ways to increased female criminality, insanity," and hysteria. From the theory that a man's heart and brain ruled his body and that the reproductive organs ruled a woman's body, it followed that if a woman pursued education she would upset the delicate balance of her body, inducing insanity, hysteria, cancer, sterility, and the onset of masculine features such as "shriveled" breasts, facial hair, and disrupted menstruation.[40]

Gunness operated in a society that valued the pious and pure woman and that feared that "true womanhood" was in danger of disappearing. The "New Woman" was "living proof of the fragility of middle-class values."[41] It was Gunness's ability to play the part of the "true woman" that allowed her to escape substantive suspicion until 1908. Appearances meant everything.

Standing behind the abuses of womenhood (women) and their profound affect in the legal system and other entities in society.

Initially, maintaining appearances proved simple for Gunness. The Gunness home in LaPorte had at one time been a brothel, and the community welcomed the Gunnesses' move there, hoping it would help to drive immorality out. The Gunness family made a "favorable impression on those about them." Peter Gunness was seen as "a thrifty and industrious farmer, who ... filled the place of a law-abiding citizen." Meanwhile, the "mistress of the house busied herself with the duties of the household, taking her part in the social and religious life of the community. ... Her piety and philanthropy even" extended to "the welfare of the orphan and homeless" in Chicago. So Belle Gunness succeeded in her role as "true woman." After Peter Gunness's death, Belle Gunness used the insurance money to make numerous improvements on the property, earning the approval of her community.[42]

A steady stream of men began to appear at Gunness's farm after her husband's death, and though this might have attracted negative attention from the community, it did not because her behavior was "ladylike." Her attempts to find a mate amused LaPorteans and they felt sorry for her unfortunate luck with retaining hired men. According to the *Argus-Bulletin*, "The men who visited her home, ... were royally entertained. She provided a bounteous board, served meals in the best of style, drove her visitors about the city, making them feel at home." In short, Gunness "maintained appearances which never breeded [*sic*] suspicion, and thereby escaped detection."[43]

After the tragic fire, LaPorteans initially hailed Gunness a heroine. The *Daily Herald* stated that "it looked as though the mother in desperate efforts to save the children had gathered them to her side and with the youngest clasped in her arms had met death bravely." She was most often referred to as a "mother" and "widow," her dominant social roles. The papers lauded Gunness as an excellent housekeeper, and credited her with having made improvements on her property.[44] These articles were, in effect, her obituary. It is interesting that LaPorteans applauded her for performing her duties as a "true woman" but said nothing about any accomplishments or interests outside her roles as mother and widow.

LaPorteans had to reframe their perception of Gunness once authorities discovered her criminal behavior. When she was a heroic mother who attempted to save her children from death, it was easy to remember things about her that made her a model of "true womanhood." Even early suspicions concerning the deaths and fires in Austin and Peter Gunness's death in LaPorte could be shrugged off—she was wearing black at the funeral so she must not be guilty of murder. However, overwhelming evidence—bodies in the yard—made her possible criminal activity impossible to ignore. Gunness was no longer a heroine and therefore could not possibly be a "true woman."

This dramatic shift in attitude is strikingly revealed in the newspapers, which called her all of the following and more: the "arch criminal of our times"; the "Modern Lucretia Borgia"; the "queen of American crime"; the "murder-priestess"; the "most fiendish murderess of the age"; the "woman Bluebeard"; the "high priestess of murder plotters"; the "Gunness Monster"; the "Butchering Widow"; "Hell's Belle"; and the "Unspeakable Mrs. Gunness."[45] The last "title" summed up the overriding horror that LaPorteans felt. What Gunness had done was indeed "unspeakable," and the fact that she was a woman made it even more disturbing. *That is always the perception of people when They found out the Crime was committed by a woman*

Ray Lamphere, on the other hand, was most often referred to by his name, with no adjectives attached to it. The very few times that his name was not used, he was called: the "prisoner," the "suspect," the "carpenter now in jail," and the "employe [sic] and the lover of Mrs. Gunness."[46] These are very flat, descriptive, nonjudgmental words for someone accused of killing a woman and her three innocent children. Before LaPorteans learned of Gunness's past, Lamphere's alleged crimes had made him the focus of open hostility. In addition, he had kept some very bad company. He frequented bars and associated with prostitutes, but he was never referred to in the same manner as Gunness. Why?

A clue to this contradiction can be found in the motives ascribed to him. Gunness had "gone against her nature"; Lamphere, according to the message hidden between the lines of the newspapers, had been the victim of a woman's wiles—the "New Woman" perhaps—and his alcoholic father's bad example. The motives given for Lamphere's actions were jealousy and "cupidity"—excessive desire. Society expected men to be aggressive—this was, after all, the age of the "strenuous life" and the glorification of "manly" sports, tycoons, and the military—and any violence they committed was far more acceptable than that committed by women. In fact, *manliness* was defined in opposition to *womanliness*. Lamphere had been obsessed with Gunness and had attempted to gain her hand in marriage. The fact that he "hounded" her was not acceptable, but some in the community could sympathize with him. That he could fall in love and not have that love returned, and then lash out in a jealous rage was understandable. Then, as the case unfolded, the story changed. Newspaper stories reported that Gunness had been "running after" Lamphere. So Lamphere was the victim of a woman who was not acting in an acceptable manner. "True women" do not literally chase after men. *Gunness* was the aggressor here. Lamphere was just another victim, though a more pathetic one because Gunness had shown more "manliness" than Lamphere. The message seemed to be that she had driven him crazy, and in order to find peace, he had to do away with her.[47]

And what about Gunness's motive for the murders that she committed? La-Porteans and others looked for an answer in contemporary theories of violent crime and contemporary views of women and what was "female." They turned to the known, placing her in a familiar framework. When she did not fit, they invented stories and scenarios that enabled them to understand the enigma before them. It is important to note that no one focused on Lamphere's sex when he was the main culprit. But Gunness's crimes were not just crimes; they were crimes committed by a woman.

Until the middle of the twentieth century, the majority of the research focusing on crime dealt with male criminals because far fewer women than men took part in criminal activity and because the majority of researchers were male. Apparently unnerved by the thought that these "gentle, passive, narcissistic, and dependent" creatures could be just as vicious as men, theorists tried to explain away the incongruity by pinning the causes on factors out of the control of women, thereby retaining the dominant image of the dutiful and loving wife, mother, or daughter.[48]

Theories concerning the etiology of female crime have advanced since the midcentury to take cultural and social factors into account. Earlier, theorists asserted that the cause of any criminal activity was rooted in the biological and psychological structure of women. "Normal" women did not commit crime. An imbalance in a woman's body could lead to an emotional imbalance that could cause a woman to act more irrationally than a "normal" woman would act—though, of course, all women were thought irrational. Most important, no one in the early years of the study of female criminality looked at the cultural construction of femininity and masculinity or the environment that these women operated in. If theorists did address a woman's environment, it was always from the standpoint of some deficiency in the woman that caused her to be impacted in a negative way, and psychological deficiencies were rooted in a woman's biology. It all went back to biology.

The first theorist to address female criminality was an "alienist" named Cesare Lombroso who, at the turn of the century, declared that the reason women were underrepresented in the criminal world was because they were not as intelligent as men.[49] Further, he found that females who did commit crimes had physical attributes often found in the male prisoners he had measured and studied. In fact, the most serious offenders, he argued, were "born criminals" who were often "more perverse than . . . their male prototypes."[50] Lombroso pointed to seven overlapping categories of female criminals.

For Lombroso, "Born criminals" had no moral compass and were lacking in "maternal affection." This decreased maternal urge, along with physical measurements that he made of the women, argued for the masculinity of the female "born criminal." She acted out of an "insatiable egotism," "greed and avarice," "love of dress and ornaments," or "religious mania."[51]

The majority of women who broke the law were "occasional criminals." They were morally superior to "born criminals" and less "perverse." These women were tempted into crime. They were usually brought into a life of crime by a man and would not have been criminal if not led into it. Another factor that produced the "occasional criminal" was higher education. Here Lombroso took contemporary gender-role expectations into account as he discussed the frustration that educated women faced when they could not find jobs that suited them and when they discovered that men found educated women unattractive.[52] Yet, the core reason behind any criminal activity would still be a woman's inherent weaknesses.

Biological factors also produced "female criminal lunatics," "hysterical offenders," and "epileptic delinquents." In the case of the "lunatics," their criminal activity ebbed and flowed according to stage of life: menopause, pregnancy, and menstruation. Women suffering from hysteria or epileptic seizures were also prone to criminal activity.[53]

Women who ignored their roles as wife and mother in favor of selfish needs and who circumvented the law to get what they wanted were "morally insane," and those who allowed their emotions to override their moral sense committed "crimes of passion."[54]

Physical measurements of female criminals linked them to criminal men in Lombroso's hierarchical structure. These women, whatever the motivating factors of their criminal behavior, were more masculine than feminine or were at least at the mercy of the inherent weaknesses of their female bodies and psyches. Those dissatisfied with Lombroso's mechanistic theories could find explanation for violent female criminality in the new theories of Sigmund Freud—though they would have needed to read German. Freudian theories held that women who were "not passive, who [were] not content with their roles as mothers and wives, [were] maladjusted." Freud stated that the underlying source of this restlessness was "penis envy." In other words, the fact that a woman was not born a man is so frustrating and traumatic that some women reject their role as "woman" and adopt that of "man." This "masculine" behavior included "attending universities, pursuing an autonomous or independent course in life, . . . joining feminist movements," or participating in criminal activity—the very behavior of the "new woman." Lombroso and Freud agreed that the root cause of female criminality is biology: female criminals are dissatisfied with being female. Irrationality and hysteria can develop and can produce behavior that runs counter to accepted norms. Freud warned that women were more apt to develop neurosis and hysteria due to the very "essence of [their] femininity."[55]

Lombroso's and Freud's theories made compelling reading for the educated reader of 1908, offering scientific explanations for the otherwise inexplicable. But the average American reading newspaper accounts of Gunness's dread deeds did not know and probably would not have sympathized with these complicated epistemologies of violence, though some observers did share the perception that criminal conduct could be the consequence of mental illness.

Some people thought that Gunness was responsible for her actions but was in the grip of some kind of "hysteria," "mania," or "insanity," echoing Lombrosian and Freudian theories. Elaine S. Abelson shows how Victorian women who were caught shoplifting remained relatively unscathed by the experience because of the medical profession's insistence that these women were not in control of their actions—that their biological monthly cycles had influenced their actions and made them irrational. It was simply the "natural constraints of the female sex" that had caused them to behave criminally. These women were in the grip of a "mania." Abelson states that "since ladies could not be called thieves, the medicalization of shoplifting provided an alternative and maintained the illusion of respectability. The individual became the focus; the crime was lost." This theory of a biology-based motive for crime "served to reinforce accepted gender roles and definitions," making even a female criminal a victim of her physiology. Women's biology was in control, not their intellect, with a resulting irrationality.[56] Although authorities had accused Gunness of committing crimes far more severe in nature than shoplifting, the same dynamics were at work when it came to explaining how a middle-class white woman could murder.

[margin note: Key]

Some declared that Gunness was in the grip of many "manias." She had a "mania for the possession of watches," a "mania for adopting children," and a "triple mania for men, blood and money." Most of all, she was possessed of a "monomania for murder." "Hysteria" was irretrievably linked to "manias" and, if the problem was not taken care of, "insanity." Lombroso asserted that "the enormity of the crimes convinces me that there must have been in her a strong inclination to hysteria."[57] Gunness was not in control of her actions.

Stated more simply, many thought her insane. A Pinkerton detective pronounced her "in every sense of the word an insane woman" with "an unquenchable thirst to kill." A "mania that was growing within her" had taken control and had led her to commit murder. The Reverend Eugene D. Daniels deemed her a "mental monstrosity" and said that "insanity may have induced the criminal state" because nothing else could explain why she would kill "her farm hands, who had no money and whose death, seemingly, could not benefit her in any way."[58] *[margin note: She killed them so she could benefit from victims]*

"Science" backed this theory. Two phrenologists came forward with their diagnosis of Gunness based on photographs of her. One of these experts, Dr. Marc Ray Hughes, professor of criminal anthropology in the Benton College of Law, asserted that the photographs showed that the "subject is mentally unstable, probably of the class of paranoiacs. I believe that if she is not dead and should be brought into a court of law it will be proved that she is insane." Dr. C. P. Bancroft, president of the Medico-Psychological Association, stated "that if a person's body is irregular or unsymmetrical, the chances are the brain will be formed badly." Bancroft believed that "Gunness had a peculiarly shaped head, a very large frame, and small feet, and her eyes were irregular. These malformations would indicate a similar malformation of mind."[59]

Other scientific observers found evidence of a "dual personality," a conflict between her "badness" and a "better nature." Thus Gunness could have been "a

[margin note: or it could have been greed and selfishness along w/other underlying factors]

moderately kind and indulgent mother at certain times and again a demon without fear of God, of man, or of the law" at other times. This dualism fit into Lombroso's theories, which held that "born criminals" have "contradictory traits"; they can often be kind and charitable—as Gunness was at times—but such traits are "intermittent and of short duration" in these women and usually benefit them in some way.[60]

Commentators focused more on Gunness's "badness" than on her "better nature." Lombroso believed that female criminals were "considerably more" vicious than male criminals at times. "It is not enough for a woman to murder an enemy; she wants to make him suffer, and she enjoys his death." The Pinkerton detective had no doubts concerning Gunness's physical strength, and he believed that she had not dismembered the bodies in order to make them easier to carry; "with a knife and cleaver, she hacked and hewed until the insanity within her was temporarily gratified." She was just as Lombroso had described her: far more vicious than necessary. James Pegler stated that "always there was the maximum of mutilation" in her killings. He said that she had a "constantly growing appetite for blood, to cut deep and watch the blood flow, to dabble the hands in it, to revel in the odor of it."[61] However, most observers eschewed Lombrosian and Freudian theories for more traditional causalities.

One approach, exemplified by a *New York Times* editorial, simply held that Gunness did not kill anyone; therefore, a woman had not killed. "In spite of the seeming evidences of the foulest kind of foul play," said the *Times*, "we still hope it will be proved that Mrs. Gunness was no murderess, but a coarse, thrifty woman who picked up occasionally an honest, if unclean, penny by disposing of cadavers for medical students of her neighborhood."[62] That the *New York Times* could place "hope" in such a bizarre theory speaks to the irrationality of those who could not bring themselves to believe that a woman could have killed anyone. The *Times* skewed the circumstances of the crime in such a way that Gunness could remain a "true woman." It "hoped" that she was merely "thrifty"—a valued characteristic—and had made a bad decision when she got involved with the disposal of cadavers for medical students.

Others believed that Gunness had indeed involved herself with disreputable people, but evil men had forced her into criminal behavior. It would not be possible, they argued, for a woman to have committed such crimes alone. Given the physically challenging nature of Gunness's method of disposing of her victims, many people registered their doubt that women had the physical strength needed for such sadistic deeds. Thus Gunness could have been only a willing or unwilling *partner*. Indeed, Cesare Lombroso personally analyzed Gunness's crimes in the *LaPorte Daily Herald*. He asserted that "a woman has not sufficient strength to commit alone a larger number of murders of young, robust men. It is therefore quite natural that there must be one or more man accomplices." The *Daily Herald* concurred: "[A]nother question that needs answering, is how were these people murdered and what help did Mrs. Gunness have, for she could not have done the jobs alone." Likewise, the *Argus-Bulletin* noted that "Helgelein was a heavy man and it seems impossible that a woman could have killed him without help." Both papers thereafter published many stories concerning some of Gunness's possible accomplices, but only Lamphere was ever charged.[63]

It is also interesting to note the source of many of these theories. Newspapers, both local and national, granted wide circulation to essentially uninformed speculations by common people. Some newspapers of that time were prone to sensationalism in an attempt to reach a wider audience. The news was often popularized, and reporters personally investigated murders in competition with the police. The sensationalism was also due to the unbelievable nature of the crimes—Gunness had violated so many social norms that anyone's guess as to why she did so was welcome. For example, in conjunction with the theory that Gunness must have had accomplices, a streetcar driver asserted that he may have let Gunness's accomplice off near her house on many occasions. The driver, a Mr. Murdock, hypothesized that perhaps this man, who often rode in his car, had "decapitated the helpless victims, dismembered the bodies, and then assisted in burying the bleeding corpses in the private graveyard." In other words, the man committed all of the violent acts and did all of the heavy lifting. Only Assistant Police Chief Schuettler of Chicago gave Gunness more credit when he stated that "she was a strong enough woman to be able to kill a man of size if she took him unawares."[64] Of course, she required the element of surprise, but Schuettler did at least recognize her strength.

The writer and detective Clifton R. Wooldridge also thought Gunness had help. He and others blamed the matrimonial agencies. A voice of the Progressive Era's campaigns against the inherent evils perceived in the industrialization of America, he fought against these agencies. He insisted that "it is the matrimonial agency, nothing else, which is directly responsible for the unbelievable horrors of the Gunness Murder Farm." Perhaps Gunness had at one time been a "true woman," but these agencies had planted an evil impulse in her that she was not strong enough to overcome. Like Lombroso's "occasional criminals," she had been led astray by others.[65] Gunness had done nothing wrong except look for a husband in the wrong manner. She had put her trust in people who sought to victimize unsuspecting men and women and in turn had also victimized *her*.

Even more bizarre, many observers found evidence of the supernatural in Gunness's crimes. Gunness was reinvented and stories ran the gamut between the influence of her father, rumored to be a magician with extraordinary powers, and the possibility that Satan possessed her. Thus, rumors about her upbringing made her appear rather exotic and in possession of supernatural powers of hypnotism. These fanciful tales provided a means of explaining her ability to murder these "young and strong" men. A woman could not have possibly done these deeds alone, but she might have been able to if she had hypnotic powers over her victims.[66]

Another theory that grew quickly was that Gunness was the reincarnation of Kate Bender, or perhaps Kate Bender herself. The legend of the Bender family, especially Kate, inspired national interest. During the early 1870s the Benders invited weary travelers into their home and then summarily killed them and stole their money. In 1873, in the face of rising suspicions, they fled, with a posse right behind them. The Benders escaped and, as far as anyone knew, were still alive in 1908, when Kate would have been fifty-seven years old.[67] The idea that Gunness was actually Bender was ludicrous, but it caught on. This formulation enabled many people to explain how two women could have killed—they were one and the same woman.

On May 11, the Daily Herald printed an anonymous letter that stated that Gunness was "descended from the same name [family] as Kate Bender," that "Kate's father was a brother to Mrs. Gunness' grandfather. I know this through my own marriage ties." It was misinformation, but the letter points up the complicated theories constructed to keep the murderesses in one demented family. Finally, on July 14, the *Daily Herald* printed a story meant to quiet the rumor that Kate Bender and Gunness were one person. George Evans Douner asserted that he had been a member of the posse sent after the Benders, and on his deathbed, he decided to set the record straight. The posse had caught the Benders and had killed the whole family in self-defense when the Benders had shot at them. The members of the posse had all promised one another to keep their actions secret. Apparently, they had actually tortured and then brutally murdered the family. They had also taken whatever valuables they found. Douner's assertions were corroborated a year later when yet another member of that posse made his own deathbed confession.[68]

The most popular theory involving the influence of the supernatural on Gunness was the belief that the house she had lived in was possessed by an evil so strong that it had driven her to murder. It was not her fault—it was the house.

The place where Gunness had chosen to live had a long and dark history. It had been built in the middle of the nineteenth century by John and Harriet Holcomb, and then it passed to Charles Drebing, a highly respected gentleman in the community. After his death, persons "less favored by the goddess of Reputation" bought it. "Strange stories of revelry and mystery had, from time to time been whispered through the community concerning its inhabitants." Josh Chaney stated that "in time, this beautiful spot acquired an unsavory reputation and it was shunned by those of the community who would otherwise naturally have acquired [purchased] it." It went through several hands, apparently becoming a brothel. The Gross family owned it in the late 1880s, until one of them committed suicide by hanging. Then Mattie Altic took possession of the house and opened another brothel. She died, alone, in 1894. Still another owner after that met tragedy there; C. M. Eddy's wife died on the farm and he promptly sold it. After he moved to Chicago, he died. (The *Daily Herald* implied a connection between the house and his death.) Gunness purchased the place in 1901.[69]

The infamy of the Gunness house is evident in many ways. On the form used for the Coroner's Inquisition into Peter Gunness's death, the coroner listed the address as simply "the old Mattie Altic place." When news of the fire appeared in the papers, the dwelling was again identified as "the Mattie Altic place."

Later, after reports of Gunness's crimes had surfaced, the newspapers referred to her home as "the death-haunted farm," the "House of Mystery," and the "house of horror."[70]

Perceptions of the house soon evolved from simply a place where tragedies and crime had occurred to being an entity itself. "The Farm" became a plague on the community. Often, instead of saying that Gunness had visited some place in the city, a writer would say that the city received a "visit from 'The Farm.'" The place where Gunness had lived became "the house of sin," and Gunness merely did its bidding. Gunness's powers and place in the minds of these writers was secondary to the influence of "The Farm." Gunness merely looked after the place, or, more to the point, was its victim. This phenomenon can be seen especially in the *Daily Herald*'s reference to psychometry, which imparted the belief that the "walls, furniture, tapestry, pictures, etc., of the home, school, church, alms-house, jail or penitentiary, bear impress of the transactions of their inhabitants and may reflect their influence on succeeding occupants." The paper theorized that people might think twice before purchasing any relics from the Gunness farm if they understood psychometry, for Gunness's possessions "transmit or reflect an ora [*sic*] of evil, though unknown and unseen." The *Daily Herald* writer went on to say, "No better fate could have befallen the Gunness residence than its utter destruction by fire, which is nature's purifying agent."[71]

At least one local minister turned to the traditional explanation that Satan had possessed Gunness. The Reverend M. L. Kirkland preached a sermon on the subject in Evansville, reported in the *Daily Herald*. Kirkland insisted that religion alone could have saved her.[72] Once again, someone stepped in to deny Gunness's responsibility for her actions. A "true woman" had not killed; a woman possessed by the devil had killed.

There were other theories, however, that assigned Gunness far more responsibility for her actions. To argue for her responsibility, though, believers of these theories had to prove Gunness "unwomanly." Gunness's real motivation was greed. These critics argued that Gunness had not behaved as a "true woman" and was, therefore, "monstrously abnormal." The *Argus-Bulletin* printed a story concerning Gunness's restlessness with her female role. Her first husband, Mads Sorenson, "was marked for his industry . . . [and] provided with lavish hand for every want of his wife, dressing her handsomely, providing her with jewels, and in every way satisfying the little ambitions so inseparably linked with womanhood." Gunness, however, was not satisfied. She had "wearied of life with him." She had "an intense longing for a new face, for the new influences which would come with a second marriage." In other words, she had wanderlust and wanted more than her husband could provide; so she killed him. She soon had a "yearning for a new home and new scenes, for new environments," and she moved on to LaPorte. She married Gunness and the two settled into a married life "where every gift of nature was in evidence, and where any couple . . . would have found the ideal place for the passing of life." But Gunness was still unsatisfied, so she killed her second husband. Even in death her husbands had taken proper care of her because Gunness "realized handsomely on the insurance policies which thoughtful husbands had provided." Though the insurance money "provided for her and her children, educating the latter, giving the home every comfort," it "was not sufficient to her mind," and she formulated "the scheme of wholesale murder." Gunness could never get enough. Her sister stated that "all she [Gunness] loved was money."[73] *Key*

Gunness's inability to be satisfied was a theme in many explanations of her crimes. A man in Washington, D.C., who claimed to have spotted Gunness, said that he could tell from her eyes that "she could never be entirely satisfied," that she had "an excess of will." A Pinkerton detective believed that Gunness had killed Olaf Limbo because "he had assumed an air of proprietorship which was displeasing to one of her masterful ways."[74]

Stories of Gunness's inherently "masculine" behavior were many. "She had a shrewd business head and quickly caught on when informed of business points which a woman is not supposed to know." One of her neighbors from Chicago said that Gunness "used to prowl about the neighborhood late at night," and Gunness's sister stated that she "was always wild." The fact that Gunness had "kill[ed] innocent victims of the opposite sex" invited comparisons to the behavior of "the normally depraved male" who did the same. Observers noted that she "ran after Lamphere" which was not "womanly" behavior. Gunness also "attended nearly all of the public sales and was a shrewd judge of cattle and sheep," and "associated entirely with men" at the sales, something a woman would never do. One woman was particularly outraged by Gunness's habit of "going into the barnyard with men," which "no woman would think" of doing. Finally, the pastor who had married Gunness to her second husband recalled that "the groom appeared to lack self-reliance, the woman directing the ceremony even to the fee which the man" had given him.[75] Gunness wanted to be the one in control, which was "unwomanly." The lesson to all women was obvious: be at peace with your role and accept it unconditionally or evil will befall you and your loved ones.

But some observers could not imagine a woman violating her social and biological roles so completely. Lombroso spoke for these skeptics in declaring that Gunness was really a man in disguise. Lombroso argued that "it is not an unusual thing in criminology to find great ferocity and great dissimulation in women." In other words, women such as Gunness often pretend to be passive, pure, and pious, but underneath this facade lurks a vicious disposition. When women "are criminal" he went on, "they are considerably more so than men." In addition, the natural maternal instinct, "which is conspicuous in the normal woman is not only suppressed, but reversed as it becomes in [female killers] a pleasure to torture their own offspring."[76] Lombroso asserted that in order for females to become criminal, they must have intelligence; and if they have that intelligence they then move up his hierarchy and become "men." His skull measurements of female criminals proved to his satisfaction the veracity of his theory; these women had the same physical characteristics as the male criminals he had studied. So Gunness was, then, essentially a man. From that essentialist argument, many people leapt to the conclusion that she *was* in fact a man.

The most obvious indication of gender is dress, and Gunness dressed like a man. Gunness would show up at farm sales "wearing a man's sealskin coat and cap. . . . Belle was very mannish looking." Mrs. Lapham of LaPorte remembered the day she saw Gunness wearing a leather belt "being of a type made for use by frontiersmen," and another woman noted Gunness's habit of wearing men's rings.[77]

Gunness not only dressed like a man, she looked like one. She had a "muscular physique," was "rugged," and her "hand was as large as that of a man her size with its muscles well-developed." She was "square jawed, black eyed, and grim visaged. She was a woman who would attract attention for her want of womanly characteristics." Her great strength was also compared to that of a man. Stories circulated that on occasion she had single-handedly lifted a calf and heavy furniture.[78]

Many people thus concluded that Gunness was actually a man masquerading as a woman. One man stated that looking at her picture, he believed that "the person who sat for [it] could easily be a man, with some operation performed in his youth which kept his voice high like a woman's and he could have fooled all the men that he married and everyone else."[79] This interpretation allowed the complete negation of the fact that a woman had killed.

Gender was erased when the *Argus-Bulletin* printed a story that theorized what would have happened had Johann Hoch—a man in Chicago who had scoured the obituaries for wealthy widows, won their trust, and then killed them—met Belle Gunness. The paper defined Hoch as a "male Gunness" and Gunness as a "female Hoch." Gender is irrelevant here. Gunness and Hoch were simply criminal beings.[80]

Not content to transform Gunness into a man, or take gender completely out of the equation, others sought to send her still further down the evolutionary scale, even below Lombroso's bottom rung of nonwhite females. Some likened Gunness to an animal, a "blood dyed human hyena," and spoke of her home as her "lair." The Reverend Daniels stated that "the outline of her profile was peculiar, especially as the forehead neared the eyes, giving to some a faint suggestion of an ape." Perhaps, Daniels concluded, Gunness had not evolved fully. Others negated Gunness's "humanness" entirely, making her a "monster," a "fiend in human form," a "she-devil," a "demon," a "ghoul," an "ogress," a "female vampire," and a "hellish harpy."[81]

The main goal of all of these theories was to allow the community to reconcile itself to the fact that a woman had killed. Whether it did so by denying that she was a "true woman," or a woman at all, or by shifting the responsibility so that she was not aware of her actions or under the influence of some evil force, the final product was the contentment that came with the knowledge that the image of the "ideal woman" was safe—safe, at least, until others cast doubt on the absolute standard of true womanhood.

This phenomenon of casting about for "logical" explanations for the crime in our midst continues today. We would all much rather believe that murderers are people—read: men—who are easy to spot. They have disheveled hair and filthy clothes, and are perpetually foaming at the mouth. They are clinically and legally "insane." The reality that it can literally be the "normal"-looking young man living next door or the innocent-looking young mother of two, is too frightening and destructive of our cultural peace. Our society has constructed roles for its members, and when people violate those ideals, they endanger the very structure of society. So we search for an explanation that makes sense and that does not threaten the status quo. As turn-of-the-century Americans searched for a means of protecting the idea of "true womanhood" and the patriarchy, contemporary Americans also attempt to explain how members of society who are supposed to be the nurturers and the caretakers can turn on the very people who are most dependent upon them, as in the Susan Smith case. The difference is that today we are able to recognize the cultural and social dynamics that are often at work, though we are hardly more comfortable as a consequence.

NOTES

1. Unless otherwise noted, the depositions of all of those involved corroborate one another. Gunness's children present in the home at the time were Myrtle, Lucy, and Philip. Coroner's Inquisition, Body of Belle Gunness, Exhibit "B," deposition of Joseph Maxson, dated 29 April 1908, 1–3, 5, filed with the Clerk's Office, 20 May 1908, State Exhibit 1, LaPorte County Historical Museum, Belle Gunness Collection (hereafter cited as LCHMBGC); Exhibit "C," deposition of William Clifford (from Coroner's Inquisition into the death of Myrtle Sorensen but included in Coroner's Inquisition, Body of Belle Gunness), dated 29 April 1908, 1–3.

2. Coroner's Inquisition, Body of Belle Gunness, Exhibit "D," deposition of William Humphrey, dated 29 April 1908, 1–4; Exhibit "E," deposition of Michael Clifford, dated 29 April 1908, 4; Exhibit "B," 4–5; Exhibit "F," deposition of Daniel Marion Hutson, dated 29 April 1908, 2.

3. *LaPorte Argus-Bulletin* (hereafter cited as *LAB*), 28 April 1908.

4. *LaPorte Daily Herald* (hereafter cited as *LDH*), 11 March 1908; *LAB*, 4, 29, 16 April 1908.

5. *LAB*, 28 April 1908; *LDH*, 28 April 1908.

6. Ibid.

7. *State of Indiana v. Ray Lamphere* (hereafter cited as *SIRL*), Charge Sheet, for the murder of Belle Gunness brought by Albert F. Smutzer, Sheriff of LaPorte County, Signed 29 April 1908 [30 April 1908], by Smutzer and Prosecutor Smith before S. E. Grover, J.P., LaPorte Circuit Court; *SIRL*, Offense Information Sheet, for the charge of the murder of Belle Gunness, 30 April 1908, filed with the Clerk's Office, 8 May 1908.

Lamphere was eventually tried on 9 November 1908 for arson, one count of accessory to murder, and four counts of first-degree murder. The jury returned a verdict on 26 November of guilty of arson, but he was found not guilty of the remaining charges. He was fined $5,000 and given a prison term of two to twenty-one years to be served in the Indiana State Prison. He was thirty-eight at the time. He died a year later on 30 December from tuberculosis. (See *SIRL*, Verdict, LaPorte Circuit Court, September Term, 1908, signed by Henry Mill, Foreman; *SIRL*, S.1061, LCHMBGC; Lillian de la Torre, *The Truth about Belle Gunness* (New York: Fawcett Publications, Gold Medal Books, 1955), 167.) *LAB*, 29 April 1908; *LDH*, 29 April 1908.

8. *LAB*, 29 April 1908.

9. *LDH*, 4 May 1908; *LAB*, 4 May 1908.

10. Coroner's Inquisition, Body of Andrew K. Helgelein, Exhibit "B," deposition of Asle K. Helgelein, dated 9 May 1908, 1–2, 13, filed with the Clerk's Office, 14 July 1908.

11. Ibid., 3–6.

12. Ibid., 6–8, 9–10.

13. Ibid., 10–11.

14. Coroner's Inquisition, Body of Andrew K. Helgelein, Exhibit "A," deposition of Coroner Mack, 1.

15. Belle Gunness to Andrew K. Helgelein, 17 September 1906 (translation), LCHMBGC; Jay Robert Nash, *Encyclopedia of World Crime: Criminal Justice, Criminology, and Law Enforcement*, vol. 2 (Wilmette, Ill.: Crime Books, 1990), 1402.

16. *LAB*, 7 May 1908.

17. *LDH*, 23 May 1908. Whether Gunness had actually died in the fire or whether the body found was that of some other woman, planted by Gunness as a decoy, was the subject of debate. There in no convincing proof either way. As late as the 1960s there was a "Gunness sighting" in California.

18. *USA Today*, 13 January 1992.

19. *LDH*, 9 May 1908; *LAB*, 12, 9 May 1908.

20. Josh Chaney, "Story Concerning Belle Gunness Mystery" (unpublished, n.d.), 17–18. Property of Judge Alban Smith, LaPorte, #89/30, LCHMBGC; "The Belle Gunness Case: As Presented to the Students of the History Department" (condensation of speech given by Judge Wirt Worden on 7 December 1938), LCHMBGC; *LAB*, 8, 9 May 1908.

21. *LAB*, 13 May 1908; *LDH*, 27 May 1908.

22. de la Torre, *Truth about Belle Gunness*, 110, 111; *LAB*, 29 April, 12 May, 30 July 1908; *St. Louis Post-Dispatch*, 7 May 1908; *LDH*, 28 April, 11 May 1908; Chaney, "Story Concerning Belle Gunness," 20, 21; de la Torre, *Truth about Belle Gunness*, 137–38, 153.

23. *LAB*, 9 May, 30 July 1908; de la Torre, *Truth about Belle Gunness*, 93; Coroner's Inquisition, Body of Belle Gunness, Exhibit "K," 3; Worden, speech 4; *LAB*, 8, 9, 12, 15, 19 May, 23 June 1908, *New York Times* [hereafter cited as *NYT*], 9 May 1908.

24. *LDH*, 11, 21 May 1908; *NYT*, 11 May 1908.

25. *NYT*, 11 May 1908; *LDH*, 11 May 1908.

26. *NYT*, 11 May 1908.

27. *LDH*, 29 June 1908; de la Torre, *Truth about Belle Gunness*, 51.

28. *LAB*, 15, 18 May 1908; *LDH*, 16, 22, 27 May 1908; de la Torre, *Truth about Belle Gunness*, 51.

29. Dorothy Rowley, *Belle Gunness—Indiana Folklore*, as reported by Norris D. Coambs, Duneland Notes, September 1977, 4, LCHMBGC; *LAB*, 1, 2 May 1908; de la Torre, *Truth about Belle Gunness*, 12; *LDH*, 8 May 1908. Gunness's original name has been listed as Bella Poulsdatter, Belle Brynhilde Paulsetter, and Brynhild Paulsdatter Storset. She was born 11 November 1859.

30. *LDH*, 7, 23 May 1908; *LAB*, 7, 2 May 1908; Rowley, *Belle Gunness*, 4.

31. According to Dr. Keith Wilson, the symptoms of arsenic poisoning—a poison that was found to be present in other Gunness victims—are diarrhea, abdominal pain, nausea, and vomiting. Victorian doctors, analyzing the symptoms of arsenic poisoning cases, often

misdiagnosed the cause of death as "gastric fever." Arsenic poisoning leads to "hemorrhage from the intestine and loss of fluids [which] result in vascular collapse with dizziness, convulsions, coma and finally death." See Keith D. Wilson, M.D., *Cause of Death: A Writer's Guide to Death, Murder and Forensic Medicine* (Cincinnati: Writer's Digest Books, 1992), 118.

32. *LAB*, 7 May 1908; *LDH*, 8 May 1908. Other sources place the total of the two policies at $8,000. I was unable to discover which amount of the two was accurate.

33. Coroner's Inquisition, Body of Peter Gunness, 18 December 1902, Testimony of Belle Gunness; Chaney, "Story Concerning Belle Gunness," 7; *LAB*, 28 April, 1, 5 May 1908.

34. For a discussion of "separate spheres" and women's progress into "man's sphere," see Carol Ruth Barkin and Mary Beth Norton, eds., *Women of America: A History* (Boston: Houghton Mifflin, 1979); Nancy F. Cott, *Grounding of Modern Feminism* (New Haven: Yale University Press, 1987); Nancy F. Cott and Elizabeth Pleck, eds., *A Heritage of Her Own: Toward a New Social History of American Women* (New York: Simon & Schuster, 1979); Ann Douglas, *The Feminization of American Culture* (New York: Knopf, 1977); Linda Kerber, "Separate Spheres, Female Worlds, Woman's Place: The Rhetoric of Women's History," *Journal of American History* 75 (June 1988): 9–39; Barbara Harris, *Beyond Her Sphere: Women and the Professions in American History* (Westport, Conn.: Greenwood Press, 1978); Mary S. Hartman and Lois Banner, eds., *Clio's Consciousness Raised: New Perspectives on the History of Women* (New York: Harper and Row, 1974).

35. Carroll Smith-Rosenberg, *Disorderly Conduct: Visions of Gender in Victorian America* (New York: Knopf, 1985), 23.

36. Ibid., 130–35, 176–77.

37. Ibid., 252, 265, 23, 24.

38. Ibid., 263; Mary P. Ryan, *Womanhood in America: From Colonial Times to the Present* 3d ed. (New York: Franklin Watts, 1983), 199. This new tactic was exemplified in the *Daily Herald*'s 15 February 1908 issue. The headline on the front page read "Women Becoming Educated Class, Predominate In Church and Philanthropic Work: Miss Laura Gregg Makes Suffrage Plea, Says Something is Wrong With Our Social Conditions When Nine-Tenths of the Inmates of Jails and Penal Institutions Are Men—Should Bring Womanhood Into Our Nation's Life." The paper offered no editorial comments on the issue or on Gregg's speech; it only reported the event.

39. Smith-Rosenberg, *Disorderly Conduct*, 265.

40. Ibid., 279, 258, 260.

41. John D'Emilio and Estelle B. Freedman, *Intimate Matters: A History of Sexuality in America* (New York: Harper and Row, 1988), 190.

42. Chaney, "Story Concerning Belle Gunness," 5, 7.

43. *LAB*, 7 May 1908.

44. *LDH*, 29, 28 April 1908; *LAB*, 28 April 1908; *NYT*, 5 May 1908.

45. *NYT*, 9 May 1908; *LDH*, 9 May 1908; *LAB*, 8, 9, 19 May 1908; *LDH*, 8, 19 May 1908; unattributed enlargements in the LCHMBGC; *LDH*, 19 May 1908.

The Gunness case even gave birth to a new verb. The *Argus-Bulletin*, when relating the story of one of Gunness's victims, stated that the victim had been "Gunnessized." See *LAB*, 11 May 1908.

46. Ibid., 7, 9, 8 May 1908; *LDH*, 12 May 1908.

47. *NYT*, 5 May 1908; *LAB*, 13, 14, 12 May 1908; Elizabeth H. and Joseph H. Pleck, eds., *The American Man* (Englewood Cliffs, N.J.: Prentice-Hall, 1980), 24, 22. Progressive Era concerns with the evils and dangers of alcohol were also exemplified in a murder case

that was tried in April 1908. A son had killed his mother with a hammer in March. Although the paper headlined the story "Son's Unnatural Crime," it also printed the following: He was a "kind and dutiful son except when under the influence of liquor." This was a man who had beat his mother to death with a hammer so that he could steal some money from her. See *LAB*, 11 April 1908. The article did not exude the same ferocity and disgust that characterized the paper's discussion of Gunness not three weeks later. LaPorte newspapers highlighted this young man's drinking problem, and Lamphere's as well, as a lesson to others; but more than that, society turned the two men into victims. Although the two were hardly leading exemplary lives, they were not "bad"; they had merely succumbed to the evils of liquor.

48. Richard Deming, *Women: The New Criminals* (Nashville: Thomas Nelson, 1977), 45; JoAnn Gennaro Gora, *The New Female Criminal: Empirical Reality or Social Myth?* (New York: Praeger, 1982), 2.

49. *Alienist* was the nineteenth-century term for a psychologist. Lombroso's assertion that men were morally superior to women was not in line with society's assertion of the moral superiority of women. This was one point of his theory that was ignored. No one questioned that deviant women were immoral, so when his theory was applied to criminal females, it made perfectly good sense.

Colin Wilson's introduction to *The New Murderers' Who's Who*, by J. H. H. Gaute and Robin Odell, forewords by Colin Wilson and Richard Whittington-Egan, Library of Crime Classics (New York: International Polygonics, 1981), Cesare Lombroso and Guglielmo Ferrero, *The Female Offender*, introduced by W. Douglas Morrison (New York: D. Appleton, 1903), 147; Rita James Simon, "Women and Crime," in *Encyclopedia of Crime and Justice*, ed. Sanford H. Kadish (New York: Free Press, 1983), 1665; Gora, *New Female Criminal*, 4.

50. Lombroso and Ferrero, *Female Offender*, 147.

51. Ibid., 152, 159, 160, 162, 164, 165.

52. Ibid., 201, 196, 204.

53. Ibid., 294, 298.

54. Ibid., 310, 244, 248.

55. Simon, "Women and Crime," 1665; *The Standard Edition of the Complete Psychological Works of Sigmund Freud*, trans. from the German under the general editorship of James Strachey, in collaboration with Anna Freud, assisted by Alix Strachey and Alan Tyson, vol. 7 (1901–1905), *A Case of Hysteria, Three Essays on Sexuality and Other Works* (London: Hogarth Press, 1953; reprint, 1968), 221 (page reference is to reprint edition).

56. Elaine S. Abelson, *When Ladies Go A-Thieving: Middle-Class Shoplifters in the Victorian Department Store* (New York: Oxford University Press, 1989), 7, 8, 12, 174, 173, 198. Abelson does not neglect to point out that this was a class issue. She states, "Middle-class women suffered from kleptomania; lower-class women who stole from stores were classified as thieves" (174). Gunness was a member of the white middle class, so this theory would apply to her.

57. *LAB*, 11, 25 May 1908; *LDH*, 7, 9 May, 4 June 1908.

58. *LDH*, 9 May 1908; *LAB*, 11, 25 May 1908.

59. *St. Louis Post-Dispatch*, 7 May 1908; *LDH*, 13 May 1908.

60. *LAB*, 9, 25 May 1908; Lombroso and Ferrero, *Female Offender*, 167, 168.

61. *LDH*, 4 June; 9 May 1908; *LAB*, 16 May 1908.

62. *NYT*, 8 May 1908.

63. *LDH*, 4 June 1908, 5 May 1908; *LAB*, 6, May 1908.

64. *LAB*, 13 May 1908; *NYT*, 5 May 1908; *LDH*, 6, 8 May 1908.

65. Clifton R. Wooldridge, *Twenty Years a Detective in the Wickedest City in the World* (Chicago: author, 1908), 165, 170.

66. *LDH*, 16, 21 May 1908; *LAB*, 12 May 1908. It was later learned that Gunness's father had been a cotter and stonemason—not a conjuror—but some LaPorteans clung to the belief that her upbringing was responsible for her actions. A dime novel published that year repeated the false story about her youth. From then on, the common belief was that Gunness's father had been a magician and that she had been his able student.

67. Kerry Segrave, *Women Serial and Mass Murderers: A Worldwide Reference, 1580 Through 1990* (Jefferson, N.C.: McFarland, 1992), 35; *NYT*, 5 May 1908.

68. *LDH*, 11, 30 May, 14 July 1908; Segrave, *Women and Serial Murderers*, 37–38; J. Gaute and Odell, *The New Murderer's Who's Who*, 51.

69. Gene McDonald, "Notes on Belle Gunness Case" (1967), LCHM, 1; Chaney, "Story Concerning Belle Gunness," 3, 4; *LDH*, 12, 14, 13 May 1908.

70. Coroner's Inquisition, Body of Peter Gunness, dated 18 December 1902; *LDH*, 28 April 1908; *NYT*, 6, 16 May 1908; *LDH*, 6 May 1908; *LAB*, 7 May 1908.

71. Chaney, "Story Concerning Belle Gunness," 13; *LDH*, 9, 14 May 1908; *LAB*, 18 July, 12 May 1908; *LDH*, 4 June 1908.

72. *LDH*, 13 May 1908.

73. Ibid., 23 May 1908; *LAB*, 7 May 1908; *LDH*, 7, 9 May 1908.

74. *LDH*, 20, 9 May 1908.

75. *LAB*, 25, 12 May 1908; *LDH*, 9, 7, 5 May 1908; Rowley, *Belle Gunness*, 6.

76. *LDH*, 4 June 1908.

77. Rowley, *Belle Gunness*, 6; *LAB*, 12, 19 May 1908.

78. Chaney, "Story Concerning Belle Gunness," 8; *LAB*, 9, 7 May 1908; Rowley, *Belle Gunness*, 6.

79. *LDH*, 20 May 1908.

80. *LAB*, 9 May 1908.

81. *LAB*, 6, 7, 9, 25 May 1908; *LDH*, 9, 13, 19, 21, 23 May 1908; *Helena Independent*, 8 May 1908.

"MY GOD! IF ONLY I COULD GET OUT OF HERE."
The midnight shriek of a young girl in the vice district of a
large city, heard by two worthy men, started a crusade which resulted
in closing up the dens of shame in that city. (See page 450.)

A young woman kidnapped into prostitution. Ernest A. Bell, *Fighting the Traffic in Young Girls* (n.p.: G. S. Ball, 1910), frontispiece.

Chapter Seventeen

Cultural Representations and Social Contexts of Rape in the Early Twentieth Century

Mary E. Odem

Over the past two decades feminist researchers and activists have challenged the dominant cultural image of rape in the United States. Popular culture has constructed a terrifying vision of an armed stranger, typically a black man, attacking his victim, typically a white woman, in dark alleys and parking lots. Numerous recent studies have shown that women are far more likely to be sexually assaulted by men they know; the assailant is usually an acquaintance, date, neighbor, or male relative and of the same racial/ethnic group as the victim.[1]

Prior to the feminist rethinking of sexual violence, stereotypes of rape in the popular press and media profoundly shaped social understandings of and legal responses to the problem in American society. This examination of rape and its representation in the early twentieth century finds that two dominant images circulated widely in newspapers, journals, films, and best-selling novels, all of which depicted rape as a violent act committed against white women by dark-skinned immigrant men or African American men. These representations had significant cultural power, but they greatly distorted the social circumstances of rape described by female victims in criminal court records, impeding any serious effort to address the problem of sexual violence during this period.

One central image of rape was constructed in the context of the great public agitation over "white slavery." Many Americans at the turn of the century believed that an underground system of "white slavery" operated in cities throughout the country, abducting young women and girls off the streets, sexually assaulting them, and then forcing them into a life of prostitution from which they could not escape. The United States district attorney for Chicago, Edwin Sims, wrote frequently about the issue in the country's leading newsmagazines, asserting that white slavery is

> a system of girl-hunting that is national and international in its scope, that it literally consumes thousands of girls—clean, innocent girls—every year; that it is operated with a cruelty, a barbarism that gives a new meaning to the word fiend; that it is an

imminent peril to every girl in the country who has a desire to get into the city and taste its excitements and its pleasures.

Historians have typically interpreted the white slavery scare as a narrative about prostitution, which was indeed a central preoccupation of middle-class reformers, public officials, writers, and social critics at the time. But white slavery is also a narrative about rape—inevitably, the route to prostitution involved a forcible assault on a young, innocent woman.[2]

The agitation over "white slavery" found expression in numerous articles, governmental reports, books, and films. Polemical tracts about white slavery flooded the American public between 1909 and 1915 under such titles as *The Great War on White Slavery* (1911), *Fighting the Traffic in Young Girls* (1910), *The Girl Who Disappears* (1911), *America's Black Traffic in White Girls* (1912), and *Modern Herodians or Slaughterers of Innocents* (1909).[3] Films such as *The Traffic in Souls* (1913) and *The Inside of the White Slave Traffic* (1913) were shown in theaters throughout the country, attracting large audiences. Social reformer and writer Reginald Wright Kauffman produced a best-selling novel about white slavery in 1910, *The House of Bondage*.[4]

The books and films told variants of the tale of an innocent, young, white woman who leaves the safety of her home and family in the country for the adventures of the city. Soon after her arrival in the city, she falls into the hands of sinister men involved in the "white slave trade" who are on the lookout for naive, unprotected girls. The main places of entrapment are movie theaters, dance halls, ice cream parlors, employment bureaus, department stores, train stations, and busy city streets. The white slaver uses a variety of devious methods to ensnare his victim. He might offer to help find lodging or employment, invite her to go out to the movies or ice cream parlor, or make a promise of marriage. If these do not work, he will resort to harsher tactics: plying the victim with alcohol, giving her a drugged drink, or using a chloroformed cloth to make her unconscious, whatever means are necessary to get her into a brothel, where she is then raped and forced to become a prostitute.

These narratives invariably portrayed white slavers as dark-skinned, foreign men, primarily as southern and eastern European immigrants. Theodore A. Bingham, a former commissioner of police in New York City, asserted that most of the men engaged in the traffic were foreigners. Jean Zimmerman, author of *America's Black Traffic in White Girls*, warned that white slavery is "carried on and exploited by a foaming pack of foreign hell hounds, . . . the moral and civic degenerates of the French, Italian, Syrian, Russian, Jewish or Chinese races." She further asserted that "an American or Englishman conducting such a business is almost entirely unknown." Clifford Roe, assistant state attorney of Illinois, wrote frequently of his dealings with the white slave trade. In his widely disseminated book *The Great War on White Slavery*, Roe asserted that in fifty of the seventy-seven cases of white slavery that had come under his jurisdiction, defendants had last names that were distinctly Jewish, French, or Italian.[5]

Kauffman's popular *House of Bondage* reinforced the image, pervasive in journalistic writings, of the dark-skinned immigrant as the rapist of young white women. In this story, chaste Mary Denbigh is lured from her Pennsylvania hometown to New York City by a Jewish procurer, Max Grossman. Kauffman described the deliberately named Grossman with graphic bigotry: "The hair on his head was black and curly. . . . His lips were thick when he did not smile and thin when he did, with teeth very white." Grossman's speech had a "quick, thick quality, and its ictus on the vowels, denoted the foreigner." Grossman, whose job is to comb the countryside looking for young female victims, sidles up to Mary on a street in her hometown, discovers that she is unhappy with her strict parents and wants to see more of the world. He offers to take her to see the sights and thrills of New York City and promises to marry her once there. But instead, when the train arrives in New York, Max takes Mary to a fancy restaurant and urges her to drink champagne. The following morning she awakens in a drugged state and discovers to her horror that she has been sexually assaulted and is now a prisoner of a brothel—another victim of the swarthy immigrant.[6]

A second dominant representation of rape—that of the black rapist—circulated in the popular press and media in the early twentieth century. The image of the black rapist first appeared widely in the South in the late nineteenth century. Although white fear of black male sexuality existed in the antebellum period, this fear greatly intensified with the emancipation of slaves and the granting of political rights to African American men after the Civil War. Many white southerners conflated the increased economic and political autonomy of African Americans with sexual aggression on the part of black men.[7]

The theme of dangerous black male sexuality appeared in numerous newspaper articles and fictional works and became a major issue in white southern politics. Prominent southern writers, politicians, educators, and religious leaders held that blacks were becoming increasingly savage and lustful now that they were no longer enslaved. In an article that appeared in the national magazine *Forum* in 1893, Bishop Atticus G. Haygood of Georgia asserted that the rape of white women by black men had increased dramatically after the Civil War. In 1901, George T. Winston, president of the North Carolina College of Agricultural and Mechanic Arts, also commented on the supposed heightened sexual criminality of black men since slavery. He provided a particularly lurid description of the black rapist: "[W]hen a knock is heard at the door, [the Southern woman] shudders with nameless horror. The black brute is lurking in the dark, a monstrous beast, crazed with lust." The belief in black-male sexual violence became so pervasive among white Americans by the early twentieth century that rape came to be referred to as the "new Negro crime."[8]

Popular fiction by southern writers further promoted the black rapist theme. Thomas Nelson Page, best known for his images of the loyal "darky" in stories of the Old South, also depicted a very different, threatening black character in Red Rock, a novel published in 1898. Set during Reconstruction, the novel portrays a devious black politician named Moses who seeks not only political power but also sexual access to white women. Moses attempts to assault a white woman and later in the novel he meets his end at the hands of lynchers.[9]

Southern novelist Thomas Dixon did more than any other fiction writer to popularize the myth of the black rapist in his best-selling novels published early in the twentieth century. Dixon, who was a prominent Baptist minister before he became a writer, used his fiction to demonstrate the supposed bestiality of African Americans and their danger to society now that they were no longer enslaved. His most popular novel, *The Clansman: An Historical Romance of the Ku Klux Klan* (1905), describes the chaos, danger, and disorder that afflicted the South during Reconstruction when black men were granted political rights. The male protagonist of the novel, southern gentleman Ben Cameron, declares that "the grant of the ballot to these millions of semi-savages and the riot of debauchery which has followed are crimes against human progress. In the climax of the book, four "black brutes" break into the home of a young white woman, Marion, who lives alone with her mother. After beating the mother, the leader of the group, Gus, brutally assaults Marion: "A single tiger spring, and the black claws of the beast sank into the soft white throat until she was still." After she regains consciousness, Marion convinces her mother that they must kill themselves in order to preserve their honor, and the two leap over a cliff to their deaths. The Ku Klux Klan, glorified as heroes in Dixon's novel, avenge the horrible crime by capturing and killing the predator. *The Clansman* found a large and enthusiastic audience; within a few months of its publication, more than a million copies had been sold. Dixon revised *The Clansman* for the theater, and the play became a popular success as it toured the South and Midwest, and even hit Broadway in 1908.[10]

Although originating in the South, the image of the black rapist acquired cultural power in the rest of the country through its circulation in books, articles, and films that reached a national audience. Perhaps most influential in disseminating the image was the film *Birth of a Nation*, first shown in 1915. Directed by D. W. Griffith, *Birth of a Nation* was based on Dixon's *Clansman*. The film version made several changes in the original story, most notably the virginal white woman leaps off the edge of a cliff to her death rather than succumb to sexual violation by a black man. Despite the changes, the plot still revolved around the theme of the monstrous black man threatening white womanhood, but now the image was depicted with even greater power and force, larger than life on the silver screen. Griffith has long been considered one of the country's greatest film directors, and of the many films he made, *Birth of a Nation* is considered his masterpiece. It enjoyed immediate and enormous success, playing to large, enthusiastic audiences in cities and towns nationwide. In spite of vigorous African American protest against it led by the NAACP, *Birth of a Nation* became the most acclaimed and financially successful film of the silent-film era. It also won the admiration and approval of the country's president. Dixon, who coauthored the script, arranged a special screening in the White House for President Woodrow Wilson, his cabinet, and their families. Wilson viewed the film with great interest and reportedly said, "It is like writing history with lightning; and my only regret is that it is all so terribly true."[11]

Such popular representations of rape had great cultural influence in American society, communicating several strong messages. The white slavery and black rapist narratives asserted that women had most to fear from strangers; that these strangers were most likely to be dark-skinned or foreign men; that only white women and girls were threatened by rape; and that women were most vulnerable to sexual assault in public places, when they left the safety of home and family to find work or seek fun and adventure in parks, movie theaters, and city streets.

And yet, the images that dominated the popular media bear little resemblance to the social circumstances of rape reported by female victims and their families to legal and law enforcement officials. To explore the social contexts of sexual violence in the early twentieth century, I have examined all of the rape prosecutions in the criminal court of Alameda County, California, for the period 1910–1920.[12] Out of a total of 120 cases, 37 were forcible assaults; the rest were cases of statutory rape that did not involve force. My analysis is based on the cases of forcible rape. These cases present a picture of sexual danger very different from that elaborated in the dominant stereotypes of rape. They indicate that women and girls were far more likely to be raped by men they knew than by strangers. Eighty-seven percent of the accused assailants knew their female victims; and the accused men were invariably of the same racial/ethnic background as their female victims. Assailants in rape cases included boyfriends, neighbors, employers, coworkers, family friends, and male relatives.[13]

Before turning to a closer examination of these records, it is important to recognize their limitations as sources. Rape trial records do not provide us with a full account of women's and girls' experiences of sexual violence. Many, if not most women and girls who were sexually assaulted did not seek legal prosecution of their assailants because of the great social stigma of rape and the grueling, humiliating treatment rape victims typically received in court. Furthermore, the case records of those who did seek prosecution present problems of interpretation. Women's accounts of rape in the transcripts were highly influenced and structured by the court context: in the intimidating environment of the courtroom, women and girls responded to specific questions posed to them by male judges and attorneys who had considerable legal authority over their lives. In spite of these limitations, the court records are still the best means that historians have for studying and understanding the experiences and circumstances of sexual violence in the past.

Alameda County lies in northern California, across the bay from San Francisco. Like many urban areas in the rest of the country, Alameda County and its principal city, Oakland, witnessed tremendous population growth and economic development in the late nineteenth and early twentieth centuries. Between 1880 and 1920, the population of Oakland increased from 34,555 to 216,260.[14] The extensive expansion of transportation, trade, and industry in northern California drew a succession of native-born and foreign-born workers to Oakland. In the late nineteenth century, native-born white Americans and northern Europeans made up the bulk of the population in the city. After the turn of the century, thousands of southern and eastern Europeans, Mexicans, Asians, and African Americans joined these earlier migrants.[15]

Virtually all of the women, men, and families involved in rape prosecutions in Alameda Superior Court were working class; that is, they and/or their spouses and parents were employed as skilled, semiskilled, or unskilled workers. Reflecting the diversity of the county's working-class population, they included native-born whites and blacks; skilled workers and common laborers; rural migrants and seasoned urban dwellers; and immigrants from Europe and Mexico.

Based on the court records, I have identified five main categories of sexual assaulters: strangers; boyfriends and dates; employers and coworkers; neighbors and family friends; and male relatives. Rapes by strangers, far less frequent than cultural stereotypes implied, constituted 13 percent of the total number of rape cases. Assaults by strange men in some instances occurred when women and girls were away from home. For example, a fourteen-year-old girl was raped when she attended a local nickelodeon one afternoon. The man employed to sell tickets took the girl into a back room, locked the door, raped her, and threatened to kill her if she told anyone. Not all stranger rapes, however, took place in public places away from home. A young white married woman, who worked at home as a housewife was sexually assaulted by a white man selling magazine subscriptions in the neighborhood. According to the woman's testimony, the salesman came into the house to discuss the magazines, then dragged her to the bedroom and raped her.[16]

The vast majority of women and girls, however, were raped by men they knew. Some by boyfriends or men they had been dating. This was so for Carrie Jones, a white woman of twenty-one years who worked as a secretary and lived with her father and cousin. She had dated Frank Martinson, a white twenty-six-year-old shipbuilder who was a long-term acquaintance of her family's. The couple ended their relationship and had not seen each other for several months when Frank showed up at the house one day when no one else was at home. He tried to persuade Carrie to have sex with him and when she refused, he beat her up and raped her.[17]

In another case, Ruby Haynes, a white teenager, had accepted a date with a young white man she met at the movie theater in Oakland. The night they met, Jason Strand took her to the beach, walked her home, and made a date to go to the movies a few days later. As they were walking home after the show, Jason pushed Ruby into a vacant lot and demanded that she have sex with him. When she refused, he threw her to the ground and raped her.[18]

Such encounters, which we now call date rape, did not fit the court's definition of forcible assault. In the eyes of court officials, Ruby had invited the assault by going out unescorted with a young man she had only recently met. She had violated what the court considered appropriate codes of conduct for respectable women and was therefore considered "fair game" for men. In commenting on this case, the judge said, "[W]herever she went and whatever she did with that man was voluntary, no force to it at all; she knew what she was going to get when she got it."[19]

A number of women and girls faced sexual assault by male employers or coworkers in their place of employment. Most of these victims were domestic servants raped by men in the households where they worked. The sexual exploitation of domestics conflicted with the prevailing belief among middle-class people that domestic work was a safe, respectable form of work and that women most often faced sexual danger in the new kinds of employment in factories, offices, restaurants, and department stores. All but one of one of the six victims of rape that occurred in the context of work were employed as domestic servants. Domestic workers were more vulnerable to sexual abuse than female wage earners in department stores, factories, and offices because they were more isolated and lacked the presence and support of fellow women workers to protect them. Often left alone in the house, they became easy targets for assault by the men who lived there. A fifteen-year-old African American girl who boarded with and worked as a domestic servant for a black couple, was raped by the man when his wife was away from home one evening. She left the house the next day and notified her father with the following letter: "Dear Papa: I am sorry that I am not going to stay with Mrs. and Mr. [Jones] because he is always so dirty, and you know [what] that means. I can tell you better when I see you. I am not going to stay here and be disgraced."[20]

A seventeen-year-old Portuguese girl, Isabelle Silva, was assaulted by the male head of the household in the home where she worked as a domestic servant. One day when his wife was away, the man followed the young woman into the barn where she was gathering eggs, knocked her to the ground and raped her. When Isabelle told her parents about the assault, they confronted the man the next day. At first he denied their accusation, then offered to pay them $100 if they agreed not to report him to the police. The Silvas refused his offer and had him arrested.[21]

Other women and girls were raped by male neighbors or family friends, and these assaults most often took place in the victims' homes. In one such case, a Slovakian woman who lived with her husband and children was raped by a family acquaintance who boarded in the household. The man, also Slovakian, assaulted the woman one night when her husband was away from home. Some men used their closeness to and knowledge of the family to take advantage of daughters or wives. For example, a man who was an old family friend visited the wife when her husband, a shipbuilder by trade, was not there. According to the woman, the man stayed and talked to her for a while and then began to make suggestive remarks and grabbed her and pinched her breasts. She tried to push him away, kicked and scratched him, but he overpowered her, carried her to a back room and raped her. In another case a thirty-eight-year-old Italian woman who was single and worked as a domestic was raped by an Italian man she had recently met. The man was an acquaintance and neighbor of her sister and brother-in-law, whose home she was visiting one day when the defendant was also there. As she got up to leave, he offered to walk her home and as they passed a vacant lot, he pushed her to the ground and raped her.[22]

A significant number of female victims of sexual assault were attacked by male family members. Such assaults account for the largest single category of rape that appeared before the Alameda criminal court. One third (32 percent) of the female victims of sexual assault had been attacked by male relatives, including fathers, stepfathers, uncles, and brothers. These cases, in particular, present a striking contrast to the dominant images of rape, which held that women and girls encountered sexual danger from strange men in public places. According to the stereotypes, it was when women and girls left the supposedly safe realm of the home that they were in trouble. But, in fact, sexual harm occurred more often in the home itself, where young women and girls faced sexual assault by male relatives in a position of authority over them.

Some young women and girls had been raped by their fathers. Fifteen-year-old Catherine Schultz had suffered sexual abuse at the hands of her father from the time she was seven years old. When her mother died several years later, her father began having sexual relations with her nearly every night. Catherine tried to stop him by locking her bedroom door; when her father threatened to climb through the window, she nailed it shut. Her father became so angry at her growing resistance, that he refused to give her any spending money and threatened to put her in a detention home. With the support and encouragement of their twenty-five-year-old housekeeper, Catherine finally reported her father to the police.[23]

In other cases, girls had been sexually abused by stepfathers, uncles, brothers, or other male relatives who were in a position of authority over the girls. One fourteen-year-old underwent the sexual abuse of her stepfather for several years. He waited until his wife was away from home to assault her. The girl hesitated to tell her mother because she was afraid of her stepfather and also feared her mother's reaction: "I didn't tell her anything about it because she has heart failure and I know when I tell her anything she gets sick." When the mother overheard her daughter warning a younger sister about the abuse, she reported her husband to the police.[24]

It is difficult to know how common sexual abuse of young women and girls was within the home. Most instances were not reported to law enforcement officials, and even fewer were prosecuted in court. Recent historical studies, however, suggest that the problem was far more general than previously believed. Linda Gordon and Paul O'Keefe found evidence of sexual abuse of girls by male relatives and guardians in 10 percent of the case records from Boston child-protection agencies between 1880 and 1930. In a study of gender relations in nineteenth-century New York, Christine Stansell has argued that "sex with girl children was woven into the fabric of life in the tenements and the streets: out-of-the-ordinary, but not extraordinary."[25]

I do not mean to suggest that the public spaces of work and recreation were free of sexual danger. Young women clearly faced assaults by male employers and coworkers in factories and offices, and by men they met at dance halls and amusement parks. But they were particularly vulnerable to sexual abuse in the home because of their greater economic and psychological dependence on male guardians and their separation from social networks outside the family on which they could rely for support. Young women and girls in families depended on the male heads of household for food and shelter. Some of the victims of familial abuse could and did work, but they rarely earned enough to support themselves independently of their families. As in Catherine Schultz's case, a father could use a daughter's economic dependence to force her compliance to his sexual demands. When Catherine resisted him, her father threatened to deprive her of spending money and to kick her out of the house.[26]

Aside from their economic dependence, most girls were raised in male-dominated households where they learned subservience to male authority. A number of the victims of familial sexual abuse did not physically resist the sexual advances of their male relatives. When questioned by judges and attorneys about their passivity, the girls said they were afraid or that the male relative had threatened to harm them if they reported the assaults. Taught at an early age to obey the orders of fathers and male adults, girls hesitated to challenge male authority even in regard to sexual abuse.[27]

A clear example is the case of a thirteen-year-old who had been sexually abused by her twenty-seven-year-old brother for several years, until an older, married sister found out and reported the offense to the police. Court officials could not understand why the girl had not reported the incident sooner or actively resisted her brother's advances. But as she explained in court, "I couldn't do anything against him, we were the only ones home." She told the judge that she was afraid of her brother, "afraid he'd get me into trouble, afraid of my father too. . . . He might put me away or something."[28]

In a similar case, a fourteen-year-old did not actively resist the sexual advances of her uncle, a man of fifty-six years. She had lived with him and her grandmother from the time she was an infant, following the death of her parents. The exchange between the girl and an attorney in court demonstrates the great difficulty young women and girls had in challenging sexual abuse by men in authority over them.

> *Attorney:* What you did, you did of your own free will?
> *A:* No, I couldn't help it.
> *Attorney:* You just told the Court that he unbuttoned one side of your panties and you unbuttoned the other side.
> *A:* Yes.
> *Attorney:* That don't look as though you were fighting very hard, did it.
> *A:* No.
> *Attorney:* You were willing?
> *A:* Yes, well yes, I was because I couldn't help it. When he come near me, I just couldn't help it, I had to do it.
> *Attorney:* Why? Were you afraid of him?
> *A:* I was, yes.
> *Attorney:* Did you want to do it?
> *A:* No, I didn't.

The uncle used his position of authority within the home to compel the girl to submit to his sexual demands. The grandmother of the girl reported in court that her son locked her out of the house when he planned to have sexual relations with his niece. He told the girl as he took her to the bedroom, "[Y]ou got to mind me. . . . I am the one that you got to mind."[29]

Given the economic, psychological, and legal factors discouraging them, it is remarkable that some girls did actively resist sexual assault by family members. Age and the support of other women apparently encouraged resistance. Catherine Schultz, for example, submitted to her father's advances until age fifteen, when she gained the courage, with the support of the family housekeeper, to report her father to the police. Another fifteen-year-old girl endured her stepfather's abuse for two years, until she finally declared to her sister that she would "shoot Papa if he tried to grab hold of her again."[30]

Considering its prevalence, it is at first difficult to understand why the sexual assault of women and girls within the home was ignored. Clearly the private nature of such offenses and the reluctance of families to report them made the problem a difficult one to address. There was, moreover, a cultural silence about sexual abuse within the family during this period. Although they must have encountered it in the course of their work, police, physicians, and court officials avoided the issue of incest, and were certainly unwilling to challenge seriously male authority within the family. The family was considered the bulwark of American social order, a place where children supposedly received protection, care, and moral instruction. The very notion of incest made a mockery of this concept of the family. Rather than address the problem, it was easier to deny it, to assume that the young women and girls who accused fathers and other male relatives of sexual assault were lying. This denial is evident in the case of Catherine Schultz. The male physician who examined Catherine criticized the family housekeeper for encouraging her to file a complaint against her father. He called the housekeeper, "a dirty liar," and accused her of putting words in the girl's mouth. "Do you realize the trouble you are causing?" he demanded to know. The court apparently shared the physician's view and eventually dismissed the charge against Catherine's father.[31]

This examination of rape prosecutions demonstrates clearly that the dominant cultural representations of rape tell us little about the actual problem of sexual violence in the early twentieth century. In fact, the white slaver and black rapist stereotypes both distorted people's understanding of the nature and causes of sexual violence and served to reinforce gender, racial, and ethnic hierarchies in American society. By focusing on the evil stranger as the source of sexual danger, especially the dangerous foreigner or black man, rape stereotypes obscured the central sources of sexual harm facing women and girls. They displaced responsibility for sexual violence away from those who committed the most serious harm: boyfriends, neighbors, fathers, and male relatives. The male-dominated family and household were rarely subjected to public scrutiny and condemnation despite a record of significant sexual abuse.

Cultural representations of rape, furthermore, reinforced white patriarchal authority and women's dependence on men by stressing that women's attempts at social autonomy, their movement into public spaces without male protection, threatened them with sexual assault by strangers. Mary Denbigh in Kauffman's white slavery novel, *The House of Bondage*, faces abduction and assault by a Jewish procurer when she tires of parental supervision and small-town life, and sets out to explore the opportunities of New York City. In the film *Birth of a Nation*, the white virgin falls prey to black rapist Gus when she strays too far from her family's home. These rape narratives warn young women that the pursuit of social autonomy leads to sexual violence and that security rests on obedience to and supervision by fathers or father figures in the home. Rape stereotypes thus served to strengthen patriarchal authority and, ironically, may have rendered women and girls more vulnerable to sexual abuse within the home.

Another destructive consequence of rape stereotypes is that they projected sexual violence onto less powerful "others" by identifying immigrant and African American men as rapists. Representations of rape contributed to damaging racial and ethnic characterizations of these groups as uncivilized, degraded, and dangerous, and justified the discrimination and harsh treatment they received within the legal system. Rape prosecutions from the Alameda County criminal court indicate that African American and immigrant men faced a disproportionate amount of scrutiny and punishment for sexual crimes. Four-fifths of the African American men prosecuted for rape in Alameda County in the early twentieth century were convicted and received the court's harshest punishment— long-term incarceration in the state prison—compared to half of the other men prosecuted for rape.

It is impossible to provide firm statistical evidence of conviction and sentencing rates for men of immigrant backgrounds because the court records do not consistently indicate the ethnicity or place of birth of male defendants. The court transcripts do, however, suggest that judges did take a defendant's ethnicity into account. Louis Albertoli, a twenty-four-year-old Italian immigrant, faced a prison sentence and then deportation for the rape of a fourteen-year-old girl who lived in his neighborhood. The young man's ethnicity clearly influenced the judge's sentencing decision. He explained that American society could not afford to tolerate the supposedly degraded customs of certain immigrant groups:

> I do not feel that we ought to have people come to this country unless they are able and willing to abide by our laws. I realize that in some foreign countries the same code of morals is not present that is present in this country. . . . [I]t is a fact that in some of the countries today a man can forcibly take his woman that he looks to and wants to have for his own and these consider it a marriage, but of course, we do not call those countries civilized, but as I said before if we permit these customs to prevail upon this soil instead of having the higher code of ethics, we would descend to the code of ethics and moral of the other communities.[32]

Other studies of sexual violence confirm the discriminatory treatment of ethnic and racial minorities in the criminal justice system. Laura Edwards found that race was one critical factor in determining the outcome of sexual assault cases in Granville County, North Carolina, in the late nineteenth century. According to Edwards, "When a white woman was involved, conviction was more likely and sentences harsher, particularly when the accused was a black man." Karen Dubinsky's study of sexual violence in Ontario from 1880 to 1929 found that men of racial and ethnic minorities were more stringently policed and punished for sexual crimes than other men.[33]

The dominant images of rape not only contributed to unfair treatment within the legal system but also fueled and justified violence directed against black and immigrant men. African American men, in particular, became the targets of extreme violence, stemming from charges of interracial rape. One of the worst instances of this type of racial violence occurred in Atlanta in 1906, when angry white mobs prowled the city smashing black businesses and attacking black people on the streets. The riot began after local newspapers reported a series of alleged rapes of white women by black men. No one bothered to investigate these spurious reports. A white man mounted a soapbox, brandishing the newspaper reporting the assaults and shouted, "Are white men going to stand for this?" The cry of "No. Save our Women. . . . Kill the [Negroes]!" was taken up and crowds began to roam the streets hunting for black men. By the end of the riot, 25 African-Americans had been killed and 150 wounded.[34]

Most lynchings did not take place on a mass scale like this, but they occurred repeatedly and usually with the same spurious justification of interracial rape. Between 1882 and 1930, at least 3,386 African Americans were killed by lynch mobs. Local white mobs carried out the burning, torture, and murder of blacks, but public leaders and law enforcement officials did little to stop or punish mob leaders and often publicly sanctioned their actions. Benjamin Tillman, a U.S. senator and former governor of South Carolina, defended the practice of lynching to his colleagues in Washington: "When stern and sad-faced white men put to death a creature in human form who has deflowered a white woman, they have avenged the greatest wrong, the blackest crime."[35]

Although the public justification for this brutal crime was the rape of white women by black men, in reality few lynchings were associated with sexual assault. Less than one-quarter (23 percent) of the known victims of lynch mobs between 1882 and 1946 were even accused of rape or attempted rape. Lynch mobs, in fact, most often directed their rage against black men who challenged white supremacy through economic success or by assertion of political rights—black political leaders, labor activists, and owners of black businesses. The primary purpose of lynching was to instill terror in blacks and to maintain the system of white supremacy in the South.[36]

Although African American men were the most likely targets of lynch mobs on false charges of interracial rape, men of other marginalized groups were also threatened. Leo Frank, a Jewish man was lynched after he was accused of raping and killing a white teenage girl who worked in the factory he managed. Educated as a mechanical engineer, twenty-nine-year-old Frank moved to Georgia from Brooklyn in 1907 to manage a pencil factory in downtown Atlanta. In 1913, one of the female workers in the factory, thirteen-year-old Mary Phagan, was found murdered and sexually assaulted in the basement of the building. Police arrested Frank for the crime and his trial became one of the most celebrated in Georgia's history. According to Joel Williamson, "The press, the pulpit, and the politicians had all painted a picture in which an innocent virginal Southern girl had been outraged by an alien Jew."[37]

Despite the weak evidence against him, Frank's trial resulted in conviction and the death sentence. Over the next year and a half, his attorneys appealed the case all the way to the Supreme Court but without success. They next pursued a campaign for executive clemency, which eventually gained the support of Georgia Governor John Slaton. Pointing to evidence unavailable to the jurors, Slaton commuted the sentence to life imprisonment. Two months later, on August 16, 1915, a group of prominent male citizens from Phagan's hometown kidnapped Frank from the state prison, took him to Marietta, the county of Phagan's birth and hung him from a tree. White furor over the Frank case led to the organization of the second Ku Klux Klan in Atlanta later that year, which was celebrated by burning a huge cross on top of Stone Mountain.[38]

Stereotypes distorted the problem of rape in the early twentieth century in another crucial way by ignoring sexual violence directed against women of color. Cultural representations defined rape as a problem that threatened white women. The narratives of white slavery and black rape typically portrayed female victims as innocent, fair-skinned young women such as Mary Denbigh in Kauffman's novel—a country girl with "blue eyes, red mouth, straight nose, pink cheeks, and abundant russet hair." The very term *white slavery* implied that only white women needed and deserved protection from sexual harm. The flip side of this image of white-female purity was an image of the inherent immorality and sensuality of women of color. In the dominant culture, African American, Latina, Asian American, and Native American women came to embody the dark, unruly, and promiscuous side of female sexuality. They were assumed to be sexually available to any man who came along and some men even denied the possibility of raping such women. Congressman A. C. Tompkins of Kentucky declared that it was impossible to force black women to have sexual relations against their will, for because of their "natural complaisance," the male is "able to easily satisfy his desire without violence." The image of the innate promiscuity of women of color grossly distorted the reality of interracial sexual relations and served to justify the women's sexual exploitation. Men, especially white men, would not be held accountable for sexual assault as long as non-white women were defined as sexually aggressive and naturally depraved.[39]

The dominant images of rape completely ignored the fact that women of color, too, faced sexual violence in the contexts of their families, neighborhoods, and workplaces. From what we know about patterns of sexual violence, minority women probably were victimized most often by men they knew: family members, neighbors, boyfriends, employers, and coworkers. In addition, women and girls faced severe forms of sexual exploitation on account of their race. The demise of slavery may have limited but clearly did not eradicate the sexual victimization of African American women by white men in the South. In fact, some southern white men responded to emancipation and the granting of political rights to African American men by assaulting black women. They used rape as a tool of racial intimidation and control of freed blacks in the South. In the Memphis race riot of 1866, a white mob attacked and killed blacks, burned their homes and schools, and raped black women at gunpoint. In 1871, the wife of a black political leader in Columbia, South Carolina, reported to a congressional committee that Ku Klux Klan members had beaten her husband and raped her to punish them for supporting the Republicans. Another woman, from Meridian, Mississippi, told the committee that Klan members had forced their way into her home, thrown her to the ground, and raped her at gunpoint.[40]

It was also common practice for white men of all ages and classes to make sexual advances to, and in some case to sexually assault, women of color. Domestic servants were most vulnerable to this type of harassment and abuse, and in the first half of the twentieth century domestic service was the primary occupation for women of color, including black, Asian American, Latina, and Native American women. In a letter that appeared in the *Independent* in 1912, a black servant who worked for a white southern family described how she resisted the aggressive advances of her male employer and was consequently fired from her job. The servant concluded that "a colored woman's virtue in this part of the country had no protection. . . . I believe nearly all white men take, and expect to take, undue liberties with their colored female servants—not only the fathers, but in many cases the sons also." Given the structure of relations between whites and blacks in the South, women who resisted such harassment could expect to be dismissed or forcibly assaulted. African American men who attempted to prevent sexual assaults of wives and daughters by white men found themselves subject to criminal arrest or physical attack. When the husband of the woman quoted above confronted the white employer for accosting his wife, the employer struck him and had him arrested. When the husband appeared in court, he was fined $25 for his bold behavior.[41]

Rape stereotypes masked the nature and sources of sexual harm facing women by defining rape strictly as a violent act committed by dark-skinned strangers against white women. They impeded any serious effort to address this problem by diverting attention away from those who posed the greatest threat to women and girls, and by completely ignoring sexual violence committed against women of color. Rape stereotypes reveal far more about the deep social anxiety and rage stemming from the disruption of gender and racial hierarchies than they do about the problem of sexual violence. Freed from the bonds of slavery, African American men and women set out to exercise their political rights, pursue work and educational opportunities, and build strong communities during and after Reconstruction. Southern and eastern Europeans migrated to the United States in increasing numbers during this period, seeking to establish a better life for themselves and their families by participating in the economic, social, and political life of this country. Women of all classes and racial/ethnic groups challenged their economic and political subordination by pursuing new avenues of employment and professional work and taking part in the suffrage, labor, and Progressive movements. Rape stereotypes justified keeping these groups in a subordinate place in the social order by asserting that African Americans and immigrants became degraded and dangerous if allowed too much freedom and autonomy, and that white women became easy targets of sexual violence if they ventured too far from patriarchal authority and control. The great disparity between the cultural representations and actual social contexts of rape in the early twentieth century should alert us to the potential dangers and distortions in dominant conceptions of sexual violence in our own time.

NOTES

1. Two of the best known of these studies are Mary Koss, "Hidden Rape: Sexual Aggression and Victimization in a National Sample of Students in Higher Education," in *Rape and Sexual Assault II*, ed. Ann Wolbert Burgess (New York: Garland, 1988), 3–25, and Diana E. H. Russell, *Sexual Exploitation: Rape, Child Sexual Abuse, and Workplace Harassment* (Beverly Hills: Sage, 1984). See also Susan Estrich, *Real Rape* (Cambridge: Harvard University Press, 1987).

2. Edwin W. Sims, "The White Slave Trade of Today," in *Fighting the Traffic in Young Girls*, ed. Ernest A. Bell (Chicago: G. S. Hall, 1910), 59. On white slavery, see Mark Connelly, *The Response to Prostitution in the Progressive Era* (Chapel Hill: University of North Carolina Press), ch. 6; Ruth Rosen, *The Lost Sisterhood: Prostitution in America, 1900– 18* (Baltimore: Johns Hopkins University Press, 1983), ch. 7.

3. Clifford G. Roe, *The Great War on White Slavery* (New York: n.p., 1911); Bell, *Fighting the Traffic in Young Girls*; Theodore A. Bingham, *The Girl That Disappears* (Boston: Gorham Press, 1911); Jean Turner Zimmermann, *America's Black Traffic in White Girls* (Chicago: n.p., 1912); Mrs. C. I. Harris, *Modern Herodians or Slaughterers of Innocents* (Portland, Ore.: Wallace, 1909).

4. "The White Slave Films," *Outlook*, January 17, 1914, 120–22; Leslie Fishbein, "From Sodom to Salvation: The Image of New York City in Films about Fallen Women, 1899– 1934," *New York History* 70 (1989): 171–90; Reginald Wright Kauffman, *The House of Bondage* (1910; reprint, Upper Saddle River, N.J.: Gregg Press, 1968).

5. Zimmerman quoted in Connelly, *Response to Prostitution*, 118; Bingham, *Girl That Disappears*; Roe, *Great War on White Slavery*; Bell, *Fighting the Traffic in Girls*, 72, 145.

6. Kauffman, *House of Bondage*, 19.

7. George Fredrickson, *The Black Image in the White Mind: The Debate on Afro-American Character and Destiny, 1817–1914* (New York: Harper and Row, 1972), ch. 9; Joel Williamson, *The Crucible of Race: Black-White Relations in the American South since Emancipation* (New York: Oxford University Press, 1984), chs. 4–6; Sandra Gunning, *Race, Rape, and Lynching: The Red Record of American Literature, 1890–1912* (New York: Oxford University Press, 1996); Martha Hodes, "The Sexualization of Reconstruction Politics: White Women and Black Men in the South after the Civil War," *Journal of the History of Sexuality* 3 (1993); Ida B. Wells, "A Red Record" and "Southern Horrors: Lynch Law in All Its Phases" in *Selected Works of Ida B. Wells*, comp. Trudier Harris (New York: Oxford University Press, 1991), 14–45, 138–52.

8. Williamson, *Crucible of Race*, 88–93, 118, quoted in Fredrickson, *Black Image in the White Mind*, 278.

9. Fredrickson, *Black Image in the White Mind*, 279–80.

10. Thomas Dixon, Jr., *The Clansman: An Historical Romance of the Ku Klux Klan* (1905; reprint, Lexington: University Press of Lexington, 1970), 291, 304; Gunning, *Rape, Race, and*

Lynching, ch. 1; Fredrickson, *Black Image in the White Mind*, 275–82; Williamson, *Crucible of Race*, 140–76.

11. Michael Rogin, " 'The Sword Became a Flashing Vision': D. W. Griffith's *The Birth of a Nation*," *Representations* 9(1985): 150–95; Lary May, *Screening Out the Past: The Birth of Mass Culture and the Motion Picture Industry* (Chicago: University of Chicago Press, 1983), 60–95; John Hope Franklin, "Birth of a Nation—Propaganda as History," *Massachusetts Review* 20 (1975): 417–33; Williamson, *Crucible of Race*, 175–76; quotation is from Rogin, " 'Sword Became a Flashing Vision,' " 151.

12. The felony trial court records from the Alameda County Superior Court contain two major sources of information on criminal prosecutions: the register of actions and the case files. The register lists the defendant's name, case number, charge, and a summary of the legal processing of each case. The case files contain the official complaint and verbatim trial transcripts from the preliminary hearings that took place in the lower courts. When discussing individual cases, I have changed the names of the alleged assailants and victims but have indicated their racial/ethnic identities when they are known.

13. Karen Dubinsky's excellent historical study of sexual violence in Ontario also finds that women and girls were far more likely to be assaulted by men they knew than by strangers. Karen Dubinsky, *Improper Advances: Rape and Heterosexual Conflict in Ontario, 1880–1929* (Chicago: University of Chicago Press, 1993).

14. U.S. Bureau of the Census, *Tenth Census of the United States, 1880: Population* (Washington, D.C.: GPO, 1883), 1:416; U.S. Bureau of the Census, *Fourteenth Census of the United States, 1920: Population* (Washington, D.C.: GPO, 1922), 3:118; Marilynn S. Johnson, *The Second Gold Rush: Oakland and the East Bay in World War II* (Berkeley: University of California Press, 1993), 13–15; Robert M. Fogelson, *The Fragmented Metropolis: Los Angeles, 1850–1930* (Cambridge: Harvard University Press, 1967), ch. 4.

15. U.S. Bureau of the Census, *Twelfth Census of the United States, 1900: Population*, Pt. 1, California (Washington, D.C.: GPO, 1904); *Thirteenth Census of the United States, 1910, Population*, vol. 2, *Reports by States*, California (Washington, D.C.: GPO, 1913); *Fourteenth Census of the United States, 1920: Population*, vol. 3, *Composition and Characteristics of the Population by States*, California (Washington, D.C.: GPO, 1922); Beth Bagwell, *Oakland: The Story of a City* (Novato, Calif.: Presidio Press, 1982), 81–90; Johnson, *Second Gold Rush*, 16–17; Fogelson, *Fragmented Metropolis*, 75–83.

16. Alameda County Superior Court, case no. 4733 (year, 1910). (Alameda cases are hereafter cited by number and year.) Alameda case no. 4733 (1910); Alameda case no. 7420 (1919).

17. Alameda case no. 7594 (1920).

18. Alameda case no. 5657 (1914).

19. Ibid.

20. Alameda case no. 5352 (1912). On the sexual exploitation of domestic workers by male employers, see Tera W. Hunter, *To 'Joy My Freedom: Southern Black Women's Lives and Labors after the Civil War* (Cambridge: Harvard University Press, 1997), 34, 106; Faye E. Dudden, *Serving Women: Household Service in Nineteenth Century America* (Middletown, Conn.: Wesleyan University Press, 1983), 214–17; David Katzman, *Seven Days a Week: Women and Domestic Service in Industrializing America* (Urbana: University of Illinois Press, 1981), 216–18; John Gillis, "Servants, Sexual Relations and the Risks of Illegitimacy in London, 1801–1900," *Feminist Studies* 5(1979): 142–73.

21. Alameda case no. 7612 (1920).

22. Alameda cases no. 4879 (1910), 7467 (1920), 993 (1919).

23. Alameda case no. 6402 (1916).

24. Alameda case no. 5572 (1913).

25. Linda Gordon and Paul O'Keefe, "Incest as a Form of Family Violence: Evidence from Historical Case Records," *Journal of Marriage and the Family* 46 (February 1984): 32; Christine Stansell, *City of Women: Sex and Class in New York, 1789–1860* (Urbana: University of Illinois Press, 1987), 182. For further discussion of sexual assaults by family members during this period, see Elizabeth Pleck, *Domestic Tyranny: The Making of American Social Policy against Family Violence from Colonial Times to the Present* (New York: Oxford University Press, 1987), 81–82.

26. Alameda case no. 6402 (1916).

27. Linda Gordon, "Incest and Resistance: Patterns of Father-Daughter Incest, 1880–1930," *Social Problems* 33 (1986): 253–67.

28. Alameda case no. 6859 (1918).

29. Alameda case no. 6574 (1917).

30. Alameda case no. 5572 (1913).

31. Alameda case no. 6402 (1916).

32. Alameda case no. 6008 (1915).

33. Laura F. Edwards, "Sexual Violence, Gender, Reconstruction, and the Extension of Patriarchy in Granville County, North Carolina," *North Carolina Historical Review* 68 (1991): 252; Dubinsky, *Improper Advances*, 82–83, 164.

34. Hunter, *To 'Joy My Freedom*, 126–28; Williamson, *Crucible of Race*, 209–23.

35. Benjamin Tillman, "Lynch Law," in *BiblioBase*, ed. Michael A. Bellesiles (Boston: Houghton Mifflin, 1998), 6.

36. Jacquelyn Dowd Hall, *Revolt against Chivalry: Jessie Daniel Ames and the Women's Campaign against Lynching* (New York: Columbia University Press, 1974), ch. 5; NAACP, *Thirty Years of Lynching in the United States, 1889–1918* (New York: NAACP, 1919); Angela Davis, "Rape, Racism, and the Myth of the Black Rapist," in *Women, Race, and Class* (New York: Random House, 1981), 172–201.

37. Williamson, *Crucible of Race*, 470.

38. Ibid., 468–72; Nancy Maclean, "The Leo Frank Case Reconsidered: Gender and Sexual Politics in the Making of Reactionary Populism," *Journal of American History* 78 (1991): 917–48; Leonard Dinnerstein, *The Leo Frank Case* (New York: Columbia University Press, 1968).

39. Kauffman, *House of Bondage*, 2; A. C. Tompkins, "The Age of Consent from a Physio-Psychological Standpoint," *Arena* 13 (July 1895): 223; Gerda Lerner, ed., *Black Women in White America: A Documentary History* (New York: Pantheon Books, 1972), 164–71; Deborah Gray White, *Ar'n't I a Woman?: Female Slaves in the Plantation South* (New York: Norton, 1987), 27–46; Patricia Hill Collins, *Black Feminist Thought: Knowledge, Consciousness, and the Politics of Empowerment* (London: Routledge, 1991), 77–78; Antonia Castaneda, "Sexual Violence in the Politics of Policies of Conquest: Amerindian Women and the Spanish Conquest of Alta California," in *Building with Our Hands: New Directions in Chicana Studies*, ed. Adela De La Torre and Beatriz M. Pesquera (Berkeley: University of California Press, 1993), 15–33.

40. Lerner, *Black Women in White America*, 172–88; Jacqueline Jones, *Labor of Love, Labor of Sorrow: Black Women, Work, and the Family from Slavery to the Present* (New York: Basic Books, 1985), 149–50. On rape as a tool of racial terror and control, see Davis, "Rape, Racism, and the Myth of the Black Rapist"; Darlene Clark Hine, "Rape and the Inner Lives of Black Women in the Middle West: Preliminary Thoughts on the Culture of

Dissemblance," *Signs* 14 (1989): 912–20; Jacquelyn Dowd Hall, " 'The Mind That Burns in Each Body.': Women, Rape and Racial Violence" in *Powers of Desire: The Politics of Sexuality*, ed. Ann Snitow et al. (New York: Monthly Review Press, 1983), 328–49; Castaneda, "Sexual Violence in the Politics and Policies of Conquest."

41. Evelyn Nakano-Glenn, "From Servitude to Service Work: Historical Continuities in the Racial Division of Paid Reproductive Labor," in *Unequal Sisters*, ed. Vicki Ruiz and Ellen Dubois (New York: Routledge, 1994), 405–35; Katzman, *Seven Days a Week*, ch. 2; Palmer, *Domesticity and Dirt* (Philadelphia: Temple University Press, 1989), 12; Lerner, *Black Women in White America*, 155–56, see also 151–55, 158–59. On sexual abuse of domestic servants, see Vicki Ruiz, "By the Day or Week: Mexicana Domestic Workers in El Paso," in *Women on the U.S.-Mexican Border*, ed. Vicki Ruiz and Susan Tiano (Boston: Allen and Unwin, 1987), 61–76; Hunter, *To 'Joy My Freedom*, 34, 106; Katzman, *Seven Days a Week*, 216–18; Palmer, *Domesticity and Dirt*, 143–45.

T. BRAUNS.

Pessary.

No. 168,711.

Patented Oct. 11, 1875.

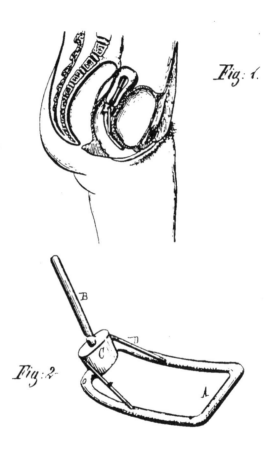

Fig: 1.

Fig: 2.

B

D

C

A

Attest.
Theo. L. Duy
Edward Barthel

Inventor.
Philo Brauns
By Atty
Thos. L. Sprogue

An example of an early American intrauterine device. Patented to correct uterine displacement, this 1875 model doubled as a contraceptive. Its size, shape, and positioning demonstrate that the comfort of the user was not the inventor's chief concern. U.S. Patent Office, patent # 168,710.

Chapter Eighteen

Violence by Design
Contraceptive Technology and the Invasion of the Female Body

Andrea Tone

On August 10, 1971, the United States Patent Office patented a new intrauterine device (IUD), the invention of Herbert W. Horne, Jr., of Brookline, Massachusetts. Horne's contraceptive, patent 3,598,115, was intended to prevent accidental uterine expulsion, a widespread problem associated with IUD use at the time. IUDs came of age in the United States in the late 1960s and were viewed, along with oral contraceptives, as one of the most exciting new birth control technologies of the decade. But, like the Pill, IUDs were not trouble-free. Many IUD users in the 1960s discovered, often when it was too late, that uterine contractions—the natural reaction of the uterus to the presence of a foreign object—had expelled their IUDs, leaving them vulnerable to pregnancy. Horne's device offered a new technology to correct this flaw.[1]

The promised efficacy of his design depended on two features: a stainless steel barb that punctured the uterus, and a balloonlike vane made of polyethylene or silico-organic rubber that expanded upon insertion, lining the uterine wall. Prior to insertion, the vane was to be rolled around the device's primary shaft, enabling the entire IUD—barb, vane, and all—to fit snugly into a standard straw-shaped insertion tube. The physician inserting the device would push the tube and its contents into the uterus, applying force so that the "barb pierces into, but not through the muscular wall and retains the device securely in place." Once the barb was hooked to the uterus, the vane would unroll and "engage" the mucous lining, generating a biochemical reaction "whose nature is not clearly known" but which, nature notwithstanding, would prevent conception all the same. And so it was that pierced by a stainless steel barb and lined with plastic, a woman's uterus was made safe from unwanted pregnancy.[2]

At one level, Horne's invention was a sound technological response to IUD troubles of the day. An IUD stapled into a woman's uterus was unlikely to free-float away. And researchers at the time knew that the more uterine contact an IUD had, the more protection it offered, making Horne's device that much more scientifically sound.

But Horne's invention was also something more dire: a technology hailed as progressive because it injured a woman's womb. It was the IUD's piercing, ballooning feature that constituted the essence of Horne's claims to scientific efficacy; it was its ability to damage women's uteri that made it a superior contraceptive in Horne's eyes.

Like most patented inventions, Horne's was never mass manufactured. We can still imagine, however, that the women for whom it was intended would have evaluated it using criteria different from Horne's. Sharing his commitment to finding an efficient contraceptive, women would likely have considered his IUD an agent of pain, not progress. They might well have wondered about the circumstances that prompted a Massachusetts man to make and patent a "breakthrough" birth control device that inflicted violence *by design*. Surely, they would have found it ironic that the price of modern birth control, as created by Horne, was mutilation and pain.

Within the gap separating an inventor's vision of progress and women's likely anguish lies a story that needs to be told. It is a story infinitely more complex than explanations that may first spring to mind: Horne was crazy; Horne was a man (no woman would invent something so gynecologically perverse); Horne, the inventor, stood alone in his indifference to the need to balance efficacy with safety and tolerance. Rather, a full history of patent number 3,598,115, takes us beyond Horne, his womb-piercing gadget, and the United States Patent Office. It demands that we look closely at the culture of invention in the 1960s and 1970s that gave rise to Horne's device—the larger political, economic, and social orbit within which support for medical contraceptives in general, and IUDs, in particular, emerged. Contextualizing invention is always important. Only when we acknowledge the inseparability of the world of scientific invention and the social and political world of medicine can we hope to answer a critical question: How could, and why would, anyone invent such a damaging instrument of reproductive control?

A close look at the myriad layers of the IUD story not only reveals new things about the history of culture and technology but also illustrates the multiple shapes violence against women have assumed over time. We think we know violence when we see it firsthand. Battery. Homicide. Rape. We know these and their visible scars well. We are less likely to recognize violence that has been rendered invisible, violence so hidden to the naked eye that it escapes comment and detection. Identifying violence in its numerous hiding spots, including blueprints for technologies designed to inflict injury against the female body, is an important step in piecing together its multifaceted history.

Early IUD Technology and Use

Contraceptive technology was neither an American nor a modern invention. Indeed, vaginal and male condoms, sponges, and suppositories are but some of the many present-day contraceptives whose origins can be traced back thousands of years. To be sure, early methods were of varying efficacy, and some did not work at all. Many undoubtedly made sexual relations between men and women awkward and uncomfortable. But this does not diminish the existence of a long history of effective fertility control that predated the innovations of the 1960s.

Women have used birth control since ancient times. The oldest guide to contraception, the *Petrie Papyrus*, an Egyptian medical papyrus dating to 1850 B.C., recommended vaginal suppositories made of crocodile dung, gum, or a mixture of honey and sodium carbonate.[3] Aristotle, writing in the fourth century B.C., noted the tendency of women of his day to coat their cervixes with olive oil before intercourse. Women in preindustrial West Africa made intravaginal plugs of crushed root; Japanese women, tampons of bamboo tissue; and women of Easter island, algae and seaweed pessaries.[4] In the United States, abortifacients, pessaries, douches, condoms, and coitus interruptus were mainstays of contraceptive practice long before oral contraceptives and IUDs became available.

Although twentieth-century physicians and manufacturers discredited traditional birth control to amass support for standardized, "scientifically engineered" contraceptives, early techniques were not devoid of contraceptive properties. Honey-based suppositories likely impeded sperm motility. And although crocodile dung probably did not, elephant dung, recommended in thirteenth-century Islamic guides, was more acidic, and thus offered women more protection. The olive oil applications of Aristotle's day likely helped prevent pregnancy too; a 1931 study by birth control expert Marie Stopes found a zero percent pregnancy rate in two thousand cases where olive oil had been the only contraception.[5] In 1936, clinician Robert Dickinson published a guide on household contraceptives in the *Journal of Contraception*, an American journal founded to promote scientific birth control. Acknowledging that "the best methods now known give security from undesired pregnancies to about 95 per cent of the women who follow carefully the *doctor's* instructions" (emphasis added), Dickinson conceded that "home-made contraceptives are better than no contraceptive." Dickinson's recommendations—cotton or lint suppositories "medicated" with olive oil, lard, or acidic fruit juices—reads like a catalogue of birth control techniques and ingredients women around the world had been using for centuries.[6]

Like other contraceptive technologies, intrauterine devices date back to antiquity. For centuries, Arabs and Turks inserted small stones into the uteri of camels before long desert trips; known to prevent camel pregnancy, this technique was likely used to inhibit human procreation at about the same time. Those who welcomed the "arrival" of IUDs in the 1960s thus celebrated not the device's recent invention but its newfound status as medically endorsed birth control. Determining why IUDs became favorable with the American medical profession for the first time only in the 1960s is important to understanding the context in which devices such as Horne's were invented.

In the United States, intrauterine devices first became popular in the late nineteenth century as a medical treatment for a wide range of gynecological disorders, from asymmetrical and prolapsed uteri to painful or excessive menstruation. Intrauterine stem pessaries, as the devices were called by gynecologists, consisted of a rubber, metal, or glass stem attached to a cup or button that held the stem upright and prevented it from becoming lost in the uterus. Favored for its numerous medical applications, the device's recognized contraceptive effect was viewed by many gynecologists to be its biggest drawback. But there were other problems too, including the difficulty of insertion and the risk of uterine perforation and infection. These shortcomings contributed to the far greater popularity of vaginal and intracervical pessaries as medical treatments for gynecological disorders.[7]

Importantly, some women eager for effective birth control bypassed the medical profession to get it, buying self-inserting IUDs or hiring a female midwife to insert them. Two stem pessaries patented in the 1890s are indicative of the first trend. One, patented in 1895 by George Gladman of Syracuse, New York, could be "readily inserted with a minimum degree of skill," and could be "worn continuously." Another pessary, patented in 1894, included both a self-insertion device and a string for self-removal. How widespread intrauterine birth control was among women is impossible to determine; as Janet Farrell Brodie has argued, the severe pain and cramping associated with their use probably ensured a small number of wearers.[8]

All the same, female use was certainly frequent enough to infuriate physicians. Mirroring larger cultural mores, most physicians opposed birth control on religious or ethical grounds; it was selfish and unhealthy, many argued, for women to try to "trick" the dictates of God and nature.[9] Until 1938, the American Medical Association officially banned members from prescribing birth control, and it took until the 1960s for most doctors to consider contraception a legitimate field of medical practice. Physician opposition to IUDs grew out of this anti-birth-control tradition, but it was also tied to women's willingness to go outside proper medical channels to acquire them. Discrediting lay healers had long been central to doctors' attempts to cement their professional status; IUD-wearing-women's flagrant transgression of the boundaries of medical authority made IUDs indicative of the very tendencies doctors wished to suppress. Gynecologist and IUD inventor Hugh Davis, explaining in 1972 enduring medical opposition to intrauterine birth control in the 1930s, 1940s, and 1950s, attributed physicians' intransigence to the IUD's established history of female, "illegitimate" use. The problem, he explained, was that most medical authorities had confused "true intrauterine contraceptive devices with the stem pessaries inserted by *quacks and granny midwives . . .* at the turn of the century" (emphasis added).[10] Before physicians professionalized contraceptive technology, the agency of women as willing wearers and inserters of IUDs contributed to the medical condemnation of intrauterine birth control.

As a contraceptive technique, IUDs first gained medical support in Germany. In 1909, Dr. Richard Richter, a surgeon in the village of Waldenberg, reported in a two-page article published in *Deutsche Medizinische Wochenschrift* his patients' successes with contraceptive IUDs he had made out of silkworm-gut shaped with bronze wire into ring form. Largely ignored at the time, Richter's findings were popularized in the 1920s by Dr. Ernst Grafenberg. A Berlin gynecologist with a large private practice, Grafenberg published widely in the late 1920s and

1930s about his clinical experiences using IUDS on more than two thousand women. The Grafenberg ring, the first IUD to be commercially manufactured as birth control, modified Richter's silkworm-gut model by substituting silver wire for bronze, creating a stiffer device more resistant to expulsion. By the mid-1930s, a handful of gynecologists across Europe and in Japan were reporting favorable results with patients using the Grafenberg ring.[11]

But most practitioners, especially those in the United States, condemned Grafenberg and his device. Invoking their authority as men of science, American obstetricians and gynecologists denounced contraceptive IUDs as a dangerous fad, the territory of abortionists, quacks, and midwives. Declaring crass commercialism to be IUD promoters' main motive, a Missouri physician complained in 1930 that "illegitimate faddists have been its strongest advocates, because the procedure has become the means of adding very substantial remuneration to their otherwise doubtful and unscrupulous practices."[12]

Other physicians sought to discredit IUDs by questioning not only the motives and training of their proponents but also the device's contraceptive attributes—a stand that, rather ironically, refuted the findings of earlier American gynecologists. Renowned obstetrician J. Whitridge Williams was one such cynic. A professor of obstetrics at the Johns Hopkins Medical School during the 1920s, Williams carried a watch chain adorned with a gold intrauterine ring. When questioned about the ring's significance, Williams would explain that he had personally extracted it from a "placenta at term." Its permanency on his chain, he believed, supplied enduring visual proof that IUDs did not work.[13]

But in fact the Grafenberg ring usually *did* work, although not without complications. The ring's rigidity and size, measuring one inch in diameter, required the cervix to be dilated to about 10 mm before insertion. With anaesthesia, dilation and insertion were pain-free but medically more complicated; without, the event inflicted agonizing pain. The ring also caused and worsened endometriosis in some women and increased all users' susceptibility to pelvic inflammatory disease, a potentially life-threatening infection of the fallopian tubes, uterus, or ovaries.

Significantly, however, American physicians typically did not latch onto these failings when they criticized IUDs. Instead, they disputed IUDs' contraceptive value, either explicitly, as did J. Whitridge Williams, or implicitly, by linking IUDs to a tradition of illegitimate female birth control practiced by and for women. Only when we recognize the connection forged in doctors' minds between intrauterine birth control and female quackery can we understand how it was even possible for IUD inventor and physician Howard Tatum to lament in 1972 gynecologists' "traditional taboo against inserting a foreign body into the uterine cavity," a taboo that had "thwarted the advance of contraceptive technology," and now had to be overcome.[14] Tatum was not alone in his evaluation. IUD inventor Charles Lalor Burdick likewise characterized early opposition to IUDs as one in which "the medical profession inveighed extensively against the practice of inserting anything into the uterus," and Hugh Davis, coinventor of the Dalkon Shield, noted that physicians had learned to regard the uterine cavity as an "inviolable sanctuary." But Tatum, Burdick, and Davis need not have worried. Even as they wrote, IUDs were on the verge of gaining a newfound respectability.[15]

The Politics and Problems of the Pill

Myriad developments encouraged wider support of contraceptive IUDs in the United States. Ironically, the most important was a rival birth control technology: oral contraceptives. The excitement surrounding their invention in the 1950s, the perceived social problems accompanying their use, and the changing role of the medical profession created by the popularity of a prescription-only birth control method, set the stage for broader acceptance of IUDs.

The Pill was largely the brainchild of physiologist Gregory Pincus, who in 1951 was asked by Margaret Sanger to undertake the invention of a foolproof birth control that would help stem population growth in underdeveloped parts of the world. Pincus received annual funds for his work from Planned Parenthood, which as early as 1948 had pledged to finance research to develop a "simple, acceptable and reliable method cheap enough for use by poverty-ridden, illiterate and backward peoples who needed it most in all countries."[16]

From its first days of sponsored research in Pincus's Worcester, Massachusetts, lab to its testing on thousands of impoverished women in Puerto Rico and Haiti (some of whom received a placebo instead of the standard 10 mg. dosage of progestin), the Pill was intended to supply critical ammunition in the war against population growth. In the 1950s and 1960s, population control was not a fringe movement. In addition to Sanger, its leading spokespersons included John D. Rockefeller III, who founded the Population Council (PC) in 1952; Dwight D. Eisenhower, one of the PC's charter members; and British biologist Sir Julian Huxley, who articulated the fear of many when he warned in a November 1959 speech that "people do not exist to live all their undernourished lives in the illiterate ignorance of an Asian village. . . . Unless population increase is drastically cut . . . mankind will be reduced to the status of a swarm of maggots on the carcass of a dead cow."[17]

Although in 1958 it was estimated that the United States, with only 6 percent of the world population, was consuming 50 percent of the world's resources, the crisis of population growth was attributed to the unchecked procreation of undesirable groups: poor, uneducated persons, particularly those in developing, politically "unstable" nations. Eugenicist sympathies drove many population controllers' concerns; Nobel prizewinner and Stanford physics professor William Shockley suggested that the threat posed by "human deterioration resulting from overbreeding among the lower classes" equaled that of nuclear war.[18]

In most population controllers' rhetoric, the entanglement of birth control politics and nuclear war was even more striking. The expansion of undesirable groups, advocates of population control opined, would fuel poverty, unrest, and the likelihood of war; thus, fear of self-annihilation through the depletion of natural resources meshed easily with Cold War anxieties about communism and nuclear extinction. An article published in 1968 by two gynecologists reveals the ways in which Cold War anxieties fueled support for medical birth control. "This is 1968," the article in *Obstetrics and Gynecology* began. "Red China exploded a hydrogen bomb . . . and, continuing an uninterrupted pattern of many centuries' duration, approximately 4 million people were doomed to death by starvation." To combat this crisis, the authors argued, medical experts must embark on a politically significant mission. "As gynecologists," they urged, "we have little influence on the decisions of governments relating to economic development or political alignments. We can only exert our influence by supporting programs of research and development in the area of human reproduction." Gynecologists, in short, must combat the population crisis with their prescription might; those who did not, contributed to the earth's ruin. "The alternatives to voluntary limitation of family size are well known," they warned. "They have been operating since time began—war, revolution, famine, and pestilence."[19]

In a Cold War climate awestruck by science's capabilities, the invention of the Pill and its approval by the Food and Drug Administration (FDA) as birth control generated an excited response. To many, its development symbolized science's redemption, a technology to stabilize a world order it simultaneously threatened to destroy. As one journalist observed, "The promise of a simple way to control population has its ironic aspect . . . at a time when mankind is crouched in fear of wholesale destruction. . . . Science . . . seems to have discovered a method to limit the reproduction of people at the very time when the world is threatened by the self-annihilation of the species." When women's desires for safe and effective birth control were weighed against the politics of population control, women's needs frequently took a back seat. As reports of the Pill's potential health hazards made the national news in the late 1960s, population controllers steadfastly championed the contraceptive's *political* utility. As Senator Bob Dole put it at a congressional hearing to determine if users of birth control pills were being properly informed of the drug's risks, "We must not frighten millions of women into disregarding the considered judgment of their physicians. . . . It is apparent at the present time the oral contraceptives are important weapons in the struggle to achieve some control over our ability to multiply ourselves into chaos."[20]

Unfortunately for votaries of population control such as Dole, the Pill never became the birth control for the masses its promoters had hoped. One obstacle to mass consumption was cost. Although average annual retail prices declined significantly within a few short years—from about $100 in 1960 to $25 in 1965, they were consistently too expensive for working-class women.[21] Prices also varied among pharmacies; one San Francisco woman complained in 1965 of having to pay as much as $84 a year for the Pill at her neighborhood drugstore. Women could get discounted pills from Planned Parenthood, whose headquarters formally approved their prescription at each of its hundred affiliates in August 1960.[22] But not every woman had easy access to a clinic, only twenty-four of which were actually dispensing Enovid, the first oral contraceptive, by early December. Those women who did, moreover, frequently found even the discounted price too high. Maurice Sagoff, executive director of the Planned Parenthood League of Massachussets, complained in 1961 to the medical director of E. G. Searle, makers of Enovid, that "even at the present consumer price of $3.50 per month . . . [Enovid] is beyond the reach of many of our low-income inquirers." Adding to the cost of prescriptions were medical costs. Pill users required an initial gynecological exam, as well as periodic checkups.[23]

But it was not price alone that cemented the Pill's middle-class identification. Also critical was birth control promoters' fear that oral contraceptives, although almost 100 percent effective when used as directed, would be misused by uneducated and poor women. Dr. Mary Steichen Calderone, medical director of Planned Parenthood, recalled an encounter with a female student at a public junior high school in New York City that supported such alarm. Observing the girl drop her handbag during a break between classes, Calderone stopped to help her pick things up, and "was astonished to see a package of birth control pills." "I asked the child," Calderone told a reporter for the *Saturday Evening Post*, "Do you really know about these things? 'Oh, yes,' she replied, 'I take them every Saturday night when I go on a date.'" As Calderone lamented, "If it weren't so funny, it would be tragic."[24]

Such widely published accounts of misuse promoted the belief that Pill effectiveness was class-specific; only middle-class women, presumed to be white, educated, and responsible, could be "trusted" to swallow a pill a night for twenty consecutive days. As Dr. Alan Guttmacher, president of Planned Parenthood, put it in 1960, "Although many modern contraceptive devices are highly effective, they are not the answer for the poor or the uneducated. They are too expensive for budgets that deal in pennies a day [and] they require intelligence and instruction." Hugh Davis, director of the Family Planning Planning Clinic at Johns Hopkins University and Dalkon Shield inventor, brought the racist and classist dimensions of such an argument into even sharper relief. Before a congressional hearing, Davis observed,

> It is especially tragic that for the individual who needs birth control the most—the poor, the disadvantaged, and the ghetto-dwelling black—the oral contraceptives carry a particularly high hazard of pregnancy as compared with methods requiring less motivation. . . . [I]t is the suburban middle-class woman who has become the chronic user of the oral contraceptives in the United States in the past decade, getting her prescription renewed month after month and year after year without missing a single tablet. Therein, in my opinion, lies the real hazard of the presently available oral contraceptives.[25]

If the Pill failed to meet population controllers' expectations, its availability nevertheless transformed the environment in which women acquired contraception, cementing physicians' role as birth control providers. Before 1960, doctors had played only a minor role supervising everyday contraceptive practice in the United States. Doctors' low profile stemmed, in part, from the AMA's birth control ban. Equally significant, and not unrelated to the absence of medical leadership, was widespread use of nonmedical birth control before and after the AMA ban was lifted in 1938. Abortifacients, homemade pessaries, condoms, coitus interruptus, pre- and postcoital douches, the rhythm method, over-the-counter spermicides—the popularity of these strategies served, in the long run, to keep the number of physicians involved in everyday birth control practice to a minimum. Diaphragms, the most medicalized form of birth control before the FDA approved the Pill for mass distribution in 1960, never gained the support of more than a minority of women. Before 1960, the proportion of women who sought physicians' advice about birth control totaled no more than 20 percent.[26]

With the Pill's arrival, physicians began serving as the exclusive gatekeepers to new contraceptive technologies. By mid-1964 oral contraceptives, available only by prescription, had become the most popular contraception in the country. An estimated 3.5 million women were taking them, constituting one-fourth of all couples practicing contraception in the United States. Women flocked to doctors' offices for Pill prescriptions because they believed they would personally benefit from a contraceptive that was more effective and simpler to use than other methods. The Pill promised almost 100 percent efficacy (compared to only 66 percent for diaphragms), and did not require direct male cooperation. The number of women who went on the Pill and the appreciative letters many sent to its inventors, suggest that most felt well served by the new technology. Many must have shared the sentiments of one Los Angeles woman, who thanked physiologist Gregory Pincus and fellow inventor, gynecologist John Rock, for permanently improving the lot of womankind. "Not since they proved Pasteur's theory on childbirth death," she wrote, "has anyone done more." A woman from Fort Plain, New York, declared oral contraceptives the birth control method that was "by far the cheapest, most convenient, and above all the most effective."[27]

But the decision by women to adopt new birth control methods entailed a trade-off. In exchange for more trustworthy contraception, women gave up some of the social control they had previously exercised as managers of their own pregnancy prevention. The patient-doctor relationship that access to new technologies necessitated made physicians the chief custodians of new technologies, confirming and heightening their professional authority as experts. Women's vulnerability to pregnancy decreased even as their dependence on doctors and the biomedical industry grew.

The medicalization of contraceptive technology, spawned largely by the popularity of oral contraceptives, had important consequences for how American society in the 1960s came to view IUDs. After 1965, when IUDs first became widely available, physicians' authority to manage female contraception, the superiority of scientifically engineered birth control (a superiority celebrated by women and scientists alike), and the image of female birth control users as patients went largely uncontested. In a sense, the "contraceptive revolution" had already occurred. The changes it had wrought made it that much easier for IUDs, yet another scientifically engineered, doctor-controlled contraceptive for women, to gain acceptance.

IUDs Come of Age

Amid the confluence, then, of several events—support for population control, the perceived inability of oral contraceptives to become a birth control for the masses, and the medicalization of contraceptive technology—IUDs came of age. As early as the 1950s, several technological advances encouraged a handful of scientists to engage in active IUD research. The availability of antibiotics in the 1940s made pelvic inflammatory disease and other IUD-related infections curable for the first time. In addition, the invention of malleable plastic enabled scientists to make IUDs with "memory," devices that would stretch into linear form before insertion but regain their original shape in the uterus. Because compressible IUDs could be inserted into an undilated cervix, they became, from a practitioner's standpoint, easier to use than models requiring anaesthesia. In 1959, the Margulies spiral, invented by gynecologist Lazar Margulies of the Mount Sinai Hospital in New York, became the first of a new generation of plastic IUDs to be tested. Margulies's invention was not only the first nonring plastic IUD, it was also the first to use a straight inserter tube. Made of polyethylene and a small amount of barium sulfate that permitted radiologic detection in the event of suspected expulsion, the spiral's tail of polyethylene beads, designed to protrude into the vagina, also enabled women to confirm the IUD's presence. Unfortunately, the length and rigidity of the tail also caused "discomfort and trauma to male partners," destining Margulies's first model to a short-lived life (although its inserter tube became a staple of IUD paraphernalia thereafter). Nonetheless, the possibilities of plastic encouraged further American IUD experimentation, as did a favorable 1959 report on the Grafenberg ring in the *American Journal of Obstetrics and Gynecology*, the first clinical evaluation of intrauterine birth control to be published in an American scientific journal.[28]

In 1961, the Population Council (PC), the most active organization in IUD promotion in the 1960s, began funding the IUD research of Margulies and fellow obstetrician Jack Lippes; with the council's financial help and institutional support, Margulies's new-and-improved spiral (the "Gynekoil") and Lippes's loop would become two of the most commercially successful IUDs of all time.[29] In 1962, the PC sponsored the First International Conference on Intra-Uterine Contraception and launched a research program that included both laboratory studies and clinical trials with promising IUDs. By July 1963, it was underwriting the costs of the insertion and medical monitoring of IUDs in 3,750 female patients at twelve medical centers across the country.[30]

IUDs first became widely available to women at Planned Parenthood clinics and other low-cost health centers in the mid-1960s. By 1965, half of Planned Parenthood's 128 affiliates were providing women with one or more models. At least initially, most IUD wearers were female patients at public clinics; the rate of adoption was highest among blacks, who were more likely than whites to rely on public health facilities for birth control. Over time, as a growing number of private doctors came to prescribe IUDs and as word of their benefits spread, IUD technology became more widely diffused. Between 1965 and 1970, adoption rates by both black and white women increased significantly—more than sixfold among whites and almost threefold among black women. By the end of 1970, more than two million women had been fitted with IUDs in the United States.[31]

By the time IUDs became widely available in the late 1960s, doctors who years earlier had been hesitant about discussing or prescribing birth control had come to accept family planning as a normal part of medical practice. A study of specialists and family practitioners in 1957 in six communities showed that half were unwilling to initiate contraception counseling and that most viewed birth control as beyond their professional scope. Studies in Georgia and California in the mid-1960s likewise found one-third to one-half of surveyed doctors unwilling to initiate a discussion of the subject.[32] A study undertaken in 1971 investigating the practices of 226 physicians in private practice revealed a dramatic shift in opinion and behavior in the space of only a few years. When asked the question "Do you provide contraceptive service to your private female patients?" 98 percent of ob-gyns, 95 percent of family physicians, and 87 percent of internists responded affirmatively. Even among Catholic physicians, the group least likely to support birth control, 78 percent replied affirmatively. Two-thirds of surveyed physicians agreed that family planning was a "routine procedure" in their medical practices.[33]

Doctors' newfound willingness to provide birth control in the late 1960s and early 1970s was matched by women's growing demand for IUDs. In Boston, one physician had to install a second telephone to handle the volume of calls he received from women eager to be fitted with this new contraception. Although some scholars have viewed such women as victims of corporate and medical manipulation, it is important to evaluate women's decisions to use IUDs in the context of birth control options at the time. By the late 1960s, evidence abounded that the Pill was not the birth control panacea for which many women had hoped. Problems from migraine headaches to nausea to strokes occupied women's discussions of birth control and framed their search for something better. The IUD seemed an alternative well worth trying, especially because it was cheaper than the Pill. In early 1966, most women could expect to pay a combined onetime insertion and device fee of thirty dollars. The IUD promised one-stop birth control; in theory, once the device was inserted, a woman need not think about contraception again. A recent study shows that even wearers of the notorious Dalkon Shield initially viewed it as a technology of sexual liberation.[34]

The dramatic escalation in the number of IUD wearers in the late 1960s and early 1970s thus must be understood as the intersection of a technological revolution and a growing demand from women for improved contraceptives. What women could not control, however, was the disparity between their objectives and those of population controllers whose dollars drove IUD invention and distribution. Women selected birth control on the basis of individual social, economic, and medical conditions that would affect their experiences with a particular method, but the proponents of IUDs typically identified prospective wearers as a monolithic group: impoverished, irresponsible, and too prolific.

Although women of all socioeconomic backgrounds appreciated the low cost of IUDs, cheapness to population controllers meant birth control for the poor. What women construed to be the simplicity of IUD contraception meant to its professional advocates a contraception whose efficacy, unlike that of the Pill, could not be altered by female behavior. Once inserted, an IUD prevented pregnancy, irrespective of female behavior, until a physician removed it; it was a technology that worked, in short, *because women could not control it*. On balance, the IUD presented population control advocates with a winning combination: a birth control method accessible to the irresponsible poor that controlled their reproduction no matter how irresponsible they were.[35]

Central to discussions of IUDs at this time was exuberant praise of female passivity. Individual IUD inventors and population control advocates relished the idea of a technology that guaranteed female passivity at every stage of the reproductive process. The very act of IUD insertion, in which female patients, half-naked, prostrate, and legs vulnerably spread, deferred to professional expertise, technology, and gynecological manipulation, was merely the first step in ushering women into a passive role. Describing his observations of IUD insertions in Hong Kong, Alan Guttmacher saw ballet in what is better described as gynecological Taylorism:

> The best IUD manipulator I have ever observed was in Hong Kong. . . . Her record was seventy-five insertions in three hours[,] . . . that is one every two minutes and twenty-four seconds. Dr. Wong kept three nurses busy helping her. One was supervising the removal of the panties of the next patient, the second nurse soothed the brow of the patient on the table and the third passed instruments to Dr. Wong. I have never seen such graceful hands, such exquisite economy of finger movement; there wasn't a false motion. I regret that I am not a choreographer, for a ballet of IUD patients with the ballerina making Dr. Wong's finger and hand movements would be a sensation.[36]

In Guttmacher's ballet, women become identical, submissive parts, passed along the continuous IUD-installment assembly line. With so little time being spent with each female patient, a comprehensive physical exam, sensitivity to women's disparate insertion needs, a medical determination of contraindications, and a full disclosure of potential IUD-related problems, would have been impossible.

The image of a device installed into the uteri of the passive poor was made more lucid by physicians and scientists such as Guttmacher, who insisted that oral contraceptives were intended for individuals; IUDs were best reserved for the masses. This seemingly nonsensical distinction rationalized treating white middle-class suburban women as individuals worthy of tailored, specialized care but assigned IUD users to an undifferentiated group and declared their individual needs, concerns, and problems less important than aggregate outcomes. In a letter to John Searle, president of G. D. Searle & Company, the makers of the first oral contraceptive, Enovid, Guttmacher revealed both his condescension toward and callous disregard for the average IUD wearer:

> . . . IUD's have special application to underdeveloped areas where two things are lacking: one, money and the other sustained motivation. No contraceptive could be

cheaper, and also, once the damn thing is in, the patient cannot change her mind. In fact we can hope she will forget that it is there and perhaps in several months wonder why she has not conceived.

I do not believe the IUD's will cut into the competitive pill market materially in industrialized, more sophisticated regions. The big difference is that the IUD's are not as effective as the pill in preventing conception. If Mrs. Astorbilt, or Mrs. Searle or Mrs. Guttmacher gets pregnant while using an IUD, there is quite a stink—the thing is no good and a lot of people will hear about it. However if you reduce the birth rate of . . . the Korean, Pakistanian or Indian population from 50 to 45 per 1,000 per year to 2, 3, or 5, this becomes an accomplishment to celebrate.[37]

Viewing IUDs as birth control for the generic masses made it easier for gynecologists designing and inserting IUDs to deem irrelevant the unique attributes and varied responses of individual wearers. As Guttmacher's letter suggests, what defined IUD efficacy in the 1960s depended entirely on who was doing the defining. Population control advocates supported a loose definition: as long as IUDs were used by poverty-stricken women, high rates of pregnancy and problems were tolerable. But irrespective of race and class, women around the world universally defined birth control efficacy as pregnancy prevention with minimal side effects. Guttmacher's words also reveal yet another layer of passivity: the agency of middle-class women versus the implied powerlessness of their poorer counterparts. If a middle-class woman gets pregnant with an IUD, "there is quite a stink"; when poverty-stricken women do, it is business as usual.

Female passivity was further reinforced in medical understandings of how IUDs prevented pregnancy. No one knew for certain, and to many, the question of causation was moot: the reasons that the IUD was efficacious were regarded as less significant than the simple fact that it was. What scientists in the late 1960s *suspected*, however, was that the introduction of an IUD caused a local inflammation and infection that made fertilization and egg implantation impossible. In 1968, the Biologic Action subcommittee of the FDA Advisory Committee on Obstetrics and Gynecology examined scientific studies on intrauterine contraception in humans, poultry, mice, rats, hamsters, rabbits, sheep, pigs, and cattle. One of its primary objectives was to determine how IUDs worked. Finding considerable variation among species, it discovered that the one cross-species characteristic of IUD use was inflammation and signs of infection in the endometrium, the lining of the female uterus. The Advisory Committee concluded that among IUD-wearing women, "bacterial contamination occurs almost universally after insertion. Chronic infiltration of the endometrium with plasma cells and lymphocytes [a group of white blood cells important to the adaptive part of the body's immune system] almost always occurs." What the committee agreed upon, in short, was that the IUD's antifertility mechanism derived from its infective, inflammatory properties which, far from being undesirable by-products of IUD use, were the very reason IUDs worked.[38]

Acknowledging that the violent response that the IUD provoked at the cellular level was the scientific basis for IUD efficacy, the committee praised the birth control method. Its report recognized that "intrauterine contraception is not quite as effective as the best oral compounds." On the other hand, "fragmentary evidence suggests that in the lowest socioeconomic group with minimum education, rates of continuation are higher with the IUD's than with the oral compounds." Situating this discovery within the broader political, economic, and social currents of the 1960s, the symbolism one is left with is inescapable. Supporting IUDs as enthusiastically as the FDA Advisory Committee did meant endorsing a technology intended—quite literally—to infect poor, ostensibly irresponsible women in order to halt their unwanted population growth.[39]

IUD Invention and the Culture of Violence

In the end, it was a small step from praise for a technology that was inherently better than traditional methods because it was scientifically engineered, effective because women could not control it, and ideal for poor and uneducated women—who were not considered individuals anyway—to Horne's uterus-piercing device. On balance, it is probably unfair to single Horne out. Although his device was certainly one of the most striking examples of contraceptive technological violence, both the rationale for its creation and the design itself incorporated decades of thinking on politics, female agency, birth control, race, and class.

Indeed, even though it might be comforting to view the scientific world, with its army of researchers, technicians, and laboratory directors as disassociated from the medical world, with its physicians, nurses, and public health officials, the IUD example tells a different story. IUD inventors were typically medical men. In the 1960s and 1970s, male gynecologists were more likely than any other group to be IUD patentees; their models, in turn, were the most frequently inserted by gynecologists nationwide. The Lippes Loop, the favored IUD of the mid-1960s, used by 200,000 women in the United States in 1966, was invented by Dr. Jack Lippes, a professor of obstetrics and gynecology at the University of Buffalo School of Medicine. The infamous Dalkon Shield, the most popular IUD in American history, was designed by Hugh Davis, a gynecologist on the faculty of the Johns Hopkins Medical School and director of its family planning program, and Davis's partner, electrical engineer Irwin Lerner. The grandaddy of them all, the Grafenberg ring, took the name of its gynecologist inventor.

It might similarly be tempting to view this medicalized culture of invention as one in which politics had no place. But here, too, evidence suggests the contrary. We have already seen how Cold War concerns conferred special urgency to the search for foolproof birth control and how the politics of class and race informed prevalent understandings of what foolproof, as a term, meant. Two agencies with a well-articulated political agenda, Planned Parenthood and the Population Council, supported the invention and promotion of IUDs. A close reading of the wording of IUD patent applications underscores the inseparability of politics and IUD invention. The application for the Margulies spiral, for instance, asserted that the device would contribute to the acceptance of IUDS "on a mass basis as is desired in certain over-populated areas of the world." Another application filed in 1970 noted the "increasing problems of overpopulation" and the "benefits which would flow from an effective intrauterine device." Yet another, filed in 1966, observed that "in developing areas of the world and generally among women from poorly educated and lower socio-economic strata, there remains a great challenge to develop effective means of contraception." Among IUD inventors, class-encumbered politics was nothing short of a driving force.[40]

Nor was Horne the only inventor to tout a technological design that demoted female IUD users to a disempowered, passive role. IUD inventors nationwide made special mention of the capability of IUDs in general, and their models in particular, to overcome an unfortunate problem: the assumed inability of poor women and women of color to use female-controlled birth control responsibly. Women of "lower socio-economic strata," wrote one inventor in his patent application, "*particularly* require devices which can be applied once and left in place." Criticizing nonintrauterine birth control, another IUD inventor warned that "all of these devices or drugs require a strict time schedule of use which too often is ignored by the *patient*, resulting in a *medically inadvisable* pregnancy." Yet another celebrated the IUD's ability to render female agency in contraception irrelevant. IUDs provided "freedom from regular intervening acts by the user," he assured. "When properly inserted," the potentially disastrous consequences of "conscious periodic acts by the user . . . are avoided."[41]

Like Horne, IUD inventors routinely invoked metaphors of violence to celebrate the power and control masculine technologies wielded over women's uteri. In so doing, they borrowed from and perpetuated a long history of medical representations of the female body that cast women's reproductive organs as a passive, natural sphere (the very anchor of all that defined "woman"), readily controlled by masculine technological might. Applied to IUDs, such a gendered account encouraged the telling of war stories in which aggressive, battle-hungry IUDs invade, irritate, infect, and finally subdue the ultimately helpless uteri. Responding to concerns in the late 1960s that small, compressible IUDs, of particular appeal to women because they produced less pain and cramping, were too easily expelled, IUD inventors championed the "staying power" of the new meaner, larger models. One was equipped with "two pairs of arms . . . stiffened with wiring springs to provide anchoring mechanisms." This model's "improved configuration," the inventor promised, will "resist expulsions." The Dalkon Shield, its very name suggesting a weapon of war, would likewise stay intact thanks to the IUD's "plurality of spurs . . . [which are] slanted in a given direction so as to impede expulsion movement of the device in that direction." The technological superiority of another, particularly large, device was attributed to the fact that it sported "substantial surface areas for uterus *wall–engaging* purposes *strategically disposed* for maximum effectiveness." Still another inventor promised that his design "will not be *unauthorizedly* expelled from the uterus" because "upon being pushed into the uterus from the insertion tube [it] will assume a self-retaining position."[42]

When such frequent and explicitly articulated expectations and perceptions of female passivity are placed within the larger context of the politics and medicine of population control, Horne's womb-piercing invention, far from being the result of a lone man's lunacy, makes sense. In the Cold War world of contraceptive research, intended female users were never considered apart from the social context in which they were likely to adopt new birth control technologies. The IUD was no exception. Designed specifically for women too poor to buy the Pill or too irresponsible to use other methods, IUDs were presumed ideal for women whose unchecked childbearing was viewed as particularly injurious to the welfare of society at large. Creating a technology to empower women was never the primary goal of invention. Rather, the chief objective of IUD research was to create a birth control in which female passivity would be technology guaranteed.

In this regard, Horne's invention fit the mold. And although his device was never manufactured, other IUDs, by-products of the same ideology of invention, were. Their diffusion eventually resulted in the Dalkon Shield disaster, in which an IUD's faulty design, hurried testing, and misleading advertising caused death, sterility, and untold suffering in women across the globe. An extraordinary example of technological violence inflicted against the female body, the Dalkon Shield catastrophe, like Horne's patent, was the unsurprising outcome of the clash between women's desires for effective, tolerable birth control and an ideology of contraceptive invention that subverted individual needs to broader political goals.[43]

NOTES

The author wishes to thank Michael Bellesiles, Paul Gilmore, Helen Rozwadowski, Joan Sokolovsky, John Tone, and Steven Usselman for their helpful comments and suggestions.

1. U.S. Patent Office, patent number 3,598,115, patented August 10, 1971.

2. Ibid., 1–2.

3. Norman E. Himes, *Medical History of Contraception* (Baltimore: Williams & Wilkins, 1936), 59–63; Linda Gordon, *Woman's Body, Woman's Right: A Social History of Birth Control in America* (New York: Penguin, 1974), 42–43.

4. A pessary is anything inserted into the vagina that physically blocks or chemically neutralizes sperm. Peter James and Nick Thorpe, *Ancient Inventions* (New York: Ballantine, 1994), 187–88; Himes, *Medical History*, 80; Gordon, *Woman's Body, Woman's Right*, 43–44.

5. Himes, *Medical History*, 63; James and Thorpe, *Ancient Inventions*, 186–87; Marie C. Stopes, "Positive and Negative Control of Conception in Its Various Technical Aspects," *Journal of State Medicine* (London) 39 (1931): 354–60; Gordon, *Woman's Body, Woman's Right*, 44.

6. Robert L. Dickinson, "Household Contraceptives," *Journal of Contraception*, February 1936, 43–45.

7. U.S. Food and Drug Administration Medical Device and Drug Advisory Committee on Obstetrics and Gynecology, *Second Report on Intrauterine Contraceptive Devices* (Washington, D.C.: U.S. Department of Health, Education, and Welfare, 1978); Howard Tatum, "Intrauterine Contraception," *American Journal of Obstetrics and Gynecology* 112 (1972): 1000; Janet Farrell Brodie, *Contraception and Abortion in Nineteenth-Century America* (Ithaca: Cornell University Press, 1994), 222.

8. Brodie, *Contraception and Abortion*, 222–24.

9. In 1899, for instance, when Dr. Edward Ill, president of the American Association of Obstetricians and Gynecologists, delivered the association's annual address in Indianapolis, he condemned women's eagerness to shirk their maternal responsibilities by using contraception. "I am sure we all have often been perplexed," he said, "by the shameless confession of a handsome and what is apparently a correct young married woman that she prevents conception; even more, that she entered the marriage bed with the distinct understanding that she desires no offspring, and does so because of the inconvenience it would give her. . . . The depth of moral degeneracy in such cases can only be imagined. I have no patience with these women, and often direct that they may return for my advice and treatment when they have decided to live a natural life and have ceased to be legitimate prostitutes." Edward Ill, "The Rights of the Unborn—The Prevention of Conception," *American Journal of Obstetrics and Diseases of Women and Children* 9 (1899): 581–82.

10. Hugh J. Davis, "Intrauterine Contraceptive Devices: Present Status and Future Prospects," *American Journal of Obstetrics and Gynecology* 114 (1972): 135.

11. Ibid., 134–35; Tatum, "Intrauterine Contraception," 1000–1001.

12. Caryl Potter, "Complications Following the Use of the Gold Spring Pessary," *American Journal of Surgery*, October 1930, 143. Other physicians concurred. According to Howard C. Clark, a Wichita, Kansas, obstetrician and gynecologist, "Illegitimate practitioners and a large number of none too scrupulous members of the medical profession advocate the use of this supposedly harmless device." Howard C. Clark, "Foreign Bodies in the Uterus," *American Journal of Surgery*, March 1938, 631.

13. Davis, "Intrauterine Contraceptive Devices," 135.

14. Tatum, "Intrauterine Contraception," 1001.

15. U.S. Patent Office, patent no. 3,312,214, patented 4 April 1967, 1; Davis, "Intrauterine Contraceptive Devices," 140.

16. Planned Parenthood Federation of America, *Research in Human Reproduction*, 9, 1948 pamphlet in Planned Parenthood Federation of America Records, Sophia Smith Collection, Smith College (hereafter cited as PPFA Records).

17. Robert Sheehan, "The Birth-Control 'Pill,' " *Fortune*, April 1958, 155; Kim Yanoshik and Judy Norsigian, "Contraception, Control, and Choice: International Perspectives," in Kathryn Strother Ratcliff, ed., *Healing Technology: Feminist Perspectives* (Ann Arbor: University of Michigan Press, 1989), 66–67; Huxley quoted in "Men or Maggots?" *Newsweek*, 30 November 1959.

18. Sheehan, "Birth-Control 'Pill,' " 155; Shockley quoted in *Kansas City Times*, 8 January 1965.

19. Charles H. Birnberg and Michael Burnhill, "Whither IUD? The Present and Future of Intrauterine Contraceptives," *Obstetrics and Gynecology* 31 (1968): 861. In the same spirit, Paul Ehrlich's 1968 forecast of doom, *The Population Bomb*, asserted the "inevitability" of nuclear war as the final chapter of a worldwide struggle over access to increasingly scarce resources. Bernard Asbell, *The Pill: A Biography of the Drug That Changed the World* (New York: Random House, 1995), 325–27.

20. Sheehan, "Birth-Control 'Pill,' " 155; U.S. Congress, Senate, Select Committee on Small Business, Subcommittee on Monopoly, *Present Status of Competition in the Pharmaceutical Industry*, 91st Cong., 2d sess., 1970, 5924–25. Similar commentary privileging political objectives over individuals' health needs appears in Nicole Grant, *The Selling of Contraception: The Dalkon Shield Case, Sexuality, and Women's Autonomy* (Columbus: Ohio State University Press, 1992), 30–35.

21. Prices derived from Steven M. Spencer, "The Birth Control Revolution," *Saturday*

Evening Post, 15 January 1966, 22; letter from William L. Searle to Mary Calderone, 16 August 1960, PPFA Records; Sheehan, "Birth-Control 'Pill,'" 222.

22. Letter to Planned Parenthood, 25 January 1965, PPFA Records; Winfield Best, "Now! Something Better Than the Pill?" *McCall's*, February 1965.

23. Letter of Dr. John Rock, December 9, 1960, and Maurice Sagoff to J. William Crosson, 16 February 1961, PPFA Records.

24. Spencer, "Birth Control Revolution," 22.

25. Alan Guttmacher, "Where Is Science Taking Us?" *Saturday Review* 43 (February 6, 1960): 50–51. Davis quoted in Grant, *Selling of Contraception*, 31.

26. Mary Ryan, "Reproduction in American History," *Journal of Interdisciplinary History* 10 (1979): 330.

27. Ruth Schwartz Cowan, *A Social History of Technology* (New York: Oxford University Press, 1997), 322; letters to Gregory Pincus, 29 June 1963, and 16 July 1964, cartons 60 and 71, Pincus Papers, Library of Congress.

28. U.S. Patent Office, patent no. 3,200,815, patented August 17, 1965; Tatum, "Intrauterine Contraception," 1001; FDA Committee, *Second Report on Intrauterine Contraceptive Devices*, 1.

29. *Population Council: 1952–1964* (New York), 41, and *The Population Council: Annual Report for the Year Ended December 31, 1966* (New York), 17, Population Council Records, Boxes 87 and 88, Rockefeller Brothers Fund, Series 4, Grants, Rockefeller Archive Center, North Tarrytown, New York.

30. Christopher Tietze, "History of Contraceptive Method," *Indian Journal of Public Health* 12 (1968): 43; "Projects on Intrauterine Devices, July, 1963," Population Council Records, Box 123, Rockefeller Brothers Fund, Series 4, Grants, Rockefeller Archive Center.

31. Charles F. Westoff, "The Modernization of U.S. Contraceptive Practice," *Family Planning Perspectives* 4 (1972): 10–12. Westoff's study, which explored trends in birth control use among married couples of child-bearing age, found a 1965 IUD adoption rate of .7 percent among whites and 1.7 among blacks, and a 1970 adoption rate of 4.8 percent among whites and 4.5 percent among blacks. These percentages included all couples of child-bearing age, even those not practicing birth control. A separate calculation of methods of contraception in 1970 by wife's education and by color, excluding couples not using birth control, revealed an IUD adoption rate of 8.4 percent among white women with a college education and 9.3 percent among black women without a high school education. These represented the highest rate in each racial group. Hugh Davis, co-inventor of the Dalkon Shield, asserted in a 1972 article that by the end of 1970, 3 million women in the United States had been fitted for IUDs. Davis, "Intrauterine Contraceptive Devices," 135. For lower estimates, see Alfred D. Sollins and Raymond L. Belsky, "Commercial Production and Distribution of Contraceptives," *Reports on Population/Family Planning* 4 (1970): 3; George Langmyhr to John G. Madry, May 13, 1970, U.S. Congress, House of Representatives, Subcommittee of the Committee on Government Operations, *Regulation of Medical Devices (Intrauterine Contraceptive Devices)*, 93d Cong., 1st sess. (Washington, D.C.: Government Printing Office, 1973), 16.

32. S. S. Spivack, "The Doctor's Role in Family Planning," *Journal of the American Medical Association* 188 (1964): 152; N. H. Wright, G. Johnson, and D. Mees, "Physicians' Attitudes in Georgia Toward Family Planning Services," *Advances in Planned Parenthood*, vol. 3 (New York: Excepta Medica Foundation, 1968), 37; J. Barnes et al., "Attitudes and Practices of Physicians Concerning Birth Control in Two California Counties," cited in Morton A. Silver, "Birth Control and the Private Physician," *Family Planning Perspectives* 4 (1972): 43.

33. Silver, "Birth Control and the Private Physician," 43. One Florida physician who had graduated from medical school in 1954 found that the Pill had transformed his practice as much as it had female patients' lives. "Early in my medical career most methods of contraception were simple and commonly available without prescription at any drugstore. The amount of time required then to adequately provide care and advice regarding contraception did not exceed 1 percent of my practice time. With the availability of oral contraceptives . . . the time spent with advice and care related to contraception suddenly skyrocketed to 20 to 25 percent." Testimony of John Madry, in U.S. Congress, House of Representatives, "Hearing before a Subcommittee of the Committee on Government Operations," *Regulation of Medical Devices (Intrauterine Contraceptive Devices)*, 93d Cong., 1st sess. (Washington, D.C.: Government Printing Office, 1973), 5–6.

34. Spencer, "Birth Control Revolution," 25; Grant, *Selling of Contraception*, 99–139.

35. In September 1965, the discovery that some gynecologists were charging as much as four hundred dollars per insertion prompted the American College of Obstetrics and Gynecologists to urge its members not to exceed a recommended fee of twenty-five dollars. Spencer, "Birth Control Revolution," 25.

36. Grant, *Selling of Contraception*, 73.

37. Guttmacher to John Searle, 29 December 1964, PPFA Records.

38. U.S. Food and Drug Administration, Advisory Committee On Obstetrics and Gynecology, *Report on Intrauterine Contraceptive Devices* (Washington, D.C.: Government Printing Office, 1968), 6, 10–17.

39. Ibid., 1, 6.

40. Patent 3,200,815, 17 August 1965, 2; Patent 3,675, 647, 11 July 1972; Patent 3,431,906, 11 March 1969, 1, U.S. Patent Office.

41. Emphasis added. Patent 3,431,906, 11 March 1969, 1; patent 3,397,691, 20 August 1968; patent number 3,675,647, 11 July 1972, 1, U.S. Patent Office.

42. Emphasis added. Patent 3,675,647, 11 July 1972, 1; patent 3,633,574, 11 January 1972, 1; patent 3,364,927, 23 January 1968, 1; patent 3,374,788, 26 March 1968, 1, U.S. Patent Office. For an excellent analysis of the gender biases of seemingly objective scientific accounts of women's reproductive organs, see Emily Martin, *The Woman in the Body: A Cultural Analysis of Reproduction* (Boston: Beacon Press, 1987).

43. Grant, *Selling of Contraception*, and Richard B. Sobol, *Bending the Law: The Story of the Dalkon Shield Bankruptcy* (Chicago: University of Chicago Press, 1991).

A cartoon from Robert F. Williams's newsletter, *The Crusader*. (*The Crusader* [July 1967]: 1.) From the Robert F. Williams papers. Used by permission of the Bentley Historical Library, University of Michigan.

Chapter Nineteen

The Monroe Rifle Club
Finding Justice in an "Ungodly and Social Jungle Called Dixie"

Craig S. Pascoe

As a race, we must work passionately
and unrelentingly for first-class
citizenship, but we must never use
second-class methods to gain it.
—Martin Luther King, Jr.[1]

God damn, the Niggers have got guns.
—A frightened older, white man in Monroe,
North Carolina (July 1961)[2]

As the young demonstrators took up their places in front of the Union County Courthouse in Monroe, North Carolina, that late Sunday afternoon in August 1961, curiosity seekers, angry white racists, and young white men expecting some excitement also began to assemble across the street. Within a short period of time the crowd had grown to more than two thousand. The picketers, comprising Freedom Riders, recently released from Mississippi jails, and local youths, had been demonstrating for more than a week at the courthouse, demanding equal opportunity and treatment for Monroe's black community. There had been no real physical violence against the picketers in the first few days, only verbal threats, intimidation, and the occasional thrown rock or bottle. Local police officials appeared unworried about the potential for racial violence and assigned only a couple of officers to the demonstrations—more to ensure that the town's new picketing laws were followed rather than to prevent any violence against the group.

In the heat of the late afternoon, the crowd of whites that gathered across from the courthouse to watch the spectacle and taunt the picketers turned belligerent when a white woman and black male demonstrators tried to get into an automobile sent to take them back to the relative safety of the black neighborhood of Newtown. When police officers confiscated a shotgun from the driver of the automobile, the crowd became incensed and started to attack the picketers. As the attack began, James Forman, one of the leaders of the demonstrations who had come to Monroe specifically to prove the validity of peaceful nonviolent protest in the face of white racist violence, turned and came face to face with the end of a shotgun barrel. The white man holding the shotgun yelled at Forman: "If you move one step, I'm going to blow your black brains back to Africa." The crowd began chanting, "Kill the nigger! Kill the nigger! Kill him!" Instead of pulling the trigger, the gunman slammed the "hot barrel" of the shotgun on Forman's head, splitting the skin and sending blood "gushing like a volcano in eruption" down his face. A second blow caused even more blood to flow from the wound. As another man wielding a knife approached Forman, he jumped into the car with some demonstrators and police officers and sped away from the melee. When Forman and the others arrived at the Monroe police department, officers placed them under arrest on charges of inciting to riot, assault, profanity, destroying personal property, and carrying concealed weapons. At that point Forman decided that nonviolence was not the answer to ending inequality against African Americans and defeating racism in the South, especially in Monroe, North Carolina.[3]

Nonviolent direct action appeared to many black leaders to be the correct tactic in the struggle for civil rights in the 1950s and 1960s. Because this method was fairly new to the civil rights movement in America, leaders worked to gain acceptance for passive resistance "through continuous non-violent workshops and constant appeals to the non-violent tradition rooted in the black church." Although nonviolence gained wide acceptance among those active in the civil rights movement, there still remained the difficulty of controlling the natural human response of self-defense when faced with imminent danger. Movement leaders like Martin Luther King, Jr., understood total acceptance of nonviolence would be difficult to achieve and conceded that "there will probably be some sporadic violence during this period of transition, and people will naturally seek to protect their property and person." King warned that "for the Negro to privately or publicly call for retaliatory violence as a strategy during this period would be the greatest tragedy that could befall us." King and other civil rights movement leaders argued that for the campaign to succeed, the "Negro southerner's campaign for equality . . . must be, and can be, contained in non-violence."[4]

Advocacy of nonviolence by the established black leadership did not mean that all black leaders fully agreed with or practiced passive resistance. Some, like Medgar Evers, admitted that they often carried weapons for self-defense against violent attacks on themselves and their families. Roy Wilkins acknowledged in his autobiography that "while I admire Reverend King's theories of overwhelming enemies with love, I don't think I could have put those theories into practice myself" if confronted with violence.[5] In Little Rock, Daisy Bates in the late 1950s recruited armed guards to protect her family from racist attacks. Martin Luther King, Jr., even faced the threat from some followers and SCLC Executive Board members who "argued the case for self-defense or retaliatory violence." They "would not initiate violence" but assured King that they "would hit back if attacked."[6]

Black author James Baldwin believed it was impossible to prevent blacks from straying from the ideals of nonviolence because blacks were "themselves produced by a civilization which has always glorified violence." Baldwin noted that only middle- and upper-class blacks would embrace nonviolence, and he held little hope for the lower classes of blacks to embrace fully the tenets of passive resistance. Nonviolence, Baldwin argued, would not be an attractive lifestyle for "every knife-wielding hoodlum outside a White Castle Diner." Baldwin also noted the irony that the same American society that viewed protective violence as the inherent right of every citizen found something horrible and disruptive when the "Negro had the gun." Kenneth B. Clark agreed with Baldwin that nonviolence "may be correct for a small minority of educated and philosophically sophisticated individuals," and it is "unlikely that it can be accepted with full understanding by the masses of Negroes."[7] Robert J. Cottrol and Raymond T. Diamond argued that outwardly "many ordinary black people" throughout the South during the civil rights movement accepted nonviolence as a tactic but maintained a firm belief in their right to self-defense and ownership of firearms to ensure their personal safety.[8]

For the nonviolence doctrine to work, the NAACP, the Southern Christian Leadership Conference (SCLC), the Congress of Racial Equality (CORE), and other civil rights organizations demanded total compliance. The black leadership feared that any display of armed resistance or violence on the part of the southern black community toward white racist aggression or physical threats would only encourage southern white racists to start a race war, one that would likely turn public sentiment away from the movement and destroy any progress made up to that point. Leading black organizations, especially the NAACP, reacted to any deviation from the Ghandian-inspired methods by members in the late 1950s by expulsion from civil rights organizations. But a growing number of African Americans believed a race war was already under way in the South.

Arguing that black men and women involved in the movement were able to control their tempers and were willing to accept the physical brutality heaped upon them by angry, snarling crowds of whites without using force in a defensive manner was to treat them as if they had superhuman willpower. True, many controlled their rage and anger, which, in itself, was a monumental effort. But, as a result of their patience, some emerged from the conflicts with psychological and physical problems that lasted for years. Black scholar Kenneth B. Clark noted that

> the natural reactions to injustice, oppression, and humiliation are bitterness and resentment. The form which such bitterness takes need not be overtly violent but the corruption of the human spirit which is involved seems inevitable. . . . [A]ny demand that the victims of oppression be required to love those who oppress them places an additional and probably intolerable psychological burden upon these victims.

On occasions some blacks, pushed to the brink of their patience by the bombings, the drive-by shootings, the lynching, the rapes, the absence of justice, and the physical harm inflicted on loved ones, often responded with force to protect themselves and their families without thinking or caring what effect their actions had on the success of the movement.[9]

In the postwar years African Americans, instead of passively accepting racist violence, exhibited an unwillingness to accept physical abuse from whites without some form of active resistance. Harvard Sitkoff pointed out that the experiences of blacks during and immediately after World War II "stimulated blacks to demand a better deal" and that many blacks "responded with a militancy" previously unseen in America. August Meier and Elliot Rudwick asserted that "advocacy of retaliatory violence, and actual instances of it, have tended to increase during periods of heightened Negro protest activity."[10] Scattered incidents of African Americans' resort to self-defense against racist violence in the South during this period have been downplayed as mere aberrations in the larger scheme of the civil rights movement.

Before the emergence of Malcolm X and his call for defensive measures and aggressive response to violence, and before the black power movement of the late 1960s, some southern blacks formed their own protective agencies and developed self-defense tactics in response to the oppressive southern environment that one indigenous civil rights leader, Robert F. Williams of Monroe, North Carolina, referred to as an "ungodly and social jungle called Dixie."[11] Williams, president of the Monroe chapter of the NAACP in North Carolina from 1957 to 1961, represents the growing tendency in the postwar South to refute the teachings of nonviolence as the only method in the struggle for equality and to confront white racist violence with violence. Williams accepted nonviolence as a tactic in the civil rights struggle but argued that "pacifism will never be accepted wholeheartedly by the masses of Negroes so long as violence is rampant in Dixie."[12]

Williams's militancy represented not only a "manifestation of an older, unsolved conflict over methods of achieving social change" but a growing frustration among poorer blacks who felt left out of the day-to-day activities of the NAACP.[13] The story of Williams's activism, the creation of the Monroe Rifle Club, a self-defense organization for the protection of the local black community, and the militancy of the Monroe NAACP also reveal an NAACP leadership that struggled against its own membership and some of its leaders who refused to follow the organization's demands that members adhere completely to the ideology of nonviolence. Williams's militant posturing and the creation of a formal self-defense organization for Monroe's black community represent an aggressive reaction to southern white violence during the increased activity of the civil rights movement. Other movements, particularly the Deacons for Defense, an African American self-defense group in Louisiana, demonstrated that Williams's activities were not just an isolated phenomenon. Clayborne Carson describes a similar self-defense organization in Lowndes County, Mississippi, where black

farmers "owned weapons and were willing to defend themselves when attacked" and often used armed guards to protect civil rights rallies.[14]

As head of the Monroe, North Carolina, NAACP in the late 1950s, Williams
gained considerable attention for his militancy and his use of the American
tradition of armed self-defense as a tactic in the struggle for civil rights.[15] He had
served in the military during World War II and, like many other black veterans,
returned home with a new sense of freedom, training in defensive and offensive
skills, and an unwillingness to "accept passively a return to the status quo of
racism."[16] James Albert Burran argued that the widespread violence against
African Americans in the South during and after the war forced them to "abandon direct forms of militance" and live in "an uneasy coexistence with whites."
And, as Numan V. Bartley noted, in the postwar years southern whites reacted
violently to any indication that the region's blacks wanted to challenge the white-
dominated social, political, and economic southern way of life. Williams, unwilling to accept the status quo passively, faced constant intimidation and threats of
violence from racist whites trying to keep him in his place.[17]

Born in 1925, Robert F. Williams grew up in rural Monroe, North Carolina,
the Union County seat of about ten thousand, twenty-five miles east of Charlotte.
Approximately three-fourths of Union County residents lived on farms where
they grew tobacco and cotton or raised chickens and dairy cattle. Situated at the
intersection of two major lines of the Seaboard railroad, many of Monroe's
residents, both white and black, worked for the railroad. Before the war, Monroe
was a mercantile center serving the needs of farmers in the surrounding area.
After the war, boosters actively campaigned to bring new industries to Monroe.
By the 1950s plastic and clothing operations, a feed-processing plant, a cotton-
seed-oil mill, and a few other small manufacturers had established factories in
the area. Town boosters proudly pointed to miles of paved streets and modern
street lighting as an indication of the town's modern spirit.[18] And white citizens
proudly proclaimed that the area had no problems between the races. But the
racial climate in Monroe, outwardly calm and peaceful, remained as oppressive
as that of "any other city in the Deep South during the 1950s and 1960s."[19]

Williams, raised in a black middle-class family, grew up in an environment
that emphasized community service and social activism. His grandfather, Sikes
Emsley Williams, was born in Union County before the Civil War into the
"ownership of the Williams family." After emancipation, Sikes attended J. C.
Smith University in nearby Charlotte. Sikes and his wife, Isabell Ellen Tomberlin,
worked as teachers in Union County's black schools. Sikes also served as a
Republican Party committeeman for Union County during Reconstruction. Robert's father, John L. Williams, worked for the Seaboard Airline Railway Company
as a boilermaker's helper in the engine repair shop, and his wages allowed the
family to have a comfortable middle-class life.[20]

Growing up in the 1930s and 1940s, Williams witnessed numerous acts of
violence against African Americans in Monroe that were representative of the
atmosphere of violence and intimidation prevalent in the South during this

period. He recalled that as a child he had witnessed one such act against an African American on the streets of Monroe:

> I remember when I was about ten years old . . . and I went into the town and I saw the chief of police [Jesse Helms, Sr.]—white man, big man who weighed about 250 pounds I suppose, and he was about seven feet tall—dragging a black woman up the street dragging her on the sidewalk by the heel, her dress up over her head, and the whites were laughing [and] the blacks were afraid. . . . I never could understand how black people could tolerate this type of thing.[21]

Williams never forgot the spectacle, especially the sight of Monroe's "emasculated black men," who, instead of coming to the aid of the woman, "hung their heads in shame and hurried silently from the cruelly bizarre sight." Other Monroe blacks, and even whites, remembered Jesse, Sr., in the same way. One Monroe native remembered that Jesse, Sr., would often beat drunks or unruly people and that he had "a nasty way of talking to people."

When Williams and other World War II black veterans returned to Monroe, they responded differently to the racial violence against the town's black community. Blacks throughout the South became increasingly unwilling to ignore violence against their own people and less likely to remain silent and cowed by the whites who terrorized them. Williams believed that the change in attitude resulted from service in the military, which taught African American veterans "what a virtue it was to fight for democracy." What Williams remembered most was that "they taught us to use arms." "So we were fresh out of the Armed Forces and we felt up to par or above, with the police and the Klan," he explained. The sense of "security and self-assurance" that black veterans gained in their military training and in combat emboldened them to defend themselves against racist violence without considering the danger or consequences.[22]

In 1947 when the Klan threatened to desecrate the body of a black veteran, Williams and other black veterans reacted aggressively and defiantly. The body of Bennie Montgomery, a black veteran who had been accused, tried, and quickly executed by the State of North Carolina for the murder of W. M. Mangum, his white boss, lay in the Harris Funeral Home awaiting burial. The local Ku Klux Klan members, angered that they had not lynched Montgomery, boasted that the body belonged to "the invisible empire" and threatened to kill the funeral home director if he allowed mourners to drape an American flag over the casket. Armed with rifles and shotguns, Williams, along with other African Americans who were mostly veterans, met the Klansmen as they drove up to the funeral home to take Montgomery's body. Facing armed African Americans willing to defend themselves, the Klansmen peaceably drove off. Williams realized that the incident "started us to understanding that we had to resist, and that resistance could be effective if we resisted in groups, and if we resisted with guns."[23]

Williams, as well as other blacks, also encountered a seemingly impenetrable barrier in the workplace. New industry in Union County in the postwar period increased the number of good-paying jobs, but black men could not find a way to break through the racial barrier to get those new jobs. Unable to find any suited to his abilities, Williams left Monroe. From 1947 to 1955, he and his wife, Mabel, moved around the country looking for work. During this time, he also attended a number of colleges, using the G.I. Bill. In 1955, the Williams family settled in California. Without any prospects for a decent job, and with his G.I. benefits exhausted, Williams enlisted in the Marines, where he hoped to learn a trade that he could use later in civilian life. The recruiter's assurance that Williams would receive training in the Information Services failed to materialize.[24]

His commanding officer informed Williams that the Marine Corps made no such guarantees, and furthermore, "the Corps doesn't allow any colored men in the Information Services." He was offered a position as a supply clerk.

Agitating for a position in the Information Services got Williams thrown into the Camp Pendleton brig on charges of refusing to march in a parade and failure to salute the American flag. He renewed his demands from inside the jail, and the Marines eventually released him after doctors at Camp Pendleton determined he suffered from a "passive-aggressive reaction." The attending doctor diagnosed Williams's unstable mental condition as probably being the result of the "subject . . . getting pushed around." Williams received a dishonorable discharge in 1955 "by reason of being [a] habitual shirker."[25] Williams returned to Monroe.

In his time away from Monroe and during his service in the Marines, Williams had experienced the kind of discrimination he thought existed only in the South, and he had soon realized that African Americans everywhere would have to struggle for equal rights and even survival. The only useful skill Williams acquired in the corps was that of self-defense, which he put into play as head of the Monroe NAACP.[26]

The Monroe NAACP, chartered in 1945, initially attracted middle- and upper-class African Americans to its ranks. In the first year, membership reached 156 and then fluctuated over the next ten years, reaching a low of 17 in 1956. By comparison, membership in other North Carolina NAACP chapters in the ten years after World War II increased by 60 percent. The majority of the most active chapters were in rural areas, where white racist terrorism remained prevalent. Like Williams, Kelly M. Alexander, Sr., state director of the NAACP, declared that the reason for the decline in membership in the Monroe chapter resulted from "pro-segregation white citizens . . . getting appeasement Negroes to . . . discourage people from joining the NAACP." Alexander also agreed that the presence of the KKK in most North Carolina communities, and intimidation and harassment by state and local police officials prevented greater participation in local NAACP chapters. But unlike Alexander, Williams believed that "appeasement Negroes" were the same upper-class and conservative black leaders who controlled the local NAACP chapter.[27]

Economic and racist pressure applied by Monroe's white community leaders and the area's white racist organizations against the Monroe NAACP prevented the chapter from retaining members. In 1956, with membership down to seventeen, chapter president Reverend T. H. Harris, along with the branch's executive committee, recommended dissolving the chapter.[28] However, chapter leaders, fearing that the black community would look unfavorably on them for that move, chose instead to pass the leadership of the chapter and its problems to someone new. Chapter members nominated Williams to be head and explained to him that he was chosen because "you're the only fool left." And because he was unemployed at the time, they reasoned that he could withstand economic coercion: "You don't have a good job to be fired from. And you don't seem to care about what else they might do to you." Only one of the chapter's leaders, Dr. Albert Perry, who had first come to the Monroe area during World War II, remained an active member. Without an executive committee, and in need of some respectable members as chapter leaders, Williams appointed Perry vice president.[29]

When Williams first tried to build up membership, he found it difficult, explaining to national headquarters:

> [I]n this section of the South today many people are willing to support the NAACP financially but are in no position to expose themselves. For some people, public gatherings have become too open and I find it necessary to visit homes and appeal directly to individuals. I admit that this is a slower method, but I'm sure that in the long run it will prove to be effective in more ways than one.

Many former NAACP members and the majority of the "social leaders of the community" no longer wanted to participate in the NAACP, so Williams turned to "the people." He recruited laborers, domestics, and especially veterans who, "just a few years out of a fox hole . . . just can't bring [themselves] around to fleeing from a white sheet." Williams selected veterans to serve as chapter officers and later concluded that "that's why the branch took on such a militant" aspect.[30]

Williams created an NAACP chapter organized and controlled not by the black community's social, economic, and religious leadership but by "poor people, the unemployed and casually employed, housemaids and janitors and porters."[31] The new membership created a very "strong and ethically responsive branch of the NAACP." Williams's self-defense tactics, as well as his demands for access to jobs in white-owned businesses and factories, and calls for the desegregation of public facilities attracted support from a large number of Monroe's black lower class. August Meier described this group as the "average Negro . . . on a dreary treadmill. Without much education, without adequate work and something for his children to aspire to," and without any interest or reason to belong to the NAACP. Many of Monroe's poor blacks had not previously participated in the organization, believing that it was for middle- and upper-class blacks. Williams's efforts to recruit them had come as a welcome surprise. Members numbered 108 by 1959. Although outwardly pleased with the growth of the Monroe NAACP, state director Alexander was apprehensive about its militancy.[32]

In 1957 and 1958, Williams's first step was a campaign against racial injustice. He planned to integrate the Monroe Public Library and encouraged a fellow veteran enrolled in a night course at the black high school to check out a book. Williams had already received permission from the head of the Union County

Library Board for African Americans to use the library on a temporary basis because the black library had been destroyed by fire. He declared that the all-white board seemed unconcerned about "niggers" using the library. The volunteer expressed amazement at not having been challenged when he entered the library, and Williams pretended not to know the reason for the lack of friction. The victory, even though not exactly a triumph through activism, helped Williams motivate blacks who had remained passive because of intense pressure from the white community.[33]

Williams and the Monroe NAACP turned next to the town's whites-only public swimming pool. Emotions in the black community ran high on the subject because several black youths had recently drowned in swollen creeks that were the only place for the blacks to swim. Arguing that Monroe's pool had been constructed during the depression with WPA funds and was a public facility, Williams asserted that African Americans could not be legally denied access. He held demonstrations and "stand-ins" at the pool. Although the initiative was unavailing, the nonviolent direct action for civil rights did manage to "arouse the wrath of the Ku Klux Klan." White racists and hooded local Klansmen countered with their own "stand-ins," hoping to scare the demonstrators into giving up. To end the controversy and the potential for violence, the city closed the pool for the rest of the summer, but not before the event had "galvanized the Klansmen into a campaign of night-riding, cross-burning and 'evangelical rallies.' "[34]

Monroe's racial violence escalated toward the end of the summer of 1957. Joyriding whites regularly sped through the black neighborhoods throwing objects at people on the street, especially women, honking horns, and firing pistols. One night a group of white fun seekers stopped a black woman and forced her to "dance at pistol point."[35] In the past, at the first sign of Klan activity in their area, blacks, especially NAACP members, grabbed their weapons and gathered in the streets to defend their homes. When NAACP members suggested to Williams that it would be a good idea to formalize the defense, he began planning.

Williams recalled that during his time in the Marines in the early 1950s, he had regularly seen civilian members of the National Rifle Association (NRA) using the military rifle range. The NRA not only received special benefits from the government, like access to rifle ranges, but was perceived as an organization of patriots who exercised the constitutional right to bear arms. Williams thought that obtaining a charter from the NRA, an association that avidly defended the doctrine of self-defense, would legitimize his group's efforts. He contacted the NRA's headquarters and "explained that he was a Marine veteran and had organized a group of ex-servicemen committed to the active preservation of their own, and their country's freedom."[36] Assuming the NRA would not issue a charter to a group of African Americans, he crafted the application to make it "look like white people" had submitted the request by listing the occupations of members of the Monroe Rifle Club as somewhat more elevated than in actuality (a dishwasher became a restaurateur; a brick mason, a contractor; a truck driver, a trucking official). The NRA issued the charter.[37]

The Monroe NAACP chapter and the Monroe Rifle Club existed as two separate entities, but the majority of NAACP members belonged to the Rifle Club and the officers of the NAACP also served as its officers. In effect, the Rifle Club became the protector of the black community and the defensive arm of the Monroe NAACP. Williams organized chapter members and others in the community, many of whom were veterans of World War II and the Korean conflict, into armed squads and established procedures to repulse Klan joyrides. The Rifle Club organized three-man defense teams; implemented a " 'snowball system' of telephone alerts"; established a communications network; dug foxholes and trenches, fortifying them with sandbags; collected weapons and ammunition; and stockpiled Molotov cocktails. Careful not to place residents in the line of friendly fire, the club set rules concerning responses to the bullets coming from Klan caravans driving through the black neighborhood: "[Y]ou couldn't fire across the street; you had to fire down the street. So when the car[s] passed they [club members] formed a line across the street, and they had tracer bullets and you could see those bullets going into the back of the car." Nobody reported being injured by the gunfire, but Williams was sure that the marauders were not unscathed.[38]

Firing weapons in the neighborhood was a dangerous practice. After a near-fatal mishap, the Rifle Club instituted a strict policy for the use of weapons in self-defense. Nervous sentries, sleeping in foxholes outside the home of Dr. Perry, almost took the life of a white newspaper delivery boy early one morning:

> We were sleeping in foxholes out on the edge of the street . . . the paper boy came in the night. . . . And this guy was sleeping in the fox hole under a blanket and this paper boy . . . threw this paper, and hit that guy. . . . [T]his guy jumped up . . . and he just start[ed] cutting loose on that boy on that bike. . . . [Y]ou could see the fire, flying off the bike where the bullets were hitting the bike. I don't know why in the world he missed that boy.[39]

The police encouraged the newspaper boy and his father to press charges against the Rifle Club, but they refused. Williams related that the boy's father "was a sharecropper white guy, [and] lived on the head Klansman's farm, and the Klansman told the farmer . . . you got to indict those niggers, and so the father asked the little boy . . . had they been bothering you. The boy said, no." The father did not take legal action, and the Klan "ran that man out of the county."[40]

Members of the Rifle Club collected M1s, Mausers, and German semiautomatic rifles, steel helmets, gas masks. They even built a rifle range for shooting practice. Many of the black women insisted that the "men teach them to shoot." NAACP members who worked as domestics also became an important part of the defensive measures; they listened in on the conversations of their white employers and passed on what they learned concerning Klan raids and rallies. Local newspapers made it even easier to monitor Klan activity because they often carried advertisements for the rallies.[41]

Occasionally, Williams and other Rifle Club members attended Klan rallies to emphasize to the Klan that they no longer feared the invisible empire. Dr. Perry boasted, "We often went to the Klan meetings. We always knew where they were going to be held because they were announced in the local paper. We would get right up in the group and take a look around. People would see us and they'd gradually move away."[42] All of these efforts became part of an intricate defense arrangement for the black neighborhood. And, because Williams went to great efforts to keep most of self-defense preparations visible to the entire community, the presence of the Rifle Club served as a warning to racist elements of the consequences if they threatened the black neighborhood.

Threats against Williams and his family and Dr. Perry increased as the racial tension in Monroe and Union County mounted. Mabel Williams, Robert's wife, described the mood of the neighborhood during the summer of 1957 as extremely wary. Rarely did black families enjoy a peaceful night's sleep. And children in the community, like Mabel's youngest son, learned at an early age how to fire weapons. White racists set up a card table on the county courthouse lawn and solicited signatures from citizens on a petition that called for the expulsion of Williams and Perry from Union County on grounds that they "were members and officials of the Communist—NAACP." The Rifle Club established a round-the-clock armed guard at Perry's house in response to telephone threats against his life. During the late summer and early fall, as many as fifty Rifle Clubbers kept vigil at night.[43]

On August 8, 1957, the *Monroe Enquirer* carried an announcement for what was described as Union County's "first Ku Klux Klan rally and cross-burning in modern times." The Klan had been actively harassing Monroe's African Americans for years but with the growing resentment among white southerners of the Supreme Court's 1954 *Brown v. Board of Education* decision, it became more active, and very public, in demanding that white southerners resist desegregation and changes to their peculiar social order. Williams's continued calls for desegregation of the pool and the very open display of the Rifle Club's fortification of the black neighborhood further inflamed racial tensions. Crowds gathered in fields outside Monroe to hear Klan speakers talk about the evils of integration, the communist conspiracy behind the civil rights movement, and the outrageous activities of some of the town's "uppity Negroes." By the end of September the KKK had held seven rallies in Union County, some with crowds estimated at five hundred to fifteen hundred.[44]

News reaching the black neighborhood of Newtown of the approach of an automobile caravan of Klan members from the Klan rally on October 4 put the Rifle Club on the alert. As fifty to sixty cars packed with Klansmen—some wearing hoods in violation of North Carolina law—reached the outskirts of the neighborhood, the Rifle Club assembled at Dr. Perry's home. Monroe police knew in advance of the Klan's intention to caravan through the neighborhood, and had stationed themselves on its outskirts in case the situation got out of hand. Williams and Perry demanded of Police Chief A. A. Mauney that he put a stop to the intimidation, but Mauney refused, saying that no laws had been broken, whereupon the two men assured the chief that Newtowners themselves would act. As the procession moved through the neighborhood, gunfire erupted from one of the lead cars. The Rifle Club responded with a volley. The Klan quickly dispersed. The notion that a group of blacks would arm themselves to repel an attack by whites was a total surprise and frightened the white community. Mauney later downplayed the incident by stating that the "negroes" were not carrying weapons and that his officers had heard only one loud noise, possibly a shot from a carbine rifle.[45]

Although Williams and the Rifle Club had been successful, their actions alienated the state and national NAACP. No whites had been injured by Rifle Club gunfire, but the fact that African Americans would aggressively react to imminent violence frightened civil rights leaders. Relations between the Monroe NAACP and the national organization were strained even further when, on October 14, 1957, the Union County grand jury indicted Dr. Perry, a devout Catholic, for having performed an abortion on a white woman. Williams declared the charge false and dismissed the indictment as an attempt to discredit Perry. Benjamin Winfield, a Rifle Club member whose assignment was to protect the Perry home during the racial unrest in the summer of 1957, believed that the Klan wanted to harm him: "Whites didn't like Perry because he was concerned about the welfare of poor blacks. . . . That's why they tried to kill him. And that's why I said that I would die along with him. I lost jobs on account of it."[46]

Soon after the Rifle Club's rout of the KKK, the Monroe city council, fearful of a wide open race war, passed an ordinance prohibiting Klan parades "without a special permit from the police chief."[47] Many in the town's white middle and upper classes did not welcome the revival of overt and violence-prone Klan activity. Although they were supportive of the Klan's defense of segregation, most were made nervous by the "tones of the Klan speakers" that emphasized a "race hatred theory" rather than a defense of "race segregation in our schools and society." They preferred the moderate and cautious leadership of North Carolina politicians like "Kerr Scott, Sam Ervin, Jr., and Luther Hodges," to the hate-filled tirades of local Klan notables. They also worried about the damage that racial strife would do to efforts to increase the county's industrial base. Soon after the Rifle Club clash with the Klan caravan, city officials and "local industrial leaders" expressed grave concern that further such incidents might "cripple greatly the program to locate new industries in the area."[48]

The Monroe NAACP under Williams also faced internal challenges. The Reverend T. H. Harris, its former president, joined the city council in condemning violence perpetrated by not only the KKK but also the "colored people" who followed Williams. Four local African American ministers alluded to Williams as an "irresponsible" person whose militancy created racial violence. Harris, as head of the black Union County Civic League, informed the council that the league "favored a 'separate but equal' policy," and believed that the NAACP under Williams and Perry had moved too quickly and aggressively to end segregation.[49]

Part of the buildup in racist activity in Monroe and the region during the late 1950s was the work of the North Carolina Knights of the Ku Klux Klan led by

James "Catfish" Cole, a self-proclaimed Baptist minister and part-time carnival huckster who interpreted the word of God as calling for segregation.[50] In January 1958, Cole's followers burned crosses in front of the homes of suspected "race traitors." They subsequently held a crusade in nearby Robeson County against the mixing of whites and Native Americans. At a Klan rally near Maxton later that month, a small group of Klan supporters encountered an estimated one thousand Lumbee Indian protesters. The Lumbees, armed with "squirrel guns and hunting knives," and one wearing a war bonnet with the inscription "Souvenir of Chimney Rock, N.C.," rushed the assembly. Sheriff's deputies fired tear gas into the crowd and all present dispersed.[51]

News of the Lumbee victory brought mixed reactions. Governor Luther H. Hodges received numerous letters supporting the Klan and condemning the Indians.[52] Harry Golden, editor of the Jewish newspaper *Carolina Israelite* (Charlotte), complained that the Lumbees had "taken the law into their own hands, and this should concern us more than the routing of a Klan meeting." Golden believed that the South's civil rights struggle would be won not through violence but through the legal methods the NAACP had used in the past. Not all whites sided with the Klan. Alabama governor James Folsom announced that "the white man has mistreated the Indian for 400 years; this is one time I am glad to see, and hope the Indians continue to beat the paleface." Williams was taken aback by the interest and support Lumbee Indians received from all sections of the country while similar events in Monroe failed to attract national attention. He attributed the disparity to the fact that Native Americans were such a small minority that their actions were not perceived as threatening to whites.[53]

Embarrassed in Robeson County, Cole moved his campaign to Monroe. Urged on by his fiery race-baiting speeches, Klan groups in the area and in nearby South Carolina stepped up their nocturnal rallies in Union County and their harassment of Monroe's black community. After rallies in late January and early February 1958, some with crowds estimated at more than seven thousand, caravans of "hooded riders drove through Monroe's Negro districts, blowing horns, shouting and sometimes firing pistols." The ordinance passed after the October 1957 clash between the Klan and the Rifle Club required that any parade or procession in Monroe be "escorted by officials of the law," and the chaperonage greatly reduced the threat of violence. Williams's self-defense tactics—the display of black citizens heavily armed, organized, and willing to defend their homes and families—motivated local officials to moderate the actions of the more violent white racists. Even so, Klan harassment continued and Klan activity increased. Williams tried to get state and federal officials to intervene.[54]

When Cole announced plans for a "personal evangelistic meeting" near Monroe, Williams warned state officials of the impact of "evangelistic meetings" and Klan rallies on Monroe's black community: "It is usually the trend that racial tension is heightened just after a Klan meeting. We attribute this to the fact that the pitch of racist attack delivered against the Negro by Klan speakers motivates the baser elements of low strata white society."[55]

Governor Hodges had clearly indicated at the beginning of his administration that he would not tolerate Klan violence. Williams wired Hodges in early February 1958 for help:

> We hope your attitude toward the K.K.K. is genuine. The Negro neighborhood here has twice been envaded [sic] by pistol-firing, screaming, hornblowing and hooded klansmen escorted by officials of the law who showed a wanton disregard for Article 15 of the U.S. Constitution. Racial violence usually follows Klan meetings in Union County. We are in no mood to be intimidated by ungodly, unamerican Klansmen. We beseech you to use your high office to avert revival of Klan action . . . violence and a meeting scheduled for Sunday here. [Request your help] that our homes and streets may not become a possible battleground.

Hodges, concerned that adverse publicity created by racial violence would hinder attempts to attract business to the state, took a firm stand against racial violence and violence-prone organizations like the KKK.[56]

The governor consulted Monroe's white business and political leaders, such as Oscar L. Richardson, a Monroe lawyer and former speaker of the North Carolina House of Representatives; Chief of Police Mauney; and Ben H. Wolfe, sheriff of Union County. (Mauney and Wolfe were the same law enforcement officials who had allowed their officers to lead Klan caravans through Monroe's black neighborhoods.) Hodges informed Williams that his office had investigated his complaints and received "information from responsible officials . . . that the statements in your telegram as to past disorders in Union County are grossly exaggerated." Robert Giles, Hodges's administrative assistant, assured Williams that the governor would "not condone violence and disorder"—any violence, "whether caused by the so-called Klan or by individuals or organizations who unthinkingly allow themselves to be provoked."[57] Hodges opposed KKK violence, but his administration would show more concern about the threat of black violence against whites and would react more quickly to it.

Klan rallies in Union County failed to attract much support through the rest of 1958. Racial tensions calmed further when a Lumberton, North Carolina, judge in March sentenced Cole to eighteen to twenty-four months on a road gang for inciting the January 18 Lumbee Indian riot.[58] White moderates deplored the violence that surrounded Klan leaders like Cole. The U.S. Klan, in an effort to stem the growing anti-KKK sentiment, tried to rekindle enthusiasm in Union County for Klan functions but received a "chilly reception" from the white community. Nonetheless, Klan activity in Monroe and the region remained below the surface of a nervous city. Although white elected officials in Monroe and the state discounted Williams's assertions of that activity and threats against his person, other whites believed Williams. Nationwide Insurance decided to cancel his automobile coverage because of the dangerous "things that have happened to Williams."[59]

In the fall of 1958, Williams tried and failed to enroll his two sons in Monroe's white public high school. He believed the attempt may have been the catalyst for the arrest in late October of two boys on charges of molesting a young white girl and the start of the "Kissing Case," which brought Williams's and the Monroe

NAACP's militant stance to national and international attention. Harry Golden, a close associate of the state and national NAACP leadership, thought that Williams's militancy and calls for self-defense, and the Monroe NAACP's earlier demands for access to the town's whites-only swimming pool and desegregation of Monroe's white schools created a "vacuum" between the two races in Monroe that prevented compromise or communication and guaranteed that racial violence would continue. Golden assured Governor Hodges that "liberal groups" and the "responsible negro leadership" in North Carolina wished to distance themselves from Williams's radical activities.[60]

In 1959, 1960, and 1961, the Monroe NAACP under Williams's leadership continued to agitate for access to swimming facilities; protested a proposed urban renewal program that meant the eradication of a large portion of the black neighborhood of Newtown; demanded that African Americans be given jobs in new industries locating in the area; campaigned for equal treatment under the law; and worked to end Klan intimidation and violence. Williams defended the militancy of the Monroe NAACP by pointing to the ongoing Klan activity in the county. Threats, assaults, and harassment of Monroe's black citizens increased. One young black man was said to have died from a "ruptured heart" when he fell onto a curb on a downtown street on a hot day while being arrested by two Monroe police officers. At a demonstration at the pool in August 1960 one of the white women in the crowd of hecklers "turned her rear end toward our group . . . and made slapping gestures with her lily white hands. . . . She invited all the 'niggers' to the domain of her behind. . . . She offered a candid shot so that the world may better understand the white mentality of this social jungle called Dixie."[61] Local and state officials countered Williams's assertions of intimidation with statements that Klan activity had ceased or had never existed in and around Monroe.

Williams's militancy increased after the acquittal in Monroe of a white man for attacking a pregnant black woman in May 1959. He openly declared that the local NAACP chapter would meet any threat to the black community with physical force:

> We cannot rely on the law. We can get no justice under the present system. If we feel that injustice is done, we must right then and there on the spot be prepared to inflict punishment on these people. Since the Federal government will not bring a halt to lynching in the South and since the so-called courts lynch our people legally, if it's necessary to stop lynching with lynching, then we must be willing to resort to this method.

An editorial in the *Charlotte Observer* confirmed the existence of Klan activity but warned that Williams's "incitement to violence is a serious, dangerous act, whether the thought be uttered by white or Negro spokesmen. Robert Williams does his people no service by his wild declarations."[62] A local white woman closely associated with the Klan telephoned Williams soon after his defiant proclamation and told him that it "wasn't Christian," that he should change his ways. Unfazed, Williams repeated his warning several times to radio stations

and newspapers, and even in a live television interview conducted by Mike
Wallace. When state and national NAACP officials demanded that Williams
retract his comments, Conrad Lynn, Williams's attorney, informed state director
Alexander that Williams "makes no apologies for his stand, which is simply that
negroes in any part of the South where the law has broken down for them, have
the common law right to defend themselves with arms."[63]

Encouraged by Alexander, Roy Wilkins, head of the national NAACP, suspended Williams soon after his inflammatory remarks, explaining in a press
release that the suspension occurred because "Mr. Williams is guilty of . . . conduct which is inimical to the best interest and welfare of the NAACP. Statements
made by him are jeopardizing the entire program of the NAACP in North
Carolina." Wilkins characterized Williams as a "tragic sort of stubbornly resent-
ful David, convinced that the Light and the Call have struck him and him only
of all the prophets and crusaders." He confided to a concerned NAACP member
that the organization "simply cannot afford to have anybody in the ranks who
talks about using violence."[64]

Wilkins saw Williams as going beyond the basic tenets of self-defense. Not
only did Williams advocate self-defense, Wilkins said, he also advocated vigilantism to punish whites committing crimes against African Americans. Wilkins
reminded critics of the suspension that the organization had long acknowledged
the right of black Americans to defend themselves against mob violence but had
taken a strong stance against vigilantism. Although supportive of self-defense,
the NAACP and other mainstream civil rights organizations feared that racist
groups like the KKK would capitalize on the specter of armed African Americans
to encourage an all-out race war in the South. Alexander noted that "it is precisely the non-violence program of the Negroes of the South that is winning us
our battle for first class citizenship. The slightest deviation from this course
would set us back another generation. it would lose the movement tremendous
support among the white Southerners, much more than appears on the surface."[65]

Wilkins received a number of letters and telegrams supporting Williams's
right to self-defense and free speech. One angry writer told Wilkins, "Negroes
have gotten tired of praying for miracles," and perhaps "it is about time we
started to use a few hand grenades, gasoline, and a few matches." Another
reminded him that the "right of self-defense is a sound principle, recognized in
law as a matter of self-preservation." Other writers criticized the NAACP for its
lack of aggressiveness or militancy in demanding equal treatment for African
Americans. And Leonard Bernstein, a white delegate from Pennsylvania to the
1959 NAACP convention, supported Williams: "[I]t's a shame that the use of the
word violence has been put in the wrong light. The lynchers are the violent
ones."[66]

In a statewide rally in Jackson, Mississippi, Wilkins addressed the issue of the
suspension. Ever since the 1954 *Brown v. Board of Education* decision, he reminded
the crowd, white resistance to federally mandated desegregation and the growing violence and intimidation against blacks willing to challenge the status quo

pushed "some desperate Negro citizens to cry out for the meeting of violence with violence. They find themselves and their loved ones hemmed in on every side. They seek justice and find her not blind, but looking closely at skin color. They read the law, and it reads all right, but it works out all wrong in their cases." "It is not surprising," he continued, that these individuals grasp violence as "the only thing left," to protect themselves. But "the NAACP has never advocated violence. It does not do so today.... We will not tolerate an NAACP official who advocates violence.... Here is no question of free speech...no question of the right of self-defense."[67]

At the 1959 NAACP annual convention in New York, Wilkins rallied support for the suspension. Speakers such as Jackie Robinson, Daisy Bates, and Martin Luther King, Jr., deplored Williams's actions and his calls for "meeting violence with violence" and urged the delegates to support the suspension.[68] The delegates overwhelmingly agreed and reconfirmed the association's commitment to nonviolence as the only workable tactic in the struggle against inequality.

Despite Williams's suspension the Monroe Rifle Club, under his guidance, went on defending the neighborhood, but it failed to prevent sporadic violence against African Americans in Monroe and Union County. Its militancy apparently increased attendance at Klan rallies: on August 1, 1959, a rally and barbecue in nearby Allen's Crossroads attracted an estimated two thousand listeners to speeches on how "the U.S. Klans as a Christian patriotic fraternal organization can save the nation from mongrelization and ruin." In his newsletter, *The Crusader*, Williams explained that in the past, "the announcement of a Klan rally electrified Negro communities. Intimidated Negroes deserted the streets at sundown, doors closed and shutters were drawn as the Klan rode and spread havoc in the name of race supremacy and white womanhood. In days long gone the powerful, feared Klan was the keeper and watchdog of this social jungle called Dixie." But now, Williams argued, Klan efforts at intimidation increased African Americans' commitment to self-defense and strengthened their conviction that self-defense was the correct tactic. The Klan "has outlived its effectiveness because it can no longer provoke panic in the Negro community.... The Klan is offering a bill of goods that it cannot deliver, namely, a frightened and cringing Negro who will passively surrender his rights."[69]

As threats of violence against the black community persisted and it became apparent that outside assistance from civil rights organizations or protection from state and federal law enforcement officials became less likely, Williams began to solicit funds to purchase additional weapons for an "armaments race with the white people of Monroe."[70] The Rifle Club already possessed weaponry sufficient for defensive purposes, but he wanted to emphasize the black community's commitment to self-defense. In addition, he believed it was important to keep the struggle in Monroe alive in the minds of outside world.

When Williams visited Harlem, he received a great deal of attention and support. Malcolm X invited Williams to his Muslim temple, where they "collected money to buy guns and ammunition for Monroe." The *Afro American* reported Williams's "plans for a national appeal for donations of $12.50," the cost of an inexpensive rifle. In response to the *Afro American* article, Williams received not only contributions of cash and weapons but requests from blacks across the nation for assistance in establishing their own rifle clubs. Conrad Lynn reported that a group in New York collected "several hundred dollars" for the arms fund and that forty rifles had been sent to Monroe. Homer King, an extremely creative businessman in the Northeast wrote of his outrage at the "disgraceful conduct of some white men in your area." King commended the Rifle Club for its willingness to use defensive armed force and offered to sell Williams tear-gas weapons for use in its arsenal—"safe, effective, and, above all, recommended by many police departments." Williams never ordered the devices.[71]

Williams utilized other methods to attract attention to the situation in Monroe. Communist sympathizers in the United States who believed they could capitalize on the racial tension in Monroe in the late 1950s, contributed cash and moral support. During the 1950s and 1960s, southern white supremacists tried to discount civil rights organizations by trying to link them with communism, often with great success. Williams never belonged to the Communist Party, but he publicly supported communist movements around the world and, in particular, praised Fidel Castro's regime. In 1960, Castro invited Williams to visit him on two separate occasions, and Williams acknowledged that people of color received better treatment in communist Cuba than they did in the democratic United States. Williams even flew a Cuban flag at his home. He fueled the already flammable situation in Monroe by his support of Castro but accomplished what he intended: more national attention on Monroe.[72]

Often, Klan spokesmen, Monroe city officials, state officials, and even civil rights leaders linked Williams's militancy to a communist conspiracy. With his support of Castro and his association with known Communists, a relationship was not difficult to imagine. One North Carolina citizen believed that Williams represented both the devil and communism at work in the state and urged Governor Terry Sanford to encourage all Christian North Carolinians to "work for Christ and God" in their battle against such evil forces. Williams explained that the Rifle Club was not associated with communism, that the organization was "a patriotic group, formed for the benefit of sportsmen, and to improve the general marksmanship of American civilians. . . . All able-bodied loyal American citizens, irrespective of race, are invited to enlist . . . and all enlisters must be willing to take an oath of allegiance to the U.S. and our great democratic Constitution."[73]

Despite the tense racial situation in Monroe, Williams continued to provoke the Klan with his appeals for weapons and attempts to attract national attention to the area. He hoped that his radical statements would highlight the potentially dangerous conditions and thereby prevent further violence against the black community. Also, perhaps, the spotlight of national publicity would compel the federal government to respond to calls for help in ending discrimination and physical attacks against the black community.

On learning that it was legal in North Carolina to carry unconcealed firearms, Williams began to wear an Army-issue .45 caliber pistol and German Luger whenever he went out in public. He later explained that many Rifle Club members began carrying weapons in public to defend themselves because the local police, state officials, and the federal government appeared reluctant to provide adequate protection. "[E]verybody in Monroe knows what we have, that we know how to use it, and that we are willing to use it. The Mayor and the Chief of Police know, and so does the Klan." The public display of arms also sent a message that Williams and the black community stood committed to their "constitutional right" to defend themselves.

The audacious wearing of weaponry created such a furor that after a black state official who had met with Williams in Monroe reported on the encounter, Hugh Cannon, Governor Sanford's executive assistant, called Williams to plead with him. Cannon assured Williams that the "governor understood that this was legal and that I had a constitutional right to protect myself," Williams recalled, but wanted him to "stop going around town and the courthouse with these guns strapped in a holster." Williams told Cannon: "[T]he only reason I was doing it [was] because we had asked for protection, and they had refused to protect us. Since they wouldn't protect us, we would protect ourselves, and we would do it with firearms."[74]

Several times from 1959 to August 1961, at the height of racial tension in Monroe, Williams wired or phoned state and federal officials, especially in law enforcement agencies, demanding government protection of blacks from the onslaughts of white racists and reporting threats against himself and his family. Telegrams also served his purposes as a way of calling attention to Monroe in a tongue-in-cheek manner. In 1961, soon after the Bay of Pigs invasion, he wired Paul Roa, the Cuban representative to the United Nations, requesting that Roa help him "convey to Mr. Adlai Stevenson: Now that the United States has proclaimed military support for people willing to rebel against oppression [the] oppressed Negroes in [the] South urgently request tanks, artillery, bombs, money, and the use of American airfields and white mercenaries to crush the racist tyrants."[75] Roa read the telegram at a session of the U.N. General Assembly.

As the civil rights movement spread through the South in 1961, racial tension increased. In Monroe, nerves became frayed and petty acts of violence were more numerous that summer as the city experienced a rash of fires believed to be the work of arsonists. And Williams's renewed efforts to integrate swimming facilities resulted in stand-offs between angry whites, demonstrators, and armed members of the Rifle Club.[76]

On June 25, Williams was transporting demonstrators to the public pool and as the car approached an intersection, he encountered a mob of whites blocking the road. Another car forced Williams's car into a ditch while three Monroe police officers watched. The other driver approached, carrying a baseball bat and making threatening gestures. Unlike many nonviolent demonstrators, Williams's group regularly carried weapons for self-defense. When the man drew near, Williams put his .45 pistol "right up in his face." As the man backed away, Williams passed his pistol to another occupant of the car and asked J. D. Blunt, one of the riders in the back seat, to hand him a carbine. Williams did not realize that as J. D. handed over the firearm he had loaded a bullet into its chamber. The crowd, estimated to be somewhere between one and two thousand, some of whom were carrying weapons, slowly began to advance on Williams, now standing by the car. Thinking that the chamber was empty, Williams pulled back the bolt to load the rifle. "When I did that he [J. D.] already had one in there so I ejected it . . . and [it] fell out right in front of the crowd of these crackers and they started looking at the bullet and they started looking at me. And they started backing up."[77]

Two of the policemen rushed up to Williams and demanded that he turn over all the weapons in the car. Williams refused, telling them that if he did, the mob would certainly lynch the blacks. As one officer reached for the carbine, Williams hit him in the chest with its butt. The other officer moved to the far side of the car and drew his revolver. The passenger in the back seat holding Williams's .45 pointed it at the second officer and told him to put his weapon back in its holster. An old man in the crowd cried out, "Oh! what is this goddamn country coming to? . . . [T]he niggers have got guns and the police can't even arrest them."[78]

Police Chief Mauney and a city council member arrived at the standoff and succeeded in clearing the road, allowing Williams and his passengers to continue on to the pool, where demonstrators were picketing. The mob followed and went on with its harassment. Williams warned city officials at the scene that if any of the mob approached too close to the demonstrators, "they are going to get shot." Williams and the officials determined that the crowd was "getting out of hand," and after some negotiations, the demonstrators left under police protection. Williams admitted that he had been frightened during the confrontation but felt certain that the weapons were what had prevented his group from being lynched.[79]

The next day Williams appeared at the FBI office in nearby Charlotte. He recounted the events and other recent acts of violence against himself, demonstrators, and Monroe's black community. Williams told of white racists pelting young demonstrators at the pool with rocks; phone threats to his family, and recent efforts to kill him by forcing his car off the road. Williams demanded that the FBI provide him protection because his constitutional rights under the Fourteenth Amendment had been violated. The agents informed him that they "could not afford private citizens protection"; he would have to go to the local authorities for assistance. Outraged, Williams told the agents that if the federal protection was not forthcoming, "he was going to have to kill white people and when he started shooting would kill all the white people he could including babies in the cradle." The only action the Charlotte FBI office took in regard to Williams's demand was to inform state law enforcement officials and the governor's office of his hysterics and threats.[80]

Because of the atmosphere in Monroe, Williams increased his campaign promoting self-defense for the black community. In the July 17, 1961, issue of the *Crusader*, he solicited contributions to "our arms fund, so that every Afro-American who desires a weapon of self-defense may have one." Williams maintained that "when violence becomes a two way proposition, then and only then will an insensate government be aroused from its lethargy." Throughout July and August gunfire in the vicinity of the black neighborhood could be heard "practically every night," and racist whites dashed through the neighborhood in their cars, firing weapons, throwing rocks and bottles, and screaming obscenities. Whenever possible, Rifle Club guards returned fire.[81] Yet, no physical injuries were reported during those hot summer nights.

White racists, convinced that the militancy of Monroe's black community was the doings of Williams, made threatening phone calls to him and his family and even approached local "colored people, offering them money and new General Motors cars to kill Robert F. Williams" (one of Monroe's active racists was Bynum Griffin, the local GM distributor). Monroe police tried that summer to prevent any more weapons from reaching Williams and the Rifle Club by stopping and searching cars driven by African American outsiders.[82]

In August 1961, a group of Freedom Riders led by Paul Brooks and James Forman converged on Monroe, intent on proving that nonviolence was more effective than Williams's self-defense tactics. Williams welcomed the group and promised that if it could "demonstrate to me that the power of love is powerful enough to overcome these savage crackers, that I too would become pacifist." John Lowry, a representative of the Freedom Riders, informed the black community that the visitors wanted "to attempt a peaceful solution" to the conflict between the races and to renew lines of communication between Williams and the "non-violent organizations active in the integration movement." Brooks and Forman were convinced that "the masses of black people in the country were [not] psychologically prepared to use aggressive violence" in response to racist threats. The Freedom Riders told reporters, " '[W]e hope non-violence can offer an answer to the economic problems of lower class blacks.' "[83]

When Forman arrived at the Williams residence, he saw a large cache of rifles in a corner of the living room. When he commented on the weapons, Williams informed him that he did not mind if the public knew about "this little arsenal." After experiencing a few nights of scattered gunfire and a constant barrage of threats and violence against the peaceable demonstrators at the courthouse, Forman and Brooks had a change of mind. The two exponents of nonviolence asked to be issued rifles for their own self-defense. One night while "we were standing out in my front yard," Williams related, "a car skidded around the corner. . . . Forman and [Brooks] fell down on their knees, man, and threw a cartridge in the chamber, I said wait a minute. . . . [W]e got discipline around here, you cats [are] worse than we are. You talking about being nonviolent. . . . We got a regulation and nobody can fire in this community until they are fired on first."[84] The car sped away without causing any trouble. Nothing amiss occurred occurred that evening, but Forman soon got the chance to experience firsthand the reality of violence in Monroe.

Jesse Helms, Jr., son of former Monroe police chief Jesse, Sr., happened to be in town during the demonstrations by the Freedom Riders. Then a reporter for WRAL in Raleigh, he interviewed Williams at his heavily fortified home. The session went badly, with Williams refusing to answer Helms's questions regarding Williams's communist leanings. Helms later declared that Williams's support in the black community was minimal and accused Williams of acting as a front for a communist conspiracy to overthrow the United States government by "instigating" violence.[85]

After two weeks of the blacks' picketing at the Union County Courthouse, Klan members and other racists began to lose control of their emotions. At the end of one day on the line, the nonviolent demonstrators marched back to the relative safety of the black neighborhood of Newtown and the Rifle Club. A crowd of whites pelted them with bricks, rocks, and bottles. One woman came out of a house along the route with a kitchen knife and yelled at the demonstrators to "not come past my house singing those damn songs." As they approached the black neighborhood, residents there protected the demonstrators by returning the volley of projectiles. A few of the marchers reported minor injuries.[86]

The next day the demonstrators returned to the courthouse in the afternoon to continue picketing. Within a short period a mob of whites, estimated at more than two thousand, had gathered, and when the demonstrators began to leave later, the crowd attacked. As soon as Williams heard about the assault, he contacted Hugh P. Cannon, Governor Terry Sanford's administrative aide, and requested help. Cannon replied that Williams and his people had "asked for violence" and that the demonstrators deserved the beatings.

As news of the attack spread, a large number of blacks congregated at the Williams home, demanding weapons and calling for retaliatory measures. Williams persuaded them to remain in the neighborhood, reminding them that "we had to wait for them to come in our community before we could fight them."[87] Cars filled with whites careered through the neighborhood, passengers sometimes firing weapons. Late in the afternoon the crowd outside the Williams home stopped a white couple, the Steagalls, and accused them of being racist agitators. Williams asserted subsequently that he held the couple inside the house for a few hours until the emotions of the blacks outside calmed enough to guarantee their safe passage out of the neighborhood.[88]

Williams, fearing local law enforcement would charge him with kidnapping the Steagalls, fled Monroe and eventually the United States. The governor meanwhile dispatched fifty-two highway patrolmen to Monroe, and the FBI assigned two special agents to assist. The FBI issued a warrant for Williams and posted "wanted flyers" that described him as a diagnosed schizophrenic and someone who, in the past, "has advocated and threatened violence."[89] The Rifle Club, without the strong presence of Williams, rapidly faded away, and state and national NAACP officials soon returned the militant Monroe NAACP chapter to the fold. Monroe's white political leaders welcomed the presence of an NAACP chapter that was administered in a "sane and responsible manner," not by someone who advocated armed self-defense. The local white leadership remained steadfast in support of segregation and political and economic dominance, and as long as the local NAACP did not challenge the status quo too much, race relations in Monroe remained calm.

Monroe's Chamber of Commerce and city officials, eager to smooth over the racial problems that had beset the town, quickly issued a resolution praising the police force for its efforts. The resolution reminded people that the "City of Monroe and Union County have always been fine places in which to live" and that "people . . . regardless of race or creed have lived together in harmony." Alluding to Williams and his followers, the resolution placed the blame for the racial strife of the previous few years on "only a few isolated individuals living in our midst who have endeavored to create strife, tension, strain, and turmoil among the various races living in this community and have accumulated a large arsenal of fire-arms and explosives." The *Monroe Enquirer* chose the "racial agitation" culminating in the "violence in Monroe" in August as the biggest story in Union County for 1961. But the newspaper considered "more significant" to Union County and Monroe "the continued vigorous buildup of industry, business, and agriculture," which increased the economic well-being of the area.[90]

White community leaders ascribed the racial violence and tension of the late 1950s and early 1960s to Robert Williams's militancy and his supposed complicity in a communist conspiracy. In addition, the absent Williams was blamed for exaggerating the influence of the KKK in Monroe and for promoting a false picture of the racial situation in Monroe to the national news media. Throughout the 1960s whenever African Americans in Monroe condemned white racism or attempted to desegregate public facilities, the white establishment held up the specter of Williams. "The implication that we are operating a secret empire [KKK] here," Mayor Fred M. Wilson explained to one national NAACP official, "is a continuation of the policy of Communist Robert Williams, and the promulgation of such an idea seems only to discourage, rather than encourage progressiveness."[91]

Although years later Williams was labeled "politically ahead of most civil rights leaders," his promotion of organized armed self-defense and his later declarations that blacks should meet "violence with violence," were, at the time, extremely unnerving to both the white community and to the leadership of the civil rights movement.[92] Martin Luther King, Jr., believed that the man's actions were not in the interest of self-defense but were obvious attempts to "initiate violence." John Dittmer believed that Williams was transformed from a "local NAACP leader to third world revolutionary" but noted that by the mid to late 1960s his advocacy of self-defense had been accepted by many African Americans who had become "unwilling to turn the other cheek." Manning Marable mistook Williams's militancy during the early period of his activism from 1956 to 1961 for the more radical declarations of the Black Panther movement and the earlier speeches of Malcolm X.[93] August Meier and Elliot Rudwick consider Williams the "most famous of that group of militants existing at the fringe of the civil rights movement, who in their complete alienation from American society articulated a revolutionary synthesis of nationalism and Marxism."[94]

Many southern whites considered Williams's calls for self-defense proof of his revolutionary intentions and ties to a communist conspiracy. Marxists, hoping that Williams's militancy was a sign of the beginnings of an African American uprising against the government, enthusiastically labeled Williams as America's newest revolutionary. But Harold Cruse argued that Williams and his advocacy of self-defense "was but a small, local manifestation" of the growing militancy of African Americans. Williams never considered "overthrowing anything, much less a capitalist system." In fact, Williams, during his leadership of the Monroe NAACP and the Rifle Club, utilized nonviolent direct action and legal methods as a tactic for gaining equal rights for Monroe's black community at the same time that he advocated self-defense. Williams proved that nonviolence "although extremely effective as a strategy, was merely that, . . . not truely a creed, a philosophy, and a way of life to protesters." Stan Levinson, a Jewish civil rights advocate, socialist, and close friend of Martin Luther King, Jr., later acknowledged that Williams's calls for violence proved effective in forcing the federal government to respond to the needs of African Americans in the South. Williams raised the tactic of violence, actually the threat of violence, Levinson confided to a friend, "to the level of a political theory." Nobody really believed him, but the possibility of violence or a race war in the South made people uneasy.[95]

Williams advocated using the American tradition of defending one's property and person, with violence if necessary. He continued to work within the legal system and employed nonviolent direct action when trying to gain equal rights for Monroe's black citizens. The idea of the Rifle Club, the elaborate system of defense, and the public pronouncements that the blacks of Monroe stood prepared to defend themselves was a self-defense tactic. Williams explained that "we have always tried to avoid a fight when we could, fighting is the last resort. You don't use weapons unless you don't have any other alternative. . . . [A] weapon is the last alternative."[96] And he always pointed out that he wanted nothing more than the protection of the black community from violence and his civil rights under the Constitution.

Soon after his return to the United States in late 1969, Williams testified before a U.S. Senate subcommittee investigating internal security. Senator Strom Thurmond of South Carolina asked Williams if he had encouraged African Americans in Monroe to "initiate a revolution." Williams replied that all he had ever advocated was

> that they resist violence, racist violence and racist oppression, that they resist it with violence, but some people thought that I had advocated revolution, but the fact was that they did not read the pamphlets very well because I'd always stipulated that I was for the support of the U.S. Constitution. . . . [T]hat we should fight for the enforcement of the Constitution.[97]

Williams spent almost eight years in exile, living most of the time in Cuba and China. However, he missed the United States and had come to believe that many of his Communist friends were just as racist as the white folks back home. When Williams returned to the United States in 1969, he faced the possibility of criminal prosecution in North Carolina on charges of kidnapping the Steagalls during the racial disturbances in Monroe in August 1961. He settled in Michigan with his family and fought extradition to North Carolina to stand trial for the alleged kidnapping. In Monroe, the Ku Klux Klan came out of hibernation and tried to organize a parade through the streets of Monroe. "The Ku Klux Klan is marching again in Monroe, The Grand Dragon, Virgil Lee Griffin, says they want 'to bring the nigger Robert Williams back so we can hang him.' That's what Police Chief Al Mauney quoted the dragon as saying, just before the Chief refused the Klan a permit to parade in the street."[98] Racism in Monroe had not changed much while Williams was away but evidently the white community leaders and public officials were in no mood to resurrect the racial tensions and violence of the late 1950s and early 1960s. Williams eventually lost his fight against extradition to North Carolina, but the Union County district attorney decided to drop the kidnapping charges. Instead of returning to hometown Monroe, Williams remained in Michigan.

In the summer of 1995, Williams attended his high school reunion in Monroe. After years of living in Michigan, Williams, diagnosed with prostate cancer, decided then to live out his days with friends and family. His friends, many former members of the Monroe Rifle Club, established a Robert Williams Relocation Fund to help him move back to Monroe and collected thousands of dollars. Former white adversaries such as the Union County district attorney expressed no objection to Williams's return.[99] But in the fall of 1996, still in Michigan, Williams died from the effects of the prostate cancer.

NOTES

Portions of research for this essay were funded by an Albert J. Beveridge Travel Grant.

1. Martin Luther King, Jr., "Hate Is Always Tragic," in Robert F. Williams, *Negroes with Guns* (New York: Marzani and Munsell, 1962), 9.

2. Williams, *Negroes with Guns*, 45; Robert F. Williams, *Oral History 588*: in Ralph Bunche Oral History Collection, Howard University, 100 (hereafter cited as Robert F. Williams Oral History 588).

3. James Forman, *The Making of Black Revolutionaries* (Seattle: Open Hand, 1990), 196.

4. Aldon Morris, *The Origins of the Civil Rights Movement: Black Communities Organizing for Change* (New York: Free Press, 1984), 62; Gloster B. Current, "Fiftieth Annual Convention—A Jubilee for Civil Rights," *Crisis* 66, no. 7 (August–September 1959): 400; Southern Regional Council, *The Federal Executive and Civil Rights* (Atlanta: Southern Regional Council, 1961), 24.

5. James Farmer, *Freedom — When?* (New York: Random House, 1965), 101; Roy Wilkins, *Standing Fast: The Autobiography of Roy Wilkins* (New York: Viking Press, 1982), 265.

6. Daisy Bates, *The Long Shadow of Little Rock: A Memoir* (New York: David McKay, 1962), 111; Herbert Shapiro, *White Violence and Black Response* (Amherst: University of Massachusetts Press, 1988), 455.

7. William Worthy, "The Possibilities and Limitations of Nonviolence," n.d., Robert F. Williams Papers, Bentley Historical Library, University of Michigan.

8. Robert J. Cottrol and Raymond T. Diamond, "The Second Amendment: Toward an Afro-Americanist Reconsideration," *Georgetown Law Journal*, 80, no. 2 (1991): 356.

9. Worthy, "The Possibilities and Limitations of Nonviolence."

10. Harvard Sitkoff, *The Struggle for Black Equality, 1954–1980* (New York: Hill and Wang, 1981), 11; August Meier and Elliott Rudwick, "Black Violence in the 20th Century: A Study in Rhetoric and Retaliation," in James A. Geschwender, ed., *The Black Revolt* (Englewood Cliffs, N.J.: Prentice-Hall, 1971), 404.

11. Robert F. Williams, interview with author, 11 March 1993; "Wait Ike Reply on Kissing Kids," *Daily Defender*, 17 November 1958; "Sends Protest to Ike," *Charlotte Observer*, 18 January 1959.

12. Kenneth O'Reilly, *"Racial Matters": The FBI's Secret File on Black America, 1960–1972* (New York: Free Press, 1989), 94; Worthy, "The Possibilities and Limitations of Nonviolence"; Taylor Branch, *Parting the Waters: America in the King Years, 1954–1963* (New York: Simon & Shuster, 1988), 23.

13. Harold Cruse, *The Crisis of the Negro Intellectual* (New York: Morrow, 1967), 399.

14. Raymond Gavins, "The NAACP in North Carolina during the Age of Segregation," in Armstead L. Robinson and Patricia Sullivan, eds., *New Directions in Civil Rights Studies* (Charlottesville: University Press of Virginia, 1991), 106; Isaac Reynolds, *Oral History 683,* in Ralph Bunche Oral History Collection, Howard University, 32; Clayborne Carson, *In Struggle: SNCC and the Black Awakening of the 1960s* (Cambridge: Harvard University Press, 1981), 164.

15. Robert F. Williams, interview with author, 11 March 1993; "Wait Ike Reply on Kissing Kids," *Daily Defender*, 17 November 1958; "Sends Protest to Ike," *Charlotte Observer*, 18 January 1959; Meier and Rudwick, "Black Violence in the 20th Century," 404; O'Reilly, *"Racial Matters,"* 94.

16. William Chafe, *The Unfinished Journey: America since World War II* (New York: Oxford University Press, 1986), 86.

17. James Albert Burran IV, "Racial Violence in the South During World War II" (Ph.D. diss., University of Tennessee at Knoxville, 1977), 12; Numan V. Bartley, *The New South, 1945–1980* (Baton Rouge: Louisiana State University Press, 1995), 76.

18. *Crusader*, 18 July 1959; Robert Carl Cohen, *Black Crusader: A Biography of Robert Franklin Williams* (Secaucus, N.J.: Lyle Stuart, 1972), 17; Andrew Herbert Myers, "When Violence Met Violence: Facts and Images of Robert F. Williams and the Black Freedom Struggle in Monroe, North Carolina" (master's thesis, University of Virginia, 1993), 8.

19. August Meier, Elliott Rudwick, and Francis L. Broderick, eds., *Black Protest Thought in the Twentieth Century* (Indianapolis: Bobbs-Merrill Educational Publishing, 1965), 360.

20. *Crusader*, 18 July 1959; Robert F. Williams Oral History 588: 1; Cohen, *Black Crusader*, 17.

21. Robert F. Williams, Oral History 588, 1.

22. Robert F. Williams, "Why I Propose to Return to Racist America," *Crusader*, 9 December 1967, 3; Ernest B. Furgurson, *Hard Right: The Rise of Jesse Helms* (New York: Norton, 1986), 39; Robert F. Williams Oral History 588, 9. Other Monroe blacks remembered Jesse Helms, Sr. (father of U.S. Senator Jesse Helms), in much the same way. "If anybody was drunk or whatever, he'd rough them up." "Some people have got a kind of nasty way of talking to people . . . that was him." Juan Williams, "Where Jesse Helms Is Coming From," *Washington Post Magazine*, 28 October 1990.

23. "Negro Confesses Brutal Murder of W. Marvin Mangum Saturday," "Montgomery Ordered Held for Trial Without Bail," "Mangum Slayer Sentenced to Die in Gas Chamber on November 15," "Montgomery Negro to Die in Gas Chamber Tomorrow," *Monroe Enquirer*, 3, 20 June, 22 August 1946, 27 March 1947; Robert F. Williams Oral History 588, 6–7.

24. FBI Memo, 7 May 1959, and FBI Report, 15 November 1955, in FBI and Michigan

State Police Files in Robert F. Williams Papers; and Robert Franklin Williams, "1957: The Swimming Pool Showdown," *Southern Exposure* 8 (summer 1980): 70.

25. Cohen, *Black Crusader*, 74; Robert F. Williams Oral History 588, 4–5; United States Naval Intelligence Report: Subject: Williams, Robert, PVT, USMC, 28 April 1955, FBI and Michigan State Police Files, Robert F. Williams Papers.

26. Williams, *Negroes with Guns*, 51; Cohen, *Black Crusader*, 83.

27. North Carolina Branch Membership Records; Monroe, N.C., Branch, and RE: Monroe, N.C., Branch, Monroe, North Carolina folder, NAACP Records, Library of Congress; Raymond Gavins, "The NAACP in North Carolina during the Age of Segregation," in Robinson and Sullivan, *New Directions in Civil Rights Studies*, 110, 111, 117; Kelly Alexander Oral History 399, in Ralph Bunche Oral History Collection, Howard University; Haywood W. Burns, *The Voices of Negro Protest in America* (New York: Oxford University Press, 1963), 31.

28. Harold Cruse, *The Crisis of the Negro Intellectual*, 351; Williams, interview with author, 11 March 1993; Cohen, *Black Crusader*, 90.

29. Julian Mayfield, "Challenge to Negro Leadership: The Case of Robert F. Williams," *Commentary*, April 1961, 297; Cohen, *Black Crusader*, 90; Robert F. Williams Oral History 588, 39; Williams, *Negroes with Guns*, 51; Marcellus C. Barksdale, "Robert F. Williams and the Indigenous Civil Rights Movement in Monroe, North Carolina, 1961," *Journal of Negro History* 69 (1984): 73.

30. Robert F. Williams to NAACP, New York, 13 March 1957, Monroe folder, NAACP Records; Williams, "1957: The Swimming Pool Showdown," 70; Robert F. Williams Oral History 588, 29; Williams, *Negroes with Guns*, 51; Mayfield, "Challenge to Negro Leadership," 298; Barksdale, "Robert F. Williams," 73; Conrad Lynn, There Is a Fountain: The Autobiography of a Civil Rights Lawyer (Westport, Conn.: Lawrence Hill, 1979), 143; Robert F. Williams Oral History 588, 39; *Crusader*, 1 August 1959, 1; *Jet Magazine*, 31 October 1957, 14.

31. Lynn, *There Is a Fountain*, 142; Forman, *Making of Black Revolutionaries*, 175; Carson, *In Struggle*, 42; August Meier and Elliott Rudwick, *Black Protest in the Sixties* (Chicago: Quadrangle Books, 1970), 17; John Nelson Truman, *People with Strength in Monroe, North Carolina* (Monroe, N.C.: Committee to Aid the Monroe Defendants, 1963), 12; Robert F. William Oral History 588, 29.

32. Truman, *People with Strength*, 12; Robert F. Williams Oral History 588, 29; Meier and Rudwick, *Black Protest in the Sixties*, 17; Monroe, North Carolina, Branch, Membership Record, Monroe folder, NAACP Records; Williams, interview with author, 11 March 1993; August Meier and John H. Bracey, Jr., "The NAACP as a Reform Movement, 1909–1965: 'To Reach the Conscience of America,' " *Journal of Southern History* 59 (1993): 4.

33. Robert F. Williams Oral History 588, 108; Cohen, *Black Crusader*, 92; Williams, *Negroes with Guns*, 51; Truman, *People with Strength*, 12; *Jet Magazine*, 31 October 1957, 14.

34. Williams, *Negroes with Guns*, 52; Williams, interview with author, 11 March 1993; "Farm Pond Claims Life of Negro Youth Sunday Morning," "8 Negro Youths Refused Admission to City Pool," *Monroe Enquirer*, 17 June, 25 July 1957; George L. Weismann, "The Kissing Case," *Nation*, 17 January 1959, 48.

35. Robert F. Williams Oral History 588, 51; Williams, "1957: The Swimming Pool Showdown," 71.

36. Robert F. Williams Oral History 588, 57; Williams, interview with author, 11 March 1993; telephone conversation with Freddie Sein, director of clubs and associations, the National Rifle Association. The NRA destroyed all records in 1971 of rifle clubs that were

no longer active. William O'Neill, *Coming Apart: An Informal History of America in the 1960s* (New York: Times Books, 1971), 161. O'Neill noted that Williams applied for the charter to get free ammunition from the government.

37. Robert F. Williams Oral History 588, 59. There was a white junior NRA Rifle Club already in Union County. "Junior Rifle Club is Organized in Monroe," *Monroe Enquirer*, 28 October 1946.

38. Timothy Buie Tyson, " 'Radio Free Dixie': Robert F. Williams and the Roots of Black Power" (Ph.D. diss., Duke University, 1994), 80; "Interviews: Robert F. Williams," *Black Scholar* 1 (1970): 3. The Monroe Rifle Club and the idea of armed intervention became closely associated with the NAACP chapter; Robert F. Williams Oral History 588, 44, 59, 149.

39. Robert F. Williams Oral History 588, 145.

40. Ibid., 147.

41. Tyson, " 'Radio Free Dixie,' " 225; Robert F. Williams Oral History 588, 33.

42. *Crusader*, 26 June 1961, 6; Forman, *Making of Black Revolutionaries*, 166.

43. Mabel Williams Oral Interview conducted by Joanne Feeney, August 1978, Bentley Historical Library, University of Michigan; Williams, *Negroes with Guns*, 54; Forman, *Making of Black Revolutionaries*, 165.

44. "Ku Klux Klan Schedules Rally and Cross Burning," "500 Attend Ku Klux Klan Rally In County Thursday," "Special Notice," "Ku Klux Klan Holds Sixth Rally in County," "Tarheel People and Places," *Monroe Enquirer*, 8, 12, 29 August, 5 September 1957; Mayfield, "Challenge to Negro Leadership," 303.

45. "Night-Riding Klan, Negroes in Near-Clash Here Friday," *Monroe Enquirer*, 7 October 1957; Robert F. Williams Oral History 588, 149.

46. "Dixie MD Denies Abortion Charge," *New York World Telegram*, 15 October 1957; Barksdale, "Robert F. Williams," 74.

47. Truman, *People with Strength*, 13; Williams, *Negroes with Guns*, 57; Williams, interview with author, 11 March 1993; "Night-Riding Klan, Negroes in Near-Clash Here Friday," "City, County Leaders Move to Ease Racial Tensions," "An Ordinance to Regulate Cavalcades . . ." *Monroe Enquirer*, 7, 10 October 1957.

48. "Tarheel People and Places," "Night-Riding Klan, Negroes in Near-Clash Here Friday," *Monroe Enquirer*, 5 September, 7 October 1957.

49. "City, County Leaders Move to Ease Racial Tensions," "Two Negro Groups Maneuver for Leadership In Affairs," *Monroe Enquirer*, 10 October, 14 November 1957.

50. Luther H. Hodges to Dana Weir, 24 January 1958, Luther Hartwell Hodges Papers, North Carolina Department of Archives and History, Raleigh, N.C.; Wyn Craig Wade, *The Fiery Cross: The Ku Klux Klan in America* (New York: Simon & Schuster, 1987), 303. Cole had never been ordained by the Baptist church and had instead held various odd jobs like carnival huckster and circus workers.

51. David M. Chalmers, *Hooded Americanism: The History of the Ku Klux Klan* (New York: New Viewpoints, 1965), 348; "North Carolina: Indian Raid," *Newsweek*, January 27, 1958, 27; "Indians: The Natives Are Restless," *Time*, 27 January 1958, 20; miscellaneous articles, *Afro American*, 30 May 1959, box 4, folder Articles 1959–1960, Robert F. Williams Papers.

52. Dana Weir to Luther H. Hodges, 19 January 1958, Luther Hartwell Hodges Papers. Ms. Weir approved of segregating whites and Native Americans because she did not believe in "love affairs between Indian maidens and white males." Ms. Weir also refused to purchase Boraxo soap because its manufacturer had sponsored two shows on CBS television portraying Native American and white love affairs.

53. "The N.C. Lumbee Indians," *Carolina Israelite*, January–February 1958; Williams, *Negroes with Guns*, 39.

54. Weismann, "The Kissing Case," 48; " 'Klan, Keep Away,' Warns Union Negro," Miscellaneous newspaper clippings, n.d., Robert F. Williams Papers; Cottrol and Diamond, "Second Amendment," 358.

55. " 'Klan, Keep Away,' Warns Union Negro," Miscellaneous newspaper clippings, n.d., Robert F. Williams Papers.

56. Robert F. Williams to Luther H. Hodges (Western Union telegram), 20 February 1958, Luther Hartwell Hodges Papers; Luther H. Hodges, *Businessman in the Statehouse: Six Years as Governor of North Carolina* (Chapel Hill: University of North Carolina Press, 1962), 123. Hodges viewed any adverse publicity caused by racial unrest as extremely harmful to the state's reputation for good relations between the races and damaging to efforts to attract business and industry to the state.

57. Robert Giles to Robert F. Williams, 21 February 1958, Luther Hartwell Hodges Papers.

58. "Klan Meeting Planned Sunday in County Fails to Come Off," "Klan Leader Cole Gets Road Sentence," "Mob Action Deplored By Klan Spokesman," *Monroe Enquirer*, 24 February, 17 March 1958, 27 April 27, 1959.

59. "Auto Insurance Cancelled for Head Of NAACP Here," "Kasper Gets Chilly Reception in Monroe," *Monroe Enquirer*, 12 May, 4 September 1958.

60. "School Board Takes Petition Under Study," "Incident in Monroe Gets Wide Attention," "Negro Pupil Transfer Request Denied by City School Board," *Monroe Enquirer*, 30 October, 20, 27 November 1958; Williams, interview with author, 11 March 1993; Weismann, "The Kissing Case," 49; Confidential to Governor Hodges from Harry Golden, 3 February 1959, Luther Hartwell Hodges Papers; Harry Golden to Burton Wolfe, 30 August 1961, Harry Golden Papers, Special Collections, University of North Carolina at Charlotte.

61. "Notes," *Crusader*, 6 August 6, 1960, 1; ibid., 27 August 1960, 2.

62. "The Robert Williams Case," *Crisis* 66, June–July 1959, 325; N.A.A.C.P. Leader Urges 'Violence,' " *New York Times*, 7 May 1959; editorial, *Charlotte Observer*, 9 May 1959.

63. Robert F. Williams Oral History 588, 144; Roy Wilkins, Complainant against Robert F. Williams, Respondent, Committee on Branches; "North Carolina State Conference of Branches [NAACP] to Roy Wilkins"; press release, 18 June 1959, Monroe folder, NAACP Records.

64. Press release, 18 June 1959, Monroe folder, NAACP Records; Roy Wilkins to P. L. Prattis, *Pittsburgh Courier*, 28 May 1959; Wilkins, *Standing Fast*, 265.

65. Roy Wilkins to James Benjamine, 8 May 1959, in Group III: A333, NAACP Records; Kelly M. Alexander to editor, *Commentary*, 7 April 1961, Kelly Alexander, Jr. Papers, Special Collections, University of North Carolina at Charlotte.

66. Tim Gray to Roy Wilkins; Afrans Society to Roy Wilkins, 11 May 1959, Herman Katzen to NAACP, 11 May 1959; James J. Adams to NAACP, 8 May 1959, Clarence Huginnie to National Board of Directors, Group III, A333, General Office File, NAACP Records; *Crusader*, 25 July 1959.

67. Address of Roy Wilkins, NAACP rally, Jackson, Mississippi, 17 May 1959, NAACP Records.

68. Louis E. Lomax, *The Negro Revolt* (New York: Harper and Row, 1962), 103.

69. *Crusader*, 1 August 1959, 1.

70. "Monroe's Militant Negro Begins Armament Race," in Unknown to J. Edgar Hoover, 20 July 1961, Robert F. Williams Papers; "Castro Fan Is Forming Rifle Club," *Charlotte Observer*, 20 July 1961.

71. Williams, interview with author, 11 March 1993; Joanne Feeney interview with Robert F. Williams, August 1978, Robert F. Williams Papers; Unknown author to Governor Terry Sanford, 20 July 1961, ibid.; "RE: Robert Franklin Williams," n.d., FBI Secret Memorandum, FBI and Michigan State Police Files, ibid.; William Worthy to Robert F. Williams, 29 September 1961, box 1, folder January–September 1961, ibid.; Homer King to Robert F. Williams, n.d., in folder Correspondence 1960, ibid.

72. W. Haywood Burns, *The Voices of Negro Protest in America* (New York: Oxford University Press, 1963), 30; Worthy, "The Possibilities and Limitations of Nonviolence"; Charlotte Office of the FBI to Director, FBI, 15 November 1955, FBI and Michigan State Police Files, Robert F. Williams Papers; "Tarheel People and Places," *Monroe Enquirer*, 5 September 1957; "Union Baptists Censure KKK," *Monroe Enquirer*, 4 November 1957; "Robert Williams Preached Violent Means for Months," *Charlotte Observer*, 29 August 1961.

73. Unknown author to Governor Terry Sanford, 20 July 1961, Robert F. Williams Papers; *Crusader*, 12 September 1959, 5.

74. Julian Mayfield, "Challenge to Negro Leadership," *Commentary*, April 1961, 302; Robert F. Williams Oral History 588: 60, 70, 71; Tyson, " 'Radio Free Dixie,' " 293.

75. "Notes," *Crusader*, 7 August 1961; Assistant Attorney General Burke Marshall to Director, FBI and Michigan State Police Files, Robert F. Williams Papers; *Crusader*, 22 April 1961; "Williams Involved in Harlem Incident," *Monroe Enquirer*, 18 May 1961.

76. "Wave of Incendiarism Hits Half-Mile Section of City," "Group of Negro Boys Seek Admission to Pool," "Negro Group Seeks Separate Swimming Facility in City," "Pageland Swimming Pool Open to Monroe People," "1961 Fire Losses in City Are Highest in History," *Monroe Enquirer*, 19, 22 June, 10, 31 July 1961, 15 January 1962.

77. Robert F. Williams Oral History 588, 98–99.

78. Ibid., 101; "Notes," *Crusader*, 10 July 1961, 2.

79. Robert F. Williams Oral History 588, 106

80. Charlotte office of the FBI to Director, FBI, 26, 28 June 1961, Charlotte FBI Internal Memorandum from A. Rosen to Mr. Belmont, 26 June 1961, FBI and Michigan State Police Files, Robert F. Williams Papers; "Notes," *Crusader*, 21 June 1961, 3.

81. "RE: Robert Franklin Williams," n.d., FBI Secret Memorandum, FBI and Michigan State Police Files, Robert F. Williams Papers; "Did You Know?" *Crusader*, 7 August 1961, 5.

82. "Notes," *Crusader*, 19 June 1961, 3, and 17 July 1961, 4.

83. Robert F. Williams Oral History 588, 110; "Notes," *Crusader*, 21 August 1961, 6; Forman, *Making of Black Revolutionaries*, 159; Carson, *In Struggle*, 42.

84. Forman, *Making of Black Revolutionaries*, 163; Robert F. Williams Oral History 588, 145.

85. Furgurson, *Hard Right*, 78.

86. Forman, *Making of Black Revolutionaries*, 191.

87. "Monroe Quiet Today Following Racial Clash," *Monroe Enquirer*, 28 August 1961; Robert F. Williams to various newspapers, in folder Papers concerning Monroe, North Carolina "kidnapping," in Robert F. Williams Papers; Robert F. Williams Oral History 588, 148.

88. "Mrs. Steagall Tells of Harrowing Experience in Kidnapping Here"; "Monroe Quiet Today Following Racial Clash," *Monroe Enquirer*, 28, 31 August 1961.

89. O'Reilly, *"Racial Matters,"* 95; " 'Wanted' Flyers out for Robert Williams," *Monroe Enquirer*, 7 September 1961.

90. "Police, Other Officers Lauded for Work in Week of Turmoil," "Significant Events of 1961 in Union County in Review," *Monroe Enquirer*, 4 September 1961, 1 January 1962.

91. "Town and Country," "Local Negroes Seek Communication Line," *Monroe Enquirer*, 25 September, 9 October 1961; Gloster B. Current to Herman Cunningham 28 August 1962, Charles A. McLean to Current, 12 September 1962; Calvin D. Banks to Morsell and Current, 14 September 1962 in Monroe File, NAACP Papers.

92. Williams, interview with author, 11 March 1993; "Prosecution Drops Case: Williams Wins Freedom," undated clipping, Robert F. Williams Papers; Robert L. Allen, *A Guide to Black Power in America: An Historical Analysis* (London: Victor Gollancz, 1970), 24.

93. Williams, *Negroes with Guns*, 15; John Dittmer, "Robert F. Williams," in *Encyclopedia of Southern Culture*, ed. Charles Reagan Wilson and William Ferris (Chapel Hill: University of North Carolina Press, 1989), 231; Manning Marable, *Race, Reform and Rebellion: The Second Reconstruction in Black America, 1945–1982* (Jackson: University Press of Mississippi, 1984), 62.

94. Meier and Rudwick, "Black Violence in the 20th Century," 404.

95. Cruse, *Crisis of the Negro Intellectual*, 352; Harold Cruse, *Rebellion or Revolution?* (New York: Morrow, 1968), 101; Calvin Trillin, "U.S. Journal: Monroe, N.C." *Enquirer Journal*, 27 October 1970; Sean Dennis Cashman, *African Americans in the Quest for Civil Rights, 1900–1990* (New York: New York University Press, 1991), 179; phone conversation between Stan Levinson and Roy Bennett, 13 June 1963, frame number 628, reel 2: Surveillance of Telephones in Stanley Levinson's Business Office, Continued, September 1, 1962 to September 30, 1963, The Martin Luther King, Jr. FBI File, Part II: The King-Levinson File (Frederick, Md.: University Publications of America, 1987).

96. Robert F. Williams Oral History 588, 107.

97. Testimony of Robert F. Williams: Hearings Before the Subcommittee to Investigate the Administration of the Internal Security Act and Other Internal Security Laws of the Committee of the Judiciary, United States Senate, February 16, 1970 (Washington, D.C.: Government Printing Office, 1971), 9.

98. "News from Southern Conference Education Fund," February 4, 1972 in folder Miscellaneous concerning Robert F. Williams in Robert F. Williams Papers, Bentley Historical Library, University of Michigan.

99. Stephanie Banchero, "Hero's Welcome," *Union Observer*, 18 August 1995, 3-u; Becky Fisher, "Civil Rights Activist Returns for Winchester Reunion," *Enquirer-Journal*, 20 August 1995, 1; "Civil Rights Activist Gets Hero's Welcome," *Charlotte Observer*, 20 August 1995, 1-b; Beverly James, "Friends Organizing Monroe Homecoming," *Charlotte Observer*, 19 March 1995, 9-b.

The fear of criminals leads many Americans to own a gun, convinced that they will be able to access and use their firearm before the attacker can use his. Mark Twain, *Roughing It* (Hartford, Conn.: American Publishing, 1872), 85.

Chapter Twenty

Armed and Dangerous
Guns in American Homes

Arthur L. Kellermann and Philip J. Cook

In *Raiders of the Lost Ark*, Indiana Jones uses a handgun to casually dispatch a huge, sword-wielding opponent. In the opening scene of *Dirty Harry*, detective Harry Callahan uses a powerful handgun to stop an armed robbery. Strong images like these are reinforced by real-life stories of citizens who have successfully used a gun to defend themselves. Although such incidents are rare, they receive widespread publicity. So do stories about Americans arming themselves in response to a crime wave or a civil disturbance.

Immediately following the Los Angeles riots of 1992, firearm sales in California surged to their highest level since the state began keeping records twenty years earlier. Gun buyers made it clear what they had in mind. A twenty-eight-year-old woman firing a .357 magnum for the first time said, "I have no one to protect me. If someone comes into my house uninvited, they're dead." A construction supervisor shopping for a .45 caliber handgun declared, "I definitely think every man has to protect himself. If they come down to my neighborhood, I'm going to protect myself, protect my street."[1]

The concept of keeping a gun for self-protection is actively reinforced by the gun industry. In the southeastern edition of the July 1992 issue of the *Ladies Home Journal*, Colt ran an ad for its "All American" line of 9 mm pistols. Over a full-color photograph of a young mother tucking her daughter into bed, the headline declared: "Self-protection is more than your right. It's your responsibility." The accompanying text built on this theme:

> You always have a right to protect yourself in your home. Even more important, you have a responsibility to be there for those who depend on you. At Colt, we believe that the safe and responsible ownership of a firearm can play an important role in personal security. Like a home fire extinguisher, it may be better to have it and not need it than to need it and not have it. For protecting yourself and your loved ones, we recommend a dependable Colt semiautomatic pistol. . . . [2]

Marketing of this sort has a powerful effect. Two-thirds of America's gun owners consider self-protection an important reason to keep a gun. Forty-two percent keep a gun in their bedroom. One-third keep at least one gun loaded at all times.[3]

It's natural to want to do everything possible to protect one's family. Its also natural, in a thunderstorm, to seek cover under the nearest tree. Bringing a handgun into the home and keeping it loaded and readily available for protection places it within reach of curious children, an angry spouse, or a depressed teenager. Anyone considering the purchase of a firearm for protection should carefully consider the overall balance of benefits and risks.[4]

How Often Are Homes the Target of Violent Crime?

Police statistics are commonly used to track community rates of violent crime, but many crimes are not reported to the police. To measure crime and violence in the United States more accurately, the U.S. Department of Justice created the National Crime Victimization Survey (NCVS). In 1991, NCVS interviewers contacted more than 83,000 people in 42,000 randomly selected households across the United States. Households that participate in the NCVS are interviewed every six months for seven consecutive interviews. Each interview serves to anchor the time frame in which respondents are asked to recall any incidents of victimization or self-defense. Strict confidentiality is assured. The survey has been progressively refined over the past twenty-five years, and it is widely regarded to be the best of its kind in the United States.[5]

NCVS data indicate that approximately nine million residential burglaries occur each year. Although most take place when no one is at home, occupied dwellings are entered approximately one million times each year. This implies an annual household victimization rate of 1 percent. One-third of these incidents result in a robbery, assault or rape.[6]

The risk of confronting an intruder is not shared equally by American households. Most of us live in relatively safe communities or neighborhoods, where the risk of household victimization is low. However, people who live in high-crime neighborhoods and those who have dangerous acquaintances face a much greater risk of victimization than those who do not. More than half of all burglaries nationwide are committed by someone known to the victim.[7]

Are Firearms Effective for Self-Defense?

When a gun is used to defend against an intruder, the victim is generally successful in foiling the crime and avoiding injury. National Crime Victimization Survey data indicate that intruders are less likely to commit a violent crime (such as rape, robbery or assault) or inflict personal injury when the victim resists with a gun.[8] However, it is not clear what we can conclude from this observation because violence is *least* likely to occur when the victim makes no attempt to resist.

Crimes that are resisted with a gun differ in at least one important respect from those that are not: the element of surprise. Intruders generally rely on

TABLE 20.1

Likelihood of Violence and Theft in Burglaries of Occupied Residences, 1979–1987, by Method of Self-Defense

Consequence	Gun	Other Weapon	Other Active Means[1]	Passive[2]	None	Total
Sample size	160	100	436	2,189	2,605	5,506
(% of total)	(3)	(2)	(8)	(40)	(47)	(100)
Violent crime %	30	55	71	44	19	34
Victim injury %	5	25	42	13	5	12
Theft %	14	14	21	17	50	33

SOURCE: Unpublished data from the National Crime Survey, 1979–1987, provided by the Bureau of Justice Statistics.
   NOTE: Each entry represents the percentage of respondents in the category defined by the type of self-defense who suffered the indicated consequence.
 [1] Hit, threw object, screamed, called police, turned on lights, etc.
 [2] Ran away, hid, held property, locked door, etc.

stealth or surprise to gain an advantage. As a result, few victims have time to reach a weapon. Although more than 40 percent of homes in America contain one or more firearms, only 3.2 percent of burglaries of occupied residences are resisted with a gun. This works out to an annual incidence of about one self-defense use per 1,300 gun-owning households.[9]

Since home invasion crimes that are resisted with a gun differ in important respects from home invasion crimes where the occupant employs another form of resistance, the available statistics simply provide no guidance about the usefulness of guns for self-defense.[10] It is often difficult to determine if a particular incident would have ended differently if a gun had not been available. In one study of 420 homicides in the home, twenty-one victims died while attempting to defend themselves with a gun.[11] All we can be sure of is that whether or not guns make resistance more effective, they are rarely used for this purpose.

Does Keeping a Gun in the Home Deter Crime?

According to one survey of incarcerated felons, many criminals consider the risk of confronting an armed homeowner at least as worrisome as the risk of arrest. However, burglary is more profitable when guns are part of the loot, a fact that undercuts any deterrent effect. Furthermore, there is evidence that some burglars arm themselves out of fear that they will confront an armed homeowner.[12]

There is little evidence that widespread ownership of guns provides effective deterrence against crime. John Henry Sloan and colleagues at the University of Washington and the University of British Columbia compared rates of crime, violence, and homicide in Vancouver, Canada (where handguns are tightly restricted), and in neighboring Seattle (where handguns are much easier to obtain) between 1980 and 1986. Although these two cities have many characteristics in common, they differ with respect to gun control and the prevalence of handgun ownership. As a result, law-abiding citizens in Vancouver have far fewer handguns to defend themselves than their counterparts in Seattle. Nontheless, during the seven-year study interval, the two cities experienced virtually identical rates of burglary and robbery, and very similar rates of simple and aggravated assault.[13]

The cities did differ, however, in one important category of crime: homicide. During the time frame of the study, the mean homicide rate in Seattle was 63 percent *higher* than the homicide rate in Vancouver. Virtually all of this difference was due to an almost fivefold higher rate of handgun homicide in Seattle.[14]

Philip Cook studied rates of robbery, gun robbery, and robbery-murder in fifty U.S. cities and found that cities with high rates of gun ownership did not have robbery rates that were lower than those noted in cities with with lower rates of gun ownership. Instead, cities with a high rate of gun ownership tended to have higher rates of gun robbery, and robbery murder.[15]

As evidence of the deterrent value of gun ownership, advocates point to the town of Kennesaw, Georgia, which enacted a symbolic ordinance that requires every adult homeowner to keep a firearm and ammunition in the home. Shortly after this ordinance took effect, household crimes in Kennesaw sharply declined. However, a subsequent analysis of Kennesaw crime data revealed that this "decline" was nothing more than the product of random, month-to-month variation in the rate of residential burglary. When household crimes in Kennesaw were viewed over a longer span of time, it was evident that the ordinance had little or no effect.[16]

Recently, the National Research Council Panel on the Understanding and Control of Violent Behavior reviewed a large amount of data on firearms and violence in the United States. Based on this evidence, the panel concluded that widespread gun availability does *not* decrease or increase the level of violence in a community. Instead, easy access to guns appears to be associated with higher rates of felony gun use, and higher rates of homicide.[17]

Is Keeping a Gun in the Home Hazardous for Members of the Household?

Firearm mishaps occur more frequently than many people realize. Arthur Kellermann and Donald Reay studied all firearm-related deaths that occurred in King County, Washington, between 1978 and 1983 and found that more than half (398 deaths) occurred in a home where the gun involved was kept.[18] Nine involved the killing of an intruder or an attacker in self-defense. During this same period, guns in the home were involved in 12 unintentional gunshot deaths, 41 criminal homicides, and 333 firearm suicides. Even after excluding firearm suicides, guns in the home were eighteen times more likely to be involved in the death of a member of the household than to be used to kill an intruder in self-defense.

Roberta Lee and colleagues conducted a three-year study of *all* gunshot injuries (nonfatal as well as fatal) that occurred in Galveston, Texas. A total of 239 shootings were identified, 110 of which (46 percent) occurred in a residence. Only two of these shootings occurred in the context of residential robbery or burglary. In one case, the resident was killed by a burglar; in the other, the burglar was wounded. During the same time frame, guns were involved in the death or injury of 96 homeowners, family members, friends, and acquaintances.[19]

A study of shootings that occurred in or around homes in Memphis, Tennessee; Seattle; and Galveston, Texas, during an eighteen-month interval (November 1992 to May 1994) identified a total of 624 incidents. Fifty-four of the shootings were unintentional, 118 were attempted or completed suicides, and 438 were assaults or homicides. Investigating police officers considered 13 cases (2.1 percent of the total) "legally justifiable" or an act of self-defense; 3 of these involved law enforcement officers acting in the line of duty. For every time a gun in the home was used to shoot an assailant or offender in self-defense, these weapons were involved in 4 unintentional shootings, 7 criminal assaults or homicides, and 11 attempted or completed suicides.[20]

Obviously, counts of bodies or wounds cannot tell the full story. A gun can be used to repel an intruder without a shot's being fired.[21] It is equally true that a gun can be used to terrify a spouse, intimidate a neighbor, or threaten suicide without inflicting physical injury. A complete analysis of the risks and benefits of keeping a gun in the home would take all of these events into consideration.

How Often Are Guns Used in Self-Defense?

Estimates of the number of times guns are used each year in self-defense vary widely. Gary Kleck and Mark Gertz extrapolated reponses to a privately commissioned poll of 4,977 households to estimate that guns are used in self-defense approximately 2.5 million times each year. Because this figure is almost twice as high as the best available estimate of the number of crimes committed each year with a firearm (1.3 million), it has been cited as proof that widespread ownership of firearms enhances public safety.[22]

Unfortunately, Kleck and Gertz's survey does not withstand close scrutiny. Eight precent of the respondents who declared they had used a gun in self-defense stated that they killed or injured the offender. If this is true, 2.4 million self-defense gun uses per year should generate 192,000 killed or injured bad guys. This figure exceeds the *total* number of gunshot injury cases treated in America's emergency departments each year.[23] Obviously, not every firearm suicide, assault, homicide, and accidental shooting is actually a self-defense shooting. It is equally improbable that more than 150,000 criminals each year obtain treatment for their gunshot wound(s) outside the American health care system. For these reasons, Kleck and Gertz's estimate can be dismissed as a gross exaggeration.

How can surveys produce such highly skewed results? The answer can be found in understanding the disproportionate impact of "false-positive" replies to surveys of rare events.[24] If, for example, the true rate of defensive gun use in the population is 0.5 percent, only five respondents out of every thousand will have an opportunity to provide a "false-negative" response to a question about defensive gun use. However, the other 995 respondents have an opportunity to provide a "false-*positive*" response to the same question.

There are many reasons that survey participants might falsely state that they had used a gun in self-defense.[25] For example, it is widely known that respondents tend to "telescope" important events from their past into a more recent frame of time. Thus, a particular event may be recalled as having occurred within the past year, when it actually took place much longer ago.

Some respondents tend to exaggerate or embellish answers. This is especially true when the action is considered desirable or heroic. Others slant their story to place themselves in a more favorable light. For example, a driver who waved his gun in a traffic dispute may depict the incident as an act of self-defense. However, motorists in surrounding vehicles may have felt otherwise. Finally, it is not far-fetched to speculate that some respondents to a survey about defensive gun use lie to advance a political agenda.[26]

Obviously, misclassification can occur in either direction (i.e., false-positives or false-negatives). But there is no reason to expect that these effects cancel each other out, especially in a study of rare events. If the true rate of defensive gun use is 0.5 percent, misclassifying 10 percent of respondents who actually used a gun in self-defense as nonusers would have little effect (i.e., the final estimate of the rate of defensive gun use would be lowered from 0.5 to 0.45 percent). However, misclassifying just 1 percent of *nonusers* as "defensive gun users" would inflate the final estimate of defense gun use threefold, from 0.5 percent to 1.5 percent! Although this exercise in arithmetic does not prove that estimates of rare events are always positively biased, it does illustrate that misclassfication has an asymetric effect. It wouldn't take many respondents who telescoped or embellished their experience to generate an inflated estimate of defensive gun use, even if false negatives also occurred.[27]

The design of the NCVS preempts the false-positive problem by limiting questions about self-defense to respondents who report that they were the victims of a crime in which they had contact with the perpetrator. Further, NCVS is designed to minimize the problem of telescoping by limiting the recall period to six months (rather than a year for most surveys) and anchoring that six-month period by the previous survey interview. Respondents are required to recall events only since the time they were previously interviewed for the survey.

Micheal Rand, a analyst with the Bureau of Justice Statistics, used NCVS data from 1993 to calculate that handguns were used to commit nearly one million crimes that year. To determine how often guns of any type are used to defend against crime, Rand pooled NCVS data from the years 1987-1993, and used these data to calculate an annual average. He found that victims used a firearm to protect people or property an average of 82,500 times per year during this seven-year span.[28]

Other researchers have reached similar conclusions. David McDowall and Brian Wiersema analyzed NCVS data from the years 1987 through 1990 and calculated that guns were used for self-defense approximately 65,000 times during each of these four years. Fewer than 1 percent of victims of violent crime (rape, robbery, or assault) reported that they used a firearm to defend themselves.[29]

Philip Cook pooled NCVS data from the years 1979–1987 and determined that only 3.2 percent of burglaries of occupied households were resisted with a gun. This finding was recently corroborated by a study of home-invasion crimes in Atlanta. During the summer of 1996, Atlanta police responded to 197 incidents in which intruders entered an occupied, single-family dwelling. Only three of the victims (1.5 percent) used a firearm to defend themselves. In six cases (3 percent of the total), the intruder reached the homeowner's gun before the homeowner did.[30]

Does Keeping a Gun in the Home Decrease a Family's Risk of Homicide?

If keeping a gun provides substantial protection against crime and violence, homes with guns should be less likely to be the scene of a homicide than comparable homes without guns. To test this hypothesis, Kellermann and colleagues at three universities conducted a large-scale, "case-control" study to examine the strength and direction of any association between gun ownership and homicide in the home.[31]

Public health researchers use the case-control method to compare the characteristics of disease or injury victims (i.e., "cases") with randomly selected individuals from the same population who do *not* have the injury or disease in question (i.e., "controls"). If a particular characteristic is observed more commonly among cases than controls, it is identified as a "risk factor" for the disease or injury in question. The degree of association between a "risk factor" and the disease is expressed as an odds ratio—the odds that a given characteristic is found among cases compared to controls.[32]

The case-control method is rarely used by criminologists, but it is a time-honored tool of public health. It has been used to study a wide variety of problems, including the link between cigarette smoking and lung cancer, the association between tampon use and toxic-shock syndrome, and high-risk behaviors and AIDS. Case-control research is particularly useful when the outcome of interest is relatively uncommon, exposure to the risk factor(s) of interest can be shown to precede the "disease," and the association is biologically plausible.[33]

Kellermann's team identified every homicide over a five-year span that occurred in the home of victims in two large metropolitan counties: King County, Washington (which includes Seattle), and Shelby County, Tennessee (which includes Memphis). Cuyahoga County, Ohio (which includes Cleveland), was added during the final 2.5 years of study. All homicides were included, whether a gun was involved or not. In more than three-fourths of cases, the victim was killed by a relative or an acquaintance. Most of the remaining victims were killed by an unidentified offender. Fewer than 4 percent were killed by a stranger.

After each homicide, a surviving family member or friend was interviewed to obtain detailed information about the victim, the family, and the home in which the homicide occurred. The characteristics of each "case" household were then compared to those of a neighboring "control" household that contained an individual of the same age range, gender, and race as the victim. Multivariate analysis was used to identify important risk factors for homicide in the home, after controlling for the effects of other variables.

Most of the study's findings came as no surprise. Households where a homicide occurred were more likely to contain an illicit drug user, an individual with a prior history of arrest, or someone who had been hit or hurt in a family fight. Living alone was also found to be an independent risk factor for homicide in the home.

After taking these risk factors into consideration, and matching case and control households on age range, gender, race, neighborhood, and socioeconomic status, the presence of a gun in the home was found to be associated with a significantly increased risk of homicide (odds ratio, 2.7; 95 percent confidence interval, 1.6 to 4.4). All of the increased risk of homicide was due to a nearly fivefold greater risk of firearm homicide. The risk of homicide by other means was not increased, or decreased, by keeping a gun in the home.

To explore the potential value of keeping a gun for protection, the authors analyzed the subset of homicides that followed *forced entry* into the home. If having a readily available firearm affords substantial protection from intruders, the risk of homicide should have been decreased in this subgroup. If, on the other hand, the association between guns in the home and homicide was due to reverse causation (i.e., people who feared harm from an intruder were more likely to keep a firearm in their home) the risk of homicide should have been particularly high in this subset. Neither proved to be true. Keeping a gun in the home was not associated with a significantly increased or decreased risk of homicide at the hands of an intruder. Instead, virtually all of the increased risk of homicide associated with gun ownership was due to homicides at the hands of a spouse, a family member, or an intimate acquaintance (adjusted odds ratio, 7.8).

Critics of this study argue that focusing on deaths ignores the nonlethal use of guns in self-defense. They contend that the households studied were not representative of the communities from which they were drawn because many of them reported problems with domestic violence, alcoholism, or drug abuse. They note that if proxy respondents for "cases" (i.e., victims) acknowledged gun ownership more readily than "control" respondents, this would bias the study's findings against guns. Others have argued that any association between gun ownership and homicide in the home is confounded by unmeasured psychological factors, criminality, or reverse causation.[34]

In fact, case-control studies can detect protective effects as readily as they can detect adverse effects. If keeping a gun in the home provides effective protection from homicide (whether the gun is fired, waved around, or simply deters unwanted entry), the risk of homicide in homes with guns should have been less than the risk of homicide in comparable homes without guns. The opposite was true.

The authors used matched-pairs analysis and multivariate statistical techniques to control for the independent effects of age, race, gender, neighborhood, socioeconomic status, family violence, prior arrests, illicit drug use, and living alone. Great care was taken to minimize the potential for misreporting by cases and controls alike. The possibility that the statistical association between gun ownership and homicide in the home is due to an unmeasured psychological factor, or reverse causation, cannot be dismissed entirely. However, the effect would have to be great to explain a nearly threefold difference in risk.

The strongest evidence of validity is independent corroboration by others. Recently, Peter Cummings and colleagues at the University of Washington reported the results of a major case-control study of the association between gun ownership and homicide or suicide. The study population was the membership of Group Health Cooperative of Puget Sound, a large health maintenance organization in the Pacific Northwest.[35]

Case subjects were 353 victims of suicide and 117 victims of homicide who died between 1980 and 1992. The risk factor of interest was purchase of a handgun from a licensed dealer. Five control subjects were matched to each case by age, gender, and zip code of residence.

In contrast to the population studied by Kellermann and colleagues, most of the cases and controls in the Cummings study were white and middle class. Instead of interviewing proxy respondents for cases and matched controls, Cummings and colleagues used Washington State Department of Licensing records to ascertain if any member of the household of a case or control legally purchased a handgun prior to the date of death. After taking a number of potentially confounding variables into consideration, the odds of homicide among persons with a history of family handgun purchase from a licensed dealer were found to be more than twice that of families that lacked a purchase history. The odds of suicide, given a history of family handgun purchase, was 1.9. These increased odds persisted for at least five years after handgun purchase.[36]

Guns and family violence appear to be a particularly deadly combination. A study of family and intimate assaults with a gun in Atlanta revealed that assaults with a firearm are twelve times more likely to end in the death of the victim than assaults involving other means.[37] An analysis of FBI homicide statistics over a twelve-year time interval revealed that twice as many women are shot and killed by their husband or an intimate acquaintance as the number killed by strangers using a gun, a knife, or any other means. When women killed with a gun, the victim was five times more likely to be a spouse, intimate acquaintance, or a family member than to be a stranger or a person of undetermined relationship. Women who live in a home where a gun is kept face an increased risk of homicide, regardless of whether they live alone or share the home with others. All of this increased risk is attributable to homicide at the hands of a spouse, intimate acquaintance, or a family member.[38]

Does Keeping a Gun in the Home Increase a Family's Risk of Suicide?

In the United States, firearm suicides are more common than firearm homicides. More Americans kill themselves with a gun than by all other methods combined. The vast majority of *nonfatal* suicide attempts in the United States involve a drug overdose, self-inflicted lacerations, or some other method, but fully 60 percent of *completed* suicides involve the use of a gun. Approximately 70 percent of firearm suicides take place in the home of the victim. Because suicide attempts with a gun are more often fatal than suicide attempts by other methods, many experts believe that the choice of a gun simply reflects the strength of the individual's intent to die. However, there is growing evidence that ease of access also plays a role.[39]

Three independent groups have conducted case-control research on the relationship between suicide and gun ownership.[40] David Brent and colleagues at the University of Pittsburgh compared a group of adolescent suicide victims to a second group of suicidal inpatients and found that guns were more likely to be kept in the homes of those who completed their attempt. They verified this observation in subsequent studies that compared the characteristics of an even larger groups of adolescent suicide victims with those of suicide attempters and nonsuicidal psychiatric inpatients. Suicide victims were much more likely to have lived in a home with a gun than members of the other two groups.[41]

Kellermann and coworkers used a different approach to study suicides in King County, Washington, and Shelby County, Tennessee. They identified households where a suicide occurred, and compared their characteristics to those of a randomly selected household in each neighborhood that was not the scene of a suicide. One or more guns in the home was found to be strongly and independently linked to an increased risk of suicide, even after the effects of alcohol, illicit drug use, living alone, and mental illness were taken into consideration. All of the increased risk of suicide in a home with guns was due to a substantially increased risk of *firearm* suicide. The risk of suicide by other means was not influenced by the presence of a gun in the home.[42]

Cummings's team found that Group Health members with a history of family handgun purchase from a licensed dealer faced an almost twofold increased risk of suicide compared with Group Health members who did not have this history. All of the increased risk of sucide was due to a threefold increased risk of firearm suicide. The risk of suicide by other means was not affected by family handgun purchase.[43]

If strength of intent is all that matters, suicidal individuals living in homes without guns would simply substitute another method to accomplish the same result, or leave the home to commit suicide by jumping, drowning, or driving into a tree. None of the studies published to date have found that the increased risk of firearm suicide among members of gun-owning households is offset by increased odds of nongun suicide among individuals who lack immediate access to a gun. At any rate, approximately 70 percent of all suicides take place in the home of the victim. As many as half of those that take place outside the home involve a firearm. Few of the guns used to commit suicide are obtained within hours or days of the attempt. Most have been kept in the home for years.[44]

Are Unintentional Gunshot Injuries a Problem?

Unintentional gunshot deaths are relatively uncommon, but they still account for a substantial percentage of firearm deaths among children aged five to fourteen. Half of unintentional shooting deaths of children occur when kids play with a loaded gun they have found in the home. Handguns are disproportionately involved.[45]

Unintentional shootings account for a substantially larger number of nonfatal woundings than fatalities.[46] Fully 85 percent of firearm sucicides and approximately 20 percent of firearm assaults end in death, but the case-fatality ratio for unintentional shootings is approximately 16 to 1. The most common injury is to a leg or arm, but some victims sustain serious gunshot wounds to the head, neck, chest, or abdomen.[47]

How Often Do Guns in the Home Fall into the Hands of Kid or Criminals?

Approximately 341,000 episodes of firearms theft occur each year.[48] Almost 80 percent are the result of burglary or theft from the home of the victim. Because most gun-owning households contain more than one firearm, many of these thefts net more than one gun. Recent estimates suggest that the annual loss of firearms to theft exceeds 500,000 weapons. The FBI's National Crime Information Center stolen-gun file contains more than two million reports. In 1994, more than 300,000 new entries were received.[49]

Joseph Sheley and James Wright recently surveyed a large number of violent juvenile offenders in detention facilities, and a similar number of inner-city high school kids. Both groups were asked about their access to firearms. Respondents reported that firearms are so common on the street that the price for most weapons is far lower than retail value. More than 50 percent of juvenile offenders reported that they had stolen one or more gun in their lives; 25 percent reported that their most recent handgun was stolen. After reviewing these data, Sheley and Wright concluded:

> If theft is indeed such an important piece of the gun supply puzzle, the approximately 72 million handguns currently possessed by legitimate private owners represent a potentially rich source for criminal handgun acquisition. Therefore, an effective gun ownership policy, of necessity, must confront the issue of firearms theft. At a minimum, there should be programs to educate the gun owning public concerning the importance of securing their firearms.[50]

Some family members knowingly supply guns to kids. When asked, "How would you go about getting a gun if you decided you wanted one?" Fifty-three percent of Sheley and Wright's student respondents answered, "Borrow from family member or friend." A third said they would "buy from a family member or friend."[51]

Peter Ash and colleagues in Atlanta interviewed a convenience sample of sixty-three incarcerated juvenile offenders to learn how, where, and why they obtained guns. Forty-two percent reported that they were given their first gun by a peer, a friend, or a relative. Ten percent acquired their first gun through theft. Another 10 percent said that they found their first gun by chance or acquired it incidentally during a burglary.[52] Perhaps one day, we will hear public service announcements that ask, "It's eight o'clock in the morning. Do you know where your gun is?"

Conclusion

There is no question that guns are occasionally used for self-defense, sometimes with spectacular results. The widespread attention these incidents receive helps sustain public demand for firearms, much as news of a big win promotes the sale of lottery tickets. Unfortunately, the rules of this game are different.

The odds that a gun in the home will be used to shoot an intruder appear to be less than the odds that it will someday be involved in a suicide or family homicide. Loaded, readily available firearms are particularly hazardous in households with children or teenagers, as well as homes marked by alcoholism, drug abuse, domestic violence, or depression. Secure storage can reduce the risk of a tragedy, but it cannot eliminate it entirely.[53]

NOTES

1. *USA Today*, June 5, 1992.

2. Jon Vernick, Stephen P. Teret, and Daniel Webster, "Regulating Firearm Advertisements That Promise Home Protection: A Public Health Intervention," *Journal of the American Medical Association* 277 (1997): 1992.

3. Time/CNN poll, December 1992; David Hemenway and Douglas Weil, "Loaded Guns in the Home: Analysis of a National Random Survey of Gun Owners," *Journal of the American Medical Association* 267 (1992): 3033–77; Philip J. Cook and Jens Ludwig, *Guns in America: Results of a Comprehensive National Survey on Firearms Ownership and Use* (Washington, D.C.: Police Foundation, 1996), 20.

4. Arthur L. Kellermann. "Gunsmoke: Changing Public Attitudes towards Smoking and Firearms," *American Journal of Public Health* 87 (1997): 910–13.

5. Wes Skogan. "The National Crime Survey Redesign," *Public Opinion Quarterly* 54 (1990): 256–72; Philip J. Cook, "The Case of the Missing Victims: Gunshot Woundings in the National Crime Survey," *Journal of Quantitative Criminology* 1 (1985): 91–102.

6. Unpublished data from the National Crime Victimization Survey, 1979–1987, provided by the Bureau of Justice Statistics. There were 6.8 million household burglaries

each year on average, of which 1 million were of occupied dwellings. Slightly more than a third (34 percent) involved a robbery, rape, or assault (attempted or successful).

7. Unpublished data from the National Crime Victimization Survey, 1979–1987, provided by the Bureau of Justice Statistics.

8. Gary Kleck, "Crime Control through the Private Use of Armed Force," *Social Problems* 35 (1988): 1–22.

9. Arthur L. Kellermann, Laurie Westphal, Lori Fischer, and Beverly Harvard, "Weapon Involvement in Home Invasion Crimes," *Journal of the American Medical Association* 273 (1995): 1759–62; Philip J. Cook, "The Technology of Personal Violence," in M. Tonry, ed., *Crime and Justice: A Review of Research* (Chicago: University of Chicago Press, 1991), 1–71.

10. Philip J. Cook, "The Relationship between Victim Resistance and Injury in Noncommercial Robbery," *Journal of Legal Studies* XV (1) (June 1986): 405–16.

11. Cook, "Technology of Personal Violence"; Arthur L. Kellermann, Frederick P. Rivara, Norman P. Rushforth, et al., "Gun Ownership as a Risk Factor for Homicide in the Home," *New England Journal of Medicine* 329 (1993): 1084–91.

12. James D. Wright and Peter H. Rossi, *The Armed Criminal in America: A Survey of Incarcerated Felons* (Hawthorne, N.Y: Aldine Press, 1986); Cook, "Technology of Personal Violence."

13. John Henry Sloan, Arthur L. Kellermann, Donald T. Reay, et al., "Handgun Regulations, Crime, Assault and Homicide: A Tale of Two Cities," *New England Journal of Medicine* 319 (1988): 1256–62.

14. Ibid.

15. Philip J. Cook, "The Effect of Gun Availability on Robbery and Robbery Murder: A Cross Section Study of Fifty Cities," *Policy Studies Review Annual* 3 (1979): 743–81.

16. Kleck, "Crime Control"; David McDowall, Brian Wiersema, and Colin Loftin, "Did Mandatory Firearm Ownership in Kennesaw Prevent Burglaries?" *Sociology and Social Research* 74 (1989): 48–51.

17. Panel on the Understanding and Control of Violent Behavior, *Understanding and Preventing Violence*, ed. Albert J. Reiss and Jeffrey A. Roth (Washington, D.C.: National Academy Press, 1993).

18. Arthur L. Kellermann and Donald T. Reay, "Protection or Peril? An Analysis of Firearm Related Deaths in the Home," *New England Journal of Medicine* 314 (1986): 1557–60.

19. Roberta K. Lee, Richard J. Waxweiler, J. G. Dobbins, T. Paschetag, "Incidence Rates of Firearm Injuries in Galveston, Texas, 1979–1981," *American Journal of Epidemiology* 134 (1991): 511–21.

20. Arthur L. Kellermann, Frederick P. Rivara, Roberta K. Lee, et al., "Firearm-Related Injuries and Deaths in the Home" (unpublished paper).

21. Gary Kleck, *Point Blank: Guns and Violence in America* (New York: Aldine de Gruyter, 1991).

22. Gary Kleck and Mark Gertz. "Armed Resistance to Crime: The Prevalence and Nature of Self-Defense with a Gun," *Journal of Criminal Law and Criminology* 86 (1995): 150–87; Donald B. Kates, Henry E. Schaffer, John K. Lattimer, George B. Murray, and Edwin W. Cassem, "Guns and Public Health: Epidemic of Violence, or Pandemic of Propaganda?" *Tennessee Law Review* 62 (1995): 513–96.

23. Joseph L. Annest, James A. Mercy, Delinda Gibson, and George W. Ryan, "National Estimates of Nonfatal Firearm-Related Injuries: Beyond the Tip of the Iceberg," *Journal of the American Medical Association* 273 (1995): 1749–54.

24. Philip J. Cook, Jens Ludwig, and David Hemenway, "The Gun Debate's New Mythical Number: How Many Defensive Gun Uses per Year?" *Journal of Policy Analysis and Management* 16 (1997): 463–69.

25. David Hemenway, "The Myth of Millions of Annual Self-Defense Gun Uses: A Case Study of Survey Overestimates of Rare Events," *Chance* 10 (1997): 6–10.

26. Cook and Ludwig, *Guns in America.*

27. Cook, Ludwig, and Hemenway, "Gun Debate's New Mythical Number."

28. Michael R. Rand, "Guns and Crime: Handgun Victimization, Firearm Self Defense, and Firearm Theft," *Crime Data Brief: U.S. Department of Justice,* NCJ-147003 (April 1994).

29. David McDowall and Brian Wiersema. "The Incidence of Civilian Defensive Firearm Use by U.S. Crime Victims, 1987 through 1990," *American Journal of Public Health* (1994): 1982–84.

30. Cook, "Technology of Personal Violence"; Kellermann et al., "Weapon Involvment."

31. Kellermann et al., "Gun Ownership."

32. James J. Schlesselman, *Case Control Studies: Design, Conduct, Analysis* (New York: Oxford University Press, 1982).

33. E. L. Wynder and E. A. Graham, "Tobacco Smoking as a Possible Etiologic Factor in Bronchogenic Carcinoma," *Journal of the American Medical Association* 143 (1950): 329–36; Mark W. Kehrberg et al., "Risk Factors for Staphylococcal Toxic-Shock Syndrome," *American Journal of Epidemiology* 114 (1981): 873–79; David Vlahov et al., "HIV Seroconversion and Disinfection of Injection Equipment among Intravenous Drug Users, Baltimore, Maryland," *Epidemiology* 2 (1991): 444–46.

34. Paul Blackman, "Guns and Homicide in the Home," *New England Journal of Medicine* 330 (1994): 366; Kates et al., "Guns and Public Health."

35. Peter Cummings et al., "The Association between the Purchase of a Handgun and Homicide or Suicide," *American Journal of Public Health* 87 (1997): 974–78.

36. Ibid.

37. Linda E. Saltzman et al., "Weapon Involvement and Injury Outcomes in Family and Intimate Assaults," *Journal of the American Medical Association* 267 (1992): 3043–47.

38. Arthur L. Kellermann and James A. Mercy, "Men, Women, and Murder: Gender-Specific Differences in Rates of Fatal Violence and Victimization," *Journal of Trauma* 33 (1992): 1–5; James E. Bailey et al., "Risk Factors for Violent Death of Women in the Home," *Archives of Internal Medicine* 157 (1997): 777–82.

39. Arthur L. Kellermann et al., "The Epidemiologic Basis for the Prevention of Firearm Injuries," *Annual Review of Public Health* 12 (1991): 17–40; Arthur L. Kellermann et al., "Suicide in the Home in Relation to Gun Ownership," *New England Journal of Medicine* 327 (1992): 467–72; James D. Wright et al., *Weapons, Crime and Violence in America: A Literature Review and Research Agenda* (Washington, D.C.: Government Printing Office, 1981), 239–44.

40. Kellermann, "Gunsmoke."

41. David A. Brent et al., "Risk Factors for Adolescent Suicide: A Comparison of Adolescent Suicide Victims with Suicidal Inpatients," *Archives of General Psychiatry* 45 (1988): 581–88; David A. Brent et al., "The Presence and Accessibility of Firearms in the Home of Adolescent Suicides: A Case-Control Study," *Journal of the American Medical Association* 266 (1991): 2989–95; David A. Brent et al., "Firearms and Adolescent Suicide: A Community-Based Case-Control Study," *American Journal of the Diseases of Children* 147 (1993): 1066–71.

42. Kellermann et al., "Suicide in the Home."

43. Cummings et al., "Association between the Purchase of a Handgun and Homicide or Suicide."

44. Kellermann et al., "Suicide in the Home."

45. Roberta K. Lee and Mary J. Harris, "Unintentional Firearm Injuries: The Price of Protection," *American Journal of Preventive Medicine* 9 (1993; supplement): 16–20; Garen J. Wintemute et al., "When Children Shoot Children: 88 Unintended Deaths in California," *Journal of the American Medical Association* 257 (1987): 3107–9; Arthur L. Kellermann et al., "Injuries Due to Firearms in Three Cities," *New England Journal of Medicine* 335 (1996): 1438–44.

46. U.S. General Accounting Office, *Accidental Shootings: Many Deaths and Injuries Caused by Firearms Could Be Prevented*, Doc. no. GAO/PEMD-91-9 (Gaithersburg, Md.: U.S. General Accounting Office, 1991); Cook, "Technology of Personal Violence."

47. Annest et al., "National Estimates of Nonfatal Firearm-Related Injuries"; Kellermann et al., "Injuries Due to Firearms."

48. Rand, "Guns and Crime."

49. Cook and Ludwig, *Guns in America*; Philip J. Cook, Susan Molliconi, and Thomas B. Cole, "Regulating Gun Markets," *Journal of Criminal Law and Criminology* 86 (1995): 59–92; Marianne W. Zawitz, "Guns Used in Crime: Firearms, Crime and Criminal Justice," *Selected Findings, Bureau of Justice Statistics*, NCJ-148201 (Washington, D.C.: U.S. Department of Justice, July 1995).

50. Joseph F. Sheley and James D.Wright, *Gun Acquisition and Possession in Selected Juvenile Samples: Research in Brief* (Washington, D.C.: U.S. Department of Justice, 1993), 10.

51. Ibid., 6.

52. Peter Ash, Arthur L. Kellermann, and Dawna Fuqua-Whitley, "Gun Acquisition and Use by Juvenile Offenders," *Journal of the American Medical Association* 275 (1996): 1754–58.

53. *STOP: Steps to Prevent Firearm Injury* (Washington, D.C.: American Academy of Pediatrics, 1994); *Clinician's Handbook of Preventive Services: Putting Prevention into Practice* (Washington, D.C.: Government Printing Office, 1994), 103–7.

Contributors

Jeffrey S. Adler is associate professor of history at the University of Florida. He is the author of *Yankee Merchants and the Making of the Urban West: The Rise and Fall of Antebellum St. Louis* (Cambridge: Cambridge University Press, 1991).

Bruce C. Baird teaches at the University of Alabama in Huntsville and is currently working on a book about dueling in the South.

Michael A. Bellesiles is director of the Violence Studies Program at Emory University. He is the author of *Revolutionary Outlaws: Ethan Allen and the Struggle for Independence on the Early American Frontier* (Charlottesville: University Press of Virginia, 1993) and is currently writing a book on the origins of American gun culture.

Lee Chambers-Schiller teaches at the University of Colorado and is the author of *Liberty, A Better Husband: Single Women in America: The Generations of 1780–1840* (New Haven, Conn.: Yale University Press, 1984).

Philip J. Cook is the ITT/Terry Sanford Professor of Public Policy at Duke University. He is the author (with Charles Clotfelter) of *Selling Hope: State Lotteries in America* (Cambridge: Harvard University Press, 1989) and (with Robert Frank) of *The Winner-Take-All Society* (New York: Free Press, 1995).

Robert R. Dykstra is professor of history and public policy at the State University of New York, Albany. A specialist in nineteenth-century American social and political history, he is the author of two books on the trans-Mississippi West, most recently *Bright Radical Star: Black Freedom and White Supremacy on the Hawkeye Frontier* (Cambridge: Harvard University Press, 1993). He is currently engaged in a long-term project on black-family demography in post–Civil War Virginia.

Laura F. Edwards teaches at the University of California at Los Angeles and is the author of *Gendered Strife and Confusion: The Political Culture of Reconstruction* (Urbana: University of Illinois Press, 1997).

Uche Egemonye is finishing her J.D. and Ph.D. degrees at Emory University.

Nicole Etcheson is assistant professor of history at the University of Texas at El Paso. She is author of *The Emerging Midwest: Upland Southerners and the Political*

Culture of the Old Northwest, 1787–1861 (Bloomington: Indiana University Press, 1996). She is currently working on a history of the Kansas civil war.

Sally E. Hadden is an assistant professor of history and law at Florida State University. Her most recent work in legal history will appear in *Law Enforcement in a New Nation: Slave Patrols and Public Authority in the Old South, 1700–1865* (Cambridge: Harvard University Press, forthcoming) and in an anthology on race and law in the nineteenth century edited by Donald Nieman and Christopher Waldrep (University of Georgia Press, forthcoming).

Evan Haefeli, currently a fellow at the Woodrow Wilson Center, is completing his dissertation at Princeton University on New Netherlands and the origins of religious pluralism. His article "Ransoming New England Captives in New France" has just appeared in *Proceedings of the French Colonial Historical Society*.

Paula K. Hinton is a Ph.D. student in the History Department at Miami University of Ohio.

Arthur L. Kellermann is director for the Center for Injury Control at the Rollins School of Public Health of Emory University. He is also professor in and chief of the Division of Emergency Medicine in the School of Medicine, and author of numerous articles that have appeared in the *New England Journal of Medicine*, the *Journal of the American Medical Association*, and the *American Journal of Public Health*.

Ann M. Little, currently a fellow at the Huntington Library, is assistant professor of history at the University of Dayton. Her article "Men on Top? The Farmer, the Minister, and Marriage in Early New England" appeared in *Pennsylvania History* in 1997. She is finishing her book *Abraham in Arms: Gender, Politics, and Power on the New England Frontier, 1620–1720*.

Laura McCall is a professor of history at Metropolitan State College of Denver and serves on the Editorial Board for the *Journal of the Early Republic*. She is currently preparing a book-length study of literary men and women in antebellum America. Her anthology, *A Shared Experience: Men, Women, and the History of Gender*, was published by NYU Press in 1998.

Catherine Ross Nickerson is assistant professor of American studies and English at Emory University, where she teaches courses on the representation of crime and violence in American culture. She is the author of a study of women's popular writing as social criticism, *The Web of Iniquity: Patterns of Gender, Crime, and Narration in Detective Fiction by American Women, 1865–1935* (forthcoming from Duke University Press). She is currently at work on a book entitled *Lizzie Borden and the Fascinations of the Past*.

Mary E. Odem is an associate professor of history and women's studies at Emory University. She is the author of *Delinquent Daughters: Protecting and Policing Adolescent Female Sexuality in the United States* (Chapel Hill: University of North

Carolina Press, 1995) and coeditor of *Confronting Rape and Sexual Assault* (Wilmington, Del.: Scholarly Resources, 1997).

Craig S. Pascoe is a Ph.D. candidate in southern history at the University of Tennessee, Knoxville. At present, he is an instructor at Georgia Southern University in Statesboro.

John C. Pettegrew teaches U.S. history at Lehigh University. He is currently completing "Brutes in Suits: The Atavistic Origins of American Masculinity, 1890–1920," a book manuscript.

Junius P. Rodriguez, associate professor of history at Eureka College, has done extensive research on antebellum slave violence in Louisiana. He served as general editor of the award-winning *Historical Encyclopedia of World Slavery*, 2 vols. (Santa Barbara: ABC-Clio, 1997).

Andrea Tone is associate professor at the Georgia Institute of Technology. She is author of *The Business of Benevolence: Industrial Paternalism in Progressive America* (Ithaca: Cornell University Press, 1997), and edited *Controlling Reproduction: An American History* (Wilmington, Del.: Scholarly Resources, 1997).

Christopher Waldrep is a member of the History Department at Eastern Illinois University. He is the author of *Night Riders: Defending Community in the Black Patch, 1890–1915* (Durham: Duke University Press, 1993) and the forthcoming *Roots of Disorder: Race and Criminal Justice in the American South, 1817–1880* (University of Illinois Press), and editor of "H-Law," an electronic journal for legal scholars.

Index